FOR VALERIE

THE POEM ITSELF

Edited, and with an introduction, by
STANLEY BURNSHAW

Associate editors: Dudley Fitts, Henri Peyre, John Frederick Nims

THE UNIVERSITY OF ARKANSAS PRESS
FAYETTEVILLE • 1995

04   03   02   01   5   4   3   2

Cover design by Ellen Beeler

☉ The paper used in this publication meets the minimum requirements of the American National Standard for Permanence of Paper for Printed Library Materials Z39.48-1984.

Library of Congress Cataloging-in-Publication Data
The poem itself / edited, and with an introduction by, Stanley Burnshaw; associate editors, Dudley Fitts, Henri Peyre, John Frederick Nims.
      p. cm.
    150 of the greatest modern French, Spanish, German, Italian, Portuguese, and Russian poems by 45 poets in the original language with English translation and commentary. Originally published: New York: Simon & Schuster, 1989.
    Includes bibliographical references.
    ISBN 1-55728-328-1
    1. Poetry, Modern—19th century.   2. Poetry, Modern—20th century.   3. Poetry, Modern—19th century—History and criticism.   4. Poetry, Modern—20th century—History and criticism.   5. Poetry—Translations into English.   I. Burnshaw, Stanley.
[PN6099.P56 1995]   94-22928
808.8´034—dc20   CIP

Acknowledgment is made to the following for permission to include the text of the poems on the pages specified

Librairie Gallimard—for the following poems copyright by Librairie Gallimard: by Paul Claudel (pp. 64, 66, 68); by Paul Valéry (pp. 70, 72, 74, 76, 78, 80); by Guillaume Apollinaire (pp. 82, 84, 86, 88, 90); by Saint-John Perse (pp. 92, 94, 96); by Louis Aragon (pp. 98, 102); by Paul Éluard (pp. 104, 106, 108); by René Char (p. 110).

Verlag Helmut Küpper—for the poems by Stefan George (pp. 122, 124, 126, 128, 131, 132).

S. Fischer Verlag—for the poems by Hugo von Hofmannsthal (pp. 134, 136, 138).

Insel-Verlag—for the poems by Rainer Maria Rilke (pp. 140, 141, 142, 144, 146, 147, 148, 149-152).

Suhrkamp Verlag—for the poems by Bertolt Brecht (pp. 156, 158).

Maria de Unamuno—for the poem by Miguel de Unamuno (pp. 168f.).

Manuel Alvarez de Lama—for the poems by Antonio Machado (pp. 172, 174, 176, 178, 180).

Francisco Jiménez Pinzón—for the poems by Juan Ramón Jiménez (pp. 182, 184, 186, 188).

León-Felipe—for his poems (pp. 190, 192).

Manuel Bandeira—for his poems (pp. 194, 196, 197).

F. Caetano-Dias—for the poems by Fernando Pessoa (pp. 198, 200).

Juan Marichal—for the poems by Pedro Salinas (pp. 202, 204, 206, 208).

Jorge Guillén—for his poems (pp. 210, 212, 214, 216).

Senhora Jorge de Lima—for the poem by Jorge de Lima (p. 218).

Georgette de Vallejo—for the poems by César Vallejo (pp. 220, 222, 224, 226).

Cecília Meireles—for her poems (pp. 228, 230).

New Directions—for the poems from *Obras Completas* by Federico García Lorca (pp. 232, 234, 236, 238, 240, 242, 243, 244, 246, 247, 248, 250, 251); Copyright © Aguilar, S.A. de Ediciones. Reprinted by permission of the New Directions Publishing Corporation, agent for the Estate of F. G. Lorca.

Rafael Alberti—for his poems (pp. 252, 254, 256, 258).

Eugenio Florit—for his poems (pp. 260, 262).

Pablo Neruda—for his poems (pp. 264, 266).

Nicola Zanichelli Editore—for the poem by Giosuè Carducci (pp. 284-286).

Arnoldo Mondadori Editore—for the following poems: by Giovanni Pascoli (p. 288), by Gabriele d'Annunzio (p. 290); by Umberto Saba (pp. 300, 302, 304); by Eugenio Montale (pp. 316, 318, 319, 320, 322, 324); by Giuseppe Ungaretti (pp. 306, 307, 308, 310, 311, 312, 314).

Giuseppe Ungaretti—for his poems on the foregoing pages.

Renato Gozzano—for the poem by Guido Gozzano (pp. 292, 294, 296).

Vallecchi Editore—for the poems by Dino Campana (pp. 297, 298).

Farrar, Straus & Giroux, Inc.—for the poem from The Selected Writings of Salvatore Quasimodo (p. 326), Copyright 1954, © 1960 by Arnoldo Mondadori Editore. Reprinted by permission of Farrar, Straus & Giroux, Inc.

NOTE: An earlier version of the discussion by Mario Praz (pp. 318 ff.) appeared in *The Criterion* (VII, iv). The commentary on pp. 134-135 is based on an essay by Andrew O. Jaszi in *The German Quarterly* (XXVI, 3).

··· CONTENTS ···

Preface . . ix

Introduction . . xi

The Three Revolutions of Modern Poetry . . xvii

FRENCH

Gérard de Nerval (1808-1855)
El desdichado	*J. W. Kneller*	2
Delfica	*J. W. Kneller*	4
Artémis	*J. W. Kneller*	6

Charles Baudelaire (1821-1867)
Correspondances	*Henri Peyre*	8
Hymne à la Beauté	*Henri Peyre*	10
Le balcon	*Henri Peyre*	12
Harmonie du soir	*Henri Peyre*	14
L'Invitation au voyage	*Henri Peyre*	16
Spleen	*Henri Peyre*	18

Arthur Rimbaud (1854-1891)
Le bateau ivre [in part]	*Henri Peyre*	20
Mémoire	*Henri Peyre*	26
Aube	*Henri Peyre*	32
Mystique	*Henri Peyre*	34

Paul Verlaine (1844-1896)
Clair de lune	*Henri Peyre*	36
Green	*Henri Peyre*	38
[Dans l'interminable...]	*Henri Peyre*	39
Bruxelles	*Henri Peyre*	40
[L'espoir luit...]	*Henri Peyre*	42
[Le ciel est...]	*Henri Peyre*	43

Stéphane Mallarmé (1842-1898)
Don du poème	*S. Burnshaw*	44
Sainte	*Henri Peyre*	46
Toast funèbre	*Henri Peyre*	48
[Le vierge, le vivace...]	*Henri Peyre*	54
Autre éventail de Mademoiselle Mallarmé	*Henri Peyre*	56
Le tombeau d'Edgar Poe	*Henri Peyre*	58

Jules Laforgue (1860-1887)
Complainte sur certains ennuis	*Henri Peyre*	60
Locutions des Pierrots	*Henri Peyre*	60
Locutions des Pierrots (XVI)	*Henri Peyre*	62
Pierrots (on a des principes)	*Henri Peyre*	62

Paul Claudel (1868-1955)
Décembre	*Henri Peyre*	64
Dissolution	*Henri Peyre*	66
L'Esprit et l'eau [fragment]	*Henri Peyre*	68

Paul Valéry (1871-1945)
La jeune parque [two sections]	*Henri Peyre*	70
La dormeuse	*Henri Peyre*	74
Le cimetière marin [in part]	*Henri Peyre*	76

Guillaume Apollinaire (1880-1918)
La chanson du mal-aimé [fragment]	*Henri Peyre*	82

Vitam impendere
  amori: I, II · · · *Henri Peyre* 86
La jolie rousse · · · *Henri Peyre* 88

Saint-John Perse (1887-1975)
Éloges. 2. [pour fêter
  une enfance] · · · *Henri Peyre* 92
Poème à l'étrangère
  (1942) [fragment] · *Henri Peyre* 94
Pluies VIII (1943) · *Henri Peyre* 96

Louis Aragon (1897-1975)
Les lilas et les roses · *J. W. Kneller* 98
Richard II Quarante· *J. W. Kneller* 102

Paul Éluard (1897-1952)
La dame de carreau · *Henri Peyre* 104
A peine défigurée · *Henri Peyre* 106
[Mon amour...] · · · *Henri Peyre* 106
[Je cache...] · · · · *Henri Peyre* 106
[Amoureuse...] · · · *Henri Peyre* 108
[Je n'ai envie que de
  t'aimer] · · · · · *Henri Peyre* 108
Le baiser · · · · · *Henri Peyre* 108
Couvre-feu · · · · · *Henri Peyre* 108

René Char (1907-1988)
Congé au vent · · *Henri Peyre* 110
Le loriot · · · · · *Henri Peyre* 110
[Mon amour...] · · · *Henri Peyre* 110

GERMAN

Friedrich Hölderlin (1770-1843)
Hyperions Schicksals-
  lied · · · · · · *H. E. Hugo* 114
An die Parzen · · · *H. E. Hugo* 116
Sonnenuntergang · · *H. E. Hugo* 118
Die Kürze · · · · · *H. E. Hugo* 119
Da ich ein Knabe
  war... · · · · · · *H. E. Hugo* 120

Stefan George (1868-1933)
Jahrestag · · · · · *C. S. Brown* 122
Der Herr der Insel · *C. S. Brown* 124
Die Fremde · · · · *C. S. Brown* 126
Franken · · · · · *C. S. Brown* 128
[Denk nicht zuviel...] · *C. S. Brown* 131
Du schlank und rein *H. E. Hugo* 132

Hugo von Hofmannsthal (1874-1929)
Die Beiden · · · · · *A. O. Jaszi* 134
Ballade des äusseren
  Lebens · · · · · · *A. O. Jaszi* 136

Der Jüngling in der
  Landschaft · · · · *A. O. Jaszi* 138

Rainer Maria Rilke (1875-1926)
Herbsttag · · · · · *Gregor Sebba* 140
Pont du Carrousel · *Gregor Sebba* 141
[Was wirst du tun,
  Gott,...] · · · · · *Gregor Sebba* 142
[Gott spricht zu jedem
  nur,...] · · · · *Gregor Sebba* 142
Leichen-Wäsche · · · *Gregor Sebba* 144
Archäischer Torso
  Apollos · · · · · *Gregor Sebba* 146
[Blumenmuskel,...] · *Gregor Sebba* 147
[Spiegel...] · · · · *Gregor Sebba* 148
Die erste Elegie
  [in part] · · · · · *Gregor Sebba* 150

Bertolt Brecht (1898-1956)
Vom ertrunkenen
  Mädchen · · · · *H. E. Hugo* 156
Grosser Dankchoral · *H. E. Hugo* 158

SPANISH AND PORTUGUESE

Rosalía Castro (1837-1885)
[Nasín cand' as pran-
tas nasen...] · · · John F. Nims 162
[Negra sombra] · · · John F. Nims 164

Miguel de Unamuno (1864-1936)
En un cementerio de
lugar castellano · · Juan Marichal 166

Antonio Machado (1875-1939)
[Yo voy soñando...] · Paul Rogers   172
[Me dijo un alba...] Paul Rogers ' 174
[Anoche cuando dor-
mía] · · · · · Paul Rogers   176
Las moscas · · · · Paul Rogers   178
[¡Soria fría!] · · · Paul Rogers   180

Juan Ramón Jiménez (1881-1958)
[No era nadie] · · Eugenio Florit 182
Octubre · · · · Eugenio Florit 184
La música · · · · Eugenio Florit 186
Los pájaros de yo sé
dónde · · · · Eugenio Florit 188

León-Felipe (1884-1967)
Pie para "El Niño de
Vallecas" de Ve-
lázquez · · · · Paul Rogers   190
Yo no soy el gran buzo Paul Rogers   192

Manuel Bandeira (1886-1968)
Profundamente · · Ernesto Da Cal 194
Tema e voltas · · · Ernesto Da Cal 196

Fernando Pessoa (1888-1935)
Autopsicografia · · Ernesto Da Cal 198

[Entre o sono e o
sonho] · · · · Ernesto Da Cal 200

Pedro Salinas (1891-1951)
[No te veo...] · · · · Julian Palley   202
Muertes · · · · · Eugenio Florit 204
[Pensar en ti...] · · · Eugenio Florit 206
El poema · · · · Eugenio Florit 208

Jorge Guillén (1893–1984)
Desnudo · · · · · Julian Palley   210
Sabor a vida · · · Julian Palley   212
Muerte a lo lejos · Julian Palley   214
Primavera delgada · Julian Palley   216

Jorge de Lima (1893-1953)
Poema de qualquer
virgem . · · · · D. Vasconcellos 218

César Vallejo (1895-1937)
Heces · · · · · Eugenio Florit 220
Ágape · · · · · · Eugenio Florit 222
Piedra negra sobre
una piedra blanca · Eugenio Florit 224
Pequeño responso a un
héroe de la Repú-
blica · · · · · Eugenio Florit 226

Cecília Meireles (1901-1964)
[De longe...] · · · Ernesto Da Cal 228
Motivo · · · · · Ernesto Da Cal 230

Federico García Lorca (1899-1936)
Preciosa y el aire · · John F. Nims 232
Romance sonámbulo · John F. Nims 237
La casada infiel · · John F. Nims 243
Romance de la pena
negra · · · · · John F. Nims 247
Despedida · · · · · John F. Nims 251

Rafael Alberti (1902-   )
Pregón submarino · *S. S. Marichal* 252
Mar · · · · · · · *S. S. Marichal* 252
El ángel de los nú-
meros · · · · · · *S. S. Marichal* 254
El ángel bueno · · · *S. S. Marichal* 256
A Luis Cernuda: Aire
del sur buscado en
Inglaterra · · · · *S. S. Marichal* 258

Eugenio Florit (1903-   )
Soneto · · · · · · *Eugenio Florit* 260
La noche · · · · · · *Eugenio Florit* 262

Pablo Neruda (1904-1973)
[Puedo escribir los ver-
sos...] · · · · · · *Paul Rogers* 264
No hay olvido · · · *Paul Rogers* 266

ITALIAN

Giacomo Leopardi (1798-1837)
La sera del dì di festa *John F. Nims* 270
A se stesso · · · · · *John F. Nims* 275
L'Infinito · · · · · *Renato Poggioli* 276
A Silvia · · · · · · *T. G. Bergin* 278

G. G. Belli (1791-1863)
Tre mmaschi e nnove
femmine · · · · · *T. G. Bergin* 282

Giosuè Carducci (1835-1907)
Alla stazione in una
mattina d'autunno · *Glauco Cambon* 284

Giovanni Pascoli (1855-1912)
Ultimo sogno · · · *Glauco Cambon* 288

Gabriele d'Annunzio (1863-1938)
Assisi · · · · · · *Glauco Cambon* 290

Guido Gozzano (1883-1916)
Totò Merùmeni · · *John F. Nims* 292

Dino Campana (1885-1932)
L'Invetriata · · · · *John F. Nims* 297
Giardino autunnale · *John F. Nims* 298

Umberto Saba (1883-1957)
La capra · · · · · *Jonathan Levy* 300
Mezzogiorno d'inver-
no · · · · · · · *John F. Nims* 302
Ulisse · · · · · · · *T. G. Bergin* 304

Giuseppe Ungaretti (1888-1970)
San Martino del Carso *Glauco Cambon* 306
Senza piú peso · · · *Glauco Cambon* 307
Alla noia · · · · · *John F. Nims* 308
Mattina · · · · · · *John F. Nims* 311
Tu ti spezzasti · · · *John F. Nims* 312

Eugenio Montale (1896–1981)
Meriggiare pallido
e assorto · · · · · *John F. Nims* 316
Arsenio · · · · · · *Mario Praz* 318
La casa dei doganieri *Glauco Cambon* 322
L'Anguilla · · · · · *John F. Nims* 324

Salvatore Quasimodo (1901-1968)
Dalla rocca di Berga-
mo alta · · · · *Wallace Fowlie* 326

Appendix

Poem by Alexander Blok *Marc Slonim* 328
A Note on the Prosodies · · · · 330
A Note on the Pronunciations · · 334
Notes on Contributors · · · · · 337

PREFACE

WAS IT irony, logic or both that led Robert Frost—for whom poetry was "that which gets lost in translation"—to coin the aptest description of this book? Taking *The Poem Itself* from my hand, he shouted "I'll give you a line!" then, spreading out two facing pages, he said "Instead of translating a foreign poem, you *discuss it into English*."

Our conversation turned to the virtues of plain prose renderings, from the three hundred works of the great Loeb Classical Library to recent Penguin collections of moderns. We also talked of an earlier comment: "For self-assurance [Frost had remarked], there should be a lingering unhappiness in reading translations." The thought had possibly played a part in the genesis of *The Poem Itself,* a work whose forthright method would change and broaden our approach to poets of foreign countries, despite or because of the mass of versified renderings coming to light each season, and some thoughtful books on the problem. For English-speaking readers at least, ours was not only an Age of Criticism but also an Age of Translation.

What relevance has this twofold fact for *The Poem Itself?* Poetry-translating had held to familiar paths, with literal renderings (prose or prose cut up into lines) at the one extreme; free-floating "adaptations" in verse at the other (e.g. *Imitations*); and what must be taken as second-hand poems in between.[1] The only break from traditional ways —the "way" of *The Poem Itself*—was not mere translation as it had been understood but, in essence, criticism of a special kind: to give readers the means for experiencing poems of a tongue they had never learned.

"Criticism, I take it," R. P. Blackmur wrote in *Language As Gesture,* "is the formal discourse of an amateur."[2] His emphasis on the final word and its unmistakable implication offer more than a sharpened

---

[1] I use this term for my own translations in verse.
[2] Harcourt Brace & Co., 1952, p. 372.

focus, summoning up Rilke's remark about works of art: "Only love can grasp and hold and fairly judge them." Not surprisingly, it took a contemporary poet (Stanley Kunitz) to perceive the relation between the discussions and the original text of *The Poem Itself* by citing the "loving care" of the introductions.[3]

To those who applaud the latest fashion, such thoughts may seem a bit odd until one steers them free from the waves of scientism temporarily roiling the seas of literary theory. Not that the fifties or sixties lacked aberrations. A critic's "inspection" of a poem, we were solemnly informed, would be quite "as careful and close as a chemical analysis." As for creative works themselves, "their explanations [would be] almost as important as the poems."[4] Roman Jakobson branded a critic who was "unconversant with linguistic methods" a flagrant anachronism.[5] Recently, alas, as Roger Shattuck notes, "a literal usurpation has begun which would depose literature and grant sovereign authority to one or more of several competing disciplines"[6]—such as structuralism, semiotics, linguistics, speech-act theory, communication-and-information theory, reader-response theory, affective stylistics, gynocriticism, intertextuality, antithetical criticism, deconstruction, as well as strained extensions of Marxist and Freudian schemas. Shattuck proposes "reciting aloud . . . as both a fruitful form of reading and a sturdy antidote." Although, as Emily Dickinson remarked, "A Pen has so many inflections and a Voice but one," getting a poem by heart still remains a most revealing and replenishing means toward possessing the poem itself.

At the present moment only two of our forty-five poets are still alive, whereas all but a few of the authors of essays continue to work with poems. With respect to these twenty-three writers, I have not attempted to bring up to date the material on the final page of this book. Thus the reader is able to know what the respective contributors had done and were doing at the time when they were engaged in "discussing" the poems they had chosen "into English."

S.B.

[3] A comment he wrote on *The Modern Hebrew Poem Itself*, Stanley Burnshaw, T. Carmi, Ezra Spicehandler, eds., Holt, Rinehart & Winston, 1965.

[4] Both quotations from Stanley Burnshaw, *The Seamless Web*, George Braziller, 1970, pp. 253, 256.

[5] *Ibid.*, p. 217.

[6] "How to Rescue Literature," *The New York Review of Books*, April 17, 1980.

INTRODUCTION

Thirty years ago in *This Quarter*, I published "A Note on Translation" which suggested that the only way one could experience the poetry of a language one did not command was by learning to hear and pronounce (if only approximately) the sounds of the originals and "simultaneously" reading literal renditions. Since the poetry inheres in the tonal language (the sounds of the poem in its original tongue), how could one possibly experience a Spanish poem in any language but Spanish, a French poem in any language but French? The "Note" appeared at a time when translators felt free to do anything: they were "re-creating originals"! Bilingual editions had not yet become familiar—nor had Frost's definition of poetry as "that which gets lost from verse and prose in translation." Before long a publisher expressed interest in my notion, and I embarked on a small anthology. But then he insisted that verse translations also be included, despite the danger of confusing and distracting the reader. And so for the time being I abandoned the project, certain as ever that mine was the only means by which a reader could begin to experience the poetry of other languages.

But my method had not gone far enough, as I discovered many years later when I found myself working on some poems by Mallarmé. My literal renditions were scrupulous, yet in certain key places a single French word could not be rendered by a single English word—pieces of two or even of three might be required. Other words, with double denotations in the French, had to be halved in English or equated by impossible compounds. And certain phrases that looked easy in the dictionaries carried quite untranslatable connotations essential as meaning. As for syntax, the reader would have to untangle it for himself. And the allusions —though at times they might hold the key to the poem, they could not even be considered, since they stand outside the purview of all translation.

What sort of experience, then, did my confident method offer? Obviously a most inadequate one: a great deal more would have to be added before an English-speaking reader could begin to experience Mallarmé. And if this were true of so familiar a poet, then it must be true of other "difficult" moderns, such as Rilke, Vallejo, Montale; it must be true to some degree of every participant in the poetic revolution of the last hundred years. The method had to be expanded, the line-by-line rendition enriched, at least with alternate equivalents where necessary and with leads where ellipsis and syntax might frustrate a reader. Other clues had also to be given: to telescoped images, private allusions, specialized symbols, systems of belief, and similar problems. And what of the poem as a work of sonal art? For a reader who wishes to hear and pronounce the original, however approximately, any number of interesting points might be signalled; not only of rime, assonance, meter, and strophe, but of graces, stops, turns, and the sonal felicities of the whole. To be faithful to its intent, the method had to be enlarged into a literal rendering plus commentary—into a discussion aimed at enabling the reader both to *understand* the poem and to begin to *experience it as a poem*.

The result of these thoughts—which can be read on pp. 44-45—fell short of its maker's ideal, yet it served to show others how a somewhat "difficult" poem in a foreign language could be made accessible to English-speaking readers through a new type of presentation. The first to examine "Don du poème" not only approved the theory and the practice but also made fruitful suggestions. When the specimen was next submitted, to other scholars and to poets, the response took the form of immediate offers to collaborate. One poet-critic thought that the discussion should be made twice as searching, but he soon saw the unwisdom of trying to analyze too much. For once the reader begins, he can plunge as deep as he wishes. The aim is to help him *into* the poem itself.

There are, of course, various ways of approaching foreign poetry; when a writer uses one, he does not thereby surrender his right to use others. Those of us who are drawn to particular poems in other languages will always be free to revivify them with English verses— and as one of this group, I applaud the practice and hail the occasional achievements. But these are personal preoccupations, and translation is of public concern. English versions of foreign writings abound, but the reader who wants to experience the poetry of other literatures must look elsewhere; the vast stock of verse translations provides no answer.

It provides no answer for several reasons. First, and overwhelming, a verse translation offers an experience in *English* poetry. It takes the reader away from the foreign literature and into his own, away from the original and into something different. The instant he departs from the words of the original, he departs from *its* poetry. For the words are the poem. Ideas can often be carried across, but poems are not made of ideas (as Degas was informed): they are made of words. Regardless of its brilliance, an English translation is always a different thing: it is always an *English* poem.

In this fact about words lies the source of all the slanderous remarks that have been made about translators, from Frost's sentence quoted above to the notorious Italian pun *traduttore-traditore* ("translator-traitor"). Says Poggioli: "Both original and translation deal with a single substance, differentiated into two unique, and incommensurable, accidents"[1]; and Nida: "There can never be a word-for-word type of correspondence which is fully meaningful or accurate."[1] When Coleridge proposed as "the infallible test of a blameless style" "its *untranslateableness* in words of the same language without injury to the meaning," he took care to "include in the *meaning* of a word not only its correspondent object, but likewise all the associations which it recalls." For every "meaningful" word is a unique totality—unique in sound, denotation, connotation, and doubtless much more.

But the order that words make is no less crucial to the translator than the words themselves. For when they appear in a sequence (as in a poem) they begin to mean in a special way—their uniquenesses act, as it were, selectively. The position that each word holds in relation to the others causes parts of its content to be magnified and other parts diminished. Yet even though some meanings recede as others come to the fore, all of them are to some degree also active—whence the multiform richness of feeling and thought conveyed (the "suggestions, ambiguities, paradoxes, levels of meaning" of current terminology). These facts may be read into Coleridge's definition of poetry as "the best words in the best order," especially into his famous remark about "a more than usual state of emotion, with more than usual order." Today we talk of the "affective" phrase or sentence, whose word arrangement differs from that of prose; we say each poem is an organization of such phrases. But some critics go further: each affective phrase is a rhythmic metaphor—a poem is a series of rhythmic metaphors which evokes a physical response in the reader's body, in his internal and external muscles. Not only the mind, but the total organism moves with and "mirrors" the rhythmic

---

[1] *On Translation*, edited by Reuben A. Brower, Harvard University Press, 1959. Renato Poggioli: "The Added Artificer," p. 138; John Nida: "Principles of Translation as Exemplified by Bible Translating," p. 13.

pattern of the words. For a translator to evoke this response by different words and word order would of course be impossible. But, all corporeal concurrences aside, could a translator even think of trying to carry across into a different language the "more than usual order" of the original words?

And yet, with all its limitations, verse translation has given us almost all we know of the poets of the rest of the world.[2] And from what we have been given we have formed our judgments. Can they be trusted? The only works we could read have been those that happened to appeal to translators who happened to succeed in turning them into English poems that happened to get published. This fortuitousness should be enough to make us suspect that the picture has been skewed; but there is more. We naturally judge the quality of a foreign poem by the quality of the English poem it inspired, even though we know such correspondence is rare. As a result, verse translation being the poorest subdivision of English verse, we must continually assure ourselves that the originals are much better—which is safe enough, but only a wishful assumption. And what of all the poetry that has never been carried across because it seemed too long or too compact or too difficult or too delicate to fashion into an English poem?

The method of *The Poem Itself* should overcome all three obstacles we have noted in verse translation. Because each word of a foreign poem is unique in itself and in its order, we ask the reader to read the original along with our English approximations (usually set in italics, with alternate meanings in parentheses and explanations in brackets). Our comments on allusion, symbol, meaning, sound, and the like will enable him to see *what* the poem is saying and *how*, though the poem itself is an unparaphrasable totality. As to how much the reader will hear of the sound of the poem, this depends on what knowledge he already has and on what effort he is willing to invest in learning to hear. This book, then, offers poems and the means toward experiencing them.

But the means vary, for each work is a unique problem: how can it best be presented in terms of this book? The extent to which each author has differed from the "model" may be judged in the varied approaches of the other 140 commentaries. Each author has, of course, been free to write in his characteristic way, and to emphasize certain things in a poem and pay little attention to others. Individuality of response is no less apparent in our way of presenting a poem than in a verse translation.

---

[2] Even when we are not aware—as, for example, when a revision of an original passage appears without acknowledgment (see p. 59).

xiv

Indeed, most of the poems in this book were chosen by the contributors themselves. But the editors have also been free to respond in their characteristic ways, and to do more than was ever intended, entirely (I like to think) out of necessity, in a collaborative undertaking dedicated to a new method.

Before inviting the reader to begin, we make five qualifications. (1) Each poem (and each unit of a long poem) is presented on a two-page spread, to enable the reader to see everything without turning pages: a few of our discussions could have used additional space. (2) Ideally each poem should be available in a recording. (3) The book makes no claim to being representative of the last hundred years—how could it be, in so few pages and with so much to choose from? Yet many of the finest poets and poems have been included. (4) The notes on "The Prosodies" and "The Pronunciations" will be most useful to the reader who recognizes the intentional brevity of the first and the avowed inadequacy of the second. Every likening of a foreign sound to an English sound is at best an approximation, often only remote. (5) We had hoped to offer a group of Russian poems. Nevertheless, our single example, with its phonetic transcription and stress marks, may indicate how a work even in an unfamiliar alphabet can be made accessible to a reader who is willing to make the leap into the poem.

Since only a few debts can be acknowledged, I record the largest: to Dudley Fitts, Henri Peyre, and John F. Nims, for their work on the Spanish and Portuguese, the French, and the Italian sections respectively, and a great deal more; and to the authors, several of whom have made contributions in addition to the pages bearing their initials. I also thank Jacques Barzun, for many thoughtful suggestions; Harry Levin, for gracious advice; John Ciardi, for the title, in particular; and the poets, publishers, and others listed on page iv for permission to present the original poems. S.B.

THE THREE REVOLUTIONS OF
MODERN POETRY

ANYONE who presumes to deal with the three revolutions of modern Western poetry must take care to define his terms, and especially "modern." I use it historically, to enclose a block of time and to suggest the cultural-philosophic climate decisive for the poets of the period. For no matter how deeply we believe a literary work to be a "linguistic system" or a "self-sustaining object" immune to time's erosions, we also know that the man who created it lived during a specific age and breathed its specific air. In the last few decades critics have given too little attention to the experiences that writers of an epoch have had in common; each author has been separated and studied as a more or less unique phenomenon. As a consequence a reader underrates the importance of the possessions and deprivations they held in common, even when these cry out to be seen and explored.

Owen Barfield, in discussing a lyric by one of the Elizabethans, observes that

part of my aesthetic experience I owe to the individual genius of the poet [and] part is due to something which I will call its "Elizabethan-ness." Needless to say, the phenomenon is not peculiar to the Elizabethan lyric. It is true of other times and places, of the poetry of the Greek Anthology, for example, of the French Pléiade, of the English Metaphysicals, or the Cavalier lyric, and it has been well named by some critic "joint-stock poetry." It arises whenever different poets work together in a kind of coterie or come under the same contemporary influence. . . .[1]

In a very broad sense, the poets whom I call modern exemplify this phenomenon of "joint-stock poetry," even though they are widely spread out in time. For the period begins with the outbreak of the Industrial Revolution and ends with the close of World War II. This is a huge block of time compared with the little ages of the Pléiade or the English Metaphysicals, and yet all the poets whom I regard as modern lived under essentially the same influence of a

---

[1] *Poetic Diction*, Faber and Faber, 1952, p. 51.

civilization that had declared war on Nature in a contest that would stop at nothing short of unconditional surrender.

This war was, of course, inevitable, man being what he is: a maker of tools and bent on mastery. Actually he had always been moving toward an open declaration, from the ancient moment when he developed the hand axe and the flint in his struggle for food and survival. The intervening preparatory stages can be traced by anyone who studies the evolution of science and technology down through what we call the Age of Reason. By that time, of course, the intellectual élite of England had ceased to be intimidated by the forces of Nature. Nature was less a mystery than a machine. But it was not until animal power had been displaced by waterpower and steampower that the war began in earnest. From that point on it was simply a question of time, one thing leading to another until the discovery and use of atomic power. The war against Nature had been confidently waged and won; and we post-moderns, of 1945-and-after, breathe the spirit of a different epoch, and we have a different terror on our minds: Now that man is victorious, how shall he stay alive?

The attitude toward the Deity shows a complementary evolution, immediately before and during the war for mastering Nature. The all-powerful Western God of the Middle Ages ceaselessly drew men's eyes from earth to heaven, and it was not till the advent of Renaissance Humanism that men could look upon their dwelling place, earth, with a certain curiosity and with growing confidence in their own capacities. The notion that men might cope with Nature without God's help became so solid that, as everyone knows, by the eighteenth century He could be looked upon as the proverbial Divine Mechanic of the Great Machine. But with the Industrial Revolution even this function was removed; He was merely to stand aside, above the battle, and to watch or urge men on to grander achievements. Max Weber made this tellingly clear in his essay on the "Protestant Ethic," tracing the development of Luther's idea of "the calling" to Calvinism's elevation of a "this-wordly asceticism" into an ideal of conduct for the godly man— "More specifically, this-wordly asceticism tended to identify spiritual salvation with business success, and so created the capitalistic spirit, which . . . retained its vitality even after its religious sources had evaporated."[1] God might be invoked by name and worshipped on

[1] Hans Speier, in *Encyclopaedia of the Social Sciences*, Macmillan, 1935, XV, p. 388.

Sundays, but as a reality, as an everliving spiritual presence in the everyday life of Western Industrial Man, He had all but disappeared. The "operational" objects for worship were things, things.

But not for everyone—especially not for the poet. The more the people around him concentrated on external reality, the more he turned inward. Industrial man was making noisome advances in his conquest of Nature; he was building more and more factories, producing more and more goods—these were the things that really mattered![1] To the poet, what mattered was his inner self: a limitless world for private exploration. As a paradigm of rejection, this is almost too tempting to be ignored by anyone with a Freudian cast of mind. But whether or not poets acted out of defensiveness, because they could not cope with their age, is irrelevant. What interests us is what happened in literature, and what happened there has unmistakable import.

Everything that the poet now experiences in this swiftly industrializing world is significant only in terms of his private reaction: this alone is worth expressing. After years of virtual absence, the first person singular returns to poetry—but with a now magisterial force and with a new assertiveness quite different from anything heard at an earlier time. Moreover, with vanguard Romantics in Germany and France, it involves something in addition to the ordinary subjective self: the subliminal mind enters literature as a necessary part of the creative intelligence. Jean Paul registered this change in a sentence that looms as a landmark in modern culture: "Our measurements of the rich territory of the Me are far too small or narrow when we omit the immense realm of the *Unconscious*, this real interior Africa in every sense."

The modern age of poetry, then, begins with these two "differences," and the greatest part of its achievement can be traced to this twofold source. For the two are really one: (1) a commitment to a subjective self (2) that is now vastly, even infinitely, expanded. Look synoptically at Western cultural history of the last hundred and fifty years, and the picture seems almost too neat to be credible—on the one hand, the province of society at large: the external reality of the whole of Nature;

---

[1] Poets were reacting and would continue to react to the concomitant effects of the Industrial Revolution more than to the Revolution itself—to changed attitudes, values, personal relations, social institutions, etc. From such alienation a few sought refuge in religion, but a great many more in the Unconscious, no doubt, in some instances, as a substitute for the divine.

on the other, the province of the poet: the internal reality of the whole psyche; and both opened up for endless exploration and exploitation.[1] The same cannot be said of the novel or the drama, but we are speaking of poetry. And we are looking down from our late point in time, from which this mainstream course of the poem is grossly clear.

Once we come close, to be sure, we encounter complexities—of date, location, temperament, for this is Western Europe and also America. The cross-currents of uneven development call to mind the painting of the Renaissance, which moved from Italy to France to the Low Countries, blooming in each place at a different period and always with characteristic change. After Romanticism burst upon France, Germany, and England, its energies centered in Paris, where it broadened and deepened into something seemingly different. But French Symbolism was merely a matured growth of Romanticism; indeed it was latent in a number of Romantic writers from the start.[2] Wordsworth's "The Simplon Pass," though published in 1845, had been written at least forty-one years earlier. The twenty-line poem ends by declaring that the woods, waterfalls, winds, rocks, crags, skies, darkness, and light

> Were all like workings of one mind, the features
> Of the same face, blossoms upon one tree,
> Characters of the great Apocalypse,
> The types and symbols of Eternity,
> Of first, and last, and midst, and without end.

18

Nobody refers to the 18th and 19th lines as "British Symbolist verse," yet how near they bring us to the heritage of Swedenborg, whose importance to French Symbolism cannot be overstated. And how far is it from Wordsworth's "types and symbols of Eternity" to Baudelaire's, in

> La nature est un temple où de vivants piliers
> Laissent parfois sortir de confuses paroles;
> L'homme y passe à travers des forêts de symboles
> Qui l'observent avec des regards familiers. . . .

(Nature is a temple where living pillars / Sometimes allow confused words to escape; / There man passes through forests of symbols / That watch him with familiar [intimate] glances. . . .)

---

[1] Is it necessary to state that poets had one attitude toward nature and that society at large had quite another? or that the use of nature by Romantic poets is a typical example of internalization?

[2] E.g., in Shelley, and in Blake. (See Louis Cazamian, *Symbolisme et Poésie*, and Henri Peyre, *Shelley et la France*, 1935.)

Though it aroused little attention when it first appeared (1857), "Correspondances" came to exert a greater impact on modern literature than any other single poem, for it epitomizes the Symbolist view that the external event is a sign of an event taking place elsewhere—the so-called vertical correspondences between the event visible to human beings and its corresponding event in the invisible world. If, then, the invisible and the visible exist in a one-to-one correspondence, the poet through his symbols can make the invisible reality available to himself and to his readers. He is no longer just a maker of rimes: he is an explorer and a wielder of vast, unsuspected powers, whose discoveries can literally bring heaven down to earth. This is not simply to paraphrase Swedenborg, but to epitomize the attitude of the typical poets of the period (including the German Goethe and the American Emerson), to whom symbols stood for profoundly important "somethings," to whom external reality was a surface to be seen through and explored for the greater reality of the truths that lie in wait there.

As for words, individual words, who could say what they might not mean and what they might not do? As components of a metaphor—which is to say, the verbalization of the symbol—they possessed more than the evocative force of which earlier poets were aware. As vehicles of the new method of discovery, they had the power to re-create reality. No wonder the Symbolist explored their suggestiveness and their reverberations—or that the successors of Symbolism would pant after pluralistic meanings. No wonder that a poet like Rimbaud tried to create a new language, or that a later poet like Mallarmé went so far as to break up ordinary relations among words in order to replace them with a new syntax of larger meanings.

And if words were to be explored for unsuspected significations and powers, the Unconscious itself would be the vastest of all possible sources. The most obvious approach was taken, of course, by Rimbaud, in his deliberate cultivation of hallucinatory states. But note the stress upon language in the closing phrase: "Then I would explain my magic sophistries with the hallucination of words." And the no-less-famous journey towards self-alienation, which succeeded at last with his victorious "Je est un autre [I is another]." But this is still relatively tame. Greater audacity was on the way—in the effort to overcome mortal limitations and to exercise superhuman power. Such so-called "angelism" was soon attempted by Rimbaud and later by others, including Mallarmé, with his infatuation with the Absolute and Nothingness; by Saint-Pol Roux, who wanted to replace the God above with the God within; by the Surrealists, who tried to transform and remake the very objects in nature. Angelism is a very far cry from Jean Paul's almost gentle fascination with the "interior Africa" of the Unconscious, but how was anyone to know what might happen when poets, in an ever more desperately rushing world of Industrialism, drove deeper and deeper into their private selves?

So much for the first two stages of modernism—Romantic and Symbolist; what of the poets who came later? French critics refer to "Three Generations of Symbolists" and suggest that Surrealism, contemporaneous with the third, was an alternate Symbolist development. When one looks at the names that distinguish these "generations," a question arises: Why label them "Symbolist"? Baudelaire and Rimbaud, as the initiators, cannot be questioned; but Mallarmé, as emblem for the second generation? and Valéry, as emblem for the third? Are these two poets legitimate exponents of Symbolism? Decidedly not in the Swedenborgian sense in which Baudelaire could take reality. But decidedly yes when one considers how Mallarmé extended the psychological and linguistic exploits of his predecessors; and how Valéry went further, with the "detached referents," the *leitmotif* use of symbols, and the concern to fathom the nature of the human mind. One has to guard against oversimple notions that inhere in the "Symbolist" label. It spreads confusion—yet it also can serve to make clear the central role of the poets of France in fostering and conditioning the poetry of the modern Western world.

The twentieth century is the French century to the extent that virtually every important Western poet was affected by Symbolist or Surrealist practices (need one point to Rilke, Yeats, Eliot, Lorca, Montale, Ungaretti, Seferis, Blok?). And the nineteenth century? The second half was also the century of France, both directly (because of the amount of excellent poetry contributed by the French) and to the extent that poets who worked independently—and even earlier (Hölderlin, Leopardi) [1]—wrote in a spirit congenial to its spirit.

---

[1] As his translator, Michael Hamburger, points out, the development in Hölderlin's poetry between 1797 and 1803 "in many ways prefigures the development of all European poetry in the next century and a half" (*Hölderlin*, Penguin Books, 1961, p. xxi). Leopardi's case is more complex. What he referred to as *noia* (spleen, tedium)

Certain Victorians may seem to stand apart, but like their peers they were also the creatures of Romanticism and, in any case, neither England nor the United States produced significant poets who consistently celebrated the values of the Industrial Age; on the contrary. There were marginal movements, of course—from the now-silent cannonading of Marinetti's "Futurists" to the sometimes memorable outcries of the socially conscious thirties and forties. But the mainstream of modern poetry is a continuous flow from the Romantic and Symbolist source, threading through not a few nations but the Western world.[1]

I

Let us look at the "revolutions," beginning with a brief characterization of each so as to review them later in terms of a new direction. From the handful of adducible examples, I take three: the first labeled somewhat approximately "syntax."

We start with Hölderlin's late hymns and fragments. Though in time of composition contemporary with the *Lyrical Ballads*, this poetry could hardly be farther away from Wordsworth's in syntax. As Michael Hamburger points out, "it combines the directness of common speech with the most daring use of ellipse and inversion, not for rhetorical but for imaginative ends," and he cites Hölderlin's own explanation of one aspect:

It is common practice to have inversions of word order within the period. But clearly much greater effects can be obtained by the inversion of the periods themselves. The logical order of periods, in which the basis (the basic period) is followed by its development, the development by its culmination, the culmination by its purpose, and the subsidiary clauses are merely appended to the main clauses to which they primarily apply—all this can only very rarely serve the poet's ends.[2]

A half century later we come upon a second and no less startling viola-

---

appears again and again in nineteenth-century European poetry—in the *ennui* of Baudelaire, for example. Sainte-Beuve's substantial essay on Leopardi's poetry appeared in the *Revue des Deux Mondes* in September 1844, and Luciano Rebay raises the question: "Is it reasonable to assume that Baudelaire could have been unaware of this essay and of all it had to tell him?"

[1] To distinguish as "modern" the period from the beginning of Romanticism to our own time is justifiable not only in poetry. See, for example, Jacques Barzun, *Darwin, Marx, Wagner*, 2nd ed., Doubleday Anchor Books, pp. 322-38 *passim*.

[2] *Hölderlin*, Penguin Books, 1961, p. xxiv.

tion of what Webster defines as "the due arrangement of word forms to show their mutual relations in a sentence." Mallarmé's syntax issues from a different system of relations, as exemplified in the following poem, "Sainte":

À la fenêtre recélant
Le santal vieux qui se dédore
De sa viole étincelant
Jadis avec flûte ou mandore,

À ce vitrage d'ostensoir
Que frôle une harpe par l'Ange
Formée avec son vol du soir
Pour la délicate phalange

Est la Sainte pâle, étalant
Le livre vieux qui se déplie
Du Magnificat ruisselant
Jadis selon vêpre et complie:

Du doigt que, sans le vieux santal
Ni le vieux livre, elle balance
Sur le plumage instrumental,
Musicienne du silence.

(At the window secretly hiding / The old sandalwood shedding its gilt / Of her viol shining / Formerly [once] with flute or mandore [mandolin],

Is the pale Saint, spreading out / The ancient book that unfolds / Of the Magnificat streaming / Formerly according to [once in] vespers and complin [nightsong]:

At this monstrance [stained-glass] window / Which is touched by a harp shaped by the Angel with his evening flight / For the delicate phalanx [bone]

Of the finger that, without the old sandalwood / Or the old book, she holds poised / Upon the instrumental plumage, / Musician of silence.)

Sixteen lines of eight syllables each—all one sentence, with five commas, one colon. No simple series of stages: beginning, middle, end. One thing runs into another, but not always the next. To get at this poem, one must read and read—and then, if one doesn't resist, certain elements may take on sudden importance. The structure is made of "presences," similar to the images bodied forth in a dream; for ordinary connectives—words like *but*, *because*, and other signs of relationship—are absent from a dream. Yet a dream communicates, often with memorable residue; and a poem of Mallarmean syntax may also be able to communicate, for the relations are held together by a logic of their own. Mallarmé's word order is often bewildering, with inversions, appositions, and what seem to be capricious displacements. But the main difficulties come from the lack of terms to denote the relations among the parts. He removed these with a will, as he removed other clues to his intention. It would be up to the reader to supply not only the morphemes and the normal word order but even an occasional verb. For Mallarmé was writing according to his new theory: "To paint, not the thing, but the effect it produces."

So far as we know, Emily Dickinson was not following any such theory when she wrote this poem, which in its own way is as nonsyntactical as "Sainte":

Further in Summer than the Birds—	Antiquest felt at Noon
Pathetic from the Grass	When August burning low
A minor Nation celebrates	Arise this Spectral Canticle
Its unobtrusive Mass—	Repose to typify—
No Ordinance be seen—	Remit as yet no Grace—
So gradual the Grace	No furrow on the Glow—
A gentle Custom it becomes—	But a Druidic difference
Enlarging loneliness.	Enhances Nature now—[1]

Charles Anderson finds this to be "her finest poem on the theme of the year going down to death and the relation of this to a belief in immortality." [2] Wherein lies the difficulty? One has to know what she is talking about; and this fact has now been supplied: the poem is called "My Cricket," for the insect that symbolized for her the mysterious moment of the year's transition from autumn into winter. Aware of this meaning, we may still find the poem as a whole indecipherable, until we surrender ourselves and are lucky enough to begin to perceive its "presences."

But revolutionary syntax does not necessarily produce difficulty. On the contrary, some of Cummings' most popular poems play havoc with the reader's expectations while communicating not with losses but with gains. Here are two familar fragments:

> (1) my father moved through dooms of love
> through sames of am through haves of give,
> singing each morning out of each night
> my father moved through depths of height. . . .
>
> My father moved through theys of we, . . .[3]

---

[1] Reprinted by permission of the publishers from *The Poems of Emily Dickinson*, edited by Thomas H. Johnson, The Belknap Press of Harvard University Press, copyright 1951, 1955, The President and Fellows of Harvard College, Cambridge, Massachusetts.

[2] *Emily Dickinson's Poetry*, Holt, Rinehart and Winston, 1960, pp. 151 f.

[3] Copyright, 1940, by E. E. Cummings. Reprinted from *Poems 1923-1954* by E. E. Cummings by permission of Harcourt, Brace & World, Inc.

(2) what if a much of a which of a wind
      gives the truth to summer's lie ; . . .

      what if a keen of a lean wind flays
      screaming hills with sleet and snow:
      strangles valleys by ropes of thing
      and stifles forests in white ago? . . .[1]

Cummings typically "makes" words by derivation: changing parts of
speech; adding prefixes or suffixes; converting verbs, pronouns, ad-
verbs, adjectives, and conjunctions into nouns. These coinages, instantly
understood, provide a strange yet natural pleasure as they extend the
usual meanings of the words. But the reader may be also led into
complex discovering, which comes on slowly, and especially so when
word order demands reconstruction:

                 to stand (alone) in some

           autumnal afternoon:
           breathing a fatal
           stillness;while

      enormous this how

           patient creature(who's
      never by never robbed of
           day)puts always on by always

           dream,is to

           taste
             not(beyond
             death and

           life)imaginable mysteries[2]

A fourth example, from the Spanish, can make its point despite
the language barrier, for its violation is of a kind we no longer notice.
As in Mallarmé and Dickinson, the words themselves are ordinary:

---

[1] *Ibid.*

[2] Copyright, 1958, by E. E. Cummings, Reprinted from *Ninety-Five Poems* by
E. E. Cummings by permission of Harcourt, Brace & World, Inc.

Without eyes, without voice,
   without shadow.
Now, without shadow.
Invisible to the world,
To everyone.
	Sin ojos, sin vos, sin
	   sombra.
	Ya, sin sombra.
	Invisible para el mundo,
	para nadie.

And you, sea, And you, fire, And you, Hastened wind of my dream.	Y tú, mar, y tú, fuego, y tú, acelerado aire de mi sueño.

"In his shorter lines," says the translator, C. M. Bowra, "Rafael Alberti often uses a highly impressionistic method of putting down the vital words without forming them into grammatical units."[1] Note: the vital words. Here lies one clue to the unriddling of poems that violate the expected pattern in the reader's mind. When one concentrates on these vital elements, the poem can begin to emerge. For there is nothing sacred or even superior in the rules of syntax; like grammar and usage, it is enthroned by custom and acceptance. Its way is not the only way of effective communication; in fact it is plainly a block in certain contexts.

2

The second revolution—in prosody—can be traced to French Symbolism, though it was never an article of its faith. Baudelaire and Mallarmé felt no need to rebel against the rigidities of French versification, with its fixed number of syllables per line, placement of caesura, perfect rime, and so on. They were fond of the prose poem, and Baudelaire could even rhapsodize about it—"musical without rhythm or rime, supple and bold enough to adapt itself to the lyric movements of the soul, to the undulations of reverie, to the somersaults of the consciousness"—but of free verse he would have none.

It was Rimbaud who violated the canons of prosody, and timidly, it seems to us today. In 1886 the first *vers libre* poem (written before 1873) was published; then a second, also by Rimbaud; then some appeared by three other poets, among them Laforgue. Finally (1889) Viélé-Griffin prefaced a book of his own with the declaration "Le vers est libre." The statement was premature; controversies continued to

---

[1] *The Creative Experiment*, Grove, n.d., p. 226.

rage between advocates of *vers libre* and the vast majority, who upheld the classic rules. But in time the *vers librists* succeeded in establishing their claims—and in the last sixty years their successors have done almost everything imaginable to the once inviolable classic line.

Readers trained only in English may marvel at the fury of this French revolution, having already known free verse in Milton, Arnold, and Whitman. But our language is tonic; every polysyllabic word has at least one fixed stress. A line of English verse is always held together to some extent by a pattern of strong and weak syllables. In ordinary French discourse, however, each syllable is about equally strong; hence, it was believed that the only way to keep a line of verse from falling apart was by constructing it with a fixed number of syllables and by tying it to another line of the same "length" by rime. *Vers librists* had therefore to show that a line could also be held together by a different pattern—by an accent of meaning. To this extent the revolution in French prosody introduced an external force. By contrast, the revolution in English prosody, if there was to be one, would have to come from within—as in fact it did with Gerard Manley Hopkins.

The impact of his new departures can hardly be exaggerated. It is apparent not only in the influence of his "sprung rhythm" upon the general sound of contemporary English verse but also in the elaboration of internal rime, assonance, and alliteration, for example. Such devices had of course been used for centuries, but Hopkins' especial way of using them has had much to do with the confidence with which twentieth-century poets have altered the basic iambic. Alongside Hopkins', the innovations of Owen and of Auden seem marginal, though they too are part of the general revolution in prosody—as was Imagist free verse and the shortlived "polyphonic prose"—as are also the yet unchristened devices in the poems of the latest magazines. We have now become so accustomed to experiments in versification that we no longer stop to appreciate that it was not always so. Yet fifty years ago they were scattered and few. One has only to compare the look of the page in anthologies of 1900 and 1960—in English, French, German, Spanish, Italian—to see how much the revolution in prosody has achieved.

Examples are scarcely needed: they are our monthly and quarterly fare. Let us look instead at some evidences of departures from the basic tradition itself, and first at the attempt to move verse in the direction of prose, which is part of a larger fascination with the blurring of distinctions among literary forms. The following stanzas come toward the close of "Poème à l'Étrangère":

Mais ce soir de grand âge et de grande patience, dans l'Été lourd d'opiates et d'obscures laitances, pour délivrer à fond d'abîme le peuple de vos lampes, ayant, homme très seul, pris par ce haut quartier de Fondations d'aveugles, de Réservoirs mis au linceul et de vallons en cage pour les morts, longeant les grilles et les lawns et tous ces beaux jardins à l'italienne

dont les maîtres un soir s'en furent épouvantés d'un parfum de sépulcre, . . .

The poet is Saint-John Perse. Paul Claudel might also serve as an example, but not Robinson Jeffers, for all his range and sonal complexity. Perhaps the French language lends itself particularly to the verse paragraph. Not that such structures are entirely absent from English, but that they tend to appear more readily in fiction and as passages rather than as works complete in themselves. Yet what one might call "prose-directed verse" is by no means lacking in English. It can be noted in the general sound of such a passage as the following by Auden, on Sigmund Freud:

> And if something of the autocratic pose,
> The paternal strictness he distrusted, still
>   Clung to his utterance and features,
>   It was a protective imitation
>
> For one who lived among enemies so long;
> If often he was wrong and at times absurd,
>   To us he is no more a person
>   Now but a whole climate of opinion. . . .[1]

One can disregard the line-breaks and read this as prose—and it is prose of a kind till the line-breaks insist and one is back again in verse. The experience differs with the work of Marianne Moore, whose poems can be scanned if not by stress then by syllable. Such verse has uniqueness of sound because it has appropriated some of the muscularities of prose:

> I, too, dislike it: there are things that are important
>   beyond all this fiddle.
>   Reading it, however, with a perfect contempt for it, one discovers in
>   it, after all, a place for the genuine.
>   Hands that can grasp, eyes
>   that can dilate, hair that can rise
>   if it must, these things are important not because a

---

[1] Copyright, 1940, by W. H. Auden. Reprinted from *The Collected Poetry of W. H. Auden* by permission of Random House, Inc.

high-sounding interpretation can be put upon them but because they are
useful. When they become so derivative as to become unintelligible,
the same thing may be said for all of us, that we
>   do not admire what
>   we cannot understand: . . .[1]

A quite contrary phenomenon in the general revolution can be
traced to the popular song. Modern French is especially rich with
examples—from Verlaine and Corbière to Apollinaire and Aragon—
and instances can also be found in English, but most often in
passages used for ironic effect. Entire poems are rare, except, of course,
for the proletarian satires of Kenneth Fearing, with their heavily
syncopated rhythms:

> But just the same, baby, and never forget,
>   it takes a neat, smart, fast, good, sweet doublecross
>   to doublecross the gentleman who doublecrossed the gentleman
>   who doublecrossed
>   your doublecrossing, doublecrossing, doublecross friend.

Or:

> And wow he died as wow he lived,
>   going whop to the office and blooie home to sleep and biff
>   got married and bam had children and oof got fired,
>   zowie did he live and zowie did he die . . .

From such jazz versification to *Un Coup de Dés* is as far as sound can
ever get from sight, and yet Mallarmé's final poem was part of the
same revolution, no doubt the most drastic attempt of all. Whether or
not we try to read it only with the silent ear, the white spaces, indenta-
tions, italics, capitals all demand to be "heard." Mallarmé read the
poem to him, said Valéry, in a low, even voice—which seems entirely
opposed to the theory expounded in the preface by the poet. As
Wallace Fowlie remarks:

By the appearance of the poem, the thought reveals its very life; its hesitations,
prolongations, designs, disappearances. Such and such a word [demands]
large print and a whole page for itself. Each word, each space, each silence has
to be apprehended.[2]

---

[1] Copyright, 1935, by Marianne Moore. Reprinted from *Collected Poems* by
Marianne Moore, by permission of the Macmillan Company.

[2] *Mallarmé*, Univ. of Chicago Press, 1953, pp. 219-20 *passim*.

An English-speaking reader who looks at *Un Coup de Dés* inevitably relates it to the typographical arrangements frequent in Cummings' poetry. But, as Norman Friedman makes clear, Cummings does not use typographic devices as part of an *attempt to equal* things, actions, feelings, or ideas. In the grasshopper poem that begins:

r-p-o-p-h-e-s-s-a-g-r

who

a)s w(e loo)k

upnowgath

PPEGORHRASS

"it is rather that the spacing is governed by the disruption and blending of syllables and the pause and emphasis of meaning which produce a figurative equivalent for the subject of the poem, as the reader reads in time."[1]

Thinking over the last few pages, a reader may object that the "what" has been omitted from discussions of the "how"—and of course *as the poem* the two are one. But must it always be declaimed that neither "form" nor "content" can exist except as terms, terms to denote ways of abstracting? Only in such an imagined sense can a poem be said to have structures of sound, syntax, and the like, for the poem is not a verbal amalgam which analysis takes apart. If critics seem to assume the contrary, it is only because they look and try to know at separated times and from separated stances. To experience a poem is a quite different action, in which critical knowing plays no part.

3

Approaching our third revolution, we face the fiercest of controversies, for this is the upheaval in poetic communication as a whole and specifically in its referents. Here we meet the end-result of the poets' decision to turn inward, to reject the world at large for their private worlds. And since the poet writes of his purely private universe, its points of reference—its objects and experiences—must inevitably be obscure, if not meaningless, to those outside. Now, poetry has to some degree always been clouded with allusions to matters of private import to the writer; nevertheless people assume that in the decent days of yore poets felt honor-bound to be understandable whereas modern

---

[1] *e.e. cummings*, Johns Hopkins Press, 1960, p. 123.

poets delight to "mean" only to themselves. Readers wishing to penetrate the obscurity may try, but the poet will not help them. He writes whatever he pleases, never caring whether his referents mean something or nothing to anyone but himself.

The charge is of course not new. Ben Johnson sneered: "Nothing is fashionable till it be deform'd; and this is to write like a gentleman." Chapman, himself no "easy" poet, had little patience with contrived obscurity, but he was careful to declare that where obscurity "shroudeth itself in the heart of the subject, uttered with fitness of figure, and expressive epithets; with that darkness will I still labour to be shadowed"—(a statement that Perse might have cited today in his Nobel Prize speech of acceptance). Samuel Johnson offered a typically sane distinction: ". . . words are only hard to those who do not understand them, and the critic ought always to enquire whether he is incommoded by the fault of the writer or by his own." And he added: "Every author does not write for every reader." This remark could have served excellently a century later in France, if poets had been willing to own up to what they were doing. But of course they were not—and they counter-attacked. "The profane multitude I hate," Chapman had said. Mallarmé preferred to use the colder word "disdain."

But is there occasion for such fire or ice? Is it not rather that a gap must grow between the vanguard and those in the rear, till the space can narrow or close? How else explain that the very same poems once thought of as "hard" can be taken as "easy" today? Not that a reader could be blamed for finding them once impossible to enter. The poems were obscure because the poet had made them so—but not out of wilful desire to be hermetic. For a writer of verse is often faced with an irreducible choice between "clarity" and "truth": he can retain one at the sacrifice of the other. Dare he allow the "understandable" statement to remain when it is not what he feels he must say? If, faced with such a choice, he decided to keep the obscure version, it is only because the clear statement is unacceptable as untrue. The literature of the past is overladen with such troubled choices, and the responsibility all too often can be traced to the limits of language itself.

Although comprehensibility is essentially a matter of such "choice," it is so only to a degree. Certain statements that are difficult for another person to follow may nevertheless continue to feel right to the poet; to alter them is to falsify. A writer of verse is likely to be compelled to let such an obscure passage stand, for poetry is feeling, and a poet, like everyone else in an uncertain situation, will act out of faith. Trusting his feelings, he must take the consequences: that his unaltered words will mean very little to most people or evoke even hostility and contempt. It is time that this much-argued problem were recognized in its context of struggle. In the last analysis, obscurity involves purely moral problems that only the poet can decide.[1]

Turning now to specific instances, we distinguish three main sources of "difficulty" whose results are visible everywhere in Western verse today. The gaps are still large, although narrower than they were at one time. But whether they will ever quite close, who would dare to predict?

The first of the three sub-revolutions was—paradoxical as it sounds— a deliberate attempt to enrich the communicative content of language by expunging the unessential words. Such removal of connectives gave rise to baffling images, yet these same images carried a new type of content in accordance with a new set of communicative principles sponsored by the high-priest Mallarmé. "To *name* an object is to do away with three-quarters of the enjoyment of the poem, which is derived from the satisfaction of guessing little by little; to *suggest* it, to *evoke* it—this is what charms the imagination," this is the ideal. Now, the difference between naming and suggesting is the difference between communicating to the reader and offering him something to unriddle. So far as Mallarmé is concerned, the poem ought to be "a mystery to which the reader will hunt the key," and his emphasis is upon the mystery; for poets who "take the thing just as it is and put it before us . . . are consequently deficient in mystery: they deprive the mind of the delicious joy of believing that it is creating." One can give the mind such joy by removing the clues, by deliberately stripping away the words that would present the thing "just as it is."

Which is precisely what Mallarmé continued to do, and with dedication unsurpassed in the history of art. He presented words and phrases as entities, almost wholly detached from other words and phrases. Words were no longer to serve as names for objects; they were to be objects in themselves. And existing as objects within the poem, they would develop new interrelations and therefore give rise to new and

---

[1] This paragraph and the four sentences that precede it first appeared in my *Early and Late Testament*, Dial Press, 1952, pp. vi-vii.

unpredictable reverberations—and to new meanings, of which the poet himself would not be aware as he watched them interacting, displaying a life of their own. This was creative writing of an altogether new kind; the poet as proverbial "maker" was now making something that had never been made before: he was disposing live materials. And these live materials produced different messages when arranged in different sequences. No wonder Mallarmé could regard them with a certain reverence. They were creations that would speak to him: as he rearranged them in the line, they would say different things, reveal new meanings, unclear and multiple, inexhaustible and ever elusive. Mallarmé had suddenly acquired a power analogous to God's, with each poem a new universe of his own making. This was angelism *par excellence;* and Mallarmé never stopped exploring its possibilities, drawing on typography, blank spaces, and everything else he could think of, as his final act of angelism bears witness in *Un Coup de Dés.*

For readers the end-results of this type of creativity are usually too bewildering to draw them in. Mallarmé might be concerned with producing "an orphic explanation of the Earth," but readers are interested only in poems that will speak to them, which is what Mallarmé's most extreme experiments quite fail to do. When faced, for example, with his sonnet "À la nue accablante tu," they must either apply themselves with immense and patient labor or throw up their hands. For the fourteen lines at first glance defy unriddling, with the subject (sepulchral shipwreck) delayed till line 5 and the main verb (abolishes) till line 8.[1] And even after studying the explications, they may flounder forever in uncertainties. Despite the fascination of the artistry and its strangeness, readers will doubt that the game was worth the striving. It is the sort of poem that may offer no future for poetry as a whole: the beginning and the end of its own tradition.

But its legacy is very much alive, having been adapted and refined by the disciple Valéry. Not the angelism, of course, but the enrichment of communicative content by detaching the image from its referent. A good example is the first quatrain of "L'Abeille":

> Quelle, et si fine, et si mortelle,
> Que soit ta pointe, blonde abeille,
> Je n'ai, sur ma tendre corbeille,
> Jeté qu'un songe de dentelle.

---

[1] Fowlie, *op. cit.,* pp. 216 f.

(However, so sharp and so deadly, / Be your point, blond bee, / I have, upon my tender basket, / Thrown only a dream of lace.)

To what does "tendre corbeille" (tender basket) refer? It is not tied to anything, it floats free in the sentence: what can it mean? This depends on the reader, on what he chooses to attach to it: only he can do the attaching. Valéry has not done it; he has left it carefully unanchored. Possibilities come to mind at once—roundness, flesh, soft curve of the body, fruit, ripeness, garden—but these are speculations, and *the* meaning remains obscure. But it is obscurity of a special kind, for the very indefiniteness of relation between image and referent sets up multiple reverberations. This vagueness thus contributes a special type of poetic pleasure which is further enriched by the resonances of such other words in the stanza as "fine," "mortelle," "blonde," "songe," "dentelle" (sharp, deadly, blond, dream, lace). One encounters such potentialities wherever indefiniteness is cultivated as an end in itself: toward enrichment. Hence we find ourselves making a paradoxical remark about this stanza, as we should about Valéry's "La Jeune Parque," whose emotionally colored words often can be taken to refer to a number of different objects at once: we say that if the images and referents were more definite, the poetry would diminish in richness.

We have traveled a long way from Pre-Symbolist communication, in which at least one clear tie can be adduced between image and referent. We are in a new universe of relations among the parts in a poem, where ties are merely suggested by images that condense a variety of meanings and hold them suspended upon others. A world in which the poet assumes that his readers will look for the meanings because they feel they are there, both beneath and within the words, and therefore also between.

This Symbolist development calls to mind other modes of compression, exemplified in such lines as Allen Tate's "We are the eyelids of defeated caves"; César Vallejo's "Poetry of the purple cheek bone / between saying and not saying"; Rilke's figure of Night, the "tender disillusioning," who is "painfully there." [1] Our best-known example is Hart Crane's "At Melville's Tomb," with its opening statement:

---

[1] Vallejo: "Poesia del pómulo morado, entre el decirlo / y el callarlo." Rilke: "sanft enttäuschende," "mühsam bevorsteht"—sometimes given in English as "mild enchantress," "wearily" (or "laboriously") "present" (or, more literally, "impending").

"Often beneath the wave, wide from this ledge / The dice of drowned men's bones he saw bequeath / An embassy," and his own explanation:

Dice bequeath an embassy, in the first place, by being ground (in this connection only, of course) in little cubes from the bones of drowned men by the action of the sea, and are finally thrown up on the sand, having "numbers" but no identification. These being the bones of dead men who never completed their voyage, it seems legitimate to refer to them as the only surviving evidence of certain messages undelivered, mute evidence of certain things, experiences that the dead mariners might have had to deliver. Dice as a symbol of chance and circumstance is also implied.

Alongside the verse of earlier periods, the modern varieties are spectacularly condensed, but not only as a result of such means as we have been noting. Certain poems are arrays of discrete details, no more conjoined than a series of cinema stills. Others come from the page with the seemingly simultaneous impact of dream, as a *Gestalt* of "presences." How classify so simple a poem as Quasimodo's "Antico Inverno"?

> Desiderio delle tue mani chiare
> nella penombra della fiamma:
> sapevano di rovere e di rose;
> di morte. Antico inverno.
>
> Cercavano il miglio gli uccelli
> ed erano subito di neve;
> così le parole.
> Un po' di sole, una raggera d'angelo,
> e poi la nebbia; e gli alberi,
> e noi fatti d'aria al mattino.[1]

(The desire for [of] your hands, transparent / in the penumbra of the flame: / they had the fragrance of oak and of roses; / of death. Ancient winter.

The birds were looking for millet / and they were suddenly of snow; / so [with] words. / A little sun, an angel's halo, / and then the mist; and the trees, / and ourselves made of air at morning.)

Largely because of the bewildering varieties of compression, critics have been busily explicating poems—sometimes to the surprise of their authors, occasionally to their dismay. But one might wonder where readers would be without such help.

---

[1] Reprinted from *Ed E' Subito Sera* by permission of Arnoldo Mondadori Editore, copyright 1942.

Our second sub-revolution can also be traced to France, specifically to a member of the Romantic generation. As early as 1837, Gérard de Nerval spoke of his desire "to compress years of anguish, dreams, and projects into a sentence, a word," but it was not till the end of his career that he succeeded—with a handful of incomparably beautiful and cryptic sonnets. Their difficulty comes not from missing links but from symbols and allusions that cannot possibly be understood without recourse to the poet's autobiographical prose writings and related materials. Take, for example, the opening of "El Desdichado." The Spanish title means "The Unfortunate One" or "The Outcast," and for some critics these meanings epitomize the poem. For others, however, the title means "The Disinherited," coming supposedly from the inscription on the shield of the mysterious knight in *Ivanhoe*. Thus a reader begins with two different keys, and his choice will affect the first line in particular:

> Je suis le Ténébreux,—le Veuf,—l'Inconsolé,
> Le Prince d'Aquitaine à la Tour abolie:
> Ma seule *Étoile* est morte,—et mon luth constellé
> Porte le Soleil noir de la *Mélancolie*.

(I am the Dark [the Shadow], the Widowed, the Unconsoled, / The Prince of Aquitania of the ruined tower: / My only *Star* is dead—and my starred lute / Bears the black Sun of *Melancholy*.)

Line 2 can be explained by Nerval's claim of descent from an old southern family whose titles of nobility were abolished in the Revolution and whose coat of arms bore Three Towers Argent. But Nerval was supposedly born under the sign of Plutus; hence "El Desdichado" is an incarnation of Plutus and the "ruined tower" can be taken to be the "castle of Plutus" or number XVI of Court de Gébelin's tarot cards, which represents a tower full of gold and falling in ruins. And so it goes —with the Star, the constellated lute, the black Sun of Melancholy: readers have more than they can manage before they reach line 5. They must ultimately depend on their own imaginative interpretations, of course, for a poem is much more than the sum of its symbols and allusions even when these can be looked up in the poet's private code-book. Nerval was writing a poem to be experienced by others as a poem. No wonder, then, that each reader becomes his own authority, once he has listened to all the scholars.

Such composition by private symbols calls to mind the case of Yeats's *A Vision*. Unlike Nerval, who could allude to myth and to public and private events simultaneously, Yeats organized a complicated system of symbols into twenty-eight "phases," comprehending the individual, history, and the universe. To what extent he thought it essential to read his poems in terms of this system, we may doubt; and in any case his work can be read without such help. But not entirely: a few symbols recur, and the poetry enlarges once they are understood. But no less important are references to persons, places, and events which have nothing to do with a code-book. Other allusions explain themselves— "Byzantium" becomes both an actual city and a symbol peculiar to this poet. On the other hand, the recurring "gyre" grows in the mind of the reader once he appreciates its symbolic force in Yeats's work as a whole.

Every artist makes use of personal symbols to the extent that he creates his own cosmology in which certain images accumulate heightened meanings. They reveal themselves in their almost obsessive recurrence as though the artist could never quite encompass all that they stand for. Such symbols, though personal, are nevertheless public, in being accessible to anyone who reads the poetry; whereas private symbols, such as those of Nerval and Yeats, must be illuminated from outside the verse. How many devoted readers of Rilke could have grasped the import of his "Angels" and "Night" and "Narcissus," for example, without the comments of scholars?

The same question may be asked in regard to our last sub-revolution, which gives rise to a poetry of "appropriated effects." Its most famous example is found of course in *The Waste Land*. Forster dubbed the conclusion a "scrap-heap of quotation," and, as everyone knows, the last eleven lines are made up entirely of original passages transplanted from five different languages. Poets have always referred to materials in the storehouse of literature, myth, and religion, but Keats's Ruth who "stood in tears amid the alien corn" and Tennyson's "Now lies the Earth all Danaë to the stars" are allusions: they are not quotations from other men's writings. Mark Van Doren takes a line from *King Lear* to entitle a poem "Down from the Waist They Are Centaurs." MacLeish goes earlier, to Villon, for "L'an trentiesme de mon aage." As J. Isaacs points out, Edith Sitwell places "O Ile leape up to my God," from *Faustus*, in her poem "Still Falls the Rain" as Marlowe himself

had done with a line from Ovid ("O lente, lente currite, noctis equi!").
Whether or not he learned it from Dante, Eliot, says Isaacs,

has taught modern poets . . . that method of incorporating a line from some
other poet, or some other language, deftly converted, deftly conveyed, its
license-plates so altered that its own proprietor would hardly recognise it. It is a
device used not for mere decoration, or even wit, but to produce reverberations
of meaning, and above all of feeling.[1]

Like the other two sub-revolutions in referents, this third one gives
rise to obscurities; but these can be clarified easily, by telling the reader
where he can find the originals. Such acknowledgment is accepted
practice in scholarly prose; why not use it for scholarly poetry as well?
For how else should a reader know, for example, that Eliot's "To purify
the dialect of the tribe" (*Little Gidding*) refers to Mallarmé's "Donner un
sens plus pur aux mots de la tribu" ("Le Tombeau d'Edgar Poe")?
How expect a reader to respond as he should to the secondary effect
unless he can experience the primary source in its context? A poet may
shrink in horror from the notion of footnotes, but this would be an odd
kind of delicacy in one who appropriates the effects of others to produce
his own. And much as he might like to believe such passages to be
self-sufficing, he knows what they owe to the original context from
which they were lifted—as he knows that reproducing them is less
a matter of creating than of editing.

4

To speak in a few pages of a century and a half of poetry is to slight
some figures and omit a great many others. We could point to angelism,
for example, in at least one poem by Frost ("I Could Give All to Time"),
perhaps in others; to appropriated effects in Stevens; to popular songs
in Brecht; to floating images in Montale; to private symbols in Alberti
—we can add case after case after case, but where do we stop?[2] And

---

[1] *The Background of Modern Poetry*, Dutton, 1958, pp. 64-69 *passim*.

[2] Example, regarding prosody: we have said nothing of such notable matters as
the "trans-sense" experiments of the Russians (*zaumni*); the study of physiological
mimicry, through the body's muscles, as a series of rhythmic metaphors; the views
of T. S. Eliot on the way a poem or a passage "may tend to realise itself first as a
particular rhythm before it reaches expression in words" in relation to Shelley's
practice (as noted by Isaacs, *op. cit.*, p. 102); the "versets" of Claudel, Whitman,
and others.

except by remarking the most striking shifts of the course, how keep track of the mainstream and its meanings?

What was once the menacing wildness of the few subsides into norms for the many. And hindsight shows why this had to happen: that an upheaval in one area would cause upheavals in others; that once a revolution had built up enough momentum, it would run its full course regardless of what it might overwhelm as it ran. Once he knew his direction, Mallarmé strove for greater and greater allusiveness and concision—compare the early (1864) and final (1887) versions of "Le Pitre Châtié"! Others in this age of discovery that was always just starting would take advantage of virtually anything novel—that something had never been done before was itself sure proof of its value. Apollinaire, at the last moment, deleted all punctuation from the proofs of *Alcools* (the verse had been punctuated in the manuscript given to the printer), with results as "new" as those he later sought by expunging all verbal connectives. No wonder he came to regard Baudelaire as limited. He was indeed, compared to his literary grandchildren—the Surrealists, for example, who tried to produce incongruous images and succeeded. What had begun as fascinated concern with multiple latent meanings could in time dispense with all notions of "primary" and "secondary," so that with Jarry all the meanings are on one plane: simultaneous, whole. We are now at the end of the line, where every meaning is equally important and true.

Such a point was bound to be reached, once the Unconscious had been opened up to dazzle all eyes with its treasures. "I believe only in what I do not see, and solely in what I feel," said Gustave Moreau. "Only inner mood seems to me eternal and undeniably sure." If undeniably sure, then all it contains must be sacred and all its productions equally true and important. Better yet: if totally laid bare and used with absolute courage, the Unconscious might bring in a new and greater reality, through the fusion of waking reality with dream.

To achieve this super-reality was, of course, the aim of the Surrealist poets gathered around André Breton, whose 1924 manifesto makes the direction appear to be quite unprecedented. But viewed historically, Surrealism was actually the last of the three stages of Unconscious exploring, begun by the Romantics and broadened by the Symbolists. Even some of its particulars had already emerged—in *Ubu Roi* (1896), in Apollinaire's startling verbal combinations (he had even used the term "surrealism" in his text for *Parade*). Dream and reality might be fused into a sur-reality by means of images bringing together the most far-fetched elements; the more they were unrelated, the greater their power in combination—such as Breton's "Eternity is searching for a wrist watch / A little before midnight by the waterfront" or "This morning the daughter of the mountain is holding upon her knees an accordion of white bats" or Eluard's "Along the walls furnished with decrepit orchestras / Darting their ears of lead toward the daylight / On guard for a caress mingled with the thunderbolt." Aragon, as one of its exponents, could refer to Surrealism as a "trial of language," but this is a very special kind of "trial." "Through the word," says Anna Balakian,

the impossible is made possible, nature can be endowed with metaphysical properties, sensuality takes on new proportions: visions dispersed on the face of the earth, going a-begging, undiscerned in their individual solitudes, are drawn to a new linguistic magnet and brought together into a new synthesis of imagery which in turn creates a new synthesis of existence. . . . language creates, it makes concrete the ineffable dream, it establishes the promised land, it enables man to discover the absolute. . . .[1]

But not just by reading, for a Surrealist poem demands active creativity on the part of the reader: he must bring to the poet's images his own thoughts, collaborating in its fulfilment. Hence the extremely compressed language and the absence of evident meaning, all within conventional syntax.

After ten years of heady activity, the movement broke up and the members went their separate ways. Was it a premature victim of menacing war and fascism in the middle thirties? or had Surrealism, after making its contribution to the later work of Eluard, Aragon, and others, quite exhausted its power for good and entered history? Today there is something incredible in its stance, particularly in the bedazzlement of some of its poets as they contemplated the Unconscious. Actually not much time was needed before scales could fall from the eyes, so that they could see that this vastest of sources was, like all human thinking, a mixture of everything that enters through the fallible organs of sense: wisdom and foolishness; truth, half-truth, and deception. One could explore and exploit it in countlessly different ways—to

---

[1] *Surrealism: the road to the absolute*, Noonday Press, 1959, p. 137.

open and lay bare was hardly enough. Writing at the time Surrealism had begun, Claudel insisted, in regard to one of its ancestors, that "The aim of poetry is not, as Baudelaire says, to plunge 'to the depths of the Infinite in quest of something new,' but rather to the depths of the definite to find the inexhaustible." Not many years later Wallace Stevens could declare that "the essential fault of Surrealism is that it invents without discovering," a distinction applicable to other movements as well.[1]

But if poetry began to retreat from its extreme position in regard to the Unconscious, it was only as a means for making a new advance: of another type, with the help of increased knowledge, and with undefensive awareness that what has been learned thus far may be only a beginning.[2] A beginning that traces its descent from earlier views of the relation of the self to the world outside, attitudes concerned less with exploring than with joining. They differ basically from notions of a physical merging with the infinite through death (as reported of Shelley and the sea), for the fusion is wholly an extension of living awareness. The wall between man and the world disappears, as in moments of mystical ecstasy, but without such union with God as the mystics avow. The "secular" quality comes through in Mallarmé's "Ma pensée se pense" (My thought thinks itself) and in Baudelaire's "What a delight to drown one's gaze in the immensity of the sky and sea . . . all those things think through me, or I through them (for in the vastness of revery, the I quickly loses itself). . . ." Roger Shattuck calls this

one of Baudelaire's most lucid moments, a purely self-reflexive perception. Henri Michaux, a poet writing eighty years later, disciplines himself to abdicate his personality and attains the same reversal of consciousness, the same simultaneous attunement: "One no longer dreams, one is dreamed."[3]

---

[1] It is as easy to mistake Surrealism's will to innovate as merely an effort to be original as it is to undervalue its achievements as a catalytic agent in twentieth-century writing: to ignore its extremely enriching effect upon writers outside the movement.

[2] E.g., *Hermès*, the journal published in France from 1933 to 1939, and recently revived; also such a work as *Connaissances par les Gouffres*, Paris, 1961, by Henri Michaux.

[3] *The Banquet Years*, Anchor Books edition, 1961, pp. 350 ff.

This is not the same thing as Rilke's

> Durch alle Wesen reicht der *eine* Raum:
> Weltinnenraum. Die Vögel fliegen still
> durch uns hindurch. O, der ich wachsen will,
> ich seh hinaus, und *in* mir wächst der Baum. . . .

(Through all things that exist [all beings] the *single* space spreads [reaches, stretches]: / World Inner Space. The birds silently fly / right through us. Oh, I who would [wants to] grow, / I look outside, and *within* me the tree grows. . . .)

for Rilke believes that external phenomena "Want us to change them entirely, within our invisible hearts, / Into—oh endlessly—into ourselves! whosoever we may be after all."[1] Yet in terms of poetry, the basic belief in the continuity of the self and the world outside is the same. Baudelaire prefigured it when he called the modern conception of pure art "a suggestive magic which contains both the subject and the object, the external world and the artist himself." It has also come to be the view of philosophers and scientists for whom "subject-and-object" are no longer valid distinctions and common-sense notions of time no longer true. The West has taken centuries to arrive at this awareness, and yet it has always suffused the act of poetic creation with a "feeling-knowledge" too large to need to be stated. Perhaps it is also found, at least in embryo, in well-known pronouncements by Romantic poets on the unity in diversity and the kinships underlying even the most recondite phenomena—except that now both the disparate and the perceiver are also one.

What happens next? What will be the course of the poetry of the post-modern period already begun? If one is not obliged to announce which grains will grow and which will not, he can dare to look into the seeds of time and timidly mutter that revolutions have often seemed to turn into their opposites. A not impossible direction, after all that has been done in the last hundred and fifty years, for what is there left to try that hasn't been tried? Little, perhaps—or perhaps a tremendous amount. But whatever the attempt, post-modern poets will not be able to reject the world at large, unless they learn ways to escape from a Nature that may be annihilated. A dozen years ago an age of anxiety gave way to an age of responsibility: its poetry cannot avert the central

---

[1] Wollen, wir sollen sie ganz im unsichtbaren Herzen verwandeln / in—o unend-lich!—in uns! Wer wir am Ende auch seien.

drive—toward a confrontation of the self that fulfills its power or dies. Poems of such general direction can be found in the books of the last century and a half, and we post-moderns begin with this heritage, one whose huge variety and complex richness are yet to be spread out and comprehended—and not by means of an essay of thirty possibly arbitrary pages.

S.B.

This essay was first published in *The Sewanee Review* (summer 1962) and republished in *Varieties of Literary Experience* (New York University Press, 1962).

FRENCH

EL DESDICHADO

Je suis le Ténébreux, — le Veuf, — l'Inconsolé,
Le Prince d'Aquitaine à la Tour abolie:
Ma seule *Étoile* est morte, — et mon luth constellé
Porte le Soleil noir de la *Mélancolie*.   4

Dans la nuit du Tombeau, Toi qui m'as consolé,
Rends-moi le Pausilippe et la mer d'Italie,
La fleur qui plaisait tant à mon cœur désolé,
Et la treille où le Pampre à la Rose s'allie.   8

Suis-je Amour ou Phébus?... Lusignan ou Biron?
Mon front est rouge encor du baiser de la Reine;
J'ai rêvé dans la Grotte où nage la Sirène ...

Et j'ai deux fois vainqueur traversé l'Achéron: 12
Modulant tour à tour sur la lyre d'Orphée
Les soupirs de la Sainte et les cris de la Fée.

(Les filles du feu. 1854)

Though he lived during the period of the Romantics, Gérard de Nerval (1808-1855) is today considered a precursor of all modern French poets, thanks to his mysterious suggestive power, his lyrical alchemy, his enigmatic symbols, and his pursuit of "dream overflowing into real life." From the point of view of literary form, one of his most important accomplishments was a revival of the sonnet; as early as 1837 he spoke of his desire to "compress years of anguish, dreams, and projects into a sentence, a word." How remarkably he succeeded may be observed in our three selections. Each line is so tightly woven as to be almost a miniature poem in itself. Each line moves to the next, not by rhetoric or eloquence, but as one vision is replaced by another.

The Spanish title *"El desdichado"*— "The Unfortunate One," "The Outcast" —epitomizes the sonnet's statement of the poet's destiny. (1) *I am the Dark (the Shadow)—the Widowed—the Unconsoled,* (2) *The Prince of Aquitania whose Tower has been destroyed* [literally *of the ruined Tower*]: (3) *My only Star is dead—and my starred lute* (4) *Bears the black Sun of Melancholy.* Of the "characters" that it has been the poet's fate to assume, the quasi-allegorical figures of the first line give way to the vague Aquitanian prince stripped of all his possessions (the French original forms line 430 of *The Waste Land*). His bereavement is explained by the death of his "only Star," the fused symbol of both his religious and erotic loves, at once the guide in his search for God and the embodiment of the various forms of his Beloved

Woman. Thus Nerval's tragic destiny is like that of the world itself, which, according to an ancient belief, would come to an end when the fire of the sun was extinguished.

Suddenly the gloom of the first quatrain gives way to the brilliant sunlight of the Bay of Naples, as he cries out to his "only Star": (5) *In my darkest night* [literally *night of the Tomb*], *you who [once] consoled me,* (6) *Give me back Posilippo and the Italian Sea,* (7) *The flower that used to please my grief-stricken heart so much,* (8) *And the arbor where the Vine and the Rose are entwined.* He implores the "Star" to bring him surcease from care (the etymological meaning assigned by some to *Posilippo*), the sunlit calm of the Italian Sea, the certain unnamed flower which was mysteriously significant for him, and the lost power he once possessed (symbolized by the union of Bacchus —the Vine—and Venus—the Rose).

Seeking now to identify the forces that control him, he asks: (9) *Am I Eros or Phoebus? . . . Lusignan or Biron?* Eros-Lusignan is contrasted with Phoebus-Biron in a question which may be understood as: "Am I essentially a lover or a poet? If a lover, have I been a successful one, like Biron, or only a lover of nymphs, like Lusignan?" Eros is paired with Lusignan, because both of them lost their loved ones—Eros lost Psyche when, disobeying his decree, she lighted her lamp to look at him; Lusignan, a mortal, lost his water-sprite wife Mélusine when, disobeying her decree, he intruded upon her on a Saturday. Phoebus, god of light and poetry, is paired with the celebrated Perigordian hero Biron, who was later immortalized in the song "*Quand Biron voulut danser.*"

The question of line 9—"Am I essentially a lover or a poet?"—is immediately answered in two images that complete the first tercet: (10) *My brow is still red with the kiss of the Queen;* (11) *I have dreamed in the Cave where the Mermaid swims.* He still feels the queen's kiss—which is to say that he is Eros rather than Phoebus. And he has dreamed in the cave of the mermaids —he is Lusignan, then, rather than Biron.

But he is Phoebus-Biron as well. Turning to this other god-and-hero pair, he begins to reflect upon his achievement. (12) *And twice a victor have I crossed the Acheron:* (13) *Modulating in turn on the Orphic lyre* (14) *The sighs of the Saint and the Fairy's cries.* He has survived death twice—twice he has crossed the River Styx—and like the Thracian poet Orpheus, who sang of his lost Eurydice, he has celebrated in verse the many forms taken by his Beloved Woman—the Star, Queen, Mermaid, Saint, and Fairy.

If few poems have been more widely praised than "*El desdichado,*" none has given rise to sharper differences in interpretation. Virtually every word has been tracked down in the hope of revealing the true meaning of this cornerstone work of Nerval's career. Is the poet's own identification of certain allusions the most dependable approach? Must one rather read the poem literally as autobiography? One may wonder what Nerval would have thought of such disputation, in view of his statement that the poems of his last two books *perdraient de leur charme à être expliqués, si la chose était possible* ("would lose their charm in being explained, if such a thing were possible"). [J.W.K.]

GÉRARD DE NERVAL

DELFICA

La connais-tu, Dafné, cette ancienne romance,
Au pied du sycomore, ou sous les lauriers blancs,
Sous l'olivier, le myrte, ou les saules tremblants,
Cette chanson d'amour qui toujours recommence? . . .   4

Reconnais-tu le *Temple* au péristyle immense,
Et les citrons amers où s'imprimaient tes dents,
Et la grotte, fatale aux hôtes imprudents,
Où du dragon vaincu dort l'antique semence? . . .   8

Ils reviendront, ces Dieux que tu pleures toujours!
Le temps va ramener l'ordre des anciens jours;
La terre a tressailli d'un souffle prophétique . . .

Cependant la sibylle au visage latin   12
Est endormie encor sous l'arc de Constantin
— Et rien n'a dérangé le sévère portique.

(Petits châteaux de Bohême. 1852)

The original title of this poem, when it first appeared in 1845, was *"Vers dorés"* ("Gilded Verses"). Later it was changed to *"Daphné"* and, finally, to *"Delfica,"* a priestess invented by the author. The epigraph of the first version —*Ultima Cumaei venit iam carminis aetas,* "Now comes the last age foretold by the Cumaean sibyl"—was replaced in the second—by *Iam redit et virgo,* "And now the virgin returns." Although abandoned in the final version, both these quotations from the opening of Virgil's "Fourth Eclogue" indicate that Gérard de Nerval wanted this sonnet to stand as a kind of oracle-poem in which Delfica would prophesy the return of pagan gods rather than the advent of Christianity, as Virgil's sibyl was interpreted by Constantine the Great to have done. Nerval repeatedly set forth his conviction that the Renaissance had prefigured a return to pagan beliefs, which would absorb Christianity without destroying it, much as Christianity had assimilated but not abolished polytheism. In a prose passage—"Isis," published with his *Les filles du feu (Daughters of Fire)*—he put this conviction in the form of a wish: "It would be so fine to rescue . . . the heroes and sages of antiquity from eternal maledictions."

"Delfica" appears to be another statement of Nerval's "syncretism," as he called his eclectic acceptance of all religions. Rather than rejecting any particular system of belief, it affirms that certain eternal forms and ideas persist in all religions and that though some of these forms may lie dormant at a particular period, they are always ready to emerge again as new religions emerge. The Delphic priestess makes such a prediction as she speaks to Daphne, the nymph beloved by Apollo, who was transformed at her own request into a laurel in order to escape his amorous designs.

(1) *Daphne, do you know that old song,* (2) *At the foot of the sycamore, or beneath the white laurels,* (3) *Under the olive, the myrtle, or the quivering willows,* (4) *That ever-recurring song of love? . . .* As they sway in the breeze, Apollo's favorite tree, Minerva's olive, Venus' myrtle, and the sycamore (a symbol of Christianity) all seem to be whispering the prophetic hymn.

But the signs are not in the heavens. They are in the temple that is filled with the mysterious presence of some pagan god—undoubtedly Apollo, since the scene is at Delphi. (5) *Do you recognize the* TEMPLE *with the immense peristyle,* (6) *And the bitter lemons marked by your teeth,* (7) *And the cave, fatal to rash visitors,* (8) *Where the conquered dragon's ancient seed is sleeping? . . .* The signs can be seen in the lemon that Daphne bites—a gesture not unlike that of the unfortunate poets in Mallarmé's "*Le guignon,*" who "bite into the golden lemon of the bitter ideal"—and in the cave that conceals the germs of this rebirth, germs which, like the seeds of the slain dragon of Cadmus, are ready to spring forth again.

The message of the signs is stated unequivocally in the three lines that follow: (9) *They will return, these gods for whom you still weep!* (10) *Time will restore the order of ancient days;* (11) *The earth has trembled with a prophetic blast (breath). . . .* Questions have now been replaced by impassioned assertions.

And yet outward appearances have not changed. The Arch of Constantine, symbol of Christianity's dominating power, stands stern and impassive, impervious to these veiled predictions: (12) *Meanwhile the Latin-faced sibyl* (13) *Still sleeps beneath the Arch of Constantine—* (14) *And nothing has disturbed the stern portico.*

The uniqueness of this sonnet lies in its combination of weighty themes with the tone and form of an almost sentimental song. The first two quatrains immediately call to mind one of the well-known arias from *Mignon—Connais-tu le pays?* ("Do you know the land?")—in which the heroine sings of a country of sunlight where there are laurel, myrtle, and lemon trees, and a large house with a tall, pillared porch. Each stanza of this aria ends with a refrain, slightly varied, " 'Tis there,' 'tis there! oh my beloved, I would go with you." To be sure, Nerval could not have known the Ambroise Thomas opera, for it was not produced until 1866, but he was familiar with Goethe's *Wilhelm Meister,* on which it is based. The theme—which was soon to reappear in Baudelaire's "*L'Invitation au voyage*" (p. 16) and "*La vie antérieure*"—is carried out with appropriate simplicity in the first eleven lines of our sonnet.

But what of the final tercet? Does it somehow "fall down"? Are readers justified who complain that the last three lines fail to combine with the first eleven to make of the poem a satisfying whole? Whatever its success as sustained art, "Delfica" has a further, historical interest: of lying almost at midpoint between Nerval's early songs and odelettes (whose mood and imagery it echoes) and the later *Chimères* (such as "*El desdichado,*" p. 2, and "*Artémis,*" p. 6), whose religious and philosophical strivings it foreshadows.

[J.W.K.]

ARTÉMIS

La Treizième revient . . . C'est encore la première;
Et c'est toujours la Seule, — ou c'est le seul moment:
Car es-tu Reine, ô Toi! la première ou dernière?
Es-tu Roi, toi le seul ou le dernier amant?   4

Aimez qui vous aima du berceau dans la bière;
Celle que j'aimai seul m'aime encore tendrement:
C'est la Mort — ou la Morte . . . O délice! ô tourment!
La rose qu'elle tient, c'est la *Rose trémière*.   8

Sainte napolitaine aux mains pleines de feux,
Rose au cœur violet, fleur de sainte Gudule:
As-tu trouvé ta Croix dans le désert des cieux?

Roses blanches, tombez! vous insultez nos Dieux,   12
Tombez, fantômes blancs, de votre ciel qui brûle:
— La sainte de l'abîme est plus sainte à mes yeux!

(*Les filles du feu*. 1854)

Regarded by many readers as the most beautiful of Nerval's sonnets, "Artemis" is surely the most difficult. And yet, although much of its incantatory effectiveness continues to elude analysis, the symbols of the poem are doubtless clearer to us today than they could have been to the author's contemporaries. Take the Artemis of the title, for example. Research leaves little question as to her intended identity. Of the several possible candidates, this Artemis is the moon deity and, specifically, the goddess of death and the lower world —Artemis-Hecate, *la sainte de l'abîme* ("the saint of the abyss") of the last line. It is to her that Nerval dedicated his meditation on death, a condensation of what was probably his final attitude toward religion.

In the opening line, life, like the shadow on a sundial, completes its span at the instant it passes from the twelfth hour to the next: (1) *The Thirteenth [hour] returns . . . It is still the first*. Depending on whether it is seen as completing a cycle or beginning a new one, it is the thirteenth hour or the first. Or is it both? In the dialectic of this poem, the words "first," "last," and "only" are synonymous: (2) *And it is still the Only one—or it is the only moment:* The poet repeats "first," "last," and "only" as a kind of exorcism to abolish the tyranny of time and to call forth the visions of the ensuing lines.

The first of these visions depicts the eternal drama of love. As we pointed out in connection with *"El desdichado"* (p. 2), Nerval loved only one woman, but she assumed a number of different forms. She is the Aurélia of the story of that name, the "only Star" of "El desdichado," and also the several figures evoked in the sonnet before us: (3) *For are you Queen, O You, [who are] the first or the last [woman]? (4) Are you King, you [who are] the sole or the last lover? (5) Love the one who loved you from the cradle to the grave; (6) The one I loved alone still loves me tenderly: (7) She is Death—or the Deceased (woman). . . . O delight! O torment! (8) The rose she holds is* THE ROSE MALLOW.

Opposite this "she"—the multiple Artemis of the poem—the poet looks at a projection of himself; and he asks whether he too is the first, the last, the unique lover, the hero of this drama. As these new figures pass before his eyes, he bids them love the eternal feminine principle that each of them embodies—to "love the one who loved you from the cradle to the grave" (5). The point of view shifts in the next line: the woman he alone loved still loves him tenderly, but she can be his only in death; indeed, she may be the incarnation of death. "Everlasting life"— the effect of *O délice!* (7) —bespeaks the certainty of this union, and "fatality"— the effect of *ô tourment!*—its opposite.

In the line that follows, the woman who will guide him in his hour of doubt bears in her hand (as she had done in *Aurélia*) a rose mallow, or hollyhock. (Etymologically, *trémière* (8) is a corruption of *trans mare:* "beyond the sea.") For Nerval, this common flower symbolizes, not Christianity, but the religions both before and beyond Christianity. Indeed, in the next five lines he repudiates Christian orthodoxy with unmistakable force: (9) *Neapolitan saint with hands full of fires [bearing light]*, (10) *Rose of the violet heart, Saint Gudula's flower:* (11) *Did you find your Cross [redemption] in the wilderness of the heavens?* (12) *White roses, fall! You insult our gods,* (13) *Fall, white phantoms, from your burning [vengeful] sky:* (14)—*The saint of the abyss is holier in my eyes.*

The "Neapolitan saint" (9), who has been identified as Rosalie of Palermo, is here related to Gudula, patron saint of Brussels, who is usually represented with a lantern—according to tradition, it went out and was then relighted by the Virgin's prayer. Nerval had originally written *sœur* ("sister") *de Sainte Gudule.* In all likelihood, he replaced *sœur* by *fleur* ("flower") not merely for reasons of euphony but also in order to achieve a subtle synthesis of the two saints. Since Rosalie is usually represented holding a flower and Gudula a lantern, Nerval, by transposing these emblems, could combine the Latin and the Nordic to form a new symbol of Christianity.

And then he asks ironically if they have found redemption "in the wilderness of the skies" (11). The answer for him is of course negative, for he proceeds to command the "white roses"—that is, all the orthodox Christian saints—to fall from their "burning" heaven—a heaven burning in the wrath of a vengeful Jehovah. It is Artemis-Hecate, the saint of the abyss, who is holier in his eyes, for she is the twofold saintliness: symbol of his pre-Christian religious faith and emblem of his eternally Beloved Woman.

One could spend hours poring over the commentaries inspired by this sonnet, some of which assert, for example, that the first line refers to "the Thirteenth woman" and the fifth to the poet's mother. Critics will doubtless continue to find new meanings for the symbols and to offer new interpretations. But one may wonder if further research will ever explain the curious enchantment of these fourteen lines, which are among the most memorable in modern French literature. [J.W.K.]

CORRESPONDANCES

La nature est un temple où de vivants piliers
Laissent parfois sortir de confuses paroles;
L'homme y passe à travers des forêts de symboles
Qui l'observent avec des regards familiers.　　　　4

Comme de longs échos qui de loin se confondent
Dans une ténébreuse et profonde unité,
Vaste comme la nuit et comme la clarté,
Les parfums, les couleurs et les sons se répondent.　　8

Il est des parfums frais comme des chairs d'enfants,
Doux comme les hautbois, verts comme les prairies,
— Et d'autres, corrompus, riches et triomphants,

Ayant l'expansion des choses infinies,　　　　12
Comme l'ambre, le musc, le benjoin et l'encens,
Qui chantent les transports de l'esprit et des sens.

(*Les fleurs du mal*. 1857)

No other poem by Baudelaire has had the impact of *"Correspondances"* upon modern literature. Yet at first it aroused little attention. There is no "Baudelairianism" here, no obsession with death or with ugliness, and the form has majestic gravity. The poet, after being portrayed in the first three *Fleurs du mal* as an accursed creature, an albatross ludicrous when forced to tread on the ground, is in this fourth poem hailed as the decipherer of correspondences: it is he who translates the secrets of the world and fuses sensations into one another. He creates the world anew.

The title recalls the Swedish mystic, Swedenborg, to whom Baudelaire had been drawn (probably through Balzac) as early as 1845. Mysterious voices respond to each other in nature; they announce a correspondence between the visible and the invisible, between matter and spirit. The title, the plural form of an abstract word (*Correspondances*) suggests the multiplicity of those correspondences, philosophical or sensuous, that conceal an underlying unity. The tone is that of a geometric theorem, formulated with prophetic assurance.

The two quatrains have the solemnity of a lofty cathedral; their sounds unroll slowly, with deep pauses at the caesura of line 1 and after the third syllable of line 4. The second quatrain introduces the notion of the senses, hence of the arts, as parallel translations of the deeper identity of essential nature.

(1) *Nature is a temple where living columns*

(2) *Sometimes murmur indistinct words [allow confused words to escape]*; (3) *There man passes through forests of symbols* (4) *That watch him with familiar glances*. (5) *Like prolonged echoes that mingle in the distance,* (6) *In a shadowy and profound unity,* (7) *Vast as night and as the light of day,* (8) *Perfumes, colors, and sounds respond to (answer to) one another.*

The more solemn assertion rises from the first quatrain. Nature is a vast ancient temple, its pillars covered with hieroglyphics. They are familiar and benevolent signs, but they are unnoticed by most passers-by and scrutinized only by the poet, whom Baudelaire characterized elsewhere as "a decipherer of analogies." The key phrase set off at the rime in line 3 (*forêts de symboles:* "forests of symbols") was to enjoy an astonishing fortune, at first to deride and later to laud the Symbolist poets. The Greek verb from which "symbol" stems means to throw, or fuse, together the sign and the object denoted by the sign. (Parable [that which has another side meaning], hyperbole [an exaggeration, thrown above], problem [thrown in front of us to be solved] are coined from the same word.) The word "symbol" has a long history; many thinkers, from Plato and St. Paul down to the moderns, have called the visible world the other face of the invisible one. This sonnet claimed for the poet the privilege of translating into evocative concrete terms the ultimate secret of things: he ceased to be a narrator or a describer; he tore off the veil that covers the true nature of objects thus to reveal the identity behind the illusory appearances, the One behind the Many, as Plato and Shelley had put it.

There is no virtuoso musical effect in the quatrains, no attempt at surprising the reader, no metaphor that fuses discordant elements. The lines have a classical beauty, their sweep is majestically and deliberately slow. An ample comparison in line 5 is prolonged further through four nasal sounds; two long abstract adjectives in line 6 delay the essential noun, *unité* ("unity"); again, a double comparison exalts, in line 7, the correspondences of the senses by linking them to the alternation of darkness and light; three nasal sounds in *um* and *on* (line 8) lengthen the distant echoes conjured up in line 5.

The grave density of the quatrains gives way to a lighter tone in the tercets. Baudelaire no longer stresses the vertical correspondences. Plunging deep into the unknown, even into the morbid, and pointing toward the realm of the spirit, he illustrates the horizontal correspondences, or synesthesia. Our senses—and, by extension, the several arts—perceive the central mystery of nature differently and render it into parallel languages, which are convertible into one another. (9) *There are perfumes, fresh as the flesh of children,* (10) *Sweet as oboe music, green as meadows,* (11) *—Others [are] corrupt, rich, and triumphant,* (12) *Having the expansion of things infinite,* (13) *Like amber, musk, benzoin, and frankincense,* (14) *Which sing the raptures of spirit and of sense.*

The last lines stress the olfactory sensations, the richest of all for so sensuous a poet as Baudelaire, the richer for some trace of corruption in them, and, as Proust was later to insist, the ones most likely to carry a whole train of associations in their wake. The end of the sonnet links —as in Baudelaire's renowned poem "*Une charogne*" ("A Carrion")—the ecstasy of the senses and that of the spirit, both closely corresponding, the former being but the reflection of the latter. In one of Baudelaire's essays, the Poet proudly declares: "I wish to illuminate things with my spirit and to project that reflection onto other spirits."　　　　[H.P.]

CHARLES BAUDELAIRE

HYMNE À LA BEAUTÉ

Viens-tu du ciel profond ou sors-tu de l'abîme,
O Beauté? ton regard, infernal et divin,
Verse confusément le bienfait et le crime,
Et l'on peut pour cela te comparer au vin.   4

Tu contiens dans ton œil le couchant et l'aurore;
Tu répands des parfums comme un soir orageux;
Tes baisers sont un philtre et ta bouche une amphore
Qui font le héros lâche et l'enfant courageux.   8

Sors-tu du gouffre noir ou descends-tu des astres?
Le Destin charmé suit tes jupons comme un chien;
Tu sèmes au hasard la joie et les désastres,
Et tu gouvernes tout et ne réponds de rien.   12

Tu marches sur des morts, Beauté, dont tu te moques;
De tes bijoux l'Horreur n'est pas le moins charmant,
Et le Meurtre, parmi tes plus chères breloques,
Sur ton ventre orgueilleux danse amoureusement.   16

L'éphémère ébloui vole vers toi, chandelle,
Crépite, flambe et dit: Bénissons ce flambeau!
L'amoureux pantelant incliné sur sa belle
A l'air d'un moribond caressant son tombeau.   20

Que tu viennes du ciel ou de l'enfer, qu'importe,
O Beauté! monstre énorme, effrayant, ingénu!
Si ton œil, ton souris, ton pied, m'ouvrent la porte
D'un Infini que j'aime et n'ai jamais connu?   24

De Satan ou de Dieu, qu'importe? Ange ou Sirène,
Qu'importe, si tu rends, — fée aux yeux de velours,
Rythme, parfum, lueur, ô mon unique reine! —
L'univers moins hideux et les instants moins lourds?   28

(Les fleurs du mal. 1857)

With Baudelaire, poetry became more than an adornment or an escape into an ideal world. He gave poetry a new dimension, by enabling men to take a bold plunge into infernal depths, from which they could rise upward once again toward the Baudelairian dream of a consoling presence, feminine or divine. Ugliness, cruelty, self-destruction, terror, are included in the Baudelairian concept of beauty. As Rilke, one of the heirs to Baudelairianism, said, "The Beautiful is nothing but the beginning of the Terrible, which we are still just able to endure [p. 150]." This twenty-first poem in the definitive edition of *Les fleurs du mal* was composed after 1857 and appeared only in 1860 in the review *L'Artiste*. It offers a curious contrast to an earlier sonnet, "*La Beauté*" ("Beauty"), in which a Greek statue seems to express an esthetics of impassive, enigmatic, motionless calm.

"*Hymne à la Beauté*" is addressed to a goddess of the nether world. From the first line, where invocations are blended with questions, the dialectics of Baudelairian beauty is stressed: it is both infernal and divine; its amphora, which is compared to the mouth of a beguiling woman, or of a Circe, pours out good and evil indiscriminately. Eroticism and art are wedded. The fourth line is awkward and serves only as a pause before the effects wrought by beauty are described in the second stanza:

(1) *Do you come from heaven's depths or rise from the pit,* (2) *O Beauty? Your gaze, infernal and divine,* (3) *Pours indiscriminately both benefaction and crime,* (4) *And [so] you can be likened to wine.* (5) *Your eye contains the twilight and the dawn;* (6) *You scatter perfumes like a stormy evening;* (7) *Your kisses are a philter and your mouth an amphora* (8) *Which make the hero cowardly and the child courageous.*

With the second section (lines 9-20), the versification becomes less regular, the images grow bolder and more sensuous: the canticle assumes the tempo of a round in which the devotees of the enchantress Beauty whirl, like priests of some Bacchic cult. The caesura in line 10 shakes the reader's expectation of regularity by cutting the line after the fifth syllable and dividing the rest into four and three syllables.

The *jupons* (10) of the all-too-human goddess recall those of a woman of the streets; men, and even Fate, are irresistibly enslaved, like dogs, by the reckless crea-

ture. She tramples upon the dead; horror is one of her jewels. Lines 15-16, with their phallic suggestion and the bold use of the word "belly," acclaim Beauty's murderous effect, beloved by the victims themselves. Like moths who live only a day, men flit around the flame that is to consume them. The very posture of the lover recalls that of a dying man in love with his own death. (9) *Do you come from blackest hell or fall from the stars?* (10) *Fate, bewitched, like a dog follows at your skirts;* (11) *You sow at random joy and disaster;* (12) *Responsible to nothing, you rule over everything.* (13) *You tread, Beauty, on dead men whom you mock;* (14) *Of your jewels Horror is not the least beguiling,* (15) *And Murder, among [one of] your dearest trinkets,* (16) *Dances voluptuously on your proud belly.* (17) *The dazzled mayfly circles toward you, candle,* (18) *Crackles, burns, and says: Come let us bless this torch!* (19) *The panting lover bending over his love* (20) *Seems like a dying man caressing his own tomb.*

The last part of the poem, which returns to the dialectics of the first stanza, asks no more questions; the worshipper of beauty no longer dallies. He has joined the mad round, consenting to his own damnation, provided that he will enter an unknown Infinite by following after Beauty. He acknowledges her as his queen. She offers man a paradise conquered through violence, a paradise into which he can escape from anguish. (21) *Whether you come from heaven or hell, what matter,* (22) *O Beauty! monster enormous, frightening, ingenuous!* (23) *[What matter] if your gaze, your smile, your foot, open for me the doors* (24) *Of an Infinite which I love and have never known?* (25) *From Satan or from God, what matter? Angel or Siren* (26) *What matter, if you make—O fairy with velvet eyes,* (27) *Rhythm, fragrance, light, O my only queen!—* (28) *The world less hideous and time less oppressive?* [H.P.]

CHARLES BAUDELAIRE

LE BALCON

Mère des souvenirs, maîtresse des maîtresses,
O toi, tous mes plaisirs! ô toi, tous mes devoirs!
Tu te rappelleras la beauté des caresses,
La douceur du foyer et le charme des soirs,   4
Mère des souvenirs, maîtresse des maîtresses!

Les soirs illuminés par l'ardeur du charbon,
Et les soirs au balcon, voilés de vapeurs roses.
Que ton sein m'était doux! que ton cœur m'était bon!   8
Nous avons dit souvent d'impérissables choses
Les soirs illuminés par l'ardeur du charbon.

Que les soleils sont beaux dans les chaudes soirées!
Que l'espace est profond! que le cœur est puissant!   12
En me penchant vers toi, reine des adorées,
Je croyais respirer le parfum de ton sang.
Que les soleils sont beaux dans les chaudes soirées!

La nuit s'épaississait ainsi qu'une cloison,   16
Et mes yeux dans le noir devinaient tes prunelles,
Et je buvais ton souffle, ô douceur! ô poison!
Et tes pieds s'endormaient dans mes mains fraternelles.
La nuit s'épaississait ainsi qu'une cloison.   20

Je sais l'art d'évoquer les minutes heureuses,
Et revis mon passé blotti dans tes genoux.
Car à quoi bon chercher tes beautés langoureuses
Ailleurs qu'en ton cher corps et qu'en ton cœur si doux?   24
Je sais l'art d'évoquer les minutes heureuses!

Ces serments, ces parfums, ces baisers infinis,
Renaîtront-ils d'un gouffre interdit à nos sondes,
Comme montent au ciel les soleils rajeunis   28
Après s'être lavés au fond des mers profondes?
— O serments! ô parfums! ô baisers infinis!

(Les fleurs du mal. 1857)

One fourth of *Les fleurs du mal* are love poems now judged to be among the deepest and most spiritual in all literature. The senses are not ignored by the poet, but eroticism is usually purified by sentiment. In woman, Baudelaire wanted to find an understanding sister, a mother, a silent presence rather than a mistress. No Don

Juan, he needed to adore rather than to conquer. The formal beauty of *"Le balcon,"* its music, its vast rocking motion, and its sumptuous finale rank it among the most perfect examples of that "abstract sensuality" (as Valéry called it) which characterizes Baudelaire.

(1) *Mother of memories, mistress of mistresses,* (2) *O you, all my pleasures! O you, all my duties!* (3) *You will remember the beauty of caresses,* (4) *The sweet warmth of the hearth, the charm of evenings,* (5) *Mother of memories, mistress of mistresses!* (6) *Evenings illumined by the glowing coals,* (7) *Evenings on the balcony, veiled in rosy mists.* (8) *How soft was your breast [to me]! how kindly your heart!* (9) *Often we said imperishable things* (10) *On evenings illuminated by the glowing coals.* (11) *How beautiful are suns in the warm evenings!* (12) *How deep is space, how powerful the heart!* (13) *As I leaned toward you, queen of the adored ones,* (14) *I thought that I inhaled the fragrance of your blood.* (15) *How beautiful are suns in the warm evening!* (16) *Night around us thickened like a wall,* (17) *And my eyes in the dark guessed the pupils of yours,* (18) *And I drank your breath, O sweetness! O poison!* (19) *And your feet fell asleep in my fraternal hands.* (20) *Night around us thickened like a wall.* (21) *I know the art of evoking happy moments,* (22) *And I relive my past [when I am] huddled in your lap.* (23) *For what is the use of seeking your languorous beauties* (24) *Anywhere but in your beloved body and in your gentle heart?* (25) *I know the art of evoking happy moments!* (26) *Those oaths (vows), those perfumes, those infinite kisses,* (27) *Will they be reborn from an abyss we never may fathom,* (28) *As rejuvenated suns climb to the skies* (29) *After bathing themselves in the depths of the seas?* (30) *O vows! O perfumes! O infinite kisses!*

"The Balcony" was inspired by Jeanne Duval, Baudelaire's "Black Venus," his "one pleasure." She becomes the beloved in general, the repository of the poet's memories and dreams. She protects and reigns over their common memories; she is addressed in litanies, as the Virgin might be. The word *caresses* is purified of all sensuousness through its being associated with the past quietly remembered and the hearth. The setting is the familiar Baudelarian one: rosy clouds as the sun sinks, watched by the lovers on the balcony; embers glowing in the hearth; few words —peace has descended upon the lovers.

The words are most usual and general: *douceur, bon, profond.* Exclamations succeed one another; the climax of the serene pleasure comes in the invocation, *reine des adorées,* ("queen of the adored ones," 13) and in the gradual sheltering by which night, becoming like a *cloison* ("wall"), keeps the outside world away. The lines oscillate from the scene outside back to the lovers united in the "sweet warmth of the hearth." Long words—*impérissables* (9), *s'épaississait* (16), *fraternelles* (19)—add to the majesty of the middle stanzas.

Suddenly the tone changes in the triumphant line 21. The poet sings proudly now, not of the charms of his mistress nor of his own ardor, but of his ability to treasure the present until it becomes the past and to conjure it up when, enshrined in another present, it has been purified. In passages such as these, Baudelaire anticipated Proust's rediscovery of the past as a source of joy and as a spur as creative as the imagination itself.

The question in lines 23-24 is rhetorical: Baudelaire will not seek in another woman what the body and heart of Jeanne Duval offer him. He will be content to relive those sovereign moments. If the poet can recapture the memory of loving promises, of woman's fragrance, and long kisses, death will be transcended and the ills of the flesh purified like suns that emerge from the seas. [H.P.]

HARMONIE DU SOIR

Voici venir les temps où vibrant sur sa tige
Chaque fleur s'évapore ainsi qu'un encensoir;
Les sons et les parfums tournent dans l'air du soir;
Valse mélancolique et langoureux vertige!⠀⠀⠀⠀⠀⠀⠀⠀4

Chaque fleur s'évapore ainsi qu'un encensoir;
Le violon frémit comme un cœur qu'on afflige;
Valse mélancolique et langoureux vertige!
Le ciel est triste et beau comme un grand reposoir.⠀⠀⠀8

Le violon frémit comme un cœur qu'on afflige,
Un cœur tendre, qui hait le néant vaste et noir!
Le ciel est triste et beau comme un grand reposoir;
Le soleil s'est noyé dans son sang qui se fige.⠀⠀⠀⠀12

Un cœur tendre, qui hait le néant vaste et noir,
Du passé lumineux recueille tout vestige!
Le soleil s'est noyé dans son sang qui se fige...
Ton souvenir en moi luit comme un ostensoir!⠀⠀⠀⠀16

⠀⠀⠀⠀⠀⠀⠀⠀⠀⠀⠀⠀(*Les fleurs du mal.* 1857)

The poetry of Baudelaire is often rich in intellectual content; critics have commented at length on the theology, the Platonic philosophy, and the esthetics of the poet. "Evening Harmony," however, does not owe its delicate beauty to any psychological originality or to any other effects of surprise. It is a masterpiece of musicality in poetry. Here and in a few similar poems, Baudelaire, anticipating the oft-quoted claim of Mallarmé and of Valéry, attempted to recapture from music the subtle and rich orchestration that it had exclusively appropriated.

The music of words and of rimes ingeniously interwoven cannot, of course, be adequately conveyed by a literal translation. (1) *Now comes the hour when stirring on its stem* (2) *Each flower exhales (fumes) like a censer;* (3) *Sounds and perfumes swirl in the evening air;* (4) *[O] melancholy waltz and languidly sensuous vertigo!* (5) *Each flower exhales like a censer;* (6) *The violin quivers like a heart distressed;* (7) *A melancholy waltz and languidly sensuous vertigo!* (8) *The sky is sad and splendid like a great altar.* (9) *The violin quivers like a heart distressed,* (10) *A tender heart, that hates the void vast and dark!* (11) *The sky is splendid and sad like a great altar;* (12) *The sun has drowned in its own congealing blood.* (13) *A tender heart, that hates the void vast and dark,* (14) *Gathers each trace of the luminous past!* (15) *The sun has drowned in its own congealing blood . . .* (16) *The memory of you shines within me like a monstrance!*

This sixteen-line poem is a *pantoum*, a

form frequently used in the poetry of the East, especially in Malaya, and one which struck the fancy of several metricians around Baudelaire, among them Banville and Leconte de Lisle. It appealed to Baudelaire because it was rare and exotic and better welded together than the sonnet, in which the tercets often differ sharply from the quatrains in meaning as well as in tempo. The constricting mold, dear to Théophile Gautier, imposes a classical distinction which can enhance the intensity of the feeling suggested. There are only ten original lines in the poem: the other six are repeated, lines 2 and 4 becoming the first and third lines of each succeeding stanza. Baudelaire was fond of such repetitions, from which Poe had derived effects which were often merely facile. There is nothing facile or weird here. Exclamation marks, frequent in Baudelaire, seem to prolong the emotions of fear of the void, of melancholy, of consolation through memory, and of devotion to his beloved, all of which were suggested through the tension and suspense. The rime scheme is *abba* then *baab*, repeated in the last eight lines. Only two rimes are used: feminine in *ige* and masculine in *oir*, both of them rare in French.

The title leads us to expect an atmosphere of evening melancholy and a musical poem that will render the correspondences among flowers diffusing their fragrance, the playing of a violin, and the swirling motion of impressions received from nature. Half of the images suggest that sorrowful vertigo which rises from external nature and gradually permeates the poet's heart. But the other set of images, religious in connotation, recalls Catholic liturgy. The *reposoirs*, which by their very name suggest repose, are altars, often strewn with flowers, erected for religious processions on such days as Corpus Christi (the second Thursday after Whitsuntide). Christ's sacrifice for the redemption of mankind is recalled in the death of the sun, drowned in its congealing blood. The two parallel threads of imagery are bound into one in the final offering of the *pantoum* to the beloved, whose memory illumines the poet like the monstrance (the French word *ostensoir*, 16, comes from the Latin verb *ostendere*, signifying "to show") or vessel of gold in which the Host is exposed.

The poem should be read slowly and gravely: the three initial *v* sounds in line 1 are like piercing arrows of pain; the evening hour is generalized and made more solemn and ominous by being called, in the plural, *les temps*, like the Biblical "days" of wrath or "days" of sadness. Line 4 felicitously evokes the melancholy of the hour and the languorous bewilderment of a heart surrendering to the distress that seizes it at night: the *v* and *l* sounds are subtly blended.

In the second stanza the adjectives are, as usually in *Les fleurs du mal*, abstract and general: *triste, beau, grand*. The heart of a too sensitive poet is "afflicted," that is, beaten repeatedly, and it moans as does the violin under the bow. But with line 8, the tone becomes more serene and the eyes turn toward the sky, which is likened to an altar.

In the third stanza, the notion of death and of the void—of the nothingness feared and yet loved by Baudelaire in such a poem as "*Le goût du néant*"—saddens the poet as the sun is drowned in its sacrificial blood. But anguish yields to the luminous memory of the woman as the *pantoum* closes: the last movement of this vertiginous and musical poem is one of joyful exultation. [H.P.]

CHARLES BAUDELAIRE

L'INVITATION AU VOYAGE

Mon enfant, ma sœur
Songe à la douceur
D'aller là-bas vivre ensemble!
   Aimer à loisir   4
   Aimer et mourir
Au pays qui te ressemble!
   Les soleils mouillés
   De ces ciels brouillés   8
Pour mon esprit ont les charmes
   Si mystérieux
   De tes traîtres yeux,
Brillant à travers leurs larmes.   12

Là, tout n'est qu'ordre et beauté,
Luxe, calme et volupté.

   Des meubles luisants,
   Polis par les ans,   16
Décoreraient notre chambre;
   Les plus rares fleurs
   Mêlant leurs odeurs
Aux vagues senteurs de l'ambre,   20
   Les riches plafonds,
   Les miroirs profonds,

   La splendeur orientale,
   Tout y parlerait   24
   A l'âme en secret
Sa douce langue natale.

Là, tout n'est qu'ordre et beauté,
Luxe, calme et volupté.   28

   Vois sur ces canaux
   Dormir ces vaisseaux
Dont l'humeur est vagabonde;
   C'est pour assouvir   32
   Ton moindre désir
Qu'ils viennent du bout du monde.
   — Les soleils couchants
   Revêtent les champs   36
Les canaux, la ville entière,
   D'hyacinthe et d'or;
   Le monde s'endort
Dans une chaude lumière.   40

Là, tout n'est qu'ordre et beauté,
Luxe, calme et volupté.

(Les fleurs du mal. 1857)

"Invitation to the Voyage" is perhaps the most famous French poem on the theme of "evasion" or escape into a land of dream and beauty. The theme was dear to the Romantics—Goethe ("Mignon"), Shelley (*Epipsychidion*), Hugo ("Chanson d'Eviradnus")—who treated it with abandon and delight. In Baudelaire's poem, however, there is profound melancholy and hardly a trace of the sensuous. Even the word *volupté* has more spiritual than carnal connotations. *Luxe* suggests repose, relief from the anguishing torments that afflicted the poet when he wrote this poem (first published in June 1855 in the *Revue des Deux Mondes*): creditors, disease, solitude, a mother whom he thought uncomprehending, a mistress whose apathy was a source of conflict. The dream of escape thus formulated was probably inspired by Baudelaire's ephemeral passion for Marie Daubrun, "La fille aux cheveux d'or," a golden-haired actress of Dutch origin to whose country he may have dreamt of escaping from the struggles of his Parisian existence.

Poetical renderings or transpositions into English of this poem have often been attempted, but the density and the evocative, tender quality of the original defy all translation. (1) *My child, my sister* (2) *Think of the sweetness* (3) *Of going yonder to live together!* (4) *To love at leisure* (5) *To love and to die* (6) *In a land that resembles you!* (7) *The humid suns* (8) *Of those cloud-blurred skies* (9) *For my spirit have the charms* (10) *So mysterious* (11) *Of your treacherous eyes,* (12) *Shining through their tears.* (13) *There, all is order, beauty,* (14) *Luxury, calm and voluptuousness.* (15) *Gleaming furniture,* (16) *Polished by the years,* (17) *Would adorn our chamber;* (18) *The rarest flowers* (19) *Mingling their fragrance* (20) *With the vague odors of amber,* (21) *The rich ceilings,* (22) *The deep mirrors,* (23) *The oriental splendor,* (24) *All would speak* (25) *To the soul secretly* (26) *In its soft native tongue.* (27) *There, all is order, beauty,* (28) *Luxury, calm and voluptuousness.* (29) *See on those canals* (30) *The vessels asleep* (31) [literally:] *Whose humor is vagabond* [whose mood is to roam]; (32) *It is to satisfy* (33) *Your slightest desire* (34) *That they come from the ends of the world.* (35) *— The setting suns* (36) *Clothe the fields* (37) *The canals, the entire city,* (38) *With hyacinth and gold;* (39) *The world drops off to sleep* (40) *In a warm glow.* (41) *There all is order, beauty,* (42) *Luxury, calm and voluptuousness.*

The felicitous simplicity, the pure beauty, and the haunting music of this celebrated poem have preserved its appeal in spite of its being much recited, translated, and sung. One can hardly find a better example of Poe's definition of poetry as "the rhythmical creation of beauty," which Baudelaire accepted. The masterful workmanship of this masterpiece is hidden behind the flowing, melodious ease of the verse.

The structure of the entire poem and of each stanza has a quality of splendor.

First, an invitation to flee toward a land of heart's desire; then the description of the indoor setting to which the poet and his mistress would be transported. The third stanza conjures up a golden vision, in the setting sun, of the fields and the harbor, apparently in Holland, where the dream of solitude would be fulfilled. Note that each stanza has twelve lines, the ninth serving as a support for the long ascending sweep and heralding the soothing descent toward the refrain. The refrain brings an interlude of serenity between the repeated caressing appeals of the lover to his love.

The entire poem is composed in *vers impairs*, lines rarely used in French poetry before Verlaine and other Symbolist poets, deeply impressed by the Baudelairian "*Invitation au voyage*," revived them as being more mysterious and subtle than lines of six, eight, or ten syllables. The pattern here consists of two lines of five syllables, each with masculine rimes and two stresses, followed by one line of seven syllables and of three stresses, prolonged by an extra syllable at the feminine rime. The combination of caesuras, shifting from the second or first to the third syllable of each of the shorter lines, is more varied than it could have been in a six- or an eight-syllable line divided into two hemistichs. Within each stanza, the sounds are ingeniously contrived: soft, melancholy in the first with *sœur, douceur,* and the humid evocation of the sounds in *mouillés, brouillés, yeux.* Nasal sounds, longer and as it were taller, suggest the ceiling, the deep and long mirrors, the ancient furniture in stanza 2. The broad *or* sounds, following a series of *v*'s at the beginning of *vois, vaisseaux, vagabonde, ville,* suggestive of the ships gliding into the sea which rocks them, expand the last stanza into an apotheosis.　　　　　　[H.P.]

CHARLES BAUDELAIRE

SPLEEN

Quand le ciel bas et lourd pèse comme un couvercle
Sur l'esprit gémissant en proie aux longs ennuis,
Et que de l'horizon embrassant tout le cercle
Il nous verse un jour noir plus triste que les nuits;   4

Quand la terre est changée en un cachot humide,
Où l'Espérance, comme une chauve-souris,
S'en va battant les murs de son aile timide
Et se cognant la tête à des plafonds pourris;   8

Quand la pluie étalant ses immenses traînées
D'une vaste prison imite les barreaux,
Et qu'un peuple muet d'infâmes araignées
Vient tendre ses filets au fond de nos cerveaux,   12

Des cloches tout à coup sautent avec furie
Et lancent vers le ciel un affreux hurlement,
Ainsi que des esprits errants et sans patrie
Qui se mettent à geindre opiniâtrement.   16

— Et de longs corbillards, sans tambours ni musique,
Défilent lentement dans mon âme; l'Espoir,
Vaincu, pleure, et l'Angoisse atroce, despotique,
Sur mon crâne incliné plante son drapeau noir.   20

(*Les fleurs du mal.* 1857)

Charles Baudelaire (1821-1867), in whom his contemporaries saw a sensuous and morbid poet, appears to our century as a classic, a profound psychologist, a master of evocative imagery and of rich music. As a poet and also as an esthetician, he stands at all the cross-roads of modern poetic achievement.

The longest section of *Les fleurs du mal,* entitled "Spleen et Idéal", contrasts the poet's aspiration after the beauty through which he hopes to transfigure life's sorrows with his temptation to despair. "Spleen" denotes a physical and nervous affliction far more intense and corrosive than the declamatory *mal du siècle* ("sickness of the age") of Baudelaire's Romantic predecessors. It is described graphically in this stark poem as a weight pressing down upon the poet's skull; elsewhere Baudelaire called it his hysteria and we know that he had tried to soothe it by the use of laudanum and other "artificial paradises." Into this intense pain there also entered a sense of the tragedy of life, of cosmic anguish with all that is wrong in the world, an insidious urge toward self-disintegration. The poet confessed repeatedly to being torn between two opposite "postulations," to being driven toward the divine and also the diabolical. Despair has seldom if ever been portrayed more memorably than in these twenty lines:

(1) *When the low and heavy sky weighs like a lid* (2) *On the groaning spirit, a prey to long tedium,* (3) *When, embracing all the horizon,* (4) *It pours upon us black day, far gloomier than nights;* (5) *When earth is changed into a humid dungeon,* (6) *In which Hope, like a bat,* (7) *Flits to and fro, beating the walls with its timid wing* (8) *And knocking its head against the rotted beams;* (9) *When the rain deploying its immense shafts* (10) *Mimics [imitates, has the look of] the bars of a vast prison,* (11) *While a silent race of loathsome (heinous) spiders* (12) *Comes and stretches their meshes into the depths of our brains,* (13) *Bells suddenly leap in frenzy* (14) *And hurl a ghastly howl toward the sky,* (15) *As would [a host of] wandering homeless spirits* (16) *Who stubbornly start their wailing.* (17) *—And long hearses, without drums or music,* (18) *Slowly file through my soul; Hope,* (19) *Vanquished, weeps, and fierce, despotic Anguish* (20) *Plants his black banner upon my drooping skull.*

The forcefulness of "Spleen" is due in large part to its inexorable, slow-moving tension and its masterful rhythm and sound. The central image is that of the poet's skull oppressed by the pain of his spleen, while correspondingly the lid of the low, heavy sky presses down upon the earth. The word "lid" (*couvercle*) occurs at the rime in line 1, the word "skull" (*crâne*) appears only in line 20.

One feels a certain majesty in the structural control. The sky, then the earth, then the rain linking the two fill, respectively, the first, second, and third stanzas, each beginning with *quand* and making use of repeated, haunting nasal sounds: *gémissant, long, embrassant,* etc. Present participles, usually avoided in French poetry as being heavy, crowd the lines, as do repetitions of harsh sounds such as *quand, que, qu'un* and alliterations of *s* (2, 3) and of *f* (11, 12, 14). Occasionally, the pause fails to coincide with the sixth syllable, as in line 6, where the limping renders the blind fluttering of the black bat Hope in the cell.

The punctuation of "Spleen" is noteworthy. Except for line 6, all the commas in the first four stanzas come at the end of the lines and these four stanzas make up one endless sentence. In the fifth stanza, on the contrary, the pauses marked by commas are multiplied. The alternate rimes in the *abab* pattern make for an effect of cumulative and imprisoning tension that enmeshes the splenetic sufferer.

A suggestion of madness runs through the poem: the *ennui* (from Latin *odium,* hatred and disgust of life) is close to the morbid dread of nothingness, alluded to elsewhere in *Les fleurs du mal.* The spider crawling in the brain of the prisoner is a symbol of mad desperation; the bells themselves seem to howl, like mad dogs, to a listless heaven. The poet's skull has sheltered lugubrious visions of funerals beneath its *couvercle,* which is also the scene of a dual between Hope and Anguish. Anguish has triumphed and in submission the victim bends his head on which the flag of bitter victory will be nailed. [H.P.]

ARTHUR RIMBAUD

LE BATEAU IVRE

Comme je descendais des Fleuves impassibles,
Je ne me sentis plus guidé par les haleurs:
Des Peaux-Rouges criards les avaient pris pour cibles,
Les ayant cloués nus aux poteaux de couleurs.   4

J'étais insoucieux de tous les équipages,
Porteur de blés flamands ou de cotons anglais.
Quand avec mes haleurs ont fini ces tapages,
Les Fleuves m'ont laissé descendre où je voulais.   8

Dans les clapotements furieux des marées,
Moi, l'autre hiver, plus sourd que les cerveaux d'enfants,
Je courus! Et les Péninsules démarrées
N'ont pas subi tohu-bohus plus triomphants.   12

Within the last fifty years "*Le bateau ivre*" has climbed to the perilous position of becoming the most famous single poem in the French language. Its every line continues to be scoured for possible ambiguities of meaning, and some of its images have already been tracked to their possible sources in Chateaubriand, Poe, Hugo, and Leconte de Lisle. The splendid rhetoric of the poem, the virtuosity of its seventeen-year-old author, and his mastery over the ample swell of twenty-five sonorous stanzas have been admired inordinately; for there are many other poems by Rimbaud that today seem more original than "The Drunken Boat." In some respects this celebrated cascade of alexandrines by a teenager who had never yet seen the sea—it was written in the summer of 1871, in his seventeenth year, when he also composed his two famous "Seer's Letters"—is a magnificent tour de force and a farewell to one phase of Rimbaud's literary past.

It may seem sacrilegious to mutilate a successful and famous work of art; but space in an anthology is parsimoniously restricted and other examples, of a different Rimbaud, must be included. Moreover, it is the conviction of this critic that our worship of "Structure" in a poem, which glibly compares it to a living organism, in which every part is functional, has gone to ridiculous lengths. "*Le bateau ivre*," like many other long poems, suffers from redundancy, a hammering of obvious and monotonous effects, an intoxication of the adolescent creator with his own coinage of images and use of rare words, and a lack of inevitability in the succession of the stanzas. We do not claim to have improved the poem by omitting most of its central part; but we believe that the truncated text offered here is adequate for a perception of the poem's originality, and that it may even encourage the reader to go to the work in its entirety.

*(1) As I sailed down impassive Rivers,
(2) I no longer felt guided by towmen: (3) Shrill
Redskins had used them for targets, (4) Having
nailed them naked to painted poles. (5) I paid
no heed to all the crews, (6) [I] Bearer of
Flemish wheat or English cotton. (7) When
the uproar ended with my towmen [dead],
(8) The Rivers let me drift as I willed.
(9) In the furious plashing of tides, (10) I, last
winter, deafer than the brains of children, (11)
I sped! and unmoored Peninsulas (12) Never
have known more triumphant disorder.*

Rimbaud at seventeen was filled with
dreams of liberation from the constraints
of family, provincial life, studies, the con-
ventions of the poetry of the past, and
political and social conservatism. He had
read illustrated stories of Redskins fight-
ing against the white intruders from the
Old World, of sweeping rivers such as the
Amazon. He dreamt of breaking loose
from all his symbolic chains, of plunging
into the elements and identifying himself
with stormy waves, unmoored peninsulas,
and of reconstructing a universe thus
atomized through his power as a visionary
poet. The drunken boat is clearly the
symbol of the child's dream of total libera-
tion. It has drifted down on streams,
indifferent to the child's complaints or
wishes. The towmen, who represented the
prudence of civilized life, have been shot
by the arrows of vociferous Indians. The
sounds in the first stanza are, at first,
in their slow and solemn motion, evocative
of a severance. The child is now freed
from adults.

The child-boat in its turn assumes a
cruel indifference to all that recalls Europe
and trade. It would seem more logical if
the word *porteur* (6) were in the plural
and referred to the other crews that the
drunken boat disregards and not to its
own cargo presumably plundered by the
Indians; but the text has it in the singular.
With line 8, the regularity of the caesuras
is broken: *m'ont laissé descendre,"* a bloc of
five syllables at the center of the line,
followed by the repetition of the *ou* sound
in *ou je voulais,* renders the new and furious
tone of the middle of the poem.

The words will be unusual ones: con-
crete, sonorous, often onomatopoeic (*cla-
potement,* 9; *démarrées,* 11; *tohu-bohus,* 12);
at times, proper nouns like *Florides,
Béhémots, Maelstroms,* reminiscent of geo-
graphical maps, Biblical monsters, or
Edgar Allan Poe. The young writer is fond
of displaying the range of his vocabulary
and the unconcern with which he can
manipulate syntax and versification—in
this respect, "*Le bateau ivre*" is the most
Hugo-like of all Rimbaud poems. With
line 9 begins the evocation of the boat
tossed about by tempests, washed pure by
the dawn on the ocean, and enraptured
by the phosphorescent seas or by the
starry night reflected on the calm waters.
Line 10 seems to offer an indication of
time: "last winter." The deafness of the
children's brains is an allusion to their
stubborn refusal to heed the commands
of their elders. *Je courus!* ("I sped!"),
breaking off the regularity of the third
stanza, sounds like the first joyful cry of
the child-boat freely speeding along.

La tempête a béni mes éveils maritimes.
Plus léger qu'un bouchon j'ai dansé sur les flots
Qu'on appelle rouleurs éternels de victimes,
Dix nuits, sans regretter l'œil niais des falots!   16

Plus douce qu'aux enfants la chair des pommes sures,
L'eau verte pénétra ma coque de sapin
Et des taches de vins bleus et des vomissures
Me lava, dispersant gouvernail et grappin.   20

Et dès lors, je me suis baigné dans le Poème
De la Mer, infusé d'astres, et lactescent,
Dévorant les azurs verts; où, flottaison blême
Et ravie, un noyé pensif parfois descend;   24

Où, teignant tout à coup les bleuités, délires
Et rhythmes lents sous les rutilements du jour,
Plus fortes que l'alcool, plus vastes que nos lyres,
Fermentent les rousseurs amères de l'amour!   28

(13) *The tempest blessed my awakenings at sea.* (14) *Lighter than a cork, I danced on the waves* (15) *[Which are] called the eternal rollers of victims,* (16) *Ten nights, without ever regretting [the absence of] the beacons' foolish eyes!* (17) *Sweeter than the flesh of tart apples to children,* (18) *Green water seeped into my firwood hull* (19-20) *And cleansed me of the blue wine-stains* (20) *And vomit, scattering rudder and grappling hook.* (21) *And, from then on, I bathed in the Poem* (22) *Of the Sea, infused with stars and growing milky white,* (23) *Devouring green azures; where a flotage [floating remnants] wan* (24) *And rapt, a pensive drowned corpse at times sinks down;* (25) *Where, suddenly dyeing the blue [depths], delirium* (26) *And slow rhythms under the red gleam of the day,* (27) *Stronger than alcohol, far vaster than our lyres,* (28) *The bitter russets [rednesses] of love ferment!*

The central part of "*Le bateau ivre*" will consist of alternate visions of tempestuous violence and serene lull. Violence domi-nates, and the boat, identified with the child, revels in it; his exultation and his greed for undergoing the most weird experiences of life, over and under the seas, appear boundless. Yet the premonition of weariness (in lines 65-72), even of the senselessness of these mad wanderings, comes over him in the very midst of his visions. The impetuous vehemence of the rhythm gives way to a more anguished and less tempestuous music as the poem unrolls. During the very months when he was composing this surprising masterpiece, Rimbaud impressed his Parisian friends, to whom he took "*Le bateau ivre*" as his first achievement, as being not only an arrogant, impulsive adolescent intoxicated with his nascent strength but also a frail child athirst for understanding and ten-derness.

Lines 13-16 are regular and ample in versification. The water with which the storm sprays the boat, when it seems to awaken at dawn to a virginal sea, is called a "benediction." The rhythm of line 14 suggests the gleeful dance of the keel on the sparkling waves, those waves which civilized men malign as hostile, rolling down over their drowned victims. Ten nights elapse thus, and the silliness of civilization is left far behind. The water, green or bluish green (18 and 23), seeps into the frail firwood of the boat. It is as pleasant to the taste as sour apples stolen from orchards are to children. Like a lustral baptism, it washes the boat-child of the coarse wine imbibed by rough sailors; and the instruments by which the ship could be steered or defended are scattered to the waves. The boat is now free to roam.

This new phase of its joyous pantheistic marriage with the star-reflecting sea is distinguished by the light, bouncing rhythm of lines 21-24, with the clearly marked breaks after *Et*, then *dès lors*, and the enjambment *Poème | De la mer* and again *blême | Et ravie*. The thought of death enters the scene with the macabre vision of the drowned corpse, pallid and *ravie* (which means both carried along by the current and enraptured by the liberation brought by death). Leconte de Lisle, whom Rimbaud admired in the early years when he wished to be a Parnassian poet, had similarly pictured a rapt, drowned young man in "*La fontaine aux lianes*" ("The Fountain among Lianas"), calm as Ophelia. Rimbaud himself had composed (in 1870) an "Ophelia" in which he addressed the pale Shakespearian heroine floating like a tall lily in the water.

After this quiet and dreamy vision of death, Rimbaud alters the tempo of the poem, multiplies rare and colorful words, complicates his syntax, dislocates the next stanza, and passes abruptly from the contemplation of death to the evocation of the "fermentation" of love in the depths of the sea. The *t* sound, cutting and sharp, recurs in every one of lines 25-28. The blending of glaring colors (*bleuités, rutilements*) with slow, vast, almost erotic rhythms renders the cosmic character of the scenes through which the drunken boat wanders. Fish and seamonsters pair and spawn among the russet weeds that color the blue water and they are more intoxicating than alcohol and the music of poetry. (This is the weaker part of the stanza, with its old-fashioned allusion to the poets' "lyres.")

J'ai vu des archipels sidéraux! et des îles
Dont les cieux délirants sont ouverts au vogueur :
— Est-ce en ces nuits sans fonds que tu dors et t'exiles,
Million d'oiseaux d'or, ô future Vigueur ? —   88

Mais, vrai, j'ai trop pleuré! Les Aubes sont navrantes.
Toute lune est atroce et tout soleil amer :
L'âcre amour m'a gonflé de torpeurs enivrantes.
O que ma quille éclate! O que j'aille à la mer!   92

Si je désire une eau d'Europe, c'est la flache
Noire et froide où vers le crépuscule embaumé
Un enfant accroupi plein de tristesses, lâche
Un bateau frêle comme un papillon de mai.   96

Je ne puis plus, baigné de vos langueurs, ô lames,
Enlever leur sillage aux porteurs de cotons,
Ni traverser l'orgueil des drapeaux et des flammes,
Ni nager sous les yeux horribles des pontons.   100

(Poésies complètes. 1895)

(85) *I have seen sidereal archipelagos! and isles* (86) *Whose delirious skies are open to the sailor:* (87) *Is it in these depthless nights that you sleep and exile yourself,* (88) *[You] million golden birds, O future Vigor?—* (89) *But, in truth, I have wept overmuch! The Dawns are heart-breaking.* (90) *Each moon is agony, each sun is bitterness:* (91) *Acrid love has swollen me with drunkening numbness.* (92) *Oh, let my keel burst! oh, let me go to sea!* (93) *If I crave Europe's waters, it is but the puddle* (94) *Black and cold, where toward the fragrant twilight* (95) *A crouching child, filled with sadnesses, launches* (96) *A boat as frail as a May butterfly.* (97) *Bathed in your languors, I am able no more, O waves,* (98) *To cut through the wake of the bearers of cotton,* (99) *Nor cross through the pride of flags and of flames,* (100) *Nor swim past the ghastly eyes of prison ships.*

In the long series of stanzas, at times monotonous, which are perforce omitted here, the boat (or the boy poet) boastfully enumerates all that he has seen: cloud-bursts, dawns, and evenings on the sea, the swell assaulting the reefs, whirlpools, and sea monsters. *J'ai vu*, ("I have seen"), he exclaims, he who had never seen the sea and could only imagine it from his reading or from the few pictures he had gazed at in some magazine. But he transcended what his eyesight might have brought him and he practiced his theory of the poet-as-seer, recreating a fantastic universe with shreds from "the baseless fabric of his vision." Despair, however, crept into his exultation at being able to see more piercingly than other men. The longing for Europe and its old battlements entered the poet's memory. Lines 85-88 offer the climax of these cosmic visions of sea and sky fused together, of archipelagos composed of islands, under madly enchanted skies, where the forlorn boat could take refuge.

The weary wanderer dreams for an instant that there, perhaps, he could find the vigor that he had possessed at the start of the poem, the "future vigor" that he would need in order to pursue his aimless visionary adventure, the new lease of ardor that birds appear to seek during their nights spent on these mysterious islands. The question itself, the only one in the poem that is punctuated by exclamation marks, is rhetorical. The boat and the poet know that the answer is negative.

Disillusionment becomes total and heartrending with line 89. *Vrai* is a familiar, childlike expression for *vraiment*. The boastfulness of the boat and of the child has collapsed: both now cry, as Rimbaud cried in a prose poem of the same period, "*Les déserts de l'amour*": "I have shed more tears than God could ever ask" and "True, at that time, I cried more than all the children in the world." The dawns, the moonlight on the sea, the glaring splendor of the sun which he had depicted in the poem, have now become inexpressibly sad, agonizing, and "bitter." The very love that had intoxicated him he now calls "acrid." A single wish remains in the wearied boat: to burst apart and to be absorbed by the sea.

The alternative is surrender. The same adolescent who has wanted to shake himself free from all the shackles of family life and who has stubbornly fled his native city now craves only the black, cold little pond to which, as a child filled with sadness, he had entrusted his frail paperboat. No other stanza in the entire poem is so richly evocative as this song of the forlorn dreams of the boy, playing near his home in the balmy twilight hour. A few adjectives are enough to conjure up the black impression, the evening fragrance, the butterfly-like frailty of his toy-ship, and the attitude of the child, crouching near the water anxiously.

Lines 93-96 seem to refer chiefly to the child. The boat again speaks in the final stanza. It confesses its powerlessness. It can no longer leap over the waves, race with the merchant ships, glide among the colorful naval vessels on the ghastly prison ships whose liberation it has once desired. Like the convicts on them, "the intractable convicts" of whom Rimbaud will speak in *Une saison en enfer* (*A Season in Hell*), the adolescent poet had attempted the revolt of an outlaw. At seventeen, he already appears to realize that no revolt can for long alter the conditions of life.   [H.P.]

ARTHUR RIMBAUD

MÉMOIRE

I

L'eau claire; comme le sel des larmes d'enfance,
L'assaut au soleil des blancheurs des corps de femme;
la soie, en foule et de lys pur, des oriflammes
sous les murs dont quelque pucelle eut la défense;   4

l'ébat des anges; — Non... le courant d'or en marche,
meut ses bras, noirs et lourds, et frais surtout, d'herbe. Elle
sombre, ayant le Ciel bleu pour ciel-de-lit, appelle
pour rideaux l'ombre de la colline et de l'arche.   8

No poem of reminiscences and of regret at the passing of childhood was ever written by a poet at an earlier age than "*Mémoire*," which Rimbaud probably composed in his eighteenth year (1872); it was published only in part in 1892 in *L'Ermitage*. In our opinion it is the most beautiful long poem by its author. It has less rhetorical intoxication than "*Le bateau ivre*." It has less inhumanity than some of the prose *Illuminations*, in which Rimbaud practiced indirect lyricism and sacrificed sensibility to imagination. It has less imperious tension than the hard, sparkling sentences of Rimbaud's poems in prose. The rimes, the suppleness of the alexandrines with their varied caesuras, the delicacy of the sensations recalled by the tender-hearted and nostalgic adolescent, the harmonious structure of the poem, with its five acts of an intimate drama, all make it formally a perfect piece. Its many obscurities are not voluntary ones, thrown at the reader like challenges or displays of the artist's superiority. They contribute to the chiaroscuro of the memories of childhood dimly and fitfully recalled by the young man, who is fearful of the solitude now in store for him.

In "*Mémoire*" Rimbaud is less the seer, whose sharp vision decomposes reality in order to recreate it according to a new order, than he is the traditional lyric poet, receptive to outside impressions, moved more by regret than by violence; no longer elated by the liberating surge that sent the boat adrift in stormy seas, but grieved by parting from childhood and from the protection of a harsh, unhappy mother. The poem is to be read as (1) autobiographical, for it tells a life-story in a discreet and a delicately transposed way; (2) symbolic, for it embodies the drama of every childhood that forsakes motherly protection and young innocence for the adventures and the hardening of the soul in the grown man; (3) impressionistic, for its sensations are airy, soft, fleeting ones, unsubstantial but haunting impressions recollected as in a dream.

The title itself is more original than "*Souvenir*" would be: memory as a "faculty" of the mind, as it was then called in psychology, as a power which stores up and transfigures the impressions and emotions of childhood, becomes creative—as it will be in Proust. This memory ranges beyond the life of the child himself and encompasses the experiences of his parents.

Water is the leitmotif of the first section, the water of the river and of tears. (Another early poem, in the curious eleven-syllable line, very close to "*Mémoire*" in tone, is entitled "*Larme*" ["Tear"].) (1) *Clear water; like the salt of childhood tears,* (2) *The assault in sunlight of the whiteness of women's bodies;* (3) *the silk, abundant and [decorated] with pure lily, of flaming banners* (4) *below walls which some maid had defended;* (5) *the frolics of angels;—No . . . the golden flowing current,* (6) *moves its arms of grass, black and heavy, and above all cool. She* (7) *dark, with blue Heaven for a canopy, summons* (8) *the shadow of the hill and of the arch for curtains.*

The scene is Charleville by the river Meuse, on whose banks Rimbaud played as a child, watched by his mother. Nearby are a bridge with several arches, a hill, banks with willows, and on Sunday afternoons, women in bright dresses walking, dignified, as in Seurat's painting of the "Grande Jatte," or lying in the sun. The first line establishes the symbolic correspondence between the river and the clear tears of a child destined to grief. The second line is more ambiguous. Does the gliding water remind him of the female bodies of the sirens whom he had read about in his Latin poets, gleaming with reverberated light, like banners floating in the breeze? Are women dressed in white, their skin pale from winter, "assaulting" the sunlight as they lie on the sunny banks of the river? (Such an interpretation would be questionable, for at this period provincial French women would hardly have exposed their bodies to the sunshine.) The purity of the tone of the poem would scarcely allow a third interpretation: that the boy was thinking of "storming" women's bodies. Here the *s* sounds and even the repetition of the same sound (in as*s*a*u*t and *s*oleil) suggest the silky gliding of the stream. Lines 3 and 4 conjure up the image of Joan of Arc, surrounded by soldiers with banners (*oriflammes* means "flames of gold") and the emblematic lilies of the French kings, besieging the walls of Orleans—it is like the event illustrated in a child's history book.

Angels haunt the boy-poet. He wonders if the swift stream might be the frolics of angels, but he repudiates this childish question in a curiously broken line(5). The identification of the river with the mother proceeds; it has heavy, consoling arms. It opposes its dark, brooding mood to the joyousness of the summer skies—as does the Mother. And again, like the Mother, whose nuptial bed is surmounted by a canopy with curtains hanging on each side, the river is sheltered by the sky above, by the falling shadows of the hill and the bridge on each side.

II

Eh! l'humide carreau tend ses bouillons limpides!
L'eau meuble d'or pâle et sans fond les couches prêtes;
Les robes vertes et déteintes des fillettes
font les saules, d'où sautent les oiseaux sans brides.   12

Plus pure qu'un louis, jaune et chaude paupière
le souci d'eau — ta foi conjugale, ô l'Épouse! —
au midi prompt, de son terne miroir, jalouse
au ciel gris de chaleur la Sphère rose et chère.   16

III

Madame se tient trop debout dans la prairie
prochaine où neigent les fils du travail; l'ombrelle
aux doigts; foulant l'ombelle; trop fière pour elle;
des enfants lisant dans la verdure fleurie   20

leur livre de maroquin rouge! Hélas, Lui, comme
mille anges blancs qui se séparent sur la route,
s'éloigne par delà la montagne! Elle, toute
froide, et noire, court! après le départ de l'homme!   24

The second section opens with a colloquial exclamation, "Eh." As in the first stanzas, Rimbaud tries to avoid the formality of traditional lyricism; he breaks the regular rhythm with bold enjambments and unexpected divisions in the lines and he uses words not usually found in the poetic language of this time. Part II presents the mother. Her daughters are around her, in their green or gray dresses (line 11); she envies and fears the sun, source of warmth and of love. Part III becomes more concrete and dramatic, almost satirical of Madame Rimbaud's tyranny when she watches over her children, whom she forces to read prayer books on Sundays, among the flowers. Her husband has deserted her, as her two sons already dream of doing. Young angels, they will cruelly vanish away and leave her desolate! (9) *See! the wet expanse spreads its clear bubbles!* (10) *The stream furnishes the prepared beds with pale, depthless gold;* (11) *The green, faded dresses of the little girls* (12) *are willows, out of which unbridled birds hop.* (13) *Purer than a gold coin, a yellow and warm eyelid* (14) *the marsh marigold—your conjugal faith, o Spouse!* — (15) *at prompt midday, envies, from its lustreless mirror,* (16) *the rosy and dear Sphere in the sky gray with heat.*

(17) *Madame holds herself too stiffly in the meadow* (18) *nearby where the sons of labor [stand white as] snow; her parasol* (19) *between her fingers; trampling the wild carrot, too proud for her;* (20) *children reading amid the flowered grass* (21) *their book bound in red morocco! Alas, He, like* (22) *a thousand white angels parting company on the road,* (23) *goes off beyond the mountain! She, all* (24) *cold, and black, runs! after the man's departure.*

Lines 9-10 start awkwardly with the vision of the river spreading over a square-shaped expanse, perhaps just before the dam that causes it to bubble. Elsewhere, the river, more peaceful, seems to be digging beds for those drowned Ophelias who haunted young Rimbaud's imagination. Little girls, perhaps the poet's two sisters, whom he was ordered to watch at their games or to accompany to church on Sundays, appear among the pale colored willows in their greenish dresses, blending with the grayness of the trees; or perhaps the willows are clad in the faded dresses of the girls.

In line 13, the Wife enters the poem, and a new symbolism invades it. The yellow flower, purer than a gold coin, warm and round as an eyelid, symbolizes, as does the color yellow, conjugal happiness: that flower and the river, beside which it grows, reflect (like an eye) the rosy (at morning and in the evening), warm, and beloved (*chère*) globe of the sun. The woman, the Spouse, is envious of the male principle (designated by the sun), whose disappearance she fears.

Suddenly with line 17 the identification of the river with the woman gives way to an almost sarcastic picture of the woman as mother, rigid and austere, walking about the meadow where the white shirts of workmen (peasants perhaps employed by her) make a snow of white dots (18).

Sheltered from the sun by her parasol, she proudly tramples upon the flowers whose height seems to rival her authority. (The lines are boldly divided with the enjambment *l'ombrelle* / *aux doigts* and the stanzas overrun one another.) The children, on a Sunday afternoon, have to read their prayer book before vespers.

But meanwhile He: the sun which is setting beyond the hill and also the husband —Rimbaud's father, an army officer who, repelled by his wife's obduracy and thirsting for freedom, had indeed disappeared one day, leaving his wife and five children behind—vanishes like a band of angels. When Arthur composed this poem, he had already run away from home several times and he was, even then, plotting his next escape. She—the river and the woman—vainly runs after the husband-sun: the sun which has set, the husband who has departed. Line 24, divided by abrupt pauses after *froide*, *noire*, and *court*, conveys the halting motion of her desperate race after the male (husband, some day children) fleeing from her tyranny.

IV

Regret des bras épais et jeunes d'herbe pure!
Or des lunes d'avril au cœur du saint lit! Joie
des chantiers riverains à l'abandon, en proie
aux soirs d'août qui faisaient germer ces pourritures!   28

Qu'elle pleure à présent sous les remparts! l'haleine
des peupliers d'en haut est pour la seule brise.
Puis, c'est la nappe, sans reflets, sans source, grise:
un vieux, dragueur, dans sa barque immobile, peine.   32

V

Jouet de cet œil d'eau morne, je n'y puis prendre,
ô canot immobile! oh! bras trop courts! ni l'une
ni l'autre fleur: ni la jaune qui m'importune,
là; ni la bleue, amie à l'eau couleur de cendre.   36

Ah! la poudre des saules qu'une aile secoue!
Les roses des roseaux dès longtemps dévorées!
Mon canot, toujours fixe; et sa chaîne tirée
Au fond de cet œil d'eau sans bords, — à quelle boue?   40

(Poésies complètes. 1895)

The sarcasm of Part III now gives way to nostalgia and desolation: desolation of the forsaken mother and of the child, now fatherless, oppressed by his mother's grief, vainly dreaming of drifting down the river towards the sea. The child dimly understands the full significance of the husband's flight for the wife, whose conjugal bed is now deprived of joy, as the April moonlight shines like an invitation to a vernal wedding. The mother's sorrow is like that of the river when the sun has set or when spring has gone and the grass along the banks is no longer thick and young. The first line (25) is divided into three segments with the two adjectives, set in the middle, that describe the lusty male as well as the grass. Line 26, made up of monosyllables, evokes the sharp crescent of the moon gleaming on the deserted bed. Then it is summer; the yards where workmen built light boats or carved wood are idle at night; dank smells fill the air; the world of nature seems to be germinating everywhere. The river is more serene, and the mother, identified with it, cries under the walls of the city (29) already mentioned in line 4. The caressing breath of the poplars is wafted away with the wind and grazes the woman's face with the derisive mimicry of a kiss. The *carreau* alluded to in line 9 no longer bubbles with life; it is now a gray, still, dreary sheet of water. On the river, an old man, his boat anchored, dredges the water, sadly and vainly attempting to purify its bottom and thus to liberate it.

(25) *Regret for the arms, thick and young, of pure grass!* (26) *Gold of April moons in the heart of the sacred bed!* *Joy* (27) *of the abandoned lumber yards on the river banks, a prey* (28) *to August evenings which made that*

putrescence germinate! (29) *Let her weep now below the ramparts! the breath* (30) *of the poplars above is for the breeze alone.* (31) *Then, the sheet of water, without reflections, without any spring, gray:* (32) *an old man, dredging, labors in his motionless boat.*

In Parts II to IV the Mother or Spouse was the central character; the son sympathized with her in her desolation. He dimly realized, as in "The Drunken Boat," how much of his mother he would some day have in him and how he would return home, defeated, resigned, avid for conventional and provincial peace. But his father's heredity lay in him, too. He had first to leave, to revolt against female domination, to roam about and away from the river banks, which had ceased to fill him with joy. The river will again become the central character in the final section, the Mother now forgotten. The first person singular *je* and *me* and *mon*—will appear for the first time. Beyond the memory of his youth and of his father's flight and of his mother's grief, the boy now looks at his own solitude, and voices his own nostalgia for another kind of life. (33) *Plaything of this eye of dismal water, I cannot reach,* (34) *O motionless boat! oh, arms too short! neither the one* (35) *nor the other flower: neither the yellow one that annoys me* (36) *there; nor the blue one, friendly to the ash-gray water.* (37) *Ah! the powder of the willows that a wing*

shakes! (38) *The roses long since devoured by the reeds!* (39) *My boat, always tied; and its chain pulled* (40) *To the depth of this eye of shoreless water,—toward what mud?*

The boy is overwhelmed by the sadness of the scene; he is torn by desperate urges to free himself, to grasp at the flowers offered to him by the river banks, by life. But he is not allowed to. His arms are too short as yet. The yellow flower, a symbol of domestic happiness, irks him; the blue flower, a symbol of tender and sentimental love, is not vivid enough for him. He is but the boy of that square of water which sadly reflects the sky; chained to it and powerless to sail down to the seas.

The last lines carry the poet's and the reader's minds back to the scene of the first stanzas. An idle exclamation of regret for the willows, color of the girls' faded dresses, from which a bird was taking flight; the roses that grow among the reeds have long ago been devoured. Arthur Rimbaud and his brother used to sit for hours in their uncle's boat, anchored or moored to the river, pretending to unmoor it by letting it drift as far as the chain would allow. Similarly, his life is tied to the mud at the bottom, to an ultimate failure: its dream of violent liberation and motion will end where it had begun.   [H.P.]

AUBE

J'ai embrassé l'aube d'été.   1

Rien ne bougeait encore au front des palais. L'eau était morte. Les camps   2
d'ombres ne quittaient pas la route du bois. J'ai marché, réveillant les haleines
vives et tièdes, et les pierreries regardèrent, et les ailes se levèrent sans bruit.

La première entreprise fut, dans le sentier déjà empli de frais et blêmes éclats, 3
une fleur qui me dit son nom.

Je ris au wasserfall blond qui s'échevela à travers les sapins : à la cime argentée 4
je reconnus la déesse.

Alors je levai un à un les voiles. Dans l'allée, en agitant les bras. Par la plaine, 5
où je l'ai dénoncée au coq, A la grand'ville, elle fuyait parmi les clochers et les
dômes, et, courant comme un mendiant sur les quais de marbre, je la chassais.

En haut de la route, près d'un bois de lauriers, je l'ai entourée avec ses voiles 6
amassés, et j'ai senti un peu son immense corps. L'aube et l'enfant tombèrent
au bas du bois.

Au réveil il était midi.   7

(*Illuminations*. 1886)

The *Illuminations* are a series of prose poems written by Rimbaud between the ages of eighteen and twenty-two (in 1872-1876 at the latest) and abandoned by him when he left Europe and gave up writing. The manuscript of those poems which have come down to us—others must have been lost—reached Verlaine and was published by a friend of his in a magazine (*La Vogue*) and then as a small volume (in 1886). Verlaine said that the title means "colored plates," and the poems are indeed a kaleidoscope of sharply outlined, colored images; but they are also hallucinations, or at least visions either having a mystical character or illuminating the subconscious mind of a boy.

In "Dawn," young Rimbaud recaptures the bright purity of nature arising from its nightly slumber. In his youthful, pantheistic impulse, he wishes not only to contemplate nature but also to embrace and possess it: nature is personified as a woman and a goddess whose veils he tears rapturously. The tone is one of grave revelation, as if the adolescent imparted a momentous secret, haltingly, panting with emotion, and surprised at his own audacity. The sentences are brief, sharply outlined, with no conjunctions or links of any other kind. "*Aube*" has the clarity of a dream-image; the motion that launches the pursuer of the dawn swiftly along groves by the roadside, amid pebbles, sleeping birds awakened, flowers, the quays, and the tall buildings of the city also has the swift fantastic rhythm of a dream.

(1) *I have embraced the summer dawn.*

(2) *Nothing was stirring as yet on the fronts of the palaces. The water was dead. The camps of shadows did not leave the road in the woods. I walked, awakening the live and warm breaths; and the precious stones watched, and wings silently rose up.*

(3) *The first venture was, on the path already filled with cool, pale light, a flower which told me its name.*

(4) *I laughed at the blond waterfall that ran dishevelling its hair through the pines: at its silver crest I recognized the goddess.*

(5) *Then I took off her veils one by one. In the path, shaking my arms. Across the plain, where I denounced her to the cock. In the big city, she fled among the bell-towers and the domes; and running like a beggar along the marble quays, I pursued her.*

(6) *At the top of the road, near a laurel grove, I enfolded her in her gathered-up veils, and I felt her vast body a little. Dawn and the child fell at the edge of the wood.*

(7) *Upon awakening, it was noon.*

Like most of the *Illuminations*, "*Aube*" is a poem of motion; a strange, and earlier, piece by Rimbaud in free verse—the first ever attempted in French—was entitled "*Mouvement*" and conveyed the ecstatic union of the boy with a youthful being of nature recomposed out of chaos into order. Description for its own sake is seldom found in Rimbaud; the elements of a scene are atomized, then reorganized by the poet's imagination.

The first line is a boy's proud, naive proclamation of his victory over the impossible: he held dawn herself in his arms. At first, nothing was stirring: the plain houses along the quays looked like palaces; only the steaming morning haze was rising from the woods; the stones, shining with dew, looked like diamonds; birds, awakened, took to flight.

Nature whispers its secrets to the young poet, who understands its motion. A flower reveals its name to him. The waterfall (*wasserfall*; Rimbaud uses the German word, which had become accepted into French) is to him—as it could have been for an early Greek poet—a creator of myths, a laughing, dishevelled goddess.

In the second part (line 5), the poem takes on an even graver tone, in its revelation of a sacred, mystical union. The poet pursues the goddess of the dawn, denounces her to the cock who will herald her appearance, chases her away from the city and up a slope where, in a laurel grove—reminiscent of Apollo and his attempt to embrace Daphne, who eluded him by changing into a laurel—the goddess and her pursuer fall into an almost sexual embrace.

But it was all a dream, child's play—like all of Rimbaud's ambitions to change the world through deranging the senses or by assigning names to inanimate objects. A tinge of disillusionment marks the last five words.   [H.P.]

MYSTIQUE

Sur la pente du talus, les anges tournent leurs robes de laine dans les herbages   1
d'acier et d'émeraude.

Des prés de flammes bondissent jusqu'au sommet du mamelon. A gauche le   2
terreau de l'arête est piétiné par tous les homicides et toutes les batailles, et
tous les bruits désastreux filent leur courbe. Derrière l'arête de droite la ligne
des orients, des progrès.

Et, tandis que la bande en haut du tableau est formée de la rumeur tournante   3
et bondissante des conques des mers et des nuits humaines,

La douceur fleurie des étoiles et du ciel et du reste descend en face du talus,   4
comme un panier, — contre notre face, et fait l'abîme fleurant et bleu là-
dessous.

(Illuminations. 1886)

It has often been said—among others, by the eminent Swiss historian of poetry, Marcel Raymond—that one of the achievements of modern French poetry has been to rival religion and to appropriate mysticism, which thus passed from the realm of the sacred to the profane. The French noun *la mystique* is more apt than the English "mysticism," for it designates a direct and immediate relationship (i.e., without any intermediary such as an established church) between a human being and the divine. A man or woman who is thus inspired by higher mysteries or who interprets them to other people is an "angel" in the etymological sense of the word—coming, as it does, from the Greek word for "messenger." The term "angelism" has therefore been used to signify a temptation to rise above the limitations of ordinary men. Both Jacques Rivière and Wallace Fowlie, in their respective critical books on Rimbaud, have stressed the "angelistic" claims to

transcendent purity entertained by the adolescent poet, who perhaps thought himself a god or a magician endowed with superhuman powers. Rivière, for a time, went so far as to proclaim him exempt from original sin!

Predecessors of Rimbaud (from Milton, Thomas Moore, and Klopstock to the French Romantics) had often portrayed angels as characters in their poetic epics; others had, as Rimbaud does here, conjured up angels as they appear in the paintings of primitive Christian artists or in Blake's engravings. This prose-poem, the title of which may be the adjective *mystique*, dear to Baudelaire, used here as a noun, graphically presents a vision similar to some medieval painting of angels. But it is not an attempt to translate painting into words; rather it is the precise, elliptic, almost realistic rendering into words—mostly substantives and verbs—of the poet's vision. Like most visionary poets, Rimbaud imposes his fantastic and ecstatic vision upon the reader through an impeccable sequence of images and with faultless logic.

(1) *On the slope of the hillock, angels whirl their woolen robes, in the grasses of steel and emerald.*

(2) *Meadows of flame leap up to the top of the mound. On the left, the earth mold of the ridge is trampled upon by all murders and all battles, and all the disastrous noises race along their own curve. Behind the crest on the right, the line of orients, of progress.*

(3) *And, while the strip at the top of the picture is made of the whirling and leaping murmur of conch shells from the seas and of human nights,*

(4) *The flowery softness of the stars, of the sky and of all else comes down opposite the bank, like a basket—close to our faces, and makes the abyss flowering and blue below.*

Like a picture, the poem is divided into several planes. First its general motif is mentioned: above a hollow or an abyss, along the slope of a hillock, as in a Sienese picture, angels, clad in long robes, dance or fly. The grass is like steel (glossy under the dew) and like emerald— Rimbaud shuns conjunctions as he does adjectives; his language, made up of meaningful and sharp substantives, has none of the soft smoothness of Lamartine, Shelley, or Musset. The meadows where the angels disport themselves along the hillock gleam under the sunlight, perhaps with a mystical glow. On the left, as in a painting of The Last Judgment, there is a confused mass of allegorical or realistic battles and murders; on the right, a line behind which something arises—Rimbaud liked the word *orient*, and in his mystical poem "*Éternité*" he uses the word *orietur*, from the same Latin verb *oriri*, "to arise." On this side of the picture are those who rise up, the blessed; and progress may originate here.

Sound, shapes, and colors are blended together. As in a primitive painting, the landscape appears at the top, with the confused murmur of the seas and all that is darkness below, but the last sentence, in contrast, shows a visitation of heaven upon earth. The stars, like a flowery basket, come down to touch us. They make the abyss below a blue depth. It is fragrant and it is also illuminated by the celestial flowers, perhaps by a rainbow thrown, like the belt of some Greek goddess, between heaven and earth.   [H.P.]

CLAIR DE LUNE

Votre âme est un paysage choisi
Que vont charmant masques et bergamasques,
Jouant du luth, et dansant, et quasi
Tristes sous leurs déguisements fantasques.   4

Tout en chantant sur le mode mineur
L'amour vainqueur et la vie opportune,
Ils n'ont pas l'air de croire à leur bonheur
Et leur chanson se mêle au clair de lune,   8

Au calme clair de lune triste et beau,
Qui fait rêver les oiseaux dans les arbres
Et sangloter d'extase les jets d'eau,
Les grands jets d'eau sveltes parmi les marbres.   12

(*Les fêtes galantes.* 1869)

Late in his own life and for twenty years after his death, Paul Verlaine (1844-1896) was the most popular of the Symbolists. His star paled, however, when a new generation found his poetry effeminate, too graceful, and too pleasing in its musical effects and transferred its admiration to Mallarmé and Rimbaud. Today, however, many signs point to the likelihood that we shall hold Verlaine in much higher estimation in the second half of our century. For he is also a tragic and mysterious poet, cursed by his demons (alcoholism, homosexuality, passive assent to his own disintegration) and torn between the most abject submission to carnal impulses and dreams of idealism and religion. *Romances sans paroles* (*Songs Without Words*, 1874), *Jadis et naguère* (*Of Old and Late*, 1885), and *Parallèlement* (*In Parallel Line*, 1889) contain many works as profound psychologically as the best

of Baudelaire. In *Sagesse* (*Wisdom*, 1881) the greatest sinner among French poets proved that he was also the most naïve and moving Catholic poet of his century.

There are many mansions in the realm of poetry. Madrigals that combine graceful elegance with sincere self-revelation, the playful evocation of masked dancers in a moonlit landscape, and the suggestion of gloom which seizes the merrymakers in the midst of their pleasures have their place in poetry as they do in music and in painting. "*Clair de lune*" ("Moonlight") was first published in 1867 and in 1869 it opened Verlaine's second volume of verse, *Fêtes galantes* (*Gallant Festivals*). The title, the themes, and the setting recall Watteau's paintings—at that time the art of the eighteenth century was very much in fashion. But "Moonlight" is no insipid, worldly, or sensuous compliment to a lady, such as an eighteenth-century poet could have ingeniously penned. It is an interpretation of that "art" in which the quest for pleasure was tinged with melancholy.

(1) *Your soul is a choice landscape* (2) *Which masks and bergamasks go delighting,* (3) *Playing the lute, and dancing, and almost* (4) *Sad under their whimsical disguises.* (5) *As they sing in a minor key* (6) *Of victorious love and propitious life,* (7) *They do not seem to believe in their good fortune* (8) *And their song mingles with the light of the moon,* (9) *With the calm, melancholy, and beautiful light of the moon,* (10) *That makes the birds dream in the trees* (11) *And the fountains sob in their ecstasy,* (12) *The tall fountains, slender, among the marbles [statues].*

The premonition of sadness (4), expressed at the very moment when a pretence of joy is made by the dancers, and invading the third stanza, aptly reflects the mood of Watteau's *Embarquement pour Cythère* (*Embarkation for Cytherea*). Seldom has Horace's well-known observation, that poetry is like painting (*ut pictura poesis*), been more convincingly illustrated. Melancholy was also part of the personality of Verlaine, who was becoming an addict to drink at the very time—aged twenty three—when he was singing this Ariel's song. And it pervades the reader also, as it suggests a cosmic sorrow, in nature itself, and symbolizes mankind's frailty. The poem shuns all declamation. Unlike the Romantics, who explained and reasoned about their sadness, Verlaine translates it with immediacy into some of the most musical verse written in French. It is no wonder that Debussy and Fauré set this poem to music.

The first stanza is filled with broad, calm, doleful *a* sounds. The lines, as often in Verlaine, are so deftly cut (3) that the regular length of the decasyllables is no longer perceived by the ear. The archaic word *quasi* at the rime, modifying the first word (*triste*) of line 4, suggests an ancient folk dance: "Bergamasks" were originally dances done by the Italian peasants of Bergamo. These scenes of masked revelers, only half sincere and reluctant to take life seriously, are, to the poet, a picture of the soul of the woman to whom the poem is addressed. Several of the phrases used here, such as *quasi, fantasques, vie opportune,* have a touch of half-humorous quaintness about them.

The moonlight glowing above the maskers and their partners in the dance is mentioned first in line 8. Here the landscape takes on the graceful stylization of a Japanese painting: the birds are dreaming in the moonlit trees, the fitful complaint of the fountains is reminiscent of lovers' ecstasies. The slender two-syllable word *sveltes* itself seems to rise like the ascending water, in the middle of the final line.   [H.P.]

PAUL VERLAINE

GREEN

Voici des fruits, des fleurs, des feuilles et des branches,
Et puis voici mon cœur, qui ne bat que pour vous.
Ne le déchirez pas avec vos deux mains blanches
Et qu'à vos yeux si beaux l'humble présent soit doux.　　4

J'arrive tout couvert encore de rosée
Que le vent du matin vient glacer à mon front.
Souffrez que ma fatigue, à vos pieds reposée,
Rêve des chers instants qui la délasseront.　　8

Sur votre jeune sein laissez rouler ma tête
Toute sonore encor de vos derniers baisers;
Laissez-la s'apaiser de la bonne tempête,
Et que je dorme un peu puisque vous reposez.　　12

(*Romances sans paroles.* 1874)

(1) *Here are fruit, flowers, leaves and branches,* (2) *And then [now] here is my heart, that beats only for you.* (3) *Do not tear it with your two white hands* (4) *And may this humble gift be sweet to your beautiful eyes.* (5) *I arrive still all covered with dew* (6) *Which the morning wind chills on my brow.* (7) *Allow my fatigue, reposing at your feet,* (8) *To dream of dear moments that will restore its calm.* (9) *Upon your young breast let me cradle my head* (10) *Still resounding with your last kisses;* (11) *Let it grow quiet after the good tempest,* (12) *And let me sleep a little since you rest.*

Verlaine, who lived at various times in England, had a fondness for English titles: "Child Wife," "Spleen," "Nevermore." This twelve-line poem is a symphony in green, figuratively speaking, for although there is not one epithet of color in it, except for the whiteness of the hands to which the heart is offered, its dominant note is one of verdant, dewy freshness. It begins as if it accompanied a bouquet of flowers and leaves offered to the woman, or to the beloved (it has been conjectured that the poem might have been addressed to Rimbaud, who fascinated Verlaine in the years 1872-1873 when *Romances sans paroles* was composed). The first line, with three substantives beginning in *f* and three clearly marked pauses, is serpentine and long. The second, cut into two parts of six syllables, each made up almost entirely of monosyllables, runs more quickly. Line 5 would be an alexandrine if the two mute *e*'s at the end of *j'arrive* and *encore* were pronounced: it is actually to be said as if it had ten or eleven syllables.

The weariness of the wandering poet hopes to find a haven of calm with his beloved. His ears still echo with the sound of kisses exchanged. Like many of Verlaine's songs, this remarkably simple poem, as fresh and young as one of Ronsard's sonnets, voices the yearning for quietude of a tormented and hunted man.

[H.P.]

[DANS L'INTERMINABLE]

Dans l'interminable
Ennui de la plaine,
La neige incertaine
Luit comme du sable.   4

Le ciel est de cuivre
Sans lueur aucune,
On croirait voir vivre
Et mourir la lune.   8

Comme des nuées
Flottent gris les chênes
Des forêts prochaines
Parmi les buées.   12

Le ciel est de cuivre
Sans lueur aucune.
On croirait voir vivre
Et mourir la lune.   16

Corneille poussive
Et vous, les loups maigres,
Par ces bises aigres
Quoi donc vous arrive?   20

Dans l'interminable
Ennui de la plaine,
La neige incertaine
Luit comme du sable.   24

(*Romances sans paroles*. 1874)

This, the eighth of the *Romances sans paroles* (the title was borrowed from Mendelssohn), is a striking example of Verlaine's attempt to reduce the intellectual content of poetry to almost nothing and to offer the reader *de la musique avant toute chose* ("Music before everything else"). In this sense, it ranks among the few perfect examples of pure poetry in the French language.

(1) *In the endless* (2) *Tedium of the plain,* (3) *The shifting snow* (4) *Glistens like sand.* (5) *The sky is copper* (6) *Without any gleam,* (7-8) *One seems to see the moon live and die.* (9) *Like clouds* (10) *The oaks* (11) *Of the nearby forests* (10) *wave grayly* (12) *Among the mists.* (13) *The sky is copper* (14) *Without any gleam.* (15-16) *One seems to see the moon live and die.* (17) *Wheezing crow* (18) *And you, lean wolves,* (19) *In these keen north winds* (20) *What happens to you?* (21) *In the endless* (22) *Tedium of the plain,* (23) *The shifting snow* (24) *Glistens like sand.*

The lines have the odd number of syllables (*vers impairs*) that Verlaine used with unequalled mastery. These five-syllable lines do not allow any padding; the adjectives must be few—and here they are suggestive of the scenery conjured up and of the poet's mood, discreetly hinted at by the word *ennui* and by the lurid copper sky, weighing upon the observer as if it were the death of the moon. The rimes are feminine, suggestive of the passivity and the dreary yet haunting monotony of the plains of northern France, which Verlaine and Rimbaud loved. Only a few oak trees seem to float, "grayish"— the adjective in line 10 is curiously used as an adverb—in that marriage of the leaden sky with the earth. With lines 17-20, the very graphic landscape assumes a visionary appearance, as if a child had asked the naïve question in line 20 (*quoi* itself is a familiar use of the interrogative). Judged as a whole, this "song without words" is a memorable achievement in literary impressionism.   [H.P.]

PAUL VERLAINE

BRUXELLES

Tournez, tournez, bons chevaux de bois,
Tournez cent tours, tournez mille tours,
Tournez souvent et tournez toujours,
Tournez, tournez au son des hautbois.   4

Le gros soldat, la plus grosse bonne
Sont sur vos dos comme dans leur chambre;
Car, en ce jour, au bois de la Cambre,
Les maîtres sont tous deux en personne.   8

Tournez, tournez, chevaux de leur cœur,
Tandis qu'autour de tous vos tournois
Clignote l'œil du filou sournois,
Tournez au son du piston vainqueur.   12

C'est ravissant comme ça vous soûle
D'aller ainsi dans ce cirque bête!
Bien dans le ventre et mal dans la tête,
Du mal en masse et du bien en foule.   16

Tournez, tournez, sans qu'il soit besoin
D'user jamais de nuls éperons,
Pour commander à vos galops ronds
Tournez, tournez, sans espoir de foin.   20

Et dépêchez, chevaux de leur âme:
Déjà, voici que la nuit qui tombe
Va réunir pigeon et colombe,
Loin de la foire et loin de madame.   24

Tournez, tournez! Le ciel en velours
D'astres en or se vêt lentement.
Voici partir l'amante et l'amant.
Tournez au son joyeux des tambours.   28

(Romances sans paroles. 1874)

It would be difficult to find a better representative of Keats's ideal of "negative capability" than Paul Verlaine, one of the most impressionable of poets. With no effort at all, he was able, as Keats urged, "to let the mind be a thoroughfare for all thoughts"—or, rather, for all impressions. Verlaine seemingly had no will of his own; he could control neither his impulses nor the promptings of the senses. Like the Impressionist painters, his contemporaries, he often merely reflected the most fugitive variations of light; he did not organize his sensations or reason from them. Often his poems betray the inner giddiness of a weak, impulsive character yielding to the outside world or to the firmer will of a friend, such as Rimbaud. This curious poem, "Brussels," reminiscent of a Flemish picture, merrily carrying the reader along with its whirling rhythm, reveals Verlaine's own awareness of his inability to withstand intoxicating temptations.

It is a masterpiece of humorous observation at a Belgian fair. The leitmotif is given in the first stanza, with *tournez* (literally "turn") seven times repeated. The soldier, the fat Flemish maid whose masters are away, the thief, are all there. It is all foolish yet irresistible. The wooden horses call to mind the spurs, the gallop, and the hay of real ones, which are not needed here where the mechanical whirling goes ever on. A suddenly imaginative glimpse of the "velvet sky" of night and the "golden stars" marks the end of the festive day. The soldier and the maid go off together as the drums seem to beat their nuptial march.

The lines have nine syllables, usually divided into units of four and five. But as in most of his *vers impairs*, Verlaine disregards the syllabic count of French versification; he writes for the ear, not the eye. For the first time in French poetry, stress has superseded syllabism.

The language of "Brussels" shows Verlaine definitely abandoning elegance in poetry. The beginning of this work is abrupt and immediate, and the words and the syntax are familiar forms of speech (lines 5-6; *clignote* in line 11, the fourth

stanza, and the ironical, implied comparison of the fat soldier and his sweetheart to the pigeon and dove, in line 23). Verlaine gave up the poetical diction that mars the less successful of Baudelaire's *Fleurs du mal*. He avoids abstract words, so important in the dignified style of the Parnassians, with whom he had associated early in his career. He makes poetry as humorous, as concrete, as prose.

(1) *Go around, go around, good wooden horses,* (2) *A hundred times around, a thousand times around,* (3) *Often around and always around,* (4) *Around, around to the oboes' sound.* (5) *The great fat soldier and the fatter maid* (6) *Are at home on your backs as if they were in their room;* (7) *For, today, to the woods of the Cambre,* (8) *In person both the masters have gone.* [The woods of the Cambre—the Bois de Boulogne of Brussels—are on the outskirts of the town, a safe distance from the city fair, where the maid and the soldier enjoy the merry-go-round.] (9) *Around, around, steeds of their heart,* (10) *While around every one of your [whirling] rounds* (11) *The eye of the sly pickpocket flickers,* (12) *Turn to the sound of the conquering trumpet.* (13) *Delightful how drunk it makes you feel,* (14) *To go around and around in this silly ring!* (15) *[It feels] good in the stomach and bad in the head,* (16) *A whole lot of bad and a crowd of good.* (17) *Go around, go around, without any need* (18) *Of ever using a single spur* (19) *To drive the circling gallops* (20) *Go around, go around, without any hope of hay.* (21) *And hurry, steeds of their soul:* (22) *Already, now, the night which is falling* (23) *Will bring the pigeon and dove together,* (24) *Far from the fair and far from Madame.* (25) *Go around, go around! The velvet sky* (26) *Slowly dresses in golden stars.* (27) *See the lover and his loved one depart.* (28) *Go around to the joyful sound of the drums.* [H.P.]

[L'ESPOIR LUIT COMME UN BRIN DE PAILLE...]

L'espoir luit comme un brin de paille dans l'étable.
Que crains-tu de la guêpe ivre de son vol fou?
Vois, le soleil toujours poudroie à quelque trou.
Que ne t'endormais-tu, le coude sur la table?   4

Pauvre âme pâle, au moins cette eau du puits glacé,
Bois-la. Puis dors après. Allons, tu vois, je reste,
Et je dorloterai les rêves de ta sieste,
Et tu chantonneras comme un enfant bercé.   8

Midi sonne. De grâce, éloignez-vous, madame.
Il dort. C'est étonnant comme les pas de femme
Résonnent au cerveau des pauvres malheureux.   11

Midi sonne. J'ai fait arroser dans la chambre.
Va, dors! L'espoir luit comme un caillou dans un creux.
Ah! quand refleuriront les roses de septembre!   14

(Sagesse. 1881)

In the early summer of 1873, Verlaine quarreled with Rimbaud, fired a revolver at him, and, as a consequence, was sentenced to two years in a Belgian prison. Rimbaud left for his mother's farm, where he composed *A Season in Hell.* Verlaine, in prison, underwent a religious crisis in the course of which he wrote many of the poems collected in *Sagesse.* His remorse and good resolutions were sincere, but his naïve faith lapsed often and finally weakened altogether.

This sonnet, the "Summer" of a group of four entitled "My Almanach for 1873," each of which represented a season, was written late in 1873 in the prison at Mons. It has none of the nobleness of the sonnets by Verlaine's "Parnassian" contemporaries; it strives for none of their sumptuous effects. Broken up into brief, familiar sentences, it seems to be uttered by a consoling mother to a sick child. One person speaks but the sonnet is a dialogue, a compact drama. The remorseful poet hopes for salvation through wisdom.

Although the poem antedates Verlaine's conversion by several months, the allusion to the stable in line 1 suggests Bethlehem and the Christ. Afflicted by his guilt, grieved at having lost both Rimbaud and his wife (the divorce took place in March 1874), Verlaine vaguely expects a redemption to illuminate his present woe.

(1) *Hope shines like a blade of straw in the stable.* (2) *What do you fear of the wasp drunk with his mad flight?* (3) *See, the sun always powders [lights up] through some opening.* (4) *Why didn't you fall asleep, your elbows on the table?* (5) *Poor pale soul, at least this water from the icy well,* (6) *Drink it. Then sleep afterwards. Come, you see, I am here.* (7) *And I shall coddle the dreams of your siesta,* (8) *And you will sing softly like a cradled child.* (9) *Noon strikes. Please, go away, Madame.* (10) *He is asleep. It is amazing how a woman's steps* (11) *Resound through the brains of poor wretches.* (12) *Noon strikes. I have had the room sprinkled with water.* (13) *Now, go to sleep. Hope shines like a pebble in a hollow.* (14) *Ah! when will September roses blossom again!* [H.P.]

PAUL VERLAINE

[LE CIEL EST, PAR-DESSUS LE TOIT]

Le ciel est, par-dessus le toit,
    Si bleu, si calme!
Un arbre, par-dessus le toit,
    Berce sa palme.   4

La cloche, dans le ciel qu'on voit,
    Doucement tinte.
Un oiseau sur l'arbre qu'on voit
    Chante sa plainte.   8

Mon Dieu, mon Dieu, la vie est là,
    Simple et tranquille.
Cette paisible rumeur-là
    Vient de la ville.   12

— Qu'as-tu fait, ô toi que voilà
    Pleurant sans cesse,
Dis, qu'as-tu fait, toi que voilà,
    De ta jeunesse?   16

(*Sagesse*. 1881)

Verlaine was charged by his contemporaries with obscurity, incoherence, decadence; and his celebrated line (in "*Langueur*") *Je suis l'Empire à la fin de la décadence* ("I am the Empire at the end of decadence") was used as a slogan by eccentric successors. But he could also be, as in this perfect poem in *Sagesse*, the simplest and clearest of classical masters. French children learn this poem by heart as they do poems of Villon and La Fontaine.

(1) *The sky, above the roof, is* (2) *So blue, so calm!* (3) *A tree, above the roof,* (4) *Waves its frond.* (5) *The bell, in the sky one sees,* (6) *Softly rings.* (7) *A bird in the tree one sees* (8) *Sings his plaint.* (9) *God, my God, life is there,* (10) *Simple and quiet.* (11) *That peaceful murmur there* (12) *Comes from the town.* (13) —*What have you done, O you in there* (14) *Ceaselessly weeping,* (15) *Say, what have you done, you in there,* (16) *With your youth?*

The speaker is in his Belgian prison. Through the bars of his cell, he sees the blue sky, calm as he wishes his own soul might be. Above the roof, a tree—as in the garden of Eden, or like the "sole Arabian tree" in the Shakespearean *The Phoenix and the Turtle*—sways its branch, which is here poetically called a "palm." In the second stanza, with impeccable order two sensations of sound (the bell tinkling and the bird singing) add to the visual sensations and are marked by the naïvely simple *qu'on voit,* which becomes a refrain.

While he hears the pleasant sound in the nearby square and dreams of the quiet domestic happiness of the families under the blue sky of this Sunday afternoon, the prisoner mechanically whispers an appeal to God. A pause separates the third stanza from the fourth. Soon he will be thirty, the age at which Villon, so often associated with Verlaine, had begun his "Testament": *En l'an trentième de mon âge | Que toutes mes hontes j'eus bues* ("In the thirtieth year of my age / When I had drunk all my shames"). Verlaine also has drunk shame to the dregs. He mourns his misspent youth. The octosyllabic lines with masculine rimes, the four-syllable lines prolonged by feminine rimes (in mute *e*), the perfection of the stanzas, the logic of the structure, and the balanced design of the whole contrast strangely with the ruin of his youth, the torment of his misdeeds, and the disarray of his feeble will. [H.P.]

STÉPHANE MALLARMÉ

DON DU POÈME

Je t'apporte l'enfant d'une nuit d'Idumée!
Noire, à l'aile saignante et pâle, déplumée,
Par le verre brûlé d'aromates et d'or,
Par les carreaux glacés, hélas! mornes encor,   4
L'aurore se jeta sur la lampe angélique.
Palmes! et quand elle a montré cette relique
A ce père essayant un sourire ennemi,
La solitude bleue et stérile a frémi.   8
O la berceuse, avec ta fille et l'innocence
De vos pieds froids, accueille une horrible naissance:
Et ta voix rappelant viole et clavecin,
Avec le doigt fané presseras-tu le sein   12
Par qui coule en blancheur sibylline la femme
Pour les lèvres que l'air du vierge azur affame?

(*Poésies*. 1887)

"Gift of the Poem" this is entitled, and the specific poem is identified in the first line: "I bring you the child of an Idumean night." For a year Stéphane Mallarmé (1842-1898) had been working upon a verse drama for the stage, named for a princess of Edomite (Idumean) ancestry. "*Hérodiade*" was to embody a new poetic theory: "To paint, not the thing, but the effect it produces"; and though the undertaking filled him with terror, he could scarcely foresee that it would remain uncompleted at his death thirty-four years later.

The setting appears in the first eight lines. The writer has been laboring at his desk throughout the night, the lamplight glistening on the window, the images of Hérodiade's world all about him. Finally at dawn something has taken form, has been completed—a poem, such as it is, has been born. He takes this child of his thought into the adjoining room where the child of his body lies sleeping with its mother. He presents it to her and asks if she will give it nourishment.

Except for the indefiniteness created by the punctuation, the setting can be literally transcribed thus: (1) *I bring you the child (offspring) of an Idumean night!* (2) *Black (dark), with wing bleeding and pale, [its feathers] plucked,* (3) *Through the window burnt with spices and gold,* (4) *Through the icy panes, alas, still bleak (dreary),* (5) *Dawn hurled itself upon the angelic lamp.*

The word *Palmes!* suddenly appears, an exclamation whose import we are left to imagine; then the description continues: (6) *Palms! and when it [dawn] showed that relic* (7) *To this father [who was] attempting a hostile smile,* (8) *The blue and sterile solitude trembled (shuddered).*

(9) *O singer (of lullabies), you who rock the cradle, with your daughter and the innocence* (10) *Of your cold feet, welcome (greet) a [this] horrible birth:* (11) *And, your voice recalling viol and harpsichord,* (12) *With your faded finger, will you press the breast* (13) *Through which in sibylline whiteness woman flows* (14) *For the lips made hungry by the virgin azure?*

This poem, like a number of others by Mallarmé, dramatizes the birth-process of art. But why does the solitude tremble? why is it sterile? And why does the father look on his offspring with animosity? Both the actions and attitudes of this poem cannot be perceived apart from Mallarmé's lifelong obsession with his own creative impotence, with his fear and his struggle against it, and with his seeming horror of the birth-process itself. The child of this nightlong labor, a pale, bleeding bird born in the icy dawn, will die if it is not nourished. But the one who gave birth to it can do nothing more for it.

It has been a strange, almost sterile birth, such as might bring into the world the strange poem of the princess Hérodiade, who rejects all human contact and for whom barrenness is the burning ideal. "Yes, it is for myself, for myself that I flower alone. . . I love the horror of being virgin . . . I want nothing human / O final joy, yes, I feel it: I am alone. . . ." Denis Saurat points out that the kings of Edom were supposedly able to reproduce without women. The poet also—and in this instance it is a blood-soaked, horrible birth. But once born, the offspring of the mind must be nourished in order to live. Brought into the world, it must be welcomed and sustained by the world.

Certain English "equivalents" in our version of this quasi-sonnet are too bare.

"Plucked" (2) is too concise for the broad, slow sounds of *déplumée*, a word which carries the further implication that a pen has been removed. "Spices" (3) lacks the exoticism and aroma of *aromates*. *Ce père* (7) means much more than "this father": it implies pity for the poor, exhausted poet with his faint, ambiguous smile. Similarly *la berceuse* (9) carries overtones of intimacy and tenderness toward the wife and mother. It might also be the lullaby itself.

A number of other elements are curiously evocative. *Noire* paired with *pâle* (2), and *lampe angélique* with the other ecclesiastical touch *relique* (5-6). The "innocence of your cold feet" (9-10). The change from the intimate pronoun *ta* (*fille*) to the more distant *vos* (*pieds*). And the breast of the nourisher-and-sustainer —it will be pressed by a finger that is "faded," "withered."

A number of the images in this poem occur elsewhere in Mallarmé, almost as his signatures (*bleue et stérile, viole et clavecin, vierge azur*); but what shall we make of *Palmes!*? A French critic found a line in Virgil containing both *palmas* and *Idumaeas*, but does this help? To some American scholar-critics the exclamation symbolizes both martyrdom and victory. Other readers suggest that the dawn threw itself suddenly, like elongated, irradiating palms, or Homeric rosy fingers—and that the very sound suggests something broad, spread-out flat, like a bird wing, to which dawn has been related implicitly (2). But perhaps *Palmes* simply occurred to Mallarmé and he retained it because he felt that he had to—much as he introduced in another poem the word "ptyx" because this pure invention struck him as being both right and necessary for his purposes.

[S.B.]

STÉPHANE MALLARMÉ

SAINTE

A la fenêtre recélant
Le santal vieux qui se dédore
De sa viole étincelant
Jadis avec flûte ou mandore,   4

Est la Sainte pâle, étalant
Le livre vieux qui se déplie
Du Magnificat ruisselant
Jadis selon vêpre et complie: 8

A ce vitrage d'ostensoir
Que frôle une harpe par l'Ange
Formée avec son vol du soir
Pour la délicate phalange   12

Du doigt que, sans le vieux santal
Ni le vieux livre, elle balance
Sur le plumage instrumental,
Musicienne du silence.   16

(*Poésies*. 1887)

This short lyric, composed (as was "*Don du poème*") in Tournon in 1865, offers few of the difficulties that irritate, or fascinate, many readers of Mallarmé's later work (composed after 1873)—rare words, syntactical intricacies, private associations, and baffling images. At first glance it seems almost Parnassian, for it appears to describe a painting, in the tradition of Horace's *ut pictura poesis*, and it is rich in substantives and free from the fluid vagueness that engulfs the Faun's sensuous afternoon dream. But "The Saint" is neither a description nor a hymn in praise of music; and its extreme conciseness demands careful attentiveness and imaginative reading (*e.g.*, a single verb carries the last two stanzas). Mallarmé rose to greater heights in other works, but nowhere else, unless it be in "*Autre éventail*" (p. 56), did he display more subtle mastery. One of his commentators, Charles Mauron, considers "*Sainte*" to be "one of the best poems that Mallarmé ever wrote, . . . a masterpiece analogous to the most astonishing of the Italian Annunciations." The condensation and brevity of the eight-syllable lines and the supreme skill with which the words are placed both in the sentence and in the stanzas make for awkwardness in translation:

(1) *At the window secretly hiding* (2) *The old sandalwood [slowly] losing (shedding) its gilt* (3) *Of her viol shining (glittering)* (4) *Formerly with flute or mandore [mandolin]* (5) *Is*

the pale Saint, spreading out (6) *The old (ancient) book that unfolds* (7) *Of the Magnificat streaming* (8) *Formerly according to vesper and complin* [*nightsong, the last liturgical prayer of the day*]: (9) *At this monstrance window* [*the stained-glass shining like a monstrance*] (10-11) *Which a harp formed by the Angel with his evening flight* [*wing*] *brushes by* ["*frôle*"] (12) *For the delicate phalanx* [*joint*] (13) *Of the finger that, without the old sandalwood* (14) *Or the old book, she holds poised (balances)* (15) *Upon the instrumental plumage,* (16) *Musician of silence.*

The figure portrayed with her ancient musical instruments, which though hidden are yet heard, and with the illuminated Magnificat, which streams with color and light and music as it did when it lay open at the vesperal service, is Saint Cecilia. Mallarmé composed the poem as a festive gift for Mme Cécile Brunet, who was named for the saint. (Mme Brunet, the godmother of the poet's daughter Geneviève, was the wife of a Provençal poet with whose group [the Félibres] Mallarmé was associated when he taught in Avignon.) Mallarmé had probably seen a reproduction of Raphael's well-known painting in the museum of Bologna, in which Saint Cecilia, with two saints on either side and the musical instruments at her feet, listens in rapture to the singing of the angels above her—the angels holding opened books before them, as in the poem. She has rejected her own instruments, preferring the "unheard" music of the angels to anything she might attempt to create. Shelley, in a letter of 1818, had expressed great admiration for the composition and the color of the painting; but it is very doubtful that Mallarmé, teacher of English though he was, had ever read that letter.

The first two stanzas are remarkable for the use—uncommon in French—of four present participles placed at the rime and for the suggestion of former times (times of religious music, stained-glass windows, and serene silence) by the repetition of *jadis* ("formerly") at the beginning of lines 4 and 8. The stained-glass window apparently depicts a window at which Cecilia sits or stands (windows held a rare fascination for Mallarmé). The Saint hides the musical instruments that the poet imagines: a viol made of sandalwood, now old and shedding its once bright gold; a flute; a four-stringed lute (mandore). She hides these objects but she spreads open the splendidly illuminated volume.

The third stanza, like the first, opens with the Saint at the window, but this is not the simple window of line 1: it is a window of stained glass that glistens with light like the liturgical vessel in which the Host is exposed (*ce vitrage d'ostensoir*). There is no verb before *vitrage:* the reader has to supply the missing words (*e.g.,* "there she sits"), for the stanza is less concrete than the first two—the poem is becoming a vision. The colors of the window stream in the evening light as the Saint's finger is about to touch an invisible harp, a harp formed by the Angel's wing in its flight. But the finger merely moves in the air above the imaginary harp (*le plumage instrumental*). It touches nothing, and the poem ends. The Saint is enshrined as the "musician of silence."

For a moment the reader may think of Keats ("Heard melodies are sweet, but those unheard / Are sweeter")—but for a moment only. For our entire poem converges and comes to rest in the final line: it ends in silence as it began in absence. Its themes are two, but the two are subsumed in Mallarmé's ever-deepening concern with "absence" in all its manifestations. "*Sainte*" is only one of the poet's memorable exaltations of the beauty and significance of ultimate Nothingness.

[H.P.]

• 47 •

STÉPHANE MALLARMÉ

TOAST FUNÈBRE

O de notre bonheur, toi, le fatal emblème!

Salut de la démence et libation blême,
Ne crois pas qu'au magique espoir du corridor
J'offre ma coupe vide où souffre un monstre d'or!   4
Ton apparition ne va pas me suffire:
Car je t'ai mis, moi-même, en un lieu de porphyre.
Le rite est pour les mains d'éteindre le flambeau
Contre le fer épais des portes du tombeau: 8
Et l'on ignore mal, élu pour notre fête
Très simple de chanter l'absence du poète,
Que ce beau monument l'enferme tout entier.
Si ce n'est que la gloire ardente du métier,   12
Jusqu'à l'heure commune et vile de la cendre,
Par le carreau qu'allume un soir fier d'y descendre,
Retourne vers les feux du pur soleil mortel!

It was customary among the ancients to write funeral elegies or to prepare collective tributes in verse as a memorial of the death of a fellow poet. The practice was revived during the Renaissance and in the nineteenth century it gave rise to a number of celebrated works, among them "Adonais" and "In Memoriam." Mallarmé's tribute to Théophile Gautier is among the most majestic and searching of such elegiac poems, for it celebrates not only an individual writer who had been beloved by his contemporaries but also The Poet in general. It was one of those poems of circumstance which moved its author to put in majestic language his most personal reflections on man's facing of death, his acceptance of Nothingness, and his spurning of all solace except for the proud awareness that art alone can transcend both life and death. Henri Mondor, Mallarmé's biographer, regards "*Toast funèbre*" as the "vertiginous summit" of the poet's achievement, and there is no doubt that it constitutes, after "*Hérodiade*" and "*L'Après-midi d'un faune*" (and long before the enigmatic "*Coup de dés*"), the most perfect of Mallarmé's long poems. The tone throughout is one of grave serenity. The difficulties of interpretation are considerable and the obscurities real, but neither are merely artificial barriers erected between the writer and his reader. They are intrinsic to the message of the poem.

Théophile Gautier, a survivor from the Romantic generation, who became the master of the Parnassians, and a friend of Mallarmé's early in the younger poet's career, died in Paris on October 23, 1872. His friends decided to publish a book in his honor, and it appeared a year later;

"Funeral Toast" was one of the eighty-three tributes of this *Tombeau*. Mallarmé had published virtually nothing since 1867, and in 1869 he was plunged into a profound personal crisis, out of which he finally emerged, with a new poetics (as exemplified in "*Hérodiade*") and a philosophic attitude that informed all the work of his subsequent career. His letters reveal how he had descended into a spiritual and intellectual inferno; refusing all belief in immortality and resurrection, he confronted Nothingness. Art alone appeared to him as the possible justification for human existence and a godless universe. "*Toast funèbre*," composed with relative swiftness, brought Mallarmé out of the gloom of his creative sterility. The poem ends with a noble hymn of faith in the consolations of his art.

After the opening line of invocation, the poem unfolds in harmonious architecture. The first fifteen lines depict the setting, the characters, and the tomb, and they reject the usual pallid comfort that other men turn to when faced by the finality of death. (1) *You, the fated (fatal) emblem of our happiness (good fortune): (2) Greeting born of madness and a pale libation, (3) Do not think that to the magical hope of the corridor (4) I offer my empty cup (glass) where a golden monster suffers (writhes)! (5) Your apparition will not suffice for me: (6) For I myself have deposited you in a place of porphyry. (7) The rite is for the hands to extinguish the torch (8) Against the thick iron of the gates of the tomb: (9-10) It is wrong not to know, [when] chosen for our very simple celebration of singing the absence of the poet, (11) That this fine monument encloses the whole of him. (12) Unless it be that the blazing glory of the craft, (13) Until the common and base (foul) hour of ashes (dust), (14) Through the pane inflamed by an evening proud of descending to it, (15) Returns toward the fires of the pure mortal sun.*

The hymn opens with a feminine rime; it will end on a masculine one, after twenty-seven couplets (*rimes plates*). The alexandrine is grave and rich, with breaks that are on the whole regular, but with an occasional striking effect of surprise, as with the *toi* of the seventh syllable.

The controlling idea is presented at the outset. Gautier will stand as the emblem, the symbol of the fortunate condition of the poet as decreed by fate *(fatal)*. The poem is a toast offered to the departed poet by his friends, and Mallarmé raises his imaginary glass; but the libation is "pale" *(blême)*, a mere gesture, and it is also a "demented" act *(démence)*, for the belief in immortality is a delusion. Firmly the speaker states his denial that death might be a passageway to another life: such a notion is only a magic, vain hope *(magique espoir, 3)*.

Looking at the golden monster in his glass—an etched figure? a reflection of twisting light?—he reasserts the vanity of pretending that the dead might still enjoy even a semblance of life. Mallarmé had already walked to the dead man's tomb (ennobled as "porphyry"); he had observed the rite of extinguishing the symbolic torch of life against its doors. How wrong it would be of him who has been elected to mourn Gautier's death not to acknowledge that nothing survives (9-11)!

Line 12, however, announces a joyful, confident creed that the rest of the work will proclaim: A poet, having practiced (as Gautier had practiced) a profession resplendent *(ardente)* with glory, instead of dissolving with the common herd into anonymous dust (13), becomes a window reflecting the evening sunlight; for his work, now part of the human heritage, acts as an influence and an example—it lives on among the *phares* ("beacons"), as Baudelaire might have said, or as Shelley declared in his elegy to Keats: Adonais "like a star / Beacons from the abode where the Eternal are."

Magnifique, total et solitaire, tel   16
Tremble de s'exhaler le faux orgueil des hommes.
Cette foule hagarde! elle annonce: Nous sommes
La triste opacité de nos spectres futurs.
Mais le blason des deuils épars sur de vains murs   20
J'ai méprisé l'horreur lucide d'une larme,
Quand, sourd même à mon vers sacré qui ne l'alarme
Quelqu'un de ces passants, fier, aveugle et muet,
Hôte de son linceul vague, se transmuait   24
En le vierge héros de l'attente posthume.
Vaste gouffre apporté dans l'amas de la brume
Par l'irascible vent des mots qu'il n'a pas dits,
Le néant à cet Homme aboli de jadis: 28
« Souvenirs d'horizons, qu'est-ce, ô toi, que la Terre? »
Hurle ce songe; et, voix dont la clarté s'altère,
L'espace a pour jouet le cri: « Je ne sais pas! »

Le Maître, par un œil profond, a, sur ses pas,   32
Apaisé de l'éden l'inquiète merveille
Dont le frisson final, dans sa voix seule, éveille.
Pour la Rose et le Lys le mystère d'un nom.
Est-il de ce destin rien qui demeure, non?   36
O vous tous, oubliez une croyance sombre.
Le splendide génie éternel n'a pas d'ombre.

The second section (13-31) shows Gautier arriving in triumph at the place where ordinary men, pale and frightened, wander about, bemoaning their mortal condition and pinning their hopes on a future existence. Gautier faces the question put to him by Nothingness. Undaunted by the abyss into which he has been plunged, he gives the reply of the agnostic.

(16) *Magnificent, total, and solitary, such [was he—unlike]* (17) *The false pride of men [that] trembles at revealing* [literally *exhaling*] *itself.* (18) *This haggard crowd! proclaims: We are* (19) *The sad opaqueness of our future ghosts.* (20) *But [once] the blazonry of mourning [was] scattered on empty walls* (21) *I scorned the lucid horror of a tear,* (22) *When, deaf even to my consecrated verse which does not startle (alarm) him* (23) *One of those passers-by, proud, blind and mute,*

(24) *A guest in (of) his [own] vague shroud, was transmuting himself* (25) *Into the virgin hero of the posthumous expectation (awaiting).* (26) *Vast gulf carried into the mass of mist* (27) *By the angry wind of the words he did not utter,* (28) *Nothingness [speaking] to this abolished Man of yore* [literally *formerly*]: (29) *"Memories of horizons, O you, what is the Earth?"* (30) *Roars (shouts, howls) this dream; and [like] a voice whose clarity falters,* (31) *Space has [takes] as its toy the [answering] cry: "I do not know."*

The three adjectives that open this passage (*magnifique, total, solitaire*), isolated by the monosyllable *tel* at the end of the line, produce an effect of surprise and awe. (*Total* suggests solidity, self-assurance, and rejection of any superhuman help.) They refer to Gautier's authentic pride (17) as opposed to the false pride of ordinary men that makes them incapable in the face of death of asserting themselves with nobility and courage. (*S'exhaler*, more eloquent than "express itself," is all but untranslatable.)

Most men (*des hommes*, 17) are a cowardly herd (18), content to remain even during their time on earth the heavy, opaque half of their postmortal condition as ghosts (19). In contrast to their attitude, Mallarmé declares his own—an affirmation introduced by the word *mais*. When the draperies and blazonries of mourning were being hung on the empty walls (20), he could feel only scorn for what he calls (in a magnificent alexandrine, of three instead of the usual four parts) "the lucid horror of a tear," alluding to the transparency of tears gliding down the cheek. Though the next four lines (22-25) are obscure, Mallarmé seems to designate Gautier as "one among those passers-by." (Elsewhere he calls Rimbaud "a considerable passer-by," referring both to his ephemeral sojourn and to his powerful influence among men of letters.) Gautier passed among them but he is now deaf and silent, inhabiting his formless (*vague*, 24) shroud. In a condensed and symmetrical combination of two nouns and two adjectives, he is called the "virgin hero" (he is entering the new life that will be lived by his work) of the "posthumous expectation" (of posterity's judgment).

Gautier is then transfigured as Man, capitalized, once alive and now (as one of Mallarmé's favorite adjectives calls him) "abolished," given back to the dust. Gautier would not utter words of pious solace (27). The vast abyss (26) of Nothingness rushes toward the newly dead man to ask him contemptuously in a dream or nightmarish cry (*hurle*, 30): What, after all, is that Earth from which he had departed, that "mere memory of horizons" he onced cherished? After these stormy lines of rising motion and wrathful declaration, the second section concludes in a line and a half that is subdued, less anguished. The deceased poet, whose voice faltered in the exhaustion of dying, still whispers an answer: four one-syllable words that are bandied about like a plaything in space—"*Je ne sais pas.*" He does not know (31). His creed is not metaphysical but esthetic.

The last section of the work defines the mission of the Poet in grave and serene words. (32) *The Master, by his deep [-searching] gaze, as he went along, has* (33) *Calmed (appeased) the restless marvel of Eden* (34) *Whose ultimate [essential] thrill (trembling) in his voice alone awakens* (35) *For the Rose and the Lily the mystery of a name.* (36) *Does anything remain of this destiny? Nothing?* (37) *O all of you, [you must] forget [such] a somber creed.* (38) *Splendid eternal genius has no shade (ghost).*

Both the fear of the ugly paraphernalia of death and mourning and the obsession with Nothingness have now been dispelled. The "Master"—Gautier; also "The Artist" as a type—walks about the gardens of the world, with eyes that see more deeply and with feelings that respond more intensely than those of other men. He is able to discover the mysterious names that define the wonders of that Eden (external nature) and thus to endow them with a personal life and meaning of their own. Such acts of creation survive his body's death (36). In lines of sculptural beauty and august fervor, the speaker urges the dead man's friends and the general world of men, that fails to heed the message of creative artists, to abandon the mistaken belief that genius can ever be eclipsed or silenced (38).

Moi, de votre désir soucieux, je veux voir,
A qui s'évanouit, hier, dans le devoir   40
Idéal que nous font les jardins de cet astre,
Survivre pour l'honneur du tranquille désastre
Une agitation solennelle par l'air
De paroles, pourpre ivre et grand calice clair,   45
Que, pluie et diamant, le regard diaphane
Resté là sur ces fleurs dont nulle ne se fane,
Isole parmi l'heure et le rayon du jour!
C'est de nos vrais bosquets déjà tout le séjour,   48
Où le poète pur a pour geste humble et large
De l'interdire au rêve, ennemi de sa charge:
Afin que le matin de son repos altier,
Quand la mort ancienne est comme pour Gautier   52
De n'ouvrir pas les yeux sacrés et de se taire,
Surgisse, de l'allée ornement tributaire,
Le sépulcre solide où gît tout ce qui nuit,
Et l'avare silence et la massive nuit.   56

(*Le tombeau de Théophile Gautier.* 1873)

After this solemn and unambiguous appeal, Mallarmé opens a long, complex, and often obscure period of nine lines. He has exalted the Artist above all other men, for the Artist disciplines the chaos of nature with creative ordering; the Artist transforms into sovereign immortality—as Gautier himself had done in his famous poem *"L'Art"*—the last thrill of the restless motion of flowers: the *frisson final.*

(39) *I, mindful of your desire, I want to see* (40-41) [*Surviving,* 42] *him who vanished yesterday, in the ideal duty that the gardens of this star assign us* [*to fulfill*], (42) *Surviving* [*in*] *for the honor of the calm disaster,* (43) *A solemn movement in the air* (44) *Of words, drunken scarlet and large clear chalice,* (45) *Which, the diaphanous gaze, rain and diamond,* (46) [*That was*] *fixed (remaining) on those flowers none of which fades,* (47) *Isolates in the hour and the rays of sunlight!*

Part of the difficulty in this passage can be traced to Mallarmé's curious fondness for inversions and appositions. Ordinary syntax would place *survivre* (42) before its indirect object two lines above: *à qui s'évanouit* ("him who vanished," 40). *Pluie et diamant* ("rain and diamond," 46) designates *regard* ("gaze"), which follows it. The tall cup of the lily (45) and the word *pourpre*—it suggests a deep red color, with which the rose seems to be drunk while its fragrance is intoxicating for others—recall *la Rose et le Lys* mentioned nine lines earlier (35). Such connections, needlessly obscured, will nevertheless be found by the reader who is (as Mallarmé contended) willing to look for the key to the mystery he has been offered.

Mindful of Gautier's friends who wish that something of him may survive his death, the speaker ventures the hope that his words will live on in a solemn motion (line 43 is one of the most splendid in the poem). *Le devoir* (40) may well be an allusion of Mallarmé's to Gautier's stoical acceptance of "the duty" that art imposes on the writer—"Carve, file, and chisel," he had advised the poet in his *"L'Art."* But *cet astre* (41) refers, not to Gautier, whom Mallarmé would not ridicule by calling a star, but to the planet Earth. *Désastre* (42) —the word originally designated the evil fate of one born under the wrong star (*astre*)—characterizes the lamented death of Gautier and the fatality of everything that lives in this world. The poet's eye, which is diaphanous (*le regard diaphane*, 46), which pierces through appearances, isolates and remains fixed upon those flowers which it singles out from among all the flowers growing at the same time and under the rays of the same sun (47). It brings them *pluie et diamant* (46; *diamant* is often used in this sense by Mallarmé and Valéry)—rain and sunshine, the peculiar nourishment that they crave; for it immortalizes these ephemeral flowers by exalting them to the plane of everlasting art, as the vase painter of Keats's Grecian Urn had immortalized the "marble men and maidens overwrought."

(48) *This is already the sole abode (place of sojourn) of our true groves,* (49) *Where the pure poet's humble and vast gesture* (50) *Is to deny access to dream, the enemy of his mission (responsibility):* (51) *So that on the morning of his lofty (proud) repose (sleep),* (52) *When ancient death is, as [now] for Gautier,* (53) *Not to open one's consecrated eyes and to keep silent,* (54) *There may arise, [as] a tributary ornament of the path,* (55) *The solid sepulchre where lies all that harms,* (56) *And miserly silence and massive night.*

The authentic (*vrais*, 48) groves are those where the beauties of nature have been transfigured by art. The pure poet watches over them. He forbids sentimental dreams of personal immortality or of solacing religious faith to enter, standing like the dragon at the gate of the Garden of Hesperides.

The last six lines return to Gautier's tomb and complete the solemn tribute by seeing in him the model of the pure poet. He is now already entering the only possible immortality: that of his works (51). Death will soon be far behind (it will be *ancienne*, 52). His tomb will stand like a tomb of the ancients (Gautier had often called himself a Pagan and a Greek), along some path among other sarcophagi that are "solid" (*solide*, from the Latin *solus;* the sarcophagi are "all of a piece"). His eyes, which had consecrated the beauty of the sentient world, are now closed and his lips are sealed. But darkness, splendidly characterized as "massive," and invidious, and greedy silence are buried in the grave: they are the only things that could bring harm. Through his verse, through the symbolic example that he has become for posterity, the poet, standing now in the true place of his abode, lives on. [H.P.]

STÉPHANE MALLARMÉ

[LE VIERGE, LE VIVACE ET LE BEL AUJOURD'HUI]

Le vierge, le vivace et le bel aujourd'hui
Va-t-il nous déchirer avec un coup d'aile ivre
Ce lac dur oublié que hante sous le givre
Le transparent glacier des vols qui n'ont pas fui!   4

Un cygne d'autrefois se souvient que c'est lui
Magnifique mais qui sans espoir se délivre
Pour n'avoir pas chanté la région où vivre
Quand du stérile hiver a resplendi l'ennui.   8

Tout son col secouera cette blanche agonie
Par l'espace infligée à l'oiseau qui le nie,
Mais non l'horreur du sol où le plumage est pris.   11

Fantôme qu'à ce lieu son pur éclat assigne,
Il s'immobilise au songe froid de mépris
Que vêt parmi l'exil inutile le Cygne.   14

(*Poésies.* 1887)

Most popular of all Mallarmé's sonnets, "*Le vierge, le vivace...*" is not only a work of surpassing beauty of language and sound; it is also an image of mystifying intent. Numerous interpretations have been put forth, many of them carefully substantiated by the words of the original. The interested reader, who may prefer a reading different from ours, would do well to remember Robert Frost's insistence that a poet is entitled to all the meanings that can be found in his poem. And a great many indeed can be found in this sonnet of The Swan.

The first stanza is both an exclamation and a question. It seizes us by the surprise of the three resplendent adjectives of the opening line, and when we come upon the *nous* of the second, we are directly involved. (1) *The virgin, the vivid and the splendid new day*—this new day bristling with life— (2) *Will it tear for us with a stroke of its drunken wing* (3) *This hard forgotten lake haunted beneath the frost* (4) *By the transparent glacier of flights that have not fled!*

Our eyes gaze at the frozen landscape before us, but we are immediately transported to time-past. (5) *A swan of former days remembers that it is he* (6) *Magnificent but who [struggles] without hope to free himself* (7) *For not having sung [of] the region in which to live* (8) *When the tediousness of sterile winter glistened.* The swan remembers the paradise of his magnificence, then his hopeless struggle to free himself—hopeless because he would not submit to necessity; he would not come to terms with reality, but clung stubbornly to his own, pure, solitary ideal.

The first tercet takes us back to time-present: the swan breaks out in a final act of resistance. (9) *His whole neck will shake off that white agony* (10) *Inflicted by space upon this bird who denies it [space],* (11) *But not the horror of the soil in which his plumage is trapped (caught).* His long neck emerges above the ice, white in the imprisoning whiteness of the snow, while his body, trapped beneath the ice, is held down by the soil that horrifies him. (12) *Phantom assigned to this place by his own pure brightness,* (13) *He stills himself in the cold dream of scorn* (14) *That the Swan wraps himself in during his useless exile.* A white ghost in the lake of ice, unable to free himself, he resorts to the only action possible for the swan that he is: scorn for his conqueror, for all that is base in the world; scorn also for himself, for having failed to do what he should have done before—reconcile the ideal with the real. This is *spleen* as Baudelaire had called it; the insidious *ennui*.

Mallarmé's art stands at its highest in this sonnet. All the rimes are in *i* or *ui*, a sound which has something of the angular sharpness of ice itself. (For Albert Thibaudet, and doubtless others, the *i* sound of all fourteen rimes evokes the vast monotony of cold, white space.) Each quatrain, perfectly formed in itself, ends with a long, dense line that seems to unfold. The effect in the first is especially notable after the almost obsessive recurrence of *v* sounds, the effect in the second is one of mournful finality (8). After the scene of struggling desperation in the first tercet, the lines begin to tighten in an ice-like gloom. But in the last three lines the swan takes on a visionary aura. He becomes a ghost proudly withdrawing within himself and from the world, the essential Swan with a capital letter, the Poet exiled among us.

The first three adjectives almost sensuously evoke the brilliant purity, restless vigor, and lovely promise of the day just born. Line 4 makes as it were a single substance of the transparent ice of the lake and of the swan. The adjective *magnifique*, set off at the beginning of line 6, instantly bodies forth the pride and proud dream once entertained by the youthful swan (and, by extension, by other birds or poets before him). Many of the words in the first tercet are thin, sharp monosyllables, hammered slowly as if to seal the swan in his *blanche agonie* ("futile struggle," the meaning of *agony* in Greek). By contrast, longer words, with an accumulation of *i*'s (*s'immobilise, l'exil inutile*) fill the last two lines, producing an impression of vast, desolate plains of ice—of the monotonous *ennui* which, as Baudelaire said, "takes on the dimensions [literally "proportions"] of immortality."

Scholars have assigned a number of sources to this sonnet, among them Gautier, Baudelaire's "Albatross," and, even more insistently, his "The Swan," the elegy of all exiles. But none is genuinely relevant, for Mallarmé's originality is unquestionable. The theme may remind some readers of the familiar Romantic view of the poet as a Moses (Vigny), a Prometheus (Goethe, Shelley) tormented by himself and by others, a martyr in a tribe which does not understand—but is this the theme? Mallarmé does not indulge in recriminating declamation: he himself, or the swan-artist whom he imagines, has evaded compromise, change, reality, "life" itself. Mallarmé was haunted by the idea of "azure" (see his early poem "*L'Azur*"), by the symbol of an eternal serenity-purity beyond all human possibility—as was Flaubert, in his dream of writing prose about no subject. Has he not congealed life itself by this insistent dreaming of unattainable perfection? Or is the final line an ambiguous warning and defiance, the "*Cygne*" merely disguising the intent of its homonym "*Signe*" ("Sign")? [H.P.]

AUTRE ÉVENTAIL DE
MADEMOISELLE MALLARMÉ

O rêveuse, pour que je plonge
Au pur délice sans chemin,
Sache, par un subtil mensonge,
Garder mon aile dans ta main.   4

Une fraîcheur de crépuscule
Te vient à chaque battement
Dont le coup prisonnier recule
L'horizon délicatement.   8

Vertige! voici que frissonne
L'espace comme un grand baiser
Qui, fou de naître pour personne
Ne peut jaillir ni s'apaiser.   12

Sens-tu le paradis farouche
Ainsi qu'un rire enseveli
Se couler du coin de ta bouche
Au fond de l'unanime pli!   16

Le sceptre des rivages roses
Stagnants sur les soirs d'or, ce l'est,
Ce blanc vol fermé que tu poses
Contre le feu d'un bracelet.   20

(*Poésies.* 1887)

The scene: Mallarmé's apartment; time: probably 1883; the actors in this brief drama: the poet, his daughter Geneviève, then nineteen, and her fan. The summer day has been hot, but now as it comes to a close, a light breeze stirs the sultry space, "like a great kiss" (10). A pink and golden sunset will soon light up the room and the girl will place her fan next to her gold or red bracelet. The atmosphere is one of family intimacy, as in a picture by Manet or Vuillard. The poem, in octosyllabic lines, might almost be taken as a garland of flowers, or a compliment, painted on a fan. Yet fans were filled with mystery and symbolic meaning for Mallarmé; he wrote two poems entitled "*Éventail*" ("Fan"), not to mention several quatrains; hence the adjective "*autre*" ("other") in the title of this one. In one of his prose writings reprinted in *Divagations*, he compared a book that is read nonchalantly by a woman at the seashore and held as a screen between the sea and her eyes to a fan—"that other paper wing conceals the site to bring back to the lips a mute painted flower, similar to the intact and annihilated word of the dream, drawn near by the motion of the fan." Mallarmé sometimes gave himself to stylistic refinement, but his preciosity never degenerated into conceit or bad taste or a search for baroque metaphors. Occasionally his poems addressed to women or written about them play on *risqué*, erotic ambiguities, but more often they raise the physical to the spiritual—as in this dramatic lyric, which is also a graceful embodiment of Mallarmé's attitude toward art.

The fan does the speaking. It addresses as *rêveuse* the poet's daughter, who holds it. She is lost in reverie—dreaming, perhaps of marriage, of the fiancé who will someday seek her, of the elegant fan that she seems to be on the verge of freeing whenever she opens it, as if it then became an angel's wing. But she holds that wing in her hand through a "subtle deception." In its rhythmical motion, the fan almost plunges into pure pathless space; like the artist, it rejects the coarser regions of life to seek the ideal. It beats the air, but like a prisoner, for the girl holds it captive; and yet it blows the stagnant air away and opens up space; and the girl behind its symbolic screen glimpses the horizon of the yet unknown country of her womanhood.

The art of this poem is exquisitely faultless; no rendering can hope to convey the musical grace of the original. The sounds (*plonge, mensonge*) are soft and rich; the adjectives felicitous and just unusual enough to create pleasurable surprise (*pur délice, subtil mensonge, coup prisonnier*). The rhythm avoids the octosyllabic danger of dividing the line mechanically into four syllables, by varying the breaks (after *sache*, 3; *délicatement*, 8, set off by its position at the rime). (1) *O dreamer, [so] that I may plunge* (2) *Into pure pathless*

delight, (3) *Know, through a subtle deceit,* (4) *How to hold my wing in your hand.* (5) *A twilight coolness* (6) *Comes to you at each beat [of my wings]* (7) *Whose captive blow pushes back* (8) *The horizon delicately.*

The next two stanzas grow suddenly impassioned—the girl is no longer placidly dreaming. (9-10) *Ecstasy* [literally *vertigo*]*! now space quivers like an immense kiss* (11) *Which, wild at being born for no one,* (12) *Can neither spring forth nor be allayed.* (13) *Do you feel the wild paradise* (14) *Like a buried laugh* (15) *Gliding from the corner of your mouth* (16) *To the depths of the unanimous fold!*

Space, opened up by the motion of the fan, quivers with the evening breeze as though it has received a kiss; and the girl's lips, revealed as the fan moves back and forth, also seem to be sketching a kiss. But the nascent kiss is for no one; it remains only half-born and unsatisfied. The tone grows more pressing in line 13: the wild paradise of voluptuous delight as yet closed to the girl is like a suppressed ("buried") laugh; it arouses her smile. She addresses that smile (15), gently sketched at the corners of her lips, to the fan now closed and held against her face: its many folds are now one—single souled ("unanimous").

(17) *The scepter of rosy shores* (18) *Stagnant on evenings of gold, this it is,* (19) *This white closed flight that you lay* (20) *Against the fire of a bracelet.* The setting sun lingers over banks of rosy cloud. The world outside and the restrained world of the girl are united once more in the humorous rime *ce l'est* that is given to *bracelet*. Geneviève has put down her "scepter"— that is, the fan, which is again captive and closed in her hand—against her glowing bracelet. She is sovereign of her world of dreams—like the artist, sovereign not of real life but of the realms of imagination.

[H.P.]

STÉPHANE MALLARMÉ

LE TOMBEAU D'EDGAR POE

Tel qu'en Lui-même enfin l'éternité le change,
Le Poète suscite avec un glaive nu
Son siècle épouvanté de n'avoir pas connu
Que la mort triomphait dans cette voix étrange!   4

Eux, comme un vil sursaut d'hydre oyant jadis l'ange
Donner un sens plus pur aux mots de la tribu
Proclamèrent très haut le sortilège bu
Dans le flot sans honneur de quelque noir mélange.   8

Du sol et de la nue hostiles, ô grief!
Si notre idée avec ne sculpte un bas-relief
Dont la tombe de Poe éblouissante s'orne   11

Calme bloc ici-bas chu d'un désastre obscur
Que ce granit du moins montre à jamais sa borne
Aux noirs vols du Blasphème épars dans le futur.   14

(Poésies. 1887)

Edgar Allan Poe died in misery in Baltimore in 1849, but within a few years Baudelaire was hailing him as his spiritual brother, and before long other important European writers were banding in a chorus of praise and vindication of America's only "accursèd poet." Not only had Poe been slanderously misunderstood; his compatriots had never seen him for what he was: a rare combination of imaginativeness and critical clarity. To most Frenchmen, Poe was primarily important as an esthetician—Mallarmé talks of "ideas bequeathed to me by my great master Poe." Such veneration continues to amaze readers of literature written in English; yet, as Eliot remarks, "No matter: if the influence of Poe upon Baudelaire, Mallarmé and Valéry was based upon misunderstanding, it was a fecund and significant misunderstanding; for the esthetic which they erected upon this dubious foundation remains valid for their own work." In 1873, a Baltimore teacher undertook to issue a Poe memorial volume (it appeared in 1877). Years later Mallarmé made a none-too-expert translation of his contribution, for an American woman who requested it.

The sonnet centers upon death, but not as Poe in his death-haunted tales speaks of it or as he wrote in "I could not love except where Death / Was mingling his with Beauty's breath." For Mallarmé, the death of Poe is far more than the triumph of a particular unfortunate over the baseness of his compatriots and his own personal weaknesses. Every artist triumphs in death, for death transforms him into his true self; it wipes out "his mortal coil" so that the work can remain henceforth untouchable.

The first line of the poem, probably the most frequently quoted in the whole range of French verse, is literally (1) *Such as into Himself at last eternity changes him.* And the next three lines bear out the claim. (2) *The Poet rouses with a bare sword* (3) *His age aghast at not having known* (4) *That death was triumphing in this strange voice.* Mallarmé rendered "un glaive nu" interpretatively as *a naked hymn*—the Poet's work is his one weapon. The next quatrain turns, from this initial statement of Mallarmé's central philosophy of life and death in relation to art, to Poe himself and to his necessary task as poet. (5) *They* ["eux" refers to "son siècle," 3], *like a hydra's vile start [a serpent's hideous twisting] on hearing, once (before), the angel* [perhaps Israfel, of Poe's poem, or Michael] (6) *Giving a purer meaning to the words of the tribe* (7) *Proclaimed aloud the spell imbibed* (8) *In the honorless flood* [Mallarmé's own rendering] *of some black brew.* Line 6 assigns to the angel the task that Mallarmé himself had undertaken (in *Little Gidding*, Eliot appropriates the words and, with characteristic change, puts them in the mouth of the spirit of poetry: "To purify the dialect of the tribe"). Instead of "hearing" the angel, Poe's contemporaries recoiled in hideous fear and contemned the purified sounds as the wild ravings of a man drunk on alcohol and other "artificial paradises."

The tercets that follow cry out, for poets and all other men of the future, the meaning that Mallarmé perceives in the fate of this accursèd poet. Line 9 remains obscure even in a literal rendering: *Out of soil and cloud, hostile, O grief.* "Grief," which usually means *grievance* (originally from the Latin *gravis*), is translated by Mallarmé as *struggle;* and it is also probably influenced by the meaning of *grief* in English. Out of that grievous conflict between the soil and the cloud—the base clay and the heavenly ideal— (10) *If our idea fails to carve a bas-relief* (11) *With which Poe's dazzling tomb is to be adorned,* (12) *Calm block fallen down here from some dim disaster,* (13) *Let this granite at least forever show (set) a limit* (14) *To the black flights of Blasphemy scattered in the future.* Out of this grievous conflict, our spirited thought must create a fitting, lasting emblem—the testament of our own belief, to be engraved upon the tomb. But if this is not done (no sculpture was actually carved; the donors failed to respond; a plain granite slab was all that could be placed as the marker), then at least this monument will stand for all time in eloquent warning. This stone block, which fell to earth from some impenetrable disaster in the sky (*astre:* "star"), now calm and immovable, will show how far the common herd can go in their attack upon the man of genius. It will silence their blasphemy in the days to come.

Few sonnets can equal this one in majesty and mastery. There is a bronze-like quality in the restraint with which the anger is controlled, a night-like aura about the images. Beneath the surface bareness, the language yields suggestive meanings with each rereading. Note, for example, the placement of *éblouissante* and *avec,* (11 and 10). Is the calm block a symbol of the dead man's career? Is its defiant presence yet another triumph of his death? The sonnet is enclosed by timelessness, from the *eternity* of the first line to the limitless *future* in the last, with the suggestion of an abundance of time in the intervening lines. It is as though with the advent of death, Poe enters upon a period of limitless existence, for the life of his true self has only begun.   [H.P.]

JULES LAFORGUE

COMPLAINTE SUR CERTAINS ENNUIS

Un couchant des Cosmogonies!
Ah! que la Vie est quotidienne...
Et, du plus vrai qu'on se souvienne
Comme on fut piètre et sans génie...

On voudrait s'avouer des choses,   5
Dont on s'étonnerait en route,
Qui feraient, une fois pour toutes!
Qu'on s'entendrait à travers poses.

On voudrait saigner le Silence,
Secouer l'exil des causeries;   10

Et non! ces dames sont aigries
Par des questions de préséance.

Elles boudent là, l'air capable.
Et sous le ciel, plus d'un s'explique,
Par quels gâchis suresthétiques   15
Ces êtres-là sont adorables.

Justement, une nous appelle,
Pour l'aider à chercher sa bague,
Perdue (où dans ce terrain vague?)
Un souvenir D'AMOUR, dit-elle!   20

Ces êtres-là sont adorables!

(Les complaintes. 1885)

LOCUTIONS DES PIERROTS

Que loin l'âme type
Qui m'a dit adieu
Parce que mes yeux
Manquaient de principes!

Elle, en ce moment   5
Elle, si pain tendre,

Oh! peut-être engendre
Quelque garnement.

Car on l'a unie
Avec un monsieur   10
Ce qu'il y a de mieux,
Mais pauvre en génie.

(L'Imitation de Notre Dame la lune. 1866)

Jules Laforgue, born in Uruguay (1860) of French parents, suffered from poverty, consumption, and a seemingly constitutional pessimism. He lived in Germany, serving as a reader to the Empress for five years, married in 1886 an English girl he had met there, and died the following year.

His irony recalls that of Tristan Corbière, at times even the morbid bitterness of Baudelaire (his pessimism was intensi-fied by his reading of Schopenhauer and Hartmann). Doubtless, if he had had time to mature, he would have acquired more depth and cast off some of the boyishness of his irony. Nevertheless his work has held fascination for poets greater than himself (Ezra Pound, T. S. Eliot, Hart Crane) and for several of the finest composers of our century (Schönberg, Honegger, Milhaud).

Tender-hearted, easily wounded by life,

eager to be understood by women and prone to idealizing them, Laforgue strained every nerve to curb his secret romanticism and to temper his sensitiveness with irony and even cynicism. He "wrung the neck of eloquence" in his verse even more determinedly than did Verlaine, and like Verlaine, he was attracted by popular ballads and by old nursery rimes. Playing skillfully with *vers impairs* (lines of odd-numbered syllables) and *vers libre* (long before it became the vogue), he dislocated traditional verse; and he also disjointed syntax and used familiar words audaciously. Hence, among enraptured idealists of the Symbolist movement and lovers of the vague and the soft, his originality is outstanding. But his range is limited (his pessimistic vein in *Le sanglot de la terre* [*Earth's Sob*], as he had intended to entitle his first volume of verse, is not represented here), and his sophistication often borders on the artificial. This poet, whom death did not allow to mature fully, has nevertheless helped others to mature. Eliot has repeatedly proclaimed the debt he incurred to Laforgue when he started writing in 1908-1909; English poets failed to touch him then, for he "was too much engrossed in working out the implications of Laforgue" (*Purpose*, 1938).

"Complaint on Certain Annoyances." (1) *A sunset of Cosmogonies!* (2) *Ah! how daily [how routine] is daily life . . .* (3) *And let us remember the most certain thing:* (4) *How paltry and lacking in genius we were . . .* (5) *We would like to confess things* (6) *Which would astonish us on the way [all the while],* (7) *Which would make us, once and for all!* (8) *Understand [hear] each other through all our pretences [posturing]:* (9) *We should like*

to bleed [drain the blood of] silence, (10) *Shake off the banishment of small talk;* (11) *But no! the ladies are bitter* (12) *About matters of precedence.* (13) *There they sit sulking, with a superior [competent] look.* (14) *And, under the sky, many a one explains to himself,* (15) *By [thanks to] what superesthetic mess* (16) *These beings are adorable.* (17) *Precisely [now], one of them calls us* (18) *To help her look for her ring,* (19) *Lost (where in this vacant lot?)* (20) *A souvenir of LOVE she says!* (21) *Oh, how adorable these creatures are.*

"Ennui" connotes boredom as well as annoying experiences with the sex whose sulking is their most charming weapon. The solitary young man would like to unburden his heart and perhaps exorcise the monsters lurking in his subconscious by confessing to a woman. But women will chatter on about nothings, fuss about frivolities (a lost ring, cherished memories). The refrain is a cynical and yet sincere expression of Laforgue's constant fascination with the Eternal Feminine.

The brief poem in five-syllable lines also rails at the respectable lady who has dismissed him because he did not behave like "a gentleman with principles." She would have nothing to do with a poet. Her own prearranged marriage was, as the middle-class ladies say, with a *monsieur tout ce qu'il y a de bien.* May she have many children and be bored for ever after! (1) *How far is the standard soul* (2) *Who bade me farewell* (3) *Because my eyes* (4) *Lacked principles!* (5) *She, at this moment* (6) *She, such tender bread,* (7) *Oh, perhaps is bringing forth* (8) *Some brat.* (9) *For she was united [wedded]* (10) *To a gentleman* (11) *Extremely eligible,* (12) *But poor in genius.* [H.P.]

JULES LAFORGUE

LOCUTIONS DES PIERROTS (XVI)

Je ne suis qu'un viveur lunaire
Qui fait des ronds dans les bassins,
Et cela, sans autre dessein
Que devenir un légendaire   4

Retroussant d'un air de défi
Mes manches de mandarin pâle,

J'arrondis ma bouche et — j'exhale
Des conseils doux de Crucifix   8

Ah! oui, devenir légendaire,
Au seuil des siècles charlatans!
Mais où sont les lunes d'antan?
Et que Dieu n'est-il à refaire?   12

PIERROTS (ON A DES PRINCIPES)

Elle disait, de son air vain fondamental:
« Je t'aime pour toi seul! » — Oh! là, là, grêle histoire;
Oui, comme l'art! Du calme, ô salaire illusoire
        Du capitaliste Idéal!   4

Elle faisait: « J'attends, me voici, je sais pas... »
Le regard pris de ces larges candeurs des lunes;
— Oh! là, là, ce n'est pas peut-être pour des prunes,
        Qu'on a fait ses classes ici-bas?   8

Mais voici qu'un beau soir, infortunée à point,
Elle meurt! — oh! là, là, bon, changement de thème!
On sait que tu dois ressusciter le troisième
        Jour, sinon en personne, du moins   12

Dans l'odeur, les verdures, les eaux des beaux mois!
Et tu iras, levant encore bien plus de dupes
Vers le Zaïmph de la Joconde, vers la Jupe!
        Il se pourra même que j'en sois.   16

(*L'Imitation de Notre Dame la lune.* 1886)

"Locutions [speeches, asides] of Pierrots, XVI:" (1) *I am only a lunar playboy* (2) *Making circles in ponds,* (3) *And this [I do], with no other design* (4) *Than to become legendary.* (5) *Tucking up with a defiant air* (6) *My pale mandarin sleeves,* (7) *I round my lips (into a circle)—and I* breathe forth (8) *Sweet Christian advice* [literally, *sweet counsels of the Crucifix*]. (9) *Ah yes! to become legendary* (10) *On the threshold of the charlatan centuries!* (11) *But where are the moons of yesteryear?* (12) *And why isn't God to be remade?*

"Pierrot (One has principles):" (1) *She*

said in her fundamentally vain way: (2) *"I love you for yourself alone!"*—Oh! come, come [that's] a pretty slim story; (3) *Yes, just like art! Let's have calm, O illusory wages [illusory return on our investment]* (4) *Of the capitalist Ideal!* (5) *She whispered: "I am waiting, here I am, I don't know . . ."* (6) *Her gaze having taken on [borrowed from] broad lunar ingenuousness;* (7) *Oh! come, come, it wasn't for nothing* [literally, *just for plums*] (8) *That we went to school down here!* (9) *But one fine evening, pertinently ill-starred [unfortunate just at the right time],* (10) *She dies!—oh, come, come now, [that's a] change of tune!* (11) *We know that you're to be reborn on the third* (12) *Day, if not in person, at least* (13) *In fragrance, verdure, and the streams of the pleasant months!* (14) *And you will go, picking up more fools* (15) *To the Zaïmph [veils] of the Gioconda, toward the Skirt!* (16) *I may even be one of those fools.*

Laforgue's most felicitous poems are those which were inspired by his ironical ballads to the moon and by his original variations on the time-honored character of Pierrot or Harlequin. In the treatment of both themes, Laforgue was the typical "modern" poet, aware that he had had many predecessors in the past and that he could both mock a hallowed literary tradition and prolong it: Mallarmé, Joyce, Proust, Thomas Mann will proceed in a similar manner. Allusion (to Villon's famous ballad on the "snows of yester-year" [line 11], to Salammbô in the second poem), reminiscences of Heine, of Verlaine, even of Watteau's clowns, can be supposed to flatter or to entertain most readers. The poet smiles at his own dream of "becoming legendary" in his turn.

The irony can be in part attributed to the poet's insolence toward what the bourgeois, the eternal butt of modern mockery, reveres: the title *Imitation*, recalling the *Imitation of Christ*, and the solemn deification of the moon as "Our Lady" are gently blasphemous; so are the allusions to the Crucifix in this poem (8) and, in the second poem, to the Resurrection on the third day (11-12). The moon fascinated Laforgue's fancy, because it has been so often celebrated by lovers and by poets, and because it suggests for him (and many moderns who came after him) not the goal for romantic aspirations of disembodied lovers but emptiness and sterility. Ambiguities are amusingly played upon by the bittersweet poet: *viveur* (1) recalls a *bon vivant*, idling around parks, but also any living creature pursuing ideals never to be reached, boastfully throwing challenges to the divine (5) and ending in meek resignation. Finally, the originality of this Laforguian irony lies in its being humorous as well as cynical: the author does not spare himself; he is a pale mandarin, a weakling, a vain dreamer whom life passes by. He wants to appear superior, yet he is wounded by life and his smile scarcely restrains tears. *"Mon cœur fait de l'esprit, le sot, pour se leurrer,"* Corbière had said ("My heart makes witticisms, the fool, to dupe itself").

The poet (the artist in Mallarmé and Picasso) sees himself as a clown whose profession it is to entertain, but whose white-faced mask expresses longing for the one consolation against the senselessness of the world: feminine tenderness. Laforgue had spurned "the celestial eternullity," as he called it, and "the Infinite, that railway station of trains which have been missed." But the feminine declaration of love for him alone and forever, in the second poem arouses his most waggish banter. He has often been duped by inadequate embodiments of the Feminine and by the enigmatic emptiness of Mona Lisas (Zaïmph is the veil of the priestess Salammbô, in Flaubert's novel, which men who dream of her yearn to touch). [H.P.]

PAUL CLAUDEL

DÉCEMBRE

Balayant la contrée et ce vallon feuillu, ta main, gagnant les terres   1
couleur de pourpre et de tan que tes yeux là-bas découvrent, s'arrête avec
eux sur ce riche brocart. Tout est coi et enveloppé; nul vert blessant, rien   2
de jeune et rien de neuf ne forfait à la construction et au chant de ces tons
pleins et sourds. Une sombre nuée occupe tout le ciel, dont, remplissant   3
de vapeur les crans irréguliers de la montagne, on dirait qu'il s'attache à
l'horizon comme par des mortaises. De la paume caresse ces larges   4
ornements que brochent les touffes de pins noirs sur l'hyacinthe des plaines,
des doigts vérifie ces détails enfoncés dans la trame et la brume de ce jour
hivernal, un rang d'arbres, un village. L'heure est certainement arrêtée;   5
comme un théâtre vide qu'emplit la mélancolie, le paysage clos semble
prêter attention à une voix si grêle que je ne la saurais ouïr.

Ces après-midis de décembre sont douces.   6

Rien encore n'y parle du tourmentant avenir. Et le passé n'est pas si peu   7-8
mort qu'il souffre que rien lui survive. De tant d'herbe et d'une si grande   9
moisson, nulle chose ne demeure que de la paille parsemée et une bourre
flétrie; une eau froide mortifie la terre retournée. Tout est fini. Entre une   10-11
année et l'autre, c'est ici la pause et la suspension. La pensée, délivrée de
son travail, se recueille dans une taciturne allégresse, et, méditant de
nouvelles entreprises, elle goûte, comme la terre, son sabbat.

(*Connaissance de L'Est.* 1900)

Paul Claudel (1868-1955) had an active career as one of the foremost French diplomats; at the same time, he composed some ten poetical dramas, which rank among the greatest of this century in any language, and several volumes of lyrical poetry and of essays. The first edition of *Connaissance de l'Est (The East I Know)*, written while he was serving as French consul in China, appeared in 1900.

(1) *Sweeping the country and this leafy valley, your hand, reaching the crimson and tan-colored earth that your eyes discover yonder, pauses with them on that rich brocade.* (2) *All is quiet (mute) and muffled; no glaring (wounding) green, nothing young and nothing new clashes with the structure and with the song of those full, deep tones.* (3) *A dark cloud occupies the whole sky which, filling the irregular notches of the mountain with vapor, seems as if it is mortised to the horizon.* (4) *With the palm of your hand, caress these broad adornments, brocaded by the tufts of black pines on the hyacinth of the plains, with your fingers, verify these details, sunk in the weft and the mist of this wintry day, a row of trees, a village.* (5) *The hour truly has stopped; like an empty theater which melancholy fills, the enclosed*

landscape seems to be attentive to [listening for]
a voice so frail that I could not hear it.

(6) *These December afternoons are sweet*
(gentle).

(7) *Nothing in them speaks as yet of the*
tormenting future. (8) *And the past is not*
so incompletely dead as to allow anything to
survive it. (9) *From so much grass and so*
great a harvest, nothing remains but scattered
straw and wilted tufts; a cold water mortifies
the ploughed earth. (10) *All is finished.*
(11) *Between one year and the next, here is*
the pause and the suspense. (12) *Thought,*
freed from its labor, gathers itself into a taciturn
joy, and, contemplating new undertakings, enjoys,
as does the earth, its sabbath.

Claudel has ranged over all forms of
lyricism, exalted and rhetorical as well as
precise and concretely interpretative, of
which *Connaissance de l'Est* offers many
samples (the title, which implies an
intellectual diplomat's attempt to under-
stand the Far East, is in itself revealing).
Many prose poems before Claudel's were
airy, over-poetical pieces which, demand-
ing neither the rime nor the rhythm of
verse, degenerated into mere facility. In
"December," on the contrary, the author
understands sensuously; he feels with his
own hand (he addresses both himself and
the reader directly as *tu*) the colors, the
design, the density, and the weight of the
landscape. The description is impeccably
organized. The poet appears to be taking
stock of everything. First the Chinese
earth, similar to a brocade, or to a grave
and tightly structured music (2), then the
cloudy sky, clinging to the mountains as
if inserted into it (3). Every visible detail,
the silky tufts of pines, as on a Chinese
painting, the mist steeping everything, is
seen and almost touched by the reader.
(4) The year is coming to a stop, while the
rebirth of the earth, with its lengthening
days, is awaited as in a melancholy, empty
theater.

Only then, in a brief second paragraph,
does the poet interpret subjectively the
impression produced by that December
landscape. In the third (lines 7 to 9), the
tone is slow, the syntax deliberately
pedestrian (with *que . . . que* repeated in 8
and the prosaic phrase *nulle chose* in 9).
The ploughed earth is literally being sub-
jected to humiliating decomposition as the
rain "mortifies" it. An atmosphere of
grave serenity fills the picture, uniting the
landscape and the mind of the gazer into
a calm sabbath, the prelude to new action
(12). [H.P.]

PAUL CLAUDEL

DISSOLUTION

Et je suis de nouveau reporté sur la mer indifférente et liquide. Quand   1-2
je serai mort, on ne me fera plus souffrir. Quand je serai enterré entre mon   3
père et ma mère, on ne me fera plus souffrir. On ne se rira plus de ce cœur   4
trop aimant. Dans l'intérieur de la terre se dissoudra le sacrement de mon   5
corps, mais mon âme, pareille au cri le plus perçant, reposera dans le sein
d'Abraham. Maintenant tout est dissous, et d'un œil appesanti je cherche en   6
vain autour de moi et le pays habituel à la route ferme sous mon pas et ce
visage cruel. Le ciel n'est plus que de la brume et l'espace de l'eau. Tu le   7-8
vois, tout est dissous, et je chercherais en vain autour de moi trait ou forme.
Rien pour horizon, que la cessation de la couleur la plus foncée. La matière   9-10
de tout est rassemblée en une seule eau, pareille à celle de ces larmes que je
sens qui coulent sur ma joue. Sa voix, pareille à celle du sommeil quand il   11
souffle de ce qu'il y a de plus sourd à l'espoir én nous. J'aurais beau chercher,   12
je ne trouve plus rien hors de moi, ni ce pays qui fut mon séjour, ni ce
visage beaucoup aimé.

(Connaissance de l'Est. 1905)

"Dissolution," the last poem in the volume *Connaissance de l'Est*, was one of a second group of poems composed between 1900 and 1905. This is no longer, like the majority of the best-known pieces, such as the "Banyan" and "The Pig," a close and scientific description of some striking feature of China. Between 1900 and 1905, Claudel had undergone a momentous personal crisis which endangered his career and his faith; a dramatized picture of the illicit love that then enraptured him is given in his greatest drama, *Partage de Midi* (*Noontide Partition*, 1905). Like its hero, Mésa, the poet had suffered cruelly, from remorse and from the person whom he had loved too ardently. He discreetly voices his despair in the brief, almost sobbing sentences of this poem, written while the sky above him, as he is sailing on the Far Eastern seas, seems to dissolve into the ocean and while his own weary heart yearns for similar dissolution.

(1) *And I am once again carried back over the indifferent and liquid sea.* (2) *When I am dead, I shall no longer be made to suffer.* (3) *When I am buried between my father and my mother, I shall no longer be made to suffer.* (4) *This too loving heart will no longer be mocked.* (5) *The sacrament of my body will dissolve in the interior of the earth, but my soul, like the most piercing of cries, will repose in Abraham's bosom.* (6) *Now everything is dissolved, and with an eye made heavy* [by sorrow] *in vain do I seek around me both the familiar land with the road firm under my steps and that cruel face.* (7) *The sky is nothing but mist and space is but water.* (8) *You see, everything is dissolved and vainly do I look for line or form around me.* (9) *Nothing for* [an]

horizon but the ending of the darkest color.
(10) All matter is gathered into one water,
similar to that of those tears which I feel
flowing down my cheek. (11) Its voice, like that
of sleep when it breathes from what is most deaf
to hope inside us. (12) It would be useless to
search [sea and sky], I find nothing outside
myself, neither that country where I sojourned,
nor that much loved face.

But for the absence of regular rhythm
and of the feeling of necessity and security
that Claudel confessed to envying in tradi-
tional verse, this prose poem is not unlike
a lyrical expression of melancholy such as
is found in the poetry of all ages. It has no
divisions into paragraphs or stanzas; the
grief is heavy, the sufferer almost prostrate
beneath it. Each sentence, supported by
neither rimes nor the regular count of
syllables, must slowly find its own solemn
music. At first, like Pascal and Rimbaud,
his greatest predecessors in the handling
of this somewhat Biblical verse, Claudel
naturally falls into a "ternary rhythm."
Et je suis | de nouveau | reporté || sur la mer
| indifférente | et liquide. || Quand je serai
mort, | on ne me fera plus | souffrir. || Such
a rhythm is better balanced and less
flatly symmetrical than a sentence regu-
larly divided into two or four segments. It
conveys the motion of the sea, the "liquid
plain," as the Latins (whom Claudel read
incessantly) called it, and it is indifferent
to the traveler's sorrow. Slowly the sen-
tences grow longer, the rhythm swells.

After the immense weariness that could
find its haven only in death, where a too
sensitive heart would be spared further
wounds, a lighter tone creeps in as the
poet imagines his soul, severed from the
body, similar to a shrill cry, seeking the
Biblical paradise. With line 6, a second
movement is ushered in: the recurring
sounds (two nasal ones in *maintenant*, the
repetition of *ou*, the *et* also repeated)
bring the traveler back to the universal
dissolution which is taking place around
him. His eyes perceive neither shape nor
outline. He assures himself (*tu*, 8) that all
is melting into that absorption of space
and sky into a watery mist. There is bitter
solace for him in such an assurance, for his
own grief also is dissolving into tears.
Slowly, heavily, they glide down his
cheek: the very syntax renders that victory
of tears over the tense, proud suffering
male (10: *celle, ces, que, qui*). In line 11 *Sa
voix* is enigmatic but it refers to *tout* and
echoes like the inarticulate heavy slumber
that seizes him who no longer will enter-
tain any hope.

The parting from China is now consum-
mated, and also the parting from the
person who, like Ysé in *Partage de Midi*,
had brought to Claudel's alter ego,
Mésa, the raptures of love and the bitter
realization that human love is ever in-
complete and leads only to thirst for divine
love. The dissolution both of his past and
of part of himself is effected.   [H.P.]

PAUL CLAUDEL

L'ESPRIT ET L'EAU [Fragment]

Salut donc, ô monde nouveau à mes yeux, ô monde maintenant total! 1

O credo entier des choses visibles et invisibles, je vous accepte avec un 2
cœur catholique!

Où que je tourne la tête. 3

J'envisage l'immense octave de la Création! 4

Le monde s'ouvre et, si large qu'en soit l'empan, mon regard le traverse 5
d'un bout à l'autre.

J'ai pesé le soleil ainsi qu'un gros mouton que deux hommes forts 6
suspendent à une perche entre leurs épaules.

J'ai recensé l'armée des Cieux et j'en ai dressé l'état. 7

Depuis les grandes Figures qui se penchent sur le vieillard Océan. 8

Jusqu'au feu le plus rare englouti dans le plus profond abîme, 9

Ainsi que le Pacifique bleu-sombre où le baleinier épie l'évent d'un 10
souffleur comme un duvet blanc.

(Cinq grandes odes. 1910)

(1) *Hail then, O world new to my eyes, O world now complete!* (2) *O entire credo of things visible and invisible. I accept you with a Catholic heart!* (3) *Wherever I turn my head* (4) *I perceive the immense octave of Creation!* (5) *The world opens up and, however wide its span may be, my glance traverses it from one end to the other.* (6) *I have weighed the sun like a fat sheep which two strong men hang from a pole between their shoulders.* (7) *I have taken the census of the heavenly armies, and I have drawn up their status.* (8) *From the great figures who bend down over old man Ocean* (9) *To the rarest fire swallowed up in the deepest abyss,* (10) *As well as the deep-blue Pacific where the whaleman watches for the blower's spouting [which is] like white down.*

If, with his indomitable Catholic faith, Claudel appears to have been all of a piece as a person, imperiously dogmatic with those whom he felt called upon to convert, as a poet he had a variety of manners and an ambitious scope equalled by no other French poet since Hugo. In *Connaissance de l'Est*, his aim was to ask the question that Mallarmé had taught him: "What does it mean?" Things answer, Claudel remarked, as did St. Thomas, only if one asks them the right question. Joy proceeds from understanding, and understanding, as Claudel again insisted, presupposes enumerating, taking stock of "the immense octave of Creation," weighing as shepherds carry and weigh an animal at the fair, interpreting the silent and tense thrust of the visible world toward the Divine.

Claudel always felt an irresistible aversion to all that is indefinite, unsubstantial, airy. He wants to reach God with the full load of all that is beautiful, indeed sacred, in the world of things. He is no disembodied mystic. He neither ignores nor scorns nature. Claudel was convinced that man is placed in nature not to be understood by it but to vanquish it. A lust for power must first drive conquerors and proud possessors (*Tête d'or*, the American business man in *L'Échange*, the builder of cathedrals in *L'Annonce faite à Marie*, Rodrigue in *Le soulier de Satin*); and then their youthful ardor for conquest will find its fulfillment in bowing in humility before God.

"Spirit and Water," the second of five long, grandiose odes published together by Claudel, celebrates water (which is the infinite, the purifying liberation, the relief of repentant tears) and the spirit that breathes over the waters, quenching man's thirst for God. This brief sample of Claudel's exalted robust lyricism offers few obstacles to interpretation. Through his faith, the poet sees the world as "total" (1): an immense concert chanting God's glory. He repudiates nothing, and his heart is catholic in the two senses of the adjective; but man must forget himself rather than know himself, or forget himself in order to commune with the world. This is not pantheism, which Claudel abhors, for Creation is not identical with God. But creation is to be praised because it is His work.

Proudly, arrogantly, the joyful poet, certain that God favored him with a sign when, converted, he bowed before Him, spans the whole of creation. Undaunted by the strangeness of some of his comparisons, familiar and Biblical in his lyricism, he proclaims his weighing of the sun, as if it were a big sheep hanging on a pole and carried by two men (6), and his recording of the stars and of their position and significance. The adjectives are not at all rare or evocative (*large, grandes, rare, profond*), and an ample comparison (preferred to metaphors by Claudel, as it also was by the Greek and Latin epic poets, whom he read assiduously) broadens the last verse into a vision of the ocean, on which the poet, like a sailor on a whaling ship, watches for the spouting of a cetacean, which will be caught by the fisherman, as rebellious souls will be caught by the Savior and brought to the service of God.

The ode from which this fragment is taken was composed in Peiping in 1906. The poet, at that time serving in the French consulate, dreams of water as a symbol of liberation. He then turns to the spirit, which pervades all, as water permeates all earth, and he hails the thrust of the spirit toward God. The unequal, unrimed lines enabled the poet to vary his form according to his inspiration and to allow for ominous, tense silences as a potential relief to lyrical eloquence. [H.P.]

PAUL VALÉRY

LA JEUNE PARQUE

[Hymne du printemps]

Écoute... N'attends plus... La renaissante année   222
A tout mon sang prédit de secrets mouvements:
Le gel cède à regret ses derniers diamants...,
Demain, sur un soupir des bontés constellées,
Le printemps vient briser les fontaines scellées: 226
L'étonnant printemps rit, viole... On ne sait d'où
Venu? Mais la candeur ruisselle à mots si doux
Qu'une tendresse prend la terre à ses entrailles...
Les arbres regonflés et recouverts d'écailles   230
Chargés de tant de bras et de trop d'horizons,
Meuvent sur le soleil leurs tonnantes toisons,
Montent dans l'air amer avec toutes leurs ailes
De feuilles par milliers qu'ils se sentent nouvelles...   234
N'entends-tu pas frémir ces noms aériens,
O Sourde!... Et dans l'espace accablé de liens,
Vibrant de bois vivace infléchi par la cime,
Pour et contre les dieux ramer l'arbre unanime,   238
La flottante forêt de qui les rudes troncs
Portent pieusement à leurs fantasques fronts,
Aux déchirants départs des archipels superbes,
Un fleuve tendre, ô mort, et caché sous les herbes?   242

(La jeune parque. 1917)

"*La jeune parque*" is without doubt the most perfect and the most difficult long poem in the French language. The difficulties stem in part from the abstractness of the underlying theme: human consciousness torn between the Absolute—which in its repose and finality is also Death—and Life, which brings the temptations of love and the raptures of vernal nature. But the difficulties can also be traced to the refined subtlety of the musical effects as well as to the author's over-elaborate work on fragments which he sought to unite into a whole. The unity of this 512-line poem, however, is somewhat artificially contrived. For posterity, "The Young Fate" will probably live as a succession of oscillating movements, the most successful of which are the monologues. In these, as in a tragedy by Racine or an opera by Gluck, melodious recitatives replace narratives as the speaker utters invocations and interrogations. Such a monologue we find in our excerpt—a hymn celebrating the untamed rush of Spring upon the young woman, the all-too-human virgin who only remotely recalls the three Fates of antiquity.

This poem of human consciousness and destiny, which ends in the rejection of death and espousal of life with its temptations, was characterized by its author as "a succession of psychological substitutions . . . and also, if one wishes, a lecture course in physiology." As always with Paul Valéry (1871-1945), the most searching efforts of the intellect are applied in a voluptuous analysis of the flesh. The heroine, frightened by love to which she might yield, is ready to offer herself to Death, if only Death will come without delay (222); otherwise Spring will flood nature and her own body with impetuous ardor.

(222) *Listen . . . Wait no more . . . The year being reborn* (223) *Prophesies secret movements to all my blood:* (224) *The ice regretfully yields its last diamonds . . .,* (225) *Tomorrow, at a sigh from the constellated kindnesses,* (226) *Spring comes and breaks the sealed-up fountains.* The metallic, glittering vocabulary faintly recalls Mallarmé's *"Hérodiade"* (see p. 44), the one true ancestor of the Young Fate. The frozen, sealed fountains will thaw when the stars (invoked earlier in the poem) favor the bountiful new season. In her imagination the girl then conjures up the Dionysian and delicious fury of Spring's invasion. (227) *Astounding spring laughs, violates (rapes) . . . No one knows whence* (228) *[It] comes? But candor* [recalling the Latin meaning of *whiteness* and of *ingenuous purity*] *streams in words so soft* (229) *That a tenderness seizes the earth in its entrails . . .* (230) *The trees filled out again and covered once more with scales* (231) *Heavy with so many arms and too many horizons,* (232) *Move their thundering fleeces against the sun,* (233) *Rise up in the bitter air with all their wings* (234) *Of leaves by the thousands which they feel [to be] new upon them.* Valéry's Spring combines mollifying tenderness with virile impetuosity. Like a centaur (there may be reminiscences of Maurice de Guérin's beautiful pantheistic prose poem *"Le centaure"* here), Spring seduces and conquers the earth.

It climbs up from the roots, through the sap and to the branches of the trees; it spurs the wind to rustle the leaves and to thunder among them (232); the wings of their branches wave in the bitter air. The scene is near the sea, and the air is salty, the wind biting. Alliterations and multiplied sonorities in *m, r, t,* evoke the sounds of these orchestrated rites of Spring (*meuvent, montent, tonnantes toisons, air amer*).

Quivering with a new impulse to become part of this dance of Spring, the Young Fate now upbraids Death, who had appeared to her previously as a serene refuge: can Death remain deaf to this revolution of nature? (235) *Do you not hear these airy names rustle,* (236) *O Deaf One! . . . And in space weighed down with shackles* [formed by the branches], (237) *Vibrating with living wood which bends at the tip,* (238) *The single-souled tree rows for and against the gods,* (239) *The floating forest whose rough trunks* (240) *Piously carry to (at) their capricious foreheads (fronts),* (241) *To (at) the rending division of superb archipelagos* [the joints from where the branches spread out capriciously, with the sap ascending from the roots up to them], (242) *A tender river, O death, and hidden under the grass?*

This sonorous and sumptuous passage is more romantic than anything else in Paul Valéry's poetry and it might almost recall Victor Hugo, whose Dionysian inspiration Valéry, the foe of "inspiration," confessed that he admired. In musical terms, it is akin to Wagner rather than to Gluck, Rameau, or Debussy. The analytical and Cartesian clarity, which Valéry professed to cherish, is not conspicuous in lines 238-242. The tree, in a thrust of its whole being, single-souled in the confused mass of its foliage, "rows" in the sea of space, eager to grow higher and to conquer that space. Its branches part above the trunk and become archipelagos. But the trunks of the trees are bathed in

[Invocation à la larme]

Je n'implorerai plus que tes faibles clartés,   280
Longtemps sur mon visage envieuse de fondre,
Très imminente larme, et seule à me répondre,
Larme qui fais trembler à mes regards humains
Une variété de funèbres chemins;   284
Tu procèdes de l'âme, orgueil du labyrinthe.
Tu me portes du cœur cette goutte contrainte,
Cette distraction de mon suc précieux
Qui vient sacrifier mes ombres sur mes yeux,   288
Tendre libation de l'arrière-pensée!
D'une grotte de crainte au fond de moi creusée
Le sel mystérieux suinte muette l'eau.
D'où nais-tu? Quel travail toujours triste et nouveau   292
Te tire avec retard, larme, de l'ombre amère?
Tu gravis mes degrés de mortelle et de mère,
Et déchirant ta route, opiniâtre faix,
Dans le temps que je vis, les lenteurs que tu fais   296
M'étouffent... Je me tais, buvant ta marche sûre...
— Qui t'appelle au secours de ma jeune blessure?

(La jeune parque. 1917)

another water: the underground stream from which its roots draw sap and vigor. That underground river, fed by the ashes of the dead and by the rotted leaves, becomes Death itself, whom the Young Fate invokes, in her attempt to elude the appeal of Spring, which overpowers her.

Spring had almost vanquished the Young Fate: she was ready to fall prey either to Death or to the sensuous intoxication of life. Her taut breast almost offered itself to imaginary lips—*Dur en moi . . . mais si doux à la bouche infinie* ("hard in me . . . but so soft to the infinite lips"). But to yield might have meant maternity, and she rebelled against transmitting life; she refused to fall into one of nature's traps (as Schopenhauer called love—a deceit contrived by the genius of our species). Rather, she preferred to appeal to the gods for help. But there was no answer.

In her abandonment, she invokes the tear that slowly distilled in her innermost caverns; and it reaches her eye, where it will cloud her vision (*faibles clartés*, 280) and yet mysteriously clarify it. ("Is there anything more mysterious than clarity?" asked Socrates in Valéry's *Eupalinos.*)

The following passage, another tragic monologue or musical recitative, is the melodious development of a question (292-298)—"Lyricism is the development of an exclamation," notes the author in his *Littérature.* Lines 280-298 are the most delicately poised and the most touching in the whole poem. (280) *Henceforth I shall implore only your faint gleams,* (281) *[You who have] long desired to melt upon my face,* (282) *Most imminent tear, and the only one to answer me,* (283) *Tear that causes to tremble before my human gaze* (284) *A variety of funereal paths;* (285) *You come from the soul, pride of the [body's] labyrinth. (286) From the heart you bear this constrained drop, (287) This deviation of my precious juice (288) Which comes to sacrifice my shadows upon my eyes, (289) Tender libation of [my] hidden thought! (290) Hollowed out of a grotto of fear in my depths, (291) The mysterious salt oozes silent water. (292) Where do you spring from? What labor ever sad and new (293) Draws you so late, O tear, from the bitter dark? (294) You climb my steps [those] of a mortal and a mother, (295) And as you tear your path, stubborn burden, (296) Through the time I live, the delays you make (298) Smother me . . . I keep silent, drinking your (inevitable) certain course . . . (298) —Who calls you to the aid of my young wound?*

The verb *pleurer* had occurred three times in the first three lines of the poem. Hearing the wind weeping, the Fate became aware of her own desire to weep, but she proudly repressed the action that would have betokened weakness (6). At last, however, that "imminent tear," which had long threatened to melt her haughty virginal intactness, forms within her; and it alone (282) answers her call for help. The tear clouds her human vision as it presents it with the variety of tragic possibilities of life always menaced by Death (284-285).

Relentlessly attentive to what takes place inside her body and her mind, the Fate describes that tear, or rather she transfigures it through ingenious and suggestive evocations. From her innermost depth it comes—from the soul, along labyrinthine ways, from the heart, where that salt drop was "constrained"—that is, distilled, and in the etymological meaning of the word, "expressed." Still playing on the pregnant ambiguities of the Latin mean-ings, Valéry sees in the tear a "distraction" (287) of the Fate's precious juice, for it is drawn in a direction different from the usual one. Line 288 alludes to the tear of self-sacrifice in the act of maternity. The tear is an offering from the depths of consciousness, a reassertion of her self-knowledge (289). That salty tear, oozing from a mysterious cavern of fear within her, is then passionately questioned. The sound *t*, struck seven times in lines 292-293, suggests the painful tearing of the pathway within her that the soothing and liberating tear, so long suppressed, must first effect. This secret labor is implicitly compared to the labor of maternity that she repudiated in lines 276-278 of the poem. Once again she invokes, in brief words, precise and acute and abounding in *t* sounds (295-297), the relief that comes to her in the act of weeping. The melodic beauty of lines such as these has been equalled in French only by certain passages in Racine and in Baudelaire.

This "canticle of the tear," as it is often called by critics, has a directness of emotion (and even some self-pity) unparalleled in French poetry. And yet, this canticle is not an elegy in which the Young Fate exhales her sorrow and contemplates her own tears. It is not a monologue but rather a dialogue. She watches herself suffering: *Je me voyais me voir* ("I saw myself seeing myself"), the Fate had declared in line 35, in typical Valéryian fashion. At the end of the poem, sleep and a confused night of dreams will cover her eyelids. And after the liberation —through these tears—of all that had been tangled like a knot within her, she will achieve control of herself. She will reject the temptation of suicide and turn in acceptance to life.   [H.P.]

PAUL VALÉRY

LA DORMEUSE

Quels secrets dans son cœur brûle ma jeune amie,
Ame par le doux masque aspirant une fleur?
De quels vains aliments sa naïve chaleur
Fait ce rayonnement d'une femme endormie?   4

Souffle, songes, silence, invincible accalmie,
Tu triomphes, ô paix plus puissante qu'un pleur,
Quand de ce plein sommeil l'onde grave et l'ampleur
Conspirent sur le sein d'une telle ennemie.   8

Dormeuse, amas doré d'ombres et d'abandons,
Ton repos redoutable est chargé de tels dons,
O biche avec langueur longue auprès d'une grappe,

Que malgré l'âme absente, occupée aux enfers,   12
Ta forme au ventre pur qu'un bras fluide drape,
Veille; ta forme veille, et mes yeux sont ouverts.

(*Charmes.* 1922)

(1) *What secrets does my young friend burn in her heart,* (2) *A soul through the sweet mask inhaling a flower?* (3) *Out of what vain nourishments does her artless warmth* (4) *Create this radiance of a sleeping woman?* (5) *Breath, dreams, silence, invincible lull,* (6) *You triumph, O peace more powerful than a tear,* (7) *When the heavy wave and the fullness of that deep sleep* (8) *Conspire on the breast of such an enemy.* (9) *[O] sleeper, golden mass of shadows and surrenders,* (10) *Your fearsome repose is laden with such gifts,* (11) *O doe languorously long beside a cluster of grapes,* (12) *That, though your soul is away, busy in infernos,* (13) *Your form with its pure belly draped by a fluid arm* (14) *Is awake, your form is awake, and my eyes are open.*

Valéry had composed several sonnets in his youth, in the early eighteen-nineties, when he was not yet very far from the Parnassian tradition, but "The Sleeper" is the only sonnet in alexandrines in *Charmes.* At first glance, it may appear merely descriptive and sculptural or pictorial, as Parnassian sonnets often were: a sleeping woman had been the subject of many works of art; and the dead Atala in Chateaubriand's prose and in Girodet's painting have often been likened to divinities asleep. This poem, however, whose theme Ronsard, Musset (in "*Rolla*") and Mallarmé (in "*Tristesse d'Été*") had also treated, is not truly descriptive or pictorial. Nor should it be read as a far-fetched allegory through which Poetic Inspiration, concealing her mysterious sources (1-4), vanquishes the poet (5-8);

the soul, or the idea of the poem, would then disappear to haunt the nether world and only the shape (and poetic form) would remain. Read in such terms, "*La dormeuse*" would turn into a pretentious and even shallow logogriph. ·

The substance of the sonnet is sensuous, fleshy. It is not a love poem—Valéry wrote scarcely any; he levelled his sarcasms at such "exercises." But it is a meditation on a real woman, contemplated, vaguely desired, and transfigured, not without preciosity and some playful artificiality, by the gazer's dream. The soul and the shape of the sleeping woman are contrasted, as the essence of all objects and persons is often contrasted with their sense-appearance; but the latter is not necessarily shallow. "The most profound part of man is his skin," reads one of Valéry's famous sayings. Inner, self-sufficing purity amounts to little without the loveliness of the form that strikes the senses. The duality in Valéry's meditation is, as always, between the ascetic or intellectual detachment from life, which closely approximates death, and the espousal of life in its changing and radiant warmth.

The sleeping woman at first appears to be inwardly burning, her fire being fed with secret and illusory nourishment, which endows her with warmth and light. Line 2 is harmonious and evocative, but hardly essential to the meaning of the quatrain: women asleep have often been compared by gallant and ungallant writers to plants (see Proust's *La Prisonnière*). *Le doux masque*, to designate the nostrils perhaps inhaling a flower's perfume, is a precious periphrasis. The broad *a* sounds (*ma, amie, âme*, followed by *amas, abandons* in line 9) suggest the long, relaxed slender, sleeping body.

S sounds, suggestive of her soft breathing, are multiplied in the second quatrain: *souffle, songes, silence, invincible*, then *puissante, sommeil, sein*. The poet interprets the impression produced on him by the sleeper: an impression of peace and of calm, which is slightly belied, however, by line 8—almost a pastiche of the Racinian manner: she might, if the poet did not transcend the erotic into the esthetic, become "an enemy," endangering the gazer's peace of mind.

But the sleeper is again transfigured into a golden and soft "abandoned" mass of beautiful details, such as those *beaux détails* of which poetry, as Valéry repeated after Voltaire, is made. Line 11 is a splendid metamorphosis of the inert body reaching for sensuous and perhaps impure joys (*aux enfers*)—it is like a doe, languidly reaching for a cluster of grapes. Alliterations of the *l* and of nasal sounds enhance its evocative beauty. Through that beauty, the poet also feels purified. He sees her now as a nude in a painting, her arm lying gracefully across her belly. Her body's shape is awake and also watches (in a half-sleep) the would-be ravisher. The word *veille* is repeated and the letter *v*, suggesting the triangle of the body covered but not concealed by the arm that protects it, occurs four times in lines 13-14. A suspense comes after the first *veille*—the contemplation of beauty with open eyes is enough for the creative delight of the poet. The observer of the sleeper, who addressed questions to himself in the quatrains, and then, more pressingly and almost sensuously, directed them to her in lines 9-13, reveals himself in the last line: "my eyes are open." He sees now with open eyes the mystery latent in the sleeping form: a self-sufficient purity, such as the Young Fate was preserving, enclosed in a graceful sensuous body.   [H.P.]

PAUL VALÉRY

LE CIMETIÈRE MARIN

Ici venu, l'avenir est paresse.   67
L'insecte net gratte la sécheresse;
Tout est brûlé, défait, reçu dans l'air
A je ne sais quelle sévère essence...   70
La vie est vaste, étant ivre d'absence,
Et l'amertume est douce, et l'esprit clair.

Les morts cachés sont bien dans cette terre   73
Qui les réchauffe et sèche leur mystère.
Midi là-haut, Midi sans mouvement
En soi se pense et convient à soi-même...   76
Tête complète et parfait diadème,
Je suis en toi le secret changement.

Paul Valéry's place among the very great poets of France is secure. His verse is wholly contained within a single volume, a "golden book," in which, like Coleridge, Keats, Baudelaire, and Mallarmé, through elimination and severity toward himself, he himself composed his own anthology. He was first attracted to poetry in his early twenties, by two masters whom he revered: Edgar Allan Poe and Mallarmé. Valéry, surprisingly (surprisingly, at least for English-speaking readers), proclaimed Poe in his first letter to Mallarmé "perhaps the most subtle artist of this century." Later, writing to the critic Albert Thibaudet, he owns that he had found in Poe "all that I needed at that time. I took from his work that delirium of lucidity which he communicates."

Actually, as a poet, Valéry stands at the opposite pole from Poe. But he admired the American as a strange philosophical mind (in *Eureka*) and as a deliberate and calculating esthetician. The artists and writers who strove hardest to act upon the sensibility and upon the nerves and senses of their public, to touch the irrational in man—Delacroix, Wagner, Poe, Baudelaire—have also been the most intellectual of all, and passionately fond of reasoning about method. Valéry belongs in their company. He often defined poetry as an activity, not of inspiration or of creation, but of combination.

His poetry itself, however, often belies his theories. Emotion is by no means absent from "The Graveyard by the Sea." This long poem, which appeared in booklet form in 1920 and in *Charmes* in 1922, is the most celebrated, though probably not the greatest, of Valéry's poems. It is to be found in all anthologies; teachers and students enjoy interpreting its subtleties. It is sacrosanct to the worshippers of the poet, who may be horrified at our mutilation of it here. Lack of space precludes our presenting all twenty-four six-line stanzas; and besides, the first stanzas and stanzas 19 to 22, ponderous and coldly over-intellectual, are, in our opinion, inferior to the best in this poem. Moreover, it seems to us that the structure and the unity of the work have been over-admired. Valéry would have been the first to smile at those who take overseriously his paradoxes on the theme of the poet as a lucid premeditating engineer à la Poe. A friend of his, Mme Lucienne Julien-Caïn, reports that he was uncertain about the order in which the stanzas should follow each other when he consented to give the poem to the *Nouvelle Revue Française* in 1920 and that he smilingly proposed to draw them by lot—he may well have done so, she adds. A great poet of the intellect, scanning its inner workings—*Je suis étant, et me voyant me voir* ("I am being, and seeing myself seeing myself,"), says his intellectual hero, Monsieur Teste—Valéry is at the same time, and perhaps even more so, the poet of voluptuously contemplated sensuousness and of melodious music. Throughout his prose writings, he insists that ideas in poetry are of a different order from the order of ideas in prose, and that sound and sense can never be disassociated without decomposing the poem itself.

"*Le cimetière marin*" is a meditation by the sea at Sète on the Mediterranean, where Valéry's family lived and died. The surface of the sea, with its waves leaping in the dazzling midday sun, is mobility itself, as is the restless mind of man, incessantly manufacturing problems and solving them. The depths of the sea are a gulf of frightening stillness, comparable to the repose of the dead, deep in the graves from which they will never rise. The noontide calm of the sea and of the dead at first tempts the poet. He feels "half in love with death" and yearns for a serene permanence from which the future is banished; the temptation of absence lures him. (67) *Now [that I have] come here, the future [stretches out in] idleness.* (68) *The sharp insect scrapes at the dryness [of the ground];* (69) *All is burned, decomposed, received [resolved] in the air* (70) *Into*

I know not what severe [rarefied] essence . . . (71) *Life is vast, being drunk with absence [nothingness],* (72) *And bitterness is sweet, and the mind clear.* (73) *The hidden dead lie easy in this earth* (74) *Which warms them again and dries up their mystery.* (75) *Noon high above, motionless noon* (74) *Within itself thinks itself and unto itself suffices . . .* (77) *O complete head and perfect diadem,* (78) *I am the secret change [taking place] in you.*

Valéry endows the decasyllabic line with a rich and grave density, breaking it diversely into 3 and 7, more often 4 and 6 syllables, and avoiding the break after the fifth syllable, which strikes French ears as a faulty alexandrine. The sounds in lines 68-70 are acute dentals, to suggest the strident scraping of the wings of the cicada, and hissing *s*'s, to convey the parched dryness of the southern red earth. Death reigns here, for all is burned into a fragrant austerity (70). The mind sheds all illusions; it will not indulge misty sentiments. It faces nothingness (absence) with a clear-sighted, sweet bitterness, as Mediterranean thinkers and poets, from Empedocles to Lucretius and Leopardi, have so often done.

In lines 73-76, the poet first expresses his envy of the dead, of their warm comfort, of their release from life's perpetual mystery. The individual "mystery" of the life of each of these dead has "dried up," withered away. Then his thought turns to the perfection of the noon hour and of a sphere which allows no corroding restlessness of man's intellect to disturb it. Line 77 is in apposition to the perfect, self-sufficient sun with its round crown of jewels, designated in the next line as *toi* (literally "thee"). The speaker, Man, a "relative" being and of constant disquietude, refuses to yield. He will choose life, change, risk, the tragic but ennobling joy of being, rather than the purity of nothingness.

Tu n'as que moi pour contenir tes craintes!   79
Mes repentirs, mes doutes, mes contraintes
Sont le défaut de ton grand diamant...
Mais dans leur nuit toute lourde de marbres,   82
Un peuple vague aux racines des arbres
A pris déjà ton parti lentement.

Ils ont fondu dans une absence épaisse,   85
L'argile rouge a bu la blanche espèce,
Le don de vivre a passé dans les fleurs!
Où sont des morts les phrases familières,   88
L'art personnel, les âmes singulières?
La larve file où se formaient des pleurs.

Les cris aigus des filles chatouillées   91
Les yeux, les dents, les paupières mouillées,
Le sein charmant qui joue avec le feu,
Le sang qui brille aux lèvres qui se rendent,   94
Les derniers dons, les doigts qui les défendent,
Tout va sous terre et rentre dans le jeu!

Except perhaps for eight lines of "*Frag-
ments du Narcisse*" (which the poet pre-
ferred to all else that he had written),
and for certain passages of "*La jeune
parque*" (pp. 7off.), Valéry wrote nothing
more beautiful than this section of "*Le
cimetière marin.*" Curiously enough, for a
poet who strove to render "the pathos of
the intellect," the pathos here is spiritual,
and also sentimental and sensuous. Not
since Ronsard has the piercing regret for
the beauties of life been so poignantly, yet
so restrainedly, expressed.

Valéry's cherished master, Mallarmé,
had been a great poet of the night and of
death—*Un peu profond ruisseau calomnié la
mort* ("a shallow brook calumnied as
death"), he called it in his *Tombeau*
("Tomb") of Verlaine. Valéry rightly
contends that he never imitated Mallarmé,
for one cannot attempt to imitate what is
perfection itself. But, like Mallarmé, he
had tried to banish chaos, disorder, pas-

sion, and even sentiment from poetry. He
hated the kind of literature that lacks
vigor and that does not grapple with a
thousand difficulties. Many of those diffi-
culties are offered to the poet by conven-
tions, such as rimes, caesuras, and rules
of versification. "Only the most naïve
people can imagine that there can exist in
the world anything more important than
a convention," was one of Valéry's favorite
paradoxes.

The strictest rules governing that most
arduous of all French verse forms, the
decasyllable, with its caesura almost al-
ways occurring after the fourth or after
the sixth syllable and its rime scheme of a
couplet preceding a quatrain (*aabccb*),
have here been joyfully imposed by the
poet upon himself. Yet few evocations of
the tragic fleetingness of sensuous love,
inevitably threatened by death, compare
with these lines 82-96.

At first, man, the thinking reed, dauntlessly opposes (*contenir*, 79) the fears that the universe or the gods of old want to instil in him. By virtue of his calling the universe perpetually into question, man is the flaw of that otherwise perfect diamond, the world; through thinking that world, he masters it. The dead, on the contrary, have aligned themselves with non-being. The marble of the tombs weighs over them. They roam about like inert ghosts in dark Elysian fields, for their dust now feeds the roots of trees. The adverb that ends line 84, set apart from the stanza, announces the next stanzas, that mourn the slow decrepitude of the dead. (79) *You have only me to contain your fears!* (80) *My repentances, my doubts, my constraints* (81) *Are the defect of your great diamond . . .* (82) *But in their night all heavy with marble,* (83) *A roaming* [in the Latin sense of *vagus*] *(shadowy) people, at (under) the roots of the trees* (84) *Have already, slowly, taken your side.*

The six lines that follow are an after-thought—and a most felicitous one. They did not appear in the early version of the poem: they grew around line 87, which had come to Valéry as an inspired line, gratuitously "given by the gods," as he somewhere speaks of it. The sumptuous flesh of those who once lived has melted, and their absence is a thick, impenetrable nothingness. The contrast of red and white is saved from artificiality by the concise, definitive little words (*a bu*, 86). The poet evokes the inflections of the voices of the dead, now stilled, their gestures and manners (*l'art personnel*, 89) their individual personalities revealed through what we commonly call their souls, their homely turns of speech, their eyes where tears of ecstasy or of grief were born, where worms now crawl undisturbed. More poignantly still, he recalls the maidens teased and thrilled by men, their shrill cries of desire blended with fear, their moist eyelids yearning to be closed with kisses, their taut breasts playing with danger while they dance or walk provocatively. Line 95 plays with the sound *d*, as the trembling fingers of the girls pretend to protect their ultimate gifts from the lover. All has perished under the avid earth. Lovers' games were but an ephemeral flash in the great, heedless play of nature. (85) *They have melted into a thick absence [impenetrable nothingness],* (86) *The red clay has drunk up the white species (kind),* (87) *The gift of life has passed into the flowers!* (88) *Where are the familiar phrases of the dead,* (89) *Their personal art (grace), their singular [peculiar to each] souls?* (90) *The larva threads his way where tears were [once] composed.* (91) *The shrill cries of girls tickled [teased by love],* (92) *The eyes, the teeth, the moist eyelids,* (93) *The charming breast that [likes to] play with fire,* (94) *The blood shining on lips that yield,* (95) *The last gifts, the fingers that defend them—* (96) *All go beneath the ground and back into the game!*

Et vous, grande âme, espérez-vous un songe 97
Qui n'aura plus ces couleurs de mensonge
Qu'aux yeux de chair l'onde et l'or font ici?
Chanterez-vous quand serez vaporeuse? 100
Allez! Tout fuit! Ma présence est poreuse,
La sainte impatience meurt aussi!

Maigre immortalité noire et dorée, 103
Consolatrice affreusement laurée,
Qui de la mort fais un sein maternel,
Le beau mensonge et la pieuse ruse! 106
Qui ne connaît, et qui ne les refuse,
Ce crâne vide et ce rire éternel!

(*Le cimetière marin.* 1920)

Rightly did Valéry confess that "The Graveyard by the Sea" was his most personal poem, laden with feelings which were intensely his own and associated with the memory of his parents buried, or to be buried, in this cemetery at Sète. The poem is also considered to be a philosophical work. Ideas count in it; they are intensely felt and poetically invested with images, rhythms, and sounds. Occasionally the weight of abstract reflection proves too much for the verse, but in the best stanzas, such as we have reprinted here, the poem is neither philosophical nor didactic.

(97) *And you, great soul, do you hope for [to find] a (some) dream* (98) *That no longer will have these illusory (lying) colors* (99) *That the wave and the gold here make for (proffer to) the eyes of flesh?* (100) *Will you still sing when you are vaporous (thin air)?* (101) *Come now! All things flee! My presence is porous,* (102) *Holy impatience also dies!* (103) *Lean immortality black and golden,* (104) *Consoler crowned with laurels, hideously,* (105) *Who makes death into a mother's breast,* (106) *What a fine lie (illusion) and what a pious trick!* (107) *Who does not know them, and who does*

not refuse (turn away from them), (108) *That empty skull and that everlasting laugh!*

The sense of these stanzas is clear. In his nostalgic regret for life's ardent joys, which are doomed to destruction in death, the speaker voices the protest of those who are dead, who have become red clay and food for trees and worms; he addresses the proud soul, that believes itself immune from the destruction of the body. He rails at the ascetic's scorn for the concrete world of sensations (*onde* and *or*, the sea and the sun) and of appearances that are supposedly delusive (98). But is it possible to sing among the shades? to sing when all the joys of creating and of understanding are gone, when the flesh is consumed? The questioning tone grows more pressing with the two verbs in the future tense and the personal pronoun omitted before the second one (100), and with the familiar dismissal of childish delusions in *Allez! Tout fuit!* (101). For I am at present in a porous envelope of flesh, and the spirit, the so-called soul, even the foolish desire for immortality, can seep out through the pores and become nothingness. (The word *sainte*, in line 102, alludes to the typical impatience of the pious for the joys of survival after death.)

Lines 103 to 108 are the most direct expression in modern poetry of the outright spurning of the gilded, insipid view of immortality to which many believers cling. The negations of Lucretius, Goethe, Vigny, and Leconte de Lisle come to mind; but Valéry's are even more ironical. In 1919, while completing this poem, he was also composing his most profound prose essay, on Leonardo da Vinci, "Note and Digression," in which he derided in similar fashion the Catholic conception, which, he thought, made the soul a very poor thing indeed. "Reason demands, and dogma imposes, the resurrection of the flesh" (*Variété*, Vol. I). He insinuated that theology too discreetly avoids discussing that carnal resurrection without which another life can hardly be tempting. Who fails to pierce through such pious lies? he asks, and who could accept a ghostly semblance of existence with no brain inside the skull and only the eternal grin of the blessed or of skeletons? With these stanzas, and with the concluding acceptance of the wind and of the sea that now grows tumultuous as the breeze and the sun glitteringly play upon it, the whole poem becomes an espousal of mobility, of the world of the relative, of sensuous appearances: a victory for romanticism, a controlled and lucid enthusiasm. And this poem is the declaration of the very same Paul Valéry who was fond of remarking that "enthusiasm is not a worthy mood for a writer."

The resort to the decasyllable, which had not often been used in modern French for a long poem, forced Valéry to eliminate all nonessentials. Every adjective is apposite and pregnant with meaning (etymological, concrete, symbolical, evocative), such as *vaporeuse, poreuse, sainte, dorée*, and the cruelly ironical ones in line 108. There are no rare words, there is no tampering with normal syntax. The music of the lines is not sonorous, as it is in Hugo when he confronts man with death and immortality; nor is it ever flat or prosaic, as it can become even in Baudelaire. It is as fluid and melodious as the best passages of Racine.

If Valéry was right in spurning the label of "philosophical poet," which too often implies pedantry, dryness, and abstraction, he is nevertheless, in lines like these, a poet for whom ideas were, as Wordsworth put it in "Tintern Abbey": "Felt in the blood, and felt along the heart." Valéry's rejection of the kind of immortality that is held out by most religious systems and his ironical denial of all illusion as to personal survival after death make him a brother of Lucretius and an ancestor of Giraudoux, Camus, and Sartre. All of them incessantly voice their faith in a humanism conceived as a stoic acceptance of man's fate; they reiterate their refusal to envy the condition of an immortal.

But Valéry is no negative thinker. His last important work, *Mon Faust* (*My Faust*), showed him—as do the concluding stanzas of "*Le cimetière marin*"—to have accepted the tumult and the unpredictability of human life and sharing the faith of ordinary men in the possibilities of their "unconquerable mind." *Le vent se lève! . . . Il faut tenter de vivre!* ("The wind is rising! . . . One must attempt to live!") is one of several exclamatory lines in the final stanza of "The Graveyard by the Sea," of this poem that is "a prolonged hesitation between sound and sense"—the definition Valéry gave (in *Rhumbs*) of every poem.   [H.P.]

GUILLAUME APOLLINAIRE

LA CHANSON DU MAL-AIMÉ [Fragment]

I

Un soir de demi-brume à Londres
Un voyou qui ressemblait à
Mon amour vint à ma rencontre
Et le regard qu'il me jeta
Me fit baisser les yeux de honte   5

II

Je suivis ce mauvais garçon
Qui sifflotait mains dans les poches
Nous semblions entre les maisons
Onde ouverte de la Mer Rouge
Lui les Hébreux moi Pharaon   10

III

Que tombent ces vagues de briques
Si tu ne fus pas bien aimée
Je suis le souverain d'Égypte
Sa sœur-épouse son armée
Si tu n'es pas l'amour unique   15

IV

Au tournant d'une rue brûlant
De tous les feux de ses façades
Plaies du brouillard sanguinolent
Où se lamentaient les façades
Une femme lui ressemblant   20

Wilhelm-Apollinaris de Kostrowitsky (1880-1918) was born in Rome of a Polish mother of noble descent and of an Italian father who preferred an adventurer's life to marriage. With not a drop of French blood in him, he became one of the most genuinely French of poets. When he was five years old, his mother took him to Monte Carlo, where he was educated in a Catholic school. At nineteen, already versed in Symbolist poetry and fond of Musset, Nerval, and Laforgue, whom his poetry will often recall, he went to live in Paris. A countess engaged him as tutor for her daughter and he traveled with them to Germany in 1901, where he met an English girl, Annie Playden, who was a governess in the same family. He courted her in vain, confided his sorrow to verse, and returned to Paris, where he soon became the friend of two Fauvist painters, Vlaminck and Derain, and (in 1904) of Picasso. Out of Apollinaire's conversations with Picasso, Max Jacob, and André Salmon at the "bateau-lavoir" in Montmartre, in 1905-1906, the modern-art movement was to emerge.

Apollinaire was not only an extraordinary art critic, who explained the intentions of the painters to themselves (in *The Cubist Painters* [1913] he drew up the manifesto of modernity in art); he was an equally clear-sighted literary critic, who boldly assigned Sade, Nerval, and Baudelaire to the positions they have occupied ever since. Leading a Bohemian life and retaining total independence from all academic conventions, he fought continually against the effete and the repetitious, advocating energy in art, and insisting (long before Freud became known in France) on the importance of sex in all human relations. His physical and intellectual appetite was voracious. *Je suis ivre d'avoir bu tout l'univers,* he declared in *Alcools* ("I am intoxicated from having drunk the whole universe"). Apollinaire read enormously, but he always imparted a novel vibration to his more traditional work (as he does in the first poem by which he is represented here). At other times, as in the last of our selections, he stood gazing into the future and pointing to uncharted lands for the poets of the future to conquer.

Apollinaire was known in his lifetime only to a restricted avant-garde circle, but since his death, his stature as a poet has grown increasingly: today he is revered as a classic, learnt by heart by schoolboys, and lectured upon at the Sorbonne. Early in World War I he volunteered for service and for a time enjoyed the gruesome adventure, which his poems celebrated along with his varied loves. In 1916, however, a shell pierced his helmet; he was trepanned soon after, just as his fanciful autobiography *Le poète assassiné* (*The Poet Murdered*) appeared. The wound had severely impaired his health. In 1918 he married "*la jolie rousse*," celebrated in our last selection, but within six months he was dead.

Anecdotes and legends have proliferated around Apollinaire—he was in love with love itself but also with a number of real women. After the idealization of pallid, ethereal creatures, languidly adored by the Symbolists, it is refreshing to come upon a poet who loves and sings with naturalness about real women. Apollinaire is seldom crude but he is often frank; tenderness and sensuousness blend felicitously in his verse. Happily for posterity, a few of his love affairs (among them his long liaison with Marie Laurencin) brought him grief, and others, like the one that gave rise to our poem, remained unfulfilled. The woman of this *chanson* (1901-1903), Annie Playden, was frightened by the advances of the young suitor, and fled. "Marriage was impossible," Apollinaire confided later, "but I suffered much, as shown by this poem, in which I believed myself ill-loved, while I was the one who loved badly."

Less than a fifth of the very long but ingeniously varied "Song of the Ill-Loved" can be given in the space available. (1) *One evening of half fog in London* (2) *A rascal who looked like* (3) *My love came up to me* (4) *And the glance he threw me* (5) *Made me drop my eyes in shame.* (6) *I followed that bad fellow* (7) *Who whistled [his] hands in his pockets* (8) *We seemed to be between rows of houses* (9) *[Like the] divided waters of the Red Sea* (10) *He the Hebrews I Pharaoh.* (11) *Let those waves of brick fall down* (12) *If you were not [once] well loved* (13) *I am the sovereign of Egypt* (14) *His sister-wife his army* (15) *If you are not the [my] only love.* (16) *At the turning of a street burning* (17) *With all the fires [lights] of its housefronts* (18) *Wounds of bleeding fog* (19) *Where the housefronts were wailing* (20) *A woman very much like her.*

This is a song, in the rhythm of popular songs, five octosyllabic lines per stanza with the stanzas running smoothly into one another. (Apollinaire is the one poet after Verlaine who was able to restore the values of pure song to the poetry of France.) As in many popular songs, the music is more important than the frequently baffling logic of the successive moods expressed. There is no punctuation —it is superfluous, Apollinaire contended: the rhythm and the breaks in the line are sufficient. The octosyllable, which can sound abrupt and monotonous because of its limited arrangement of the caesuras, is wielded by him with superb skill. At times the lines are suspended on a preposition (2) and the rimes are mere assonances (1, 3, and 5). Typically poetic diction, which had become rarefied with the Symbolists, is trampled under foot almost insolently. Scholarly allusions to the Bible, to Egyptian, and to Indian figures alternate with words of everyday life (*voyou, mauvais*

V

C'était son regard d'inhumaine
La cicatrice à son cou nu
Sortit saoule d'une taverne
Au moment où je reconnus
La fausseté de l'amour même   25

VI

Lorsqu'il fut de retour enfin
Dans sa patrie le sage Ulysse
Son vieux chien de lui se souvint
Près d'un tapis de haute lisse
Sa femme attendait qu'il revînt   30

VII

L'époux royal de Sacontale
Las de vaincre se réjouit
Quand il la retrouva plus pâle
D'attente et d'amour yeux pâlis
Caressant sa gazelle mâle   35

VIII

J'ai pensé à ces rois heureux
Lorsque le faux amour et celle
Dont je suis encore amoureux
Heurtant leurs ombres infidèles
Me rendirent si malheureux   40

(*Alcools.* 1913)

garçon, 2, 6) and playfully boastful exclamations (11-15). The profound sentiment of distress expressed here—reminiscent of Thomas de Quincey's gloomy peregrinations along Oxford Street—is touched with irony.

The theme is half wrapped in mist. Apollinaire's love for the English girl is personified as a real being or a ghost—a scoundrel roaming and whistling in the metropolis. It is the poet's "Doppelgänger," his spiritual counterpart, who, like Musset's vision in "*Nuit de décembre*," resembled him "like a brother" even while he frightened him. He flees from this image of his uglier self, which seems to blaspheme against the truth of his love. The allusion to the row of red bricks is mock heroic and it brings on a strange train of thought: his love was and is true; the only love; as true as it is that he is not the Pharaoh or Pharoah's sister-spouse. In the reddish glare of the twilight inside the houses, made lurid by the fog, a face appears which then recalls his love.

(21) *It was her [cold] inhuman glance* (22) *The scar on her bare neck* (23) *[She] came out drunk from some tavern* (24) *At the instant when I recognized* (25) *The falsity of love itself* (26) *When at last he was home*

again (27) *In his own land wise Ulysses* (28) *His aged dog remembered him* (29) *Nearby a rug [woven in] a high warp* (30) *His wife awaited his return* (31) *Shakuntala's royal husband* (32) *Tired of conquering rejoiced* (33) *When he found her paler* (34) *From waiting and her eyes faded from love* (35) *Stroking her male gazelle* (36) *I have thought of those happy kings* (37) *When the [this] false love and she* (38) *With whom I am still in love* (39) *Their faithless shadows jostling [each other]* (40) *Made me so miserable.*

These stanzas are unashamedly sentimental. Behind the corpulence and the Rabelaisian appetite that made Apollinaire proverbial among painters and poets, there lurked a very tender soul. He played at eroticism when it was enhanced by gracefulness and, more than any other modern, he did much to inaugurate the rehabilitation of Sade as the boldest discoverer of the rôle of desire in most human relationships. But he could never stomach Maupassant or Zola. In a letter from his army days, September 14, 1915, he confessed that he could not approve of writers who contemplated the vices or the ugliness of mankind without smiling; smiling was for him a manner of "remedying in a way our misery, veiling it with intelligent grace, even if one were immediately to sob over it." There was more of Musset in Apollinaire than modern anti-romantics are willing to admit.

With youthful persistence he tried to force himself upon Miss Playden after she had returned to her parents and resumed her life in a rigid Puritan background. She fled from his fits of anger and finally settled in America, forbidding him ever to write to her again. The scene of the poem is laid in London—like many a Frenchman, Apollinaire had been impressed by De Quincey's encounter, on Oxford Street, with a girl called Ann. (Musset and Baudelaire had both adapted the *Confessions of an Opium Eater*.) In the fifth stanza he is reminded, by the passing vision of a woman with a scar on her neck, coming out of a pub, of the English girl's cold, blue, "inhuman" eyes. That vagrant woman, probably ready to trade venal love, confirms him in his vituperation against all loves, at least those which he is destined to know and to suffer from. Here, as earlier, the feminine rimes (*inhumaine—taverne—même*) are merely assonances. The tone in lines 21-25 is vivid and dramatic, and in the last line of the stanza the pause after the fourth syllable, *la fausseté*, engraves the meaning like a maxim.

His woeful fate is then imaginatively contrasted with that of Ulysses and of an oriental sovereign, not without a trace of the pedantry one often finds in Apollinaire, whose sincerity was strengthened by the thought that others had felt like him before or had found a fate happier than his own as an "accursèd poet." Lines 26-30, inspired by the *Odyssey's* famous recognition scene of Ulysses and his dog, are among the most harmonious of the poem. Dushmantra, a legendary sovereign of India, was Shakuntala's husband; his wife became one of the hallowed Indian widows, celebrated in a drama by the

fifth-century poet Kalidasa (and also, in French literature, by Gautier). The vignette suggested in three lines (32-35), with the multiplication of the *a*'s (ten times), the graceful gesture of the queen stroking her gazelle (*mâle;* and indeed *Sacontale* may well have been brought here solely by the rime), is again vividly pictorial. Then the poet's memory, which had wandered afar in the past, is brought back to his own, unhappier, plight. The casual apparition on the London street of a false love, recalling the true one by whom he had been rejected (in another manuscript in Apollinaire's hand, two lines conjuring up De Quincey, drinking "the sweet and chaste poison," followed line 35), plunges him into sorrow. But the singing of his pain through fifty-one more stanzas soothes him in the end—as the old French saying has it, "Who sings his sorrow charms it."

With the fifteenth stanza, the tone changes. The sentimental melancholy of the opening verses vanishes, and Apollinaire sings one of the gayest *aubades* in the language, inviting girls to be merry like the spring in the wooded valleys. Then, following his freely roaming fancy, he interpolates another—more bawdy—song, addressed by the Zaporogan Cossacks to the Sultan of Constantinople to spurn his advances. The sharp pain of Apollinaire's grief when he was ill-loved recurs as he playfully describes the seven swords that have wounded his heart. Finally the long, meandering elegy ends, with the forsaken lover wandering through Paris, on one of those Sundays which he loved, with its street organs and café terraces, turning in his nostalgia *vers toi, toi que j'ai tant aimée* ("towards you, you whom I loved so much"). The poem is a series of semi-musical variations on several themes, half-disconnected, diverse as its author's changing moods. [H.P.]

VITAM IMPENDERE AMORI

I

L'amour est mort entre tes bras
Te souviens-tu de sa rencontre
Il est mort tu la referas
Il s'en revient à ta rencontre   4

Encore un printemps de passé
Je songe à ce qu'il eut de tendre
Adieu saison qui finissez   7
Vous nous reviendrez aussi tendre

II

O ma jeunesse abandonnée
Comme une guirlande fanée
Voici que s'en vient la saison
Et des dédains et du soupçon   12

Le paysage est fait de toiles
Il coule un faux fleuve de sang
Et sous l'arbre fleuri d'étoiles
Un clown est l'unique passant   16

Un froid rayon poudroie et joue
Sur les décors et sur ta joue
Un coup de revolver un cri
Dans l'ombre un portrait a souri   20

La vitre du cadre est brisée
Un air qu'on ne peut définir
Hésite entre son et pensée
Entre avenir et souvenir   24

O ma jeunesse abandonnée
Comme une guirlande fanée
Voici que s'en vient la saison
Des regrets et de la raison   28

(*Vitam impendere amori.* 1917)

These two delicate and tenderly nostalgic songs are among the finest in this vein (the tradition of Musset and Verlaine) in twentieth-century French poetry and the most discreetly tragic—they were inspired by the poet's prolonged love for the painter Marie Laurencin. He met her soon after his unsuccessful courtship of the English girl who haunts the "*Chanson du mal-aimé,*" and their liaison lasted from 1907 to 1913, when the petulant painter, who had charmed and exasperated Apollinaire, finally preferred a German husband to him. Her blend of naïveté, in part contrived (as was her talent as a painter), and the elusiveness with which she drew away from her avid but sentimental lover long kept Apollinaire fascinated, if not faithful.

The Latin title ("to devote life to love") was coined after a well-known phrase from the fourth satire of Juvenal, *Vitam impendere vero,* which Jean-Jacques Rousseau had adopted as his motto when he decided to make total sincerity the rule of his life and writings. I—(1) *Love has died in your arms* (2) *Do you recall meeting it* (3) *It has died you will do so again [meet it]* (4) *It comes back to meet you* (5) *Another spring is now past* (6) *I dream of the tenderness it had* (7) *Adieu season which is ending* (8) *You will come back to us just as tender.*

The first of these songs is not yet touched with tragic melancholy. Love has died, but only for a time, extinguished by too much reality and by what Paul Valéry, in "*Anne,*" gracefully alluded to as "*la vigueur et les gestes étranges / Que pour tuer l'amour inventent les amants* ("the vigor and the strange gestures / That lovers invent to kill love"). But love will emerge, reborn out of new desire. The first quatrain is built on the word *rencontre* and the second on the adjective *tendre*. Tenderness is the melancholy but half-consoling note of the poem. The encounter (*la* in line 3 refers to the feminine substantive, *rencontre;* the phrase, *tu la referas*, echoes like a consolation offered to a child who has lost its favorite toy) is the encounter of love which the poet made in the woman's arms, then allowed to escape. All is over now. But another spring is not far behind, and another love may meet him on the path of his life. The brief song is as pure and as airy as any in modern or in old French. The phrase *il s'en revient* has a faintly archaic flavor.

II—(9) *O my youth now abandoned* (10) *Like a faded garland* (11) *Now is the season coming* (12) *Of both disdains and suspicion* (13) *The scenery is made of canvases* (14) *A fake stream of blood is running* (15) *And under the tree flowering with stars* (16) *A clown is the only passer-by* (17) *A cold ray powders and plays* (18) *On the settings and on your cheek* (19) *A pistol shot a cry* (20) *In the dark a portrait has smiled* (21) *The glass of the frame is broken* (22) *An air (melody) which cannot be defined* (23) *Hovers between sound and thought* (24) *Between the future and memory* (25) *O my youth [now] abandoned* (26) *Like a faded garland* (27) *Now is the season coming* (28) *Of both regrets and reason.*

The second of these songs is tinged with somewhat bitter regret. Its faded garlands recall Nerval's "*Sylvie*" and Watteau's melancholy clowns, of whom Verlaine already had dreamt. Apollinaire, now nearing thirty, casts a backward glance at his youthful years, which were sacrificed to vain loves. The impetuous oaths and promises of the youthful lovers have now yielded to disdain and to mutual suspicion.

Lines 13 to 24 may be read as delicate allusions to her paintings, and to the circus scenes that Seurat, Degas, Picasso,

and Marie herself liked to render on their canvases. Like those stylized paintings, reminiscent of a theatrical set, their love was in part make-believe; they were but actors on a stage, shooting toy pistols under a cold light (13-20). But the two tragic comedians shattered the glass frame of their illusions. A tune of bygone days echoes; is its mournful meaning to be heeded (23)? Its music would bring solace, if one could forget the meaning behind it (line 23: hesitation between sound and thought). One is tempted to welcome the future and to forget, but the melancholy of the past is also seductive (24).

In the last quatrain, resignation creeps into the poet's spirit: the hour has rung for the sweetness of regrets, for reasonableness and wisdom. Apollinaire echoed Musset's favorite claims for ever loving and ever changing from one woman to another: reasonableness, *la raison*, may emerge from such passions, and the truest pleasure of love is not to love, but to have loved.

Whereas rhetoric often crept into the poems of Musset and Baudelaire that Apollinaire seems to echo, and their posturing as infelicitous lovers pursued by fate or by their own demon verged on the dramatic, Apollinaire remained more simple in his sentimental complaints, almost detached in watching himself amusedly as though he were someone else. In these airy songs, he stripped French poetry of all traces of rhetoric. He eschewed the rare words and the intricate syntax of the Symbolists. He played like a delicate musician with one of the most difficult lines in French, the octosyllable with its limited variety of caesuras. The break in the middle (as in 1, 4, 12, 25) can easily become mechanical; it has to be varied with the caesura after the third syllable (3, 20, 28), or after the fifth (lines 8, 11), or after the sixth (19). As a metrician, Apollinaire owed much to Verlaine. [H.P.]

GUILLAUME APOLLINAIRE

LA JOLIE ROUSSE

Me voici devant tous un homme plein de sens
Connaissant la vie et de la mort ce qu'un vivant peut connaître
Ayant éprouvé les douleurs et les joies de l'amour
Ayant su quelquefois imposer ses idées
Connaissant plusieurs langages
Ayant pas mal voyagé
Ayant vu la guerre dans l'Artillerie et l'Infanterie
Blessé à la tête trépané sous le chloroforme   8
Ayant perdu ses meilleurs amis dans l'effroyable lutte
Je sais d'ancien et de nouveau autant qu'un homme seul pourrait
           des deux savoir
Et sans m'inquiéter aujourd'hui de cette guerre
Entre nous et pour nous mes amis   12
Je juge cette longue querelle de la tradition et de l'invention
           De l'Ordre et de l'Aventure

Vous dont la bouche est faite à l'image de celle de Dieu
Bouche qui est l'ordre même   16
Soyez indulgents quand vous nous comparez
A ceux qui furent la perfection de l'ordre
Nous qui quêtons partout l'aventure

Nous ne sommes pas vos ennemis   20
Nous voulons vous donner de vastes et d'étranges domaines
Où le mystère en fleurs s'offre à qui veut le cueillir

"The Pretty Redhead": (1) *Here am I in everyone's eyes a man full of sense* (2) *Knowing life and what a living [man] is able to know of death* (3) *Having experienced the sorrows and the joys of love* (4) *Having known at times how to impose his ideas* (5) *Versed in several languages* (6) *Having traveled quite a little* (7) *Having seen war in the Artillery and in the Infantry* (8) *Wounded in the head trepanned under chloroform* (9) *Having lost his best friends in the fearful struggle* (10) *I know of the old and the new as much as a single man alone could know of both* (11) *And without concerning myself today with this war* (12) *Between us and for us my friends* (13) *I judge this long quarrrel of tradition and of invention* (14) *Of Order and Adventure.*

(15) *You whose mouth is made in the image of God's* (16) *Mouth which is order itself* (17) *Be lenient when you compare us* (18) *To those who were the perfection of order* (19) *We who seek adventure everywhere.*

(20) *We are not your enemies* (21) *We want to give you vast and strange domains* (22) *Where flowering mystery offers itself to whoever wishes to pluck it.*

Through one of his facets, the Proteus that Apollinaire was looked back to gracefully tender French poets whom he liked to echo, or to popular songs of haunting musical beauty, such as those which the German Romantics had brilliantly revived with their *Lieder*. But the great significance of Apollinaire in modern poetics and esthetics comes from the other aspect of his talent: he was also the poet of adventure against tradition, the champion of Cubism and the precursor of Surrealism, the experimenter with new themes and new techniques. Around 1908-1912, he was the first to understand that a cleavage was taking place which was to relegate Symbolism to the past, to acclaim new influences on modern letters (Jarry, Rimbaud), and to enable Picasso, Juan Gris, the Douanier Rousseau, the Russian Ballet company, Stravinsky, and many others to become aware of their true revolutionary mission. Apollinaire left two manifestoes which have remained the charter of modern views on art: *Les peintres cubistes*, 1913, and a posthumous article in the *Mercure de France* (December 1, 1918), "*L'Esprit nouveau et les poètes.*" Along with these epoch-making prose declarations, the beautiful and grave "*La jolie rousse*" may be read as Apollinaire's poetic testament.

Characteristically, the title given to this testament designates a young woman, Jacqueline Kolb, whom the poet loved in the last year of World War I and whose flaming hair he admired. Apollinaire married Jacqueline on May 2nd, with Picasso and the art-dealer Vollard as his witnesses. On November 9th he was dead.

"*La jolie rousse*" is no old-fashioned poetical art. It does not utter pontifical decrees or didactically admonish the poet of the future not to stray from the narrow path to Parnassus. In typical fashion, Apollinaire mocks his own gravity at the end; he practices the precepts first offered. The poem turns into a flamboyant love-song, experiments with lines of unequal length, and disposes the lines ingeniously on the page. The volume from which this, his last piece, is drawn was entitled *Calligrams*.

The opening is solemn. The rhythm plays around the mold of the twelve-syllable line (as in 1 and 11) but avoids the monotony of a succession of alexandrines. At times, a much shorter line cuts in as a surprise and the tone becomes familiar (6); at other moments, a long line, further lengthened by nasal sounds (*ancien, autant*, 10; *longue, tradition invention, aventure*, 13), generates an ominous suspense. Rimes occur in the last stanzas, when the grave poem grows fanciful and starts to sing. "The Pretty Redhead" is the statement of a man aware of the nearness of his end; he has indulged many eccentricities and knows that his more conservative contemporaries have branded him as a dangerous destroyer of tradition.

There is nothing obscure in this testament; Apollinaire did away with punctuation but retained a normal syntax and did not strive to alter the meaning of words. The key terms are *connaître* and *savoir*, the former suggesting intuitive and empirical procedures, the second a more laborious and systematic effort at accumulating knowledge. Apollinaire was indeed widely read in several languages and explored many hidden byways of literature, even the "Inferno" of Aretino and of Sade. He was also a theoretical esthetician, with a lucid intellect, fully aware of the need for appreciating the best in a national tradition. To his friend André Billy, in the last year of his own life, Apollinaire confided, in words which stand as an apt commentary on this manifesto-poem: "I have never destroyed, but on the contrary I attempted to reconstruct. The classical line had been disrupted before me, who utilized it often, so often that I gave the octosyllable, among others, a new lease of life. In the arts likewise, I have not destroyed, but tried to help new schools

Il y a là des feux nouveaux des couleurs jamais vues
Mille phantasmes impondérables   24
Auxquels il faut donner de la réalité
Nous voulons explorer la bonté contrée énorme où tout se tait
Il y a aussi le temps qu'on peut chasser ou faire revenir
Pitié pour nous qui combattons toujours aux frontières   28
De l'illimité et de l'avenir
Pitié pour nos erreurs pitié pour nos péchés

Voici que revient l'été la saison violente
Et ma jeunesse est morte ainsi que le printemps   32
O Soleil c'est le temps de la Raison ardente
                    Et j'attends
Pour la suivre toujours la forme noble et douce
Qu'elle prend afin que je l'aime seulement   36
Elle vient et m'attire ainsi qu'un fer l'aimant
                    Elle a l'aspect charmant
                    D'une adorable rousse

Ses cheveux sont d'or on dirait   40
Un bel éclair qui durerait
Ou ces flammes qui se pavanent
Dans les roses-thé qui se fanent

Mais riez riez de moi   44
Hommes de partout surtout gens d'ici
Car il y a tant de choses que je n'ose vous dire
Tant de choses que vous ne me laisseriez pas dire
Ayez pitié de moi

(Calligrammes. 1918)

live, without harming the past ones. . . .
God bear witness to me that I wished only
to annex new domains to arts and letters,
without ever refusing to acknowledge the
merits of true masterpieces of the past or
of the present."

(23) *There are new fires and colors never
seen before* (24) *A thousand imponderable
phantasms* (25) *To which reality must be given*
(26) *We want to explore goodness [kindness]
that huge country where all is silent* (27) *There
is also time which can be driven away or
brought back* (28) *Pity us who are always
fighting at the frontiers* (29) *Of the limitless
and of the future* (30) *Have pity on our
mistakes have pity on our sins*

(31) *Here is summer returning [again] the
violent season* (32) *And my youth is dead as the
spring* (33) *O Sun this is the time of ardent
[burning] Reason* (34) *And I wait* (35) *To
follow her always the noble and sweet form*
(36) *Which she assumes that I may love only
her* (37) *She comes and draws me as the
magnet [draws] iron* (38) *She has the charm-
ing appearance* (39) *Of an adorable redhead*

(40) *Her hair is of gold one would say*
(41) *A beautiful flash of lightning that endures*
(42) *Or those flames which [proudly] strut
[as in a pavan]* (43) *In fading tea roses*

(44) *But laugh laugh at me* (45) *Men from
everywhere and especially from here [local
people]* (46) *For there are so many things*

which I dare not tell you (47) *So many things which you would not let me say* (48) *Have pity on me*

The middle-class public, the traditionalists, the *bien-pensants* ("right-thinking people"), often decry the eccentrics (be they the Impressionists, the Symbolists, the Cubists) whom their successors will one day revere. They boast complacently of being the only true heirs to the French tradition; their mouth, which rounds itself proudly to pronounce the word *ordre*, is they claim, God's own. They like to crush the rebels of art by comparing them unfairly to the classics of twenty-five centuries and of ten different lands. Apollinaire proclaimed his reverence for the classics, but he wished to be true to their spirit of adventure that had made them the innovators of their own day and the classics ever since. The third stanza suggestively mentions several of the new lands which, in his prose essays and in the most famous long poem of *Calligrams*, "*Les collines*," he was proud of having charted: mystery, new colors (reminiscent of Arthur Rimbaud), the phantasms of dreams (soon to become the favorite theme of the Surrealists), kindness or goodness (for realistic and naturalistic literature had too long fed on monstrosities, drabness, a bitter view of man's vices unredeemed by any charity (26), and the relativity of time (27). To these he was to add, in his last prose essays, the miracles of modern science and even of technology, which he thought should not frighten "futuristic" poets. "Great poets and great artists have as a social function to renew incessantly the appearance that nature assumes in man's eyes." His "*Collines*" is the most eloquent plea made since Shelley and Hugo for the poet as a prophet.

Lines 31 and 33 have often been quoted as vindicating Apollinaire's claims: he seems to herald the summer, the violent, mature era of his century, the marriage, which he advocates, of French Reason with new emotional and even subconscious forces. But the poet cannot deal with didactic abstractions. His ideal is embodied in living symbols, and this poetical art ends in a graceful song to his fiancée, the red-haired Jacqueline. Lines 36-39 swing capriciously, with rimes and assonances. The poet recaptures the light grace of his early octosyllabic love-songs to laud the red hair, which he compares to flames proudly illuminating fading tea roses (42-43). He returns to his earnest, imploring mood to beg the light, flippant public (of Paris in particular, *gens d'ici*) to have pity instead of derision for their prophet-poets. Much of what Apollinaire has to say will be interred with his bones because of the incomprehension of the public.

As a creator, Apollinaire must probably be judged to have been less powerfully imaginative than Rimbaud and Claudel and less intent than Mallarmé or Valéry upon extracting the very essence of poetry from all that might dilute it. His long poems, "*Chanson du mal-aimé*," "*Les collines*," and even the most touching of them all, "*La maison des morts*" ("The House of the Dead"), move too slowly, wander concentrically, and lack the felicitous inevitability of very great poetic language. His was the talent of a pioneer, who defined poets as perpetual inventors. He, a Slav and an Italian who had elected French as his language, proclaimed at the very time when he was composing "*La jolie rousse*": "The French are carrying poetry to all nations. . . . All other languages seem to be silent so that the universe may better listen to the voice of the new French poets." [H.P.]

ÉLOGES. 2. [POUR FÊTER UNE ENFANCE]

Et les servantes de ma mère, grandes filles luisantes... Et nos paupières   1
fabuleuses... O

   clartés! ô faveurs!   2

   Appelant toute chose, je récitai qu'elle était grande, appelant toute bête,   3
qu'elle était belle et bonne.

O mes plus grandes   4

fleurs voraces, parmi la feuille rouge, à dévorer tous mes plus beaux   5

   insectes verts! les bouquets au jardin sentaient le cimetière de famille. Et   6
une très petite sœur était morte: j'avais eu, qui sent bon, son cercueil d'acajou
entre les glaces de trois chambres.

   Et il ne fallait pas tuer l'oiseau-mouche d'un caillou...   7

   Mais la terre se courbait dans nos jeux comme fait la servante, celle qui a   8
droit à une chaise si l'on se tient dans la maison.

                                          (*Éloges.* 1911)

Saint-John Perse (Alexis Léger), long a mysterious figure in French literature, for he had published little before 1941 and was admired by only a happy few, has achieved fame in recent years as one of the leading poets of our mid-century. His verse has enjoyed the rare distinction of being translated in entirety by gifted writers in England and the United States, among them T. S. Eliot, who prefaced and translated *Anabase* (1930). Perse was born in 1887 on a little island off Guadeloupe, where his family had long been settled. At the age of eleven, he was sent to France to finish his schooling. He met Paul Claudel, Francis Jammes and, later, Paul Valéry; published *Éloges* (1911); and contributed to the *Nouvelle Revue Française;* and in 1914 entered the diplomatic service. After serving for several years in China and traveling widely in Asia, he became Permanent Secretary of the French Foreign Office. A stubborn opponent of Nazi policies, Perse left France in 1940 to escape persecution by the Germans and the Vichy government. For the last twenty years he has lived in retirement in Washington, D.C., and (except for *Éloges* and *Anabase*, 1924) his books of poetry have all been published in New York in bilingual editions: *Pluies* (1943), *Neiges* (1944), *Vents* (1946), *Amers* (1957).

Many lyrical poems of past ages were "laudations" or praises addressed to the gods, litanies to the Virgin, graces to a divine Being or to Nature, in appreciation of the bounties of this world and of the promises of the next, or to a loved person in response to what Blake called "the lineaments of gratified desire." Claudel and, even more notably, Saint-John Perse, have revived this poetic form, which sings, in orderly raptures and carefully controlled cascades of enumerations, the author's wonder in the presence of external phenomena. Such a world appears even more enchanting when seen through the eyes of the boy the poet once was. Saint-John Perse's childhood on the island that belonged to his family, among Hindu servants and devotees of the sea and of sailing, among volcanoes, cyclones, and wild vegetation, must have been a fabulous one. *Éloges* (represented here by a fragment) is a long monologue in praise of that fantastic world recaptured, "a long, single sentence without break and forever unintelligible," as the poet somewhere amusingly characterizes all his poetry.

(1) *And my mother's maids, tall, shining girls . . . And our fabulous eyelids . . . O* (2) *brightness! O favors!* (3) *Calling each thing, I recited that it was great, calling each beast, that it was beautiful and kind.* (4) *O my biggest* (5) *voracious flowers, among the red leafage, [ready] to devour all my most beautiful* (6) *green insects! The clusters of flowers in the garden smelled of the family cemetery. And a very little sister had died: I had had, with its fragrance* [literally, *which smells good*] *her mahogany coffin between the mirrors of three rooms.* (7) *And one must not kill the hummingbird with a stone . . .* (8) *But the earth crouched down in our games [being humbly primitive] as does the maid servant, the one who has the right to a chair when the family stays indoors.*

The theme is the bliss of a child's discovery of the strange world around him, through a kaleidoscopic succession of visions: the colored maids with their shining skin, who had been imported from Asia after the African slave trade had been discontinued; then the voracious red flowers that snapped up the wonderfully colored insects; the smell of the boxwood and the cypresses of the churchyard.

This vision brings back the fleeting memory of a sister who had died very young and of the odor of the wood of which her coffin, now lying in the central room upstairs, was made. The parental injunction not to throw stones at birds and the piles of sand and holes in the earth made by the children at play are then recalled, with the dignified but surprising comparison of the earth to a maid servant crouching humbly even when she had the right to use a chair in the house.

These glimpses of childhood memories are introduced, in tones reminiscent of Rimbaud's ecstatic exclamations ("O seasons! O castles!"), in lines 1 and 2 by the allusion to "fabulous" eyelids, that is, to the power children have of seeing everything with eyes sharper and more easily irradiated by these splendors than the dulled eyes of adults.

The prose poem, admirably used by Rimbaud and by Claudel, is carried to perfection by Saint-John Perse; it never becomes declamatory or monotonous. Effects of surprise are obtained, as in 1-2 and 5-6, through long pauses delaying the cymbal stroke of the substantives; *clartés, fleurs, insectes.* A few syntactical devices, which the poet will later use more abundantly, scarcely detract from the luminous clarity of this evocation: *voraces . . . à dévorer* in line 5 (*à* is the author's favorite preposition) here replaces an entire phrase (*si voraces qu'elles pouvaient dévorer*), and the inversion of the relative clause inserted before the noun (*son cercueil*, governing the relative pronoun *qui* in *qui sent bon*, as if the fragrance were projected before one could realize where it came from). Such a mode of writing has the effect of imparting the one enduring impression left by that death: the fragrance of the wood.

[H.P.]

POÈME À L'ÉTRANGÈRE (1942)

Mais ce soir de grand âge et de grande patience, dans l'Été lourd d'opiates 1
et d'obscures laitances, pour délivrer à fond d'abîme le peuple de vos lampes,
ayant, homme très seul, pris par ce haut quartier de Fondations d'aveugles,
de Réservoirs mis au linceul et de vallons en cage pour les morts, longeant
les grilles et les lawns et tous ces beaux jardins à l'italienne —
dont les maîtres un soir s'en furent épouvantés d'un parfum de sépulcre, 2

je m'en vais, ô mémoire! à mon pas d'homme libre, sans horde ni tribu, 3
parmi le chant des sabliers, et, le front nu, lauré d'abeilles de phosphore, au
bas du ciel très vaste d'acier vert comme en un fond de mer, sifflant mon
peuple de sibylles, sifflant mon peuple d'incrédules, je flatte encore en songe,
de la main, parmi tant d'êtres invisibles,
ma chienne d'Europe qui fut blanche et, plus que moi, poète. 4

(Œuvre poétique. 1953)

The poetry of Saint-John Perse has often been characterized, not un-justly, as haughtily impersonal. Everything in it is indeed exalted to the level of an elaborate ritual, as if a ceremonious diplomat were initiating humble mortals into a hallowed protocol, or an Asiatic high-priest were cataloguing the sumptuous offerings laid upon an altar for some divinity of the desert. The words are rich and rare, not pretentiously and languidly vaporous as in Symbolist poetry but, rather, sculptural and Parnassian, often drawn from the three disciplines most familiar to the author: botany, equestrian science, and nautical sport. But behind the colorful veil of the poet's verbal embroidery and the haunting cadences of his chant, it is not difficult to experience the impact of restrained but communicative emotions.

When in 1940, Saint-John Perse, who had worked hard as a diplomat to preserve European peace against the ambitions of a Hitlerian Germany, had to flee persecution at the hands of the temporary victors, he joined the long train of writers who had been exiles (since the time of Ovid) and the still longer train of poets who had always felt like exiles on this earth from their "land of heart's desire." *Toujours il y eut cette clameur, toujours il y eut cette fureur* ("There has always been this clamor, there has always been this furor"), said Perse in *Exile*, resorting to his familiar device of varying the last substantive in a refrain. (*Splendeur* and *grandeur* were the symmetrical words preceeding *fureur*.) He became a permanent resident of the American capital, whose sultry summers, noble mansions, and lawns, and sea-coast vapors he conjured up in symbolic imagery as no American-born poet had ever done.

Our fragment comes at the very end of

"*Poème à l'étrangère*" ("Poem to a Foreign Lady"), the most nostalgic and least impersonal of Perse's works. (1) *But this evening of great age [advanced years, but also age calling for greatness in men] and great patience, in the Summer heavy with opiates and dim milt* [the substance in male fish, recalling the whiteness of milk, by which roe is fertilized], *in order to free from their deepest abyss the people of your lamps* [people now painfully studying events and at a loss as to how to act in the war then afflicting the United States also], *having walked, a very solitary man, through that high district of Foundations for the blind, of enshrouded Reservoirs* [covered over by foliage as by a shroud] *and encaged valleys for the dead, skirting the gates and the lawns and all those beautiful Italian-style gardens, (2) whose owners left one evening, aghast at an odor of the sepulcher, (3) I go my way, O memory! with the stride of a free man, without either horde or tribe, amid the song of the hour glasses and, my forehead bare, laureled with phosphorescent bees, at the foot of the vast, steel-green sky as on a floor of the sea, whistling for my people of Sibyls, whistling for my incredulous people, I still stroke in dream with my hand, among so many invisible beings, (4) my dog in Europe who was white and, more than I, a poet.*

The poet's solitariness as he walks around embassy gardens, water reservoirs, cemeteries, and manor houses now deserted by their owners, who were afraid of the sepulchral past weighing upon them, fills the long mournful opening stanza. But within him, the exile carries his memories of Europe and his creative power of bringing that past back to life. Thereby he is assured his spiritual freedom; he is almost glad to have severed ties with "horde and tribe" (3), to be free from the pressure of other men for whom clocks ("hour glasses") do not sing as they do for him. He has relinquished honors, having given up hats with gold braid (his "forehead" is "bare"); only phosphorescent insects fluttering around him in the summer evening crown him—and in a novel manner. They may well be fireflies, and the jewel-like effects of their lights recall phosphorescent bees. Beneath the oppressive sky that has the greenness of a sea-floor, he whistles to call those Sibyls: the fireflies thus transfigured seem to be heralding light in the spiritual darkness of the world at war and to be warning the faithless ones (*incrédules*) who refuse to hear the voices of the future. Seized by nostalgic memories of what was dear to him in his now forsaken European world, he stretches out his hand to pat the gentle female dog he left behind. She is more of a poet than he, for she is freer in her fancy and not oppressed by the dire events that force the poet to brood on the turmoil of the world.

The prose-verse is much less regular than that of Rimbaud or of Claudel. Perse's sentences are often long and sinuous. They teem with parentheses and at times they resound with the eloquence of rather elaborate periods. Their syntax is extremely complex. Not seldom an entire poem will conclude on a detached line of anti-climactic surprise.   [H.P.]

PLUIES VIII (1943)

... la banyan de la pluie perd ses assises sur la Ville. Au vent du ciel la chose   1
errante et telle

   Qu'elle s'en vint vivre parmi nous!... Et vous ne nierez pas, soudain, que   2
tout nous vienne à rien

   Qui veut savoir ce qu'il advient des pluies en marche sur la terre, s'en vienne   3
vivre sur mon toit, parmi les signes et présages.

   Promesses non tenues! Inlassables semailles! Et fumées que voilà sur la   4
chaussée des hommes!

   Vienne l'éclair, ha! qui nous quitte!... Et nous reconduirons aux portes de   5
la Ville

   les hautes Pluies en marche sous l'Avril, les hautes Pluies en marche sous
le fouet comme un Ordre de Flagellants.

(Œuvre poétique. 1953)

A long with works like the "*Poème à l'étrangère,*" in which tender longings haunted the poet during the first months of his bitter exile in the United States, when the New World seemed to disassociate itself from the struggles and sufferings of the Old, Saint-John Perse's American poems included elemental evocations of the West and the South, of rains and snows pelting the cities, and of winds howling over the plains. *Pluies (Rains,* 1943), *Neiges (Snows,* 1944), *Vents (Winds,* 1946), and *Amers (Sea-Marks,* 1957) are the titles of his epic of man embracing the universe. There is joy in his pilgrim-like rediscovery of America and of the world, even humor in his evocation of library galleries, of the virgin earth of the West, of long-legged women "like the iron ornaments of very high style," and of the main streets of cities along which they rush, as the New Year dawns, these "new girls, wearing, under nylon, the fresh almond of their sex" (*Vents,* II, i).

But the war years held many a day of wrath for him and for the other exiles who bemoaned the lack of understanding around them and the passing of European glory. The rains that the poet invokes are the tropical rains he had observed in Georgia, whipping and "flagellating" the countryside and its inhabitants, the huge drops falling on the parched earth in columns suggesting the multiple stems of the banyan tree. The raindrops are also the manna from Heaven—Perse never invokes God and his earth is not otherwise visited by Heaven—that may wash away all the treasured possessions of men, rows of books, museums, the whole legacy of history. "Wash" was the refrain of Part VII of *Pluies,* a dramatic prayer to waters to wash away all the litter of knowledge oppressing bookish men. The tone grows quieter as the prophetic poet returns to the splendid image of the cloud as a tree whose roots lower themselves to earth to become new pillars: "The banyan of rain takes its assizes over the City" was the striking opening of *Pluies* (*Rains*). As is customary with him, Perse alters only one essential word in this refrain: *prend* becomes *perd* in the line that opens our selection. Since the word "assizes" suggests a court of justice and a final doom inflicted upon a corrupt or blind world as well as a layer of masonry or a firm seat, and is as rare in the original as it may sound in translation, it had best be retained here.

(1) *The banyan of the rain loses its assizes over the City. To the wind of heaven [it is] the wandering thing and such* (2) *As came to live among us!* . . . *And you will not deny*, *suddenly* [modifies the verb that follows: *comes*, as adverbs often do in Perse's syntax] *that all comes to naught for us.* [The cloud has shed its form in the sky; the wind has taken it away: it has come to nothing, like everything else that happens in the world of men.] (3) *Let him who wants to know what happens to rains marching over (against) the earth, come and live on my roof, among the signs and omens.* (4) *Unkept promises! Indefatigable sowings! And smokes (steam) there on roads (causeways, roadbeds) [built] by men.* (5) *Let the lightning come, ha! which leaves us!* . . . *And we shall escort back to the City gates* (6) *The tall Rains marching (fleeing) under April, the tall Rains fleeing under the whip, like an Order of Flagellants.*

The beauty of such poetry lies in its exact yet sumptuously evocative language —Perse has wielded rare words with more mastery than any other French poet since Hugo. His birth in a remote part of the world, where the French tongue was cherished as the shrine of an entire culture and cultivated with perspicuous care, may account, at least in part, for the distinctiveness of his language. The syntax resorts to mannerisms: optative moods (2, 5), questions and addresses to an imaginary reader (3), exclamations (4), relative pronouns separated from their antecedents (5), periphrastic turns (the cloud, wandering in the sky after it has brought the rain, poetically designated in line 1), comparisons of natural phenomena to religious groups of men and women who flagellated themselves in lurid processions at the end of the Middle Ages (6). This is learned, some will say Byzantine, poetry, rich in allusions, stylized and at times hieratic in its splendor, yet it burns with restrained fervor and with adoration for the most precious goods of the world: those which are concrete and real.

Perse is the only French poet since Claudel to have embraced the whole world and to have given a voice to all the elements: "cosmic" and "epic" are the adjectives most often used to describe his verse. At the same time, he has curbed his sonorous rhetoric and he has cherished density; in 1956 he confided to some of his admirers that his poetry was made of "subtractions and omissions." In his eyes, the French poet must avail himself of the advantages afforded him by the relative poverty and abstractness of his tongue and resort to secret analogies and correspondences, even if some obscurity is thereby engendered. [H.P.]

LOUIS ARAGON

LES LILAS ET LES ROSES

O mois des floraisons mois des métamorphoses
Mai qui fut sans nuage et Juin poignardé
Je n'oublierai jamais les lilas ni les roses
Ni ceux que le printemps dans ses plis a gardés   4

Je n'oublierai jamais l'illusion tragique
Le cortège les cris la foule et le soleil
Les chars chargés d'amour les dons de la Belgique
L'air qui tremble et la route à ce bourdon d'abeilles   8
Le triomphe imprudent qui prime la querelle
Le sang que préfigure en carmin le baiser
Et ceux qui vont mourir debout dans les tourelles
Entourés de lilas par un peuple grisé   12

Je n'oublierai jamais les jardins de la France
Semblables aux missels des siècles disparus
Ni le trouble des soirs l'énigme du silence
Les roses tout le long du chemin parcouru   16
Le démenti des fleurs au vent de la panique
Aux soldats qui passaient sur l'aile de la peur
Aux vélos délirants aux canons ironiques
Au pitoyable accoutrement des faux campeurs   20

Mais je ne sais pourquoi ce tourbillon d'images
Me ramène toujours au même point d'arrêt
A Sainte-Marthe Un général De noirs ramages
Une villa normande au bord de la forêt   24
Tout se tait L'ennemi dans l'ombre se repose
On nous a dit ce soir que Paris s'est rendu
Je n'oublierai jamais les lilas ni les roses
Et ni les deux amours que nous avons perdus   28

Bouquets du premier jour lilas lilas des Flandres
Douceur de l'ombre dont la mort farde les joues
Et vous bouquets de la retraite roses tendres
Couleur de l'incendie au loin roses d'Anjou   32

(*Le crève-cœur.* 1940)

This poem was written in July 1940, one month after the fall of France in World War II. Its subject and most of its images will be clear from a reading of our translation. We shall respect the absence of punctuation in the original. (1) *O month of blossoming month of metamorphoses* (2) *May that was cloudless and June stabbed to death* (3) *I'll never forget the lilacs or the roses* (4) *Nor those that spring has kept in its folds*

(5) *I'll never forget the tragic illusion* (6) *The column the cries the crowd and the sun* (7) *The tanks laden with love the gifts from Belgium* (8) *The quivering air and the road with the humming of bees* (8) *The rash triumphing before the battle [had begun]* (10) *The ruby kiss prefiguring the blood* (11) *And those who are going to die standing in the turrets* (12) *Garlanded with lilacs by an intoxicated people*

(13) *I'll never forget the gardens of France* (14) *Like the missals of centuries long past* (15) *Nor the confusion of the evenings the riddle of the silence* (16) *The roses all along the road we traveled through* (17) *The lie [contradiction] of [given by] the flowers to the winds of panic* (18) *To the soldiers passing on wings of fear* (19) *To the delirious bikes to the ironic cannons* (20) *To the pitiful garb of the false campers*

(21) *But I don't know why this whirl of images* (22) *Always brings me back to the same stopping place* (23) *At Sainte-Marthe A general Dark foliage* (24) *A Norman villa at the edge of the forest* (25) *All is quiet The enemy rests in the shade* (26) *They told us that night that Paris surrendered* (27) *I'll never forget the lilacs nor the roses* (28) *Nor the two loves that we have lost*

(29) *Bouquets of the first day lilacs lilacs of Flanders* (30) *Softness of the shade with which death paints our cheeks* (31) *And you bouquets of the retreat delicate roses* (32) *Color of the distant fire roses of Anjou.*

Born in 1897, Louis Aragon entered the world of letters after the First World War, in which he had fought and been decorated for bravery. He became one of the early enthusiasts of Dadaism, the bitter revolt that set out to reexamine all literary values and to deride everything that was rhetorically, sentimentally, and artificially "literary." Dadaism proved to be an important movement, but it was short lived; and by 1922 Aragon collaborated with André Breton in the founding of Surrealism. There was a good deal of mystification in his early Surrealist poems, but they also bore witness to an earnest endeavor to change man through a rebirth of the sense of wonder and a new contact with the "infinite" within. *Qui est là? Ah, très bien — faites entrer l'infini* ("Who is there? Ah, very good—show the infinite in!").

The poet, however, scored his finest success during his Surrealist years (he also joined the Communist Party at that time, hoping for a political and social renovation) as a writer of prose. *Le paysan de Paris* (1926, *The Peasant of Paris*) is a beautiful, free narrative interspersed with reflections on the need to reintegrate the senses and the imagination into our over-rationalized modern way of life. With remarkable, not to say perilous, facility, Aragon wrote poetical-social novels: *Les cloches de Bâle* (1934, *The Bells of Basel*), *Les beaux quartiers* (1936, *The Fine Quarters*), and a nostalgic, semi-autobiographical portrayal of his own youth, *Aurélien* (1944).

Mobilized into the military once again in 1939-1940, he took part in the retreat of the French Army from Belgium to the Loire River, in May and June of 1940, and he also published in the journals of Occupied France a number of poems that stirred the humiliated and anguished French people to their depths: in *Le crève-cœur* (1940, *Heartbreak*), *Les yeux d'Elsa* (1942, *Elsa's Eyes*), and a fierce, poetic satire of the Vichy régime, *Musée Grévin* (1943).

The case of Louis Aragon is one of the most controversial in contemporary French letters. Aside from political matters, he has been a source of disagreement among critics on purely literary grounds. Some consider him one of the most gifted writers of his generation. Others call him an elegant failure—a *précieux* who, for reasons of his own, has refused to write the poetry for which he is best suited by nature.

"The Lilacs and the Roses" is the type of poem that could give rise to such widely divergent views. There is a great deal of Victor Hugo in Aragon, of the *écho sonore*, of the self-appointed voice of the people. He prescribed as a vehicle for this rôle, a return to the short verse chronicle, which, during the Middle Ages, passed from mouth to mouth. That he was successful in giving to the masses verses about themselves which they could recite to each other is attested to by many anecdotes of occupied France and by the great success of *Le crève-cœur*, in which our poem was published.

But in writing occasional verse, has Aragon condemned himself to future oblivion? A study of the form and subject matter of "The Lilacs and the Roses" may lead to an answer. The first thing that strikes the reader—apart from the absence of punctuation, a rather studied negligence in professedly popular poetry —is its most rigorously traditional versification. There are some exceptions, to be sure. Five lines (20, 23, 29, 30, 31) do not carry a stress at the sixth syllable; but this practice was already common during the Romantic period. In nine instances out of a possible sixteen, a singular rimes with a plural; but this is only the consequence of a principle long defended by theorists, though ignored by poets before Aragon wrote his essay *Rime in 1940*, which maintains that riming should be for the ear and not necessarily for the eye: the endings of two riming words need not be spelled identically.

Familiar rhythms and rimes are used here to convey familiar scenes in a poem whose structure, one must add, has been designed with great attention to symmetry. Two quatrains, one at the beginning and one at the end, form a kind of frame within which the changing images of the three eight-line stanzas are enclosed. The subject-matter is remarkably consistent with the form. In the opening four lines, there is a clear statement of the poem's theme: the lilacs, flowers of a sunny May, symbolizing the false optimism of the French people, as they cheered their forces rushing to the Albert Canal in a futile counter-offensive thrust; the roses, flowers of a dreadful June, standing for the tragic realization of the error, as these same people saw their country "stabbed to death" and their soldiers fallen.

There is a readily discernible order in the images that follow this opening statement, and each of the next three stanzas possesses an unmistakable unity. In the first, we see the images associated with the "tragic illusion," the month of May, and the lilacs: the columns; the crowds; the tanks laden with love (probably a reference to the girls who climbed aboard the tanks to kiss the soldiers); the gifts donated by the Belgian people; the buzzing of the bees; the lipstick on the cheeks (9-10); the tankmen standing amid lilacs in their turrets. In the next stanza, we find the transition, the tragic irony of the misunderstood signs: the confusion; the enigmatic silence; the soldiers rushing by "on wings of fear"; the frantic, panic-stricken bicyclists; the ineffective cannons, ironic because they were fleeing instead of firing; the sorry rigs of the refugees from Paris who flooded the highways, ill-equipped to pitch a tent for the night. In the last of the three longer stanzas, the kaleidoscope of mental pictures stops at a scene at Sainte-Marthe, a hamlet near Evreux, in Normandy, on the night of June 14, 1940, when Paris fell. The final quatrain recapitulates the statement of the first, as the scenes of the longer stanzas give way to the symbolism of the shorter ones, in which they are enclosed.

Among all these familiar images there are some that are not altogether clear. In what way, for example, do gardens resemble ancient missals? Is it because the well-ordered, colorful plots call to mind medieval illuminated manuscripts, or the bright covers of the prayer books themselves? What or who are the "two loves" in line 28? Do they refer to the two great passions of which Aragon has so often written, his patriotism and his love for Elsa Triolet, his wife? This does not appear probable in the context of the poem. Might they refer to the opening verses of a popular song, *J'ai deux amours, / Mon pays et Paris* ("I have two loves, / My country and Paris")? Or did the poet mean, as seems somewhat more likely, the lost illusions symbolized by the two flowers: the lilacs, false harbinger of victory, and the roses, false interpreters of defeat? The "lilacs of Flanders" seem appropriate in the last stanza, since the May columns advanced through that region in their abortive attempt to turn the German flank. But why the "roses of Anjou"? Surely Aragon is not referring to any specific rose of that name. Since the Armistice was signed at Compiègne, northeast of Paris, and the poet was at Javerlhac, in the Dordogne, when he wrote the poem, the former duchy in western France has no special significance in this context. Could this be the only region outside the Normandy retreat area that would fit the rime? At any event, the poem is not without stylistic negligences.

It has been said that Aragon's artistic temperament compels him, in spite of himself, to assume a tone of condescension towards the very people for whom he says he writes, and that elegances of style create dissonances in this professedly proletarian verse. On the other hand it could be argued that regardless of certain minor flaws, the formal excellence of "The Lilacs and the Roses" takes it out of the category of banal, popular, national poetry and makes of it one of our century's more expressive war poems, which will long move even those who have not been through the scenes it describes.   [J.W.K.]

RICHARD II QUARANTE

Ma patrie est comme une barque
Qu'abandonnèrent ses haleurs
Et je ressemble à ce monarque
Plus malheureux que le malheur
Qui restait roi de ses douleurs   5

Vivre n'est plus qu'un stratagème
Le vent sait mal sécher les pleurs
Il faut haïr tout ce que j'aime
Ce que je n'ai plus donnez-leur
Je reste roi de mes douleurs   10

Le cœur peut s'arrêter de battre
Le sang peut couler sans chaleur
Deux et deux ne fassent plus quatre
Au Pigeon-Vole des voleurs
Je reste roi de mes douleurs   15

Que le soleil meure ou renaisse
Le ciel a perdu ses couleurs
Tendre Paris de ma jeunesse
Adieu printemps du Quai-aux-Fleurs
Je reste roi de mes douleurs   20

Fuyez les bois et les fontaines
Taisez-vous oiseaux querelleurs
Vos chants sont mis en quarantaine
C'est le règne de l'oiseleur
Je reste roi de mes douleurs   25

Il est un temps pour la souffrance
Quand Jeanne vint à Vaucouleurs
Ah coupez en morceaux la France
Le jour avait cette pâleur
Je reste roi de mes douleurs   30

(*Le crève-cœur*. 1940)

"Richard II Forty" was written at Carcassonne in September 1940, two months after the composition of "The Lilacs and the Roses." The earlier poem reflects the first impact of France's humiliating defeat; this one gives voice to a bitter hopelessness, and abandonment of all human values. The title and the refrain at the end of each stanza were inspired by Shakespeare's *Richard II*, Act IV, Scene I, where the king laments: "You may my glories and my state depose / But not my griefs. Still I am king of those." What appealed to Aragon in Shakespeare's subtle interpretation of this ruler's character was not, of course, his weakness or lack of devotion to royal business; it was his plight as prisoner in Flint Castle, where he saw himself as the victim of his own people's treason. The poet in 1940 has survived the crushing military downfall only to suffer even more intensely from the enemy's domination— "the reign of the bird-catcher"— and from the knowledge that his country has been betrayed by treacherous Frenchmen.

Since here as elsewhere in Aragon's poetry the absence of punctuation creates no difficulties of interpretation, we shall respect this omission in our translation. (1) *My country is like a boat* (2) *Abandoned by its haulers (crew)* (3) *And I am like that monarch* (4) *Unhappier than misfortune* (5) *Who still was king of his sorrows*

(6) *Living is but a stratagem now* (7) *Winds fail to dry our tears* (8) *I must hate all that I love* (9) *Let them have what I have lost* (10) *Still I am king of my sorrows*

(11) *The heart may cease to beat* (12) *The blood may flow without heat* (13) *Let two and two not make four* (14) *As robbers play at children's games* (15) *Still I am king of my sorrows*

(16) *Let the sun die or be reborn* (17) *The sky has lost its colors* (18) *Sweet Paris of my youth* (19) *Farewell [to] springs on the flowering quays* (20) *Still I am king of my sorrows*

(21) *Shun the woods and fountains* (22) *Be still [you] scolding birds* (23) *Your songs are put in quarantine* (24) *The bird-catcher reigns these days* (25) *Still I am king of my sorrows*

(26) *There's a time for suffering* (27) *When Joan came to Vaucouleurs* (28) *Oh cut France to shreds* (29) *The day was just as pallid* (30) *Still I am king of my sorrows*.

The fundamental theme is stated in the first stanza: France, forsaken by its leaders, is like a boat adrift; the poet resembles that monarch who was king of nothing but his sorrows. In the variations that follow, each stanza stresses one aspect of life during the Nazi Occupation: possessions and emotional attachments are to be forsaken; rules are to be violated in the thieves' game; nature's beauty is to be ignored; men, like birds hiding from the fowler, must live in silence and abandon their usual habitats; France is to be torn to shreds. However, in the final stanza a glimmer of optimism appears; for the situation seemed just as hopeless on the day that the Maid of Orleans related her visions to Robert de Vaudricourt, governor of Vaucouleurs, who, finally convinced, recommended her to Charles VII.

The form of "*Richard II Quarante*" is remarkably consistent with the ideas it expresses. One of the essential formal features of the poem is an insistent repetition of sounds. The rime scheme, for example, follows the pattern *ababb, cbcbb, dbdbb*, etc., and all the rimes are very rich (fon*taines*, quaran*taines;* souf*france, France;* re*naisse,* jeun*esse*). The dominant rime in -*leur*, which marks the end of each stanza, lends strong harmonic emphasis to the somber message of the refrain. Throughout the poem the frequent recurrence of the *s*'s underlines effectively the bitterness in the poet's words.

Needless to say, such formal beauty is lost in translation. Moreover, our renderings of *Quai-aux-Fleurs* and *Pigeon-Vole* are only vague approximations of what are, in the original, very precise images. The *Quai aux Fleurs*, in the Island of the City, near Notre Dame Cathedral, is covered with flower stalls which make it one of the most picturesque spots in Paris. There is of course, no English equivalent for its French name. In *Pigeon-Vole* there is a pregnancy of expression which merits some explanation. This is a children's game, somewhat like "Simon Says." Whenever the child who is acting as leader precedes the command "*Vole!*" ("Fly!") with the word "*Pigeon*" or with the name of any other creature capable of flight, his comrades must raise their hands. Otherwise the children must keep their hands down. Aragon could be alluding, in an ironic way, to the nature of the authority under the German régime with its *Heil Hitler!* salute. He may also be playing on the word *voler*, which means not only "to fly" but also "to steal." Taking into consideration the fifth stanza, in which he compares the enemy to a bird-catcher, we may assume a voluntary ambiguity here. [J.W.K.]

PAUL ÉLUARD

LA DAME DE CARREAU

Tout jeune, j'ai ouvert mes bras à la pureté. Ce ne fut qu'un battement d'ailes   1
au ciel de mon éternité, qu'un battement de cœur amoureux qui bat dans les
poitrines conquises. Je ne pouvais plus tomber.

Aimant l'amour. En vérité, la lumière m'éblouit. J'en garde assez en moi   2
pour regarder la nuit, toute la nuit, toutes les nuits.

Toutes les vierges sont différentes. Je rêve toujours d'une vierge.   3

A l'école, elle est au banc devant moi, en tablier noir. Quand elle se retourne   4
pour me demander la solution d'un problème, l'innocence de ses yeux me
confond à un tel point que, prenant mon trouble en pitié, elle passe ses bras
autour de mon cou.

Ailleurs, elle me quitte. Elle monte sur un bateau. Nous sommes presque   5
étrangers l'un à l'autre, mais sa jeunesse est si grande que son baiser ne me
surprend point...

Une fois, le monde allait finir et nous ignorions tout de notre amour. Elle   6
a cherché mes lèvres avec des mouvements de tête lents et caressants. J'ai bien
cru, cette nuit-là, que je la ramènerais au jour.

Et c'est toujours le même aveu, la même jeunesse, les mêmes yeux purs,   7
le même geste ingénu de ses bras autour de mon cou, la même caresse, la
même révélation.

Mais ce n'est jamais la même femme.   8

Les cartes ont dit que je la rencontrerai dans la vie, mais sans la reconnaître.   9

Aimant l'amour.   10

(*Le dessous d'une vie ou la pyramide humaine.* 1926)

After fighting a lung disease in his youth and being gassed in World War I, Paul Éluard (1897-1952) turned to Dadaism as to a bitter refuge against the absurdity of wars and of a literature which had stooped to carrying nationalist propaganda. Then he joined the Surrealist group, of which André Breton was the theorist and jealous guardian. In time, however, he broke away from the too rigid doctrines of Surrealism and, during World War II, he joined the Communist Party, along with his close friend, Picasso. But his participation in the Surrealist movement left Éluard with a keen interest in the poetry of dreams and in rendering in verse *la vie immédiate*—subconscious visions and images in their pristine form. He also shared André Breton's fervor in proclaiming that love should be restored as the chief theme of poetry and that woman should be lauded by all Surrealists as the interpreter of mysteries.

More than any other modern French poet, Éluard sought to break away from the isolation of Romantic and Symbolist authors. He repudiated poetry of complacent self-contemplation which bemoans the writer's solitude. "Art and poetry," he said, "are meaningful only as means of knocking down the barriers that stand between the world and myself and also between others and myself." Again in 1946, after he and Aragon had written deeply moving verse inspired by their country's woes, he declared: "The poet must never gaze at himself; his mirror is others." For Éluard, love was a force of attraction (as the Greek word *eros* also implied) drawing two people together in carnal caresses out of which a new and deeper understanding is born. Thus the lover moves from *I* to *you*. "To love you returns me to all men," he sang in a poem to one of the women he celebrated.

"The Queen of Diamonds" is among the very few prose poems of Éluard. The title is an allusion to prophecies which the Surrealists were at that time fond of reading in cards or in coincidences. The queen, who appears in the poem perennially virginal, is first a schoolgirl, then a traveler on a ship, and then, when he dreams of the end of the world, a consoling vision. Such visions favor men in love with love itself (*amans amare*, as St. Augustine said of himself in his *Confessions*). Every paragraph conjures up a different picture, as in a series of chaste hallucinations. The rhythm does not attempt to approximate that of poetry. The sentences are direct, imperiously forcing upon the reader the reality of the poet's dreams of what Verlaine had called "an unknown woman whom I love and who loves me / And who is not quite the same every time / Yet not quite another, and who loves me and understands me."

(1) *Quite young, I opened my arms to purity. It was only a beating of wings in the sky of my eternity, only the beating of a loving heart that beats in breasts conquered* [by love]. *I could not fall any more.* (2) *Loving love. In truth, the light dazzles me. I retain in me enough of it to look at the night, the whole night, all nights.* (3) *All virgins are different. I always dream of a virgin.* (4) *At school, she is seated in front of me, in a black smock. When she turns around to ask me for the answer to a problem, the innocence of her eyes so disconcerts me that, taking pity on my agitation (confusion), she puts her arms around my neck.* (5) *Elsewhere, she leaves me. She gets on a ship. We are almost strangers to each other, but her youthfulness is so great that her kiss does not surprise me.* [Two lines which add little to the poem are omitted here.] (6) *Once, the world was going to end and we knew nothing about our love. She sought my lips with slow and caressing motions of her head. I truly thought that night that I would bring her back to daylight.* (7) *And it is always the same confession, the same youthfulness, the same pure eyes, the same ingenuous gesture of her arms around my neck, the same caress, the same revelation.* (8) *But it is never the same woman.* (9) *The cards have said that I would meet her in life, but without recognizing her.* (10) *In love with love.*

The end of the poem is touched with melancholy. For this embodiment of a Pure Eternal Feminine appears real only in the poet's dreams: she is but a phantom of the night. For him to "bring her back to daylight" (6) is as impossible as for Orpheus to resist casting a backward glance at Eurydice. Such love is nostalgic aspiration rather than selfish possession.

[H.P.]

A PEINE DÉFIGURÉE

Adieu tristesse
Bonjour tristesse
Tu es inscrite dans les lignes du plafond
Tu es inscrite dans les yeux que j'aime
Tu n'es pas tout à fait la misère   5
Car les lèvres les plus pauvres te
    dénoncent
Par un sourire   8

Bonjour tristesse
Amour des corps aimables
Puissance de l'amour
Dont l'amabilité surgit   12
Comme un monstre sans corps
Tête désappointée
Tristesse beau visage

    (*La vie immédiate*. 1932)

[MON AMOUR...]

Mon amour pour avoir figuré mes désirs
Mis tes lèvres au ciel de tes mots comme
    un astre

Tes baisers dans la nuit vivante   3
Et le sillage de tes bras autour de moi
Comme une flamme en signe de
    conquête
Mes rêves sont au monde
Clairs et perpétuels

Et quand tu n'es pas là
Je rêve que je dors je rêve que je rêve

    (*L'Amour la poésie*. 1929)

[JE CACHE LES SOMBRES TRÉSORS]

Je cache les sombres trésors
Des retraites inconnues
Le cœur des forêts le sommeil
D'une fusée ardente   4
L'horizon nocturne
Qui me couronne
Je vais la tête la première
Saluant d'un secret nouveau   8
La naissance des images

    (*L'Amour la poésie*. 1929)

É luard, like the other Surrealists, was fundamentally an optimist: he was confident that ways could be found or devised to alter man's fate and to accomplish the "miracle" of a loving couple challenging the misery of the world. But like all men, he knew moments of dejection, and the title of his early (1926) volume *Capitale de la douleur* evokes the images of a metropolis of sorrow. "*A peine défigurée*" ("Scarcely Disfigured") alludes to the slight alteration made upon a fair face by the intrusion of sorrow. Sorrow was rejected, but it returns, and one is wiser to welcome it as the faithful companion of love. (1) *Farewell sadness* (2) *Good morning sadness* (3) *You are inscribed in the lines of the ceiling* (4) *You are inscribed in the eyes that I love* (5) *You are not quite misery* (6) *For the poorest lips reveal (betray, proclaim, denounce) you* (7) *Through (by) a smile* (8) *Good morning sadness* (9) *Love of lovable bodies* (10) *Power of love* (11) *Whose lovableness* [the word is stronger than mere *amiability*] *leaps up* (12) *Like a monster without a body* (13) *Disappointed head* (14) *Sadness fair face*.

Sadness was often invoked by the

Romantics, but this invocation is notable for the intimacy of its tone. A series of parallels enumerates some of the refuges where sadness hides: bodily love, love that deems itself independent of the body (a monster), a slightly disfigured face. But sadness has its own beauty and, like Keats's melancholy, it "dwells with Beauty —Beauty that must die."

Love had been derided by Mallarmé and Valéry as a fit subject for poetry; there are few, if any, heroines in Sartre and Camus. Éluard, however (along with Giraudoux, who sang the praises of *jeunes filles* in many a page of prose), celebrates an almost Petrarchan cult of woman. His verse makes frequent allusion to the hair, eyelid, lips, and breasts of women; and kisses are exchanged—but with a strange chastity. Éluard seems to have found most satisfying "the harmonies of absence," as he calls them, for they make dreaming easier and desire more imaginative. In such love poetry there is no possessiveness in the man, no coquettish cruelty in the woman. All is stylized; both seem to have become actors of some cosmic drama through which liberating forces will be unleashed into our captive world. Even during World War II, when Éluard was hunted down as one of the most courageous writers of the Resistance and when he witnessed untold suffering among his countrymen, he remained, like Aragon, the devotee of the love of woman as the first step toward the love of other men and the love of freedom: *Et parce que nous nous aimons / Nous voulons libérer les autres / De leur solitude glacée /* ("And because we love each other / We want to free others / From their icy solitude").

The second poem ("*Mon amour...*) is made up of unequal, unrimed lines of frail music. Connections, conjunctions, and linking phrases are absent. The com-parisons are simple. The woman's love, embodying and creating anew the desires of her lover, is compared to a star and to a flame. She is more "a phantom of delight" than a real person; her arms are the wake of a flying creature around him. Through her the poet can dream, always and "clearly." The world is cleared of its darkness and lightened of its weight through her tenderness. (1) *My love because you have presented my desires [become the image of my desires] (2) Placed your lips like a star in the sky of your words (3) Your kisses in the living night (4) And the wake of your arms around me (5) Like a flame as a sign of victory (6) My dreams are to the world (7) Clear and perpetual (8) And when you are not here (9) I dream that I sleep I dream that I dream.*

Our third selection is on poetry, often associated with love, as it is in the title of the book from which it comes. (1) *I hide the dark treasures (2) Of unknown retreats (3) The heart of forests the slumber (4) Of an ardent (burning) rocket (5) The nocturnal horizon (6) That crowns me (7) I press forward (8) Hailing with a new secret (9) The birth of images.* For Éluard, as for Breton and Pierre Reverdy, images are the soul of poetry; but Éluard's images do not aim at surprising and they are seldom elaborately rare. They spring in the poet's mind as he walks among other men and feels a new secret bond between them and himself (7-9). Alone he heaps up treasures of sensations, of exploration of his deeper self. He penetrates to the heart of symbolic forests (those of sleep, illuminated by the glowing rocket of dream), his head crowned by the luminous night that he has pierced: the night of dark truths. "Somber," wrote Éluard in *Poetic Evidence*, "are the truths that appear in the work of true poets; but truths they are, and almost all else is but lies." [H.P.]

[AMOUREUSE...]

Amoureuse au secret derrière ton sourire
Toute nue les mots d'amour
Découvrent tes seins et ton cou
Et tes hanches et tes paupières   4
Découvrent toutes les caresses
Pour que les baisers dans tes yeux
Ne montrent que toi toute entière

        (*L'Amour la poésie*. 1929)

[JE N'AI ENVIE QUE DE T'AIMER]

Je n'ai envie que de t'aimer
Un orage emplit la vallée
Un poisson la rivière   3

Je t'ai faite à la taille de ma solitude
Le monde entier pour se cacher
Des jours des nuits pour se comprendre

Pour ne plus rien voir dans tes yeux
Que ce que je pense de toi   8
Et d'un monde à ton image

Et des jours et des nuits réglés par tes
    paupières

        (*Les yeux fertiles*. 1936)

LE BAISER

Toute tiède encore du linge annulé
Tu fermes les yeux et tu bouges
Comme bouge un chant qui naît
Vaguement mais de partout

Odorante et savoureuse   4
Tu dépasses sans te perdre
Les frontières de ton corps

Tu as enjambé le temps
Te voici femme nouvelle   8
Révélée à l'infini

    (*Une longue réflexion amoureuse*. 1945)

COUVRE-FEU

Que voulez-vous la porte était gardée
Que voulez-vous nous étions enfermés
Que voulez-vous la rue était barrée
Que voulez-vous la ville était matée   4
Que voulez-vous elle était affamée
Que voulez-vous nous étions désarmés
Que voulez-vous la nuit était tombée
Que voulez-vous nous nous sommes
    aimés

        (*Poésie et vérité*. 1942)

É luard abhorred all that was ornamental and rhetorical in poetry; he wished to be understood even by the workmen of Saint-Denis, among whom he had been born. By simple language and evocative imagery, these concise love-songs carry an energy that is immediately conveyed to the reader. The key words of the first poem are *découvrent* (which means both "uncover" and "discover") and *montrent* ("show"). There are few adjectives, few connectives. The poet works his magic through "caressing" words that unveil the woman's body. Enigmatic, with a secret behind her smile, she will reveal her entire self when gently kissed on her eyelids. A strange, almost statue-like purity pervades lines that might have been sensuous: (1) *Loving one (amorous one) remaining secret behind your smile* (2) *When naked the words of love* (3) *Discover-uncover your breasts and your neck* (4) *And your hips and your eyelids* (5) *Discover [gradually perceive] all the caresses* (6) *So that the kisses in your eyes* (7) *Show none but you entire.* Éluard's verse often remains cryptic under its appearance of clarity but here the meaning seems to be that kisses on the eyelids of the woman will reveal her totally in a secret and almost spiritual vibration.

The second poem is again a hymn, almost a grateful prayer to the loved one: she is his creation, for all love is born of the imagination and of the molding power of desire. She is his mirror (Éluard's most frequent image) and the mirror of the world, which is reflected in her eyes and controlled by them. (1) *My sole desire is to love you* (2) *One storm fills the valley* (3) *One fish the river* (4) *I have created you to the size of my solitude* (5) *The whole world [for us] to hide in* (6) *Days nights to understand each other* (7) *So as to see nothing more in your eyes* (8) *But what I think of you* (9) *And of a world in your image* (10) *And days and nights governed by your eyelids.* The first three lines compare the woman to nature. The words seem lightened of all weight, yet they have a crystal-like substance.

In "The Kiss," the vision of the woman is more precise, the evocation is at first more sensuous. (1) *Still all warm from the linen annulled* (2) *You close your eyes and you stir* (3) *As stirs a song which is born* (4) *Vaguely but from everywhere.* She has just thrown off the bed clothes and a mysterious, ubiquitous song seems to quiver in her warm body. But the tercet soon transcends the eroticism with which Éluard deftly plays. Two evocative adjectives— of fragrance and delectation—transfigure the woman. She vanquishes time by becoming, in the feigned death of love, a new woman. She touches an infinite. (5) *Odorous and delectable* (6) *You transcend without losing (ceasing to be) yourself* (7) *The frontiers (limits) of your body* (8) *You have stepped over time* (9) *Here you are a new woman* (10) *Revealed to the infinite.*

"Curfew" is one of the poems that thousands of Frenchmen recited during World War II (the longest and best known was his *"Liberté"*). In the popularity of these verses, Éluard's dream of the poet's rôle was fulfilled, for a few years earlier he had prophesied: "Today the solitude of poets is breaking down. They are now men among men, they have brothers." Most of the war poems are grave or tragic, though they never depart from the simplicity of language and the exquisite balance for which Éluard is admired as a classic. This one is gently humorous in its progression toward the surprise of the last line. (1) *So what the door was guarded* (2) *So what we were shut in* (3) *So what the street was blocked* (4) *So what the town was brought to heel* (5) *So what it was starved* (6) *So what we were disarmed* (7) *So what night had fallen* (8) *So what we loved each other.* [H.P.]

RENÉ CHAR

CONGÉ AU VENT

A flancs de coteau du village bivouaquent des champs fournis de mimosas. 1
A l'époque de la cueillette, il arrive que, loin de leur endroit, on fasse la 2
rencontre extrêmement odorante d'une fille dont les bras se sont occupés durant
la journée aux fragiles branches. Pareille à une lampe dont l'auréole de clarté 3
serait de parfum, elle s'en va, le dos tourné au soleil couchant.

Il serait sacrilège de lui adresser la parole. 4

L'espadrille foulant l'herbe, cédez-lui le pas du chemin. Peut-être aurez- 5
vous la chance de distinguer sur ses lèvres la chimère de l'humidité de la Nuit? 6

LE LORIOT

3 septembre 1939.

Le Loriot entra dans la capitale de l'aube.
L'épée de son chant ferma le lit triste.
Tout à jamais prit fin.

(*Seuls demeurent.* 1945)

[MON AMOUR À LA ROBE DE PHARE BLEU]

Mon amour à la robe de phare bleu
je baise la fièvre de ton visage
où couche la lumière qui jouit en
secret.

J'aime et je sanglote. Je suis vivant 4
et c'est ton cœur cette Étoile du
Matin

à la durée victorieuse qui rougit
avant
de rompre le combat des
Constellations.

Hors de toi, que ma chair devienne
la voile
qui répugne au vent. 9

(*Le poème pulverisé.* 1947)

René Char, born (1907) in L'Isle-sur-Sorgue, is a Provençal whose poetical affinities are with both the early Greek philosophers, especially Heraclitus, and the Surrealists, with whom he was first associated. He has been hailed by many, among others by Albert Camus, as the greatest French poet born in this century. Char's is the most difficult poetry since Mallarmé's, not because of syntax or an attempt to express profound or esoteric ideas, but because he tries to make language and rhythm approximate the experience from which the poem issued. Among the commentators on his work, the most helpful is Georges Mounin (to whom we are indebted).

(1) *Up along the village hillside fields filled with mimosa keep watch.* (2) *At gathering time, it happens that, far from them [from their place], you make the extremely fragrant encounter of a girl whose arms have been busied all day with the fragile branches.* (3) *Like a lamp whose luminous halo is perfume, she goes her way, her back turned to the setting sun.* (4) *It would be sacrilegious to speak to her.* (5) *Your sandal trampling the grass, yield her the way.* (6) *Will you perhaps have the [good] fortune to distinguish [perceive with discrimination] on her lips the chimera of Night's humidity?*

Simplicity, clarity of outline, gravity, nobleness of sentiment, define the impression produced by this poem. Its extreme conciseness and the omission of links between the glimpses of the poet's vision account for its obscurity. The sentences are short; imperious, like edicts; definitive, like statements of sensations. The· title, "Dismissing the Wind," suggests that the wind itself has been given leave by the poet or has ceased blowing, so that the integrity of the vision may be respected. Near a village of southern France, seemingly guarded ("bivouac" is from the German *Beiwache,* "to watch by") by yellow mimosa trees, a girl, fragrant with the flowers she has been picking, goes by —sculptural as a Greek goddess or an Italian peasant in a Corot painting. The setting sun behind her crowns her with its gold (*auréole* suggests the Latin *aurum:* "gold," from which it derives); her halo is made of fragrance. She inspires respect, as though within her she contained the mysteries of the earth. In your dreams, says the poet to him who respectfully yields her the path, you may receive a kiss from that picker of mimosa when

humid, wintry night follows the setting sun. (Mimosas are picked in winter.)

"The Oriole" is explained by its date: World War II has just begun; the lights are out over Europe; the poet could dimly foretell the woes he and others were to endure. (He became a heroic fighter in the Resistance.) A bird sang on the tops (*capitale* suggests the "head" or "summit") of the village houses. Its joyful song pierced the sky like the lightning of a sword. The comfort of peace, symbolized by the bed, is now sadly ravished by the sword-like bird call. (1) *The oriole entered the capital of the dawn.* (3) *The sword of its song closed the sad bed.* (3) *Everything was forever ended.*

The third poem is closer to the love poetry of Éluard, in collaboration with whom Char published a volume in 1930. It is passionately tender and respectful and noble as well. The rare and striking images, free from preciosity, link the loved woman with the sky and sea. Her gown is a blue beacon; light almost erotically enjoys her beauty, it dwells and sleeps on her face. The second stanza condenses the poet's feelings. The woman is the morning star, victorious over stellar struggles. Men in Char's poetry are often pictured as *debout* ("standing") by the side of the woman "who breathes," whose heart seems to beat in harmony with the earth. (1) *My love with the dress of a blue beacon* (2) *I kiss the fever of your face* (3) *where the light sleeps in secret enjoyment.* (4) *I love and I sob, I am alive* (5) *and that Morning Star is your heart* (6) *[star] of victorious continuance that blushed before* (7) *breaking off the battle of Constellations.* (8) *Away from you, may my flesh become the sail* (9) *That turns in repugnance from the wind.* The brief poem ends on a cry of fidelity: deprived of her, may his flesh lose its strength and bend, like a sail, sickened by the wind.   [H.P.]

GERMAN

FRIEDRICH HÖLDERLIN

HYPERIONS SCHICKSALSLIED

Ihr wandelt droben im Licht
Auf weichem Boden, selige Genien!
Glänzende Götterlüfte
   Rühren euch leicht,   4
     Wie die Finger der Künstlerin
     Heilige Saiten.

Schicksallos, wie der schlafende
Säugling, atmen die Himmlischen;   8
Keusch bewahrt
  In bescheidener Knospe,
    Blühet ewig
     Ihnen der Geist,   12
      Und die seligen Augen
      Blicken in stiller
      Ewiger Klarheit.

Doch uns ist gegeben,   16
Auf keiner Stätte zu ruhn,
Es schwinden, es fallen
Die leidenden Menschen
  Blindlings von einer   20
  Stunde zur andern,
    Wie Wasser von Klippe
    Zu Klippe geworfen,
      Jahr lang ins Ungewisse hinab.   24

Friedrich Hölderlin's career (1770-1843) is almost a paradigm for the tragic Romantic artist. Born in the same year as Hegel, Beethoven, and Wordsworth, he went from one distasteful task to another until his twenty-fifth year, when he found congenial work as tutor in the home of a Frankfurt banker. But he was compelled to relinquish this position (1798) because of a reciprocated passion for his employer's wife (Suzette Gontard, the beautiful Diotima of his epistolary novel *Hyperion*).

He moved to Homburg and spent brief periods in Switzerland and France. Then he returned unexpectedly to his mother's house, insane, at the age of thirty-two. He improved sufficiently to get a job as librarian (1804), but by 1806 his madness (probably schizophrenia) forced his withdrawal from the world throughout the remaining thirty-seven years of his life.

"Hyperion's Song of Fate" is sung by the melancholy hero of the novel, a young Greek involved in his country's struggle against Turkey in 1770. Like Hölderlin, Hyperion yearns to invigorate modern Germany with the spirit of ancient Greece; and even this short poem reflects the polarity familiar to Greek epic and tragedy. On the one hand are the gods, serene and beautiful; on the other, men, "creatures of the day," as Aeschylus described them.

The poem begins with a direct address to the gods. (1) *You move [dwell] above in the light* (2) *On soft ground, blessed genii.* (3) *Luminous (shining) divine breezes* (4) *Touch you lightly,* (5) *As the fingers of the artist* [female harpist] (6) *[Touch] sacred strings.* (7) *Fateless, like a (the) sleeping* (8) *Babe (nursling), the heavenly ones breathe;* (9) *Chastely preserved* (10) *In modest bud,* (11) *Eternally blossoms* (12) *For them the spirit,* (13) *And the blessed eyes* (14) *Gaze in still* (15) *Eternal clarity.*

No prose translation can begin to suggest the patterns of sound in these two stanzas. In the first four lines aspirated *ch* sounds occur four times, but they do not recur before line 16. The five occurrences of *sch* (the sound of English *sh*) in the first seventeen lines are all bunched together in lines 7-10. Such patterns of sound help to give form to Hölderlin's free verse, as well as to suggest the peace of the heavenly light above.

Stanza three brings us down sharply to our perilous mortality. If lightness belongs to the gods, weight is ours. (16) *But to us it is given (granted)* (17) *To rest at no place.* (19) *Suffering mankind* (18) *Dwindles, falls* (20) *Blindly from one* (21) *Hour to another* (22-23) *Like water thrown* ["geworfen," 23] *from cliff to cliff* (24) *Forever* [literally *year-long*] *down into the unknown.*

Stony harshness and the perpetual flux of descending torrents—such is the world in which human beings must work out their destiny, while the holy spirits "move" blissfully in the light above, on soft ground. They dwell "up there" (*droben*); but for

humanity the key word in the lyric is "down" (*hinab*). Even the slanting typography of these long stanzas suggests the falling of man from the world of the genii down into his own, into uncertainty, the abyss of the unknown.

Hölderlin's free verse—free of both time and meter and emphasizing cadence and imagery—was in part the outcome of his studies of Greek classic poetry, chiefly of the complex meters of Pindar. Reading the German poem aloud, one can hardly fail to respond to the richness of the rhythmical variety within single lines, where double and triple feet succeed each other in no discernible pattern. The "freedom" of Hölderlin's meters, notable in many of his lyrics, militated against his reputation among his contemporaries. To be sure, it was not until our own century that Stefan George and his followers rescued Hölderlin from literary oblivion. By bringing him back into the main tradition, they presented the reading public with one of Germany's greatest Hellenists and finest poets.

Hölderlin wrote frequently on the central theme of "Hyperion's Song of Fate," on the eternal conflict between man's demand for a moral universe and the ironic response of the gods, who look down upon humanity's plaintive requests with serene detachment. It is both human tragedy and divine comedy. The deities "up there" are *schicksallos*, "fateless"; unlike man, they are free, Hölderlin takes care to inform us. Yet this "Song of Fate" is sung by one who has been especially named—after the Titan who was the son of Heaven and Earth (Uranus and Ge) and the father of the Sun, Moon, and Dawn (Helios, Selene, and Eos). Hölderlin's Hyperion, of course, knows no such divine antecedents as he stands in his modern Promethean loneliness, looking up at the bright gods whose blessed eyes gaze in eternal clarity. [H.E.H.]

FRIEDRICH HÖLDERLIN

AN DIE PARZEN

Nur Einen Sommer gönnt, ihr Gewaltigen!
Und einen Herbst zu reifem Gesange mir,
  Daß williger mein Herz, vom süßen
    Spiele gesättiget, dann mir sterbe.   4

Die Seele, der im Leben ihr göttlich Recht
Nicht ward, sie ruht auch drunten im Orkus nicht;
  Doch ist mir einst das Heilge, das am
    Herzen mir liegt, das Gedicht, gelungen,   8

Willkommen dann, o Stille der Schattenwelt!
Zufrieden bin ich, wenn auch mein Saitenspiel
  Mich nicht hinab geleitet; Einmal
    Lebt ich, wie Götter, und mehr bedarfs nicht.   12

(*Sämmtliche Werke.* 1826)

R eaders familiar with the circumstances of Hölderlin's career may find it difficult to disassociate these lines from the period of their composition. "To the Fates" was written some time before Hölderlin's thirtieth year (1800) and before he left Frankfurt. The time of his happiness was already drawing near its end. Hence the poignancy of these almost prescient words addressed "To the Fates," the three ominous deities—Clotho, Lachesis, and Atropos—who controlled man's destiny and the length of his life, and who were variously portrayed as hideous crones or meditative maidens.

Hölderlin's cry recalls Lear's "O, let me not be mad, not mad, sweet heaven!" "*An die Parzen*" goes even further as an emblematic representation of human mortality. Hölderlin faces the inescapable fact of eventual annihilation with the sense of a noble task to be accomplished.

(1) *Grant me only one summer, ye mighty ones!* (2) *And one autumn for ripe song* (3) *So that my heart more willingly with sweet* (4) *Playing* [as on a lyre] *sated, then may die.* (5-6) *The soul which in life has not received its divine[ly appointed] right does not rest below in Orcus, either.* [Literally, *The soul to which in life its divine right was not (accorded), it also rests not below in Orcus*— Hades, Dis, Tartarus: the nether world, abode of the dead]. (7-8) *But once I have achieved the sacred [thing] that my heart is intent on, the poem,* (9) *Welcome then, O peace of the world of shadows (shades)!* (10) *I shall be* [literally *am*] *content, even though my lyre* (11) *Does not accompany* [also: *guide*] *me down: once* (12) *I [shall have] lived like gods, and no more is needed.*

The poem begins with an entreaty and ends with a paean of acceptance: the movement of ideas is essentially dialectical. A number of critics have pointed to a

Hegel-like construction in many of Hölderlin's lyrics (the poet and the philosopher studied together at the University of Tübingen in 1790, when they were both twenty). The Hegelian pattern —thesis, antithesis, and synthesis—of "To the Fates" may be roughly characterized as follows: THESIS: the poet pleads for more time to live, that he may achieve fulfilment; ANTITHESIS: without this boon, non-existence is unendurable; SYNTHESIS: the true after-life will take place once he has fulfilled his potentialities as a poet.

Such a triadic form also resembles the Pindaric ode, in which the Greek poet's strophe, antistrophe, and epode frequently presents a conflict in thought followed by its resolution. If these observations sound academic, the reader should be reminded of Hölderlin's belief in his rôle as poet-prophet-seer, which he shared with Pindar.

The rhythms of "To the Fates," though apparently free, conform precisely to one of the complex meters (the Alcaic) employed by the classical writers whom Hölderlin strove to emulate and which he very frequently used:

$$\breve{\mathrm{U}} - \mathrm{U} - \bar{\mathrm{U}} - \mathrm{U}\,\mathrm{U} - \mathrm{U} -$$
$$\breve{\mathrm{U}} - \mathrm{U} - \bar{\mathrm{U}} - \mathrm{U}\,\mathrm{U} - \mathrm{U} -$$
$$\breve{\mathrm{U}} - \mathrm{U} - \bar{\mathrm{U}} - \mathrm{U} - \mathrm{U}$$
$$- \mathrm{U}\,\mathrm{U} - \mathrm{U}\,\mathrm{U} - \mathrm{U} - \mathrm{U}$$

His grafting of classical quantities onto German qualities, where stressed and unstressed syllables replace the Greek long and short, was not mere metrical experimentation. Hölderlin believed that it was his task to instill through poetry the spirit of ancient Hellas into modern Germany; and perhaps Greek meters, along with Greek myths and values, could assist in this necessary undertaking!

The emotional progression throughout this short poem is worth observing: from the impassioned hortatory (stanza 1) through the proud statement of poetic craft (stanza 2) to the final triumphant cadence in the last four lines. The relationship of human beings to the gods—never far from Hölderlin's thought—is suggested by the *Gewaltigen* ("mighty, powerful ones"), the divine right (*göttlich Recht*) of the soul, and the concluding line, in which he asserts his claim to the condition of the gods themselves (*Lebt ich, wie Götter*). One is reminded of what the authors of Greek tragic drama asserted again and again of men who coveted the condition of the gods, who were guilty of *hubris*, the excessive pride and insolence that sends them to their eventual destruction.

A quatrain which Hölderlin wrote many years later, in one of those moments of lucidity which from time to time interrupted the insanity of the last decade, returns to the contrast of this world with the next, of life with death. But now the mood is utter defeat; in the last line, he is weary of existence:

Das Angenehme dieser Welt hab ich genossen,
Die Jugendstunden sind, wie lang! wie lang! verflossen,
April und Mai und Julius sind ferne,
Ich bin nichts mehr, ich lebe nicht mehr gerne!

(1) *The pleasant things of this world have I enjoyed,* (2) *The hours of youth have passed [away] so long! so long ago!* (3) *April and May and July are far away,* (4) *I am nothing more, I do not live gladly any more.* [H.E.H.]

FRIEDRICH HÖLDERLIN

SONNENUNTERGANG

Wo bist du? trunken dämmert die Seele mir
Von aller deiner Wonne; denn eben ists,
Daß ich gelauscht, wie, goldner Töne
Voll, der entzückende Sonnenjüngling   4

Sein Abendlied auf himmlischer Leier spielt';
Es tönten rings die Wälder und Hügel nach.
Doch fern ist er zu frommen Völkern,
Die ihn noch ehren, hinweggegangen.   8

(Sämmtliche Werke. 1826)

This short lyric, "Sunset," like "*Die Kürze*," which follows, takes place at a special time of day. The later eighteenth and early nineteenth centuries were to find twilight increasingly congenial for artistic purposes. Wakefulness is about to give way to sleep. Each day's life moves on toward its miniature death.

Hölderlin's syntactical inversions, difficult even in German, make a literal translation conspicuously cumbersome. Like all poets, he was interested in the position of images and phrases within each line and the timing of their impact upon the reader. (1) *Where are you? my soul is in twilight* [literally *my soul twilights*—German can say *it twilights* ("es dämmert"), exactly as English says *it rains*], *intoxicated* (2) *With all your rapture; for it was just now* (3) *That I listened (heard) how, full of golden sounds,* (4) *The entrancing youthful sun-god* (5) *Was playing his evening song on (a) heavenly lyre;* (6) *The woods and hills around re-echoed [it].* (7-8) *But he has gone far away to pious people who still honor him.*

Peculiarities of word order are doubtlessly intensified by the poet's allegiance to classic Greek metrics. The eight lines adhere to the Alcaic strophe.

The theme is one that he never abandoned: the modern world, specifically Germany, is moribund because it has lost the inspiration of ancient Greece. Apollo, god of sun and light, sings his brief song, which is heard by the poet. Apollo flees, a departure coincident with the departure of the day, which he illuminates with his "golden sounds." The *frommen Völkern* ("pious peoples," 7) may refer to the modern Greeks, even though at the end of *Hyperion* Hölderlin sadly acknowledged the greatness of the gap between past Greek ideals and present Greek realities.

The sonal elements of the poem accord with its sparseness of imagery. The monosyllabic question in line 1 is answered with equal brevity at the beginning of lines 7 and 8, to trail off with the lengthy *hinweggegangen* ("gone far away"). *Sonnenjüngling* (literally "sun-youth"), the key word in the poem, supplies the predominant tonal values in this richly sonorous poem.   [H.E.H.]

FRIEDRICH HÖLDERLIN

DIE KÜRZE

« Warum bist du so kurz? liebst du, wie vormals, denn
    Nun nicht mehr den Gesang? fandst du, als Jüngling, doch,
        In den Tagen der Hoffnung,
            Wenn du sangest, das Ende nie! »   4

Wie mein Glück, ist mein Lied. — Willst du im Abendrot
    Froh dich baden? hinweg ists! und die Erd ist kalt,
        Und der Vogel der Nacht schwirrt
            Unbequem vor das Auge dir.   8

(Sämmtliche Werke. 1826)

"Why are you so brief?" This question, with which "Brevity" begins, makes the reader the partner to some unresolved emotional struggle. The entire lyric hangs, as it were, upon four questions: three raised by the anonymous audience and one given in the form of a cryptic answer. The poet asks the reader to understand the brevity of his writing in terms of an "evening" experience, for the reader as well as the poet. Like "*Sonnenuntergang*" (at the left), "*Die Kürze*" is a twilight song.

The elliptical suspension of the German clauses in this eight-line poem makes straightforward literal translation inadvisable. To make sense in English, one must transpose and interpolate, thus: (1-2) "*Why are you so brief? do you now no longer love song, then, as you formerly did?* [Literally *do you love, as before, then, now no longer song?*]—*yet, as a youth, you never found* (3) *In the days of hope,* (4) *The end, when you sang!*" (5) *As my bliss, so is my song.— In the sunset's glow* [literally *evening-red*] *would you* (6) *Bathe joyfully? It is gone, and the earth is cold,* (7) *And the bird of night whirrs* (8) *Uncomfortably before your eyes.*

["Unbequem" also has the force of *troublesomely, inopportunely.*]

The first clause in line 5—"Like my happiness (fortune, fate), is my song"— seems to act as the fulcrum in a dialectical interchange involving youth and age, inexperience and maturity, days of hope and close of day *(Abendrot)*. The evening-red of the sunset's glow also bears suggestions of comfort and warmth, but the world, the earth, is "cold." And the poem ends with a curiously evocative finality as the transient bird of night whirrs disconcertingly past our eyes, for the owl is not only the symbol of Athene, goddess of wisdom, and consequently the scholar's patron bird, but also the bird of evil omen and the harbinger of death.

"Brevity" as verse is epitomized, as it were, by two sets of monosyllables, one at the beginning of line 5 and the other at the end of line 6, each containing a full clause and a bit beyond it. The metrical structure for what might seem to the modern reader to be free verse is actually a Greek stanzaic pattern, the third Asclepiadean. Consequently, the two stanzas are metrically identical.   [H.E.H.]

FRIEDRICH HÖLDERLIN

DA ICH EIN KNABE WAR...

Da ich ein Knabe war,
  Rettet' ein Gott mich oft
    Vom Geschrei und der Rute der Menschen,
      Da spielt ich sicher und gut   4
        Mit den Blumen des Hains,
          Und die Lüftchen des Himmels
            Spielten mit mir.

Und wie du das Herz   8
Der Pflanzen erfreust,
Wenn sie entgegen dir
Die zarten Arme strecken,

So hast du mein Herz erfreut,   12
Vater Helios! und, wie Endymion,
War ich dein Liebling,
Heilige Luna!

O all ihr treuen   16
Freundlichen Götter!
Daß ihr wüßtet,
Wie euch meine Seele geliebt!

Zwar damals rief ich noch nicht   20
Euch mit Namen, auch ihr
Nanntet mich nie, wie die Menschen sich nennen,
Als kennten sie sich.

Doch kannt ich euch besser,   24
Als ich je die Menschen gekannt,
Ich verstand die Stille des Aethers,
Der Menschen Worte verstand ich nie.

Mich erzog der Wohllaut   28
des säuselnden Hains
Und lieben lernt ich
Unter den Blumen.

Im Arme der Götter wuchs ich groß.   32

(Gedichte von Friedrich Hölderlin. 1826)

Notably simpler than our foregoing selections from Hölderlin, "When I Was a Boy . . ." treats a theme common in Romantic verse: the formative childhood years of the poet nurtured by nature, by perhaps even supernatural forces. Our first four Hölderlin poems reverberated with strong emotion. Except for the apostrophe in the third stanza, "*Da ich ein Knabe war . . .*" is quietly reflective and almost elegically muted.

(1) *When I was a boy,* (2) *Often a god rescued me* (3) *From the noise (clamor) and the rod [punishment] of men,* (4) *Then I played securely and well* (5) *With the flowers of the grove (woods),* (6) *And the little breezes of heaven* (7) *Played with me.*

Having made this factual statement, Hölderlin talks directly to his beloved Hellenic gods throughout the next five stanzas. (8-9) *And as you delight the heart of the plants,* (10) *When towards you they* (11) *Stretch their tender arms.*

(12) *So have you delighted my heart,* (13) *Father Helios!* [sun-god, son of Hyperion and brother of the moon] *and like Endymion* [the handsome youth eternally asleep on Mount Latmus; he attracted the moon goddess (Selene, Luna), who kissed him], (14) *I was your darling,* (15) *Holy Luna!*

(16) *O all you faithful* (17) *Friendly gods!* (18) *If only you knew* (19) *How my soul loved you!*

(20) *True, at that time I did not call you yet* (21) *By name, [and] you too* (22) *Did not call me (name me), as men call each other* (23) *As if they knew each other.*

(24) *But I have known you better* (25) *Than I ever knew mankind.* (26) *I understood the stillness of the ether;* (27) *I never understood the words of men.*

(28) *I was taught by the pleasant sound (the harmony)* (29) *Of the rustling (whispering) grove,* (30) *And I learned to love* (31) *Among the flowers.*

(32) *In the arms of the gods I grew up.*

The verse is free, virtually conversational in tone: brief lines and a simple, almost childlike vocabulary. The longer lines appear to outline a thematic development. First the poet recoils from the distractions and punishments of men. Then the gods invest their sympathy in this new Endymion. Hölderlin expresses love for these benefactors, and he asserts the immediate rapport between poet and deities, in contrast with the merely nominalistic relationship he shares with human beings. An understanding of the world above is his special ability, a knowledge of that "stillness of the ether" (26) which supplants the clamor of men. Finally, divine arms have nestled him to provide sanctuary when a human hand is raised against him. Just as plants raise their "arms" to the light of the sun (which is their "god"), so the poet raises his arms to the god (which is his sun).

This poem, which was written before 1799, offers a significant contrast to "Hyperion's Song of Fate" (p. 114). Here both the celestial and earthly habitations are congenial, and only mankind is alien.

As one reads the poem aloud, one is led to speculate on the source of the slowness with which stanza five begins. Is it, perhaps, the predominance of *m*, *n*, and *ch* sounds? *Zwar damals rief ich noch nicht/ Euch mit Namen, auch ihr/Nanntet mich nie, wie Menschen sich nennen,/ Als kennten sie sich.* [H.E.H.]

JAHRESTAG

O schwester nimm den krug aus grauem thon·
Begleite mich! denn du vergassest nicht
Was wir in frommer wiederholung pflegten.
Heut sind es sieben sommer dass wirs hörten   4
Als wir am brunnen schöpfend uns besprachen:
Uns starb am selben tag der bräutigam.
Wir wollen an der quelle wo zwei pappeln
Mit einer fichte in den wiesen stehn   8
Im krug aus grauem thone wasser holen.

*(Die Bücher der Hirten- und Preisgedichte, der Sagen und
Sänge, und der hängenden Gärten. 1895)*

Probably the most important endowment of Stefan George (1868-1933) was a remarkable gift for language. Before he was ten he had invented a complete private language of his own, in which, as he tells us in the poem *Ursprünge* ("Beginnings"), he could be sole master of his own world. Later, he designed his own Romance language, in which he published two poems. His father was wise and rich enough to let the son devote his life to the development of his gifts and interests. The clearest evidence of George's linguistic and literary culture is his five hundred pages of excellent verse translations from seven languages, including a complete version of Baudelaire's *Les fleurs du mal.*

During an early visit to Paris (see "*Franken,*" p. 128) George came under the influence of French Symbolism, and the greater part of his esthetic ideas are in agreement with the goals of the Symbolists. These ideas were amply developed in his journal, *Blätter für die Kunst* (*Pages for Art,* 1892-1919), which served as the organ for the closely knit "circle" of George and his disciples. He differed from the Symbolists in his total rejection of free verse and his insistence on compressing his thoughts into predetermined poetic forms. His ideal was one of condensation, perfect formal control, and almost ascetic severity. Even in his early poetry, where he was sometimes ornate and splendid, he knew that what he was doing was not what he really wanted to do. In a little poem entitled *Die Spange* ("The Clasp," 1891), he says that he would like to make his clasp of cool, polished steel, but there is no such metal at his disposal; *therefore* he will make it of fire-red gold encrusted with gorgeous gems. Later, he found his steel and polished it. The unique flavor of George's work is the result of a great gift for language kept under severe discipline.

The same self-control—or self-denial—appears in other aspects of his work. He stuck to the simple stanzas and blank verse which had long been traditional in German poetry, studiously avoiding the more intricate imported forms. Though he translated all Shakespeare's sonnets and many others ranging from Dante and Petrarch to Rossetti and Rimbaud, he never wrote a single sonnet of his own. His syntax is tightened by his habit of dropping logically unnecessary words, even though they may be required by the normal idiom of the language. Similarly, he reduced punctuation to the bare minimum needed for intelligibility, and occasionally below that minimum. He used a mark of his own—a centered period—for most purposes. He rejected the German practice of capitalizing all nouns. The only luxury he allowed himself was the use of his own private typeface. The poems reprinted here reproduce the poet's punctuation and capitalization, but for obvious reasons they are not printed in his special type.

For a long time George was interested only in poetry and wrote only for his own exclusive circle. Later, he came to think of himself as something of a leader and prophet—as in his strange deification of the boy he called Maximin—and to address a larger public. Like Nietzsche, he preached doctrines which could be easily perverted into Hitlerism, and the Nazis were not slow to use this fact. When they came into power, they sought to make him their poet and prophet. George hesitated briefly. Then he silently withdrew to Switzerland, where, after refusing a needed operation, he soon died.

George's typical restraint is well illustrated by "Anniversary," in which the whole effect is one of directness and simplicity. (1) *O sister, take the pitcher of gray clay (earthenware); (2) Accompany me! for you have not forgotten (3) What we have been accustomed [to do] in pious (reverent) repeti-* *tion. (4) Today it is seven summers since we heard it (5) As we were talking together while drawing [water] at the spring: (6) Our fiancés died on the same day. (7) We will [go] to the spring, where two poplars (8) Stand with a spruce in the meadow, (9) To fetch water in the pitcher of gray clay.*

The basic experience is one of quiet, dignified grief, and this is communicated by the use of language which is at the same time elevated and direct. There is no English equivalent for *bräutigam* (6) that does not violate this tone: *fiancé* smacks of the society-page, *betrothed* is too archaic and literary, and *intended* is, of course, too vulgarly coy. The poet maintains his tone perfectly, and the precision and compression of the language create the impression of a grief that is restrained and ritualized rather than effusive.

The details used in the poem have both a positive and a negative function—they are highly specific without being in any way restrictive. A pitcher of gray clay gives a clear, concrete mental image, but does not imply any particular time or place, nor do the poplar and spruce (7-8), which are widely distributed. By using only such non-restrictive details, George makes the experience simultaneously individual and universal.

Though written in strict unrimed iambic pentameter, the poem carries a hint of rime in the agreement of the final consonants: every line except the second ends with a nasal, and seven of the nine lines end with *n*. The return in the last line of a phrase from the first is combined with this consonant-rime as a device of sound to tie the poem together and make it a single unit.   [c.s.b.]

DER HERR DER INSEL

Die fischer überliefern dass im süden
Auf einer insel reich an zimmt und öl
Und edlen steinen die im sande glitzern
Ein vogel war der wenn am boden fussend   4
Mit seinem schnabel hoher stämme krone
Zerpflücken konnte   wenn er seine flügel
Gefärbt wie mit dem saft der Tyrer-schnecke
Zu schwerem niedrem flug erhoben: habe   8
Er einer dunklen wolke gleichgesehn.
Des tages sei er im gehölz verschwunden
Des abends aber an den strand gekommen
Im kühlen windeshauch von salz und tang   12
Die süsse stimme hebend dass delfine
Die freunde des gesanges näher schwammen
Im meer voll goldner federn goldner funken.
So habe er seit urbeginn gelebt   16
Gescheiterte nur hätten ihn erblickt.
Denn als zum erstenmal die weissen segel
Der menschen sich mit günstigem geleit
Dem eiland zugedreht sei er zum hügel   20
Die ganze teure stätte zu beschaun gestiegen
Verbreitet habe er die grossen schwingen
Verscheidend in gedämpften schmerzeslauten.

(*Die Bücher der Hirten- und Preisgedichte, der Sagen und Sänge, und der hängenden Gärten.* 1895)

Several of George's best poems deal with primitive nature, before or at the time of the arrival of man. Always it is seen as a world different from that of civilization and incompatible with it, though neither world is idealized at the expense of the other. In this poem, "The Lord (Master) of the Island," we have all the spices and jewels of a typically romanticized nature, but they are combined with an element of the grotesque that gives the picture interest and—paradoxically—a certain realism and credibility.

(1) *Fishermen report (hand down a tradition) that, in the south,* (2) *On an island rich in cinnamon and [olive] oil* (3) *And precious stones that glitter (glisten, sparkle) in the sand,* (4) *There was a bird that, if (when) lit (perching) on the ground,* (5-6) *Could pluck to pieces with his beak the tops of high trees* [or, alternatively, *the crowns of exalted families*]; *if (when) he had raised his wings,* (7) *Colored as if with the juice of the Tyrian*

snail, (8) *For heavy, low flight, it was said that* (9) *He looked like a dark cloud.* The subjunctive, translated *it was said that* in this sentence, runs on through the poem as a constant reminder, not always translatable without overemphasis, that the poet is simply reporting the tradition without vouching for it himself.

(10) *In the daytime he would disappear in the wood (copse),* (11) *But in the evening [he would] come to the beach,* (12) *In the cool breeze of salt and seaweed* (13) *Raising his sweet voice so that dolphins,* (14) *The lovers (friends) of song, would swim closer* (15) *In a sea full of golden scales, golden sparks (glints).* (16) *Thus he had lived since the first (primeval, aboriginal) beginning.* (17) *Only shipwrecked men had caught a glimpse of him.* (18) *For, when for the first time the white sails* (19) *Of human beings, with propitious guidance,* (20-21) *Turned towards the island, he climbed to the hill to gaze over the whole beloved (dear) place.* (22) *He spread out his great pinions,* (23) *Passing away (dying) with subdued (muffled) moans (sounds) of grief.*

A few individual points call for comment. The ambiguity in line 5 is probably unintentional, since it offers no real multiple meaning; but we cannot resolve the problem, for both readings draw support from other parts of the poem. A bird able to stand on the ground and dismember treetops would be huge (9, 22), and would tend to walk rather than fly (21). But the gems glittering in the sand (3) and the implication of shipwrecks near the island (17) support the other reading. George perhaps intended one meaning and did not realize the possibility of the other. Thus the reader is left to his own choice.

The general strictness of the blank verse makes the extra foot in line 21 particularly effective in suggesting the slow, heavy-hearted last journey to the hill-top.

The island of the poem is something primeval and legendary, outside historical time, and the poet uses various suggestions of antiquity to reinforce this impression. The description of the dolphins as lovers of song (14) is an allusion that carries the mind back to Greek legend. When the poet Arion was about to be thrown overboard by sailors (who planned to steal his wealth), he got permission to sing a last song. This song attracted a school of dolphins, and when, at its conclusion, the poet leaped overboard, one of them carried him safely to shore. This association with antiquity is reinforced in the next line by an entirely different type of suggestion. *Federn* (15) normally means "feathers," but here the word is clearly used in the archaic sense of "(fish)scales." In general, the archaisms in George's vocabulary seem to be a reflection of the peasant and rural tradition of his family rather than a bookish affectation. This one, however, serves a definite function in its suggestion of ancient times. The next line (16) tells us that the bird has lived there since the very beginning—*seit Urbeginn.* In the second chapter of *The Magic Mountain,* Thomas Mann has a fine passage on the impressive sound and the remote associations of this prefix *ur-*, which is also the "great" of "great-grandfather."

The concentration of these suggestions of antiquity into the lines (14-16) immediately preceding the breaking in of man and his world (17 to the end) serves to heighten both the contrast and the pathos of this irruption. [C.S.B.]

STEFAN GEORGE

DIE FREMDE

Sie kam allein aus fernen gauen
Ihr haus umging das volk mit grauen
Sie sott und buk und sagte wahr
Sie sang im mond mit offenem haar.   4

Am kirchtag trug sie bunten staat
Damit sie oft zur luke trat . .
Dann ward ihr lächeln süss und herb
Gatten und brüdern zum verderb.   8

Und übers jahr als sie im dunkel
Einst attich suchte und ranunkel
Da sah man wie sie sank im torf —
Und andere schwuren dass vorm dorf   12

Sie auf dem mitten weg verschwand . .
Sie liess das knäblein nur als pfand
So schwarz wie nacht so bleich wie lein
Das sie gebar im hornungschein.

(*Der Teppich des Lebens und die Lieder von
Traum und Tod, mit einem Vorspiel.* 1899)

With a light touch, in relaxed quatrains reminiscent of German folk-song, George celebrates the passage of "The Stranger Woman"—the outsider—through a commonplace little village and through the lives of its inhabitants.

(1) *She came alone, from far away.* (2) *The [local] people avoided her house with horror.* (3) *She boiled and baked and prophesied (told fortunes);* (4) *She sang in the moon[light] with loose (unbound, flowing) hair.* (5) *On a feast-day (fair-day) she wore gay finery* (6) *In which she often went to her dormer window.* (7) *Then her smile became sweet and tart [dry, as of wine],* (8) *To the ruin of husbands and brothers.* (9) *And after a year, when, in the dark, she* (10) *Was once looking for dwarf-elder and crowfoot (buttercups, ranun-*

culus), (11) *Someone saw how she sank into the peat—*(12) *And others swore that, outside the village,* (13) *She vanished in the middle of the road.* (14) *She left behind as pledge (forfeit) only her little boy,* (15) *As black as night, as pale as linen,* (16) *Whom she had borne in the light of February.*

This stranger is not merely from far away in a geographical sense. She comes from, and still inhabits, a physical and moral world utterly alien to that of the villagers. What she sings in the moonlight (4) is doubtless incantations to give power to her charms and potions, whose ingredients have to be gathered at night (9). Instead of going to church in her Sunday clothes, she shows off in them at her window in order to lure men into her house (5-8). Whether she sank into the bog (11) or vanished on the highway (13), her disappearance was a deliberate act as unfathomable as her arrival. Even the child whom she abandoned, with his striking combination of coal-black hair and linen-white complexion (15), bears the mark of her alien world and seems to owe nothing to his unknown—and probably local and ordinary—father. Is there some special superstition connected with the fact that he was born in February and the month is called by its old folk-name, *Hornung*, or is this statement simply used to intensify the general aura of mystery that surrounds her? Or does George expect his reader to be enough of a philologist to know that in the early Germanic languages the word also had the meaning of "bastard"?

The poet begins his account as a disinterested observer—"the local people avoided her house"(2) — but he soon begins to speak from the point of view of the villagers whose lives the stranger has disrupted. (This disruption is formally reflected in the breaking down of the stanza as a closed entity, when line 12 logically goes with the final stanza.) In the identification of the men whom the stranger seduces as "husbands and brothers" (8), the poet is momentarily one of the outraged wives and sisters—and one suspects that it was these same women who themselves made use of the stranger in her capacity as fortune-teller. The shifting points of view lead the reader to the ambivalent position of the villagers, who regard the stranger with fascinated misgivings. This attitude is as interesting as the woman herself, and would be entirely adequate as the subject of the poem. But the stranger's point of view is present, too, though never stated. It is suggested throughout by the light, carefree swing of the verse itself, which does not match the feelings of the villagers, but is perfect for her.

Yet one cannot help suspecting that the stranger is a symbol as well as a gypsy. One critic says that she represents the disrupting influence of woman in general as seen by a poet of homosexual tendencies. Another, somewhat more plausibly, suggests that she is the artist, improvident and rootless, scandalizing and fascinating conventional people, and leaving behind a strange creation wished off on a world that may not want it. This view leads one on to speculations beyond the end of the poem. After the first excitement and relief, when the villagers realized that the stranger was really gone for good, what did they think? When their dominant passions—the lust of the men and the curiosity of the women—were frustrated by her absence, did they realize that they actually needed her? And if so, did they admit it to each other? If she is the artist, did they cherish her legacy—her child— after she was gone? And if she is the artist, how much irony is intended in the portrait?

Such speculations and allegorical interpretations are tempting, but none of them is either certain or necessary. The essential effect is that the reader is left, like the villagers, unable either to ignore the stranger or fully to comprehend her.

[C.S.B.]

STEFAN GEORGE

FRANKEN

Es war am schlimmsten kreuzweg meiner fahrt:
Dort aus dem abgrund züngelnd giftige flammen ·
Hier die gemiednen gaue wo der ekel
Mir schwoll vor allem was man pries und übte ·   4
Ich ihrer und sie meiner götter lachten.
Wo ist dein dichter · arm und prahlend volk?
Nicht einer ist hier: Dieser lebt verwiesen
Und Jenem weht schon frost ums wirre haupt.   8

Da lud von Westen märchenruf . . so klang
Das lob des ahnen seiner ewig jungen
Grossmütigen erde deren ruhm ihn glühen
Und not auch fern ihn weinen liess · der mutter   12
Der fremden unerkannten und verjagten . .
Ein rauschen bot dem erben gruss als lockend
In freundlichkeit und fülle sich die ebnen
Der Maas und Marne unterm frühlicht dehnten.   16

Und in der heitren anmut stadt · der gärten
Wehmütigem reiz · bei nachtbestrahlten türmen
Verzauberten gewölbs umgab mich jugend
Im taumel aller dinge die mir teuer —   20
Da schirmten held und sänger das Geheimnis:
VILLIERS sich hoch genug für einen thron ·
VERLAINE in fall und busse fromm und kindlich
Und für sein denkbild blutend: MALLARMÉ.   24

Mag traum und ferne uns als speise stärken —
Luft die wir atmen bringt nur der Lebendige.
So dank ich freunde euch die dort noch singen
Und väter die ich seit zur gruft geleitet . . .   28
Wie oft noch spät da ich schon grund gewonnen
In trüber heimat streitend und des sieges
Noch ungewiss · lieh neue kraft dies flüstern:
RETURNENT FRANC EN FRANCE DULCE TERRE.

(*Der siebente Ring*. 1907)

In this poem George describes his visit to Paris in 1889, as a youth of twenty-one, and tells what it meant to him both then and later. As an intensely personal account of his intellectual and artistic awakening, it contains a number of semi-private allusions that must be understood before the poem can be approached as a poem.

First of all, the title is not "France," but "The Franks," or "Land of the Franks." The old Frankish kingdom extended far into what is now Germany—Charlemagne's capital was at Aachen (Aix-la-Chapelle) —and the poet does not see himself as a German influenced by France, but as a wanderer coming at last to his ancestral and spiritual home.

(1) *It was at the worst crossroads of my journey:* (2) *There [on one path], venomous flames licking up from the abyss;* (3-4) *Here [on the other], the avoided (shunned) regions where my gorge rose (nausea swelled within me) at everything that people praised and practiced.* (5) *I derided their gods, and they mine.* (6) *Where is your poet (artist), poor and boastful tribe (nation)?* (7) *Not one is here: the One lives in banishment,* (8) *And frost is already blowing about the Other's confused head.* When George went to Paris, the great landscape and mythological painter Arnold Böcklin was already an old man and had long lived in Italy. His "banishment" was voluntary, but George sees him as driven out by conditions which made life in German regions (he was actually born in Switzerland) impossible for him. In a poem addressed to Böcklin, George says that the painter withdrew from humiliating condescensions, taking the jewel of his art away until his people, cured of their blindness, should ask for it. At this same time, insanity was already closing in on Nietzsche; it became final during the following year. George's poems to Böcklin and Nietzsche, placed shortly before "*Franken*" in the same volume, make it clear that they are the men here alluded to as "the One" and "the Other."

(9) *Then a legendary (fabulous) call summoned [me] from the west—thus sounded* (10) *My ancestor's praise of his eternally young,* (11-12) *Magnanimous land, whose glory made him glow, and [whose] need [made him] weep, even from afar—the mother* (13) *Of foreigners, of the unrecognized and hounded-out.* The ancestor is George's grandfather, who told the young poet a great deal about his own home in Lorraine. (14) *A murmur gave the heir a greeting, as alluringly,* (15) *In friendship and plenty, the plains* (16) *Of the Meuse and Marne [rivers] stretched out under the early light.*

(17) *And in the city of gay charm—the gardens'* (18) *Melancholy grace (attraction)— with towers in the radiant night,* (19) *With enchanted arches (vaults), youth surrounded me* (20) *In the ecstasy (intoxication) of all things which [are] dear to me.* (21) *There hero and singer guarded (shielded, defended) the Mystery—*(22) *Villiers, [who thought] himself high enough for a throne,* (23) *Verlaine, in fall and atonement innocent (pious) and child-like,* (24) *And, bleeding for his idea (monument), Mallarmé.* Villiers de l'Isle-Adam, the author of *Axël*, lived in austere poverty, but with a pride of ancestry which once led him to assert his claim to the throne of Greece. George did not know him personally, but went to his funeral in Paris—see line 28, below. In 1889, Verlaine had served his two years' sentence for the shooting of Rimbaud, and Mallarmé was already famous for his struggle to maintain a level of absolute perfection in his poems.

(25) *Though dream and distance may serve as food to strengthen us,* (26) *Only a living Man brings the air we breathe.* (27) *Therefore I thank you, friends who still sing there* (28) *And fathers whom I have since accompanied to the grave.* (29) *How often even of late, when I had already gained ground* (30-31) *struggling in [my] gloomy home[land] and not yet*

certain of victory, this whisper has lent /me/ new strength: (32) "*The Franks turn back to the sweet land of France.*" This last line is in Old French. It ought to be from the *Song of Roland* (and one German commentator blandly states that it is), but there is actually no such line in that poem. Since similar ideas are expressed there several times, George's line might be a very loose recollection, or it may be from some other work in Old French. It is also entirely possible that George composed the line himself when he was reading Old French literature during his stay in Paris. Whether he found it or made it up, he certainly applied it to himself at that time. Thus by its language the line is appropriate to the general theme of the Franks; but it is also a mental keepsake of his visit, and a talisman and promise against the discouragements of a poet in the hostile surroundings described in the first stanza.

The entire poem is both concise and evocative. Again and again a simple phrase carries with it a wealth of allusion or implication. For example, the statement that the poets "guarded the Mystery" (21) suggests the high priests of a cult who are charged with protecting its mysteries and holy things from profanation by the uninitiated. It is probably also an allusion to Mallarmé's contention—frequently echoed in his group—that poetry is entitled to its mysteries, that difficulty and obscurity can serve to protect the poet from the stupid, vulgar, or merely incompetent reader.

There is a strange evocation in the *nacht-bestrahlten türmen* (18). A *Strahl* is a beam of light, and *bestrahlt* is "shone upon, lighted up." But these towers are not artificially illuminated, or moonlit. They are, literally, "towers shone upon by the night" itself—a phrase which conveys the visual image of a tower faintly visible in the surrounding darkness, but which also carries a further suggestion of the night's benevolence and sponsorship. The translation "towers in the radiant night" was used above because it comes closer to the suggestion of the phrase than does a stricter version of the words.

The language itself is as concentrated as are the images and suggestions. Words not strictly necessary, or necessary words that can be supplied mentally, are suppressed. In line 5 there is an unusual arrangement to make it possible to use *lachten* only once; and the normal idiom calls for a preposition with it: to laugh "at" (*über*) something. George prefers a rarer construction without the preposition. The compression in lines 11-12 can be readily seen from the necessity of supplying words (in square brackets) which are omitted in the original. What the poem actually says here is "whose glory made him glow and need even afar him weep."

There are many other instances of a conciseness and concentration going even beyond George's ordinary usage. Such compression gives weight and a slow movement to the poem, but it is also effective in another way. The poet spent only a few months in Paris, but those months were crowded and crucial for his poetic development. By the use of richly evocative imagery and lines packed tight with meaning, he makes the poem reflect the wonder and excitement—and the concentrated significance—of the experience it describes.   [C.S.B.]

[DENK NICHT ZUVIEL VON DEM WAS KEINER WEISS!]

Denk nicht zuviel von dem was keiner weiss!
Unhebbar ist der lebenbilder sinn:
Der wildschwan den du schossest den im hof
Du kurz noch hieltest mit zerbrochnem flügel   4
Er mahnte—sagtest du—an fernes wesen
Verwandtes dir das du in ihm vernichtet.
Er siechte ohne dank für deine pflege
Und ohne groll . . doch als sein ende kam   8
Schalt dich sein brechend auge dass du ihn
Um-triebst in einen neuen kreis der dinge.

(Der Stern des Bundes. 1914)

Certain events seem loaded with a symbolic meaning that can never be precisely defined, and in this short, untitled poem George describes such a happening.

(1) *Do not think too much about what no one knows!* (2) *The meaning of the images* [or *symbols:* "lebenbilder" is literally *life-pictures,* and the poem itself raises the question of whether the things we see in life should be considered as symbols] *in life cannot be settled:* (3-4) *The wild swan that you shot, that you just briefly kept in the yard with a shattered wing—*(5-6) *He reminded [you], you said, of something distant, related to you, that you [had] destroyed in him.* (7) *He languished without thanks for your care* (8) *And without resentment (rancor); but when his end came* (9-10) *His dying (fading) eye rebuked you because you drove him into a new sphere (cycle) of things.*

The flat statement of the first two lines, with its didactic rhetorical generalization, is almost the opposite of poetry as George and most modern poets practice it. It seems intended to be ineffective. The incident of the swan is given as a series of simple facts interrupted by a vague feeling of the "you"—the intimate pronoun *du*— of the poem. This feeling is too tenuous to be translated except as a recollection of "something," but *wesen* (5), which includes such possibilities as "being, existence, creature, condition, essence," is actually more forceful and less general than "something." At the end the poet (or speaker in the poem) adds his own slight speculation, an interpretation of the swan's dying look. Slight as they are, the vague feeling of "you" and the final comment of the poet are enough to insure that when the reader finishes the poem he will reject the opening admonition and go on to think much—if not "too much"—about what meaning may lie behind the simple facts. Thus the poem suggests and achieves—in short, "means"—the opposite of what it directly says.   [C.S.B.]

STEFAN GEORGE

DU SCHLANK UND REIN WIE EINE FLAMME

Du schlank und rein wie eine flamme
Du wie der morgen zart und licht
Du blühend reis vom edlen stamme
Du wie ein quell geheim und schlicht   4

Begleitest mich auf sonnigen matten
Umschauerst mich im abendrauch
Erleuchtest meinen weg im schatten
Du kühler wind du heisser hauch   8

Du bist mein wunsch und mein gedanke
Ich atme dich mit jeder luft
Ich schlürfe dich mit jedem tranke
Ich küsse dich mit jedem duft   12

Du blühend reis vom edlen stamme
Du wie ein quell geheim und schlicht
Du schlank und rein wie eine flamme
Du wie der morgen zart und licht.   16

(*Das neue Reich*. 1929)

This untitled work was published as part of George's cycle of poems *The New Kingdom*. The subject of the lyric was doubtless the short-lived, exceptionally beautiful adolescent boy, Maximilian Kronberger, who was renamed "Maximin" by George and his circle. Maximin was virtually deified by the poet and his followers to become the embodiment of the ideal of ancient Greece: plastic beauty raised to an absolute, canonic apogee; the perfect blend of the physical and the spiritual. Moreover, George made the youth the incarnation of aristocratic and "German" qualities in a modern civilization whose democratic internationalization he found increasingly abhorrent. George composed this impassioned apostrophe some two decades after Maximin's death, but for him the youth's brief sojourn on earth was an unforgettable reminder of native nobility in the midst of bourgeois vulgarity, of the elite figure who stands above the masses.

Whence this brief poem's intensity? It offers neither setting nor dramatic situation; only a sustained outpouring of affection. Here passion takes recourse to natural rather than man-made objects; and in this the poem departs from much of George's verse, for, like the French Parnassians and Symbolists, he exhibited a frequent fondness for jewels, statues, fountains, and the like. The first stanza of the lyric draws on elemental materials— a flame, the morning, a tree with boughs, a spring. And these are recapitulated in the final quatrain.

The first stanza: (1) *You slender (slim) and pure as a flame* (2) *You like the morning tender (delicate) and light (bright)* (3) *You blooming (flourishing) twig (branch) from a noble stem (line)*, (4) *You like a spring (source), hidden (mysterious) and simple (unadorned).*

Stanza two shifts from attributes to a feeling of the beloved youth's presence throughout the day (midday sun, evening fog, shadow of night): (5) *[You] accompany me [are about me] on sunny meadows*, (6) *[You are the light] shudder about me in the evening haze* [the untranslatable "umschauern" denotes the uncanny feeling of dark, cool breezes; "Abendrauch" is the smoky haze after sunset; "Rauch," literally *smoke*], (7) *You light up my path in the shadow*, (8) *You cool wind, you hot breath (breeze).*

(9) *You are my desire and my thought*, (10) *I breathe you in with every [breath of] air*, (11) *I sip you in with every drink (swallow)*, (12) *I kiss you with every scent.* Note the sensuous, erotic strength of this expression of longing, underlined by the concreteness of the verbs in this stanza as compared to the more quiet verbs in the second stanza and to the absence of verbs in the first.

The reprise (stanza four) reorders the lines of the first stanzas (1, 2, 3, 4 become 3, 4, 1, 2) to compose a different system of adoration and to produce a symmetrical ending on the opening lines, an invocation of the qualities of the youth: "slender," "pure," "tender," "light." For this is a love poem; specifically a highly erotic poem; more specifically, a lyric of homosexual love. The imagery that the poet devotes to his beloved in lines 3 and 4 (13 and 14) is masculine: branch from a noble trunk, hidden fountainhead. . . .

How does George create an atmosphere in which the two persons are tightly bound, to the exclusion of the rest of the world? He concentrates on *Du* and *Ich* ("you" and "I") and related pronouns: *dich, mein, mich* ("you, mine, me"). The latter, possessives or accusatives, emphasize how much the two persons own each other or what they do to each other. *Du*, the intimate "thou," which modern English reserves for discourse with the deity, resounds eleven times.

The sonal appeal of the poem is not easy to describe. Nevertheless, one cannot fail to be struck by the boldness of the initial sounds in twelve of the sixteen lines—ten are begun by *Du*, three are begun by *Ich*. Assonance and alliteration are also apparent—for example, *schlank, flamme, rein, eine* (1); *ein geheim* (4); *mich, matten* (5); *umschauerst mich im; umschauerst, abendrauch* (6); *meinem, im* (7); *heisser, hauch* (8).

The meter is rigorously iambic except in line 5, but of course it is not mechanically scanned by all readers. Some, for instance, stress the initial *Du*, followed by a pause, which in some cases (lines 2 and 4) gives the rest of the line an anapaestic-trochaic character:

Dú | wie der mórgen zárt und lícht
Dú | wie ein quéll gehéim und schlícht

We know, however, that George himself read his lines in an even, almost hieratic way—"Free rhythms," he wrote, means as much as "white blackness"—"whoever cannot move very well in rhythm, let him stride out unfettered." "Most rigorous measure [rhythm] is at the same time utmost freedom," he remarked, and elsewhere he declared that the poet seeks out the most rigorous restrictions because in their observance he attain highest mastery and freedom of expression.   [H.E.H.]

DIE BEIDEN

Sie trug den Becher in der Hand
— Ihr Kinn und Mund glich seinem Rand —,
So leicht und sicher war ihr Gang,
Kein Tropfen aus dem Becher sprang.   4

So leicht und fest war seine Hand:
Er ritt auf einem jungen Pferde,
Und mit nachlässiger Gebärde
Erzwang er, daß es zitternd stand.   8

Jedoch, wenn er aus ihrer Hand
Den leichten Becher nehmen sollte,
So war es beiden allzu schwer:
Denn beide bebten sie so sehr,   12
Daß keine Hand die andre fand
Und dunkler Wein am Boden rollte.

(Ausgewählte Gedichte. 1904)

The first stanza of *Die Beiden* ("The Two") introduces "her," as she carries a goblet of wine: (1) *She bore the cup in her hand* (2) *—Her chin and mouth were like its rim—* (3) *So light and sure was her gait,* (4) *Not a drop spilled (sprang) from the cup.*

The second stanza is devoted to "him": (5) *So light and firm was his hand* [perhaps no less so than hers]: (6) *He rode upon a young horse,* (7) *And with a careless [casual] gesture* (8) *He forced it to halt quivering.*

The lack of a *dass* ("that") at the beginning of 4 reflects the striving of the structural elements toward autonomy. As a result the poem speaks with almost classical aloofness; it expresses not the feelings of the writer but of the two persons. Moreover, in contrast to the central German lyric tradition, the words of the

poem fail to fuse with the acts they describe. But though the words seem to be separated from the acts, there is hardly any distance between these acts and the emotions that they express. Indeed, "expression," as Hofmannsthal understood it, called for so intimate a conjoining of body and spirit that only a Philistine could deny their union. "*Die Beiden*," then, presents clear contours and distinct entities while at the same time blurring them by an all-pervading unity. It is both "classical" and "romantic"—in this respect not unlike Rilke's so-called objective poems and a number of works by George.

With the second stanza the actions have moved almost too far in the direction of autonomy, when a strong *jedoch* ("however") reintroduces unity. But another separateness returns: the act of handing over the cup miscarries, and the wine is spilled. (9) *However, when from her hand* (10) *He was to take the light cup,* (11) *This was too difficult (heavy) for both [of them]:* (12) *Because both trembled so much* (13) *That neither hand found the other* (14) *And dark wine rolled upon the ground.*

The word *Gebärde* ("gesture"), in the very center of the poem (7), fascinated Hofmannsthal and his fellow poets. They used it to suggest the expressive element in human action as contrasted with purposiveness. It is not *what* a person does that is expressive but *how* he does it. For example, the act of halting the horse is esthetically irrelevant as a means to an end (as Valéry put it, the means is consumed by the end). But the *how* of this same act—the man's ability to cause his powerful horse to quiver merely by making a casual gesture—speaks the language of "expression" eloquently. Note that it is not the verb but the adverb that suggests the way in which an act is performed. "With a careless gesture" is of course an adverbial phrase and in the subsequent "quivering" the adverbial force is unmistakable.

At first glance "*Die Beiden*" resembles a sonnet, but it is also a lyric with a plot and as such a kind of ballad. To achieve the utmost in "expression," the poet reduces the plot to the minimum, and this minimum serves as the raw material in which the feelings of the two people are embodied. Each of the stanzas leads up to *Gebärde*, gaining in intensity; and the same principle of intensification is at work in the poem as a whole.

To understand the meaning of *Gebärde* the reader must recognize that to Hofmannsthal there was no symbolic significance in the act when viewed merely as a means to a concrete everyday objec-

tive. Hence, the act of handing over the cup had finally to be deprived of its purpose by being deflected from its goal. In everyday terms the spilling of the wine means that the two people have failed to bring about their union. But this spilling of the wine is also a symbolic shedding of blood and as such means that union has been effected, in spite of all. These two persons who are doomed to separateness by the failure of their act in terms of purpose are also, by dint of this same failure, joined all the more closely in the fulfilment of another—and to Hofmannsthal, more meaningful—kind of union: in the harmony and beauty of the gesture they perform together.

Nothing could be more sophisticated than the stance of this poem, whose gesture—on the surface so naïve—derives its perfection from the very failure of the surface act to which this gesture can be traced. For poetry at the end of the last century had come to feed on the agony of life—a tendency of which Hofmannsthal was well aware and in which he had begun to participate. Only a few years after the publication of "*Die Beiden*," when he was in his mid-twenties, and recognized as one of the most gifted writers in German, Hofmannsthal (Vienna: 1874-1929) turned from poetry to other forms. He is remembered today as an outstanding essayist and an important force in the drama—author of a number of distinguished tragedies (of which *Der Turm* is probably his most significant), adaptor of plays of Sophocles, Calderón, and Molière, for the Max Reinhardt theatre, and writer of comedies, of which *Der Schwierige* is considered one of the finest written in German and *Der Rosenkavalier* is best known to Americans because of the musical setting by Richard Strauss.   [A.O.J.]

BALLADE DES ÄUSSEREN LEBENS

Und Kinder wachsen auf mit tiefen Augen,
Die von nichts wissen, wachsen auf und sterben,
Und alle Menschen gehen ihre Wege.

Und süße Früchte werden aus den herben   4
Und fallen nachts wie tote Vögel nieder
Und liegen wenig Tage und verderben.

Und immer weht der Wind, und immer wieder
Vernehmen wir und reden viele Worte   8
Und spüren Lust und Müdigkeit der Glieder.

Und Straßen laufen durch das Gras, und Orte
Sind da und dort, voll Fackeln, Bäumen, Teichen,
Und drohende, und totenhaft verdorrte . . .   12

Wozu sind diese aufgebaut? und gleichen
Einander nie? und sind unzählig viele?
Was wechselt Lachen, Weinen und Erbleichen?

Was frommt das alles uns und diese Spiele,   16
Die wir doch groß und ewig einsam sind
Und wandernd nimmer suchen irgend Ziele?

Was frommts, dergleichen viel gesehen haben?
Und dennoch sagt der viel, der « Abend » sagt,   20
Ein Wort, daraus Tiefsinn und Trauer rinnt

Wie schwerer Honig aus den hohlen Waben.

(*Ausgewählte Gedichte.* 1903)

Nothing could be less dramatic than this "Ballad of Outer Life." Instead of moving steadily to a climax, the poem presents a monotonous repetition: half of the lines start with a coordinating "and," and almost each "and" introduces a new story! Yet this new story is always the same—the meaninglessness of outer life. Death, decay, is the end of everything— and because this end is so near, each story is only a line or two long. By line 10 the plot is no longer strong enough to fill a whole line: coordinate clauses are about to give way to a mere tired listing of unrelated things. "Torches, trees, ponds" are "here and there" in a space that itself lacks an organizing principle. There is no going on, as the three dots (12) suggest;

and the ballad proper comes to a close: (1) *And children grow up with deep eyes* (2) *Who know of nothing, grow up and die,* (3) *And all people go their ways.* (4) *And the bitter fruits become sweet* (5) *And fall down at night like dead birds* (6) *And lie a few days and spoil.* (7) *And always the wind blows, and again and again* (8) *We hear and speak many words* (9) *And feel [the] pleasure and weariness of our limbs.* (10) *And streets run through the grass, and places* (11) *Are here and there, full of torches, trees, ponds,* (12) *And menacing ones and death-like withered ones.* . . . Most of the verbs are intransitive, and the others lack the power to reach out: the children, for example, know of "nothing."

Enumeration continues as five rhetorical questions sum up once more the futility of everything: (13) *Why are these raised up? and resemble* (14) *Each other never? and are countlessly many?* (15) *Why do laughing, crying, and turning pale alternate?* The five questions are essentially the same question: there is no true difference among laughing, crying, and turning pale; for all motion is at a standstill, viewed in the aspect of outer life.

The next question, however, is vital enough to require an entire tercet: (16) *Of what use is all this to us and all these games* (17) *Who are (after all) great and eternally lonely* (18) *And, wandering, never seek any goals?* The "us" is the poet of the *fin de siècle*, the blessed-accursed, the king-beggar, who lives and views existence by the principle of art: in terms of the motion that seeks no goal, because art is its own goal—to paraphrase Rilke, it leads straight to heaven because it leads nowhere.

(19) *Of what use is it to have seen many*

such things? the poem asks, and the answer must be read carefully: (20) *And nevertheless* ["dennoch"] *he says much who says "evening,"* (21) *A word from which deep meaning and sadness run* (22) *Like heavy honey from the hollow comb.*

The word "evening" is a container-word —not of denotation but of emotion, of emotion composed of all the feelings, of depth and sadness and sweetness; of the emotion transcendent. To say "evening" therefore means to write poetry. We can now see what the two statements of the poem linked by *dennoch* (20) communicate: Outer life is futile; nevertheless this outer life as reflected in poetry is "much." In lines 1-19 Hofmannsthal *seems* to be saying that this transformation could never take place; and at this point the reader should remind himself that, according to Hofmannsthal, words used referentially must be distinguished fundamentally from the same words used poetically. Thus Hofmannsthal's ballad can be called dreary and decadent only if the words that compose it are understood as being carriers of a life content. But when the words are understood poetically, they convey a quite different meaning. Every word here, every *and*, every dead bird, every tiredness of limb, must be read as a poetic word—as what Hofmannsthal called a dreamlike *Bruderwort* ("brother word") to the same word used referentially. As such it is a bearer of poetic delight—of depth, sadness, sweetness. Every word in this ballad is poetry, for every word says "evening," or, to quote St. John of the Cross, is full of "the knowledge of the evening." [A.O.J.]

DER JÜNGLING IN DER LANDSCHAFT

Die Gärtner legten ihre Beete frei,
Und viele Bettler waren überall
Mit schwarzverbundnen Augen und mit Krücken —
Doch auch mit Harfen und den neuen Blumen,   4
Dem starken Duft der schwachen Frühlingsblumen.

Die nackten Bäume ließen alles frei:
Man sah den Fluß hinab und sah den Markt,
Und viele Kinder spielen längs den Teichen.   8
Durch diese Landschaft ging er langsam hin
Und fühlte ihre Macht und wußte — daß
Auf ihn die Weltgeschicke sich bezogen.

Auf jene fremden Kinder ging er zu   12
Und war bereit, an unbekannter Schwelle
Ein neues Leben dienend hinzubringen.
Ihm fiel nicht ein, den Reichtum seiner Seele,
Die frühern Wege und Erinnerung   16
Verschlungner Finger und getauschter Seelen
Für mehr als nichtigen Besitz zu achten.

Der Duft der Blumen redete ihm nur
Von fremder Schönheit — und die neue Luft   20
Nahm er stillatmend ein, doch ohne Sehnsucht:
Nur daß er dienen durfte, freute ihn.

(Ausgewählte Gedichte. 1903)

A youth walks through a landscape that is renewed by spring, and as he does so, experiences an inner renewal himself. (1) *The gardeners uncovered (laid free) their [flower] beds,* (2) *And many beggars were everywhere* (3) *With eyes bandaged in black and with crutches—*(4) *But also with harps and the new flowers,* (5) *(With) the strong fragrance of the frail (weak) spring flowers.* This is no realistic description but a vision—what would beggars be doing in a fine park? Line 6 repeats the important "free." Thus the first line of the second stanza reads like a new beginning; the poet strives to "free" the meaning of the vision—through *Sinnbilder,* "significant pictures": symbols. Not until line 11 is abstract statement substituted for imagery: every person is involved in the destinies of everyone else. (6) *The naked trees* [the buds are just beginning] *left everything free:* (7) *One could see (saw) down the river* and (saw) the market (8) And many children playing along the ponds. (9) Through this landscape he walked slowly (10) And felt its power and knew—that (11) He was involved ["sich beziehen auf": have bearing on, relate to] in the destinies of the world.

The youth enters the poem quietly: all emphasis falls on the landscape whose power he feels and obeys. The subject er ("he") in line 9 is an unstressed syllable and it is preceded by "this" landscape. This landscape abounds in water (ancient symbol of life), human activity, children. Not until line 11 does a strong accent fall on ihn ("him"). As though suddenly quickened, the youth awakens to a new life and from now on becomes the conscious, active protagonist. (12) Towards those strange (unfamiliar) children he walked (13) And was ready, upon an unknown threshold, (14) To spend a new life in service ["dienend hinzubringen": serving to spend]. The lack of emphasis on the three syllables at the beginning of 12 and 13 suggests the urgency with which the youth hastens toward his goal, but the three strong stresses that follow in each case dam up his feelings (and the reader's) almost painfully until these feelings are finally released in line 14.

Once the youth has made contact with the invisible forces, (stanza 2), the emphasis (stanza 3) shifts from the outer scene to the inner, from landscape to mind, from space to time. Accordingly, stanza 3, in contrast to the preceding one, is filled with abstract concepts. Those few which seem concrete are mostly used metaphorically and stand for inner realities.

Now that the poem has reached its climax, the journey through time turns backwards. Line 15 opens up into an extended image: (15) It did not occur to him [to consider: "zu achten," which appears in 18] the wealth of his soul, (16) His earlier paths and the memory (17) Of intertwined fingers and interchanged souls (18) More than worthless possession.

This picture of the past has exquisite formal balance and harmony. "Intertwined fingers" and "interchanged souls" correspond in poetic meaning: the first is the visible embodiment of the second. Moreover, they equal each other in rhythmic structure, and thus seem to rest in a state of equilibrium on either side of the conjunction. Similarly, the rhythm of 16 parallels that of 17. But too much harmony is inimical to life: the total impression we get is one of perfection coupled with sterility. The youth rejects his past, and the last stanza offers a rededication to service: (19) The fragrance of the flowers spoke to him only (20) Of strange beauty—, and the new air (21) He inhaled ["einnehmen": take, take in] breathing quietly, but without longing: (22) Only that he was allowed to serve made him glad. The word "longing" seems out of place in this context. No one can long for what he already has in abundance. And suddenly we realize that there are two landscapes in this poem (we also understand the stress on "this" in 9). The one, with its enchanting flowers, its fragrance, and its harps, is an evocation of the youth's past, of estheticism in all its "beauty—which was barren" (as Hofmannsthal says elsewhere). The other, with its water, beggars, human activity, and children, is an embodiment of the new spirit to which the youth has awakened. In this poem the two landscapes exist side by side; the boundary line between them is fluid because the poet's mind is the place where past, present, and future meet. [A.O.J.]

RAINER MARIA RILKE

HERBSTTAG

Herr: es ist Zeit. Der Sommer war sehr groß.
Leg deinen Schatten auf die Sonnenuhren,
und auf den Fluren laß die Winde los.

Befiehl den letzten Früchten voll zu sein;   4
gieb ihnen noch zwei südlichere Tage,
dränge sie zur Vollendung hin und jage
die letzte Süße in den schweren Wein.

Wer jetzt kein Haus hat, baut sich keines mehr.   8
Wer jetzt allein ist, wird es lange bleiben,
wird wachen, lesen, lange Briefe schreiben
und wird in den Alleen hin und her
unruhig wandern, wenn die Blätter treiben.   12

(*Das Buch der Bilder*. 1906)

R ainer Maria Rilke (1875-1926), born
in Prague, is the greatest lyric poet
of the German language since Goethe.
His deeply musical verse—it can dazzle
with effortless virtuosity—ranges from the
classical simplicity of "*Herbsttag*" to the
late, difficult *Duino Elegies* and *Sonnets to
Orpheus*, which opened new realms of
feeling and gave the German language a
new dimension. Rilke also wrote a sub-
stantial body of poetry in French.

"*Herbsttag*" ("Autumn Day") expresses
the urge and fear of those last hot days
just before the autumn chill:

(1) *Lord: It is time. The summer was (has
been) very great.* (2) *Lay Thy shadow upon
the sun dials* (3) *and on the (open) fields
(meadows) let loose (unleash) the winds.*
(4) *Command the last fruits to be (become)
full (ripe);* (5) *give them another two
southerly days,* (6) *urge them on towards per-
fection [fulfilment], and drive (chase)* (7) *the
last (final) sweetness into the heavy wine.*

(8) *Who now has no house, builds himself none
any more.* (9) *Who now is alone, will long re-
main so,* (10) *will wake, read, write long letters*
(11-12) *and will restlessly wander up and down
the tree-lined avenues when the leaves are swirling.*

In his celebrated critical work *Laokoon*
(1766), Lessing showed how a great poet,
Homer, avoids the tedium of description
by turning description into an account of
action (Hephaistos making the shield of
Achilles). In "*Herbsttag*" Rilke expresses
the urgency of those outwardly quiet last
summer days by reverently reminding the
Lord of the action He now must take:
"Lay Thy shadow . . . Unleash the winds . . .
Command . . . give . . . urge . . . drive . . ."

The stanzas lengthen like the autumn
nights (three lines, four, then five), and so
do the sentences. The last stanza turns
from nature to man, who will be restless
and lonely once the time of ripening and
of the harvest of life has come and gone.

[G.S.]

RAINER MARIA RILKE

PONT DU CARROUSEL

Der blinde Mann, der auf der Brücke steht,
grau wie ein Markstein namenloser Reiche,
er ist vielleicht das Ding, das immer gleiche,
um das von fern die Sternenstunde geht,   4
und der Gestirne stiller Mittelpunkt.
Denn alles um ihn irrt und rinnt und prunkt.

Er ist der unbewegliche Gerechte,
in viele wirre Wege hingestellt;   8
der dunkle Eingang in die Unterwelt
bei einem oberflächlichen Geschlechte.

(Das Buch der Bilder. 1906)

The Pont du Carrousel is an old stone bridge in Paris. As you look down upon it, you see people hurrying back and forth, tracking a tangled web of invisible pathways. In its center stands that gray figure which might be of stone but isn't: (1) *The blind man who stands on the bridge,* (2) *gray as a boundary stone of nameless realms,* (3) *he is perhaps that thing, the ever same one,* (4) *around which from afar the star-hour revolves,* (5) *and [he, the beggar] the constellations' still center-point.* (6) *For everything around him strays and streams and shows magnificence.*

(7) *He is the immovable Righteous One,* (8) *set down into (in the midst of) many tangled paths;* (9) *the somber entrance to the netherworld* (10) *among a superficial race of men.*

A carousel is a model of the universe: gleaming things revolve around a drab, immobile center. It is also an object of showy splendor in the fair-ground's noisy confusion. The gray beggar is the only thing that stands still on Merry-go-round Bridge.

Above him, the stars circling "on their metalled ways" (T. S. Eliot); beneath them, the milling crowds. The beggar, out of communication both with man and with the heavens he cannot see, marks the entrance to the netherworld of poverty, deprivation, stillness, righteousness, reality. The "superficial race" hurries by, blind to what it passes.

In one of his *Geschichten vom lieben Gott (Stories of God)* Rilke explains why God desires that there be poor people. It seems that when He was fashioning man, Adam in his eagerness to live suddenly wiggled out of His hands: and when God looked down one God-moment or human eternity later, the earth was already swarming with men so gorgeously, so grotesquely attired that He could no longer make out man's original shape. This is why God is trying to make some human creature so desperately poor that he can no longer cover his nakedness; for then only will God know man as He created him. *Denn Armut ist ein grosser Glanz aus innen,* as Rilke says elsewhere ("Poverty is a great radiance from within").   [G.S.]

[WAS WIRST DU TUN, GOTT, WENN ICH STERBE?]

Was wirst du tun, Gott, wenn ich sterbe?
Ich bin dein Krug (wenn ich zerscherbe?)
Ich bin dein Trank (wenn ich verderbe?)
Bin dein Gewand und dein Gewerbe,
mit mir verlierst du deinen Sinn.   5

Nach mir hast du kein Haus, darin
dich Worte, nah und warm, begrüßen.
Es fällt von deinen müden Füßen   8
Die Samtsandale, die ich bin.

Dein großer Mantel läßt dich los.
Dein Blick, den ich mit meiner Wange
warm, wie mit einem Pfühl, empfange,
wird kommen, wird mich suchen, lange—
und legt beim Sonnenuntergange   13
sich fremden Steinen in den Schooß.

Was wirst du tun, Gott? Ich bin bange.

(Das Stunden-Buch. Erstes Buch. 1905)

[GOTT SPRICHT ZU JEDEM NUR, EH ER IHN MACHT]

Gott spricht zu jedem nur, eh er
        ihn macht,
dann geht er schweigend mit ihm
        aus der Nacht.
Aber die Worte, eh jeder beginnt,
diese wolkigen Worte, sind: 4

Von deinen Sinnen hinausgesandt,
geh bis an deiner Sehnsucht Rand;
gieb mir Gewand.

Hinter den Dingen wachse als Brand,
daß ihre Schatten, ausgespannt,
immer mich ganz bedecken.   10

Laß dir alles geschehn: Schönheit
        und Schrecken.
Man muß nur gehn: Kein Gefühl
        ist das fernste.   12
Laß dich von mir nicht trennen.
Nah ist das Land,
das sie das Leben nennen.

Du wirst es erkennen   16
an seinem Ernste.

Gieb mir die Hand.

(Das Stunden-Buch. Erstes Buch. 1905)

The first of these two poems from Rilke's *Book of Hours* (he wrote them in 1899) opens with a startling question: (1) *What wilt Thou do, God, when I die?* (2) *I am Thy jug (what if I am smashed into sherds?)* (3) *I am Thy drink (what if I spoil?)* (4) *I am Thy garment and Thy trade,* (5) *with me [in losing me] Thou losest Thy meaning.* (6) *After me [after I die] Thou hast no house wherein* (7) *words, near and warm, greet Thee.* (8) *From Thy tired feet falls* (9) *the velvet sandal that I am.*

(10) *Thy great mantle lets Thee go.* (11) *Thy glance, which I with my cheek* (12) *warmly, as with a pillow, [now] receive,* (13) *will come, will seek me, long—*(14) *and will lie [literally lies] down at sunset* (15) *in the lap of (unresponding) stranger-rocks.* (16) *What wilt Thou do, God? I am fearful.*

Death is a loss to man; but does it make God poor and helpless? The theologians are not worried: God has done quite well so far. The psychologists will call the poem's last line a transparent way of saying: I fear death. And indeed, this dread was an obsession with Rilke when he wrote this early work. But is there nothing more to be found in the poem?

This God is surely not Pascal's "God of Abraham, Isaac, and Jacob." It is a God searching for partnership and love among His own creation. Man, individual man, is God's "business," the task that makes Him meaningful while it lasts. God's glance goes searching through the whole of creation, longing for that warm cheek that receives it as a soft cushion receives the tired head. Failing to find man, God's glance will have to rest disconsolately in the "lap" (an ironic word here) of the hard "stranger-rocks," symbols of nature that has not been infused with meaning by man.

The second poem ("*Gott spricht . . .*") elucidates this God-man relationship. It is conceived with extraordinary boldness:

(1) *God speaks to everyone only before He makes him,* (2) *then He walks silently with him out of the night.* (3) *But the words, before everyone begins,* (4) *those cloudy words, are:* (5) *"By thy senses sent forth,* (6) *go right to the rim of thy longing;* (7) *give Me garment (clothe Me).*

(8) *Behind the things, grow as (a) conflagration,* (9) *so that their shadow, stretched out,* (10) *always wholly cover Me.*

(11) *Let everything happen to thee: beauty and terror.* (12) *One must merely (simply) go: No feeling is the farthest [one].* (13) *Let* *thyself not be separated from Me.* (14) *Close-by is the land* (15) *that they call life.* (16) *Thou wilt recognize it* (17) *by its seriousness.*

(18) *Give Me thy hand."*

God's "cloud-like" words are spoken to man before he enters life; they tell him that he will have to go through that life alone. God will not speak to him then. But He will be there, waiting "to be clothed." For without man, "the things" —rocks, trees, houses, dogs, clouds, jugs— are mere numb objects; man's "fiery" passion must transform them into "things" that cast a far-flung shadow like a mantle (lines 4 and 10 of "*Was wirst du tun . . .*") over the silent God.

The metaphor is rather wild, but it expresses what Rilke, in his late poems, meant by his cardinal concept of "using" (*brauchen*). Man needs and uses "things" to support him in his loneliness; he takes them into his world of feeling and meaning where the object transcends its status and becomes a felt "thing." Even God becomes God only as man takes Him into his passionate feeling, and forms, and transforms Him.

There is an undertow of anxiety in God's words (13) as He gets ready to rise and begin the walk towards life: Fear that man might go through life cold, dull, unyielding to longing (this would be separation); fear, too, that He might be left shivering without the "garment" for which he depends on man. It is almost as if God dreaded that joint walk towards life more than does unborn man's apprehensive yet expectant soul. [G.S.]

RAINER MARIA RILKE

LEICHEN-WÄSCHE

Sie hatten sich an ihn gewöhnt. Doch als
die Küchenlampe kam und unruhig brannte
im dunkeln Luftzug, war der Unbekannte
ganz unbekannt. Sie wuschen seinen Hals,   4

und da sie nichts von seinem Schicksal wußten,
so logen sie ein anderes zusamm,
fortwährend waschend. Eine mußte husten
und ließ solang den schweren Essigschwamm   8

auf dem Gesicht. Da gab es eine Pause
auch für die zweite. Aus der harten Bürste
klopften die Tropfen; während seine grause
gekrampfte Hand dem ganzen Hause   12
beweisen wollte, daß ihn nicht mehr dürste.

Und er bewies. Sie nahmen wie betreten
eiliger jetzt mit einem kurzen Huster
die Arbeit auf, so daß an den Tapeten   16
ihr krummer Schatten in dem stummen Muster

sich wand und wälzte wie in einem Netze,
bis daß die Waschenden zu Ende kamen.
Die Nacht im vorhanglosen Fensterrahmen   20
war rücksichtlos. Und einer ohne Namen
lag bar und reinlich da und gab Gesetze.

(*Der Neuen Gedichte anderer Teil.* 1908)

Two women have been called in to
wash a corpse. It is getting dark.
They bring a kerosene lamp with them,
finish their task, and go.
  (1) *They had got used to him. But when*
(2) *the kitchen lamp came and burned un-
quietly (unevenly)* (3) *in the dark air draft,
the Unknown one was* (4) *wholly unknown.
They washed his throat,* (5) *and since they
knew nothing of his fate (life story),* (6) *they
trumped up (made up from lies) another one,*
(7) *washing all the while. One had to cough*
(8) *and while doing so left the heavy vinegar
sponge* (9) *upon the [his] face. This meant
a pause* (10) *for the second one [the other
woman] too. From the hard brush* (11) *the
drops fell tapping; while his grisly* (12-13)
*cramped hand wished to prove to the whole
house that he was no longer thirsty.*
  (14) *And he proved [it]. They resumed, as
if embarrassed,* (15) *more hurriedly now,
with a short cough,* (16) *[they resumed] their*

work, *so that on the wallpaper* (17-18) *their crooked (bent) shadow writhed and wallowed as if in a net,* (19) *until the washing women came to the end.* (20) *The night in the curtainless window frame* (21) *was ruthless. And a nameless one* (22) *lay there bare and cleanly and gave laws.*

"*Leichen-Wäsche*" ("Washing the Corpse") describes an eery scene in curiously repressed matter-of-fact language. There is tension between the irregular spoken rhythm and the underlying regular iambic meter. The three metrical exceptions (2, 10, 15) underline disquieting words: *únruhig* ("unquiet"), *klópften die Trópfen* ("the knocking sound"), and the tripping *eiliger jétzt* ("more hurriedly now"). Sentences run past line and stanza endings while the rime scheme pursues its own independent course. Only at the climactic points (13 and 22) do sentence, stanza, and rime-group simultaneously come to a stop. It is as if the language were straining against something that struggles for recognition—the fact that the corpse changes. The two women do not know what they are doing: the corpse is the master.

A man has died in a shabby furnished room, a lodger (the German word would be *Zimmerherr*, "rooming gentleman" or "room master"), one of those who come and go, and nobody cares who they are so long as they pay the rent. The two women called in to wash the corpse know nothing about him. As darkness falls, the pale body suddenly looks unfamiliar, "quite unknown" (4), in a deeper, more disturbing sense. The women start chattering to overcome this strangeness. The story they tell is made of whole cloth, but for them it has a familiar, comforting ring. Now they pause for a moment. The slow knock of falling drops accentuates a silence in which the corpse suddenly takes on the semblance of the crucified Christ, sponge at the mouth, the hand cramped in agony. There is an almost unbearably brutal description of the Crucifixion earlier in the book from which "*Leichen-Wäsche*" is taken: the executioners, "greedily" trying not to let the man on the cross die too quickly, hold up "the vinegary gall to His fading cough." This is what the washing women unwittingly mimic. But it is all a grotesque misunderstanding, the corpse seems to say: I am past thirsting. Take the sponge off my face. This is death.

The only horror word in the poem—*graus* ("grisly")—stands at this turning point. The corpse's grisly hand is *frozen* in death. Seeing it, the women can no longer pretend. They hastily start working again, "with a short cough" that once more mocks the Crucifixion. Like giant fish caught in a net, their shadows move awkwardly in the wallpaper pattern. Now the women are gone: the body lies alone. Brutal night blacks out the world in the window. "Bare and cleanly," the corpse lies in state, nameless, "laying down the law." For washing the corpse is a symbolic act like a coronation, though in the reverse sense: the majesty of Death is established, not by clothing the body with the insignia of rank and power, but by stripping and washing away the last vestiges of life.   [G.S.]

RAINER MARIA RILKE

ARCHÄISCHER TORSO APOLLOS

Wir kannten nicht sein unerhörtes Haupt,
darin die Augenäpfel reiften. Aber
sein Torso glüht noch wie ein Kandelaber,
in dem sein Schauen, nur zurückgeschraubt,   4

sich hält und glänzt. Sonst könnte nicht der Bug
der Brust dich blenden, und im leisen Drehen
der Lenden könnte nicht ein Lächeln gehen
zu jener Mitte, die die Zeugung trug.   8

Sonst stünde dieser Stein entstellt und kurz
unter der Schultern durchsichtigem Sturz
und flimmerte nicht so wie Raubtierfelle;

und bräche nicht aus allen seinen Rändern   12
aus wie ein Stern: denn da ist keine Stelle,
die dich nicht sieht. Du mußt dein Leben ändern.

(*Der Neuen Gedichte anderer Teil.* 1908)

W*e did not know his unheard-of (unbeliev-able) head* (2) *wherein the eye-apples ripened. But* (3) *his torso still glows like a candelabrum* (4) *in which his gaze, merely turned down low* [like the flames of a candelabrum, no longer visible but still sending out an afterglow] (5) *holds on and gleams. Else the curve* (6) *of the chest could not blind you, and in the slight twist* (7) *of the loins there could not go a smile [there would not be a smile, going]* (8) *towards that center that bore procreation [the genitals].* (9) *Else this stone would be standing disfigured and short* (10) *under the shoulders' transparent fall (plunge)* (11) *and [it] would not glint like the fell (skin) of beasts of prey;* (12) *and would not break out from all its [sharp] edges* (13) *like a star: For here [on this torso] is no place* (14) *that does not see you. You must change your life.*

The sonnet does not describe the "Archaic Torso of Apollo." It states its impact upon the beholder: an immediate confrontation, almost a collision, with a work of art that defies even mutilation. The interplay of internal and end rimes (6-7) beautifully reflects the characteristic turn of the body: *blenden—Drehen—Lenden—gehen* ("blind—twist—loins—go") as the line gracefully breaks between substantive and attribute (*Drehen | der Lenden*).

Head and limbs have been broken off, but the stone's vitality, controlled and firmly contained where the sculptor's hand shaped it, "erupts" at the rough broken surfaces "like a star." The lost eyes' gaze is all-present in the marble: every spot you look at looks at *you.* Confronted with such overwhelming beauty, such power over time and destruction, only one attitude is possible, and the last line proclaims it: You must become essential like this stone; nothing less will do.   [G.S.]

[BLUMENMUSKEL, DER DER ANEMONE]

Blumenmuskel, der der Anemone
Wiesenmorgen nach und nach erschließt,
bis in ihren Schooß das polyphone
Licht der lauten Himmel sich ergießt,   4

in den stillen Blütenstern gespannter
Muskel des unendlichen Empfangs,
manchmal s o von Fülle übermannter,
daß der Ruhewink des Untergangs   8

kaum vermag die weitzurückgeschnellten
Blätterränder dir zurückzugeben:
du, Entschluß und Kraft von w i e v i e l Welten!

Wir, Gewaltsamen, wir währen länger.   12
Aber w a n n, in welchem aller Leben,
sind wir endlich offen und Empfänger?

(*Die Sonette an Orpheus.* 1923)

The anemone flings out its petals to the rising sun. The muscle in the calyx moves them in tune with signals from another world:

(1-2) *Flower-muscle, which little by little opens (unlocks, releases) the anemone's meadow-morning,* (3) *until into her lap the polyphonic* (4) *light of the loud heavens (sky) pours down,* —(6) *muscle of infinite receiving,* (5) *braced in the still star-blossom,* (7) *at times so overcome by fullness* (8) *that the restward call of the sunset* (9–10) *can barely return to you the far-outflung petal-edges:* (11) *you, decision and strength (power) of how many worlds!* (12) *We, the violent, we last longer.* (13) *But when, in which of all our lives,* (14) *are we (will we be) at last open and receivers?*

The first eleven lines are an apostrophe, almost a hymn, to the anemone's hidden muscle through which the world above transmits its command to the still blossom below. The light of the "loud" (jubilant) skies is "polyphonic"; one recalls the great opening scene in Goethe's *Faust II*, where the sleeping woods and fields also awaken to the "meadow-morning" as they "hear" the tumultuous rise of the Sun (the thundering horses of Helios). The anemone yields utterly to the cosmic impact, so overwhelmed that at "the restward call of evening" (J. B. Leishman's beautiful translation) it barely succeeds in regaining control over itself. "We, the violent" are more durable; we can and do impose our will upon nature and creature. But when, in which of the transformations that man may yet undergo, will we be at peace and in tune with the created worlds? Rilke's own poetry gives an unexpected answer to this question; for, unlike his great counterpart, Stefan George, who is a poet of will, and forceful to the point of violence, Rilke is "open and a receiver"—as this very *Blumenmuskel* sonnet reveals.   [G.S.]

[SPIEGEL: NOCH NIE HAT MAN WISSEND BESCHRIEBEN]

Spiegel: noch nie hat man wissend beschrieben,
was ihr in euerem Wesen seid.
Ihr, wie mit lauter Löchern von Sieben
erfüllten Zwischenräume der Zeit.   4

Ihr, noch des leeren Saales Verschwender —,
wenn es dämmert, wie Wälder weit...
Und der Lüster geht wie ein Sechzehn-Ender
durch eure Unbetretbarkeit.   8

Manchmal seid ihr voll Malerei.
Einige scheinen i n euch gegangen —,
andere schicktet ihr scheu vorbei.

Aber die Schönste wird bleiben —, bis   12
drüben in ihre enthaltenen Wangen
eindrang der klare gelöste Narziß.

(*Die Sonette an Orpheus.* 1923)

The third poem in the second part of Rilke's *Sonnets to Orpheus* offers to define, not mirrors, but the "essence" of them:

(1) *Mirrors: Never yet has anyone knowingly described* (2) *what you in your essence are.* (3-4) *You, interstices of time, all filled as with holes of sieves.* (5) *You, squanderers even of the empty hall—,* (6) *when dusk falls, wide as woods (wide as woods when twilight broods)* . . . (7) *And the candelabrum (chandelier) goes like a sixteen-pointer* (8) *through your unenterability.*

(9) *Sometimes you are full of images* [literally *of painting*]. (10) *Some [persons] seem (to have) gone into you—,* (11) *others you shyly sent past.* (12) *But the fairest one will stay until* (13) *over there [in the mirror] into her abstaining cheeks* (14) *[there] has penetrated the clear, dissolved (limpid) Narcissus.*

What are mirrors? The key word is in line 8: *Unbetretbarkeit* ("unenterability").

Mirrors are full of familiar things to which they give no access. They have space in abundance: they "squander" it (like the space of the empty hall) even when there is nobody to see the image. But this is not the same as experienced, enterable space. The mirror-space is non-space; it is to space as the holes are to the solid parts of the sieve.

This empty, unenterable space wholly fills the "interstices of time." As we look in the mirror, time stands still. We are no longer acting in the palpable unity of time-space. We are observing: we divide ourselves into the actor and the observer who watches his hand (is it *his* hand?) move in the unenterable space before him. As actors we produce change, consequences; only in our awareness of change are we "in time." Mirror images leave no tracks. They move in timeless stillness.

Mirrors, like sieves, discriminate. They

take into their stillness the pictorial, poetic qualities of things: the abundance of the empty hall, widening into the boundlessness of woods that stretch away and lose themselves in the dusk; the candelabrum proudly carrying its stag's crown. —

How do we see ourselves? We see our body, our limbs, but we cannot see that which makes up our individuality: our face, our eyes, our expression. Looking into a mirror for the first time, we see what we never saw before, and we begin to know what we look like. (Only the blind man knows, by the same process by which he knows what other people look like. The seeing man sees others but is blind to himself.)

When we look in the mirror we see what we look like, but we do not see ourselves. We see a stranger. Narcissus does not love himself: he loves that stranger in the unenterable mirror-space. The "fairest one" will remain before the mirror, gazing at the beauty it reflects (hers, that went into it), until Narcissus, limpid and free, passes "over yonder" into the glass and makes her mirrored image seem to come alive. Looking in the mirror is giving and receiving and giving again. Angels, says Rilke in his "Second Elegy," are "Mirrors: drawing the Angel's out-pouring beauty back into his own face."

The distance between "Herbsttag" and this sonnet marks the span of Rilke's development. His growth was astoundingly rapid. The "late" Rilke is the Rilke of the Sonnets to Orpheus and the Duino Elegies, both published in 1923; but the first of the elegies was written in 1912, at the age of only thirty-seven. At that time Rilke was already popular, beloved, and famous (the critics, though, "discovered" him much later). There is sometimes a cloying, almost embarrassingly naked sentiment in the works that first established him, in the Book of Hours, the Stories of God, The Song of the Love and Death of Cornet Christopher Rilke (a bittersweet virtuoso piece that has sold over a million copies). But his curve rose fast. The Notebooks of Malte Laurids Brigge, drenched with the fear of dying, mark the end of a period. The great New Poems mark the climax of another. Under the impact of Rodin's art and attitude towards art, Rilke had become the language-sculptor who fashions "the things" in all their truth; nothing must be applied or brought to them: it is all in them, in their detail, their hidden dimensions. This is the Rilke who taught us to "see" essences: The Dog, The Leprose King, Blue Hydrangea, Lady Before the Mirror, The Beggar, Unicorn, Buddha. In the essences he "saw," there was always Death, not the personal death that horrifies Malte, but Death at the root, behind, and in the very constitution of "the things." The "late" Rilke rose to his ultimate insight into the condition of true poetry: the poet is Orpheus, descended to the dead, eating with them of their food, to return transformed and "knowing" so that he may "render the unending praise." This is what the Sonnets to Orpheus say. The Mirror Sonnet begins: "Mirrors: no one yet has knowingly described your essence"; it is an "Orphic" song of knowledge and praise.   [G.S.]

RAINER MARIA RILKE

DIE ERSTE ELEGIE

Wer, wenn ich schriee, hörte mich denn aus der Engel
Ordnungen? und gesetzt selbst, es nähme
einer mich plötzlich ans Herz: ich verginge von seinem
stärkeren Dasein. Denn das Schöne ist nichts   4
als des Schrecklichen Anfang, den wir noch grade ertragen,
und wir bewundern es so, weil es gelassen verschmäht,
uns zu zerstören. Ein jeder Engel ist schrecklich.
Und so verhalt ich mich denn und verschlucke den Lockruf   8
dunkelen Schluchzens. Ach, wen vermögen
wir denn zu brauchen? Engel nicht, Menschen nicht,
und die findigen Tiere merken es schon,
daß wir nicht sehr verläßlich zu Haus sind   12
in der gedeuteten Welt. Es bleibt uns vielleicht
irgendein Baum an dem Abhang, daß wir ihn täglich
wiedersähen; es bleibt uns die Straße von gestern
und das verzogene Treusein einer Gewohnheit,   16
der es bei uns gefiel, und so blieb sie und ging nicht.
O und die Nacht, die Nacht, wenn der Wind voller Weltraum
uns am Angesicht zehrt —, wem bliebe sie nicht, die ersehnte,
sanft enttäuschende, welche dem einzelnen Herzen   20
mühsam bevorsteht. Ist sie den Liebenden leichter?
Ach, sie verdecken sich nur mit einander ihr Los.
Weisst du's n o c h nicht? Wirf aus den Armen die Leere
zu den Räumen hinzu, die wir atmen; vielleicht daß die Vögel   24
die erweiterte Luft fühlen mit innigerm Flug.

Ja, die Frühlinge brauchten dich wohl. Es muteten manche
Sterne dir zu, daß du sie spürtest. Es hob
sich eine Woge heran im Vergangenen, oder   28

The first of Rilke's *Duineser Elegien*
(*Duino Elegies*) is ninety-four lines
long. We give lines 1-68 in literal transla-
tion with some explanations in square
brackets. The comment that follows the
translation offers a condensed paraphrase
of "The First Elegy" as a whole.

(1) *Who, if I screamed [in anguish] would
hear me among the angels'* (2-3) *orders? and,
suppose, even if one of them took me suddenly
to his heart [if he embraced me]:—I should
perish by his* (4) *stronger existence. For the
Beautiful is nothing* (5) *but the beginning
[the first feel] of the Terrible, which we are*

da du vorüberkamst am geöffneten Fenster,
gab eine Geige sich hin. Das alles war Auftrag.
Aber bewältigtest du's? Warst du nicht immer
noch von Erwartung zerstreut, als kündigte alles   32
eine Geliebte dir an? (Wo willst du sie bergen,
da doch die großen fremden Gedanken bei dir
aus und ein gehn und öfters bleiben bei Nacht.)
Sehnt es dich aber, so singe die Liebenden; lange   36
noch nicht unsterblich genug ist ihr berühmtes Gefühl.
Jene, du neidest sie fast, Verlassenen, die du
so viel liebender fandst als die Gestillten. Beginn
immer von neuem die nie zu erreichende Preisung;   40
denk: es erhält sich der Held, selbst der Untergang war ihm
nur ein Vorwand, zu sein: seine letzte Geburt.
Aber die Liebenden nimmt die erschöpfte Natur
in sich zurück, als wären nicht zweimal die Kräfte,   44

still just able to endure, (6) and we admire it
so because it serenely disdains (7) to destroy
us. Each and every angel is terrible.

(8) And so I curb myself and swallow down
the call-note (9) of deep-dark sobbing. Alas,
whom (10) can we use [at all, to share our
aloneness]? Not angels, not men, (11) and
even the sharp (shrewd) animals notice per-
fectly well (12) that we are not very reliably
at home (13) in the interpreted world. [We
must interpret the world to understand it, the
animals understand it instinctively.] Perhaps
there remains to us (14) some tree on the
hillside, to be daily (15) seen again; there
remains for us yesterday's street (16) and the
pampered loyalty of a habit [the capricious
loyalty of a pampered habit] (17) that liked
being with us, and so it stayed and did not go
away.

(18) Oh, and the night, the night, when the
wind full of world-space (19) feeds on our
faces—for whom would she not remain, the
longed-for, (20-21) the gently disappointing
one, which the single (lone) heart wearily
[wearisomely] has before it? Is she [night]
easier on lovers? (22) Alas, in their together-
ness they merely cover up their lot [of irremediable
separation]. (23) Don't you know it yet?
Fling out of your arms the [deceptive embrace's]
emptiness; (24) add it to the spaces we inhale;

maybe the birds (25) will feel the more
spacious air [and respond] with more heart-felt
flight.

(26) Yes, the springtimes [in years past]
did need you. (27) Some stars put it to you
to feel them (their presence). There rose up
(28) towards you a wave in [the realm of] the
past, or (29) as you went by the opened
window, (30) a violin would [caressingly]
yield. All this was an order [a task imposed
upon you]. (31) But did you master the task?
Were you not all the time (32) still expectantly
distracted, as if everything were heralding [the
coming to you of] (33) a loved one? (Where
would you keep her, (34) considering that
(the) great stranger-thoughts (35) go in and
out at your place [frequent your heart and mind]
and often stay through the night.) (36) But if
you are yearning, sing [praise] the [celebrated]
lovers; (37) their renowned feeling is far from
being immortal enough. (38) [Praise] Those
—you almost envy them—forsaken ones, whom
you (39) found so much more loving than the
quieted ones [whose love was returned.] Begin
(40) ever anew the never achievable song of
praise; (41) consider: the Hero preserves
himself—even his ruin was for him (42) just
a pretext for being: his final birth. (43) But
the lovers—exhausted nature takes them (44) back
into herself, as if she had not the strength again

dieses zu leisten. Hast du der Gaspara Stampa
denn genügend gedacht, daß irgend ein Mädchen,
dem der Geliebte entging, am gesteigerten Beispiel
dieser Liebenden fühlt: daß ich würde wie sie?   48
Sollen nicht endlich uns diese ältesten Schmerzen
fruchtbarer werden? Ist es nicht Zeit, daß wir liebend
uns vom Geliebten befrein und es bebend bestehn:
wie der Pfeil die Sehne besteht, um gesammelt im Absprung   52
m e h r zu sein als er selbst. Denn Bleiben ist nirgends.

Stimmen, Stimmen. Höre, mein Herz, wie sonst nur
Heilige hörten: daß sie der riesige Ruf
aufhob vom Boden; sie aber knieten,   56
Unmögliche, weiter und achtetens nicht:
S o waren sie hörend. Nicht daß du G o t t e s ertrügest
die Stimme, bei weitem. Aber das Wehende höre,
die ununterbrochene Nachricht, die aus Stille sich bildet.   60
Er rauscht jetzt von jenen jungen Toten zu dir.
Wo immer du eintratst, redete nicht in Kirchen
zu Rom und Neapel ruhig ihr Schicksal dich an?
Oder es trug eine Inschrift sich erhaben dir auf,   64
wie neulich die Tafel in Santa Maria Formosa.
Was sie mir wollen? leise soll ich des Unrechts
Anschein abtun, der ihrer Geister
reine Bewegung manchmal ein wenig behindert.   68

*　*　*　*

(Die Duineser Elegien. 1923)

(45-46) *to achieve this [giving the lovers a second existence, an immortal one like the Hero's]. And have you paid enough tribute to Gaspara Stampa to make some girl* (47-48) *whose lover slipped from her, feel at (in the face of) this heightened (more intense) example of a loving one: Would that I became like her?* (49) *Shall these most ancient sufferings not at long last* (50) *become more fruitful to us? Is it not time for us* (51) *to free ourselves lovingly from the beloved one, and tremblingly to endure it:* (52) *as the arrow endures the string, to be—in the concentrated leap-off—* (53) *more than itself. For staying is nowhere.*

(54) *Voices, voices. Listen, my heart, as only* (55) *saints have listened: [so intently] that the gigantic call [of God]* (56) *lifted them off the ground; but they continued kneeling,*

(57) *the impossible ones, and paid no attention to it [the miracle].* (58) *Thus [so intently] were they listeners. Not that you could endure God's* (59) *voice, far from it. But do hear the wind-like,* (60) *the uninterrupted message that is forming out of the stillness (silence).* (61) *Now it comes rustling (murmuring) to you from those young dead ones.*

(62) *Did not, wherever you entered churches at Rome and (at) Naples, their fate calmly speak to you?* (64) *Or an inscription solemnly (sublimely) imposed itself [as a trust] upon you,* (65) *as, lately, that tablet in Santa Maria Formosa.* (66-67) *What they [who died young] now want of me?—that I gently dispose of the semblance of wrong which at times a little hinders their spirits' pure motion.*

*　*　*　*

The *Duino Elegies,* Rilke's greatest work, are exceedingly difficult for anyone who comes upon them for the first time. Even the German reader must struggle with their uncommon use of common words, with their sentences that tear open to let displaced parts of speech press into the gap, with their obscure allusions and mystifying or wildly farfetched metaphors (when fully understood, they will appear wonderfully apt and illuminating). But the deepest difficulty, and the source of all others, lies in the strangeness of the experience into which they lead us. Out of them rises a unique image of life, death, and love, a world of heart-felt correspondences.

The way to the "Elegies," Rilke suggested, is not through elucidation. One must try and reach out to those "farthest feelings" (p. 142, second poem, l. 12) that are almost beyond the sayable. Their language of "lyrical totals," of "condensation and abbreviation" (Rilke's terms), is the language of new experience, and has to be learned.

The "First Elegy," simpler in design than others, asks: Where can we, alone and insecure in our fleeting existence, find support? And how can we become more than ourselves? For what we are is not enough, by far.

We cannot turn to the Angels. Who are they, those "almost deadly birds of the soul," "dawn-red ridges of all creation," "spaces of being, shields of bliss, tumults of tempestuously rapt feeling, and suddenly, singly, *Mirrors,*" as the "Second Elegy" calls them? They are the triumphant accomplishment of creation in whom "the Visible," the transient, "the things," are gloriously transformed into the greater reality and surpassing strength of "the Invisible"; while "we, where we feel, evaporate." Were the Angel to take but one step towards us, our heart would leap up to him in one lethal upbeat

("Second Elegy"). There is no refuge in the Angel (1-7).

Nor can we turn to fellow-man, for there is no such thing as fellowship. Even in the embrace of love are we utterly alone. And the animals, secure in their instinctive knowledge of the world, refuse to make common cause with us groping ones. There is pitifully little left we can turn to—perhaps some insignificant but remembered, revisited thing, some small, capricious habit, comforting because it stays and does not choose to desert us. Even the night we long for disappoints us, whether we face it alone or with the beloved one. For love does not make the lovers one; it merely covers up their separateness (8-25).

But are not we ourselves, perhaps, needed? Have we not at times been called upon in a vague, allusive, easily missed yet unmistakable way? For ". . . our task is to stamp this provisional transient earth into ourselves so deeply, so hurtfully and passionately, that its essence may be 'invisibly' resurrected in us" (Rilke—in a letter to his Polish translator). This is what those questioning calls of spring, of a melody, of a star, meant to say. But we did not listen. We were still waiting for the wrong thing, for the impossible, for a beloved one to come and end our loneliness. And so we mistook these urgings for signs heralding her advent. Yet we could not have kept her if she had come, for whenever the "great, strange thoughts" enter and stay, our heart is full, since these "great thoughts," and not love, are the task of our lives (26-35). Our yearning for love should rather make us praise *die Liebenden* ("the loving ones"), a term by which Rilke means those exceedingly rare women who so loved and who were so cruelly deserted that in their very ruin they found strength to create a memorial to their grief: Louise Labé in her sonnets (1555), the Portuguese nun Marianna Alcoforado (born 1640) in her famous letters—Rilke had translated both—and Gaspara Stampa, an Italian, who died young and heartbroken in 1554, and whose sonnets are now all but forgotten. The memory of these tragic loves must be kept alive by "praise"; for whereas the hero's ruin is but the beginning of his immortality (in Greek myth, the dying hero is transposed to the stars in "his last birth"), the great loving ones fall into oblivion as if the effort of producing such heroic strength had exhausted nature. There has not been one like them since these three died. Perhaps Gaspara's example will rouse some girl to renounce her lover, "lovingly" and of her free will, so that, beyond herself in her grief (and yet enduring it) she will become "*more* than herself," like her predecessors and the heroes and the saints (26-53).

"Voices, voices"—our heart, no longer distracted, hears them if it listens with the superhuman concentration of those kneeling saints whom "God's gigantic call" bodily lifted from the ground (the mystical levitation), and who kneeled in the air and did not know it. What *we* hear is *not* God's voice—how could we endure it when even the Angel is terrible beyond our enduring? What we may hear is silence endlessly forming into "the uninterrupted message" now wafting towards us, breath-like, from the dead. It comes from those who died in childhood or youth and left us in grief. They want us to understand that there was no injustice in their dying so young. They are still not "weaned from earth," and any bitterness that galls our grief will slightly hamper "their spirits' pure motion" towards eternity (59-69).

Here our selection breaks off; we summarize the concluding two sections of the "Elegy,"—which speak of those who died early:

To them "it is strange not to inhabit the earth any longer," not to practice barely acquired habits, not to be what one was in the mother's "infinitely anxious hands," to omit even one's proper name "like a broken toy"; strange to stop wishing, to see all earthly relations "loosely fluttering in space." To those young ones, being dead is "arduous and full of catching up" so that they máy in time "feel a bit of eternity." But do not we, the living, make too strong a distinction between life and death? Angels, it is said, often do not know whether they walk among the living or the dead. The eternal current unceasingly roars through both these realms, unceasingly rushing human beings of all ages from one to the other, its voice outsounding the voice of life and the voice of death.

The last, brief section (86-95) takes us back to the "Elegy's" main theme, in a bold, inevitable curve. The early-departed may need us now, but soon they will grow away from their earthly origins. It is *we* who need *them*: we need the deep sorrow of their passing. For our "blessed progress" often springs from deepest lament, as the Greek myth of Linos may teach us. Music, it says, first penetrated a numb, silent world when the death of this "almost divine youth" so shook space that its emptiness began to swing "with that vibration which now / ravishes us, and comforts, and helps."

Rilke said that the "Elegies" and the "Sonnets to Orpheus" were "dictated" to him. The "First Elegy" was written in January 1912 at Duino Castle, near Trieste (hence the name); a voice, out of a raging storm, had given him the opening line. The "Elegies" are the work of a consciousness which passionately rejects the distinction between life and death, between a here and a beyond, between sorrow and joy. Man is transient, perishable, fleeting, like all the "visible" and earthly. But man's consciousness stands "vertically" upon this fleeting, beloved earth, capable of grasping the "visible" with such deep, hurtful passion that its essence will be "invisibly" resurrected in him.

This statement of Rilke's, quoted once before (p. 153), holds the key to the "Elegies": they "show us engaged in this work" of rescuing the "visible" from transience; for "we are these transformers of the earth; our whole existence, the flights and the plunges of our love, everything makes us capable of this task," as he says in the same statement.

It is above all the poet's task. The "Ninth Elegy" asks: "Are we perhaps *here* to say: House, Bridge, Fountain, Door, Jug . . ."? This *saying* is not description. It is an act of establishment.

We now see why in Rilke's "thing" poems (p. 149) death is both at the root and in the very structure of things. The fleetingness of "things" is both their death and their life. And this is why true song is lament (*Klage*), a song of sorrow. But just as death is an aspect of all life, so sorrow is the well-spring of joy. The "Tenth [last] Elegy" says this in a magnificent image. Lament (personified) is leading one who died in his youth through the ancient Land of Sorrowing into Deathland. As they reach the foot of the Mountains of Primordial Grief, she reverently shows him a small spring that rises there: the source of Joy. The dead one will silently go into those silent mountains. But Joy will descend down to the living and there she will become a broad, carrying river.   [G.S.]

BERTOLT BRECHT

VOM ERTRUNKENEN MÄDCHEN

Als sie ertrunken war und hinunterschwamm
Von den Bächen in die grösseren Flüsse,
Schien der Opal des Himmels sehr wundersam,
Als ob er die Leiche begütigen müsse.   4

Tang und Algen hielten sich an ihr ein,
So dass sie langsam viel schwerer ward.
Kühl die Fische schwammen an ihrem Bein,
Pflanzen und Tiere beschwerten noch ihre letzte Fahrt.   8

Und der Himmel ward abends dunkel wie Rauch
Und hielt nachts mit den Sternen das Licht in Schwebe.
Aber früh war es hell, dass es auch
Noch für sie Morgen und Abend gebe.   12

Als ihr bleicher Leib im Wasser verfaulet war,
Geschah es (sehr langsam), dass Gott sie allmählich vergass,
Erst ihr Gesicht, dann die Hände und ganz zuletzt erst ihr Haar.
Dann ward sie Aas in Flüssen mit vielem Aas.   16

(*Die Hauspostille.* 1927)

More than forty plays and operas have established Bertolt Brecht (1898-1956) as one of our century's most provocative playwrights. Countless essays have been written about his programmatic views—his "epic theatre" and its requirement of a "powerful movement in social life," which for Brecht meant Marxism; his *Lehrstücke* ("teaching pieces") and their unequivocally didactic theatricalism; his insistence upon maintaining for the spectator a cold sense of dramatic artifice. His internationally successful *Dreigroschenoper* (*Three-Penny Opera*), first produced in 1928, with music by Kurt Weill, exemplifies his method of "transfiguring" available material—it was based on John Gay's *The Beggar's Opera* (1728)—in an ironic blend of past history and present social problems.

Themes of death, decay, and drowning reappear constantly in Bertolt Brecht's poetry, especially in verses written in the nineteen-twenties, before his radical nihilism was replaced by Marxist ideology. The purportedly inexorable processes of history as set forth in dialectical materialism brought him at least a measure of philosophic assurance, for his "proletarian" folk-songs and the ballads he composed for the Loyalists in the Spanish Civil War ring with an underlying faith in human possibilities. "*Vom ertrunkenen Mädchen*" and "*Grosser Dankchoral*" (p.158), however, date from his pre-Marxist period. Each of these poems defines in its own way a different contour of the same unqualified pessimism.

(1) *When she was drowned and floated down*
(2) *From the creeks into the larger rivers,*

(3) *The opal of heaven [the sun] shone most marvelously,* (4) *As if it felt compelled to appease the corpse.* (5) *Seaweed and algae clung to her,* (6) *So that slowly she became much heavier.* (7) *Cold the fish swam on her leg,* (8) *Plants and animals burdened even her last journey.* (9) *And the sky in the evening became as dark as smoke* (10) *And at night held the light in suspension with the stars.*

(11) *But [in the] early [hours] it [the sky] was light, so that* (12) *There would still be morning and evening even for her.* (13) *When her pale body had rotted in the water,* (14) *It happened (very slowly), that God gradually forgot her,* (15) *First her face, then her hands and only at the very last her hair.* (16) *Then she became carrion in the rivers with lots of carrion.*

As a literary phenomenon, the elegy for a drowned young maiden dates back at least to classical Greek times, and since then it has reappeared frequently, with numerous though not dissimilar variations: the setting itself is enough to evoke a strong emotional response in the reader. The pathos of "About the Drowned Girl" is especially acute because the poem portrays a universe devoid of all human meaning—life and death are merely events to be chronicled with other natural events. Even the behavior of the sun (3-4) stops short of compassion or concern. Plants and animals offer nothing but encumbrances to her desolate voyage.

Brecht offers a final commentary on the emptiness of the world by bodying forth a deity that exists in a state of unmindfulness of the human race. This is not necessarily a matter of malevolence but of gradual forgetfulness. And this divine lapse of memory— from face to hands and then to hair—seems to parallel the actual physical processes of corruption, until we come to the final line of the poem and the repetition of the small, horrifying word *Aas* ("carrion").

The poet's eye moves with detached,

almost ironic nonchalance throughout the four stanzas: from heaven to earth, from day to night, from the divine being to the human. The flat, conversational tone of Brecht's verse, seemingly so devoid of both poetical devices and impassioned responses, is quietly deceptive. By being deliberately unemotional, by offering no judgment upon the scene, the poet paradoxically achieves an immense emotional force. (This "method" of detached observation is also frequently found in the plays of this writer.)

"About the Drowned Girl" unites metrical casualness with riming restrictiveness. Readers familiar with Kurt Weill's musical setting for this poem will not be surprised to learn that many lyrics in Brecht's operas and operettas have a comparable metrical looseness, where the musical— more specifically, the jazz — syncopations play against the rhythms of speech. Here the length of the lines varies from nine to fifteen syllables; there is no discernibly repetitive pattern of rising or falling, of double or triple feet. The word order is that of quite ordinary prose—there is neither assonance nor alliteration. Indeed the elegiac scene is so unexalted that the reader is likely to miss Brecht's subtle employment of poetic devices: the "opal of heaven" (3), that gazes strangely at the girl; the personification of the plants and weeds that embrace her in a loveless world; the action of God in the final stanza. God is not really present as are the objects in this world that He may have created. He merely forgets, as though He had never actually remembered.

The most evident poetic graces are reserved for the last line of the poem. *Flüssen* recalls the *Flüsse* of line 2. The flat sound of *Aas* in the middle of the line recurs at the very end, as though to hammer home the theme that all life ends in death, dissolution, and rotting. [H.E.H.]

BERTOLT BRECHT

GROSSER DANKCHORAL

Lobet die Nacht und die Finsternis, die euch umfangen!
Kommet zuhauf
Schaut in den Himmel hinauf:
Schon ist der Tag vergangen.   4

Lobet das Gras und die Tiere, die neben euch leben und sterben!
Sehet, wie ihr
Lebet das Gras und das Tier
Und es muss auch mit euch sterben.   8

Lobet den Baum, der aus Aas aufwächst jauchzend zum Himmel!
Lobet das Aas
Lobet den Baum, der es frass
Aber auch lobet den Himmel.   12

Lobet von Herzen das schlechte Gedächtnis des Himmels!
Und dass er nicht
Weiss euren Nam' noch Gesicht
Niemand weiss, dass ihr noch da seid.   16

Lobet die Kälte, die Finsternis und das Verderben!
Schauet hinan:
Es kommet nicht auf euch an
Und ihr könnt unbesorgt sterben.   20

(*Die Hauspostille.* 1927)

Brecht's *"Grosser Dankchoral"* ("Great Hymn of Thanksgiving") is a masterful example of sustained, bitter irony. The tone of the verse is Biblical, reminiscent of some of the Psalms; and the poem also reminds one of Luther's great hymns, though Brecht dissolves the Christian, Protestant world-view into nihilism. Part of the power of *"Grosser Dankchoral"* derives from its conjoining of traditional, even orthodox, form with subject matter that is revolutionary in skepticism, a method frequently employed by Brecht. During his exile under the Nazi regime, for example, he composed a series of verses to be sung to the tune of the Martin Rinckart-Johann Sebastian Bach chorale *Nun danket alle Gott, | Mit Herzen, Mund und Händen* ("Now let us all thank God, | With heart, mouth and hands"). Brecht's parody begins, *Nun danket alle Gott, | Dass Er uns Hitler sandte* ("Now let us all thank God, | That he sent us Hitler").

(1) *Praise ye the night and the darkness, that enfold you!* (2) *Come together* (3) *Gaze up to Heaven:* (4) *Already the day is gone for you.* (5) *Praise ye the grass and the beasts, that live and die beside you!* (6) *Behold, like you* (7) *Lives the grass and the beast* (8) *And it too must die with you.* (9) *Praise ye the*

tree, that grows up out of carrion exulting to Heaven! (10) *Praise ye the carrion* (11) *Praise ye the tree, that ate it [carrion; ate* scarcely catches the force of *frass* (a form of *fressen*): *fressen* is reserved for animals, the milder *essen* for people] (12) *But also praise ye Heaven.* (13) *Praise ye from your hearts the bad memory of Heaven!* (14-15) *And that it knows neither your name nor your face.* (16) *No one knows, that you are still there.* (17) *Praise ye the cold, the darkness and the corruption [of the grave]!* (18) *Lift up your eyes* [literally *Look upward*]: (19) *It [really] does not depend on you* (20) *And you can die without worrying.*

The opening stanza gives only the barest clue to what becomes the major idea in the poem: the indifference of the universe, and of God and Heaven, to the fate of mankind and, specifically, of individual man. The day is gone, and we will go (17) to darkness, cold, and decay. The theme of death soon enters, of the eventual demise of man and of all animate and inanimate nature. With the third stanza, Brecht turns to one of his favorite substantives, *Aas* ("carrion"), almost as if he found in this repellent monosyllable all that is emblematic of the miserable human condition.

Stanzas one and five repeat the exhortation to gaze upward, and the presence of four important words in each reinforces the formal unity of the hymn: *Lobet, Finsternis, kommet,* and *schaut.* The three interior quatrains progress carefully from grass through animals and trees up to heaven, as the poet's eye makes it slow ascent. The ironic shift in lines 12-13 reveals the message: man's melancholy benediction is directed toward a deity that ignores him; not with overt hostility but with something more terrible: indifference. This is the same world that Brecht portrayed in *"Vom ertrunkenen Mädchen"* (p. 156), but the condition of that young victim is now universalized to include

our own. The emotional climax of the poem is achieved through an interesting technical device. The hortatory *Lobet* ("Praise ye") opens each stanza with a long line ranging up to seventeen syllables (5), but in the third stanza *Lobet* is repeated three times, reinforcing the bitterness when the fourth command is uttered.

Man's meaningless anonymity while he is alive, his unacknowledged existence in an indifferent world, brings the poem to a conclusion of bitter consolation. We recall Rilke's reiterated theme, *der eigene Tod* ("One's own death"), in which individual death, the fruit of individual life, is opposed to modern *Massentod* ("mass-produced death"). Rilke's possible mysticism afforded an answer, albeit clothed in mystery; God's existence—now as neighbor, now as distant deity—guarantees, if only dimly, that death, like birth, is meaningful. Not so with Brecht: For him there is no meaning. There is only the comfort in the fact that man does not have to find a meaning and is not responsible for its absence. This is Housman's "I, a stranger and afraid / In a world I never made" carried to such an extreme that it becomes a vindication as well as a consolation.

But Brecht rejects even this possibility of giving the human situation true significance, and his rejection is carried by a shift in tone. The parodied liturgical language gives way to easy colloquialism, which turns what might otherwise be an exculpation of man for the evil of the world into a rebuke for his concern about it.—Don't worry about the problem of evil! Just mind your own business—which is not running the universe or passing judgment upon it, but dying. And the grim word *sterben* ("die") brings this paean of un-thanksgiving to its dismal close.

[H.E.H.]

SPANISH AND

PORTUGUESE

ROSALÍA CASTRO

[NASÍN CAND' AS PRANTAS NASEN]

Nasín cand' as prantas nasen,
No mes das froles nasín,
Nunha alborada mainiña,
Nunha alborada d'abril.   4
Por eso me chaman Rosa,
Mais á do triste sorrir,
Con espiñas para todos,
Sin ningunha para ti.   8
Dés que te quixen, ingrato,
Todo acabou para min,
Que eras ti para min todo,
Miña groria e meu vivir.   12
¿De qué, pois, te queixas, Mauro?
¿De qué, pois, te queixas, di,
Cando sabes que morrera
Por te contemplar felís?   16
Duro cravo me encravaches
Con ese teu maldesir,
Con ese teu pedir tolo
Que non sei qué quer de min,
Pois dinche canto dar puden
Avariciosa de ti.   22

O meu coraçón che mando
C'unha chave para ó abrir;
Nin eu teño máis que darche,
Nin ti máis que me pedir.   26

(*Cantares gallegos.* 1863)

Though Rosalía Castro (1837-1885) is not widely known outside her homeland, her poetry has received the highest praise. "The best written in Spain in the nineteenth century," says Salvador de Madariaga. And Gerald Brenan is even convinced that if she had written in Castilian instead of the dialect of her native Galicia, she would be recognized as "the greatest woman poet of modern times."

Rosalía Castro did not give titles to her poems. The first one here—"I Was Born When the Plants Are Born"—opens in a tone of childlike sweetness as Rosa, who is speaking, is identified with an April world of gentleness and beauty. (1) *I was born when the plants are born,* (2) *in the month of* flowers I was born, (3) on a dawn soft and gentle, (4) on an April dawn. (Maina—"soft" or "gentle"—is caressed by the affectionate diminutive -iña, which Rosalía Castro was fond of using.) The relation between the girl and her vernal world is more explicit in (5) That's why they call me Rosa—and immediately a sadder note is heard: (6) but she of the mournful smile. It becomes clear that Rosa has reason for grief, but since the mournful smile is mentioned before we know why, it would seem to evidence some characteristic melancholy. (7) I'm a thorny Rose for others, (8) not a single thorn for you.

Her love for Mauro is first revealed through an image in harmony with what has gone before—a love the more precious since she is a girl others find aloof or unresponsive. (9) When I came to love you—ungrateful you!— (10) all was over for me; (11) you became my all in all, (12) my bliss [glory] and my existence. In these lines expression through imagery is abandoned before the frankness and urgency of her feelings, impatient of artifice. The poem returns to metaphor only passingly, in one colloquial line (17) and in the concluding lyric. Instead, we have an almost painfully realistic account of the source of the lovers' discord. It is largely this candor that protects the floral opening from a charge of softness, just as it is the memory of that April sweetness, and the final quatrain, that save the central part of the poem from harshness.

(13) Of what, then, are you complaining, Mauro?—and, with pleading insistence, (14) Of what, then, are you complaining, tell me, (15) when you know that I would die (16) just to see you happy? (17) It's a sharp knife you drive into me [literally: a harsh nail: nail can mean "sorrow" in Spanish, but the idiom does not carry over well into English] (18) with this bitter tongue of yours [maldesir implies slander and suggests that Mauro is talking cruelly of her to others] (19) and with this insane demanding (20) for I don't know what you want, (21) since I gave you all I could give, (22) thirsting, hungering [literally: covetous] for you. All this is painful and unromantically mean—like a problem for an Advice to the Lovelorn column. The man does not cut a good figure; the girl is at her wits' end, her tone close to exasperation. But even so her love is no less constant; she hardly complains of the lover, even to him, though it seems that he complains, and publicly, of her. Perhaps she feels some abasement in admitting that she was "greedy" for him: upon this admission a silence follows.

But then she bursts sweetly and passionately into song. The italics of the fiñal quatrain set it apart in tone from the rest of the poem, make it like one of the little love-songs that have flourished in Galicia and all Spain for centuries. (23) My heart I send you (24) with a key to open it; (25) I have nothing more to give you, (26) nor you any more to ask. Lines that with their valentine imagery of heart and key return to the tone of the beginning. But the little love-song has accumulated an emphasis and content from the intervening lines that it would never carry in itself. A rare combination of romance and grating realism, the poem is about more than a series of quarrels between lovers. Without specifying its wider theme, we can see it related to aspects of a human cycle that could be described (in one of many ways) as innocence, disenchantment, and recovery.

[The pronunciation of her poems is generally as in Spanish. But x is pronounced sh (quixen, for example, is kée-shen); and nh is a nasal ng as in sung or gong (unha is oong-a; not oon-ga).] [J.F.N.]

[NEGRA SOMBRA]

Cando penso que te fuche,
Negra sombra que me asombras,
Ao pê dos meus cabezales
Tornas facéndome mofa.   4

Cando maxino que ês ida
No mesmo sol te me amostras,
I-eres a estrela que brila,
I-eres o vento que zoa.   8

Si cantan, ês ti que cantas;
Si choran, ês ti que choras,
I-ês o marmurio d'o río,
I-ês a noite i-ês a aurora.   12

En todo estás e ti ês todo,
Pra min i-en min mesma moras;
Nin me abandonarás nunca,
Sombra que sempre me asombras.   16

(*Follas novas.* 1880)

Expressed long before in medieval poetry, the Galician mood of *morriña* —the passionate dark longing for something loved and absent—found its most eloquent voice in Rosalía Castro. "Black Gloom" ("*Negra sombra*"), as this poem might be called—the verses were originally untitled—has no sharply focused visual imagery; sound and rhythm constitute its physical being and have most claim on our attention. The black shadow, or gloom, of inescapable melancholy clings to the very words—*negra sombra*—with their identical length and accent—an effect found also in the first two words of the poem. Galicians have been heard to say that their word for shadow is not *sombra* but *soma*, in which case Rosalía Castro, in choosing the darker and weightier word, is more poet than philologist.

(1) *When I think that you have gone,* (2) *black gloom that over-glooms me,* (3) *at my bedside* (4) *you return to deride me.* This phrasing of course loses the poetry, which lies in the richness and appropriateness of the sound and the rhythm of the palpitating eight-syllable lines with their varying stresses: in the first two lines starkly on the first, third, and seventh syllables; almost undefined in the shuffling third line; a bit off-beat in the mocking fourth, with stresses on the first, *fourth*, and seventh syllable—a mockery sharpened by the repetition, in *mofa*, of sounds heard just before. Rhythm and position of *Cando penso* and *negra sombra* may relate

the two: thinking also is a kind of gloom. And *asombras*, which here means "fill with gloom," is the more menacing because of its commoner meaning of "frighten" or "amaze."

(5) *When I imagine that you have gone* (6) *in the very sunlight you appear to me*, (7) *and you are the star that shines*, (8) *and you are the wind that sighs.* The *think* of line 1 has become the more forced *imagine*, and the apparition of the *sombra* in full sunlight is more disconcerting than in the dark bedroom. *Sol* bears the strongest accent in its line, pregnant with incredulity and dismay. Noticeable too is the little echo of sound (*rela, rila*) in *estrela* and *brila* (7), as the presence of the shadow spreads from the sun to another kind of light and then into the moving atmosphere itself, the air of life—to invade, in the following stanza, very different spheres of nature and human activity.

(9) *If they sing, it is you that sing;* (10) *if they weep, it is you that weep;* (11) *and you are the murmuring of the river,* (12) *and you are the night and you are the dawn.* The two *y*'s ("and's") begin lines in this stanza exactly as in the preceding one, followed by a final weary *and* in the middle of line 12.

The fourth stanza makes a universal presence of a sorrow so widely detected. (13) *You are in everything and you are everything. Estás* and *és* (*eres*) are forms of *estar* and *ser*, the two verbs rendered in English by *to be*; the first indicates location or accidental quality, the second existence—so here the meaning deepens. (14) *For*

me and in my (very) self you live—the sorrow is taken so to heart by the poet that it seems as if all sorrow had made her its victim and were rooted deep within her. The meaning is dramatized not only by the repetition of sound but by the nature of the sound repeated: humming nasals deep within the resonant chambers of the head (Plato in the *Cratylus* called *n* an "internal sound"—appropriate in such words as ἔνδον, *inside*) deep in our physical being, so that the line can be read between closed teeth. It is not fanciful that the deep *m*'s and *n*'s are expressive in a statement about the *sombra* as felt within, whereas the more external clipped *t*'s of the line above, with its two elided syllables, are adequate for a statement. The same sounds recur relentlessly in the last two lines: (15) *and you will abandon me never,* (16) *gloom that always over-glooms me.*

In the last of these, which looks into an endless future, sound and rhythm are particularly significant, with the three violent stresses on words so similar, so that the double gloom, gloom as fact and agent, are identified with foreverness—the very form of the line involves us in that clinging presence. The last word—for the movement of invasive gloom—is stronger, since it is the final assonance in the series of *o-a* (e.g., *mofa*) in the even-numbered lines throughout. The poem is without verbal extravagances: not one unusual word, not one inversion. In an age when so many poets were declaiming, Rosalía Castro (like Sappho) dared to use natural speech. [J.F.N.]

EN UN CEMENTERIO DE LUGAR CASTELLANO

Miguel de Unamuno (1864-1936) was already a famous author and public figure when he published his first book of poems, *Poesías*, 1907. Professor of Greek at Salamanca (Spain's oldest university) since 1891, and its Rector since 1901, Unamuno had become the leader of his own intellectual generation: *el campeador* Unamuno, as the young Ortega y Gasset called him (Unamuno "the champion," in the traditional meaning of this term, as applied, for instance, to the Cid). His leadership was due, first of all, to his prodigious activity. Salamanca, a marginal university since the founding of the Central University at Madrid in the 1820's, was transformed by Unamuno's presence and action into a place of intellectual pilgrimage. Many a young Spanish philosopher or writer would go to there to meet Unamuno, to listen to his constant monologuing on eternal human problems. But one did not have to take the train for Salamanca to hear Unamuno's voice. It was becoming increasingly familiar in the provincial daily newspapers, and not only in Peninsular Spain: it was reaching also into the Spanish-speaking lands beyond the sea, and many Latin-American intellectuals would be drawn to Salamanca while visiting Spain.

In the Spanish-speaking world of the twentieth century, Unamuno was, in a sense, a man-center of culture, like Voltaire in the eighteenth, or Goethe in the early nineteenth. His influence was, of course, the result of his ideological action, of his insistence upon speaking as a Man, not only as a Spaniard. His approach to Spanish problems—indeed, his own political activity—was based on a new transcendentalism: *el hombre es lo que hemos de buscar en nuestra alma* ("Man is what we must look for in our soul"). Unamuno wanted Spaniards to stop considering themselves as picturesque and peculiar individuals, as members of an "odd" human community; and their first gesture of liberation from their intellectual localism must be, he said, *lanzarse de la patria chica a la humanidad* ("to jump from one's own birthplace into mankind"). That is why Unamuno's voice seemed at first so abstract and remote to many Spaniards, and even foreign; indeed, one famous historian (a man fairly representative of Spanish intellectual life of the 1890's) spoke of Unamuno's ignorance of the Castilian language!

This apparent remoteness of ideas and style was also, in part, a result of Unamuno's religious orientation, of his emphasis on spiritual problems completely alien to his Spanish fellow-writers. Let us remember that he belonged to a deeply anti-clerical generation, to the first group of Spanish writers whose sensitivity was avowedly non-religious. His manner of dress—he spurned ties and the conventional shirt, and wore a black vest that made him look like a Protestant minister —reflected accurately his originality within his Spain: he was the rare and almost foreign voice that spoke in the name of Man. But soon all of Spain and all of Latin America got accustomed to that powerful voice, to that splendid sermonizing; and when Unamuno died in 1936 many felt, with Ortega y Gasset, that his death left the Hispanic countries in a sad silence, the silence that marks the absence of a transcendental voice. But his mission had been accomplished. As he said of another European author, *ha cambiado más almas que pueda cambiar la mayor batalla* ("[he] has changed more souls than any great battle could possibly change"). No Spanish-speaking writer coming after him could avoid the impact of his soul-searching, of his view of literature as a transcendental activity: *la literatura no es una especialidad* ("literature is not a specialist's occupation"), that is, literature must at all times be concerned with the whole of man.

Unamuno had begun late to write poems—*apenas escribí versos hasta pasar de los treinta años*, he remarked in a letter written in 1906 ("I hardly wrote verses before my thirties")—and he called them *versos de otoño*, "autumn verses." In a sense this was a historically accurate definition of his poetry and its impact on the literary life of Spain of the years before World War I. Unamuno's themes and metrics, his rhythm and vocabulary, seemed utterly behind the times. Of course he was more than merely aware of the oddity of his poetry: he contrasted disdainfully his own *eternismo* ("eternalness") with the *modernista* school. Spanish poetry was dominated at that time by the founder of *modernismo*, the Central American Rubén Darío, and his followers. Their literary influence, especially in the first decade of the century, rested on their opposition to the prosaic tendencies of the 1880's and on their rhetorical enthusiasm, their exaltation of all concrete forms, verbal and other (thus, Darío proclaimed that *la mejor musa es la de carne y hueso*—"the best Muse is flesh and bone"). Darío considered Unamuno a true poetical creator—and it should be noted that Unamuno influenced Darío's last poems—even before 1907. But Unamuno's entrance into Spanish poetry was not unanimously welcomed; and he was right in claiming that his obsessive meditation upon man's fate gave his poetry its rather shocking "quaintness." Unamuno's younger fellow-poets were equally right in placing him outside their own chosen lineage, namely French Symbolism: a fact not denied by Unamuno, for he stated, in his 1907 *Credo poético*, "poetry is something that is not music . . . your work is like the sculptor's" (*algo que no es música es la poesía . . . de escultor es tu tarea*). And truly his verses are not music, at least not Symbolist music, since they are somehow rigid and have a certain monotony of rhythm and rime—"a sort of spoken song, of prayer, is verse," as he put it: *una especie de canto hablado, de rezo, es el verso*.

His characteristic fusion of Parnassian stonework with religious chant has another "autumnal" significance, autobiographical rather than historical. The writing of verse gave Unamuno a momentary peace and a sense of durable achievement. For Unamuno, prose was always the imperative but nevertheless dissolving release of the self. Poetry, on the contrary, gave permanence to the temporal forms of the self: *Aquí quedáis mis momentos;—con el ritmo aquí os fijé* ("Here, my moments you remain;—I fixed you here with rhythm"); *el hueso del universo sobre compás se sustenta* ("on rhythm the bone of the universe rests"). It is not surprising, therefore, to see Unamuno the poet seeking constantly for the places and the landscapes where that *compás* ("rhythm") is manifest: *los paisajes son apaciguadores* ("landscapes are peace-giving").

"*En un cementerio de lugar castellano*" ("In a Castilian Village Cemetery") is Unamuno's most famous single poem. It was written in 1913, after a visit to the ruined and abandoned graveyard near Arévalo Castle, and contributed to *David*, a literary review planned by Díez-Canedo and Salinas; but the magazine did not materialize, and the poem remained unpublished until 1922, when it appeared

Corral de muertos, entre pobres tapias,
hechas también de barro,
pobre corral donde la hoz no siega,
sólo una cruz en el desierto campo
señala tu destino.   5

Junto a esas tapias buscan el amparo
del hostigo del cierzo las ovejas
al pasar trashumantes en rebaño,
y en ellas rompen de la vana historia,
como las olas, los rumores vanos.   10

Como un islote en junio
te ciñe el mar dorado
de las espigas que a la brisa ondean,
y canta sobre ti la alondra el canto
de la cosecha.   15

Cuando baja en la lluvia el cielo al campo,
baja también sobre la santa hierba
donde la hoz no corta,
de tu rincón ¡pobre corral de muertos!,
y sienten en sus huesos el reclamo
del riego de la vida.   21

Salvan tus cercas de mampuesto y barro
las aladas semillas,
o te las llevan con piedad los pájaros,
y crecen escondidas amapolas,
clavelinas, magarzas, brezos, cardos,
entre arrumbadas cruces,
no más que de las aves libre pasto.   28

Cavan tan sólo en tu maleza brava,
corral sagrado,
para de un alma que sufrió en el mundo
sembrar el grano;
luego, sobre esa siembra,
¡barbecho largo!   34

in the verse epilogue of *Andanzas y vi-siones españolas* (*Spanish Walks and Visions*). At once it became a favorite with many readers: there they found the clearest voice of Unamuno the poet, the quiet music of his Castilian meditations. In *"En un cementerio de lugar castellano"* the stone-like wording of other Unamunian poems lost its odd appearance: it was still the Unamunian poetical language, but the vigor of the images was fused with a feeling of serene surrender, of *la dulce y santa calma* ("the sweet and holy quietness") that he had looked for in his *andanzas*. Unamuno's poem became, in a way, the Spanish counterpart to Paul Valéry's "*Le cimetière marin*" (see pp. 76 ff.): its stark lines and themes contrasted with the artistic and intellectual complexity of the French poem. There is also the contrast between the two cemeteries—at Arévalo and at Sète. The Spaniard's choice of an abandoned graveyard—in his description of the walls "poor" (*pobres*) suggests their half-ruined condition—is very revealing: Unamuno felt there, more than in any other place (much more, of course, than in a well-kept cemetery), the presence of God's receiving hand, the refuge and repose of embattled man. Similarly, in his poem "*En la mano de Dios*" ("In God's Hand") he tells God that at death man's heart *duerme al sol en tu mano poderosa* ("sleeps under the sun in your powerful hand") *libre de la losa del pensamiento* ("free from the gravestone of thought"). In Unamuno's Castilian graveyard the very fact of its ruined condition makes it a symbol of the peaceful sleep offered by God to man.

The poem has sixty lines; it combines the three metrical units that Unamuno used most frequently (lines of eleven, seven, and five syllables). The even lines end with an assonance in *a-o* (*barro, campo, amparo, rebaño, vanos, dorado, canto, reclamo, cardos*). The two main themes—the impenetrable solitude of the dead and the counting of the sheep by the Sovereign Shepherd—are not allotted the same number of stanzas. Unamuno has written many pages on the second theme, the need that God has of men, in his essays and even in his fiction (the novel *Niebla* [*Mist*] plays with the parallel character-author, man-God, and their mutual dependence). In particular, his famous and controversial book *The Tragic Sense of Life* (1913) portrays God as a suffering and doubting being, always trying to assert His own reality; the creation of man is God's effort toward His own completion. In the poem "*Aldebarán*" (1908) Unamuno asks the star: *¿Eres un ojo del Señor en vela . . . escudriñando las tinieblas y contando los mundos de su rebaño?* ("Are you an eye of God in his vigil . . . prying into the darkness and counting the worlds of his herd?"). Rainer Maria Rilke writes on a similar theme, in the two poems presented on pages 142-143 of this collection.

The first theme occupies the first seven stanzas:

(1)*Corral of the dead, between poor walls,* (2) *also made of clay,* (3) *poor corral where the scythe does not reap,* (4) *only a cross, in the deserted fields,* (5) *marks your fate [fated place in the nature of things].*

(6-7) *Near these walls the sheep* ["las ovejas," 7] *seek shelter / from the lash of the north wind* (8) *as they go by in their nomadic flock;* (9-10) *and there [on these walls] break, like waves, the worthless rumors of history.*

(11) *Like a jutting rock in June* (12) *you are surrounded by the golden sea* (13) *of spikes waving in the breeze,* (14) *and above you the lark sings the song* (15) *of harvest.*

(16) *When heaven falls in rain upon the fields* (17) *it falls also upon the blessed grass* (18) *where the scythe does not cut,* (19) *[the blessed grass] of your corner, poor corral of the dead!* (20) *And they [the dead] feel in their bones the lure* (21) *of life's watering.*

(22) *Over your walls of rubblework and clay pass* (23) *the winged seeds,* (24) *or they are brought to you mercifully by the birds;* (25) *and there grow hidden poppies,* (26) *pinks, camomile, heather, thistles,* (27) *among the discarded crosses,* (28) *to be the birds' free pasture.*

(29) *They dig only in your fierce thicket,* (30) *blessed corral,* (31) *when a soul that suffered in the world* (32) *is sown as grain;* (33) *then, on this sown field,* (34) *[there is a long period of] a lasting fallow.*

Cerca de ti el camino de los vivos,
no como tú, con tapias, no cercado,
por donde van y vienen,
ya riendo o llorando,
¡rompiendo con sus risas o sus lloros
el silencio inmortal de tu cercado!   40

Después que lento el sol tomó ya tierra,
y sube al cielo el páramo
a la hora del recuerdo,
al toque de oraciones y descanso,
la tosca cruz de piedra
de tus tapias de barro
queda, como un guardián que nunca duerme,
de la campiña el sueño vigilando.   48

No hay cruz sobre la iglesia de los vivos,
en torno de la cual duerme el poblado;
la cruz, cual perro fiel, ampara el sueño
de los muertos al cielo acorralados.
¡Y desde el cielo de la noche, Cristo,
el Pastor Soberano,
con infinitos ojos centelleantes
recuenta las ovejas del rebaño!   56

Pobre corral de muertos entre tapias
hechas del mismo barro,
sólo una cruz distingue tu destino
en la desierta soledad del campo!   60

(Andanzas y visiones españolas. 1922)

---

(35) *Close to you, [runs, is] the path (road)
of the living,* (36) *but not like you and (with)
your walls, not enclosed;* (37) *and along it
they come and go,* (38) *laughing at times or
weeping,* (39) *breaking with their laughter or
their tears* (40) *the immortal silence of your
enclosure.*

The last two lines and 9-10 epitomize
Unamuno's theme in the first part of the
poem: the fragile wall of the cemetery,
made of the same poor clay as the clay
of the dead, though impinged upon by
the voices of the living, stands as the
immutable reality of the dead. In "*Alde-
barán*" Unamuno ends his anxious ques-
tioning of a distant star by concluding *de
eternidad es tu silencio prenda* ("of eternity is
your silence a token"). The Arévalo
cemetery is surrounded by life itself—and
Unamuno emphasizes the diverse and
repeated visits of the living to the dead's
domain—, but like the star Aldebaran it
never gives its secret away, it keeps a
perennial and reassuring silence.

The sheep, stopping near the cemetery
in their annual southward pilgrimage, are
like lark and rain, like men and flying
seeds, signs of life's rhythmical movement

—and even of the flow of history, if the reader recalls Unamuno's frequent, almost obsessive allusions to the struggle between sheepherders and peasants in Castilian country. But "history" and "noise" are exact synonyms in Unamuno's language, and "sheep" are usually the equivalent of *los hombres que no meten ruido* ("men who do not make noise"), men outside history. Moreover, the Arévalo cemetery, with its grazing sheep, gave Unamuno, in the excursion mentioned above, the initial main image of the poem: the graveyard as corral of the dead.

The sheep will also be a linking-image with the second part of the poem: (41) *After the sun has slowly landed* (42) *and the barren plain climbs to heaven (the sky)* (43) *at the hour of remembrance,* (44) *at the toll (bell) of prayers and rest,* (45) *the crude (rough) stone cross* (46) *of your walls of clay* (47) *stands as a guardian that never sleeps,* (48) *vigilant (watching) over the sleep of the countryside.*

(49) *There is no cross on the church of the living* (50) *around which the village sleeps;* (51) *the cross, like a faithful dog, protects the sleep* (52) *of the dead, corralled in heaven.* (53) *And from the heaven of night (night sky), Christ,* (54) *the Sovereign Shepherd,* (55) *with numberless twinkling eyes* (56) *counts the sheep of the flock.*

(57) *Poor corral of the dead between (within) walls* (58) *made of the same clay,* (59) *only*

a cross marks your fate (60) *in the lonely solitude of the fields.*

The poet, as was indicated before, uses a constant symbol: the divine eye regarding —and always counting!—His creatures. Unamuno's God needs men in order to be sure of His own existence, and it might be said that in the night of His heaven He is as anxious as are the eyes who seek Him from earth. That is why the ending of line 52 is so strikingly Unamunian. Let us consider very briefly the verb itself, *acorralar*, keeping in mind Unamuno's subtle use of Spanish. *Acorralar* is, of course, as in English, "to confine"; and also, as in colloquial American, "to capture," "to get." But it means in addition, particularly when referring to disputes or debates, "to silence one's opponent." And, finally, the word *corral* signifies, in maritime vocabulary, (*a*) a fence used by fishermen to enclose their catch, and (*b*) a small sea-wall where waves break. "Corralled into heaven" acquires, thus, a multiplicity of connected Unamunian meanings: the dead are confined (and, obviously, protected) by God, but their coming to the corral was not voluntary. And their "immortal silence" marks the end of all questioning debates for them. Just in the same way, the waves of history and of harvest break uselessly on the walls of the corral of the dead.   [J.M.]

ANTONIO MACHADO

[YO VOY SOÑANDO CAMINOS]

Yo voy soñando caminos
de la tarde. ¡Las colinas
doradas, los verdes pinos,
las polvorientas encinas! ...   4
¿A dónde el camino irá?
Yo voy cantando, viajero
a lo largo del sendero...
— La tarde cayendo está —.   8
« En el corazón tenía
la espina de una pasión;
logré arrancármela un día:
ya no siento el corazón. »   12

Y todo el campo un momento
se queda, mudo y sombrío,
meditando. Suena el viento
en los álamos del río.   16

La tarde más se obscurece;
y el camino que serpea
y débilmente blanquea,
se enturbia y desaparece.   20

Mi cantar vuelve a plañir:
« Aguda espina dorada,
quién te pudiera· sentir
en el corazón clavada ».   24

(*Soledades.* 1903)

B efore discussing this poem, it may be useful to say a word about the theoretical views of the author, whom many regard as one of the greatest Spanish poets of our time (Antonio Machado was born in Seville, 1875, and died in Collioure, France, 1939). On one occasion he said that for him "the poetic element" was not "the word for its phonic value, nor color, nor line, nor a complex of sensations, but a deep palpitation of the spirit." On another occasion he defined poetry as "the essential word in time," and again as "the dialogue of a man with his time." If we add one more element of prime importance in his poetic theory, intuition, we can attempt a definition of the poet as Machado would have him: a man whose inner being is in contact with the world of his time, deriving inspiration from the deepest experience of life, and who *intuitively* rises above his temporality by means of the word; that is, by means of the verbal expression he gives to his spiritual experience.

Turning now to our poem, we observe, first, that it has no title, which is true of a very considerable number of Machado's poetic compositions. In the life of every sensitive person there is much spiritual experience ("palpitation of the spirit") which cannot be given a name or a title. The present poem, and some that follow, deals with such an experience.

The opening lines set the time of the action, late afternoon, a favorite hour with Machado, who was a great walker and regularly chose this time for strolling along the solitary country roads: (1) *I go dreaming roads [roadways]* (2) *of the afternoon. The hills* (3) *golden, the green pines,* (4) *the dusty oaks* . . . The next line suggests the mystery that life held for him: what is its purpose? to what end do we live? The word "road" is symbolic of life: (5) *Where does the road go [lead to]?* Having asked this question, omnipresent with him, the poet tells us that he is a traveler along this road: (6) *I go singing, [a] traveler* (7) *along the way [road]* . . . Machado was the poet of the late afternoon, of the twilight hours, which for him symbolized the autumn of life. The line that follows is not only a parenthesis to point up this moment of the day; the poet tells us, too, that as a traveler along the road of life he has nearly reached its end: (8) *—The evening is falling [it grows late]—*. And now comes his song, announced two lines earlier: (9) *"In my heart I had* (10) *the thorn [pain] of a passion,* (11) *I succeeded in pulling it out one day:* (12) *[Now] I no longer feel my heart."*

The tearing out of a thorn ought to mean escape or release from pain. But is this a song of joy or regret? We do not know yet, for the poet says only that his heart is left without feeling. And even nature seems to pause to ponder this question: (13) *And all the countryside [for]* (14) *a moment* (15) *remains [stands], quiet and somber,* (15) *meditating. The wind sounds* (16) *in the poplars of [by] the river.* (17) *The evening grows darker;* (18) *and the road that winds* (19) *and feebly shows white,* (20) *grows dim and disappears.* It is in this moment of melancholy beauty, this symbolic setting of nightfall, when light changes to darkness—and life passes to that which is beyond—that the poet's song breaks forth again. And now we learn that it is not one of joy, but of bitterness, the mournful plaint of one who has forever lost something that once gave meaning to life: (21) *My song returns to moan:* (22) *"[Oh] sharp, golden thorn,* (23) *would that I might feel you* (24) *thrust [fixed] in my heart [again]."*

Some commentators have thought that the poet strolls this late-afternoon road dreaming of some lost love that has left his heart senseless and dead. It may be so; but the "thorn of a passion" may well stand for other sorrows in the poet's life —the loss of faith in the accepted beliefs of mankind, a youth never lived to the full and now gone beyond recall, the loss of an ideal, some betrayal of trust, or one of many other things. It is not possible to know, and for the sake of the poem it does not matter, for the uncertainty lends its own charm. Also, in reading Machado it is always necessary to keep in mind that his symbols may have multiple meanings. In one of the many bits of advice to the would-be poet he says: *Da doble luz a tu verso, | para leído de frente | y al sesgo* ("Give double meaning to your verse, | so it may be read forward | and sideways"). [P.P.R.]

ANTONIO MACHADO

[ME DIJO UN ALBA DE LA PRIMAVERA]

Me dijo un alba de la primavera:
Yo florecí en tu corazón sombrío
ha muchos años, caminante viejo
que no cortas las flores del camino.   4

Tu corazón de sombra, ¿acaso guarda
el viejo aroma de mis viejos lirios?
¿Perfuman aún mis rosas la alba frente
del hada de tu sueño adamantino?   8

Respondí a la mañana:
Sólo tienen cristal los sueños míos.
Yo no conozco el hada de mis sueños;
ni sé si está mi corazón florido.   12

Pero si aguardas la mañana pura
que ha de romper el vaso cristalino,
quizás el hada te dará tus rosas,
mi corazón tus lirios.   16

(Soledades, galerías y otros poemas. 1907)

A spring dawn said to me: (2) I flowered
in your somber heart (3) many years ago,
old traveler (4) [you] who do not cut the
flowers of [along] the road. (5) Your dark
[melancholy] heart, does it [still] keep per-
chance (6) the old aroma of my old lilies?
(7) Do my roses still perfume the white brow
(8) of the fairy of your adamantine dream?

Now comes the poet's turn to speak:
(9) I replied to the morning: (10) My dreams
are only crystal [glass]. (11) I do not know
the fairy of my dreams; (12) nor do I know if
my heart is in flower. (13) But if you will
wait for the pure morning (14) which is to
break the crystalline vase [cup], (15) perhaps
the fairy will give you [back] your roses,
(16) [and] my heart your lilies.

The first thing we notice about this
poem is that it is a dialogue between the

poet and a springtime morning. This kind
of dialogue is frequent in Machado: he
often personifies, and communes with,
various elements of nature or conceptual
abstractions. Thus we frequently find him
in intimate converse with the morning,
the afternoon, the night, a fountain, a
mountain range, water, sorrow, or beauty.

There are several words in Spanish for
"dawn," but the poet has chosen to begin
with *alba*, which has the connotation of
white and, by extension, that of innocence
or purity (cf. *alba frente*, "white brow,"
7). And this lovely spring dawn recalls to
the poet that once, years ago, in his youth
(the morning of his life) he had in him
the beautiful flowers of hopes and expecta-
tions. Does the scent of those lilies of long
ago still linger? And what has happened

to the ancient roses? Do they still rest on the innocent brow of the fairy (moving spirit) of his once diamond-bright dreams? But the poet, now a melancholy old traveler on the road of life, no longer plucks the flowers along the way; that is, he no longer entertains dreams of beauty. He has been disillusioned by time and life. He answers that his dreams of now are only glass.

To understand this statement and the two lines that follow, we must seek elsewhere in Machado's work. In other poems he equates dreams and recollections. On several occasions he makes clear the distinction between glass and mirror. In one place he speaks of the "profound mirror of my dreams [recollections]" *(el profundo / espejo de mis sueños)*, and again of "the magic mirror of my dreams" *(los mágicos cristales de mi sueño)*— magic, or wonder-working, in that it reflects the past. In still a third place we find these lines: *Al espejo del fondo de mi casa / una mano fatal / va rayando el azogue, y todo pasa / por él como la luz por el cristal* ("A fatal hand [time with its inevitable disillusionments] is scratching away the mercury from the mirror [kept] within my house, and everything passes through it like light through glass [nothing is reflected, retained]." This brings us very close to our poem. What Machado is saying in lines 10, 11, and 12 is that he cannot recall from the past the "fairy" of his youthful dreams, nor does he even know her; and he does not remember that the lovely flowers mentioned by the dawn ever existed at all.

The poet's answer is somber, but it does not fall into complete pessimism. There is hope, *perhaps;* hope that on some future morning the lilies and the roses will be recovered. However, that "pure morning" which is to "break the crystalline cup [of life]" is the moment when the soul (if there is one) will pass into the Beyond (if there is one). Then, *perhaps*—and this is the big word in the last stanza—all questions will be answered, and beauty will return to those who have lost it among the disillusionments of life. But this is no more than the statement of a beautiful hope, a "perhaps"; for Machado is sure neither of the soul nor of an after-life. Even so, death, with whatever lies beyond, is a release from a present life become wearisome.

A nice touch in this poem is the subtle self-dramatization. Dawn, an aspect of the poet himself, evokes the disillusioned past to which answer is made. Thus the poet, in replying that his memory is no mirror and that nothing of the past is reflected in it, not only engages himself in dialogue, but is able in the last stanza to make for himself a profession of hope, however slight, that in some future time beauty will be restored to his soul; that is, that this life with its unanswerable questions is not all.   [P.P.R.]

ANTONIO MACHADO

[ANOCHE CUANDO DORMÍA]

Anoche cuando dormía
soñé, ¡bendita ilusión!
que una fontana fluía
dentro de mi corazón.   4

Di, ¿por qué acequia escondida,
agua, vienes hasta mí,
manantial de nueva vida
de donde nunca bebí?   8

Anoche cuando dormía
soñé, ¡bendita ilusión!
que una colmena tenía
dentro de mi corazón;   12
y las doradas abejas
iban fabricando en él,
con las amarguras viejas,
blanca cera y dulce miel.   16

Anoche cuando dormía
soñé, ¡bendita ilusión!
que un ardiente sol lucía
dentro de mi corazón.   20

Era ardiente porque daba
calores de rojo hogar,
y era sol porque alumbraba
y porque hacía llorar.   24

Anoche cuando dormía
soñé, ¡bendita ilusión!
que era Dios lo que tenía
dentro de mi corazón.   28

(*Soledades, galerías y otros poemas.* 1907)

In this poem of resigned agnosticism the poet tells us *today*, while he is awake, of his visions of *last night*. They are progressive in beauty, from the pure water of a clear welling spring, crystalline source of new life, through busy golden bees engaged in creating beauty out of whatever is at hand, even out of sorrows and sufferings, to the bright light of the sun, symbolic of divinity, of God, in whom Machado wanted to believe but could not, whom he sought but never found:

El Dios que todos buscamos | y que nunca encontraremos ("The God whom we all seek | and whom we never shall find"). And it should be noticed that the poet tells his dreams without bitterness, but as the beautiful experience they were:

(1) *Last night when I was sleeping* (2) *I dreamed, [Oh] blessed vision!* (3) *that a fountain was flowing* (4) *within my heart.* (5) *Say, by what hidden channel,* (6) *water, do you come to me,* (7) *spring [source] of a new life* (8) *from which I never drank?* (9) *Last night when I lay sleeping* (10) *I dreamed, [Oh] blessed vision!* (11) *that I had a hive* (12) *within my heart;* (13) *and the golden bees* (14) *were making in it* [i.e., in my heart] (15) *out of old bitternesses,* (16) *white wax and new honey.* (17) *Last night when I lay sleeping* (18) *I dreamed, [Oh] blessed vision!* (19) *that a burning sun shone* (20) *within my heart.* (21) *It was burning because it gave [off]* (22) *the glowings of [glowed like] a red hearth,* (23) *and it was sun because it lighted up [illuminated]* (24) *and because it made [one, me] weep.* (25) *Last night when I lay sleeping* (26) *I dreamed, [Oh] blessed vision!* (27) *that God was what [it was God] I held* (28) *within my heart.*

The fountain in the first stanza is a familiar poetic image and may suggest many things, such as freshness, coolness, music, gaiety, and even purity. The Spanish word *fontana*, however, is better rendered as "spring," the "source" (*manantial*) of pure fresh water welling up from the bosom of the earth through some "hidden channel." The fountain proper (*fuente* in Spanish) is a common companion of Machado's poetic dialogues and is nearly always a symbol of sadness and melancholy. But the *fontana* mentioned here is, as the poet says, a "source of new life," though, sadly, one from which he has never drunk. What is this new life? It could be a life without bitterness, without disillusionment, without frustrated dreams and hopes; it could be the life of a simple and credulous faith which the poet longs to accept, but whose acceptance has been made impossible for him by life itself.

Stanza 3 introduces a second vision, with images that occur repeatedly in Machado's poetry. The "hive" is a center of fruitful activity and industry (*Colmenares de mis sueños, | ¿ya no labráis?* "Hives of my dreams, | are you no longer busy?") where the bees, usually golden (*las doradas | abejas de mis sueños,* "the golden bees of my dreams"; *abejicas de oro,* "little golden bees"; *los enjambres de oro,* "the golden swarms"), are busy making things of beauty, symbolized by "white wax and new honey," out of "old bitternesses." In Machado the idea that spiritual values—sensitive feeling, understanding, joy, beauty—may come from sorrow and pain, is common: *De cuántas flores amargas | he sacado blanca cera* ("From how many bitter flowers | have I drawn white wax"); *La nueva miel labramos | con dolores viejos* ("We make new honey | out of old sorrows"). We have already found this same thought given expression in an earlier poem: *Oh, sharp golden thorn | would that I might feel you | fixed in my heart again.*

The third vision is that of a sun which shone within his heart and "glowed like a red hearth." It was sun, not because it glowed, but because it illuminated (made clear) everything and because it brought tears to the eyes that looked at it or beheld what it lighted up. In Machado's poetic landscapes the sun occurs often and is always a thing of beauty (*The sun, this beauty | that is the sun! . . .*) On one occasion it is even the illuminator of dreams: *The red sun of a dream appears in the East. | Light in [one's, our] dreams.* But only in our poem does the sun become a "Divine Light" like that of Dante's vision, a light toward which the soul strives throughout an entire life.　　　　　[P.P.R.]

LAS MOSCAS

Vosotras, las familiares,
inevitables golosas,
vosotras, moscas vulgares,
me evocáis todas las cosas.   4

¡Oh, viejas moscas voraces
como abejas en abril,
viejas moscas pertinaces
sobre mi calva infantil!   8

¡Moscas del primer hastío
en el salón familiar,
las claras tardes de estío
en que yo empecé a soñar!   12

Y en la aborrecida escuela,
raudas moscas divertidas,
perseguidas
por amor de lo que vuela,   16

— que todo es volar — sonoras,
rebotando en los cristales
en los días otoñales...
Moscas de todas las horas,   20

de infancia y adolescencia,
de mi juventud dorada;
de esta segunda inocencia,
que da en no creer en nada,   24

de siempre... Moscas vulgares,
que de puro familiares
no tendréis digno cantor:
yo sé que os habéis posado   28

sobre el juguete encantado,
sobre el librote cerrado,
sobre la carta de amor,
sobre los párpados yertos   32
de los muertos.

Inevitables golosas,
que ni labráis como abejas,
ni brilláis como mariposas;   36
pequeñitas, revoltosas,
vosotras, amigas viejas,
me evocáis todas las cosas.

(*Soledades, galerías y otros poemas.* 1907)

The title of this poem is "Flies."
Robert Burns wrote one about a
mouse. In each case the poet addresses the
subject of his verses, and in each case he
passes from the personal to the universal.
(1) *You, familiar,* (2) *inevitable [unavoidable] greedy [things], you common flies,* (4) *you remind me of everything.* (5) *Oh, [you] old flies, voracious* (6) *as bees in April,* (7) *persistent [stubborn] old flies* (8) *upon my infant baldness!* (9) *Flies of the [my] first boredom* (10) *in the family parlor,* (11) *[on] bright summer afternoons* (12) *in which I began to dream!* (13) *And in the hated school,* (14) *swift [impetuous] funny flies,* (15) *pursued* (16) *by love of that which flies,* (17) *—for flying is everything—[you] noisy [things],* (18) *beating against the window panes* (19) *on autumn days . . .* (20) *Flies of all hours [times],* (21) *of [my] infancy and adolescence,* (22) *of my golden youth;* (23) *of this second innocence,* (24) *which has taken to [insists on] believing in nothing,* (25) *of always . . . [You] common flies,* (26) *who out of sheer familiarity* (27) *will not have a worthy singer:* (28) *[but] I know that you have lit* (29) *upon the [child's] enchanted toy,* (30) *upon the great closed book,* (31) *upon the love letter,* (32) *upon the rigid eyelids* (33) *of the dead.* (34) *[You] inevitable greedy [things],* (35) *who neither*

toil like bees, (36) *nor shine like butterflies;* (37) *tiny, mischievous [little things],* (38) *you, old friends,* (39) *you remind me of everything.*

Beneath the humor of these lines is the poet's awareness that the common house-flies embrace not only his own life, but human life in general. He begins by addressing them as the inevitable, greedy little things they are, and then immediately invests them with a poetic quality by stating that they remind him of everything. This "everything" is at first his own life span, beginning with earliest infancy, when they crawled over his hairless baby head. And who does not remember with the poet those hot summer afternoons when the boredom of childhood was intensified by the monotonous buzzing of the flies? Or the dull classroom hours when childish attention was diverted by their swift darting?

With lines 15, 16, and 17 the author moves them to a still higher poetic plane. If we rephrase these lines to read "impelled by love of flying—for flying is everything," we get a better idea of what the poet is saying: flying, soaring, dreaming, thinking beyond the commonplace, are what is important, what is worthwhile. Now the poet repeats that flies are reminders of his life and all its moments, from infancy through adolescence and golden (dream-filled) youth to what he calls his second infancy, that disillusioned maturity that doubts everything. Once more he addresses the flies to tell them

that because they are so common they will never have a worthy singer.

But *he* is willing to sing them, because he understands them and knows what they mean. And here, in six remarkable lines (28-33), the poet passes from individual experience to experience in general and makes the flies embrace all human life: he knows that they have lit upon the enchanted toy that brings such wonder and delight to the child; upon the great book, symbol of man's accumulated knowledge, product of his study and thought; upon the love letter, carrier of the tenderest human emotions; and finally upon the lifeless lids of the dead. These verses hold literally the beginning and the end of human experience; and it is of this that the poet is reminded as he contemplates the lowly housefly, a creature that has rarely, if ever, soared in verse or fancy as has the industrious little bee or the bright, brilliant butterfly.

It is impossible to carry over the sonic values of a poem from one language to another, but attention may be called here to an interesting detail. Though he was a skillful rimer when he wished to be, Machado rejected rime as simple poetic ornamentation. Rime should serve the idea. For example, in line 15, the *pie quebrado* ("broken foot" or short line), with its quick repetition of the rime of the preceeding line, produces a hammer-like emphasis. This is even more effective in line 33, where the same device is used to drive home the finality of death. [P.P.R.]

ANTONIO MACHADO

[¡SORIA FRÍA!]

¡Soria fría, *Soria pura*,
cabeza de Extremadura,
con su castillo guerrero
arruinado, sobre el Duero;   4
con sus murallas roídas
y sus casas denegridas!

¡Muerta ciudad de señores
soldados o cazadores;   8
de portales con escudos
de cien linajes hidalgos,
y de famélicos galgos,
de galgos flacos y agudos,   12
que pululan
por las sórdidas callejas,
y a la medianoche ululan,
cuando graznan las cornejas!   16

¡Soria fría! La campana
de la Audiencia da la una.
Soria, ciudad castellana,
¡tan bella! bajo la luna.   20

(*Campos de Castilla.* 1912)

This is part six of a longer poem entitled "*Campos de Soria*" ("Sorian Countryside"). For its full appreciation it is necessary to know what Castile and Soria meant to the author.

Though born in Andalusia, the sunny southern part of Spain, Antonio Machado was to become the poet of the high Castilian plateau. Circumstances took him, in his early childhood, to Madrid and, in his maturity, to the ancient Castilian city of Soria, where he went as a teacher of French in 1907. He put it this way:

Nadie elige su amor. Llevóme un día
mi destino a los grises calvijares
donde ahuyenta al caer la nieve fría
las sombras de los muertos encinares.

No one chooses his love. I was carried one day /
by my destiny to the gray open spaces / where
the cold snow, on falling, puts to flight / the
dark shadows of the holm oak groves.

Soria is located in a desolate part of Castile on the west bank of the Duero river, a stream often sung by Machado because of its connection with this city: "the father river, / which furrows the cold wastes of Castile" and eternally "traces its crossbow arch around Soria." From his verses we know, too, what the region was like: "the land of Soria is arid and cold"; "Soria of the blue mountains / and violet-tinted wastes." And for Castile he had such epithets as "miserable Castile" and "austere land," and left us this stark picture of a bleakness that extends even to the lives of the inhabitants:

¡Oh tierra triste y noble,
la de los altos llanos y yermos y roquedas,

de campos sin arados, regatos ni arboledas;
decrépitas ciudades, caminos sin mesones,
y atónitos palurdos sin danzas ni
     canciones.

Oh sad and noble land, | [land] of the high
plains and wildernesses and rocky wastes, |
of fields without plows, brooks or groves; |
decrepit cities, roads without inns, | and wonder-
struck bumpkins without dances or songs.

The first year in Soria was one of
profound loneliness, and Machado spent
many solitary hours in long walks over the
countryside. But the cold and naked region
became forever a part of his being; and
when in the following year he met and
loved Leonor, whom he was soon to marry,
Castile and Soria lost some of their
austerity. In later years, living elsewhere
in Spain, he sang of Soria, "My heart is
where it was born / not to life, but to
love, near the Duero . . ."

Against this background we can now
turn to one of the most beautiful lyric
poems in Spanish. In the first five parts
of the longer poem the poet describes the
lands about Soria as they appear in the
different seasons of the year. Then he
pauses for a description of the city itself:
(1) *Soria cold,* "*Soria pure,* (2) *head of*
Extremadura," (3) *with its warlike castle*
(4) *in ruins, upon the Duero;* (5) *with its*
crumbling walls, (6) *and its [age-] blackened*
houses! (7) *Dead city of men* (8) *[who were]*
soldiers or hunters; (9) *of portals with escutch-*
eons (10) *of a hundred hidalgo families,*
(11) *of starving greyhounds [dogs],* (12) *of*
gaunt sharp dogs (13) *that pululate* (14) *in*
the sordid alleys, (15) *and at midnight*
ululate, (16) *when the night-owl croaks!*
(17) *Cold Soria! The bell* (18) *in the*
Courthouse strikes one. (19) *Soria, Castilian*
city, (20) *so beautiful under the moon!*

In the first two lines the poet quotes the
legend on the city's coat-of-arms ("Soria
pura, cabeza de Extremadura"), thus
hailing Soria as "head," that is, chief city

of Extremadura and endowing it with a
degree of dignity and historical impor-
tance. In the Middle Ages, during the wars
against the Moors and other hostile
peoples, an area of Castile bordering on
enemy territory was called Extremadura.
But Soria's hour of glory passed long ago;
and now, these many centuries, its castle
and its walls have been in ruins, and its
houses are black with the patina of ages.
It is a decrepit city of *señores;* that is, of
men who were lords, but not feudal lords,
for Soria was a free city and attached to
the crown. Among these *señores* were a few
great lords, but mostly they were strong,
rude men whose pleasures were the hunt
and war. When they got money they
bought property, carved escutcheons over
their doorways, and called themselves
hidalgos. The *hidalgos* were the bottom-rung
nobility of Castile. Today their coats-of-
arms over many of Soria's portals recall a
once illustrious, even seignorial, past, while
in the squalid alleys the dogs—sharp be-
cause they are gaunt and thin—breed by
day and howl by night. But, decrepit and
cold—above all cold—Soria, a city of Cas-
tile, is so beautiful in the light of the moon.

This poem's lyric qualities can hardly
be brought over into English. The clear,
strong articulation of the Spanish vowels
gives them a beauty not easily reproducible
in Northern tongues. However, some idea
of the musicality of the first two lines may
be got by tampering with the last word
in line 2:

> *Soria cold,* "*Soria pure,*
> *head of Extremadure*" . . .

Line 13 is a *pie quebrado,* or short line.
Its *four* syllables, with their alliterative
repetition of the vowel *u* and the liquid *l,*
not only have a strong lyrical emphasis,
but leave the ear demanding an early
completion of the rime, which comes
two verses later and at the end of an
eight-syllable line.   [P.P.R.]

JUAN RAMÓN JIMÉNEZ

[NO ERA NADIE]

— No era nadie. El agua. — ¿Nadie?
¿Que no es nadie el agua? — No
hay nadie. Es la flor. — ¿No hay nadie?
Pero ¿no es nadie la flor?   4

— No hay nadie. Era el viento. — ¿Nadie?
¿No es el viento nadie? — No
hay nadie. Ilusión. — ¿No hay nadie?
¿Y no es nadie la ilusión?   8

(*Jardines lejanos.* 1904)

One of the recurring characteristics of the poetry of Jiménez (1881-1958), especially in his first books, is the use of words that rhythmically or sonally produce musical effects, thus relating the atmosphere, color, or sonority of the poems to other arts, chiefly music and painting. This particular poem, a very early one, is an example of this tendency. It is in octosyllabic lines, a rhythm that could be noted thus:

No͡e : ra : na : die͡el : a : gua : Na :die :
Que : no͡es : na : die͡el : a : gua : no : ∧

a falling four-stress rhythm somewhat like that of Poe's "The Haunted Palace:"

Ín the greénest óf your válleys
Bý good ángels tenantéd ∧

"No era nadie" is governed by the word *nadie* ("no one"), which is its dominant, and which appears in all of its eight lines. It is a dialogue. One of the speakers may be taken to represent a realistic point of view, inasmuch as he affirms that wind, water, flower, and "illusion" are *nadie*. The other speaker, whom we may call "the poet," contradicts each of the realist's assertions by affirming, interrogatively, that these things are not *nadie:* that is to say, they have a life of their own, even a soul or a being. This attitude is one of the main trends in Jiménez's thought: the personification of the world about us, from wild flower to star.

(1) "*It was no one. Water.*" "*No one?* (2) *Is the water no one?*" "*There* (3) *is no one. The flower.*" "*Is there no one?* (4) *But is the flower no one?*"

(5) "*There is no one. It was the wind.*" "*No one?* (6) *Is the wind no one?*" "*No.* (7) *one. Illusion.*" "*There is no one?* (8) *And is illusion no one?*"

The mood is established at the beginning by the negative statement *No era nadie* ("It was no one"). Moreover, the dialogue form enforces a dramatic tone, a suggestion of incident: the speakers, let us say, have been disturbed by a noise outside the room, and one of them, the "realist," goes out to ascertain the cause, and returns with the assurance that it was *Nadie. El agua.* ("No, there was no one out there.

It was just the water.") The "poet" knows better than this because he understands a different and superior reality.

The two stanzas employ a parallel construction in the use of the key word *nadie:* twice in lines 1, 3, 5, 7, and only once in 2, 4, 6, and 8. Moreover, this parallelism is also interior, or "strophic": each line of the first stanza has its correlative in the second. Another kind of balance, that of the conflict between affirmation and denial, sustains the eight lines.

We note also that the conflict is not stated absolutely, as it would have been if the "poet" had said: "No, water *is* somebody; the flower *is* somebody," and so on. Rather, it is expressed indirectly by the use of rhetorical questions that balance the emphatic *No*'s similarly placed in the first two lines of each stanza, and that soften, as though by a kind of echo, the insistence of these denials. The opposition between the two approaches to the issue is further emphasized by the ending of lines 2 and 6 with a *no* carrying over into the following line (enjambment), whereas all the other lines end in a question. Also, there is a gradation from what is most real and tangible, in the first stanza—"water," "flower"—to the less tangible, in the second—"wind," "illusion".

The reader is naturally expected to share the point of view of the second speaker, that the things mentioned are *alguien* ("somebody"), but he is assenting to what is really a mystery implied, not emphatically stated, by the riddling questions. This mystery is implicit even in the handling of the tenses—*era* ("it was"), says the first speaker, and *es* ("it is"), says the second—, where the present tense used by the "poet" is like a secondary affirmation embodied in his questions.

Also characteristic of Jiménez is the lack of ornament. The nouns and verbs are unmodified. Thus, *agua, flor, viento, ilusión* stand stripped, four isolated phenomena gradually emerging in the poem, each with the persistent echo of *nadie* placed before and after to create, by negation and affirmation, a patterned frame. A maximum of force in a minimum of words, where repetition itself—*water* (1, 2), *flower* (3, 4), *wind* (5, 6), *illusion* (7, 8)—achieves a semantic discrimination.

[E.F.]

JUAN RAMÓN JIMÉNEZ

OCTUBRE

Estaba echado yo en la tierra, enfrente
del infinito campo de Castilla,
que el otoño envolvía en la amarilla
dulzura de su claro sol poniente.   4

Lento, el arado, paralelamente
abría el haza oscura, y la sencilla
mano abierta dejaba la semilla
en su entraña partida honradamente.   8

Pensé arrancarme el corazón, y echarlo,
pleno de su sentir alto y profundo,
al ancho surco del terruño tierno;
a ver si con romperlo y con sembrarlo   12
la primavera le mostraba al mundo
el árbol puro del amor eterno.

(Sonetos espirituales. 1916)

This sonnet appeared in the volume that closes the first period in the work of Juan Ramón Jiménez. It offers, in its octet and sestet, two landscapes, the first of which is impersonal except for the "yo" *(I)* in the opening line: (1) *I was lying down (resting) on the ground (earth), facing* (2) *the infinite countryside of Castile* (3) *which autumn was wrapping (swaddling) in the yellow* (4) *sweetness (mellowness) of its clear setting sun.* (5) *Slowly the plow, in parallel lines,* (6) *was breaking the dark soil, and the simple (unassuming)* (7) *open hand was leaving the seed* (8) *in its honorably splitted (broken) entrails.* Up to this moment the poet is there, watching the Castilian landscape where the lonely figure, the sower, is laboring. Note that this figure is not presented to our eyes, but is symbolized, as it were, by his plow *(el arado)* and

by his hand *(la mano).* Throughout these eight lines we sense a slow *(lento)* movement: the sower and the lazy passing of the hour progress, as it were, in a horizontal line, suggested by the imperfect tense of the verbs *(estaba, envolvía, abría, dejaba)* and by the adverbs *(paralelamente, honradamente),* which in Spanish seem longer drawn out than their English equivalents.

The sestet presents a different perception of the landscape. (9) *I thought of tearing off (drawing off) my heart, and tossing (hurling, casting) it,* (10) *full of its high and deep feeling,* (11) *(in)to the wide furrow in the tender soil (ground);* (12) *to see if by breaking it and sowing it* (13) *spring would show to the world* (14) *the pure tree of eternal love.*

The contrast is sharply made at the beginning of line 9 by the use of *pensar* ("to think") in its past-perfect tense (*pensé*), immediately after the *honradamente* and accompanied by the noun *corazón* ("heart"). The two words stress the last syllable, like an arrow shot into the air. The other verbs are used in the infinitive mode (*echar, romper, sembrar*). Thus the horizontal *lento* of the first eight lines has now changed to a vertical, energetic movement.

Moreover, the poet presently enters the poem in the very personal *pensé* ("I thought"). From now on he will be the axis of the poem. Placed between earth and sky, he himself will be the center of the world: his heart is full of high and deep feeling. He goes upward like a wing and downward like a root. (These two symbols—wing and root—appear in diverse forms in Jiménez's poems, just as they appeared in those of José Martí, the Cuban poet, much admired and read by Jiménez, who was one of the forerunners of the Spanish Modernist movement.)

The poet is thus a hypothetical center between earth and sky. He wishes to eternalize himself. He wishes to sow. The sower, in a way, eternalizes himself in his seed; the poet wishes to sow, not any seed, not a tree, but his own heart, because he knows that from an autumn sowing, spring will bring to the world a new kind of tree, grown from his heart—the tree of eternal love.

This Castilian landscape is seen by an Andalusian who feels identified with it, not because it is Castilian but because of the universality of his feeling. And although it is Castilian, it does not possess —as in Unamuno or Machado—the force, the vigorous character, of that land. Here the *infinito campo de Castilla* ("the limitless landscape of Castile") is softened by the light, not of midday but of the setting sun, near dusk. The melancholy mood is achieved partly by the use of a favorite Jiménez color-word, yellow. This is the softness that is suddenly changed by the irruption of *pensé*, a word that thus becomes the very center of the poem.

Unlike our simple and brief first poem by Jiménez, "October" is involved, ornamented. Most of the nouns are accompanied by an epithet; only six stand alone—and these are the most important ones in the poem—*tierra* ("earth"), *otoño* ("autumn"), *semilla* ("seed"), *corazón* ("heart"), *primavera* ("spring"), *mundo* ("world"). Around these the whole poem rotates. And, finally, we may note that the poem projects an ideal passing from autumn (3) to spring (13); a passing that, naturally, does not actually take place, because the *deseo* ("wish") of the author has remained in his *pensamiento* ("thought"). The sonnet thus creates a mood of impotence, of frustration.　　　　　[E.F.]

LA MÚSICA

De pronto, surtidor
de un pecho que se parte,
el chorro apasionado rompe
la sombra — como una mujer   4
que abriera los balcones sollozando,
desnuda, a las estrellas, con afán
de un morirse sin causa,
que fuera loca vida inmensa. —   8

Y ya no vuelve nunca más,
— mujer o agua —,
aunque queda en nosotros, estallando,
real e inexistente,   12
sin poderse parar.

(*Belleza*. 1923)

L*a música*" ("Music") was written shortly after the publication in 1916 of *Diario de un poeta reciencasado (Diary of a Newlywed Poet)*, a book in which Jiménez developed a new style in a verse form freer than any he had used before.

Like many other poets, Juan Ramón had been steadily involved with the fine arts; painting (which he practiced in early youth) and music in particular have left their impress upon his work. Criticism invariably points approvingly to the unusual musicality and color of his verse, but their presence also makes the task of the translator exceptionally difficult. The difficulty is apparent even when one attempts to make a strictly literal translation:

(1) *Suddenly, like a jet of water* (2) *[which has sprung] out of a split breast (chest),* (3) *the passionate spurt (stream) breaks* (4) *the shadow—like a woman* (5) *who* would *[fling]* open the balcony windows: sobbing (6) and naked, to the stars, in her strong eagerness (7) for her own dying without [any] reason (cause) (8) and which would [turn out to] be [for her] an immense, mad life. (9) And which does not come back any more (10) —[the] woman or [the] water— (11) although it remains within us, bursting forth (12) real and nonexistent, (13) unable to stop.

In the opening lines, music and water are identified as one. Music pours out, bursts forth, swiftly—in song—from the heart, as if it were a woman bursting open her balcony windows in the night to the stars. Woman and water thus have become identified; and music—which was first compared to a jet of water—loses this single meaning to become both water and woman. (It is interesting to note that music, water, and woman are constant themes of Jiménez's verse; the duality woman-poetry may be considered the essence of his lyrical thought.)

"*La música*" differs sharply from another poem by Jiménez which begins with the question: *What happens to a piece of music/ when its sound ceases?*—a poem that recalls to readers of Shelley his famous "Music when soft voices die. . . ." The mood is melancholy and soft in both poems, and their sounds linger in the reader's memory. "*La música*," on the other hand, bursts forth violently, rapidly, even aggressively. Its uplifting opening line *De pronto, surtidor* is echoed in a series of strong, swift words—*chorro, apasionado, rompe, abriera, afán, loca, nunca, más, estallando*—whose movement is upward like that of the jet of water in the first line.

The second stanza, of only five lines, also begins with an upward movement. Its *Y ya no vuelve nunca más* ("And which does not come back any more") refers to the music or the song pouring out of the breast of the person who is singing. And it ends in another swift line: *sin poderse parar* ("unable to stop"). Note that in this stanza both the first and last lines end in a word stressed on the last syllable —*más, parar*—reflecting the stress of the *surtidor* of line 1, which also falls on the last syllable.

Because of its atmosphere of urgency, the poem has not been composed in a regular verse form, in an organized pattern of lines or stanza; and yet it moves with a carefully measured interior rhythm, in a more or less free verse. Very evident is the recurrence of enjambment, as between lines 1 and 2, 3 and 4, 6 and 7, all of them adding to the speed of the little piece. But it is the abrupt, jagged motion that is most striking—a quick force, almost sexual in its immediacy, that admirably conveys the latent meaning of the poem. The *surtidor* is a creating jet, beautiful, instant, and ruthless. There are no modulations, no transitions; the strong music bursts from the page.   [E.F.]

LOS PÁJAROS DE YO SÉ DÓNDE

Toda la noche,   1
los pájaros han estado
cantándome sus colores.

(No los colores   4
de sus alas matutinas
con el fresco de los soles.

No los colores   7
de sus pechos vespertinos
al rescoldo de los soles.

No los colores   10
de sus picos cotidianos
que se apagan por la noche,
como se apagan   13
los colores conocidos
de las hojas y las flores.)

Otros colores,   16
el paraíso primero
que perdió del todo el hombre,
el paraíso   19
que las flores y los pájaros
inmensamente conocen.

Flores y pájaros   22
que van y vienen oliendo,
volando por todo el orbe.

Otros colores,   25
el paraíso sin cambio
que el hombre en sueños recorre.

Toda la noche,   28
los pájaros han estado
cantándome los colores.

Otros colores   31
que tienen en su otro mundo
y que sacan por la noche.

Unos colores   34
que he visto bien despierto
y que están yo sé bien dónde.

Yo sé de dónde   37
los pájaros han venido
a cantarme por la noche.

Yo sé de dónde   40
pasando vientos y olas,
a cantarme mis colores.

(*Tercera antolojía poética*. 1957)

This poem represents the last phase of Jiménez's work, composed in America and appropriately entitled *En el otro costado* ("On the Other Shore"). It is one of the group called *Canciones de la Florida* ("Florida Songs"), written in Miami in the years 1938-1940.

(1) *All night long* (2) *the birds have been* (3) *singing their colors to me.* (4) *(Not the colors* (5) *of their morning wings* (6) *in the cool air of suns rising.* (7) *Not the colors* (8) *of their evening breasts* (9) *in the embers of suns setting.* (10) *Not the colors* (11) *of their everyday beaks* (12) *extinguished at night,* (13-15) *as the familiar colors of leaves and flowers are extinguished.)* (16) *Other colors,* (17) *[of the] primeval paradise* (18) *completely lost by man,* (19) *the paradise* (2) *that flowers and birds* (21) *so enormously know.* (22) *Flowers and birds* (23) *that come and go perfuming,* (24) *flying around [encircling] the whole orb.* (25) *Other colors,* (26) *[of]*

the unchangeable paradise (27) *that man travels in his dreams.* (28) *All night long* (29) *the birds have been* (30) *singing the colors to me.* (31) *Other colors* (32) *which they have in their other world* (33) *and which they bring out at night.* (34) *Some colors* (35) *I have seen, quite awake,* (36) *and where they are I well know.* (37) *I know whence* (38) *the birds have come* (39) *to sing for me in the night.* (40) *I know whence,* (41) *crossing the winds and the waves,* (42) *[they came] to sing my colors to me.*

This is a nocturne. The poet, awake, enjoys the songs of the birds; but by a very interesting transference of sense perception (synesthesia) he hears the birds in terms of their color. In a foreign land, homesick for his own country, he knows whence these birds have come; they cannot be the alien, American birds; they are from his distant land. Besides, the song that they sing—the colors to which he is listening— is not of this moment, this reality; it belongs to a time that is passed.

The poem opens with its main theme: the birds have been singing their colors all night long, and the poet has been listening. Stanzas 2, 3, and 4 present parenthetically thoughts of color at sunrise, sunset, and nightfall—colors that fade with fading light; and they are rejected because they are real, natural colors. For the colors heard by the poet are other (*otros*) colors. And at this word *otros* the poem's turning point appears, for these other colors can be identified only with those in his remembered past. The distance—and the difference—between the two worlds, of reality and memory, are happily expressed by *otros* in its emphatic

position at the opening of lines 16, 25, and 31.

A poet is one who knows things, who sees, hears, feels what others can not. That is why Jiménez introduces himself in an indirect way, so to speak: it is only *cantándome* ("singing to me") in stanzas 1 and 8—two points upon which the whole weight of the poem rests—until the moment of personal recognition, namely, the emergence of the *knowledge* of the poet (in the last three stanzas, with their insistent repetition of *yo sé, yo sé bien*). That is why he can also say that he knows whence the birds have come: in such an idealization of his own past, induced by absence and exile, the colors that he now is listening to are the very ones that he used to know; the colors of his own birds that he remembers so poignantly. Note, in this connection, the change in the possessive pronoun: *sus* ("their"), line 3, becomes *mis* ("my") in the last line: by the end of the poem the poet has become totally identified with the singing birds around him. They sing all night in his mind.

The ternary pattern recalls the form of a very well-known poem by St. John of the Cross, "The Fount that Freely Flows," although that poem uses lines of eleven and five syllables. Moreover, St. John's cry, *How well I know the fount that flows,/ Although it's night,* is clearly echoed in the present poem. A binding element is achieved by Jiménez in a play on two words, *noche* ("night") and *colores* ("colors"), which are related by the assonance of *o* and *e*—the same vowels, incidentally, that dominate the poem by St. John.

[E.F.]

LEÓN-FELIPE

PIE PARA « EL NIÑO DE VALLECAS »
DE VELÁZQUEZ

Bacía... Yelmo... Halo...
Este es el orden, Sancho.

De aquí no se va nadie.
Mientras esta cabeza rota
del Niño de Vallecas exista,
de aquí no se va nadie. Nadie.   4
Ni el místico ni el suicida.

Antes hay que deshacer este entuerto,
antes hay que resolver este enigma.
Y hay que resolverlo entre todos,   8
y hay que resolverlo sin cobardía,
sin huir
con unas alas de percalina
o haciendo un agujero   12
en la tarima.
De aquí no se va nadie. Nadie.
Ni el místico ni el suicida.

Y es inútil,   16
inútil toda huida
(ni por abajo
ni por arriba).
Se vuelve siempre. Siempre.   20
Hasta que un día (¡un buen día!)
el yelmo de Mambrino
— halo ya, no yelmo ni bacía —
se acomode a las sienes de Sancho   24
y a las tuyas y a las mías
como pintiparado,
como hecho a la medida.
Entonces iremos todos   28
por las bambalinas.
Tú, y yo, y Sancho, y el Niño de Vallecas
y el místico y el suicida.

(*Versos y oraciones de caminante, Libro II.* 1929)

León-Felipe, pseudonym of León Felipe Camino Galicia: born in Zamora, Spain, in 1884.

The title of this poem can be rendered as "Caption for *The Child of Vallecas* of Velázquez," but "Moral Caption" gives us a better idea of what the poet has in mind. *The Child of Vallecas*, one of Velázquez's well-known paintings, represents a young dwarf with misshapen body and idiotic mind, perhaps the most pathetic of those abnormal and deformed creatures kept at the court of Philip IV for the diversion of the king and his nobles.

The epigraph, *Basin . . . Helmet . . . Halo . . . / This is the order, Sancho*, is an imaginary remark assigned by the poet to Don Quixote, who captured a brass *basin* from a barber and thought himself possessor of the famous *helmet* of the wicked giant Mambrino. On the courageous and idealistic knight's head the crude basin has become for the poet a *halo*, symbol of the highest virtue and courage. But Don Quixote is addressing Sancho Panza, his squire and his earthly and materialistic opposite.

The moral obligation of every human being, stated in the opening line, carries greater force by being an assertion rather than a command: (1) *From here no one goes away [leaves]*. The word *here* means, of course, this life, the world we live in; or, in a more precisely moral sense, our responsibility in this life. (2) *While this broken [deformed] head* (3) *of the Child of Vallecas exists*, (4) *no one goes away. No one.* (5) *Neither the mystic nor the suicide.* The Child of Vallecas, with his physical and mental deformities, symbolizes all the injustices and sufferings of humanity, and it is not unlikely that in referring to the "broken" or deformed head the poet is thinking as much of the idiot brain within

the oversized skull. The repetition of "no one" and the words of line 5 emphasize the poet's insistence that the responsibility for righting the world's wrongs falls upon each individual within the entire range of humanity: from the suicide, at one extreme, who selfishly takes his own life, to the mystic at the other, who strives, with equal selfishness, for his private salvation.

Before we leave this life, or before we can think of ourselves only, there are tasks to be done: (6) *First it is necessary to undo this wrong [injustice]*, (7) *first it is necessary to resolve this enigma [problem]*. (8) *And it is necessary to resolve it among [us] all*, (9) *and it is necessary to resolve it without cowardice*, (10) *without fleeing* (11) *on percaline wings* (12) *or by making* (13) *a hole in the platform [stage]*. (14) *From here no one goes away. No one.* (15) *Neither the mystic nor the suicide.* (16) *And it is useless*, (17) *useless all flight* (18) *(either upward* (19) *or downward)*. There is no escaping our responsibility: (20) *One always comes back. Always.* And now the poet asserts his insistent hope, perhaps his belief, that finally there will come a time when justice shall prevail upon the earth, when the golden ideal, the transformation of a brass barber's bowl into a halo, will have been accomplished: (21) *Until one day (a fine day!)* (22) *Mambrino's helmet* (23) *— halo now, not helmet or basin—* (24) *fits Sancho's temples* (25) *and yours, and mine*, (26) *as [if expressly] suited [to them]* (27) *as if made to measure.* When this happens, then, and only then, may we leave this life or turn to our own affairs. And here (28 ff.) the author reintroduces the earlier figure of human life as a stage on which we are actors: (28) *Then we shall all go* (29) *through the wings.* (30) *You, and I, and Sancho*, (30) *and the mystic, and the suicide.* [P.P.R.]

LEÓN-FELIPE

YO NO SOY EL GRAN BUZO

A Pablo Neruda, mi viejo amigo, el Gran Buzo

Y alguien dirá mañana:
pero este poeta no bajó nunca hasta el fondo del mar,
ni escarbó en la tierra profunda de los tejones y los topos...
No visitó las galerías subterráneas   4
ni caminó por las fibras oscuras de la madera,
no perforó la carne ni taladró los huesos,
no llegó hasta los intestinos y las vísceras,
no se filtró por el canal de las arterias   8
ni navegó con la espiroqueta por la sangre hasta morder el
    corazón helado de los hombres...
Pero vió el gusano en la copa del árbol,
la nube de langostas en la torre,
las aguas lustrales rojas y estancadas,   12
la plegaria amarilla,
la baba verde en los belfos de los sacristanes epilépticos...
Vió el sapo en la cúpula,
la polilla en la mesa del altar,   16
el comején en el Arca
y el gorgojo en la mitra...
Vió el ojo torcido y guiñón del arzobispo y dijo:
la luz se está ahogando en la sombra seca del pozo   20
y hay que salvarla con una maroma de lágrimas.

(Llamadme publicano. 1950)

This poem lies about midway between the hopeful exhortations of León-Felipe's early period and the bitter disillusionment of his present period. The poem is representative of the kind that has given him a great following among Spanish-speaking peoples; the kind that brings out large audiences when he recites.

The dedication reads, in English, "To my old friend Pablo Neruda, the Great Diver." *Buzo* means one who dives deep; for example, a deep-sea diver. The title of the poem is, then, "I Am Not the Great Diver" and in the lines that follow, the poet is not only contrasting himself with his friend, whom he regards as a poet diving far below the surface in his examination and interpretation of human experience, but he is also anticipating the possible charge that his own poetry lacks profundity. At the same time he defends what he considers his poetic mission: to speak out against evil.

(1) *And someone will say tomorrow:* (2) *But*

this poet has never descended to the bottom of the sea, (3) *nor scratched [dug] in the deep earth of badgers and moles . . .* (4) *He has not visited subterranean galleries* (5) *or traveled along the dark fibers of wood,* (6) *he has not penetrated flesh or drilled into bones,* (7) *he has not reached the intestines and the viscera,* (8) *he has not filtered into the canals of the arteries* (9) *or sailed with the spirochete along the blood until biting the frozen heart of men . . .*

Anticipating that some future reader may make these charges against him, the poet retorts: (10) *But he did see the worm in the tree top,* (11) *the cloud of locusts in the tower,* (12) *the lustral waters [now become] red and stagnant,* (13) *the yellow prayer,* (14) *the green slaver on the thick lips of epileptic sacristans . . .* (15) *He saw the toad in the cupola,* (16) *the moth on the altar table,* (17) *the termite in the Ark* (18) *and the weevil on the miter . . .* (19) *He saw the sly and winking eye of the archbishop and said:* (20) *The light is dying in the dry shadow of the well* (20) *and we must save it with a rope of tears.*

León-Felipe's poetic language is seldom obscure. His images are original, but usually easy to grasp. So, when he tells us that he is not "The Great Diver," he is saying in fairly plain language that it is dark at the bottom of the sea and under the earth and inside the body, where the vital organs are; that one must go down or penetrate in order to know what is there, and that in this darkness of depths and interiors there is moral sickness. Finally, he is implying that other poets, Pablo Neruda, for example, may perhaps have probed more deeply and, with a poetic language of greater subtlety, written what some would call a "deeper" poetry.

In his retort the poet tries to justify himself. He seems to say: "If deeper, more penetrating poets have exposed what is in the depths, I, also a poet with a mission, have used my talents and plain words to point out the evil that is all about us here

above. I have called it by name and I have cried out against it".

León-Felipe is to a certain degree a poet of humility. He often uses the phrase *Yo no soy nadie,* "I am nobody," by which he means, "I am just one of very, very many." But his is not the humility of the meek; rather it is that of the Jeremiah of the denunciations who, making himself the servant of God (as the poet is the servant of Right), fulminates against wickedness. What distinguishes León-Felipe is a conviction that everyone has a moral obligation to fight against evil and that too many lack the courage to perform this duty. This courage is not wanting in him.

It is not necessary to look for other than the obvious in the words "tree" and "tower." These are tall objects, well above the ground, which all may see. However, the poet calls our attention to the infection in them. The "lustral (or purification) waters" and the "yellow prayer" stand for what is accepted in life as spiritually salutary. (The word "yellow" refers not only to the faded parchment on which the prayer is written, but also to the hypocrisy with which it is uttered.) With "epileptic sacristans" we are brought close to people who are foul in body and soul.

With lines 15 to 19 the poet is telling us that there is corruption in high and holy places, in places where we do not expect or wish to find it. The symbols are easily recognizable.

The language up to this point is plain and carries more evangelical fire than modern poetic subtlety; the last two lines contain a pair of striking images, "the dry shadow of the well," in which the light is drowning, and the "rope of tears" with which it may be saved. The word "light" is symbolic of all that is lofty and noble and decent in life, of all the values that man has been taught to believe in and live for, and of his hopes that some day this will be a better world. [P.P.R.]

PROFUNDAMENTE

Quando ontem adormeci
Na noite de São João
Havia alegria e rumor
Estrondos de bombas luzes de
    Bengala   4
Vozes cantigas e risos
Ao pé das fogueiras acesas.

No meio da noite despertei
Não ouvi mais vozes nem risos 8
Apenas balões
Passavam errantes
Silenciosamente
Apenas de vez em quando   12
O ruído de um bonde
Cortava o silêncio
Como um túnel.
Onde estavam os que há pouco 16
Dançavam
Cantavam
E riam
Ao pé das fogueiras acesas?   20

— Estavam todos dormindo

Estavam todos deitados
Dormindo
Profundamente.   24

* * * *

Quando eu tinha seis anos
Não pude ver o fim da festa de
    São João
Porque adormeci   27
Hoje não ouço mais as vozes
    daquêle tempo
Minha avó
Meu avó   30
Totônio Rodrigues
Tomásia
Rosa
Onde estão todos êles?   34

— Estão todos dormindo
Estão todos deitados   36
Dormindo
Profundamente.

(*Libertinagem.* 1930)

When I fell asleep yesterday (2) On Saint John's Eve (3) There was gaiety and noise, (4) Rumblings of fireworks, Roman candles, (5) Voices, songs, and laughter (6) Around the lighted bonfires.

(7) In the middle of the night I woke up. (8) I did not hear any more voices or laughing; (9) Only [some] balloons (10) Went by erratic[ally], (11) Silently; (12) Only from time to time (13) The clangor of a streetcar (14) Cut the silence (15) As a tunnel [with its sudden noise cuts the "silence" of a riding train]. (16) Where were those who a little while ago (17) Were dancing, (18) Singing (19) And laughing (20) Around the lighted bonfire?

(21) —They were all sleeping, (22) They were all lying down, (23) Sleeping (24) Profoundly.

(25) When I was six years old (26) I could not see the end of Saint John's Eve merrymaking (27) Because I fell asleep. (28) Today I cannot hear any more the voices of that time. (29) My grandmother (30) My grandfather (31) Totônio Rodrigues (32) Tomásia (33) Rosa (34) Where are all of them?

(35) —They are all sleeping, (36) They are all lying down, (37) Sleeping (38) Profoundly.

The *ubi sunt?* ("where are they?") theme, probably as old as poetry itself, is related here to an evocation of a childhood experience. As a six-year old, the speaker had looked forward to all the fun that awaited him on the night of Saint John's Eve (when children may stay up very late and share fully in the adults' merriment), only to fall asleep when the fiesta was at its best. When he awoke, in the middle of the night, all the gaiety was over, everyone had gone to bed; and instead of the festive noise, all he could hear was the usual nightsounds of the city and all he could see were some stray balloons still wandering in the air to remind him of all he had missed. Many years later, on approaching middle age, he relives the childhood experience: his yesterday is now yesteryear; the time perspective has turned into a symbol of anguish. He asks the same *ubi sunt* question. In the childhood midnight the familiar voices of the merrymakers were quieted by sleep, and today other familiar voices have been quieted by death—They are all sleeping; they are all lying down, sleeping profoundly (35-38).

Bandeira treats these standard ideas of transitoriness, time, and death in an almost conversational tone, without rhetoric or other ornament. The language, like the form, is direct and unpretentious. The poem as it were unrolls, as though the speaker were addressing himself rather than an audience, as though he were thinking aloud in the spontaneously simple language of inner thought. Hence the absence of poetical trappings (there is only one comparison in the whole poem and it is incidental: 12-15). Rather than dress the poem, the poet presents the natural nakedness of this particular lyric intuition as it came to his heart and mind.

This mode of expression is characteristic of Manuel Bandeira (born 1886), who has been called the John the Baptist of contemporary poetry in Brazil—and not with-

out reason. In more ways than one, he was a forerunner of the "Modernista" movement, that started in 1922 in Saõ Paulo. Preaching complete freedom, even from grammar and dictionary rules, he was the first to raise a banner against all the complicated technical devices of the native Parnassian and Symbolist poets. The bareness of his style risked leading poetry into prosaic plainness; but, as this poem makes evident, the apparent simplicity hides a subtle artistry. For despite its flowing freedom, "*Profundamente*" is carefully constructed according to a parallelism between the actions and emotional responses of the child and of the middle-aging man. The two worlds combine in an extended image which is the entire poem. Each element in the first has its counterpart in the second, even though these counterparts arise as suggestions in the reader's imagination in the wake of line 28. Indeed, the true poem is created in this wake—the undelineated counterparts in mature life to the child's falling asleep when the fiesta was at its height; waking up in the middle of the night when the event itself was already irretrievable; and listening for familiar voices that no longer sound.

In a poem intended as a statement of principles ("*Poética*"), Bandeira declared that "all rhythms are legitimate, above all those which cannot be numbered" (*inumeráveis*)—those completely free from any "rules" of metre. For all its freedom in versification and its lack of any ascertainable metrical pattern, "*Profundamente*" has nevertheless an interior rhythm produced by the alternation of long and short lines and by the recurrence of lines with the same number of syllables. (For example, lines of six syllables: 9, 10, 11, etc.; of seven syllables: 25, 34, 35, 36, etc.; of eight syllables: 2, 4, 12, 16, 20, etc.; of nine syllables: 3, 6, 8, etc.)   [E.G.D.]

TEMA E VOLTAS

Mas para quê
Tanto sofrimento
Se nos céus há o lento
Deslizar da noite?   4

Mas para quê
Tanto sofrimento
Se lá fora o vento
É um canto na noite?   8

Mas para quê
Tanto sofrimento
Se agora, ao relento
Cheira a flor da noite?   12

Mas para quê
Tanto sofrimento
Se o meu pensamento
É livre na noite?   16

(Obras completas. 1948)

B*ut why should there be* (2) *So much suffering* (3) *If in [on] the sky there is the slow* (4) *Gliding (sliding) of the night?* (5) *But why should there be* (6) *So much suffering* (7) *If out there the wind* (8) *Is a song in the night?* (9) *But why should there be* (10) *So much suffering* (11) *If now, with the dew,* (12) *The night-flower exudes fragrance* [literally *smells*]*?* (13) *But why should there be* (14) *So much suffering,* (15) *If my thoughts [my soul]* (16) *Are free in the night?*

Faithful to its title, "Theme and Variations" uses a common theme *(tema)* in the first two lines of each quatrain—they are taken from a children's folk-song—and introduces variations *(voltas)* in the last two. The variations are narrowly restricted, since all the fourth lines end with the same word *(noite,* "night") and every third line is linked to the same final word in the line above with which it rimes *(sofrimento: lento, vento, relento, pensamento).* In fact, the third line and four syllables of the fourth are all that Bandeira has available for his variations. And yet the melodic result is surprisingly effective, suggesting a delicate Verlainian echo that haunts the ear.

"Suffering" and "night" are the two poles of the poem, which the strophic structure confronts and contrasts. But while "suffering" remains unaltered "night" changes from stanza to stanza, evoking in each of them a different aspect or impression of nightly serenity: each creates an emotional climate contrary to the idea of suffering. Bandeira begins with a time perception translated into visual terms—the slow sliding of the night across the sky. The next variation is one of sound—the singing of the wind. In the third, the calm of nocturnal beauty is perceived through the sense of smell—the nightflower exudes fragrance. Finally, the speaker transcends physical sensations, his mind and spirit freed from all earthly suffering, in the unbounded beauty of the night. The poem is simultaneously static and dynamic. The night is timeless, immovable; the variations create a dynamic pattern that develops in delicate waves until, in the last stanza, the speaker is overwhelmed and liberated by the placid infinitude.

The poem calls to mind Portuguese lyrics of the sixteenth century, when poems were often composed of original variations upon a "given" two lines from a well-known source. It also calls to mind another Bandeira poem on night ("*Noite morta,*" "Dead of Night") which is poles apart from this almost classical creation, but which has in common with it a feeling of "eternalness" (6-8) that Bandeira associates with the night:

Noite morta.
Junto ao poste de iluminação
Os sapos engolem mosquitos.

Ninguém passa na estrada.   4
Nem um bêbado.

No entanto há seguramente por ela uma procissão de sombras.
Sombras de todos os que passaram.
Os que ainda vivem e os que já morreram.   8

O córrego chora.
A voz da noite. . .

(Não desta noite, mas de outra maior.)

(1) *Dead of night.* | *Beside the lamp post* | *The toads are swallowing mosquitoes.* (4-5) *Nobody passes in the street.* | *Not even a drunkard.* (6-8) *And yet there is surely a procession of shadows.* | *Shadows of all those who have passed.* | *Of those who are still alive and those already dead.* (9-11) *The gutter weeps [in its bed, streaming with water].* | *The voice of the night . . .* | *(Not of this night, but of another [that is] larger.* [E.G.D.]

FERNANDO PESSOA

AUTOPSICOGRAFIA

O poeta é um fingidor.
Finge tão completamente
Que chega a fingir que é dor
A dor que deveras sente.   4

E os que lêem o que escreve
Na dor lida sentem bem
Não as duas que êle teve
Mas só a que êles não têm.   8

E assim nas calhas de roda
Gira, a entreter a razão
Esse comboio de corda
Que se chama o coração.

(*Poesias.* 1958)

The poet is a feigner [simulator; Latin *fingere:* "to form, shape, invent, feign"]. (2) *He feigns so completely* (3) *That he even feigns that he is suffering* (4) *The pains that he is really experiencing.*

(5) *And those who read what he writes,* (6) *As they read, sharply feel* (7-8) *Not his double pain, but their single one* [literally *Not the two pains that he had but only the one they do not*].

(9) *And so, upon its toy tracks,* (10) *Runs around, diverting reason,* (11) *The wound-up mechanical train* [the toy train operated by a wound-up cord] (12) *That goes by the name of heart.*

As its ironical pseudo-scientific Greek title indicates, this poem expresses Pessoa's idea of the relationship of the poetic experience to truth. The writer attempts, by means of an imaginative "graph" of his own psyche, to present the essence of the creative process. His starting point is the Nietzschean idea that "only the poet who is capable of lying, consciously and voluntarily, is capable of telling the truth." But what is the "poetic lie" ultimately? This is what Pessoa hopes to answer.

His criterion of poetic, as contrasted with ordinary, truth seems to be "feigning" —that is, giving a mental existence to something neither actual nor real in objective existence. But this is not simply an imposture which the poet creates and to which he himself may fall victim in self-deception. For Pessoa, the only truth in poetry is that which the poet may arrive at after eliminating all sentimental accessories, all accretions of emotional and sentient experiences in everyday life. And this much the poet can accomplish during the gestation period, through voluntary self-control and through conscious exclusion of such "objective" truth, until he reaches the point at which he is able to simulate that other truth which is a genuine act of knowledge and a true vision of the world. The resulting poem, then, to use the words of MacLeish, does not "mean" any more, but simply "is"; if achieved, the poem is "equal to: not true."

Pessoa says elsewhere, "To simulate is to know oneself," and during his short life he carried this dramatic adventure to remarkable lengths. In his effort to annihilate his own "objective" truth through feigning, he projected himself into four different poet-personalities: his own and a trio of respectively individual qualities —"Alberto de Campos," "Alberto Caeiro," "Ricardo Reis" (the reader familiar with Antonio Machado may recall his alter egos, "Abel Martín" and "Juan de Mairena"). Pessoa did not intend these three names as pseudonyms. He called them his "heteronyms," for they were autonomous entities in both nature and mode of expression. He defined them psychologically and biographically, and at times even engaged in polemics with them.

"*Autopsicografia*," like all of Pessoa's poetry, moves in the realm of interior life and aims at nonrational intuition. A kind of abstract emotion infuses the writer's lucid intellectuality until it becomes as moving and intense as the immediate emotions of the heart; it becomes almost like the toy train itself, perpetually running around reason.

In another poem, Pessoa speaks of the anguishing "pain [he] experienced while simulating the pain [he] had in [his] soul."

According to lines 5-8 of our poem, however, the reader will not experience either of these two pains felt by the poet, but a third one: a single pain, through which the poem "is," and which is not in either of the poet's twofold pains. This single pain experienced—but not felt—by the reader constitutes the revelation given by that other and special truth which the poem contains.

During his lifetime (1888-1935; he was born and died in Lisbon), Fernando Pessoa published only four booklets of English verse and a thin volume of Portuguese (*Mensagem*, 1934). Since then several volumes of Pessoa's uncollected and unpublished work have been issued, and he is now regarded as the outstanding member of the first Portuguese poetic generation of our century, a generation which began propitiously with futurism (in the review *Orpheus*, 1913) and reached full fruition with the "modernista" group (centered around the review *Presença*, 1927). Pessoa acted as the influential link between the two movements. An Anglo-Saxon by education (he spent twelve years in South Africa, from the age of five), he was nevertheless fully Lusitanian in spirit. His prophetic bent and pre-occupation with the mystical, irrational, religious, and occult relate him to Blok, Yeats, Unamuno, Rilke, and George, and like some of them, he was obsessed by the nature and meaning of personal identity. Multiplying his voice in a conscious process of alienation, he never ceased searching for his ultimate "I."   [E.G.D.]

FERNANDO PESSOA

[ENTRE O SONO E O SONHO]

Entre o sono e o sonho
Entre mim e o que em mim
É o quem eu me suponho,
Corre um rio sem fim.   4

Passou por outras margens,
Diversas mais além,
Naquelas várias viagens
Que todo o rio tem.   8

Chegou onde hoje habito
A casa que hoje sou.
Passa, se eu me medito;
Se desperto, passou.   12

E quem me sinto e morre
No que me liga a mim
Dorme onde o rio corre —
Esse rio sem fim.

(*Poesias*. 1958)

*etween sleep and dream, (2) Between me
and [that which is] in me, (3) The Who
I assume to be, (4) An endless river flows.*

*(5) It passed by other banks, (6) Diverse
and way off yonder, (7) In those different
travels (courses) (8) That every river takes.*

*(9) It arrived where I dwell, (10) The
house I am today. (11) It passes, if I muse
on me; (12) If I awake, it passed away,*

*(13) And [he] who[m] I feel [to be], and [he
who] dies (14) In that which links me to
myself, (15) Slumbers where the river flows—
(16) That river without end.*

In this untitled poem, Pessoa voices his
preoccupation with the meaning of human
existence and the multiple essence of
human personality. Faintly echoing
Hamlet in the first line, the poem begins
by making a river flow *between* sleep and
dream, which are for Pessoa symbols of
two parts of his own self. This river,
which meanders through the entire poem,
entering it in the first stanza and flowing
out and into infinity at the end, asserts its
wavy presence repeatedly (*corre, passou,
viagens, chegou, passa, passou, corre*; 4, 5, 7,
9, 11, 12). The two similar phrases in
lines 4 and 15-16 reinforce the effect. In
marked contrast are the presences of the
poet's self, in lines 2-3 and 13-14-15. The
first—*me and that which is in me*—parallel
sleep and dream. But what is the third
self, dying *in that which*, supposedly across
the river, *links* the egos of sleep and dream?

Is it a bridge-ego of a sort, which sleeps on the bed of the river ("onde o rio corre")?

We can merely surmise the meaning of Pessoa's interpretation of the mystery of being. Is this river the "river of life" that Jorge Manrique (1440-1479) described, which ends in the sea of death? Is it death itself? Or perhaps both life and death? It comes from very far away and it has no end; it separates two zones of the poet's personality at the same time that a third both dies above it and sleeps beneath it. It arrived in the past at the house where he dwells in the present, a house which the poet identifies with himself (and perhaps yet another "I"). And it runs (*passa*, 11) only when he "ponders himself," but if he awakes (present tense) from that form of dreaming, he finds that it passed away (preterit: *passou*, 12). Possibly this river, without beginning or end and simultaneously static and dynamic, this river which so pervades a man's mysteriously multiple existence, is God—ever-present and ineffable. Is Pessoa, who was long preoccupied with the mystical, irrational, religious, and occult—his French translator, Armand Guibert, called him the "mystic of agnosticism"—trying to analyze God?

The extremely individual nature of Pessoa's imagination, combined with his ability to clothe it in language and symbols of poignant simplicity, makes this poem, like many others by him, a beguiling challenge. On first reading, it seems to lend itself to easy interpretation; sustained by the power of highly controlled rime and meter, it casts an almost simple charm on the reader's attention. But on closer examination, one sees that it is revelatory writing—the product of the mystic intuition of a metaphysically tormented spirit, who is trying to give artistic form to cryptic and contradictory visions, visions whose very nature demands not only vagueness and ambiguity but violations of established syntax as well. For example, Pessoa makes reflexives of three non-reflexive verbs, to produce unexpected effects that are essential to the thought: *me suponho, me medito, me sinto* (3, 11, 13) —"I assume myself," "I muse on me," "I sense myself."

The fact that it challenges the reader to unseal its riddle while at the same time withholding its meaning does not prevent us from enjoying "*Entre o sono e o sonho*" as a beautifully achieved work of art. The language of poetry is by nature oracular or sibylline, a fact that is widely recognized and accepted today. Possibly the very elusiveness of Pessoa's poem is a substantial factor in its impact. As Ortega y Gasset observed in this general connection, anything that can be expressed adequately and completely in prose is not worth turning into poetry.   [E.G.D.]

PEDRO SALINAS

[NO TE VEO]

No te veo. Bien sé
que estás aquí, detrás
de una frágil pared
de ladrillos y cal, bien al alcance   4
de mi voz, si llamara.
Pero no llamaré.
Te llamaré mañana,
cuando, al no verte ya   8
me imagine que sigues
aquí cerca, a mi lado,
y que basta hoy la voz
que ayer no quise dar.   12
Mañana... cuando estés
allá detrás de una
frágil pared de vientos,
de cielos y de años.

(*Presagios.* 1923)

I *don't see you. I know well* (2) *that you are here, behind* (3) *a fragile wall* (4) *of bricks and mortar, well within range* (5) *of my voice, should I call.*

"I don't see you," says the speaker, "but I know that you are there, behind a real (though fragile) wall; that should I need you, you would come. The mere fact of your physical presence is enough; the certainty of your responding to my call is sufficient. I do not desire you now, because you are attainable, because I am certain of your love and your response."

(6) *But I will not call.* "But now I need not call out to you. I am content in the knowledge of your presence and your love. I am content with the memory of your face, your voice, your body; knowing that you are waiting, existing, *being there*

for me; the need is not urgent, our love can wait."

(7) *I will call you tomorrow,* (8) *when, no longer seeing you,* (9) *I shall imagine that you are always* (10) *here, nearby, at my side,* (11) *and that today the word is enough* (12) *that yesterday I would not pronounce* [literally *give*]. "Yes, tomorrow there will be time enough for our love. And I am certain that tomorrow you will be there still, behind that real wall [real because it can be destroyed] that separates us. And tomorrow I shall say to myself: 'Today I need only pronounce that word, your name; need only call to you with the phrase that yesterday I didn't feel like saying . . . And surely you will be there, at my side, waiting, as always, for my love, my voice'."

(13) *Tomorrow . . . when you are* (14) *there*

behind a (15) *fragile wall of winds,* (16) *skies, and years.* "But tomorrow . . . What if tomorrow you are not behind a wall of brick and mortar, but behind an unreal [but indestructible] wall of winds and years? What if we are separated—finally, irrevocably—by one of a thousand contingencies: by physical separation; by the failure of our love; by war; by sickness; by death? If, seeking you behind a fragile wall of skies and years—death—I call to you, what good *then* will be the phrase that yesterday I refrained from speaking?"

In this poem, as in many others of Salinas (1891-1951), the compelling love of the poet is threatened by the shadow of nothingness. He lives and loves on the edge of an abyss of skies and years—*le néant hante l'être* (Sartre: "Nothingness haunts being"). This is the only troubling note in his otherwise fervent and unmixed devotion.

The achievement of Salinas lies in his saying so much with so little. There is no rime; there are no allusions. The meter is irregular, based generally on the seven-syllable line. There is hardly the suggestion of a metaphor (15, 16). There are no learned or difficult words. There is no landscape, no recollected event, no symbol. There are only the simplest phrases (*I don't see you; I will call to you tomorrow*). Yet out of this simplicity the poet creates the rich and highly nuanced world of his love.

There are two significant transitions: the first from present to future time (10, 11, 12), where the word *hoy* ("today") is projected into the future; the second, from his attitude of confidence in the future to the sudden specter of loss and nothingness (12-16). Their abruptness heightens the immediacy of these transitions. His only other technical devices are the delicate enjambments, the frequent pauses, and the stronger caesuras marked by an occasional full stop (1 and 6). These are the devices of natural conversation, modulated to a soft and indefinable music, a music that must be lost in translation.

[J.P.]

PEDRO SALINAS

MUERTES

Primero te olvidé en tu voz.
Si ahora hablases aquí,
a mi lado,
preguntaría yo: « ¿Quién es? »   4

Luego, se me olvidó de ti tu paso.
Si una sombra se esquiva
entre el viento, de carne,
ya no sé si eres tú.   8

Te deshojaste toda lentamente,
delante de un invierno: la sonrisa,
la mirada, el color del traje, el número
de los zapatos.   12

Te deshojaste aún más:
se te cayó tu carne, tu cuerpo.
Y me quedó tu nombre, siete letras, de ti.
Y tú, viviendo,   16
desesperadamente agonizante,
en ellas, con alma y cuerpo.
Tu esqueleto, sus trazos,
tu voz, tu risa, siete letras, ellas.   20
Y decirlas tu solo cuerpo ya.

Se me olvidó tu nombre.
Las siete letras andan desatadas;
no se conocen.   24
Pasan anuncios en tranvías; letras
se encienden en colores a la noche,
van en sobres diciendo
otros nombres.   28
Por allí andarás tú,
disuelta ya, deshecha e imposible.
Andarás tú, tu nombre, que eras tú,
ascendido   32
hasta unos cielos tontos,
en una gloria abstracta de alfabeto.

(Fábula y signo. 1931)

Fábula y signo was Salinas' third book, following Presagios (1923) and Seguro azar (1929). In it we note an intensification of the personal element—the tú (you), the woman to whom most of these poems were written; or, if no particular woman, perhaps a love "intellectualized," but not coldly so.

The important thing in this poetry is the *idea* of love, the *idea* of woman; but the *idea* is deeply and passionately apprehended by the poet. In the present poem, for example, forgetfulness means death: when we forget someone, we kill him in ourselves, and this killing implies a real death in the exterior world.

The title is "Deaths." (1) *First I forgot you in your voice.* (2) *If you were to speak here, now,* (3) *beside me,* (4) *I'd ask, "Who is it?"* (5) *Next, it was your step that I forgot.* (6-7) *If a shadow of flesh draws back* [withdraws; the word order is marked by a rather elegantly artificial *tmesis: If a shadow withdraws into the wind, of flesh]/ into the wind,* (8) *I no longer know if it is you.* (9) *You stripped yourself of petals, slowly,* (10) *before a winter: [your] smile,* (11) *[your] look, the color of [your] dress, the size [número: size-number]* (12) *of [your] shoes.* (13) *You stripped yourself of petals even more:* (14) *your flesh fell from you, your body.* (15) *Only your name remained to me, seven letters, [only that much] of you.* (16) *But you [are] living [still],* (17) *desperately agonizing* (18) *in them, body and soul.* (19) *Your skeleton, their tracery;* (20) *your voice, your laughter: seven letters, those [seven].* (21) *Now your body is only the pronouncing of them.* (22) *I forgot your name.* (23) *The seven letters walk by, unrelated;* (24) *they do not know each other.* (25) *Streetcar advertisements pass by; letters* (26) *flare up in colors at night;* (27) *[letters] go [by] on envelopes saying* (28) *other people's names.* (29) *And there you will be,* (30) *undone, destroyed, and impossible (incredible).* (31) *You will be there, you, your name that used to be you,* (32) *gone up* (33) *into some absurd Heaven* (34) *in an abstract alphabet glory.*

The poem is composed of lines of irregular length, with seven- and eight-syllable verses predominating. The rime is irregular, too; but the occasional assonances emphasize interrelations of mood and idea—for example, the *a-o* of 3, 5, 12; *e-o* (14, 16, 18); *o-e* (22, 24, 26, 28) with two internal assonances, *colores* (26) and *sobres* (27).

In structure, the poem is made up of five "episodes," or movements, which express four modes of "forgetting"—that is to say, four deaths. First her voice is forgotten (1-4); then her footstep (5-8); then the whole body, leaving only her name (9-12); then her name (22); and after these four acts of forgetting, the poet creates an almost surrealistic procession of the seven letters of her name, dissociated, each one living for itself in streetcar advertisements and electric signs and on envelopes.

The woman, in the letters of her name, is dispersed, fragmented; the pieces circulate desperately, reuniting at last for a comic ascension into an alphabetical paradise. The original *You*-ness of the *tú*, the beloved woman, has become, in these progressive acts of forgetting, a kind of literal-literature abstraction, a Dadaist collage.   [E.F.]

PEDRO SALINAS

[PENSAR EN TI ESTA NOCHE]

Pensar en ti esta noche
no era pensarte con mi pensamiento,
yo solo, desde mí. Te iba pensando
conmigo extensamente, el ancho mundo.   4

El gran sueño del campo, las estrellas,
callado el mar, las hierbas invisibles,
sólo presentes en perfumes secos,
todo,   8
de Aldebarán al grillo, te pensaba.

¡Qué sosegadamente
se hacía la concordia
entre las piedras, los luceros,   12
el agua muda, la arboleda trémula,
todo lo inanimado,
y el alma mía
dedicándolo a ti! Todo acudía   16
dócil a mi llamada, a tu servicio,
ascendido a intención y a fuerza amante.
Concurrían las luces y las sombras
a la luz de quererte; concurrían   20
el gran silencio, por la tierra, plano,
suaves voces de nube, por el cielo,
al cántico hacia ti que en mí cantaba.
Una conformidad de mundo y ser,   24
de afán y tiempo, inverosímil tregua,
se entraba en mí, como la dicha entra
cuando llega sin prisa, beso a beso.
Y casi   28
dejé de amarte por amarte más,
en más que en mí, inmensamente confiando
este empleo de amar a la gran noche
errante por el tiempo y ya cargada   32
de misión, misionera
de un amor vuelto estrellas, calma, mundo,
salvado ya del miedo
al cadáver que queda si se olvida.

(Razón de amor. 1936)

Razón de amor (*Love's reason*) and *La Voz a ti debida* (*The Voice due you*) are the heart of Salinas' poetry. The latter is his great poem of love, and one of the most important love poems in contemporary European literature; the former incorporates some of the most intensely lyric of his poems; and together the two books compose a hymn to love, a liturgical Sequence, as it were. This is the poetry of a wholesome love, healthy and sound; a love that is affirmative, happily innocent of complications and deviations. Or let us say that such complications as arise are of the metaphysical order, springing from Salinas' preoccupation with the reduction of sensation to idea, with the transformation of real time into an ideal abstraction of time. The problems are difficult, but the solution is inevitably poetical.

(1) *To think of you tonight* (2) *was not to think of you with my thought,* (3-4) *I, alone, from out of myself. The wide world was thinking of you, with me, prolongedly.* (5) *The great sleep of the fields, the stars,* (6) *the silent sea, the invisible grass,* (7-8) *present only in [its] dry perfume, everything,* (9) *from Aldebaran to the cricket, was [were] thinking of you.* (10) *How calmly* (11) *a harmony emerged (was found)* (12) *between the stones, the stars,* (13) *the still water, the trembling grove,* (14) *all inanimate things,* (15) *and my soul* (16) *offering all of it to you! Everything responded* (17) *docilely to my call, to serve you,* (18) *risen to purpose and [in] loving strength!* (19) *Light and shade combined to meet* (20) *in the light of loving you; combined [also]* (21) *the vast silence level on the earth,* (22) *the soft cloud voices of the sky,* (23) *in the canticle of You that was singing itself into me.* (24) *A concord of world and being,* (25) *of time and desire [anxiety], an improbable truce,* (26) *entered me as happiness enters* (27) *when it arrives without haste, kiss by kiss.* (28) *Almost, I*

(29) *stopped loving you, for loving you the more,* (30) *in more than myself, immensely entrusting* (31) *the observance of loving [you] to the huge night* (32) *wandering through time, charged now* (33) *with a mission, emissary* (34) *of a love transformed into stars, stillness, world,* (35) *saved now from the terror* (36) *of the corpse that remains when we forget.*

Here we have the vigorous individual affirmation related to the universal: the poet, thinking of his loved one, imagines that everything is thinking of her at the same time. As we saw in a poem commented upon before—"*Muertes,*" from *Fábula y signo*—forgetting someone is an act of killing. It follows, then, that thinking of someone is a life-giving act, a saving from death and oblivion. These two poems combine handsomely in a metaphysical idea.

"To Think of You Tonight . . ." is composed of two short stanzas followed by an uninterrupted flow to the end. The first stanza establishes the fact of meditation (3, 4); the second amplifies the idea, expanding it into the great unity of Nature, of the universe, the key point being placed at the word *todo* ("everything," 8). From here on the development is clear enough; although it should be noted that at line 15, *y el alma mía* ("and my soul"), we come to another key point, the idea that it is through the poet's spirit, his individual power to love, that the miracle of universal love is made possible. The thought takes on a fine strangeness at the end, where the poet leaves to the night the task ("observance") of loving (30, 31) and withdraws into, or identifies himself with, the night. The stars, the stillness, the whole world— these themselves have become love, and it is they that save the loved one from the dark.   [E.F.]

PEDRO SALINAS

EL POEMA

Y ahora, aquí está frente a mí.
Tantas luchas que ha costado,
tantos afanes en vela,
tantos bordes de fracaso   4
junto a este esplendor sereno
ya son nada, se olvidaron.
Él queda, y en él, el mundo,
la rosa, la piedra, el pájaro,   8
aquéllos, los del principio,
de este final asombrados.
¡Tan claros que se veían,
y aún se podía aclararlos!   12
Están mejor; una luz
que el sol no sabe, unos rayos
los iluminan, sin noche,
para siempre revelados.   16
Las claridades de ahora
lucen más que las de mayo.
Si allí estaban, ahora aquí;
a más transparencia alzados.   20
¡Qué naturales parecen,
qué sencillo el gran milagro!
En esta luz del poema,
todo,   24
desde el más nocturno beso
al cenital esplendor,
todo está mucho más claro.

(*Todo más claro y otros poemas.* 1949)

This is the fourth and last poem of a group called "*Todo más claro*," which gives its title to Salinas' book published in 1949. The verse in this collection was written between 1937 and 1947, when the author was "far away from [his] native land, though it is always and increasingly in [his] love and [his] dreams; living in the hospitable United States, clinging to [his] language as to an incomparable treasure," as he observes in his preface. Thus it is a work of Salinas' maturity, a summary, as it were, of his poetical thought. It reflects his struggle to "make everything clearer" (*todo más claro*), since "poetry is the work of love and clarity combined." Clarity and love are not always to be found in a young poet, but they almost always appear in the poet whom age has ripened. Accordingly, in this small volume the major themes are love and the actuality of the visible world—preoccupations that deepen and intensify in Salinas' last poems.

"*El poema*," like the other three poems in the group, is in the octosyllabic line so often used by Salinas. It is the meter of the Spanish *romance*, or ballad, with an *a-o* assonance broken only at line 24 (a single word), and with the assonanced rimes in the even verses (2-4, 6-8, etc.). This rime is broken before and after line 24: the key words *poema* ("poem") and *beso* ("kiss") thus stand guard, so to speak, over that other key word *todo*. ("everything"), which is repeated in the last line.

(1) *And now, here it stands before me.* (2) *So many struggles it has cost [me]!* (3) *so much anxious staying awake!* (4) *So many riskings of failure!* (5) *[And yet,] in the light of this serene splendor,* (6) *they are nothing, they are forgotten.* / (7) *It [the poem] remains; and, in it, world,* (8) *rose, rock, bird,* (9) *those elemental things,* (10) *astonished in the presence of this finality.* (11) *They seemed so clear to us!* (12) *But they could be made clearer.* (13) *[Now] they are better: a light* (14-15) *not known to the sun illumines them with its rays, beyond night,* (16) *revealed for ever.* (17) *The clarities of Now* (18) *shine even more than those of May.* (19) *If they were there before, they are here now,* (20) *exalted in a greater lucidity.* (21) *How natural they seem,* (22) *how simple the great miracle!* (23) *In this poem-light,* (24) *everything—* (25) *from the most noctural kiss* (26) *to the splendor of the zenith—* (27) *everything is clearer.*

At the beginning of these four poems in the group "*Todo más claro*," the author stated that he was trying to "describe a road to the poem." He has found the road, and now he is face to face with the poem. Just as women forget their labor pains after childbirth, he has forgotten all the trouble that the poem cost him (6). The poem stands by itself; and in its autonomous radiance (13-16) the essential realities of this world (symbolized by the rose, the rock, the bird) shine transfigured. The realities of this world—for Pedro Salinas is a poet of the world of actuality: his transformations of reality into essence and abstraction never lose the touch of the world's shapes and textures. In this poem, for instance, what is "real" is the radiance.

In the first of the four poems he gave us the *data*, material things shrouded in mystery. In the second, he was searching darkly, like a blindfolded man groping towards the light. In the third, it is Language (*santas palabras*, "blessed words") that comes to aid him. Finally, in the poem we are discussing, the work of art appears, realized, revealed (16) in its own abstract light. "Everything is clear"; we need search no further. Everything is the more clear, it may be, because the poet himself was unconsciously nearing death: that is to say, the ultimate clarification.

[E.F.]

DESNUDO

Blancos, rosas. Azules casi en veta,
Retraídos, mentales.
Puntos de luz latente dan señales
De una sombra secreta.   4

Pero el color, infiel a la penumbra,
Se consolida en masa.
Yacente en el verano de la casa,
Una forma se alumbra.   8

Claridad aguzada entre perfiles,
De tan puros tranquilos,
Que cortan y aniquilan con sus filos
Las confusiones viles.   12

Desnuda está la carne. Su evidencia
Se resuelve en reposo.
Monotonía justa, prodigioso
Colmo de la presencia.   16

¡Plenitud inmediata, sin ambiente,
Del cuerpo femenino!
Ningún primor: ni voz ni flor. ¿Destino?
¡Oh absoluto Presente!   20

(Cántico: primera edición completa. 1950)

D*esnudo* ("Nude") is a poem of emergence from nothingness to Being; it conveys, in precise and measured terms, an almost childlike wonder at the miracle and perfection of existence. In this it resembles certain of Guillén's longer poems, among them *"Más allá"* ("Beyond"), the initial poem of *Cántico*. *"Más allá"* describes an awakening, a slow emergence from chaos, a gradual awareness of an identification with surrounding objects. The Romantic *I* has disappeared from the poet's world-view; his individuality fuses with what the Existentialists call *L'être en soi* ("being-in-itself"), to achieve fulfilment. The first part of *"Más allá"* ends with the words:
> Reality invents me.
> I am its legend. Hail!

Guillén's principal theme is delight in being, but his own being is dependent on exterior reality, the *beyond*. Likewise in the short poem *"Beato sillón"* ("Blessed Armchair") it is the chair that links him to the physical universe and allows him to transcend it.

In *"Desnudo"* this reality takes the form of a woman's body, a perfect creation, which emerges at first only in its most abstract form: color.

(1) *Whites, pinks. Blues almost in veins,* (2) *Fugitive, mental.* (3) *Points of latent light give signs* (4) *Of hidden shadow.*

The colors are "fugitive and mental": they are still almost abstract, ideas not yet coalesced into reality. The body's contour is suggested at first only by "fugitive points of light": chaos is still dominant.

(5) *But the color, disloyal to its half-shadow,* (6) *Consolidates itself into a mass.* (7) *Lying in the house's summer,* (8) *A form lights up.* (9) *Clarity sharpened between profiles,* (10) *So pure [and] quiet,* (11) *That they cut and annihilate with their edges* (12) *The base confusions.*

The poetry of Jorge Guillén (1893–1984) is of clarity above all, or of the triumph of clarity: light, bright contours, tactile and visual certainty. The "pure and quiet profiles" annihilate the "base confusions." Chaos is abhorred as nothingness; only the clear outline of being is desired.

(13) *The flesh is naked. Its evidence* (14) *Melts into repose.* (15) *The right monotone, prodigious* (16) *Over-measure of presence.*

The form is clear now; it takes on a human quality, repose. The physical presence of the beloved, the exactly "right monotone," is of prodigious—almost unbearable—intensity.

(17) *Immediate abundance, without ambient,* (18) *Of the female body!* (19) *No beauty: neither voice nor flower. Destiny?* (20) *Oh absolute Present!*

The female body needs no *ambiente*, no atmosphere, no additional beauty, voice or flower, to set it off. It is its own realization. It is perfect not in its promise (future? children?) but in its "absolute present." *Presencia, presente, plenitud inmediata:* again the poet sings the moment, the *now*, its sufficiency and abundance.

The movement of this poem is slow, considered, measured. The eleven- and seven-syllable lines are frequently broken with pauses. The slow movement is intended to sugest the gradual appearance of the desired reality, the woman's body, its process of becoming, its coming into being. The rime, in *abba, bccb,* etc., is consonantal, that is, both consonants and vowels rime. The structure and rime add strength and texture to the statement of an emotion (recollected, certainly, in tranquillity) which might otherwise lose itself in a spontaneous outburst, or in diffuseness.

[J.P.]

JORGE GUILLÉN

SABOR A VIDA

Hay ya cielo por el aire
   Que se respira.
Respiro, floto en venturas,
   Por alegrías.   4

Las alegrías de un hombre
Se ahondan fuera esparcidas.
Yo soy feliz en los árboles,
En el calor, en la umbría.   8

¿Aventuras? No las caza
   Mi cacería.
Tengo con el mismo sol
   La eterna cita.   12

¡Actualidad! Tan fugaz
En su cogollo y su miga,
Regala a mi lentitud
El sumo sabor a vida.   16

¡Lenta el alma, lentos pasos
   En compañía!
¡La gloria posible nunca,
   Nunca abolida!   20

(Cántico: primera edición completa. 1950)

"Sabor" (the English *savor*) means "taste," and the title suggest a taste not of but *like* life: lifetaste. Delight in the moment, in pure being, is of the essence in Jorge Guillén's work. Until recently (in 1957 he issued a new volume of poetry called *Clamor. Maremagnum*) that work consisted primarily in a single book, *Cántico*, which was originally published in 1928, but was reissued, expanded, and revised three times thereafter: 1936, 1945, and 1950. The last edition is considered by the author definitive and final. His poetry combines a tight classical form with a brilliantly complex style, a metaphorical density and daring that recall not only Mallarmé but also the great baroque poet Luis de Góngora (1561-1627), yet which somehow achieve a freshness and clarity not reminiscent of either of his predecessors, in a poetry dedicated to the celebration of immediate delight, of joy in living, in being alive.

Breath, air, sky, joy are mentioned in the first lines of "*Sabor a vida*" to set its theme of expanding intoxication with the sufficiency of the present: (1) *There is a sky in the air* (2) *That breathes.* (3) *I breathe, I float in hazards* ["ventura" suggests both *chance* and "viento," *wind*], (4) *Through joys.* (5) *The joys of a man* (6) *Deepen and scatter abroad.* (7) *I am content with the trees,* (8) *In the heat, in the shade.* (9) *Adventures? They are not hounded* (10) *By my hunters.* (11) *I have with the sun itself* (12) *A date for ever.*

Both *ventura* and *aventura* come from the Latin *advenire*, but in Spanish the first has come to mean "chance," "luck," whereas the second (the English *adventure*) suggests an unusual personal experience. Our poet says that he would abandon himself to *ventura* ("chance"), but that he does not seek *aventura* ("excitement"). (The alliterated assonance of "hounded" and "hunters" is intended to suggest that of *caza* and *cacería*.) Here the poet does not seek exotic joys; he finds his felicity in the familiar manifestations of nature: the sun, the shade, the air, the moment. To state these things is not enough: he makes abstractions (*joys, sky, fortune, the present*) concrete and tangible; this is his personal vision of reality, where there is harmony and order, where doubts become certainties. The *sky breathes;* the *joys deepen and scatter;* and *the present:*

(13) *The present! so elusive* (14) *In its pith and marrow,* (15) *Rewards my loitering* (16) *With the uttermost taste of life.* (17) *Slow is the soul, slow are footsteps* (18) *In company!* (19) *Glory possible never,* (20) *Never abolished!*

The present is *elusive in its pith and marrow,* and it *rewards my loitering:* this kind of metaphor, the concretization of the abstraction, is frequent in Guillén's work, and he uses it with unusual precision and daring. The finale is *fortissimo:* the poet is enjoying the sound of his own footsteps, perhaps relishing his solitude, his own company (*compañía* could also refer to a friend or beloved). The present, the moment, rises to an ecstatic intensity, and the poem ends on a suggestive inversion, where instead of *never possible glory*, we see that the poet means *a possibility of glory never abolished.*

The present! Guillén's celebration of the moment, of Being, of Becoming, has led some critics, not without justification, to point out his nexus with Existentialism, which emphasizes lived experience over philosophical abstraction, Being above Essence. But Guillén is not, strictly speaking, an Existentialist poet, because he seems untroubled, in the poems of *Cántico*, by the anguish, the dread before nothingness, the problem of choice and responsibility which are the concern of the Existentialist philosophers. His is a poetry not of nothingness but of Being, of its fullness and immediacy.

A word about the versification: there are five quatrains, three of which have the alternate line short. The two quatrains of four full lines (the normal eight-syllable Spanish line) provide a movement suggesting strophe and antistrophe, and also act as a base, lending solidity to the whole. The assonantal rime, so difficult to reproduce in English, is maintained on the vowels *i* and *a* throughout: *respira, alegría, esparcidas, umbría*, etc.   [J.P.]

JORGE GUILLÉN

MUERTE A LO LEJOS

Je soutenais l'éclat de la mort toute pure.
— VALÉRY*

Alguna vez me angustia una certeza,
Y ante mí se estremece mi futuro.
Acechándole está de pronto un muro
Del arrabal final en que tropieza   4

La luz del campo. ¿Mas habrá tristeza
Si la desnuda el sol? No, no hay apuro
Todavía. Lo urgente es el maduro
Fruto. La mano ya lo descorteza.   8

...Y un día entre los días el más triste
Será. Tenderse deberá la mano   10
Sin afán. Y acatando el inminente

Poder diré sin lágrimas: embiste,   12
Justa fatalidad. El muro cano
Va a imponerme su ley, no su accidente.

(*Cántico: primera edición completa.* 1950)

A suggestive paradox opens this sonnet ("*Muerte a lo lejos*," literally "Death in the distance"). (1) *At times I am troubled by a certainty.* One is usually troubled by doubts or fears, seldom by a *certainty.* The poet is anguished by the only certainty, death. (2) *And there before me trembles my future.* The poet is not afraid; he does not tremble. But his "future (death) trembles before his eyes"—the physical reaction usually inspired by the object is transferred to the object itself, thereby softening the image of fear, without losing it altogether.

(3) *And lying in wait is suddenly a wall* (4) *Of the final suburb on which is cast* (5) *The field's light* . . . Death suddenly takes a more concrete form: a cemetery wall in a city suburb. The poet visualizes himself buried within the walls: death's inescapable reality, our future. Yet its terror is softened by the presence—also inescapable—of sunlight and countryside.

(5) *But will there be sorrow* (6) *If the sun reveals it? No, there is no anxiety* (7) *Yet.* . . . Should the image of death—the loss of light, forms, love—inspire sadness? No need to dwell on it yet, because:

(7) *What is urgent is the ripe* (8) *Fruit. The hand already peels it.* Why be anxious about death in the midst of life? "What is urgent": what deserves the concentration of our being is life in its infinite variety: knowledge, nature, love, art, the

keen presence of the moment, the air that fills our lungs, our senses that drink the expanding, multiform, multicolored world; there is too much to learn, to see, to hear, to touch; our lifetime is a moment, our bit of light a second of eternity; why waste it contemplating the *after*life, the unknown and unknowable? Better enjoy the fruit that the "hand now peels."

(9) . . . *And of all these days the saddest day* (10) *Will come. The hand should offer itself* (11) *Without fear.* . . . But the image remains, as it should, of our death, the "saddest day." The poet refuses to dwell on it morbidly, but neither will he blindly deny it. Light implies dark, birth implies death. It is part of the scheme of the universe; one depends on the other, and a joyful acceptance of light and birth implies the acceptance of its cycle and conclusion. "The hand should offer itself without fear." He will not resist; there should be a calm yielding to necessity, symbolized by the hand's quiet gesture. ("And I consent to dying with joyful, clear, and pure will, for it is madness that a man should wish to live when God wants him to die." These words, translated into prose, are by the fifteenth-century poet Jorge Manrique, from his famous "*Coplas a la muerté de su padre.*" Guillén's sonnet is clearly in the Castilian tradition of Manrique—serenity, resignation, clarity—but without the religious emphasis of the medieval poet.)

(11) *And revering the imminent* (12) *Power I shall say without tears: Come,* (13) *Just fatality. The white wall* (14) *Will impose on me its law, not its accident.* "When death comes I will accept it without tears: because it is just; because there is no preference, and all men suffer it equally; and above all because it is part of the *law* of the universe. It is not an accident [*accidente* suggests the philosophical idea of an incidental quality, not a happening]; it is not gratuitous or capricious; it is inevitable and right, part of the world's symmetry." That symmetry may be fearful, but more fearful still would be no rest, no end: the contemplation of eternal existence (and the suffering that existence implies) is more terrible. The poet then faces the inevitable, like Jorge Manrique, *con voluntad placentera:* "with serene accord".   [J.P.]

* "Je soutenais l'éclat de la mort toute pure": I sustained the splendor of pure death. — Valéry.

PRIMAVERA DELGADA

Cuando el espacio sin perfil resume
  Con una nube
Su vasta indecisión a la deriva,
  — ¿Dónde la orilla? —   4
Mientras el río con el rumbo en curva
  Se perpetúa
Buscando sesgo a sesgo, dibujante,
  Su desenlace,   8
Mientras el agua duramente verde
  Niega sus peces
Bajo el profundo equívoco reflejo
  De un aire trémulo...   12
Cuando conduce la mañana, lentas,
  Sus alamedas
Gracias a las estelas vibradoras
  Entre las frondas,   16
A favor del avance sinuoso
  Que pone en coro
La ondulación suavísima del cielo
  Sobre su viento   20
Con el curso tan ágil de las pompas,
  Que agudas bogan...
¡Primavera delgada entre los remos
  De los barqueros!   24

(*Cántico: primera edición completa.* 1950)

The title itself is a metaphor of an abstraction, the personification of a season: "Slender Spring." ("Spring" has several connotations in English, but in Spanish *primavera* is unambiguous.) *Delgada*, like its English equivalent, suggests youth and a rebirth. The personification conveys the image of the miracle of renascent nature in a Spring day. The poem lyrically endows a moment with immortality. A simple event—boating on a river—is given transcendence by a series of lovely metaphors involving river, sky, water, morning, poplars, oars, and spring. These intricate metaphors are sometimes ambiguous in themselves and in their interrelation, but the ambiguity—always a source of richness in poetry—sharpens the apprehension of an experience that is both dreamlike and permanent.

(1) *When profileless space sums up* (2) *With a cloud* (3) *Its vast indecision on the course,*

(4) *Where the shore?* "Profileless space" is metaphorical because it indirectly bestows human or, at any rate, visual qualities upon space. "Space sums up its indecisive course by a cloud," *i.e.*, the cloud is symbolic of the lack of direction implied in "space." The use of the word *deriva* ("course") suggests the as yet unmentioned river.

(5) *While the river with its curved route* (6) *Perpetuates itself* (7) *Seeking, stroke by stroke, [like an] artist,* (8) *Its conclusion*—. The river explores its bed, seeking its own dénouement. The extending rivulets, part of the water's movement, are compared to an artist's strokes with brush or pencil that also "seek the conclusion" of a sketch or painting.

(9) *While the opaquely [hard] green water* (10) *Denies its fish* (11) *Beneath the equivocal deep reflection* (12) *Of tremulous air.* . . . The deep opaque green of the water "denies its fish" to the observer above. Why "equivocal" reflection? Because the ripples in the water distort the reflected image of the air above.

(13) *When morning conducts, slowly,* (14) *Its poplar groves,* (15) *Thanks to the vibrating wake* (16) *Between the fronds*—. "Lentas" is an adjective, modifying "alamedas," but it has the force of an adverb. But our translation misses the suggestion of "slow poplar groves"—perhaps a vision of lethargically swaying trees. "Morning conducts its poplars, thanks to the vibrating wake between the fronds"—*morning* is personified; moreover, the boat's wake

helps it (morning) to lead the poplars: an extremely complex image.

(17) *Seconding the sinuous advance* (18) *Which puts in tune* (19) *The gentle undulation of the sky* (20) *Over its wind* (21) *With the agile course of the bubbles* (22) *That intently row,* (23) *Slender spring among the oars* (24) *Of the boatmen!* Why "seconding the sinuous advance" (the river)? Perhaps "the morning conducts its groves 'in favor of' the river" because nature is united in helping the river move toward its destination. The river "puts in tune" (in concord, in harmony) the sky's undulation and the rhythmic oarstrokes, which themselves are metaphorically suggested by the word *pompas* ("bubbles"), leaving us with an image of a stream of bubbles created by each plunge of the oar. The poem ends with an apostrophe, evoking the image of "slender spring" among the oars.

The series of clauses are connected by adverbial conjunctions (*when, while*) or prepositions (*under, in favor of, with*), the whole suggesting the river's leisurely movement, its "sinuous advance." The repetition of *when* and *while* seems to arrest time, affirming the supremacy of the moment. The delicate music of the assonant rime, which intensifies the dreamlike quality of the verse, is untranslatable; it is achieved by terminal vowel-rimes on the alternating eleven- and five-syllable lines, *e.g.*,

> Cuando el espacio sin perfil resume
> Con una nube . . .

[J.P.]

POEMA DE QUALQUER VIRGEM

As gerações da virgem estão tatuadas no ventre escorreito,
porque a virgem representa tudo o que há de vir.
Há arco-íris tatuados nas mãos, há Babeis tatuadas nos braços.
A virgem tem o corpo tatuado por Deus porque é a semente do mundo que há de vir.
Não há um milímetro do corpo, sem desenho e sem plantas futuras.
Não há um poro sem tatuagem: por isso a virgem é tão bela.
Vamos lêr a virgem, vamos conhecer o futuro: reparai que não são
enfeites, ó homens de vista curta. Olhai: são tatuagens dentro   8
de tatuagens, são gerações saindo de gerações.
Quem tatuou a virgem? Foi Deus no dia da Queda.
Vêde a serpente tatuada nela. Véde o anjo tatuado nela.
Vêde uma cruz tatuada nela. Vêde, senhores, que não pagareis nada. E' o supremo
espetáculo meus senhores. Ensinarei os mistérios, as letras simbólicas até o ômega.
Vinde vêr o trabalho admirável gravado no corpo da virgem: a história do mundo,
a estratosfera habitada, o mágico Tin-Ka-Lu viajando na lua. Porque a virgem
é admirável e tem trato. Vinde senhores que não pagareis nada. A imagem da
inocência, da volúpia, do crime, da bondade, as representações incríveis estão no
dorso da virgem, no pescoço, na face. Vão sair tumultos das tatuagens. E' um
momento muito sério, senhores. Vão sair grandes revoltas. Há um mar tatuado
na virgem, com os sete dias da criação, com o dilúvio, com a morte. Vinde senhores,
que não pagareis nada.   12

Senhores, hoje há espetáculo no mundo.
Vamos vêr a virgem, a virgem tatuada, a virgem tatuada por Deus.
Ela está nua e ao mesmo tempo vestida de tatuagens.
Meus senhores a virgem vai se desdobrar em milênios.   16
Há intuições nas tatuagens, há poemas, há mistérios.
E' por isso que o espetáculo é bonito. E' por isso que a virgem vos atrai.
Vinde, senhores!

(*Túnica inconsútil.* 1938)

The "Poem of Any Virgin" belongs to the third period of Jorge de Lima (1893-1953), which was characterized by a deepening of his Catholicism. Like most of his contemporaries, he had begun as a Parnassian, but with the inauguration of the Modern Movement in 1922, he turned to free verse and prose poems. At this time he also wrote a number of works on Negro themes, inspired by the northeastern region of Brazil where he was born. Religious inspiration is clearly discernible in these regional poems, but he had still to discard the popular conception of Catholicism. In his third period, religion became the *motive*; when in his fourth he reached his highest art (with *Invenção de Orfeu*), it became the *theme*. Transfigured by visions of transcendency, he enriched his language with religious and Biblical symbolism, mingling the universes of the visible with the invisible world.

Unlike this last, introspective work, where meanings are often inaccessible, the "Poem of Any Virgin" speaks out clearly —in the ringing phrases of a side show at a circus.

(1) *The generations of the virgin are tattooed on her unblemished belly,* (2) *for the virgin represents all that is to be.* (3) *Rainbows are tattooed on her hands, Towers of Babel on her arms.* (4) *The virgin's body is tattooed by God because she is the source of the world to be.* (5) *There is not a particle of her body without designs and future plans.* (6) *Not a pore without tattooings: that is why the virgin is so beautiful.* (7) *Come, let us read the virgin, let us learn the future: note that they [the tattooings] are not* (8) *mere adornments, O men of short sight. See, there are tattooings within* (9) *tattooings, there are generations issuing from generations.* (10) *Who tattooed the virgin? It was God on the day of the Fall.* (11) *See the serpent tattooed on her. See the angel tattooed on her.* (12) *See the Cross tattooed on her. Look, gentlemen, there is nothing to pay. This is the supreme spectacle, gentlemen. I will explain the mysteries, the symbolical letters even to omega. Come and see the marvelous work etched on the virgin's body: the history of the world, the inhabited stratosphere, the magician Tim-Ka-Lu taking a journey in the moon. For the virgin is marvelous and contains everything. Come gentlemen, there is nothing to pay. The image of innocence, of lust, of crime, of goodness,* *all these incredible pictures are on the virgin's back, on her neck, on her face. Disorders are about to issue from the tattooings. The moment is extremely grave, gentlemen. Great revolts are in the making. There is a sea tattooed on the virgin, with the seven days of creation, with the flood, with death. Come, gentlemen, there is nothing to pay.* (13) *Gentlemen, today there is a spectacle on earth.* (14) *Come and see the virgin, the tattooed virgin, the virgin tattooed by God.* (15) *She is naked and at the same time clothed with tattooings.* (16) *Gentlemen, the virgin is going to unfold through millenniums.* (17) *There are meanings in her tattooings, there are poems, there are mysteries.* (18) *That is why the show is beautiful. That is why the virgin attracts you.* (19) *Come, gentlemen!*

Woman is the essence of creation, the source of life itself. "And Adam called his wife's name Eve, because she was the mother of all living" (Genesis, iii:20). The Virgin bears tattoo marks on her belly as the seal impressed by God. God predestined her to conceive and bear virgins; and they, in turn, will conceive new beings, generation begetting generation. Why did God tattoo the Virgin, and why on the day of the Fall? Because she had allowed herself to be seduced by the serpent: she had sinned. God in his wrath tattooed her and said: "I will greatly multiply thy sorrow and thy conception; in sorrow thou shalt bring forth children." Therefore the serpent is tattooed upon the Virgin's body as the sign of sin; therefore innocence, lust, crime, and goodness are tattooed on her back, her neck, her face. A world of procreation is etched upon her body. Within her she carries both life and death, and out of her will issue all sorts of men: evil-doers, criminals, saints. Come let us look on the Virgin, who is like a symbol, naked and beautiful. Young and desirable, she is the body of fruitfulness. In the beauty of her form lies the mystery of creation. [D.V.]

HECES

Esta tarde llueve como nunca; y no
tengo ganas de vivir, corazón.

Esta tarde es dulce. Por qué no ha de ser?
Viste gracia y pena; viste de mujer.   4

Esta tarde en Lima llueve. Y yo recuerdo
las cavernas crueles de mi ingratitud;
mi bloque de hielo sobre su amapola,
más fuerte que su « No seas así! »   8

Mis violentas flores negras; y la bárbara
y enorme pedrada; y el trecho glacial.
Y pondrá el silencio de su dignidad
con óleos quemantes el punto final.   12

Por eso esta tarde, como nunca, voy
con este buho, con este corazón.

Y otras pasan; y viéndome tan triste,
toman un poquito de ti   16
en la abrupta arruga de mi hondo dolor.

Esta tarde llueve, llueve mucho. ¡Y no
tengo ganas de vivir, corazón!

(*Los heraldos negros*. 1918)

The anguished sadness of Vallejo's poetry is expressed in a highly personal way, colloquial in many instances, strange and unusual always. This poem is a typical example. The *donnée* is a rainy afternoon in Lima, the Peruvian capital, tormented by memories of a beloved woman who has put the *punto final*, the irrevocable last period, to an unsuccessful love affair. The lonely speaker's heart is heavy; it is like a mute, brooding owl. Near the end of the meditation (15-17) the gloom is somewhat lightened by the passing by of certain women who "take a little" of the protagonist's grief; but the last two lines bring back his despair.

Heces, the title, means literally the sediment left in the bottom of a glass that has contained liquid; figuratively, it evokes the bitterness of that sediment, the cup of grief that must be drained to the last drop. (1) *It rains this afternoon as never before, and I* (2) *do not wish to live [do not feel like living], O my heart.* (3) *This is a gentle afternoon. Why not?* (4) *It is dressed in grace and grief; dressed like a woman.*

(5) *It is raining this afternoon in Lima. And I remember* (6) *the cruel caverns of my ingratitude;* (7) *my block of ice [weighing] upon her poppy,* (8) *harsher than her "You mustn't be like that!"* (9) *My violent black flowers; the savage,* (10) *enormous blow of stone, the glacial distance [between us].* (11) *The silence of her withdrawn-ness will put [write],* (12) *in burning oil, the final period.* (13) *That is why this afternoon, as never before, I bear [go with, suffer]* (14) *this owl, this heart of mine.* (15) *Other women pass me by and, seeing me so sad,* (16) *take a little bit of you* (17) *from the wrenched furrow of my inner grief.* (18) *It's raining this afternoon, raining so hard; and I do not* (19) *wish to live, O my heart!*

The poem opens and concludes with couplets (1-2, 18-19) in which the connection between the exterior (afternoon rain) and the interior (the speaker's sad heart) is established. Three terms—"I," rain, heart—fix the mood. There is a difference between the first couplet and the last: at the beginning, the statement is effected by a comparison ((*llueve como nunca:* "it rains as it never did before"), but at the end this comparison disappears and the statement is absolute: *llueve, llueve mucho* ("it's raining so hard"). These four lines frame the poem. In lines 3 and 4 we encounter a kind of happiness; but the "grace and grief" follow immediately, bringing memories of the beloved woman. (*Gracia y pena* oddly echoes the Angelic Salutation: *gratiâ plena;* though this is probably no more than an unconscious evocation.)

At first we have "woman" generalized, but from *una mujer*, or *la mujer* ("a woman," "woman") we pass to the particular woman who was the speaker's love. The "I" is now tormented by bitter memories of his own ingratitude, his cruelty. In the eight lines that follow the diction is unpleasant, even bitter; the speaker seems to be punishing himself for his attitude towards "her." Note such words as *cavernas crueles* ("cruel caverns"), *bloque de*

hielo ("block of ice"), *violentas flores negras* ("violent black flowers"), *bárbara y enorme pedrada* ("savage, enormous blow of stone"), *trecho glacial* ("glacial distance"), *óleos quemantes* ("burning oil[s]"). In line 7 the seemingly rather obscure and certainly brutal *mi bloque de hielo sobre su amapola* ("my block of ice upon her poppy") may perhaps mean the (momentary) cold indifference of the man to the red blossom of the woman's ardor; but it is worth noting that *amapola* is a more "poetic" word than the English "poppy," though its connotations may be no richer, and that in this situation it contrasts tellingly with *hielo* ("ice").

After this tormented evocation the mood softens to melancholy. "Afternoon," "rain," "heart," are again mentioned. The passing of the other women (*y otras pasan*) eases the lover's grief, since we are told that they *toman un poquito de ti* (16)—, they "take a little bit of you," O [my] heart: that is, these women help him forget for a time his *hondo dolor* (17), his deep, bitter grief. To little avail, however: at the end of the poem (18-19) he repeats the first lines, returning to the threefold idea of afternoon rain, grieving lover, heart. The poem concludes with the simple, sad phrase *No tengo ganas de vivir* ("I do not wish to live," or, better because more colloquially, "I don't feel like [going on] living." It is this colloquial tone combining with the unexpected music—both harsh and tender—that gives the poem its impact. There is "form," certainly: the verses are almost all hendecasyllabic; and the rime (assonant, 1-2; 13-14-17 and elsewhere; consonant, 3-4) is interestingly worked out. But in Vallejo, "form" is incidental; what counts, as with so many modern poets, is the dramatic intensity, achieved not only by word-music, but by word-dissonance as well.

[E.F.]

ÁGAPE

Hoy no ha venido nadie a preguntar;
ni me han pedido en esta tarde nada.   2

No he visto ni una flor de cementerio
en tan alegre procesión de luces.
Perdóname, Señor: qué poco he muerto!   5

En esta tarde todos, todos pasan
sin preguntarme ni pedirme nada.   7

Y no sé qué se olvidan y se queda
mal en mis manos, como cosa ajena.   9

He salido a la puerta,
y me da ganas de gritar a todos:
Si echan de menos algo, aquí se queda!   12

Porque en todas las tardes de esta vida,
yo no sé con qué puertas dan a un rostro,   14
y algo ajeno se toma el alma mía.

Hoy no ha venido nadie;
y hoy he muerto qué poco en esta tarde!

(*Los heraldos negros.* 1918)

The title [Greek ἀγάπη, "brotherly love"] refers to the love-feast, the ceremonial supper, of the primitive Christians. Even during his last years, when his outlook had become exaltedly revolutionary, Vallejo (1895-1937) never lost the religious strain that is notable in his early work; and here, it gives the poem its connotative richness.

The theme is brotherly love, the "charity" of I Cor. xiii. As in "*Heces,*" the agonist is alone; but here he is transfigured by his burning desire to give himself to others. Because he can not satisfy this desire, because there is no one who will ask for or receive his gift, he complains that he has not "died enough"; and for this failure he asks God's forgiveness.

(1) *Nobody came today to ask me questions,* (2) *nor has anyone asked me for anything this afternoon.* (3) *I have not seen a single graveyard flower* (4) *in all this gay procession of lights.* (5) *Forgive me, Lord: how little have I died!* (6) *Everyone, everyone passes by this afternoon* (7) *without asking me questions, without asking anything of me.* (8) *And I do not know what they have forgotten that remains* (9) *wrong in my hands, like an alien thing.* (10) *I come to the door,* (11) *I would shout at everyone:* (12) *"If you miss anything, here*

it is!" (13) *All the afternoons of my life,* (14) *I can not say what doors they slam in my face;* (15) *and something alien is taken by my soul.* (16) *Nobody came today;* (17) *and I have died this afternoon so little!"*

The mood is set at the beginning by the words *nadie* ("no one") and *nada* ("nothing"), which establish the "I" in a kind of vacuum. The external world is gay enough (4-5) in that procession of lights that includes not a single flower of sadness. It is precisely because of this happiness that the passers-by do not stop to ask anything of (from) the "I." (In Spanish there are two different verbs of asking: *preguntar*, to ask questions, and *pedir*, to ask *for* something.) Thus we have a contrast between the merry passers-by outside the house and the sad figure of the "I," who is begging to give, and to whom no one pays any attention. In lines 10-12 there is a climax: the "I" tells us, "I come to the door, I feel like shouting to everyone."

The need to shout, to share his feelings with the indifferent transients, is really only shouting for shouting's sake: he knows quite well that no one will answer him. Yet the longing to give himself, to communicate himself, is so strong that even his desire, he thinks, makes him absorb something from the others—something left *mal* ("wrong, idle, useless") in his hands. (The word "afternoon" is less obscure than idiosyncratic: Vallejo very often refers to his life as "afternoon.") He is rejected; the door is slammed in his face. Curiously, the beggar is not the one who passes by and who might be expected to call at the door; it is the householder, the "I," who opens the door and *begs to give himself* to the crowd. This is an effective inversion of the usual situation, and it gives the poem its impetus.

The piece ends with a play of language characteristic of Vallejo. He says (17) *Hoy he muerto qué poco.* The more natural way of expressing this idea would have been, as in line 5, *qué poco he muerto* ("how little have I died," or "I have died [this afternoon] so little"); but the twist of syntax gives us "[This afternoon] *how little* have I died!", or, ambiguously, "I have died *how little* this afternoon!".

Like "*Heces,*" this poem is free in rime and stanza structure. Except for lines 10 and 15, which are seven-syllable, the verse is hendecasyllabic. Line 17, indeed, is a classically stressed (*muér, pó, tár*) hendecasyllable, wholly formal. In his later poems Vallejo freed himself more and more from the classical structure, but in "*Ágape*" and "*Heces*" he still adheres to it.   [E.F.]

CÉSAR VALLEJO

PIEDRA NEGRA SOBRE UNA PIEDRA BLANCA

Me moriré en París con aguacero,
un día del cual tengo ya el recuerdo.
Me moriré en Paris — y no me corro —
tal vez un jueves, como es hoy, de otoño.   4

Jueves será, porque hoy, jueves, que proso
estos versos, los húmeros me he puesto
a la mala y, jamás como hoy, me he vuelto,
con todo mi camino, a verme solo.   8

César Vallejo ha muerto, le pegaban
todos sin que él les haga nada;
le daban duro con un palo y duro

también con una soga; son testigos   12
los días jueves y los huesos húmeros,
la soledad, la lluvia, los caminos...

(*Poemas humanos*. 1939)

"*Piedra negra sobre una piedra blanca*"
("Black Stone upon a White Stone")
recalls the ancient practice of memorial-
izing a fortunate event with a white stone,
an unfortunate one with a black. Since
this sonnet is about the poet's death, the
intent of the title seems clearly ironical.
But is it? The first quatrain immediately
suggests "*Heces*" (p. 220), whose setting
is also a rainy afternoon; but between the
writing of the two poems, important years
had elapsed in Vallejo's life. "*Heces*"
appeared in a book issued in his native
Peru in 1918; "*Piedra negra . . .*" was
written between 1923, when he left Lima
for Europe, and his death in Paris four-
teen years later. When one reflects upon
the unjust accusation, prosecution, and
imprisonment that he suffered in his
native country soon after his first book

appeared, and the extreme poverty of
his ensuing years in Spain and France,
one is tempted to read the "black stone"
of the title as Vallejo's sorrowful salute to
his anticipated moment of good fortune:
release by death from the misery of living.
But his poetry is too complex ever to be
pinned down to a single interpretation.
The title may even be regarded as being
in itself a tiny poem serving as epigraph
to the sonnet that follows it.

(1) *I shall die in Paris at a time of heavy
showers* [literally *I shall die in Paris with
heavy showers*], (2) *on a day of which I
already possess the memory.* (3) *I shall die in
Paris—and I'm not dismayed—* (4) *perhaps
on a Thursday, like today, in the autumn.*
(5) *It shall be a Thursday, because today,
Thursday, as I prose* [Vallejo uses *prosar*, a
curiously medieval term for the composing

of poetry] (6) *these lines, my forearms ache badly* ["húmeros," humerus; "me he puesto a la mala" has the colloquial force of *have gone bad*], (7-8) *and, never before, in all my life* ["camino" means *road;* thus, *in all the road of my life*], *have I felt myself so lonely as [I do] today,* (9) *César Vallejo is dead; everybody kept hitting him* (10) *even though he has done nothing to them* [literally *without his doing them . . .*]; (11) *they hit (beat) him hard with a stick (club), and hard,* (12) *also, with a rope; his witnesses are* (13) *the Thursdays and the bones of his arms,* (14) *the loneliness, the rain, the roads . . .*

The mood of the poem is, as it were, enclosed by the *aguacero* ("heavy showers") and the *lluvia* ("rain") of the first and last lines respectively. It is rain, autumnal sadness, melancholy, grief—the kind of mood that occurs often enough in lyric poetry and very frequently in the work of Vallejo. What makes "*Piedra negra . . .*" different is not this mood but the poetic freshness of its expression.

The poem is in the form of a free sonnet, free in that the riming is assonanced and irregularly ordered. All the lines but one are hendecasyllabic, and the exception (10) embodies a typical oddity of Vallejo's style—the use of *haga nada*, a present subjunctive, instead of *hiciera nada*, the conditional that the Spanish reader would normally expect. The consequence is a twofold shock: in the surprising verb form and in the brevity of the line, which is short by at least one syllable. The expression *sin que* ("without"), which immediately precedes *él les haga nada* ("he does nothing to them"), adds a third touch of the unexpected—and *le pegaban* ("they

used to hit him") is a past tense followed by a present!

Vallejo's use of time in this poem would make an interesting study in itself. The present moment is projected as a paradigm of that future day on which he will die. It will be (he says) the same day—of rain, aching bones, loneliness. "I shall die" (*me moriré*, 1) in the past: "on a day of which I already possess the memory" (2); that is, although the day is not yet here, it is nonetheless already preserved in his memory as an event of his past. Time also declares itself in *César Vallejo ha muerto* ("César Vallejo is dead," 9), which is the dividing point between the two parts of the poem; all that follows belongs to his future, imagined as past.

One or two other typical Vallejo touches are worth noting. *Los húmeros me he puesto a la mala* (6-7) is a curiously conversational way of describing the pain in his forearms; *ponerse a la mala* means to be in a bad mood or state of mind. This offhand characterization of his physical pain contrasts sharply with the grave phrasing of his pain of loneliness: *con todo mi camino* (8). Because of its place in the word order, it suggests "the entire road" of the speaker's life. Six lines later *camino* ("road") changes to *caminos* ("roads"), and it is the final word of the poem. Did Vallejo add three dots to convey the thought that there was more than a single road in his past?—or in the future?—or that the roads will not actually end, even in death? Whatever the interpretation, the calm certainty that informs the entire poem is suddenly shaken by the final suggestion of its opposite.   [E.F.]

CÉSAR VALLEJO

PEQUEÑO RESPONSO A UN HÉROE DE LA REPÚBLICA

Un libro quedó al borde de su cintura muerta,
un libro retoñaba de su cadáver muerto.
Se llevaron al héroe,
y corpórea y aciaga entró su boca en nuestro aliento;   4
sudamos todos, el ombligo a cuestas;
caminantes las lunas nos seguían;
también sudaba de tristeza el muerto.

Y un libro, en la batalla de Toledo,   8
un libro, atrás un libro, arriba un libro, retoñaba del cadáver.

Poesía del pómulo morado, entre el decirlo
y el callarlo,
poesía en la carta moral que acompañara   12
a su corazón.
Quedóse el libro y nada más, que no hay
insectos en la tumba,
y quedó al borde de su manga el aire remojándose   16
y haciéndose gaseoso, infinito.

Todos sudamos, el ombligo a cuestas,
también sudaba de tristeza el muerto
y un libro, yo lo vi sentidamente,   20
un libro, atrás un libro, arriba un libro
retoñó del cadáver exabrupto.

10 septiembre 1937

(España, aparta de mí este cáliz. 1940)

This poem is one of fifteen written by Vallejo in 1937, when he traveled to Spain and experienced at first hand the horrors of that country's Civil War. What he saw and heard affected him profoundly; and his poems must also have borne profound meanings to the soldiers of the Republican Army of the East, some of whom set up and printed them on paper which they themselves made. Three years after his death the work was published in Mexico, with a title taken from Christ's words in the garden of Gethsemane: "O my Father, if it be possible, let this cup pass from me" (Matthew xxvi:39). In the judgment of many critics, this final volume by Vallejo, *España, aparta de mí este cáliz* ("O Spain, turn aside from me this cup"), contains much of the finest writing inspired by the agony of Spain.

The poem is called "*Pequeño responso a un héroe de la República*" ("A brief funeral liturgy for a hero of the Republic"). A *responso*, a responsory led by a priest, is used here in a purely secular way. This is not a liturgy, but a succession of pictorial images that narrate an event. (1) *A book was lying (remained) at the edge of his dead waist,* (2) *a book was sprouting from his dead corpse.* (3) *They carried the hero away,* (4) *and his carnal and ill-fated mouth entered our breath;* (5) *all of us sweated, our navels a burden;* (6) *the wandering moons were following us;* (7) *the dead man, too, was sweating from grief.* (8) *And a book, at the Battle of Toledo,* (9) *A book, a book behind, a book above, was sprouting from the corpse.* The stanza that follows defines this book in a series of condensed suggestions. (10) *Poetry of the purple cheek bone, [a poetry that is half way] between saying* (11) *and not saying,* (12) *poetry in the moral message that had accompanied* (13) *his heart.* (14) *The book remained and nothing else* [the body has been taken away], *for there are no* (15) *insects in the tomb,* (16) *And [now all that] remained there at the edge of his sleeve [was] the air soaking itself [with his blood]* (17) *and becoming vaporous, infinite.* The last stanza returns to the images of the first, but with a sudden definitive ending. (18) *All of us sweated, our navels a burden,* (19) *the dead man also sweated from grief* (20) *and a book, I saw it with emotion* [literally *feelingly*], (21) *a book, a book behind, a book above,* (22) *sprouted from the corpse violently.*

This is a small ritual for a man who is now as it were doubly dead—*cadáver muerto* ("dead corpse")—but whose book, that fell with him on the battlefield, insists on staying alive. It is already sending out shoots to spread the message that was once in his heart. From everywhere it asserts the meaning of his life and death; its enduring message grows. In lines 2 and 9 the verb (*retoñaba*) has the force of continuing action ("was sprouting"), but in the last line the action has been accomplished (*retoñó*). This definitive effect is intensified by *exabrupto* ("violent"). But does this final word refer to "sprouted" only? or to the book? or to the "corpse" that is now "dead"? Does it touch all three?

Attempts to illuminate other obscurities in this poem would doubtless end in asking further questions. Line 6 could read: *we were wandering and the moons were following us.* Line 5, for example, (literally "we all sweated, our navels on our shoulders, or back") we have translated as "our navels a burden." Why navel? Is it because this organ, through which the unborn child is nourished, is still the center of our bodies? Does the line then suggest that we bore away with us the very center of our lives, after the hero's breath had entered our breath? Lines 10-13 ("poetry of the purple cheek bones") evokes for this reader, at least, the moment between saying and being silenced: the poetry that he was bearing in his heart as he performed his last rite of sacrifice. But what of lines 14-15? Are insects made present by negation, in the manner of Keats's "And no birds sing"? And what of the *responso* itself: is the dead man in some way answering?   [E.F.]

CECÍLIA MEIRELES

[DE LONGE TE HEI DE AMAR]

De longe te hei de amar
— da tranqüila distância
em que o amor é saudade
e o desejo, constância.   4

Do divino lugar
onde o bem da existência
é ser eternidade
e parecer ausência.   8

Quem precisa explicar
o momento e a fragrância
da Rosa, que persuade
sem nenhuma arrogância?   12

E, no fundo do mar
a Estrela, sem violência
cumpre a sua verdade
alheia à transparência.   16

(*Canções*. 1956)

From afar I shall love you, (2) —*from that calm distance* (3) *from which love is (becomes) longing* (4) *and passion, perseverance.* I shall love you from that distant place in my heart from where I can look at you without being troubled by love, from that distant place where love becomes an untarnished desire, a longing for love, and where lustful desire, a perishable feeling, turns into an unfailing, constant faith.

(5) *From that divine place* (6) *where the joy (virtue) of existence* (7) *is that, being eternity,* (8) *it appears to be absence.* I shall love you from that divine place, the soul, where life, while apparently depriving us of the presence of the beloved, grants us its best gift: everlasting love.

(9) *Who needs to explain* (10) *the moment and the fragrance* (11) *of the Rose, which persuades* (12) *without any arrogance?* Does the absolute yet transitory perfection of the rose—a fleeting instant of time and of fragrance—which is humbly self evident, need to be explained? Isn't the rose itself its own explanation?

(13) *And, at the bottom of the sea* (14) *the Star, without violence,* (15) *fulfills its truth* (16) *oblivious of transparency.* Similarly, the reflection of a star at the bottom of the sea: its presence there softly evinces the beauty and significance of the star, even though it is not the star at all and only its image—a reflection in the water.

The work is untitled. Like the other poems in the book *Canções* (Songs), it was offered as simply another song, a song of love in the most rarefied sense. It is pervaded, as is the whole volume, by the writer's desire to give poetical expression to a feeling of sublimated love, free from the urge for carnal possession that enslaves the lover to the physical presence of the beloved, a love that aspires to the divine and eternal—a love that is pure contemplation, quite unrelated to time and space. This is a love that, in the best Lusitanian tradition, fulfills itself in *saudade* ("longing," 3) from afar, an experience more pleasurable than love itself. All this the poem says in the first eight lines with a minimum of imagery and a maximum of musical suggestion.

The theme—the contemplation of beauty as an end in itself—is further developed in the third and fourth stanzas. Cecília Meireles does not hesitate to evoke the Rose and the Star, though these two poetical objects have long been threadbare from use and abuse. In her hands, they recover freshness; we almost begin to feel that we are meeting these two lyric commonplaces for the first time. For the old cliché of the Rose as the symbol of beauty's transitoriness is transformed into "the moment and the fragrance of the Rose, which *persuades without arrogance*" (10-12). And the Star "fulfills" itself through the action of something other than itself—the reflection of light upon water. Unlike the first two stanzas, in which the thought is set forth declaratively, the third and fourth project their meanings through oblique suggestions. The Rose and the Star lie at a tangent to the core of the thought.

The pattern of meter and rime—four quatrains of heptasyllables in an *abcb* rime —is actually a shortened form of the *romance* (folk ballad) of the Iberian countries. But instead of the customary assonance, we find rich rime almost throughout. In addition, the poet applies a rime scheme to the entire architecture of the song, treating the four stanzas as though they were individual lines and combining them in a closer *abab* (1: *distância—constância;* 2: *existência—ausência;* 3: *fragrância—arrogância;* 4: *violência—transparência*). And to top that, she creates another interstanzaic rime by linking all the quatrains in their first and third lines (1: *amar, lugar, explicar, mar;* 3: *saudade, eternidade, persuade, verdade*). Despite these involved technical devices, the poem glides smoothly and softly, with a melody that, in a musical language like Portuguese, is inevitably natural.

Cecília Meireles, one of the most distinctive of living Portuguese poets, was born in Rio de Janeiro in 1901. She began her literary career under the influence of French Symbolism, but she soon cast it off to return to the Iberian tradition, in which she has asserted her unequivocally personal art. Author of many volumes of verse, she has also contributed to other branches of literature. Her essays on literary subjects, folklore, and educational problems are brilliant, and she is considered an authority on children's literature. She has traveled and lectured on Brazilian belles lettres in the United States, Europe, and Asia.   [E.G.D.]

CECÍLIA MEIRELES

MOTIVO

Eu canto porque o instante existe
e a minha vida está completa.
Não sou alegre nem sou triste:
sou poeta.   4

Irmão das coisas fugidias,
não sinto gôzo nem tormento.
Atravesso noites e dias
no vento.   8

Se desmorono ou edifico,
se permaneço ou me desfaço,
— não sei, não sei. Não sei se fico
ou passo.   12

Sei que canto. E a canção é tudo.
Tem sangue eterno e asa ritmada.
E un dia sei que estarei mudo:
— mais nada.   16

(*Viagem*. 1939)

I *sing because the moment exists* (2) *and
my life is complete.* (3) *I am neither happy
nor sad:* (4) *I am a poet.*

(5) *A brother of fleeting things,* (6) *I do not
feel either joy or torture.* (7) *I traverse nights
and days* (8) *in the wind.*

(9) *Whether I demolish (crumble) or build,*
(10) *whether I remain or dissolve,* (11) *—I do
not know, I do not know. I do not [even] know
whether I am staying* (12) *or [simply]
passing.*

(13) *I do know that I sing. And the song
is everything (all that counts).* (14) *It has
eternal blood and rhythmed wing.* (15) *And
I know that one day I shall be muted:* (16)
—that's all (nothing more).

"Motive" expresses the inescapability
of total surrender to the creative urge,
the unavoidable nature of an inner motiva-
tion. Meireles *sings* because when the
moment, the poetical ecstasy, arrives, it
comes to her with a compelling inevitable-
ness: she must burst into song. When she
reaches this completion, this plenitude,
she is on a sphere above and beyond the
happiness or *sadness* of daily life. She is
entranced, dwelling in a world which
transcends common experience. *She is a
poet.*

As such, she is in *brotherhood* with all that
is *fleeting, evanescent, vague,* for the essence
of poetry is precisely that *momentariness* of
the emotive "charge" which experience
and objects suddenly acquire for the crea-
tive person and which impel him to seek
fulfillment—through giving concrete ex-

pression to the abstract vision. In her abandonment, she enters a world in which *joy* and *torture* cease to have meaning. She *takes flight in the wind*; she travels against time, *cutting athwart nights and days*. In that dreamy flight, she is not sure of the meaning of action, either, for ordinary notions and values have no value in this new world of experience.

She *does not know whether she demolishes or builds*. She loses herself to such an extent that her very sense of identity escapes her; and she is not even aware whether her self *remains*, or *dissolves* into her vision; she *does not care whether she is staying or passing*.

The only thing she is sure of is her *singing, and that is all that matters: the poem*. If it is achieved, it will fly and sing forever, alive with its own *eternal blood* and its *rhythmed wing*. And this everlasting life of her song is everything to her, for she *knows that one day* age or death will *silence her*. She will sing *no more—that's all she knows*—she will go into *nothingness* ("nada").

Thus, with remarkable economy and with almost no rhetoric, Meireles succeeds in conveying the fundamental testimony of the poet, a summary statement of his *raison d'être*. Her own creative experience takes on here a universal value. This she underlines by assuming the masculine form ("poeta," "mudo") and avoiding "poetisa" (*poetess*), a term not especially flattering to a real woman-poet. There are almost no metaphors. Only in the last stanza, a fraction of an image is to be found (*the song . . . has eternal blood and rhythmed wing*) which suggests, in a vague and oblique way, that the poem becomes a "singing bird." This vagueness makes it possible for us to associate the image with the poet herself, who also *sings* and *flies in the wind*. The other three stanzas are bare of imagery. Instead, the writer uses a series of antitheses as a linking structural element (1: *moment-life, happy-sad;* 2: *joy-torture, nights-days;* 3: *demolish-build, remain-dissolve, staying-passing*) which reiterates the essentially ambivalent nature of the creative experience. Additional structure is achieved ("and by structure we don't mean mechanics of rime and meter, but the organic interrelation of all the component elements"—Robert Penn Warren) by successive yet unobtrusive repetitions of words at the beginning of clauses ("Não *sou* alegre nem *sou* triste: *sou* poeta, 3-4; *não sei, não sei. Não sei,* 11; *Sei que,* 13-15). These anaphoric passages effectively project the conflict of emotions in the poet as she gropes for a definition of her impulse. The beginning and the end of the poem are joined in a statement that constitutes the core: *I sing . . . I know that I sing* (1, 13).

The last line ("—mais nada") is charged with multiple meanings, all emerging simultaneously as an inevitable close, all of them valid yet contradictory —a master stroke of poetic ambiguity. According to the punctuation, the line seems to complete the thought of the preceding verse: *I know that one day I shall be muted:—that's all [I know]*. But it can also be taken to complete the whole last stanza. Again, it can be the closing remark in the entire poem:—*that's all [I have to say]*. One may also interpret it as meaning *nothing more;* and in this sense it opens a horizon of *nothingness* ("nada") that expresses the metaphysical anguish of the poet confronted with her ultimate silence, which for her is death.

[E.G.D.]

FEDERICO GARCÍA LORCA

PRECIOSA Y EL AIRE

Su luna de pergamino
Preciosa tocando viene
por un anfibio sendero
de cristales y laureles.   4
El silencio sin estrellas,
huyendo del sonsonete,
cae donde el mar bate y canta
su noche llena de peces.   8
En los picos de la sierra
los carabineros duermen
guardando las blancas torres
donde viven los ingleses.   12

Four of our five poems of García Lorca are taken from his *Romancero gitano*, or *Gypsy Ballad-Book* (1928). In Lorca's poetic world the gypsy is a key figure: passionate, sensitive, mysterious—persecuted for centuries by the stolid forces of law and order. But Lorca resented attempts to identify him with an exclusively gypsy world: interviewed some years after writing the book, he said it was "an Andalusian song in which the gypsies serve as a sort of refrain," and even before the collection came out he protested in a letter to Jorge Guillén: "I'm getting a bit tired of [talk of] my gypsy myth. The gypsies are a theme. And that's all. I could be the same poet if I were writing about sewing needles or views of irrigation projects. Besides, gypsyism gives me an air of lack of culture, of lack of education, an air of being a primitive poet, which you know very well I am not. I don't want to be pigeonholed."

Deeply influenced by the folk poetry of Spain, Lorca wrote these poems in one of the oldest of popular rhythms, the eight-syllable ballad line—not to be thought of as corresponding to English lines of four iambic or trochaic feet, since in the Spanish line there is no pattern of accents: only the seventh syllable is accented regularly. The stanzas do not rime, but all the even-numbered lines are linked by assonance. Throughout "Preciosa and the Air," for example, the two final vowel sounds are *e-e*, as in *viene, laureles*. The Spanish reader hears in Lorca's ballads the energetic rhythms long familiar, but he is aware at the same time of something new and strange.

Instead of using the strong but monotonous drive of the old octosyllables, line after line, Lorca constructs his poem clearly in quatrains, each tending to be a unit, like the little *coplas* or folk-songs of the people. (Occasionally we find a six-line unit, as in lines 37-42, here indicated by the line-numbering.) These units follow each other with amazing variety. In the first quatrain of "Preciosa," for example, the gypsy girl, partly mythologized by the moon emblem and a symbolic path between two kinds of life, comes dancing into the poem. The second quatrain is a lyric evocation of the mysteriously stirring environment. The third is matter-of-fact;

it has almost the quality of "sung prose" for which Lorca praises the lyrics of *cante jondo*—though later we come to realize that it has significant ironies. The fourth quatrain, in contrast, is pure fancy, baroque luxuriance. These dazzling changes of focus and tone are found, not always to the same degree, throughout our four poems from *Romancero gitano*.

Perhaps it will help to think of this poem (and the "Sleepwalking Ballad", p. 237) as a sort of ballet of images. There are such individual figures as the frightened girl, hulking San Cristobalón, and the impeccable English consul. There are the three *carabineros* and the sportive gypsies, who are only waves of the sea. We can imagine dancers for the Silence and the Night, the Sea and the Olive-trees. The poet is their choreographer; the poem is what they do. Seeing such a ballet, one would feel in general what it was about.

Though the story is reminiscent of the pursuit of Daphne by Apollo and of Orithya by the wind-god Boreas, Lorca wrote a friend that "this is a myth I invented myself." Preciosa, the gypsy girl, has the same name and nature as the charming fifteen-year-old of Cervantes' *La Gitanilla*, who is a model of chastity (gypsy women, at least in Spain, are famously so). Lorca seems to have remembered many details from Cervantes: there also the heroine plays the tambourine enchantingly, is threatened by "los aires," sings of an old god with his "flattering and loving tongues," and even mentions "San Cristóbal gigante." San Cristobalón, big St. Christopher, half-pagan, half-Christian, dear to Spanish folklore and gypsy mythology, is a kind of Pan figure, an ancient roguish fertility god likely to make a victim, soon or late, of youth and innocence. Preciosa escapes by having recourse to the artificial sanctions of the civilized world—the world of policemen

and rich foreigners, of soothing milk and immaculate white mansions. But though it saves her, she does not surrender to it. There will be another night, and Preciosa, like most Preciosas of the world, may not escape the furious dark deity. The conflict here between innocence and sex is a cosmic one: earth and sea are convulsed in sympathy—though in sympathy with which of the participants we are not told. If indeed there is a moral, Lorca does not formulate it.

(1-2) *Preciosa comes playing her moon of parchment* (3) *along an amphibious path* (4) *of crystal waters and laurels*. The dead-white mottled disk of the tambourine resembles the full moon, but, more than that, the image suggests Diana and virginity. Preciosa on her amphibious path is between two kinds of life: the clear crystal and Daphne's laurel are not fortuitous. (5) *The starless silence*, (6) *fleeing before her strumming*, (7) *falls where the sea beats and sings* (8) *its night [that is] full of fishes*. Suddenly the universe around the girl has dimension: height, depth, and distance. Like the darkness of the sea, it is teeming with vibrant life. The sea "sings" its night: gladly proclaims, in a musical surging, its vital mystery. (9) *On the peaks of the sierra* (10) *the special police are sleeping* (11) *guarding the white towers* (12) *where the Englishmen live*. Here is another world, refined and alien, the world of constraint and law. Lifted above the dark sea-world, guarded by special police (*carabineros* are generally customs police or revenue men—and as such the natural enemies of the gypsies—but here they seem to have another assignment); a world of aloof whitewashed houses inhabited by foreigners. The English, an actual part of the Andalusian scene, who have given their names to many famous Spanish wines, still represent a different and more "proper" world than that of the gypsies with which they are now

Y los gitanos del agua
levantan por distraerse
glorietas de caracolas
y ramas de pino verde.   16

*

Su luna de pergamino
Preciosa tocando viene.
Al verla se ha levantado
el viento que nunca duerme.   20
San Cristobalón desnudo,
lleno de lenguas celestes,
mira a la niña tocando
una dulce gaita ausente.   24

— Niña, deja que levante
tu vestido para verte.
Abre en mis dedos antiguos
la rosa azul de tu vientre.   28

*

Preciosa tira el pandero
y corre sin detenerse.
El viento-hombrón la persigue
con una espada caliente.   32

Frunce su rumor el mar.
Los olivos palidecen.
Cantan las flautas de umbría
y el liso gong de la nieve.   36

¡Preciosa, corre, Preciosa,
que te coge el viento verde!
¡Preciosa, corre, Preciosa!
¡Míralo por dónde viene!
Sátiro de estrellas bajas
con sus lenguas relucientes.   42

*

Preciosa, llena de miedo,
entra en la casa que tiene,
más arriba de los pinos,
el cónsul de los ingleses.   46

contrasted. (13) *And the gypsies of the water* (14) *are raising for their amusement* (15) *arbors made of seashells* (16) *and boughs of green pine.* Lorca may be writing of actual gypsies here, but it seems likelier that he is comparing the waves of the sea to gypsies. The waves, like the gypsies, are engaged in work that is utterly useless: instead of solid white houses that the police can guard, they are building their fanciful arbors, for pure pleasure—and building them with the natural materials of sea and earth, working with seashells and the green pine boughs that the foreigners would not bother with.

The two opening lines are repeated as Preciosa, who first came into the poem out of nowhere, now reappears against this rich and varied background. (19) *On seeing her has uprisen* (20) *the wind that* [unlike the policemen] *never sleeps.* In his talk on *cante jondo*, Lorca says that in Spanish folk-poetry the wind is often imagined as a giant that busies himself knocking down the stars, etc. Barea reminds us that the wind of this poem is "the hot exciting wind that blows on the Andalusian seashore by night and rips all covers from desire." (21) *Big St. Christopher, naked,* (22) *full of heavenly tongues,* (23) *looks at the girl,* [he] *playing* (24) *a sweet and faraway tune.* Lengua ("tongue") means, as in English, both speech and its physical organ; *celeste* ("celestial") can also mean "skyblue," if there is anything we care to make of that meaning. The persuasive physical impulse that the pagan saint embodies is as omnipresent as air. What he is playing is a sort of bagpipes, a wind instrument for the wind-god. Why is he playing mournful numbers (*ausente*, "absent, faraway, sad") rather than the sportive ditty we might expect? Perhaps because his rôle in the poem—witness the outcome—is by no means a merry one. It is taxing to be a natural force, and he has frustrations of his own. The compliment he now pays the girl is abrupt and frank, not far removed from what the Spaniards call *piropos*, the compliments lounging males are likely to murmur even today toward a passing señorita. (25) *Girl, let me lift up* (26) *your dress so I can see you.* (27) *In my ancient fingers open* (28) *the blue rose of your belly.* The image is veiled and softened by *blue*, with its suggestions of coolness, remoteness, purity.

(29) *Preciosa lets fly her tambourine* (30) *and* takes to her heels without stopping. (31) *The wind-giant pursues her* (32) *with a fiery sword.* This third section of the poem is all flight and pursuit; nature herself is involved in the excitement. (33) *The sea makes a frown of its murmur*—literally, *wrinkles* its murmur: an image of some concentration, with the corrugations of the sea seen as wrinkles of a frowning brow. What the sea wrinkles is not its brow or its surface, but the constant murmur which its surface makes and is. (34) *The olive trees turn pale.* (35) *The flutes of the shady places sing* (36) *and the sleek gong of the snow.* Sea and land, shady lowlands, and the smooth snowfields of the sierra take part in the drama. One might relate each of these details to pursuer or pursued, but the poet does not seem to insist on such schematic correspondences.

(37) *Preciosa, run, Preciosa,* (38) *he'll catch you, the green wind!* As an earth-god, the wind is green, but "verde" also means *free, improper,* or *lustful:* an old man is called "verde" if he is amorous beyond what seems proper to his age. Preciosa is again (39) urged to hurry: (40) *Look at him, where he's coming!* Some readers might hear in this line a burlesque echo of the old ballads that announce their hero with: *Helo, helo por do viene!* ("Lo, lo, where he comes!"). Big St. Christopher now becomes explicitly a pagan fertility deity: (41) *A satyr of low [earthy, etc.] stars* (42) *with his tongues a-glitter [or a-dazzle].* The tongues, which before were *heavenly* and seemed to refer especially to his gifts of eloquence, become more physical as the eroticism of the old wind-god burns high.

In the next three quatrains we leave the fabulous for the factual: Preciosa might be any young girl fleeing an imaginary terror. Perhaps there is nothing in the poem that insists her bugaboo is anything more than the product of a young girl's imagination. But even if that were true, it would not essentially change

Asustados por los gritos
tres carabineros vienen,
sus negras capas ceñidas
y los gorros en las sienes.   50

El inglés da a la gitana
un vaso de tibia leche,
y una copa de ginebra
que Preciosa no se bebe.   54

Y mientras cuenta, llorando,
su aventura a aquella gente,
en las tejas de pizarra
el viento, furioso, muerde.   58

(*Romancero gitano*. 1928)

the meaning of the poem—she is fleeing a reality of one sort or another, of ancient myth or modern psyche. (43) *Preciosa, full of fear,* (44, 46) *goes into the house that the consul of the English has* (45) *up over the pine trees. Over* the pine trees, which have been earlier associated with the night-and-water world of the gypsies. The English consul, presumably the most English of the English, stands for a world of decorum and law—convention as against nature; he is alien because what he represents is alien to the natural world. He is protected by the powers of civilized repression, who now appear, alarmed at the uproar in Preciosa's wake, and, unlike the naked giant, tightly wrapped in the dark trappings of their office. (47) *Frightened by the outcries* (48) *three policemen arrive,* (49) *their black capes wrapped around them* (50) *and their hats [pulled down] on their temples.* Meanwhile, in lines that have been described by at least one Spanish critic, though not disparagingly, as "rimed prose": (51) *The Englishman gives the gypsy*—it is the first time she has been called that, and the contrast between the two races, two natures, two attitudes to reality, is emphatic in the line— (52) *a tumbler of lukewarm milk,* (53) *and a glass of gin* (54) *which Preciosa does not drink.* It

is not clear from the syntax whether Preciosa refuses only the gin, or both milk and gin. Probably (unlike Proserpina) she refuses all sustenance, and by her refusal shows her incompatibility with a world which has temporarily given her shelter. The point is not that the consul, well intentioned but perhaps rather stiff, offers the wrong drink; the point is that there is nothing he and his world of whitewashed towers can give this frightened creature who has come from the rich and stirring dark. (55) *And while she recounts, in tears,* (56) *her adventure to those people,* (57) *at the slates of the roof* (58) *the wind, in a rage, is gnawing:* a natural force frustrated, at least temporarily, by the hostile world of law. Big St. Christopher still, or merely the wind in the eaves? And what of Preciosa when she emerges, as she must —propelled, as likely as not, by her natural enemies, the special policemen who safeguard the world of convention? But what may happen later is no part of the poem; García Lorca has simply presented his myth, his vivid little ballet, for us to make of what we will. What we will, that is, if we observe with the respect and care they deserve the data he has so carefully set before us.   [J.F.N.]

FEDERICO GARCÍA LORCA

ROMANCE SONÁMBULO

The poet Rafael Alberti wrote García Lorca that he considered his "Sleep-walking Ballad" beyond doubt the best ballad in modern Spanish literature—full of chilling secrets, of mysteries deep in the blood. And Salvador Dalí, when he heard it read by the poet, is reported to have marvelled, in what Lorca called his *olive-colored voice*, "It seems to have a story, but actually it has none."

What Dalí probably meant is that the poem certainly implies a story, but that the mere story, striking as it is, is far from being the poem. Actual events are perceived through a haze of dream or enchantment, and thus is achieved such a vision of those events as a sleepwalker might be imagined as having, or a participant who, unable to face their brutal reality, withdraws into a "green" world of hallucination.

The story is clear enough. A mortally wounded gypsy smuggler, the police hard on his heels, makes his way very late at night to the house of the girl who has long been expecting him. He asks help of her father, whom he finds for some reason in a state of shock. The two men ascend to the terraces of the roof, the balustrades stark in the moonlight. There the girl, who had waited so long in vain, yearning toward the green distance of forest and sea, is floating on the moonlit surface of the pool, apparently a suicide. The spell is ruffled but not really broken by the clamorous arrival of the police.

A narrative poet might simply have told the story, as dramatic as any old Scottish or Spanish ballad. But Lorca is fascinated less by the events than by the memories, imaginations, and passions of those involved—all highly suggestive human beings in an almost intolerable state of crisis. The poet's own fevered imagination fuses and completes that of the others, so that often when he is speaking for himself he is speaking also for them. In whose mind, for example, is the refrain of the poem at any given time? All the characters need, and love, and are doomed by "greenness," but the poet, more than any of his creations, is haunted by the spell and mystery of green.

The characters, all living under the malefic and beautiful enchantment of the moon, are in a way sleepwalkers: the mortally wounded smuggler, bleeding his life away; the old father, so dazed with grief that he is no longer himself; the girl, now dead, who mad with longing for hope's green world cast herself into the green death of the cistern—even, in a lesser way, the drunken policemen who come lurching up to the door.

The assonance throughout is a rich *a-a*: ra*ma*s, *pla*ta, etc. The poem opens with a line of untranslatable allure; it is suggested that the reader leave it in Spanish. A kind of nonsense line, it means much and means nothing. Not even the syntax is clear. It may be, as one critic reports, part of a popular Andalusian folk song. It may have been suggested by a nursery rime or by one of the songs children sing at their games. (Lorca was interested in both.) It is, at any rate, incantation rather than statement. (1) "Verde" means *green;* "te quiero" means both *I love you* and *I want*

Verde que te quiero verde.
Verde viento. Verdes ramas.
El barco sobre la mar
y el caballo en la montaña.   4
Con la sombra en la cintura
ella sueña en su baranda,
verde carne, pelo verde,
con ojos de fría plata.   8
Verde que te quiero verde.
Bajo la luna gitana,
las cosas la están mirando
y ella no puede mirarlas.   12

                 *

Verde que te quiero verde.
Grandes estrellas de escarcha
vienen con el pez de sombra
que abre el camino del alba.   16
La higuera frota su viento
con la lija de sus ramas,

y el monte, gato garduño,
eriza sus pitas agrias.   20
Pero ¿quién vendrá? ¿Y por dónde...?
Ella sigue en su baranda,
verde carne, pelo verde,
soñando en la mar amarga.   24

                 *

— Compadre, quiero cambiar
mi caballo por su casa,
mi montura por su espejo,
mi cuchillo por su manta.
Compadre, vengo sangrando,
desde los puertos de Cabra.   30
— Si yo pudiera, mocito,
este trato se cerraba.
Pero yo ya no soy yo,
ni mi casa es ya mi casa.   34

you. "Que" we would probably not put into English at all: it means something like *the fact is that*, and is little more than a rhetorically intensive expletive. Instead of (1) *Green, I love you green,* or *Green, I want you [to be] green*—that is, I want life in its rankness and richness as it is—or anything of the sort, the reader would do well to let the Spanish words dwell in his imagination, noting that the line is made up, predominantly, of the same few sounds repeated, and that none is harsh, sharp, or sibilant. An incantation. (2) *Green wind. Green branches.* On first reading we may not know why these images are conjured up. The branches are literally green; the wind (green for a different reason in "Preciosa and the Air," p. 232) is green here only because of where it blows.

Friends report that the poet read these first two lines with a certain elevation of tone, followed by a pause. Then, in a lower voice, as if shifting to another and more familiar level of reality: (3) *The ship on the sea* (4) *and the horse on the mountain.* For a Spanish ear the music of these lines lies in the repeated two syllables of *verde,* together with the strong mono-syllabic *mar* that closes the third line with an accent—as rarely happens in this rhythm. The mention of ship and horse may seem haphazard at first, mere details of Andalusian life. But, as having particular and ominous relevance to the life of the smuggler, they must have been prominent in the minds of all involved.

After these hallucinatory lines with their as yet unaccounted for primal images of ship and horse ("obviously" Freudian), we are given, through imagery that dwells on sex and death, a more graphic picture: the drowned girl floating face upward on the rooftop pool. (5) *With a shadow upon her waist* (6) *she dreams on her baranda*—a "baranda" is regularly a *railing,* like that on a stair or a balcony, but in this Andalusian usage it is a railed roof-terrace, open to the moonlight and with space for a cistern or reservoir. Here in a greenish radiance by the green water, she has been waiting many nights, staring into the distance, looking for a horse on the mountain, dreaming of a ship on the sea. (7) *Green flesh, tresses green* (8) *with eyes of chilly silver*—flesh pale-green in the shimmer of moon and water; hair only imagined as green in this green ensemble, or because of the moon's green lustre on it, or because dead things turn green, or because it is now actually green with the weeds and water-plants of the pool. Cold and hueless, her eyes. In the context the refrain "Verde que te quiero verde" (9) patently invites meanings beyond whatever meaning it had originally: love for the good green things of the world, wind and boughs and sea and mountain, has become either ironic or all-embracing. It accepts the green of life and death in their totality with a kind of sighing forth of the death-wish so strong in Lorca's characters. (10) *Under the moon of the gypsies* ("gypsy moon" is as common in Spanish songs as "harvest moon" or "southern moon" is in American; there is thought to be a special affinity between gypsies and the moon, as between them and all mysterious forces) (11) *things are looking at her* (12) *but she cannot return their glances.*

Again the refrain (13) "Verde que te quiero verde," with its accumulating resonances. The following lines evoke, in somewhat mysterious imagery, the hour before dawn, when the stars are keen and cold and deeper darkness floats like a great looming fish in the waters of night; or perhaps the fish is the luminous hover of misty light in the east preceding dawn. (14) *Great stars of frost* (15) *come with the fish of shadow* (16) *that opens the road of dawn.* The four lines that follow show, in images of attrition and menace, both the sharp wind that predicts the dawn and the mountain like a crouched and angry cat, the vegetation on its skyline bristling against the greying heavens. (17) *The figtree is chafing its wind* (18) *with the sandpaper of its branches,* (19) *and the mountain, furtive cat,* (20) *is bristling its acrid cactus* [the *pita* is a cactus-like Mexican plant now widespread in southern Spain]. These eight lines turn from the vision of the dead girl to the eerie, beautiful, and ominous background against which the human drama runs its course. Suddenly there is a stir of activity: (21) *But who is it coming? Which way?* (22) *On her terrace she continues,* (23) *green flesh, tresses green,* (24) *dreaming of the bitter sea.* "Soñar en" means to dream *of;* the *bitter sea* may be not only the sea of the smuggler, the sea that has kept him away from her, but also the great sea of human grief. And the line may be telling us too that she is dreaming *in* the bitter flood of moonlight.

The person dramatically introduced by the question of four lines above begins to speak abruptly out of the darkness. This whole section (lines 25-52) is in dialogue. Though it can be divided into quatrains, it falls more naturally into the six-line units indicated by the line-numbering. (25) *"Friend, I'd like to exchange* (26) *my horse for your home,* (27) *my saddle for your mirror,* (28) *my knife for your blanket"*—the properties of his dangerous, vagrant, and now ebbing life for those of the settled householder. (29) *"Friend, I come bleeding* (30) *from the mountain-passes of Cabra"*—in the sierra between Granada and Córdoba, where the terrain would offer special advantages to revenue men or the Guardia Civil on the lookout for smugglers.

(31) *"If I could, young man,"* replies the father, hinting at his daughter's death, (32) *"I'd have closed the deal already.* (33) *But I'm not myself any longer,* (34) *nor my house my house any more."* The wounded gypsy,

— Compadre, quiero morir
decentemente en mi cama.
De acero, si puede ser,
con las sábanas de holanda.
¿No ves la herida que tengo
desde el pecho a la garganta?   40
— Trescientas rosas morenas
lleva tu pechera blanca.
Tu sangre rezuma y huele
alrededor de tu faja.
Pero yo ya no soy yo,
ni mi casa es ya mi casa.   46
— Dejadme subir al menos
hasta las altas barandas;
¡dejadme subir!, dejadme
hasta las verdes barandas.
Barandales de la luna
por donde retumba el agua.   52

*

Ya suben los dos compadres
hacia las altas barandas.
Dejando un rastro de sangre.
Dejando un rastro de lágrimas.   56
Temblaban en los tejados
farolillos de hojalata.
Mil panderos de cristal
herían la madrugada.   60

*

Verde que te quiero verde,
verde viento, verdes ramas.
Los dos compadres subieron.
El largo viento dejaba   64
en la boca un raro gusto
de hiel, de menta y de albahaca.
¡Compadre! ¿Dónde está, díme,
dónde está tu niña amarga?   68
¡Cuántas veces te esperó!
¡Cuántas veces te esperara,
cara fresca, negro pelo,
en esta verde baranda!   72

not comprehending, and desiring, at least in death, the status of respectability he has never achieved in life, continues to appeal: (35) *"Friend, I'd like to die* (36) *respectably in my bed. (37) An iron bed, if possible"*—the bed of a man of property—

(38) *"with sheets of fine linen.* (39) *Don't you see the wound I have* (40) *from my breast to my throat?"* One may feel that the imagery in these lines refers not to one but to both of the great themes of the poem: to love as well as to death.

The father describes the wound with a certain gypsy eloquence not unlike the Celtic poeticisms of Synge, with whose work Lorca was familiar: (41) *"Three hundred dark-red roses* (42) *your white shirt-front bears.* (43) *Your blood is oozing, reeking* (44) *all around your sash."* Even the appeal of the terrible wound, he tries to say, can mean nothing to him now: (45) *"But I'm not myself any longer,* (46) *nor my house my house any more."*

(47) *"Let me go up, at least,"* the wounded man pleads, (48) *"as far as the high porches;* (49) *let me go up, oh let me,* (50) *as far as the green porches"*—the speaker is not aware of the meaning *green* has taken on; for him *green* is still the greenish moonlight and the pool of water; for us it is that, and so much more— (51) *"Balustrades of the moon* (52) *where the sound of water echoes."*

The eight lines that follow are the most literal, the least dreamlike of the poem: there is no reference to the suspense of the climb that leads to the terrible discovery on the roof. (53) *Now the two companions go up* (54) *toward the high porches.* (55) *Leaving a trail of blood.* (56) *Leaving a trail of tears.* The young man streaming blood; the father weeping. When they reach the roof, we are told so by images of what is to be seen and heard there: (58) *Little lanterns of plated tin* (57) *were shimmering on the rooftops.* We cannot insist on any one meaning: reading the lines, some Spaniards will see real little lanterns here and there on the roofs; other will see the lights of the town, like lanterns over the roofs; others will see the reflections of the moon twinkling on the metal fittings or trim or "flashing" of the roof. So with the lines that follow: probably they refer

to windowpanes reflecting back sharply the first light of dawn, but they might be the thin stirrings, like glass against glass, of the city coming to life. (59) *A thousand glass tambourines* (60) *were wounding the [early] dawn.* Whatever exactly suggested the images to Lorca, they evoke the sudden sparkle and expanse of the open rooftop —before the new arrivals there fasten their eyes on the tragic spectacle.

Before they do, we again have, as if for escape or reassurance, a withdrawal from the world with its sharp edges of glass and tin into the mystery of the refrain, which can be felt here in many ways, according to the resonances it might have had in the mind of the dead girl, or of the dying smuggler, or of the father, or in the mind of the poet and his reader, where its richest meaning ought to lie. (61) "Verde que te quiero verde," (62) *green wind, green branches.* (63) *The two companions went up.* [There is a suggestion of fatality achieved and terrors to be revealed in the completed past tense of "subieron," as contrasted with the present tense of "ya suben" (53).] On the roof: (64) *The long wind was leaving* (65) *in the mouth a strange taste* (66) *of gall, of mint, and of basil.* A wind crisp with mint and basil, bitter with gall—the scent of three green things, sweet and bitter mixed, as greenness is rendered in a more intimate and physical sense than sight.

(67) *"Friend!* [the young man cries out, with what may now be apprehension in his voice], *where is she, tell me,* (68) *your bitter girl, where is she?"* "Amarga," *bitter,* combines notions of wry, austere, melancholy, brooding—effects of the *bitter sea* (24) in which the girl was dreaming. Again the grief-stricken father answers indirectly: (69) *"How often she waited for you!* (70) *How often she'd be waiting,* (71) *complexion fresh, black hair,* (72) *on this green open terrace."*

There is no further reference to the two

Sobre el rostro del aljibe
se mecía la gitana.
Verde carne, pelo verde,
con ojos de fría plata.   76
Un carámbano de luna
la sostiene sobre el agua.
La noche se puso íntima

como una pequeña plaza.
Guardias civiles borrachos
en la puerta golpeaban.   82
Verde que te quiero verde.
Verde viento. Verdes ramas.
El barco sobre la mar.
Y el caballo en la montaña.   86

(*Romancero gitano*. 1928)

beholders: all eyes fasten forever on what is to be seen. We too are lost so completely in what they perceive that we have no eyes for them.

(73) *On the face of the pool* (74) *the gypsy girl was swaying.* Then lines 7 and 8 are repeated from the beginning of the poem; there they were mysterious; here they are stark: (75) *Green flesh, tresses green,* (76) *with eyes of chilly silver.* The moon's influence over the girl and the world of the poem now becomes as palpable as possible: the moonlight in which she lies seems to solidify into (77) *an icicle of moon* that (78) *holds her on [the surface of] the water*—as the green influence of the moon holds together the distraught and wandering imagery of the poem. Before the wide eyes of the gazers, swaying with grief and weakness, tormented with memories and the might-have-been, the whole world shrinks to the small area of the rooftop.

(79) *The night became intimate,* (80) *like a very little plaza.* Lorca is thinking of the tiny and silent Andalusian plazas, just room for a tree or two and perhaps a bench, quite cut off by their high walls from the noises of town. He says nothing about the feelings of the two gazers here, but he shows the force of those feelings by showing how it shrank the whole external world to this one point of intensity. Isolated intensity, so that there is no evidence that the two take any notice when the police pound on the door. Since dawn has already been mentioned, some readers think that this *night* (79) must be the following night, and that twenty-four hours pass in a sort of daze as the two bereaved ones stare at the pool. Unlikely: this is not the kind of poem that watches the clock. And even if dawn is breaking, there is still probably enough darkness on the roof to be called night.

(81) *Drunken, the Guardia Civil* (82) *were hammering on the door.* The continuous past tense of "golpeaban" is significant; it suggest that they had been pounding for some time before anyone took notice of them. If anyone ever did—the poem itself does not, but withdraws again into its tragic and rapt refrain. The last four lines are the same as the first four, but now we know all they mean. (83) "Verde que te quiero verde." (84) *Green wind. Green branches.* (85) *The ship on the sea.* (86) *And the horse on the mountain.* The green world is no longer merely the living world of wind and boughs and ships and horses, but also the tragic world where love and death are one forever beneath the embittered beauty of the moon.   [J.F.N.]

LA CASADA INFIEL

Y que yo me la llevé al río   2
creyendo que era mozuela,
pero tenía marido.   4
Fué la noche de Santiago
y casi por compromiso.

Known and quoted even by many who would be unaware of its origin, "The Unfaithful Wife"—which might more accurately be called "The Gypsy Lover"—has become the most famous of Lorca's poems. "As was to be feared," laments Diaz-Plaja: for its popularity, which Lorca himself came to regret, is due less to its poetic merits than to its vivid eroticism and to the frankness with which it depicts not only the code of the gypsy but that of the "average Spanish male" (says Barea) in his rôle as lover. The poem turns on an ethical decision: the gypsy's renunciation of the girl he has just made love to, on the grounds that she was not the virgin she professed to be. Professor Trend believes that "the point of the poem is the high gypsy standard of manners . . . the gypsy considers that he has acted correctly." Other readers, even among Lorca's countrymen, think the gypsy hypocritical: he finds a high-sounding pretext to get rid of a girl he has now finished with.

The assonance is in *i-o* (*río*, *marido*, etc.), a rare combination, occurring only here in the *Gypsy Ballad-Book* and infrequently elsewhere. The two vowels, one high, one deep, are at opposite ends of the vocal scale, so that their combination is achieved with more strain than the *e-e* or the *a-a* of our foregoing poems. But Christoph Eich, in his excellent study, is perhaps over-subtle in finding the whole theme echoed in this vocalic tension between the vigorous and masculine *i* and the passive and feminine *o*.

This poem too is constructed in quatrains. The first three lines are puzzling until we notice that the assonance, which regularly begins in the second line, here opens immediately with *río*. This and the three-line unit indicate that the first line has been dropped. The poet begins in mid-sentence, with an *and*, to plunge us immediately into the center of things, leaving certain preliminaries to be understood. (2) . . . *And so I took her down to the river* (3) *believing that she was a virgin*, (4) *but she had a husband*. Here is the theme of the poem and the grievance of the lover, to which he will return at the end. Meanwhile, the unpleasant truth does not seem to interfere with his love-making.

(5) *It was the night of the Feast of St. James*—July 25th, the great mid-summer fiesta, with revelry likely to lead to such episodes as the poem is concerned with. St. James is no ordinary saint: he is the Patron of Spain, and what happens on his night ought to have a particularly Spanish sanction. The man also has a special obligation, on this night, to live up to his code. He begins by insinuating that the idea was not really his, but the woman's. He went to the river (6) *and almost by obligation*—simply to fulfill his

Se apagaron los faroles
y se encendieron los grillos.   8
En las últimas esquinas
toqué sus pechos dormidos,
y se me abrieron de pronto
como ramos de jacintos.   12
El almidón de su enagua
me sonaba en el oído
como una pieza de seda
rasgada por diez cuchillos.   16
Sin luz de plata en sus copas
los árboles han crecido,
y un horizonte de perros
ladra muy lejos del río.   20

   Pasadas las zarzamoras,
los juncos y los espinos,
bajo su mata de pelo
hice un hoyo sobre el limo.   24
Yo me quité la corbata.
Ella se quitó el vestido.
Yo el cinturón con revólver.
Ella sus cuatro corpiños.   28
Ni nardos ni caracolas
tienen el cutis tan fino,
ni los cristales con luna
relumbran con ese brillo.   32
Sus muslos se me escapaban
como peces sorprendidos,
la mitad llenos de lumbre,
la mitad llenos de frío.   36
Aquella noche corrí
el mejor de los caminos,
montado en potra de nácar
sin bridas y sin estribos.   40
No quiero decir, por hombre,
las cosas que ella me dijo.
La luz del entendimiento
me hace ser muy comedido.   44
Sucia de besos y arena,

maculine rôle and do the lady a favor. He shows no further reluctance, however, until the experience is completed to his satisfaction—and then his scruples promptly return.

(7) *The street lamps were extinguished* (8) *and the crickets came afire:* artificial civilization gives way to spontaneous nature. Perhaps the crickets *came afire* in the sense of striking up their music, or perhaps they are really fireflies—a meaning the Royal Spanish Academy would not approve for "grillo," but which the gypsy may have given it anyway, expecially since Lorca needed a word with *i-o* for his assonance. In these lines and the following most of our senses are engaged in the world of the poem—the poet, Lorca believes, has to be a professor of the five senses.

(9) *On the last corners [of town]* (10) *I touched her sleeping breasts,* (11) *and they blossomed for me promptly* (12) *like sprays of hyacinth.* In contrast with the lyric images of awakening and fragrant blossoming are the more prosaic and violent lines that follow: (13) *The starch of her slip* (14) *was sounding in my ear* (15) *like a piece of silk* (16) *slitted by ten knives*—the fingers or fingernails of the gypsy. A close-up— which the following quatrain widens impressively to the farthest horizons of the moonless night, horizons delimited at this hour by night-sounds only. (17) *Without silver light in their foliage* (18) *the trees loomed up (larger)*—as they seem to do on the darkest nights— (19) *and, in what is probably the most evocative image of the poem, a horizon of dogs* (20) *barks very far from the river.* After the various past tenses of the preceding lines (*they blossomed, was sounding, have loomed*), *barks* brings us to an actual present: time stops for a moment and we stop with it among the many sensations of the wide exciting darkness.

(21) *Having passed the blackberry bushes,* (22) *the rushes and the hawthorn,* (23) *under* her cover of hair (24) *I scooped a trough in the mud.* (25) *I took off my necktie.* (26) *She took off her dress.* (27) *I my belt with revolver.* (28) *She her underthings, four.* The blunt one-line sentences, whether their tone is fumbling urgency or mechanical compulsion, make a pattern not duplicated in the gypsy ballads. After this direct prose, the gypsy is moved to metaphor to praise her beauty: (29) *Neither tuberoses nor seashells* (30) *have a skin so lovely,* (31) *nor crystal pools by moonlight* (32) *glow with that glow of hers.* [For *pools* we might read *mirrors* or *glass*—"cristales" could mean any of these.] Again we have sense reinforcing sense: the gypsy has been looking; now he touches, and finds both struggle and surrender, ardor and reluctance. (33) *Her thighs eluded me* (34) *like fish seized by surprise,* (35) *half, they were [filled with] fire,* (36) *half, they were [filled with] cold.* The speaker relies increasingly on metaphor as his passion quickens: first flowers, mother-of-pearl, moonlit waters, then the more sustained image of the struggling fish, and now, for the sensuous climax of the poem, all metaphor, with only the mother-of-pearl to relate the image to physical details mentioned before: (37) *That night I went riding* (38) *of all roads the best one,* (39) *mounted on a filly of pearl* (40) *without reins and without stirrups.* (Vivanco points out, quite rightly, that these lines would not have their effect in isolation; they derive much of their force from the lines that precede.)

Fatigue or disillusionment apparently followed fast; at least the immediate "No quiero" seems to imply a more generally negative attitude than mere unwillingness to speak. (41) *I don't want to say, as a man,* (42) *the things she said to me.* (43) *The light of my mother-wit* (44) *makes me discreet indeed.* A rather hollow gallantry, this pledge not to tell when he has already told everything, and will add in a moment that she is (45) *Dirty with kisses and sand.*

yo me la llevé del río.
Con el aire se batían
las espadas de los lirios.   48

　　Me porté como quien soy.
Como un gitano legítimo.
La regalé un costurero
grande, de raso pajizo,   52
y no quise enamorarme
porque teniendo marido
me dijo que era mozuela
cuando la llevaba al río.   56

(*Romancero gitano*. 1928)

Readers who lack sympathy with the gypsy lover will find in these statements evidence of his insincerity: he seems like one of those lovers who promise silence but let all be known, by winks and hints, in barbershop and tavern. (46) *I took her back from the river* echoes the beginning and recalls the reason for his rejection. Conflict between the two lately so taken up with each other is implied in the apparently marginal image: (48) *The swordblades of the iris* (47) *were waging war with the air.* This is the only time in the poem when nature is not at harmony with itself.

Recently carried away by feeling, the gypsy is now all control and reason; no hero of Corneille ever stood up more stoutly for *l'amour raisonnable.* He can choose to fall in love or not—or so he says. His manhood has been gulled and insulted by the woman's deception in promising him what a woman can give only once; nothing for it but manfully to insult her in return. (49) *I behaved like the man I am.* (50) *Like a regular gypsy.* And he pays her, by his standards generously, for her services, in this way showing her what kind of woman he takes her to be. (51) *I gave her a sewing-basket,* (52) *large-size, of straw-colored satin,* (53) *and I chose not to fall in love,* (54) *because though she had a husband* (56) *she told me she was a virgin* (57) *when I took her down to the river.* [J.F.N.]

FEDERICO GARCÍA LORCA

ROMANCE DE LA PENA NEGRA

Las piquetas de los gallos
cavan buscando la aurora,
cuando por el monte oscuro
baja Soledad Montoya.   4

Cobre amarillo, su carne
huele a caballo y a sombra.
Yunques ahumados sus pechos,
gimen canciones redondas.   8

Pena negra is literally "black grief."
Negro can be used for things terrible
in any way (much as we speak of a
"black day"); *frío negro*, for example,
means "terrible cold." But *black* also has a
sort of talismanic power for García Lorca.
In his essay on *duende* (the Andalusian term
for that mysterious power "that all may
feel and no philosophy may explain") he
quotes approvingly a comment he once
overheard at a concert of Manuel de
Falla's music: "Whatever has black
sounds has real inspiration"—for these
black sounds, he adds, are the mystery
and very root of art. There is something
almost divine or inspired, then, about a
grief so pure and deep as to be a *black*
grief.

Constructed mainly in quatrains, some-
where this poem has a six-line unit; it
would seem to come most naturally in
lines 9-14. The assonance of the even-
numbered lines is in *o-a* (*aurora, horas,*
etc.). Like the "Sleepwalking Ballad"
(p. 237), this one too opens in the myster-
ious hours before dawn, again described
in a metaphor. (1) *The pickaxes of the
roosters* (2) *are digging looking for dawn*—on
the descriptive level this is clear and vivid:
by synesthesia a sharp searching sound
becomes a sharp searching implement
(like the rooster's beak) chipping away at
the darkness. The whole poem is about a
search; the initial image is keyed to that
theme. Since the bitter woe would appear

to be related to some frustration in love,
we might ask ourselves if the rooster image
has reference to sex also. And does the
idea of digging suggest, as Vivanco
wonders, a gravedigger theme? Certainly
the poem has presages of death: the
warning about the runaway horse, the
imagery of jet-blackness (31-34). It is never
easy to set limits to the range of suggestion;
all we can say is that the first meaning is
obviously intended and that Lorca was
probably not unaware of the others, which
reinforce certain meanings to be brought
out in the body of the poem. It is cock-
crow, then, but not dawn (3) *When down
the dark mountain* (4) *comes Soledad Mon-
toya.* She *comes:* no tense except the vivid
present is used anywhere in her poem.
The mountain, with its aura of mystery,
difficulty, loneliness, suffering, is not mere
locale: it is the state of soul in which the
girl has been living. Her surname *Montoya*
is the clue to her gypsy blood. *Soledad*
("Solitude") is an abbreviation of *María de
la Soledad* ("Our Lady of Solitude")—only
the fact that it is a common Spanish
name saves it from being almost too
allegorical for this figure of lonely grief.

(5) *Yellow copper her flesh*, firm, vivid
even in darkness; (6) *it smells of horse and
shadow*—of rich warm animal vigor as
well as haven and peace: the ardor and
solace Soledad is capable of giving the
man she loves. (7) *Smoky anvils her breasts*,
(8) *they are sighing rounded songs*. The dark

— Soledad, ¿por quién preguntas
sin compaña y a estas horas?
— Pregunte por quien pregunte,
díme: ¿a ti qué se te importa?
Vengo a buscar lo que busco,
mi alegría y mi persona.   14
— Soledad de mis pesares,
caballo que se desboca
al fin encuentra la mar
y se lo tragan las olas.   18
— No me recuerdes el mar
que la pena negra brota
en las tierras de aceituna
bajo el rumor de las hojas.   22
— ¡Soledad, qué pena tienes!
¡Qué pena tan lastimosa!
Lloras zumo de limón

agrio de espera y de boca.   26
— ¡Qué pena tan grande! Corro
mi casa como una loca,
mis dos trenzas por el suelo,
de la cocina a la alcoba.   30
¡Qué pena! Me estoy poniendo
de azabache carne y ropa.
¡Ay, mis camisas de hilo!
¡Ay, mis muslos de amapola!   34
— Soledad, lava tu cuerpo
con agua de las alondras,
y deja tu corazón
en paz, Soledad Montoya.   38

*

Por abajo canta el río:
volante de cielo y hojas.
Con flores de calabaza

skin of the gypsy and the shape of the rounded end of the conventional anvil are visual justification for line 7, but more important here are the connotations, in *smoky anvils*, of such qualities as strength and endurance: an anvil is a place of fire and blows and painful forging. The gypsy has been so tortured with love and longing that the very sighs of her heaving breasts have lyric intensity. The songs are round songs because they are so deeply felt, so physical, that the music is inseparable from the rounded breasts.

The voice that now suddenly addresses the girl is that of the poet, who more than once sees himself as a character in his poetic world and talks with his creations; in one poem a character in trouble even appeals to Lorca by name: "Ay, Federico García, call the Guardia Civil!"

Lorca, who speaks as if he did not know what was going on in the mind of his character, begins to question her; some ardent agitation in the girl makes the question reasonable. (9) *"Soledad, whom are you looking for* [literally *asking for*] (10) *all alone, and at such an hour?"* The girl, in her passion, answers bluntly:

(11) *"Looking! Whomever I'm looking for,* (12) *tell me, what's it to you?"* But defiant as she is, she admits she's in search of someone or something: (13) *"I come looking for what I'm looking for,* (14) *my happiness and my self."* Here she defines the object of her search as openly as she ever does: her happiness through her fulfillment as a person—a fulfillment that will be achieved, it seems implied, through her love for another. But though unhappiness in love may be the immediate cause of her mysterious grief, it is by no means the whole story. The last lines of the poem make it clear that this is some obscure racial sorrow, deeper than any single cause can account for: it has no adequate motive and no probable cure.

Seeing from her attitude the lengths to which Soledad is likely to go, the poet's reply is an affectionate warning, which, mindful of her irritability, he softens by putting in the form of a proverb: (15) *Soledad of my sorrows*—a colloquial expression of fond exasperation, such as a mother might use to a misbehaving child— (16) *the horse that runs away* (17) *comes at last to the sea* (18) *and the waves engulf it.*

But the girl rejects the warning by deliberately misunderstanding it: the sea has nothing to do with her sorrow, which has some unspecified but easily imagined relationship with events that took place in the olive groves: (19) *Don't speak to me of the sea* (20) *for the bitter woe wells up* (21) *in the lands of the olive* (22) *under the sound of the leaves.* Again the reference is not merely geographical: the mention of the fertility of earth points to a likely source — as far as there is one — of her own barren sorrow.

Again the poet's sympathetic voice, all wonder and concern: (23) *Soledad, what a grief you feel!* (24) *What a grief that calls for pity!* (25) *What you weep is essence of lemon* (26) *bitter with longing for lips.* Literally translated, line 26 makes impossible English: *bitter with waiting and mouth.* The poet, while divining a reason for her grief, remembers her earlier defiance and is not so direct as he might be in describing it. But the meaning is clear: her tears are bitter as lemon because of something related to waiting, something related to lips.

Touched by his sympathetic insight, Soledad gives vent to her longest and fullest revelation of her state and behavior: (27) *What a mighty grief! I run* (28) *through my house like a woman crazed,* (29) *my two braids on the floor* (30) *from the kitchen to the bedroom.* The same restlessness that has driven her out on the mountainside at night keeps her in continual mad agitation, as she rushes, hair down, back and forth between the rooms most tormenting with memories. (31) *What a grief! I'm becoming* (32) *of jet, my flesh, my clothing.* (33) *Alas for my linen blouses!* (34) *Alas for my thighs, like poppy!* Soledad feels not only that in her distraught condition she is careless of her clothes; she feels that even her vivid flesh, the color of copper and poppies, is turning in the absence of love hard and black as jet, black as her grief

itself. This is her final despairing cry, this mention of her thighs, fine and silky as the petals of a flower—a common sexual symbol in Lorca. (In his essay on Góngora's imagery, he says that his great predecessor displays in his poetry "a floral sexuality.")

As Soledad, overcome, sinks into silence, the poet gives, not too hopefully, two final bits of advice. The first is figurative, a sort of white-magic formula for achieving innocence and peace through lucid ablutions: (35) *Soledad, bathe your body* (36) *in water of the larks*—leave your heated world of smoky midnight passions and animal rankness, tears bitter as lemon and black grief—leave it, if possible, for the sweet morning world where larks bathe their wings in the fresh dew of the meadows. Symbolic ablutions to purify her from the grime of her passion, to prepare to live, in effect, another kind of life. Having spoken figuratively, the poet now becomes direct: (37) *and leave your heart* (38) *in peace, Soledad Montoya.* Literally, *leave your heart in peace;* but "dejar en paz" is the colloquial *leave alone! Leave your heart alone,* he says; for the gypsy is exacerbating her sufferings. Though the poet uses her name affectionately, the way it echoes in its lonely sonority as his voice falls silent recalls the fierce and passionate figure we first saw striding down the mountainside before dawn, and implies that she cannot be other than she is—pure-blooded gypsy alone with her corrosive and ennobling grief.

The voices have ceased. What we are given after a pause is a morning vision of a world quite unlike Soledad's bitter world of jet and lemon. (39) *Down below,* farthest from the dark mountain, *sings the river;* (40) *a wheeling of heaven and leaves—* the one reflected, the other reflected or floating in its eddies. (41) *With blossoms of squash and gourd* (42) *the new day makes a crown.*

In this brilliant picture the new day

la nueva luz se corona.   42
¡Oh pena de los gitanos!
Pena limpia y siempre sola.
¡Oh pena de cauce oculto
y madrugada remota!   46

(*Romancero gitano*. 1928)

is seen as *luz* ("light"); the blossoms with which it crowns itself might be literally part of the sparkling scene, but more probably they are images for the golden radiance in the east. A world of bright water and song, of blue and green reflections, of yellow flowers and the fresh splendor of dawn. Though some of the images (the song, the flowers—but not the same flowers) have been used for the world of gypsy grief, the whole effect of freshness and sparkle presents another aspect of life, an aspect which immediately suggests to the poet that individuals as darkly passionate as Soledad can never be at home there.

The last lines of the poem deny, for such as Soledad, the possibility of such a dawn. And destroy such theories as those of the scholar who holds that the poet is trying to straighten out a "morally erring" woman! (43) *Oh grief of the gypsies!* (44) *Grief pure and forever lonely.* (45) *Oh grief whose source is hidden* (46) *and whose [chance of] dawn remote!* The sorrow of Soledad, then, is more than a personal sorrow; it is the age-old racial sorrow of a passionate and mysterious people persecuted from time immemorial. This ancient sorrow is clean, pure, noble; it exists independent of this or that occasion. It is *sola;* it cannot be divulged or shared. Nor need it be limited to the gypsies; it is rather the "cosmic loneliness of man" that can be ascribed to no specific cause and look to no likely solution.

In the figure of Soledad Montoya, perhaps the most memorable in this gypsy gallery, the poet has created an embodi-

ment of *cante jondo* itself, the tragic and mysterious "deep song" of Andalusia. Turning to the speech he delivered in Granada in 1922, a few years before these ballads were written, on the theme of *cante jondo*, we find striking similarities with the poem: there is almost a formula for the great figure that Lorca was to bring to life a few years later. The following paragraph of summary and quotation will show how many links there are between discourse and poem.

It was the gypsies who gave definite form to *cante jondo:* we owe them "the creation of these songs, soul of our soul; we owe them the construction of these lyric springs [*cauces*] whence escape all the sorrows and ritual gestures of the race." They are songs that permit the most infinite gradations of Sorrow and Grief (*Pena*); their common basis is Love and Death. At the root of all is a terrible hidden questioning—a questioning for which no answers can ever be found. The songs, always at one extreme or another, without "middle tone," either present a deep emotional problem which has no solution, or resolve it with Death. They are always sung in a night that has no dawning. "Woman, heart of the world, is everywhere in these poems . . . Woman in the *cante jondo* is called Grief [*Pena*]." In the *coplas*, or songs of the *cante jondo*, Grief becomes flesh and takes on human form: that of a dark woman who wishes the impossible—to hunt birds with nets of wind. Grief becomes flesh: this is what we see in Soledad Montoya.   [J.F.N.]

FEDERICO GARCÍA LORCA

DESPEDIDA

Si muero,
dejad el balcón abierto.

El niño come naranjas.
(Desde mi balcón lo veo.)   4

El segador siega el trigo.
(Desde mi balcón lo siento.)

¡Si muero,
dejad el balcón abierto!   8

(*Canciones.* 1927)

"Farewell" belongs to a little group published as "*Trasmundo*" ("After-life") in *Canciones* (1927). (1) *If I die,* (2) *leave the balcony open.* (3) *The boy is eating oranges.* (4) *(From my balcony I see him.)* (5) *The sickleman sickles the wheat.* (6) *(From my balcony I hear him.)* (7) *If I die,* (8) *leave the balcony open!* For one critic, this is a serene acceptance of death. For a second, it is no such thing, since it admits no kind of life except a prolongation of the present one.

Perhaps it is not about death at all, but about life as seen by one now leaving it: convinced at least of the desirability of earth, he says nothing about what is beyond. Of the many possible images of human life he gives two: one for the care-free joy of childhood, one for the significant labor of maturity. In parentheses, to indicate that his perception is another kind of reality, and to mark too his separation (a sick man's), he affirms his participation in the great drama of the world—seeing what he can see, hearing what he can hear. After his contemplation of the two images, doubled exclamation marks at the end show that his acceptance is even more eager than before. The request about the balcony is a rhetorical flourish, not to be taken literally: all it means is that even against the fact of imminent death, life is wholly desirable.

The way to read such a poem is to let it suggest not *a meaning* but *meanings;* to let it be, as Jorge Guillén says it is, at once clear and mysterious. Not "modern" in form; but reminiscent of the medieval Gallego-Portuguese lyrics, it handles gracefully its interplay of balance and variation, its imagery at once simple and symbolic, and the shifting cadences of its eight-syllable lines—contrasting, for example, a simple rhythm for the boy and the apples with a more complex, swaying rhythm for the sickleman. Everywhere, variety achieved by the simplest means.

[J.F.N.]

PREGÓN SUBMARINO

¡Tan bien como yo estaría
en una huerta del mar,
contigo, hortelana mía!

En un carrito, tirado   4
por un salmón, ¡qué alegría
vender bajo el mar salado,
amor, tu mercadería!

— ¡Algas frescas de la mar   8
algas, algas!

(*Marinero en tierra*. 1925)

MAR

En las noches, te veo
como una colgadura
del mirabel del sueño.

Asomadas a ella,   4
velas como pañuelos
me van diciendo adiós
a mí, que estoy durmiendo.

(*Marinero en tierra*. 1925)

No young poet of the Spanish Twenties exemplified the experimental, joyful quality of those years more than Rafael Alberti. He combined with rare skill the refinement of his elders (Juan Ramón Jiménez, for instance) and the simplicity of traditional rhythms and themes. His direct, candid songs, set against a background of Spanish land and sea, couple with his glittering, Góngora-sounding sonnets to give Alberti's poetic voice an echo-like quality; but one feels an authenticity of emotion entirely his own. His first book, *Marinero en tierra* (1925), won him the National Prize for Literature; Rafael Alberti was thus, at twenty-three, an established poet.

The book was welcomed by Juan Ramón Jiménez, his fellow Andalusian, as the expression of a "new and very Andalusian" voice (*nueva, andalucísima*), and by all the critics as an example of natural virtuosity. It should be borne in mind that when Alberti's book appeared there were many important poets in Spain, each of them with a new and singular style. They recognized Alberti's voice, however, as a totally new kind of poetry. First of all, his Andalusia was a new poetic theme. It is true that Jiménez had created the "Universal Andalusia"—that is, an Andalusia liberated from the traditional *Carmen*-like descriptions of gypsy life and similar local debasements—but Alberti's Andalusia seemed even more "universal" because it was more stylized, and above all more joyful, more *grácil* (to use Jiménez's own term: "subtle-light"). Thus, his was an old theme—nothing is older than the Andalusian idea in Spanish poetry—with a new, original approach. In his poetry the ancient tragedy of bullfighting, for example, becomes a delightful dancing game between the youthful bull and the equally young bullfighter—a golden sparrow, half-flying over the arena.

Alberti's power of stylization, and hence of universalization, was the result of his fusion of the popular forms already mentioned with the *ultraístas'* method of unexpected juxtapositions. The *ultraísmo* current was at that time emphasizing the freedom of the poet as regards words and images, going against, in a sense, the deep-rooted Spanish feeling of the immutability of verbal entities and patterns. That Alberti should have been at the same time an obvious traditionalist (with his mastery of folk-song metrics) and a striking innovator is a clear indication of his originality. Juan Ramón Jiménez speaks of a *golpe* in explaining Alberti's success: and indeed *Marinero en tierra* was a joyful, assertive poetical *golpe* ("blow") on the doors of Spanish poetry. But with no aspiration to rule or to destroy. His gay rebellion was immediately accepted by his elders in power.

"*Pregón submarino*" belongs to a series of short poems written in the concise, rhythmically neat style of traditional songs, each one a vivid impression bound to the whole by the thread of the sea. In the indigo-blue waters of Alberti's sea there are no storms or treasons. The ocean is the element of carefree adventure that Baudelaire's *enfant amoureux des cartes et des stampes* dreams of in the opening lines of "*Le voyage*," a vast ocean equal to his "vast appetite." In Baudelaire the child's attraction for the unknown results in the *amer savoir*, the "bitter knowing," of the man; but Alberti's child sailor is attracted by known, familiar shores. He is back from the voyage when he starts to dream. There is no bitterness in *Marinero en tierra* (*Sailor Ashore*) because in this harmonic world, joyfully growing, asserting its existence, the somber side of the ocean becomes transformed: the salty waters are sweet because saltpeter becomes air (*cielo:* "sky-heaven") in this rising mood. On Alberti's sea appear foam horses, blue bulls, green mermaids. Away from it the child sailor dreams of an "orchard lost under the sea," a paradise lost where he would live with a young mermaid, the orchard-maiden in "*Pregón submarino*" ("Hawker's Cry under the Sea"):

(1) *How happy I would be* (2) *in a sea*

orchard (3) *with you, my orchard-maiden!* (4) *In a little cart pulled* (5) *by a salmon, what joy* (6) *to sell under the salty sea,* (7) *Love, your wares.* (8) —*Fresh seaweed from the sea,* (9) *seaweed, seaweed!*

The poem is in the traditional eight-syllable verse of the *romance*, the Spanish ballad. The rime follows the pattern of many folk-songs: only the odd verses correspond. The change of rime in the last two lines with the repetion of words and sounds in *a-a* answers to a change of persons: it is the mermaid who speaks now.

Like so many traditional songs, this poem conveys an impression of fanciful frolic, of freshness, of poetry created by *homo ludens*. The classical mermaid—Siren or Lorelei—is to be feared; but Alberti's, a child, a "Christian mermaid," is quite devoid of fatal power, and her voice does not attract man to certain death. A farm-girl, a gardener of the "salty valleys," she offers her ware: seaweed, oranges from the undersea orchards, and she sings the joyful, sweet advent of life.

The transition from wish to fulfillment is not always a smooth process for Alberti's child sailor. Sometimes his song becomes a lament, and he takes refuge in the "navigable beds of sleep" because in them he can easily reach the faraway sea. This is the situation in "*Mar*" ("Sea"). (1) *At night I see you* (2) *like a canopy* (3) *of sleep's sunflower.* (4) *Peeking out of it* (5) *sails like handkerchiefs* (6) *are saying goodbye to me* (7) *while I go on sleeping.*

In this poem, written in the seven-syllable verse of the Spanish folk-song (with an assonant rime in *e-o* in lines 1, 3, 5, and 7 [*veo, sueño, pañuelos, durmiendo*]) the image of the sea is projected over the bed's canopy, small and attainable. But here the impulse to dream is too strong: the sleeper-voyager is carried away from the beloved image, while the sea, left behind, signals a sad farewell with its sails.

[s.s.m.]

RAFAEL ALBERTI

EL ÁNGEL DE LOS NÚMEROS

Vírgenes con escuadras
y compases, velando
las celestes pizarras.   3

Y el ángel de los números,
pensativo, volando
del 1 al 2, del 2
al 3, del 3 al 4.   7

Tizas frías y esponjas
rayaban y borraban
la luz de los espacios.   10

Ni sol, luna, ni estrellas,
ni el repentino verde
del rayo y el relámpago,
ni el aire. Sólo nieblas.   14

Vírgenes sin escuadras,
sin compases, llorando.   16

Y en las muertas pizarras,
el ángel de los números,
sin vida, amortajado
sobre el 1 y el 2,   20
sobre el 3, sobre el 4...

(Sobre los ángeles. 1929)

An adolescent Ulysses, Rafael Alberti moved swiftly in his poetic adventure, avoiding the danger of dwelling too long at any one stage. After the success of *Marinero en tierra* he cries "Death to the sea!" and embarks on an inland voyage. He has turned his old values upside down, but he seems unable to establish himself in a senseless world. *Sobre los ángeles* (*About Angels*), Alberti's masterpiece, bears witness to the poet's constant effort to recreate his own identity in an alien *milieu*. He remains within the tradition of form and imagery by choosing angels as the protagonists of his book, but now he makes increasing use of the style and subject-matter of Surrealism. The world is now apprehended as an infinite space of mist and crumbling ruins; and the poet, himself a lost angel, fights against the invading forces of disintegration and chaos.

In *"El ángel de los números"* ("The Angel of Numbers") we witness the inevitable death of Harmony at the hands of total disorder:

(1) *Virgins with T-squares* (2) *and compasses, in a vigil over* (3) *the celestial blackboards.*

(4) *And the angel of numbers,* (5) *thoughtful, flying* (6) *from 1 to 2, from 2 to 3, from 3 to 4.*

(8) *Cold chalks and sponges* (9) *rasping and erasing* (10) *the light of spaces.*

(11) *Nor sun, moon, nor stars,* (12) *nor the sudden green* (13) *of thunderbolt and lightning,* (14) *nor air. Only mist.*

(15) *Virgins without squares,* (16) *without compasses, weeping.*

(17) *And upon the dead blackboard,* (18) *the angel of numbers,* (19) *lifeless, shrouded* (20) *above the 1 and the 2,* (21) *above the 3, above the 4. . . .*

The twenty-one seven-syllable lines fall roughly into three divisions of seven lines. At irregular intervals there is a rime-like repetition of *a-o* at the end of the line. In the first section, all is well in the celestial spheres, where the angel moves slowly, thoughtfully, about his orderly work, measuring, counting, while watchful Muse-virgins hold his instruments and symbols. The images of blackboard, chalk, sponges, erasers, give a tangible dimension to an otherwise limitless space by evoking memories of childhood days in the classroom. The second section (11-13) describes the cold harsh attack on light by the elements of chaos: nothing is left but fog. The third section repeats the first, but with variations (*y compases, volando* becomes *sin compases, llorando,* 15-16). These variations, however, are significant: Death has put an end to the angel's harmonious operations. The destruction of light and order is also indicated by a different rhythmic flow: there is a new, abrupt stop at the end of the second line (18); and in the last two verses (20-21) the numerals are uttered in a staccato movement, quite unlike the dancing verses of the first section.

This poem of violence and destruction does not convey an altogether tragical impression. The repetition of sounds muffles the tragic note (though at the same time it makes the few changes the more significant and poignant); and in the second part, the brutality of the attack is attenuated by the scarcity of verbs: there are only two (*rayaban* and *borraban,* 9), and these are in the imperfect tense—the tense of description rather than of action—, thus investing the destruction with an aura of inevitability. Life and movement are no more; but the dead angel, resting on his numerals, seems still to be a symbol of harmony.   [S.S.M.]

RAFAEL ALBERTI

EL ÁNGEL BUENO

Vino el que yo quería,
el que yo llamaba.

No aquel que barre cielos sin defensas,
luceros sin cabañas,   4
lunas sin patria,
nieves.
Nieves de esas caídas de una mano,
un nombre,   8
un sueño,
una frente.

No aquel que a sus cabellos
ató la muerte.   12

El que yo quería.

Sin arañar los aires,
sin herir hojas ni mover cristales.

Aquel que a sus cabellos   16
ató el silencio.

Para sin lastimarme,
cavar una ribera de luz dulce en mi pecho
y hacerme el alma navegable.   20

(Sobre los ángeles. 1929)

There are times when the forces of destruction seem to prevail: the Angels of War, of Wrath, of Envy, of Revenge, of Cruelty, of Darkness are joined in their victory by those representing the disintegration of matter, the Angels of Sand, of Ashes, of Mildew. After the attack of the Ashy Angel, who hurls himself down from the heavens in his foggy boat, the world, jolting from side to side, rolls dead into nothingness. There is no possible defense against these obscure forces, because their very existence is connected with the crisis through which man is going. In fact, they are the symbols of different stages in this long crisis. Thus, the boundless, crumbling world of *Sobre los ángeles* shrinks sometimes into the limited space of the bedroom where man fights against the demons of nightmare, the Sleepwalking Angels. Their eyes, *los invisibles ojos de las alcobas* ("the invisible eyes of bedrooms") sink like incandescent needles into the walls. And to the west of the poet's dream, the False Angel plants his tent to make [him] "walk among the knots of roots—and the bone-like dwellings of worms" (*para que yo anduviera entre los* nudos de la raíces—y las viviendas óseas de los gusanos), and to make [him] "bite the petrified light of the brightest stars" (y mordiera la luz petrificada de los astros).

But not everything is death and ruin. The innocence of life comes back in the "Three Remembrances of Heaven," placed at a time when creation was in the stage "before harp, rain or world." Also, in the midst of nightmare, the Good Angel comes three times to comfort man.

This poem, El ángel bueno, is an account of the third visit: (1) There came the one I wanted (2) the one I called. (3) Not the one who sweeps away defenseless skies, (4) bright stars without shelter, (5) moons without country, (6) snows. (7) Snows of the kind that fall from a hand, (8) a name, (9) a dream, (10) a forehead. (11) Not he who to his hair (12) tied death. (13) The one I wanted. (14) Without scoring the airs, (15) without wounding the leaves nor moving the windowpanes. (16) The one who to his hair (17) tied silence. (18) So as to dig ["cavar," 19] without hurting me, (19) a bank of sweet light in my breast (20) and make my soul navigable.

In its twenty lines three perfectly classical endecasílabos (eleven-syllable lines) mix with the short, irregular lines of traditional songs. And at the end, the long verses of fourteen and nineteen syllables seem to mark the poet's intent of drawing away from accepted patterns. There is no rime, but the vowel e at the end of lines occurs frequently. Some repetitions are reminiscent of traditional forms (el que yo quería, aquel que a sus cabellos ató): their function is to underline the difference between this Angel and the Bad one, the one who destroys even the most subtle matter, that snow falling from a hand which perhaps could have started the creative process.

Throughout this book we feel the echo of Gustavo Adolfo Bécquer (1836-1870), his soothing music (here most clearly heard in lines 14 and 15) in contrast with the harshness of Surrealistic discordant rhythms. The mano de nieve ("snow hand") in Bécquer's famous "Rima VII" is the symbol of the poet's power to awaken song from nature where it waits, esperando la mano de nieve que sabe arrancarla [la música]—Bécquer speaks of an abandoned harp, "waiting for the snow hand that knows how to extract [music] from it". For Alberti, these snows, these latent powers of creation, are killed by the Bad Angel: and that is why todo un siglo es un arpa en abandono. After the first two lines Alberti speaks again of the disintegrating powers which are his obsession. Only at the end of the poem does he speak of the visit of the Good Angel, whose halo is not death but comforting silence. The Angel comes without scratching, without wounding, without hurting. Without is repeated six times and contributes thus to mark the great contrast between the two angels. The Good one moves lightly, almost in bodiless fashion. He comes sin herir los fanales—nocturnos de la alcoba—por la ciudad del aire ("without wounding the nocturnal lights of the bedroom through the city of air"). He seems to be pure air, and with him comes back the possibility of movement and creation. But then, cinco manos de ceniza—cayeron sobre mi cuerpo—cuando inmóvil resbalaba sobre los cinco navegables rios—que dan, almas corrientes, voz al sueño ("five ashen hands, fell over my body, when motionless it slid over the five navigable rivers which give, flowing souls, a voice to sleep").

Alberti's poem depicts a still world that recovers its capacity of motion and of creation when the Good Angel arrives, because he opens within the poet's heart corredores anchos, largos—que sorben todos los mares ("long and broad corridors that suck in all the seas"). And poet and man can again embark on the adventure of dreams. [S.S.M.]

A LUIS CERNUDA: AIRE DEL SUR
BUSCADO EN INGLATERRA

Si el aire se dijera un día:
                 — Estoy cansado,
rendido de mi nombre... Ya no quiero
ni mi inicial para firmar el bucle
del clavel, el rizado de la rosa,   4
el plieguecillo fino del arroyo,
el gracioso volante de la mar y el hoyuelo
que ríe en la mejilla de la vela...

Desorientado, subo de las blandas,   8
dormidas superficies
que dan casa a mi sueño.
Fluyo de las paradas enredaderas, calo
los ciegos ajimeces de las torres;   12
tuerzo, ya pura delgadez, las calles
de afiladas esquinas, penetrando,
roto y herido de los quicios, hondos
zaguanes que se van a verdes patios   16
donde el agua elevada me recuerda,
dulce y desesperada, mi deseo...

Busco y busco llamarme
¿con qué nueva palabra, de qué modo?   20
¿No hay soplo, no hay aliento,
respiración capaz de poner alas
a esa desconocida voz que me denomine?

Desalentado, busco y busco un signo,   24
un algo o alguien que me sustituya,
que sea como yo y en la memoria
fresca de todo aquello, susceptible
de tenue cuna y cálido susurro,   28
perdure con el mismo
temblor, el mismo hálito
que tuve la primera
mañana en que al nacer, la luz me dijo: 32
— Vuela. Tú eres el aire.

Si el aire se dijera un día eso...

                        (Pleamar. 1944)

Like other Spanish poets of his generation, Alberti left his country at the end of the Civil War (1939). Exile, though a painful human experience, did not affect the writing of all of these men; but Alberti was so obsessed by the disastrous outcome of the war and the death of many friends that he feared he would never be able to write again. After 1940, however, he gradually recovered his creative strength and became the poet of exile. Away from his land, there is no solace in life, in nature: everything points to the lost world, which thus becomes a new and veritable Paradise Lost. The poet's only hope now is to reach—almost to invent— his homeland by means of his verses. Thus Alberti embarks on his last adventure, the remembrance of things past and the identification of his creative force with his Spanish roots. This poetry is a process of personal and collective survival.

This is the mood of Poem 9 of *Pleamar*, addressed to Luis Cernuda, another Andalusian poet, exiled in England: *Aire del sur buscado en Inglaterra* ("Looking for a Southern air in England"). (1) *If the air were to say to itself one day: "I am tired,* (2) *dead tired of my name . . . I no longer want* (3) *my initials to sign the curl* (4) *of the carnation, the ripples of the rose,* (5) *the small fine fold of the brook,* (6) *the graceful ruffle of the sea and the dimple* (7) *laughing in the sail's cheek. . . .* (8) *Astray [disoriented], I rise from the soft* (9) *sleeping surfaces* (10) *that house my sleep.* (11) *I flow from the still vines, I pierce through* (12) *the blind mullioned windows of the towers;* (13) *I turn, already pure leanness, into the streets* (14) *with their sharp corners, penetrating,* (15) *broken and wounded by the doorjambs, the deep* (16) *vestibules leading to green patios* (17) *where the water, rising [lifted: as of a fountain], reminds me,* (18) *sweetly and desperately, of my desire. . . .* (19) *I try and try to [find a] name [for] myself,* (20) *with what new word, in what way?* (21) *Is there no*

gust of wind, no breath, (22) *no respiration able to give wings* (23) *to that unknown word* ["voz": voice, word] *that will name me?* (24) *Discouraged, I look and look for a sign,* (25) *a something or someone to replace me,* (26) *that might resemble me, and, in the recent memory* (27-28) *of all these things [the scenes and images recalled], instinct with soft cradle and warm humming,* (29) *might endure with the very same* (30) *flutter, the same breath* (31) *that I took that first* (32) *morning, when I was born and the light said to me:* (33) *'Fly. You are air.' "* (34) *If one day the air were to say that . . .*

The poem is divided into sections of eight, eleven, five, and ten verses, with one final verse almost identical with the first. There is a clear intention to break conventional patterns: no rime; and many of the lines are torn in half by a pause and move into the next line as though following the rhythm of a disturbed voice. The prevailing eleven-syllable line of the Spanish elegy is broken up at sparse, uneven intervals.

The poem itself is presented in the form of a conjecture: if the air felt as the poet does now, lost and disheartened, it might very well fail in its attempts to move. The winding investigation takes us stumbling through a painful labyrinth to the tranquil enclosed patios, where the perennial rising of the water in the fountain repeats the doomed, useless rising of the air (8-10). Air and poet seek a new name, or perhaps a new way of self-evocation. Alberti realizes that identity and inspiration are linked, that he will not completely recover his poetic voice unless his former self, rooted in the Spanish soil of his childhood, restores to him his first wings. Alberti's dominant element, his permanent fixation is Air: poetry for him is always a world in flight. This poem is an exile's prayer for the restored grace of his Element. [s.s.m.]

SONETO

Habréis de conocer que estuve vivo
por una sombra que tendrá mi frente.
Sólo en mi frente la inquietud presente
que hoy guardo en mí, de mi dolor cautivo.   4

Blanca la faz, sin el ardor lascivo,
sin el sueño prendiéndose a la mente.
Ya sobre mí, callado eternamente,
la rosa de papel y el verde olivo.   8

Qué sueño sin ensueños torcedores,
abierta el alma a trémulas caricias
y sobre el corazón fijas las manos.

Qué lejana la voz de los amores.   12
Con qué sabor la boca a las delicias
de los altos serenos oceános.

(*Doble acento.* 1937)

The matter of this untitled *soneto* ("sonnet") may at first remind the reader of the theme of César Vallejo's "Piedra negra sobre una piedra blanca" (p. 224), for in each of these poems the writer speaks of himself as of one already dead. But there all similarity ends; the methods and metrical forms of the two poems have as little in common as their emotional overtones and their settings. If Vallejo talks of this newly dead self with intense subjectivity, Florit may be said to take an almost objective view. He looks upon his body as an interested observer might look upon it at some unspecified future date. Moreover, the thought as a whole has been projected into the future; the single reference to the present (*hoy,* "nowadays," 4) pulls time back from the future only for a moment, and then merely to enable the writer to speak of his present grief. The poem as an entity moves forward from the death-in-the-future to an "even more future" date when the speaker will have achieved serenity.

The words are addressed to the people who will be present at the death scene. (1) *You will notice (become aware) that I had been alive* (2) *from a shadow that my forehead will show.* (3) *Only in my forehead [should be] the restlessness present* (4) *that nowadays I keep within me, [I] a prisoner of my own grief.* (5) *My* [literally *the*] *face [shall be] white, without any lascivious burning,* (6) *without dreams clinging to my thought.* (7) *Now [at that time of death there will lie] upon me, forever silenced,* (8) *a paper rose and a green olive branch.*

The sestet of the sonnet introduces a shift in mood, as the speaker reflects upon his future state. (9) *Oh, such sleep without disturbing dreams* ["Qué sueño" means literally *What a sleep!*], (10) *the soul opened to tremulous caresses* (11) *and my hands fixed upon my breast* [literally *heart*]. (12) *How far away now is the voice of my loves!* (13) *Oh, the taste in my mouth of the delights* (14) *of lofty, serene oceans!*

The people observing the body will note the presence of a shadow on the dead man's forehead. It is the only sign of his suffering; it creates the only moment of anguish in the entire poem, for it is the only thought "located" in the present: everything else suggests future restfulness and the movement of restfulness towards serenity. The face will be pallid, for with death the body sheds the burning flush of desire. And thought will at last be liberated from the dreams that trouble the living mind. Both conditions are evoked, not by picturing anything new, but by canceling out the old—through the double use of *sin* ("without") in lines 5 and 6. Indeed, the only suggestion of anything new appears in the two decorative symbols that will be placed upon the body: a rose recalling the dead man's memories of youth and spring, and an olive branch of peace. But the rose is of paper: youth and spring are irrecoverable; all that remains is their abstract idea. The olive branch, however, is alive, and as such it resembles the peace of the body it ornaments.

The last six lines of this strictly formal sonnet describe the wished-for serenity through suggested contrasts. The body of the dead man is immobile, his hands fixed upon his breast, but his soul has already opened to the delights of "tremulous caresses." The voices of his bygone loves, of those whom his lips had once known, are now far away; but he is already alive to a new union as his mouth tastes the waters of eternity.   [E.F.]

[Eugenio Florit was born of a Cuban mother and a Spanish father in Madrid in 1903. Fifteen years later he moved with his family to Cuba, where he remained until 1940. Upon graduation from the University of Havana, he found employment in the State Department, and for several years after his arrival in the United States (1940) he served in the Cuban Consulate in New York. Five years later he became a member of the faculty of Barnard College, Columbia University, where he continued to teach as Professor of Spanish language and literature.

His poems have been published in the following volumes: 32 *poemas breves*, 1927; *Trópico*, 1930; *Doble acento* 1937; *Reino*, 1938; *Cuatro poemas*, 1940; *Poema mío* [collected poems], 1946; and *Asonante final y otros poemas*, 1956. A volume of his selected poems, *Antología poética*, appeared in 1956.]

EUGENIO FLORIT

LA NOCHE

Ya, Señor, sé lo que dicen
las estrellas de tu cielo;
que sus puntas de diamante
me lo vienen escribiendo.   4

Ya, por páginas de aire,
las letras caen. Yo atiendo,
ojos altos, muda boca
y callado pensamiento.   8

Y qué clara la escritura
dentro de la noche, dentro
del corazón anheloso
de recibir este fuego   12

que baja de tus abismos,
va iluminando mi sueño
y mata la carne y deja
al alma en su puro hueso.   16

Lo que dicen tus estrellas
me tiene, Señor, despierto
a más altas claridades,
a más disparados vuelos,   20

a un no sé de cauteloso,
a un sí sé de goce trémulo,
(alas de una mariposa
agitadas por el suelo).   24

Y en el suelo desangrándose
se pierde la voz del cielo
hasta que se llega al alma
por la puerta del deseo.   28

Paloma de las estrellas,
ala en aire, flecha, hierro
en el blanco de la fragua
de tu amor. En el desvelo   32

de tantas luces agudas
todo va lejos, huyendo;
todo, menos Tú, Señor;
que ya sé cómo me hablas   36
por las estrellas del cielo.

(*Asonante final y otros poemas.* 1956)

To anyone who knows the verses of St. Teresa of Avila or the minor poems of St. John of the Cross, this twentieth-century meditation on "Night" (or "The Night") will have a familiar ring. Like many of the religious poems in the Spanish tradition, "*La noche*" uses the eight-syllable line of the popular ballad, or *romance*, to communicate a wholly personal religious vision. Moreover, the imagery of "*La noche*" is symbolic in the traditional mystic manner. Yet the central thought of the poem presents no difficulty, deriving, indeed, from no more remote a source than Psalm XIX: "The heavens declare the glory of God." As the speaker (or poet) gazes at the stars, his mind fills with a series of ideas in which he perceives a connection between the lights in the sky and the voice of God.

(1) *Now, O Lord, I know the meaning* (2) *of the stars in Thy sky* [literally *what the stars in Thy sky are saying*]; (3) *for their diamond points* (4) *are writing it down for me.* (5) *Now, through the pages of the air,* (6) *the letters fall.* [*And*] *I listen,* (7) *with lifted eyes, muted mouth,* (8) *and silent thought.* (9) *And how clear* [*is*] *the writing* (10) *within*

the night, within (11) *my heart [which is] so eager* (12) *to receive this fire* (13) *that falls from Thy abysses* (14) *[that] keeps illumining (lighting up) my dreams* (15) *and kills the flesh and leaves* (16) *the soul in its pure bone [naked core].* (17) *That which Thy stars are saying* (18) *keeps me O Lord, alert* (19) *to [even] loftier brilliances (glories, splendors),* (22) *to swifter flights,* (21) *to an I-know-not-what cautiousness* [literally *to an I-do-not-know of cautious*], (22) *to an I-know-what quivering joy* [literally *to an I-know of quivering joy*], (23) *([like the] wings of a butterfly* (24) *fluttering on the ground.)* (25) *And [also] on the ground, bleeding,* (26) *the voice of the sky vanishes* (27) *until it reaches the soul* (28) *through the door of desire.* (29) *Dove of the stars [stars in the shape of a dove],* (30) *wing on air, arrow, brand* (31) *in the white [heat] of the forge* (32) *of Thy love. In the watchfulness* (33) *of so many sharp lights,* (34) *everything goes far off, fleeing;* (35) *everything except Thee, O Lord;* (36) *for now I know how Thou speakest to me* (37) *through the stars in the sky.*

The first four lines set forth the general statement. The speaker knows the meaning of the messages that the stars are writing with their diamond points of light. But this light is more than light: it is fire (12) borne from the abyss of timelessness, fire which not only illumines his dreams but "kills the flesh" (15). By extinguishing all material and earthly desire, it places his soul in a pure state of separation from the body—the soul is *en su puro hueso* ("in its pure bone"), an image reminiscent of the contrasts and paradoxes of Spanish mystical verse with "bone" or "core" denoting pure essence. Once the cleansing fire has laid the soul naked, the speaker becomes capable of penetrating more deeply into "that which Thy stars are saying" (17). And this deepened understanding alerts him to a new experience—of ecstasy—suggested by such terms as *más altas claridades* ("loftier, higher brilliancies or glories," 19) and *más disparados vuelos* ("swifter flights," 20). It is also expressed by an indefinable uncertainty (21-22): *un no sé de cauteloso,* a hitherto unknown sense of fearfulness or cautiousness, and *un sí sé de goce trémulo,* a hitherto unknown quivering of delight which makes him think of the wings of a butterfly lying on the ground.

The butterfly image leads to a new idea. The message of the heavens (*cielo*: there is only one word in Spanish for both "heaven" and "sky") also lies upon the ground; it lies there bleeding, wasting, until such moment as a soul in its desire opens its doors to receive it (25-28). The lines that immediately follow introduce a new series of rhapsodic ideas, projected by the "dove of the stars"—stars in the shape of a dove, wings in flight, and a brand or dart glows with the white heat of heavenly love as it pierces the enraptured soul. The stars are no longer fixed in the sky; they are flying downward to earth, flying as doves would fly, the dove of the Holy Ghost. Thus the poem ends with its simple intimation that the starry sky may be sufficient to arouse both the mystical knowledge and love of God.   [E.F.]

[PUEDO ESCRIBIR LOS VERSOS...]

Puedo escribir los versos más tristes esta noche.

Escribir, por ejemplo: « La noche está estrellada,
y tiritan, azules, los astros, a lo lejos ».

El viento de la noche gira en el cielo y canta.   4

Puedo escribir los versos más tristes esta noche.
Yo la quise, y a veces ella también me quiso.

En las noches como ésta la tuve entre mis brazos.
La besé tantas veces bajo el cielo infinito.   8

Ella me quiso, a veces yo también la quería.
Cómo no haber amado sus grandes ojos fijos.

Puedo escribir los versos más tristes esta noche.
Pensar que no la tengo. Sentir que la he perdido.   12

Oir la noche inmensa, más inmensa sin ella.
Y el verso cae al alma como al pasto el rocío.

Qué importa que mi amor no pudiera guardarla.
La noche está estrellada y ella no está conmigo.   16

Eso es todo. A lo lejos alguien canta. A lo lejos.
Mi alma no se contenta con haberla perdido.

Como para acercarla mi mirada la busca.
Mi corazón la busca, y ella no está conmigo.   20

La misma noche que hace blanquear los mismos árboles.
Nosotros, los de entonces, ya no somos los mismos.

Ya no la quiero, es cierto, pero cuánto la quise.
Mi voz buscaba el viento para tocar su oído.   24

De otro. Será de otro. Como antes de mis besos.
Su voz, su cuerpo claro. Sus ojos infinitos.

Ya no la quiero, es cierto, pero tal vez la quiero.
Es tan corto el amor, y es tan largo el olvido.   28

Porque en noches como ésta la tuve entre mis brazos,
mi alma no se contenta con haberla perdido.

Aunque éste sea el último dolor que ella me causa,
y éstos sean los últimos versos que yo le escribo.   32

(*Veinte poemas de amor y una canción desesperada.* 1924)

[**P**ablo Neruda: born in Temuco, Chile, in 1904.] This is the last of twenty poems which deal with the aftermath of the poet's love for a woman no longer with him. In the early poems, he reviews their love from its beginning, passing back and forth from the recollection of her to his present solitude, to his awareness that this love is a thing of the past. Her absence is permanent and his loneliness is inescapable. The poet submerges himself in the sadness produced by his awareness of this: (1) *I can write the saddest verses tonight.* This declaration is followed by two pretty but rather ordinary lines. The author knows this and puts them in quotation marks: (2) *Write, for example:* "*The night is starry,* (3) *and the stars, blue, shiver in the distance.*" But his mood does not permit him to toy with such verses. He is too much preoccupied with his own state and immediate surroundings: (4) *The wind of the night gyrates in the sky and sings.* Once more he tells us what he could write if he were so minded, and follows with some of the causes of his sadness: (5) *I can write the saddest verses tonight.* (6) *I loved her and at times she also loved me.* (7) *On nights like this I held her in my arms.* (8) *I kissed her so many times under the infinite sky.* (9) *She loved me, [and] at times I also would love her.* (10) *How [was it possible] not to have loved her great steady [serene] eyes?* Again, and for the last time, the poet restates his initial theme, and follows with an elaboration of lines 6-10: (11) *I can write the saddest verses tonight.* (12) *To think that I do not have her. To feel that I have lost her.* (13) *To hear the immense night, more immense without her.* (14) *And the [my] verse falls on the soul like dew on the grass.* The important thing, the thing that matters, is that she is not with him, that their love is over: (15) *What does it matter that my love could not keep her?* (16) *The night is starry and she is not with me.* (17) *That is all. In the distance someone sings. In the distance.* The distant singing intensifies his solitude, and his soul rebels against being alone: (18) *My soul is not content with having lost her.* (19) *As if to bring her near, my look seeks for her. My heart seeks for her, and she is not with me.* (21) *[It is] the same [kind of] night that makes the same trees appear white.* (22) *We, of then, are no longer the same.*

In his struggle to forget, the poet finds little comfort in the inescapable fact that change and the passing of time make recapture of the past impossible. But he does try to give himself courage: (23) *I no longer love her, that is true, but how much I did love her!* Before he has finished saying he no longer loves her, he has fallen back into the sickness from which he was trying to save himself. So once again we follow him into the past: (24) *My voice sought out the wind to touch her ear.* Then comes a bitter realization: (25) *Another's. She is another's. As [she was] before my kisses.* (26) *Her voice, her clear body. Her infinite eyes.* He fights this thought by declaring again that he does not love her; but with worse results than before, because he confesses to loving her still: (27) *I no longer love her, it is true, but perhaps I do love her.* (28) *Love is so short, and forgetting is [takes] so long.* And with his last lines he surrenders to this fact and to his sadness: (29) *Because on nights like this I held her in my arms,* (30) *my soul is not content with having lost her.* (31) *Although this be the last sorrow she causes me,* (32) *and these be the last verses I shall write to her.* [P.P.R.]

PABLO NERUDA

NO HAY OLVIDO (SONATA)

Si me preguntáis en dónde he estado
debo decir « Sucede ».
Debo de hablar del suelo que oscurecen las piedras,
del río que durando se destruye: 4
no sé sino las cosas que los pájaros pierden,
el mar dejado atrás, o mi hermana llorando.
Por qué tantas regiones, por qué un día
se junta con un día? Por qué una negra noche   8
se acumula en la boca? Por qué muertos?
Si me preguntáis de dónde vengo, tengo que conversar
    con cosas rotas,
con utensilios demasiado amargos,
con grandes bestias a menudo podridas   12
y con mi acongojado corazón.

No son recuerdos los que se han cruzado
ni es la paloma amarillenta que duerme en el olvido,
sino caras con lágrimas,   16
dedos en la garganta,
y lo que se desploma de las hojas:
la oscuridad de un día transcurrido,
de un día alimentado con nuestra triste sangre.   20

He aquí violetas, golondrinas,
todo cuanto nos gusta y aparece
en las dulces tarjetas de larga cola
por donde se pasean el tiempo y la dulzura.   24

Pero no penetremos más allá de esos dientes,
no mordamos las cáscaras que el silencio acumula,
porque no sé qué contestar:
hay tantos muertos,   28
y tantos malecones que el sol rojo partía,
y tantas cabezas que golpean los buques,
y tantas manos que han encerrado besos,
y tantas cosas que quiero olvidar.   32

(Residencia en la tierra (1925-1935). 1935)

This poem is a sort of *ars poetica* in which the poet describes his approach to the subject matter. He calls it a sonata. On many occasions Neruda imitated musical forms: one poem is called a symphony, another a serenata, a third is a barcarolle; there are several sonatas, chants, songs, a hymn, and a tango.

In his use of symbols Neruda deliberately broke with their traditional meanings. Some are concrete, but many are intentionally obscure, as we shall see in "There Is No Forgetting."

(1) *If you ask me where I have been* (2) *I must say "It happens."* (3) *I must speak of the ground which the stones obscure,* (4) *of the river that enduring destroys itself:* (5) *I know only the things that birds lose,* (6) *the sea left behind, or my sister weeping.* (7) *Why [are there] so many regions, why [does] a day* (8) *join with a day? Why [does] a dark night* (9) *accumulate in the mouth? Why [are there] dead [people]?* (10) *If you ask me where I come from, I [shall] have to converse with broken things,* (11) *with utensils too bitter,* (12) *with great beasts [animals] often putrid* (13) *and with my afflicted heart.* (14) *They are not memories those [things] that have crossed [in my mind],* (15) *nor is the yellowish dove that sleeps in forgetfulness,* (16) *but faces with tears [are],* (17) *fingers at the throat,* (18) *and that which drops from the leaves:* (19) *the darkness of a day elapsed,* (20) *of a day nourished with our sad blood.* (21) *Here are violets, swallows,* (22) *everything that pleases us and [that] appears* (23) *on sweet and fancy [picture] cards* (24) *where time and sweetness promenade [walk].* (25) *But let us not penetrate beyond those teeth,* (26) *let us not bite [through] the rind that silence accumulates,* (27) *because I do [shall] not know what to answer:* (28) *there are so many dead,* (29) *there are so many dikes [seawalls] that the red sun split [cracked],* (30) *and so many heads that beat [strike against] the boats,* (31) *and so many hands that have enclosed kisses,* (32) *and so many things I want to forget.*

Neruda's intuitive conception of the world is one of continuous disintegration and destruction. In the first two lines he seems to pick up the thought of an earlier poem: *Sucede que me canso de ser hombre* ("It happens that I am weary of being a man"), that is, weary of the decay and falsifications of modern civilization. But he must write about these matters, of the ground darkened by stones (elemental matter), of the perpetual destruction of life and things ("of the river that lasting destroys itself"), of that which is past and forgotten ("the sea left behind"), and of present sorrow ("my sister weeping"). He feels himself alone in the great solitudes of the world ("Why are there so many regions?") and the depressing mysteries of life and civilization (7, 8, 9). He must speak, if you ask him, of utensils (a suggestive image only) that are "too bitter," of animals often decayed, and of his grieving heart.

The things that cross in his mind are not memories (14), not even the "yellowish dove" (symbol of passing life, life that is past, 15). But "faces with tears" (16) and terrible "fingers at the throat" (17) are remembered, and so is the day that has elapsed and "which is nourished with our sad blood," that is, with our unhappiness and pain (19, 20).

There are, however, beautiful things in life: violets and swallows (the swallow is a symbol of things we like, of things seen in dreams and flights of fancy). But, the poet says, let us not go beyond these things, "let us not penetrate beyond those teeth" (i.e., that smile, those pleasant things), let us not bite into the pleasing rind accumulated by silence, for if we do he will not then know what to answer, because there is so much death (28), so much destruction (29), so much suffering (30, 31), and so many things that he wishes to forget (32), but that he will have to remember because there is no forgetting, and to write about because that is his poetic mission. [In the interpretation of this poem I have made some use of Amado Alonso's *Poesía y estilo de Pablo Neruda*, 1940.]   [P.P.R.]

ITALIAN

LA SERA DEL DÌ DI FESTA

Dolce e chiara è la notte e senza vento,
E queta sovra i tetti e in mezzo agli orti
Posa la luna, e di lontan rivela
Serena ogni montagna. O donna mia,   4

Giacomo Leopardi (1798-1837), the greatest Italian poet of recent centuries, held views of man's condition that were bleak indeed. "My pleasure," he wrote in a letter of May 6, 1825, "is in discovering ever more clearly . . . the misery of men and things, and of freezing with horror as I speculate on this unhappy and terrible mystery of life. . . ." Subjected in his provincial town to well-meant but rigid parental custody, Leopardi felt, at eighteen, that his health had been ruined forever by the philological studies which consumed his youth. Sensitive and in need of the affection of women, he was attractive to few: a hunchback and semi-invalid to whom at times any change of light or breath of air was painful. Out of these experiences he generalized his own sufferings into a philosophy of despair. But though the poet insisted that life was nothing but boredom and pain, the poetry had different and more dazzling insights— as if the pessimism were some black shadow thrown by a splendid sun. Leopardi's attitude, as the critic De Sanctis has observed, was not so much a denial of life as the supreme sensation of its value. No other poet has insisted more strongly on man's drive toward the infinite; none has been more passionately moved to look from confinement to liberation: from a crooked body, a straitened house, a meager village into endless vistas of time, space, and eternity. No poet since Lucretius, said one of his biographers, has been so great a poet of the sky.

This longing for the infinite, the keynote of Leopardi's poetry, determines not only theme and attitude but even imagery and diction. What is limited and "real," he felt, was farthest from the infinite; there are no present joys, nothing but joys remembered or joys desired. Man is happiest in his illusions, since there his imagination, tending toward the illimitable, has freest play. Man's imagination, indeed, is the "prime fount of human happiness," creating for itself the infinity not available in the "real" world. We cannot hope to know the infinite, but we can be sure that its deadly opposite is the definite, the delimited, the here and now. Leopardi, for whom the definite was antipoetic, built much of his esthetic theory on the notion of the vague or indefinite, which, leaving the mind free to range to infinity, "delights and satisfies the soul more than anything else possible on this earth," as he wrote (p. 473) in his wonderful four-thousand page *Zibaldone* (*Miscellany* or *Notebook*) in which he insisted later

(p. 971) that "The smallest confused idea is always greater than a grand, completely clear one." Leopardi was completely clear as to why he loved the vague, but we may wonder how much he was influenced too by the fact that the Italian word for "vague" (*vago*) means also "beautiful," "desirous," or "desirable."

Hence Leopardi's fondness for memories of childhood, a time in which our impressions and ideas are vague, hazy, undefined—of the nature, in short, of the infinite. So profound are these impressions that the keenest feelings of later life may be nothing but the stirrings of these depths. Since what is present and limited cannot in itself be poetic but can become so in our memory, remembrance for Leopardi is essential to all poetic feeling. His preference for the vague and indefinite (those springboards to infinity) determines too what his favorite images will be: such things as distant mountains in the moonlight, songs fading away in the dark, lost splendors of antiquity. It affected too his vocabulary, one of the simplest a great poet ever had, distilled by his researches into a dozen languages and by the care with which he rejected (as his manuscripts show) a score of words to settle finally on the simplest. The words that he found "most poetic" were those which (unlike scientific terms, which terminate) come trailing accessory images in addition to the ones they signify. Of these Leopardi preferred words for things whose limits cannot be grasped: words for extent of space or time (like "faraway," "ancient," "future," "eternal") or words of multitude or abundance. He liked words relating to night, which effaces the outlines of things. He liked such expressions as "last" or "never again," rich in suggestions of infinity, or whatever evokes it by contrast, like "death," "mortal," "unreturning." He liked words for anything ended or doomed to end: "lost," "finished," "quenched." All contrasts between the finite and the infinite (a hedge against vast space, etc.) he found "sublime and moving."

These preferences in imagery and diction are evident in "*La sera del dì di festa*" ("The Evening of the Fiesta"), written probably in 1820. The word *dì* for "day," instead of the ordinary *giorno*, is somewhat poetic; Leopardi compares such a word to fruits preserved in all their freshness to delight us out of season. (1) *Tender and clear is the night and without wind,* (2) *And silent over the roofs and among the gardens* (3) *Pauses the moon, and faraway reveals* (4) *Serene every mountain.* With Leopardi, so much of whose poetry lies in the way that sound and rhythm vitalize the meaning, it is particularly important to remember that our English words are in no way a poetic equivalent of the original. Here, for example, the effect is in the perfect clarity of the long vowels that carry the melody: with no bunching of consonants to interfere with their continuity. The three opening accents (*dólce-chiára-nótte*) are rich and rounded (like the English sounds *awe-ah-awe*); these are hushed into the repeated *en*'s of *senza vento*. The lines move smoothly as final vowels are muted before vowels that follow: *dolce e* and *notte e* are pronounced about as if there were one *e* sound at the end, not two. In line 2 the soft *e*'s of *senza vento* prevail up to the final *agli orti* (pronounced *ahl' yáwrtee*), in which the *ah-awe* pick up the opening notes of the poem. The common Italian word for "quiet" is *quieta* (*kwee-áy-tah*); Leopardi prefers *queta* (*kwáy-tah*)—the rarer and quieter form without the diphthongal ripple. Line 3 goes back to the sounds of line 1, but introduces also *u* and the purer *e* of *rivela*. How wide the moonlight spreads as the sounds of *luna* are diffused and echoed in *lontan!* *Serena* serenely prolongs the *e* of the preceding *rivela* instead of inaugurating a new vowel sequence. Appropriately, the first rugged sounds of

Già tace ogni sentiero, e pei balconi
Rara traluce la notturna lampa:
Tu dormi, che t'accolse agevol sonno
Nelle tue chete stanze; e non ti morde   8
Cura nessuna; e già non sai nè pensi
Quanta piaga m'apristi in mezzo al petto.
Tu dormi: io questo ciel, che sì benigno
Appare in vista, a salutar m'affaccio,   12
E l'antica natura onnipossente,
Che mi fece all'affanno. A te la speme
Nego, mi disse, anche la speme; e d'altro
Non brillin gli occhi tuoi se non di pianto.   16
Questo dì fu solenne: or da' trastulli
Prendi riposo; e forse ti rimembra
In sogno a quanti oggi piacesti, e quanti
Piacquero a te: non io, non già, ch'io speri,   20
Al pensier ti ricorro. Intanto io chieggo
Quanto a viver mi resti, e qui per terra
Mi getto, e grido, e fremo. Oh giorni orrendi
In così verde etate! Ahi, per la via   24
Odo non lunge il solitario canto
Dell'artigian, che riede a tarda notte,
Dopo i sollazzi, al suo povero ostello;
E fieramente mi si stringe il core,   28
A pensar come tutto al mondo passa,
E quasi orma non lascia. Ecco è fuggito

the passage are in the consonants of *ogni montagna* (*áwn-yee mawn-táhn-yah*), which reverberate more hollowly the opening vowels. Syntax too is expressive in the simple spellbound sentence, strung together with its five *e*'s ("and" s), with all adjectives preceding their nouns, as if the qualities of things (the softness of the night, the calmness of the moon, the serenity of the mountains) were felt before the things themselves, which are almost disembodied in the atmosphere. Sound and image are one: we see, we hear, we feel the kind of night it is in the soft windless air, the clarity of the vast moonlit vistas, the silence which so prevails that it seems centered in the moon itself. So much in lines so simple.

Probably no great poet has been devoted to nature in itself. Leopardi's interest is limited to seeing in it some image for his own moods and preoccupations. So now the profound quiet is thrilled by a human cry, the passion of which we cannot at once account for. (4) *O my lady*—one is tempted to hear the Shakespearean *O mistress mine*, since the words would render one of Leopardi's most characteristic practices: the use of words and phrases from earlier poets as an integral part of his vocabulary. (5) *Now every path is hushed; through balcony-windows* (6) *Rare* (scattered, far apart) shine the nocturnal lamp[s]. Fiestas, brief moments of revelry in the humdrum life of the village, greatly affected Leopardi, who found in their flare of gaiety and the darkness that followed a parable of man's career. The feast itself he never describes; always the darkness before, the darkness after.

The love for which Leopardi longed in vain is in his thoughts as he contemplates a scene both charming and forlorn. (7) You are asleep, for easy slumber took you (8) In your quiet rooms; and (9) No care consumes you ["ti morde," 8] and you little know nor imagine (10) How great a wound you opened in the middle of my breast [in my very heart]. In mezzo a ("in the middle of") is the same expression that in line 2 was used of the moon above the gardens: the wound is as central a fact in the poet's life as the moon itself in its moon-bathed world. All details emphasize the contrast between the healthy girl and her melancholy poet. Line 10 uses sound for a quite different effect from that of the first lines: the heavy quanta piaga is thrust deeper by the forceful p's that follow. (11) You are asleep; I (12) show myself to greet (11) this heaven, that so benignant (12) Seems to the view (13) And ancient nature the omnipotent, (14) Which made me for affliction. (15) "I deny (14) you hope," (15) she told me, "even hope; and with [anything] else (16) but tears may not your eyes be bright." But if the girl is luckier in her euphoria, the poet has his lonely grandeur: his mission is to face not flattering semblances but the terrible truth of things in a world in which he does not have even the solace of false hope. Such reflections bring Leopardi close to what was always a danger for his poetry: a tendency to philosophize which sometimes interrupts the lyric impetus for the sake of gloomy ruminations about fate. Entries in the Zibaldone show that he was aware

of the danger (at least for others): "A poetry that reasons?—as well to speak of a reasoning beast [p. 18]!" This present poem, one of his best, has only a few such obtrusions; in the lines translated above one feels just an edge of harangue. (17) This day was gala: now from [its] diversions (18) You take [your] rest, and perhaps you remember (19) In dream how many you pleased today, and how many (20) Pleased you—and then, wistfully but with immediate candor from a heart that has no illusions—not I, not that I hope to, (21) Come to your mind again. Meanwhile I ask (22) How long I have yet to live, and here on the ground (23) Fling myself, and exclaim, and shiver. This is not rhetoric; the poet's papers show that he was forced to such extremes in fits of grief. Oh dreadful days (24) In so green a season [youth: which should be "green"—both bright and hopeful]!

With the song of the wayfarer we are again under the spell of the night. Leopardi was sensitive to the poignancy of the singing voice, and especially to its dying fall in the wastes of darkness: like the holiday itself it became an image of man's life. In the Zibaldone (50-51) he describes: "My sorrow on hearing late on the night of some holiday the singing of farmers on the roads. The infinity of the past which I thought of, musing on the Romans fallen so low after such clamor and so many great events, which I sadly compared with that profound quiet and silence of the night, brought home to me by the contrast of that peasant song." (24) Ah, on the road (25) I hear not far away [near now, but fading soon] the lonely song (26) Of the journeyman returning late at night, (27) After his pleasures, to his poor abode— and this at once sets up vibrations wide as the night itself: (28) And fiercely my heart contracts, (29) To think how all things in the world pass by, (30) And leave hardly

Il dì festivo, ed al festivo il giorno
Volgar succede, e se ne porta il tempo   32
Ogni umano accidente. Or dov'è il suono
Di que' popoli antichi? or dov'è il grido
De' nostri avi famosi, e il grande impero
Di quella Roma, e l'armi, e il fragorio   36
Che n'andò per la terra e l'oceano?
Tutto è pace e silenzio, e tutto posa
Il mondo, e più di lor non si ragiona.
Nella mia prima età, quando s'aspetta   40
Bramosamente il dì festivo, or poscia
Ch'egli era spento, io doloroso, in veglia,
Premea le piume; ed alla tarda notte
Un canto che s'udia per li sentieri   44
Lontanando morire a poco a poco,
Già similmente mi stringeva il core.

(*Canti.* 1835)

---

a trace. See, it has fled, (31–32) *The festive day and [on its heels] the common* ["Volgar," 32] *workday succeeds and time carries away* (33) *Every human affair.* To Leopardi, the philosophical meaning of *accidente* ("accident") would suggest that nothing human has real existence of its own. (33) *Now where is the sound* (34) *Of those nations of long ago? Now where is the cry* ["grido," *cry* and also *fame* here] (35) *Of our famous ancestors, and the mighty empire* (36) *Of that Rome, and the [clash of victorious] arms, and the uproar* (37) *That traveled over land and sea?* Where is it now, the worldwide roar of Rome? Our answer is in the opening image of the poem: silence and the night. All that tumult annulled by a great stillness—annulled as utterly as the brief fiesta of a little town. (38) *All is peace and silence, and it all comes to a close,* (39) *[That] world, and no talk of them any longer.* Since for Leopardi the deepest experiences were those remembered from childhood, he now confirms his present mood by memories of another night after another holiday,

in which, as a child gay and straight of limb, he participated more vividly, and of another song sent dying on the night. After the splendor and hubbub of the Roman imagery, this passage begins quietly; such changes of tone, like those between movements of a quartet, are among the wonders of Leopardi's poetry. (40) *In my earliest days, [at an age] when one awaits* (41) *Longingly for [some] holiday, [and] then when* (42) *It was over* ["spento," *extinguished,* is used of things once bright or warm], *I sad of heart, wide awake,* (43) *Lay on my bed* [literally *pressed the down*]; *and in the deep of night* (44) *A song that was heard along the paths* (45) *Going farther away, to die little by little,* (46) *Once in just such a way clutched at my heart.* The waves of dwindling sound are echoed in the syllables of *lontanando* (*lon-ta-nán-do*), and then in the duller farther sounds of *a poco a poco.* At least twice, feeling for the perfect equivalent, Leopardi in his *Zibaldone* had tried various combinations of these words. [J.F.N.]

GIACOMO LEOPARDI

A SE STESSO

Or poserai per sempre,
Stanco mio cor. Perì l'inganno estremo,
Ch'eterno io mi credei. Perì. Ben sento,
In noi di cari inganni,   4
Non che la speme, il desiderio è spento.
Posa per sempre. Assai
Palpitasti. Non val cosa nessuna
I moti tuoi, nè di sospiri è degna   8
La terra. Amaro e noia
La vita, altro mai nulla; e fango è il mondo.
T'acqueta omai. Dispera
L'ultima volta. Al gener nostro il fato   12
Non donò che il morire. Omai disprezza
Te, la natura, il brutto
Poter che, ascoso, a comun danno impera,
E l'infinita vanità del tutto.   16

(*Canti.* 1835)

"Certainly love and death are the only
beautiful things in the world,"
wrote Leopardi to a pretty lady with whom
he was lucklessly in love, "and by all
means the only ones worth desiring."
When a few months later this love, "the
last deceit," had faded, he felt that only
death was left, and in "*A se stesso*" ("To
Himself") he turned his back forever on
the vanity of vanities. What is most
remarkable here is the way the poet's ex-
haustion finds a voice in every cadence of
the poem—so stark and stripped of
imagery. Leopardi's characteristic melody
is that of the flowing period; but here the
rhythms are jagged, the sentences short:
three words, two words, one word. There
are many pauses (as if the despondent poet
had stopped for breath) in the very middle
of the lines, many words (*Assai* / *palpitasti.*)
drooping listlessly over the brink of the
line. (1) *Now you will rest forever,* (2) *My
weary heart. The last deceit has perished,*
(3) *Which I believed eternal. Perished. Indeed
I feel* (4) *That in us [my heart and me]*
(5) *Not just the hope but the [very] desire of
dear illusions* ["cari inganni," 4] *has gone
dead.* (6) *Rest forever. Enough* (7) *You strove*
[literally *palpitated*]. *Nothing compensates*
(8) *Your throbbings, nor is the earth* ["terra,"
9] *worth sighs.* (9) *Bitterness and ennui*
(10) *Is life, never anything else; and mud the
world.* (11) *Be quiet now. Despair* (12) *For
the last time. To our sort [humankind], fate*
(13) *Gave but [one gift], to die. Now hold in
scorn* (14) *Yourself, [and] nature, the foul*
(15) *Power that, in hiding, rules to the common
bane (hurt)* (16) *And the infinite vanity of
everything.*   [J.F.N.]

GIACOMO LEOPARDI

L'INFINITO

Sempre caro mi fu quest'ermo colle,
E questa siepe, che da tanta parte
Dell'ultimo orizzonte il guardo esclude.
Ma sedendo e mirando, interminati   4
Spazi di là da quella, e sovrumani
Silenzi, e profondissima quiete
Io nel pensier mi fingo; ove per poco
Il cor non si spaura. E come il vento   8
Odo stormir tra queste piante, io quello
Infinito silenzio a questa voce
Vo comparando: e mi sovvien l'eterno,
E le morte stagioni, e la presente   12
E viva, e il suon di lei. Così tra questa
Immensità s'annega il pensier mio:
E il naufragar m'è dolce in questo mare.

(*Versi.* 1826)

"The Infinite" was written in September, 1819. About two years later Leopardi refers to it in his *Zibaldone* (1430-31) as follows: "In regard to the sensations which are pleasing by virtue of the indefinite alone, see my idyll on *L'Infinito*, and picture to yourself a country terrain dipping so sharply that at a certain distance the eye cannot reach the valley; and a row of trees, whose ending is lost to sight, either because of the length of the row, or because it is running down hill, etc. A factory, a tower, etc., seen so that it seems to stand alone above the horizon, which is out of sight, produces a most effective and sublime contrast between the finite and the indefinite, etc."

Most commentators on *"L'Infinito"* saddle its readers with information about the topographical identity of the "lonely hill" (*ermo colle*, 1) of the poem. Although we hardly need to be told the name of that modest landmark (it is Monte Tabor), we should know something about its location, which is in the immediate surroundings of the poet's home town. Recanati, like other places in the Marche, lies on a slope between the Adriatic Sea below and the peaks of the Apennines in the distance. Thus the hill should command an unobstructed view of the sea alone. But, at least in the spot where the poet liked to sit and muse—rather than to stand and gaze—the hill is not a lookout, since a hedgerow prevents the beholder from enjoying the full vista enclosed within "the farthest horizon" (*ultimo orizzonte*, 3) and the skyline. All this is suggested in the preliminary lines, which convey the stance of both poet and poem. (1) *Always dear to me was this lonely hill,* (2) *And this hedge, which from so great a part* (3) *Of the farthest horizon excludes the view.* The poem unfolds by calling forth the unobstructed vision that the obstructed panorama helped the poet to fashion within his mind. (4) *But sitting [here] and gazing, boundless* (5) *Spaces beyond that [hedge], and more than human* (6) *Silences, and profoundest quiet* (7) *I in my mind imagine (create); wherefore* (8) *The heart is almost* ["per poco," 7] *filled with fear.*

Beyond the hidden panorama, beyond that vast yet limited expanse of land and water—which, were it not for the screening fence, he could fully encompass with his physical eyes—the poet contemplates with the eyes of the spirit a limitless expanse, one that stretches far beyond the boundaries of earth and sky. And it is because he is blocked from seeing a visible and finite space that the poet is able to see an invisible and infinite one—which he conceives in plural terms, as an endless succession of spaces beyond spaces. Then, almost without transition, he shifts from the intuition of infinity to that of eternity, from those boundless spaces (*interminati Spazi*, 4-5) into a timelessness without sound or voice, into what he calls, still in plural terms, "the superhuman silences" (*sovrumani Silenzi*, 5-6) of the universe. This shift hints at a further intuition: that the silence of eternity may be even more overwhelming for man than the void of infinity. Yet Leopardi called this poem an idyll—and idyllic it is in its self-possession and calm. There is nothing here of Pascal's "the silence of those infinite spaces terrifies me" (*le silence de ces espaces infinis m'effraie*). Leopardi is content with an understatement: with the moderate claim that the imagined silence of the universe *almost* fills his heart with fear (8).

It is this pagan and classical restraint that makes it possible for him to balance and compare that deafening and everlasting silence with the ephemeral whisper of the wind passing by; that enables him to see in his imagination at once eternity and time, the past and the present, all the seasons now dead and the single one that is now alive. (8) *And as* (9) *I hear the wind* ["vento," 8] *rustle among these shrubs, that* (10) *Infinite silence to this voice* (11) *I* ["io," 9] *go on comparing: and [memory of] the eternal (eternity) comes to mind,* (12) *And the dead seasons, and the present* (13) *And living one, and the sound of it.* Eternity and time merge anew in an infinity which the poet suggests—again in terms of space—through the image of a sea into which his thought and his whole being now willingly lose themselves in quest of peace. (13) *So within this* (14) *Immensity my thought is drowned:* (15) *And foundering is sweet to me in this sea.*

The artistic greatness of "*L'Infinito*" arises from its fusion of sublimity of vision and simplicity of statement. The sense of cosmic awe which is the mood of the poem is fostered by the interplay of enjambments (*interminati/Spazi; sovrumani/Silenzi*) and diaeresis (the separate and distinct pronunciation of adjacent vowels—*profondissima qui-e-te*). The first device quickens the rhythm, the second slows it up, combining in an effect of breathless agony and lingering anguish. Yet the most telling device of the poem is to be seen in its use of the humble pronoun *this*, which appears no less than six times in fifteen lines, normally marking the ordinary, finite objects of the poet's direct experience: the hill and the hedge, the trees and the wind, which are all part of the season and the landscape. It is with the other pronoun *that* that the poet marks instead the incommensurable, inaudible, and invisible reality which his mind has bodied forth. But in the last line the poet transfers the pronoun *this* from the first sphere to the second, and prefixes it to the infinity of *both* space and time in the image of "this sea" (in which it is sweet to be foundered). It is by such a slight grammatical change that for an instant Leopardi makes familiar and almost dear to the heart of man the alien metaphysical vision of a universe ruled by laws other than those of life and death.　　　　[R.P.]

A SILVIA

Silvia, rimembri ancora
Quel tempo della tua vita mortale,
Quando beltà splendea
Negli occhi tuoi ridenti e fuggitivi,   4
E tu, lieta e pensosa, il limitare
Di gioventù salivi?

Sonavan le quiete
Stanze, e le vie dintorno,   8
Al tuo perpetuo canto,
Allor che all'opre femminili intenta
Sedevi, assai contenta
Di quel vago avvenir che in mente avevi.   12
Era il maggio odoroso: e tu solevi
Così menare il giorno.

Io gli studi leggiadri
Talor lasciando e le sudate carte,   16
Ove il tempo mio primo
E di me si spendea la miglior parte,
D'in su i veroni del paterno ostello
Porgea gli orecchi al suon della tua voce,   20
Ed alla man veloce
Che percorrea la faticosa tela.
Mirava il ciel sereno,
Le vie dorate e gli orti,   24
E quinci il mar da lungi, e quindi il monte.
Lingua mortal non dice
Quel ch'io sentiva in seno.

Che pensieri soavi,   28
Che speranze, che cori, o Silvia mia!
Quale allor ci apparia
La vita umana e il fato!
Quando sovviemmi di cotanta speme,   32
Un affetto mi preme
Acerbo e sconsolato,
E tornami a doler di mia sventura.
O natura, o natura,   36
Perchè non rendi poi

Quel che prometti allor? perchè di tanto
Inganni i figli tuoi?

Tu pria che l'erbe inaridisse il verno,   40
Da chiuso morbo combattuta e vinta,
Perivi, o tenerella. E non vedevi
Il fior degli anni tuoi;
Non ti molceva il core   44

Written in Pisa in 1828, "To Silvia" first appeared in the Florentine edition of Leopardi's poems in 1831. The Silvia to whom it is addressed is identified with Teresa Fattorini, daughter of the coachman of the Leopardi family, who died in 1818 at the age of twenty-one, the poet being at that time twenty years old. It is not necessary to believe that the young Leopardi was in any sense in love with Silvia. He must of course have been moved by the thought of her death, and it is natural that he should dwell upon her fate and inevitably compare it with his own. Ten years after Silvia's death, Leopardi recalled the distant summer when in his lonely, studious, melancholy adolescence he first became aware of the peasant girl, gay and serious, whose singing had relieved the tension of his youth. It was to be her last summer. In a sense the poem fits the traditional (Wordsworthian) view of poetry as emotion recollected in tranquillity, and it would have pleased Poe, who thought the death of a young and beautiful woman the most appropriate subject for a poet. Like most of Leopardi's lyrics, "To Silvia" is essentially simple, with little intellectual subtlety, its effect lying in the choice of words and the mournful cadence of its music.

(1) *Silvia, do you still remember* (2) *That time of your mortal life* (3) *When beauty was resplendent* (4) *In your smiling, elusive eyes* (5-6) *And you, happy and pensive, were mounting the threshold of youth?*

(7-8) *The quiet rooms and lanes around reechoed* (9) *With your perpetual song,* (10) *When, intent upon a woman's tasks,* (11) *You would sit, supremely content* (12) *With that smiling future you were thinking of.* (13) *It was the fragrant Maytime; and you were accustomed* (14) *To spend the day like this.* (15-16) *From time to time then I, leaving my happy studies and my toil-worn notes,* (17-18) *Whereon were spent my early days and the best part of me,* (19) *From the balconies of my paternal home* (20) *Would turn my ears toward the sound of your voice* (21) *And toward your nimble hand* (21) *Swiftly traversing the toilsome thread[s].* (23) *I looked upon the serene sky,* (24) *The golden roads and the gardens,* (25) *And this way the distant sea, and that way the mountain.* (26) *Mortal tongue cannot* [literally *does not*] *say* (27) *What I felt in my breast.*

(28) *What gentle thoughts,* (29) *What hopes, what hearts [feelings], my Silvia!* (30) *How [happy] it seemed to us then,* (31) *Human life and fate!* (32) *When I remember so much hope,* (33) *A feeling oppresses me,* (34) *Bitter and disconsolate,* (35) *And grief for my ill lot comes back to me.* (36) *O nature, nature,* (37) *Why do you not redeem later* (38) *What you promise then? Why so greatly* (39) *Do you deceive your children?* (40) *You, before winter withered the shrubs* (41) *Assailed and conquered by a hidden ill,* (42) *Perished, O tender girl. And you were not to see* (43) *The flower of your years;* (44) *Nor did it soothe your heart,* (45) *Sweet praise now of your black hair,* (46) *Now of your glances, loving and shy;* (47) *Nor did your companions*

La dolce lode or delle negre chiome,
Or degli sguardi innamorati e schivi;
Nè teco le compagne ai dì festivi
Ragionavan d'amore.   48

Anche peria fra poco
La speranza mia dolce: agli anni miei
Anche negaro i fati
La giovanezza. Ahi come,   52
Come passata sei,
Cara compagna dell'età mia nova,
Mia lacrimata speme!
Questo è quel mondo? questi   56
I diletti, l'amor, l'opre, gli eventi
Onde cotanto ragionammo insieme?
Questa la sorte dell'umane genti?
All'apparir del vero   60
Tu, misera, cadesti: e con la mano
La fredda morte ed una tomba ignuda
Mostravi di lontano.

                    (*Canti.* 1831)

with you on festive days (48) Discourse of love.
   (49) So perished soon (50) My own sweet
hope: to my years (51) Also the fates denied
(52) Youth. Alas, how, (53) How fled you
are, (54) Dear companion of my early days,
(55) My lamented hope! (56) This is the
world? and these (57) The delights, the love,
the deeds, the events (58) Of which we spoke
so much together? (59) This is the lot of
mankind? (60) At the first sight of truth
(61) You, hapless one [my hope], fell; and
with your hand pointed to ["mostravi," 63]
(62) Cold death and a bare tomb (63) From afar.
   In the first stanza, in which the poet
addresses the dead Silvia as if she could
still hear him, the word *fuggitivi* not only
describes the glances of a girl too shy to
meet the eyes of another; it also suggests
how ephemeral her smiling adolescence
was to be. Silvia is *lieta e pensosa* ("happy
and pensive"): at her age happiness is
natural, but *pensosa* reveals that, to the
poet's eye, at least, she is uncertain of her

future and may indeed have had some
premonition of her early death.
   In the two stanzas that follow, Leopardi
builds up, with complete naturalness, a
comparison between Silvia and himself,
as they were in that "fragrant May" of a
decade past. As Silvia's day is occupied
with her womanly tasks and yet she finds
happiness in her work, so too the young
man, toiling over his books and his
studies (on which, he observes with a cer-
tain regret, his best years were spent) yet
finds his occupation "happy"; his reflec-
tive moments of rest between bouts with
his work blend with Silvia's song and the
exhilarant promise of nature around
them. The town of Recanati lies under
the mountains; from the balconies of
Leopardi's house the sea is visible in the
distance. So the labors of the young people
and their hopeful expectations merge in
the golden landscape (23-27), a symbol of
the anticipated future.

The next stanza is one of transition; the poet returns from memory of that springtime to the realization of a present sad and disheartening. Nature has failed again to redeem her promises—the use of the present tense in lines 37-39 indicates that the poet is bitterly aware that this is her constant practice. Nature always deceives her children. In lines 40-48 he illustrates this melancholy principle: Silvia was never to know the fulness of life that seemed almost within her grasp in that long-ago Maytime. She was to wither and die even before the flowers and shrubs of that summer had perished under the winter chill. *Tenerella* (42) is a most effective diminutive, stressing unobtrusively the innocence of the girl and her helplessness in the face of the "hidden ill" (*chiuso morbo*, 41). She was never to know even the first delights of youthful love, the simple compliments of a suitor, the girlish confidences of her companions.

The poet, to be sure, still lives, but in the last stanza he tacitly shifts his comparison: Silvia is now compared not to himself but to his youthful hope. This hope, this happy illusion, ten years ago as confident as Silvia, has withered away like the girl, at the first touch of reality (*del vero*, "the truth," 60), here equated with death. Nature has betrayed Silvia as life has betrayed Leopardi. Looking back on his hope, now personified, he can see that its only function was the bitterly ironic one of pointing the way to death and a tomb as yet unoccupied. The poem is typical of many of Leopardi's lyrics in that its theme is the futility of hope, the death of illusion, the betrayal of aspiration. It contains also an example of the poet's illogical pessimism, which runs through his *canti*: after all, if life has turned sour for the poet, isn't Silvia better off dead? She would have been cheated anyway. Should we not, as Housman does in "To an Athlete Dying Young," rather congratulate her on slipping off with illusion still intact? Leopardi is not primarily concerned with logic, nor indeed does the reader of this poem, if he be at all sensitive, care much about contradiction. Pity for the dead girl, compassion for the disillusioned poet, blend to create a mood of melancholy and sadness for the lot of mankind.

It is in the form of a *canzone*, or, as we should say, an ode, a favorite lyric pattern since the days of Dante and Petrarch. Like the traditional *canzoni*, it is made up of seven- and eleven-syllable lines; it differs from the traditional form in that the pattern is not the same in all stanzas. The rime scheme too is "free"; the poet seems to rime at will, although the last line of each stanza always has a rime. This is the first of Leopardi's *canti* to be written in the free style; the earlier ones follow the tradition of uniformity among the stanzas. The dramatic juxtaposition of short and long lines and the recurrent but unpredictable rimes make for a music meaningful and subtle.

Apart from what has been said about specific words in the commentary above, it should be noted that in the original there is the characteristic Leopardian mixture of straightforward, almost colloquial syntax with a choice of words of traditionally "poetic" connotation. Leopardi makes constant use of such poetic verb forms as *splendea* (for *splendeva*), *apparia* (for *appariva*), and *negaro* (for *negarono*). *Speme* (for *speranza*, "hope"), of line 32, is a Latinism never used in prose. Such a phrase as *paterno ostello* ("paternal lodging") could in the hands of another poet seem affected indeed. Leopardi's lyric vocabulary, rather limited and highly stylized, confers on the substance of his verse a kind of classical dignity, a dimension of the permanent.   [T.G.B.]

TRE MMASCHI E NNOVE FEMMINE

De fijji sce n'aveva una duzzina,
Ma pperantro l'ha ttutti assistemati.
Giujjo et Llesandro se sò ffatti frati,
Agusto sta in galerra a Tterrascina,   4

Creria morze l'antr'anno, Sarafina
Ha ppijjato un pittore de Frascati,
Verginia sta a sservì co ccert'abbati
Che la tiengheno come una reggina.   8

Filumena è ffattora a Ssant'Urbano,
Briscita annò ppe bbalia co un'ingresa,
E Amaglia scappò vvia co un ciarlatano:

Poi viè Fferminia c'aricama in oro;   12
E ll'antre dua, che ssò Ccrèofa e Tterresa,
Nun hann'arte, ma ccampeno da loro.

(*Sonetti romaneschi.* 1887)

To appreciate the scope and force of the work of G. G. Belli (1791-1863), one should read at least a few hundred of his sonnets, for one aspect of his greatness is surely his exuberant fecundity. "I have intended to leave a monument of what is today the people [*plebe* also means "masses"] of Rome," he wrote in the introduction to his *Sonetti romaneschi*. And he succeeded perhaps even beyond his hopes. So sharply drawn and so realistically set forth are his characters (countless in number) that the poet himself, as if terrified by what he had created, left instructions in his will that his vernacular poems be destroyed. Belli is in fact in a class with such life-breathing, large-scale creators as Balzac or Tolstoi; he too has created or re-created a world; in his case, more accurately, a city. He might well be regarded as a novelist save for the essentially lyric vigor that characterizes his tone and the mastery of his choice instrument, which is the sonnet. Belli wrote well over 2000 sonnets in *romano*, all dedicated to portrayal of life in Papal Rome of the mid-nineteenth century; the streets, squares, and landmarks of the city, and the customs, vices, and mentality of its people.

At once both passionate and cynical, naive and disillusioned, shocking and ingratiating, the *plebe romana* ("working class of Rome," we would say) lives an eternal life in Belli's pages, enlarged a little by the magic of art, and surcharged, as it were, by a penetrating humor that ranges from the casual to the ferocious; a humor that still characterizes the *romano*, but in the sonnets is sharpened by the poet's skill and underlined by his temperamental pessimism which, to be sure, is Roman too.

"My book," he tells us, "is one to take up and put down as one does with simple amusements. . . . Each page is the beginning of the book and each page is its end." Belli's "mask" is the Roman *popolano*, man of the street (and back street at that), whose language, strictly speaking, is not Italian but *romano* or *romanesco*, the speech of Rome. Works in dialect are normally excluded from histories of literature, manuals, and anthologies of Italian letters. But just as the genius of Burns compelled readers to overlook the fact that he wrote in a dialect—rather indeed to rejoice in it—so it is with Belli, who has brought his dialect into the mainstream of Italian literature.

The Roman speech, a language in its own right, differs from standard Italian (based on Tuscan) in various ways. It has its own phonetic features: almost consistent doubling of consonants, certain assimilations (*nn* for *nd*, for example), frequent substitution of *r* for the Tuscan *l*, simple vowels where standard Italian has diphthongs (*boni* for *buoni*), numerous apocopations (*so'* for *sono*). Morphologically, it contains some verb forms not found in the standard language and it has a number of purely local words. The effect of spoken Roman on the non-Roman Italian ear is faintly comic and at the same time seductive; perhaps a little like the impression the speech of our deep South makes on the Northern ear, though it should be noted that *romano* is urban and has no connotation of the rustic. Belli's language has its own peculiarities. For one thing it abounds in distortions of words, often with punning intent (*madrimonio, Culiseo*), making frequent use of Latin

phrases and words naturally current in a city dominated by the clergy. Furthermore, the poet's speech is constantly and uncompromisingly indecent; and this characteristic has inevitably limited his audience. Without attempting to justify obscenity, we must recognize that with Belli it becomes a genuine instrument of his art.

"Three Boys and Nine Girls" may serve to illustrate the poet's skill in tucking *multa* (and what a heterogeneous *multa!*) in *parvo*. (1) *Kids—she had a dozen of 'em,* (2) *but somehow she's got 'em all settled.* [*Sistemati* (in the dialect *assistemati*) has a subtly comic value here, meaning *to set up, arrange, put in order, settle*, with implications of tidiness and planning.] (3) *Jule and Alex have gone for monks,* (4) *Gus is in the pen at Terracina,* (5) *Clelia died last year* [*sistemata* indeed!*], Sary* (6) *has picked up a painter from Frascati,* (7) *Virginia is in service with some abbots* (8) *who treat her like a queen.* (9) *Filumena is housekeeper at San Urbano,* (10) *Bridey went off as wet nurse to an Englishwoman,* (11) *and Amaglia ran off with a shill.* (12) *Then comes Ferminia, she does gold embroidery:* (13) *and there's two others: Cleofe and Terry.* (14) *They don't have no trade. But they support themselves.*

In fourteen lines we have met an equal number of characters, for the subject of the main verb—I take it as feminine—has certainly done a remarkable job of settling her brood, and the narrator, surely a female friend, has drawn an effective self-portrait in her casual recital of the destinies of the children. Admirable again is the use of comic—or is it pathetic?—juxtaposition: two brothers monks, one in jail; with underlying casual irreverence, for it is all the same to the narrator. And as for Cleofe and Terry; we can guess how they support themselves. [T.G.B.]

ALLA STAZIONE IN UNA MATTINA D'AUTUNNO

Oh quei fanali come s'inseguono
accidiosi là dietro gli alberi,
tra i rami stillanti di pioggia
sbadigliando la luce su 'l fango!　　　　4

Flebile, acuta, stridula fischia
la vaporiera da presso. Plumbeo
il cielo e il mattino d'autunno
come un grande fantasma n'è intorno.　　8

Dove e a che move questa, che affrettasi
a' carri foschi, ravvolta e tacita
gente? a che ignoti dolori
o tormenti di speme lontana?　　　　12

Tu pur pensosa, Lidia, la tessera
al secco taglio dài de la guardia,
e al tempo incalzante i begli anni
dài, gl'istanti gioiti e i ricordi.　　　16

Van lungo il nero convoglio e vengono
incappucciati di nero i vigili,
com' ombre; una fioca lanterna
hanno, e mazze di ferro: ed i ferrei　　20

freni tentati rendono un lugubre
rintocco lungo: di fondo a l'anima
un' eco di tedio risponde
doloroso, che spasimo pare.　　　　24

E gli sportelli sbattuti al chiudere
paion oltraggi: scherno par l'ultimo
appello che rapido suona:
grossa scroscia su' vetri la pioggia.　　28

Although Giosuè Carducci (born in 1835) had won the Nobel Prize and had achieved international recognition as the leading poet of the new Italy, his prestige has waned considerably since his death in 1907. To be sure, much of his work served as the vehicle for short-lived polemics and the touting of his favorite themes: the lost glory of Rome, the virtues and joys of classical paganism, the legends of the medieval city-states, the legacy of Dante—themes all suggested by his fiery-hearted republican patriotism and his impassioned partisanship in Italy's epic struggle for independence. Certain of his odes, however, soar beyond the world of provincial officialdom and plaster myth. Probably his authentic voice as a poet is heard in a few simple lyrics and in the impressionistic "At the Station on a Morning in Autumn." This poem, which has been compared to Monet's painting *À la Gare St.-Lazare*, anticipates in its tone and technique the twentieth-century idiom of Montale (pp. 316-325). Contemporary in setting but timeless in theme, this sad farewell to a departing lady goes beyond mere incident to deal with love and with life itself, both lost forever in the urgency of time. The poem is made up of objects heard and observed; out of them the mood and meaning seem to arise quite naturally.

[In the *Odi barbare* (1877-89) from which it comes, Carducci went back to certain rhythms of classical Greece and Rome, but used them, as he knew, "barbarously"—disregarding *length* of syllable, on which they were grounded, in favor of *accent*. This poem is written in the alcaic stanza, that of Horace's well-known "*Vides ut alta stet nive candidum. . . .*" The first half of the first line of each stanza has five syllables, with accents generally on the second and fourth (*Oh | quéi fă | nálĭ*), but not always so (*Flé | bĭle͡ ă | cútă*—here and elsewhere two vowels together, often slurred in speech, generally count as one). The second half of the line has six syllables, in principle two dactyls but not always so in practice (*cómĕ s'ĭn | séguŏnŏ*). The second line is the same as the first. The third is something like a single syllable followed by four

trochees: (*tra͡ĭ | rámĭ | stĭllán | tĭ dĭ | piŏggiă*). The fourth corresponds to two dactyls followed by two trochees, but Carducci gives us such lines as *sbădĭglián | dŏ lă lú | cĕ sŭ'l | fángŏ*.

Though the attempts to graft quantitative (length) meters on an accentual language were no more lasting in Italian than in English, in this poem, where the system is probably best used, Carducci achieves some remarkable effects: note how the accent hammers down on the second syllable of *sbattuti* ("slammed," 25) when strict meter would have it on the first syllable; and how the accent is hurried in *rapido*, two lines further, with its stress on the first syllable where the meter would have stressed the second.

J.F.N.]

(1) *Oh those lamps, how they trudge* (2) *sluggish there behind the trees,* (3) *among the branches dripping with rain* (4) *yawning their light on the mud!* (5) *Plaintive, sharp, shrill, whistles* (6) *the engine near by. Leaden* (7) *the sky, and the autumn morning* (8) *like a huge ghost is surrounding us.* (9-11) *Where and to what end do these cloaked, silent people move, hurrying toward the gloomy cars? To what unknown griefs* (12) *or harrowing of distant hopes?* (13-14) *You too—sunk, in thought, Lydia, give your ticket to the dry punching of the conductor,* (15-16) *and to impatient time give the lovely years, the enjoyed moments and the memories.* (17-18) *Black-hooded along the black train come and go the watchful brakemen,* (19) *like shades; a dim lantern* (20) *they have, and iron sledges: and the iron* (21-22) *brakes respond to the testing with a long-drawn knell: from the depth of the soul* (23) *an echo of ennui answers* (24) *lamenting, and seems like agony.* (25) *And the carriage doors slammed shut* (26) *seem like insults: like mockery seems the last* (27) *call that hastily rings:* (28) *thick crashes the rain on the window.* (29) *Already the monster,*

Già il mostro, conscio di sua metallica
anima, sbuffa, crolla, ansa, i fiammei
occhi sbarra; immane pe 'l buio
gitta il fischio che sfida lo spazio.   32

Va l'empio mostro; con traino orribile
sbattendo l'ale gli amor miei portasi.
Ahi, la bianca faccia e 'l bel velo
salutando scompar ne la tènebra.   36

O viso dolce di pallor roseo,
o stellanti occhi di pace, o candida
tra' floridi ricci inchinata
pura fronte con atto soave!   40

Fremea la vita nel tepid' aere,
fremea l'estate quando mi arrisero;
e il giovine sole di giugno
si piacea di baciar luminoso   44

in tra i riflessi del crin castanei
la molle guancia: come un' aureola
più belli del sole i miei sogni
ricingean la persona gentile.   48

Sotto la pioggia, tra la caligine
torno ora, e ad esse vorrei confondermi;
barcollo com' ebro, e mi tocco,
non anch'io fossi dunque un fantasma.   52

Oh qual caduta di foglie, gelida,
continua, muta, greve, su l'anima!
io credo che solo, che eterno,
che per tutto nel mondo è novembre.   56

Meglio a chi 'l senso smarrí de l'essere,
meglio quest' ombra, questa caligine:
io voglio io voglio adagiarmi
in un tedio che duri infinito.   60

(*Odi barbare.* 1877)

---

aware of its metallic (30-31) *soul, blows,
shakes, pants, opens its fiery eyes; immense
through the gloom* (32) *it hurls its whistle
that challenges space.* (33) *The evil monster
goes; with a horrible dragging* (34) *flapping
its wings it carries off my love.* (35) *Alas, the
white face and lovely veil* (36) *saying good-bye
disappear in the darkness.* (37) *O sweet face
of rose-lit pallor,* (38) *O starry eyes of peace,
O white* (39-40) *pure forehead gently bending
among clustered curls!* (41) *Life throbbed in
the warm air,* (42) *summer throbbed when*

they smiled at me; (43) *and the young sun of June,* (44) *brilliant, delighted in kissing* (45) *amid reflections of light-brown hair,* (46) *the soft cheek: like a halo* (47) *more splendid than the sun, my dreams* (48) *encompassed the slim figure.* (49) *In the rain, into the fog* (50) *I now return, and I wish I could merge with them;* (51) *I reel like a drunken man, and I touch myself* (52) *[to make sure] that I too am not, then, just another phantom.* (53) *Oh what a fall of leaves, cold,* (54) *continuous, silent, heavy, on the soul!* (55) *I think that alone, that forever,* (56) *that all over the world is November.* (57) *Better, for him who lost the sense of being,* (58) *better this shadow, this mist:* (59) *I want to I want to lie down* (60) *in a tedium lasting forever.*

Pause and stress, with alliteration or internal rime, are the more expressive in a poem without rime—particularly in lines 13-32, which evoke in counterpoint the noises of the departing train, the punching of tickets, the testing of brakes, the slamming of doors, etc., as a sequence of psychological reverberations, building cumulatively to a sense of inexorable loss. The ear cannot ignore such sound-effects as *tessera . . . taglio . . . tempo* (13-15) *lugubre . . . lungo* (21-22), *spasimo . . . sportelli . . . sbattuti* (24-25), *grossa . . . scroscia . . . pioggia* (28). The sharp plosive sounds, reinforced by strong pauses and run-on lines (20; 29-32), set up an accelerating rhythm not only mechanical but human in its physiological or psychological overtones of panting, sobbing, and pounding of the heart—the more so as most of the sequences culminate in some word referring to the psyche: *tedio* ("ennui"), *lugubre* ("mournful"), *oltraggi* ("insults"), *sfida* ("defies," "challenges"). Then, after the gentle interval of happiness remembered

(37-48), a foil to the dismal scene, the pace of the verse slows to funereal monotony in the last two stanzas, where the falling leaves are evoked by insistence of internal pause and syntactic repetition.

November is the month of the dead, and a ritual burial is enacted; when the heart-rending separation is completed, leaves drift deeper on the poet's soul. Spiritual deprivation, emptiness, loss of the sense of reality itself—these are the epilogue. One realizes now that the train was a hearse ("gloomy cars" . . . "black train") with its attendant crowd of mourners, its pallbearers ("the black-hooded brakemen"), its funeral torches (the "lamps" and the "dim lantern"), and its tolling bell. The juxtaposition of *guardia* ("conductor") and *tempo* ("time") makes the ticket-taker a figure of Fate; the rain is a cosmic weeping; the locomotive becomes a smoky-winged demon of hell.

Both in its mechanical and demoniacal aspects, the train's "soul" contrasts with the poet's own *anima*, which grieves (22), finally dies, and is buried (54)—the one word, according to the context, developing its own ironies. Poetic unity is strengthened by the correlation between the steam, the autumnal fog, the ghostly feeling which possesses the travelers, and finally the poet's own consciousness. With its last stanza ("in a tedium lasting forever"), the poem returns to the note struck at the beginning by the yawning lamps, and the lugubrious circle is closed. A piece of personal, not official history, this is a poem not likely to be lost on ears attuned to Baudelaire and Eliot, whose work, in its *spleen* and metropolitan imagery, it strikingly resembles. [G.C.]

ULTIMO SOGNO

Da un immoto fragor di carriaggi
ferrei, moventi verso l'infinito
tra schiocchi acuti e fremiti selvaggi...
un silenzio improvviso. Ero guarito.   4

Era spirato il nembo del mio male
in un alito. Un muovere di ciglia;
e vidi la mia madre al capezzale:
io la guardava senza meraviglia.   8

Libero!... inerte sì, forse, quand' io
le mani al petto sciogliere volessi:
ma non volevo. Udivasi un fruscìo
sottile, assiduo, quasi di cipressi;   12

quasi d'un fiume che cercasse il mare
inesistente, in un immenso piano:
io ne seguiva il vano sussurrare,
sempre lo stesso, sempre più lontano.   16

(*Myricae.* 1892)

Giovanni Pascoli (1855-1912), like d'Annunzio, had begun his career as a close follower of the fiery classicist Carducci, but his gentler nature led him to a Virgilian pastoral reminiscent of Wordsworth or Frost. He was at his best in poems inspired by Italian country life and by his personal sorrows. He can draw vivid sketches, experimenting with sound, color, and tone in a way that anticipates the Crepuscolari (see below, p. 293) and Montale, but his elegies incline to the sentimental and he indulges in excessive onomatopoeia. These flaws are absent from "*Ultimo sogno,*" a poem worthy of Leopardi in gravity and strength. It is a "last dream," or rather an "ultimate dream," a dream of last things: of death.

Not nightmare but liberation. The poet has experienced a recovery from the "illness" and "evil" (*mio male*) of life, a recovery that came as an awakening in the midst of sleep.

(1) *From a motionless roar of wagons* (2) *of iron, moving on towards infinity,* (3) *among sharp crashes and wild vibrations . . .* (4) *a sudden silence. I had recovered (was healed).* (5) *The stormcloud of my illness (evil) had spent itself* (6) *in a soft breath. A movement of my eyelids;* (7) *and I saw my mother at my bedside:* (8) *I was looking at her without amazement.* (9) *Free! . . . powerless, perhaps, had I* (10) *wished to unfold my hands on my breast:* (11) *but I did not wish to. A rustling was heard* (12) *thin, insistent, as though of cypresses;* (13) *as though of a river seeking*

the sea (14) *that does not exist, on an enormous plain:* (15) *I followed its vain whispering,* (16) *always the same, always more remote.*

Seeing his dead mother is a confirmation of such a crucial transition, beyond sorrow and wonder itself; the climactic vision emerges from an initial roar of vehicles to be resolved in a ceaseless murmur of trees and water, so that the awe is transfigured into a softer mystery, and the impression of what is heard prevails over that of what is seen. But the visual experience has its turn, for along with the exclamation in which it culminates (9) it constitutes the focus of the poem, the defining element at the center of the indefinite sounds. Such function is neatly clinched by the tense-shift from the dominant mood of unlimited duration in the past (*Ero guarito . . . Era spirato,* 4-5) to that single verb which expresses time-limited action (*e vidi,* 7) and then back to indefinite past continuity (*io la guardava,* 8). This is a passage to a new state, for the verbs before the turning point imply a past within the past, while those following the definite "I saw" suggest contemporaneity in the past. The movement from indefiniteness to definition to a soothing indefiniteness is enhanced by the lack of verbs in the initial clause, for after it the explanatory "I had recovered (and was healed)" (4) begins to give shape to form and perception, and a climax is reached in the verb of focused consciousness *e vidi* ("and I saw," 7), to be transcended in the verbless utterance *Libero!* ("Free!" 9) as a further awareness, almost an ecstasy. One might also notice that the opening word is *da* ("from"), a preposition denoting separation, derivation, or emergence, and that the whole poem comes to rest in the final word *lontano* ("far away"). It is as if the dreamer, awakening to death, had arrived at an infinite peace, but kept moving on with that river which still seeks an unreachable sea—recalling Leopardi's image of shipwreck at the close of "*L'Infinito*" (p. 276).

The rolling wagons (1) vaguely evoke a column of emigrants, a hearse, a military convoy: some ineluctable situation. The balancing contrast between *immoto* ("steady" and "motionless") and *moventi* ("moving")—perhaps more forceful in the Italian—contributes to the ambiguous atmosphere of dream. In itself the unexpected explanation "I had recovered" explains very little, for we know nothing of any previous illness of the dreamer. But he assumes it as a matter of course and thereby intimates that the illness was life itself. In line 5 we find another pregnant expression: *era spirato,* which refers literally to the exhalation of one's last breath. But since this refers to the "stormcloud" of illness and not to the dreamer's own self, death is both suggested and denied: it has destroyed only the anguish of existence. *Spirato, nembo,* and *alito* here are related by the theme of moving air: breath and winds of varying intensities, from softness to violence to a final softness. In line 8, the negative expression "without amazement" deepens the very idea of the wonder it denies. The unquestioning lucidity of dream, or dream-waking, makes for uncanny acceptance. Thus we are introduced to the passive awareness of line 9, with the violent contrast of freedom and paralysis in the juxtaposition of "Free!" and "powerless, perhaps." Here the only exclamation of the poem is a weird gesture of unqualified assertion that gives relief to, but does not break, the dominant tone. This is not the freedom of action, but of a transcendental perception beyond anxiety; and the sibilant sounds of the third and fourth quatrains (*volessi . . . fruscìo . . . assiduo . . . cipressi . . . cercasse . . . sussurrare . . . stesso*) bear this out, superseding as they do the clangorous tumult of the opening. [G.C.]

ASSISI

Assisi, nella tua pace profonda
l'anima sempre intesa alle sue mire
non s'allentò; ma sol si finse l'ire
del Tescio quando il greto aspro s'inonda.   4

Torcesi la riviera sitibonda
che è bianca del furor del suo sitire.
Come fiamme anelanti di salire
sorgon gli ulivi dalla tòrta sponda.   8

A lungo biancheggiar vidi, nel fresco
fiato della preghiera vesperale,
le tortuosità desiderose.

Anche vidi la carne di Francesco,   12
affocata dal dèmone carnale,
sanguinar su le spine delle rose.

(Elettra. 1903)

An exuberant writer, Gabriele d'Annunzio (1863-1938) deserves to be known for some of his remarkable lyrical verse rather than for the sumptuous rhetoric of his plays or the overblown sensuality of his novels. His flamboyant personality dominated the nineties and the early decades of this century in Italy, carrying literary paganism far beyond the limits touched by his admired model, Carducci. In view of this, it is exciting to see what he does with St. Francis of Assisi in this smooth sonnet from the *Città del silenzio* series, made up of several poems on the silent charm of Italian towns that have outlived their medieval and Renaissance glories. Although d'Annunzio had much more of Nietzsche than of the seraphic saint in his make-up, he referred to the latter at several points in his work. His major collections of verse, published around the turn of the century, take their general title *Laudi* (*Songs of Praise*) from the Franciscan *laudes*, and the third volume (*Alcyone*) contains pantheistic addresses to the olive-tree or to the ear of wheat, intentionally worded after the refrain of St. Francis' *Cantico delle creature.* He did something of the sort even with the austere Dante, so totally unlike him, when he inserted in his poems quotations from well-known episodes of the *Commedia.* The result varies—but at times is convincing.

"Assisi," which belongs to the second volume of *Laudi*, is particularly successful because instead of trying to recapture the chaste folk-poetry of St. Francis, it evokes the suffering saint from the landscape itself. It does this in a highly personal way which we must call baroque or expressionist. The unfailing association of Assisi in the general mind is with serenity, but the eager d'Annunzio breaks into this peace with the turmoil of his own sensual yearning, and at once everything is distorted into an erotic fury; we get an imagined flood, a madly thirsting river-bed, flamelike olive trees à la Van Gogh, spirals of desire, and Francis himself tortured by the carnal demon: a Bernini statue, a Jesuit counter-reformation painting, or perhaps a Munch. The poem, therefore, is not an act of surrender to Assisi and its great poet-saint, but a violent appropriation; and the clash is frankly stated at the outset by the forcefully egocentric poet. This frankness, averting pretense and insincerity, saves the day for d'Annunzio. By focusing on the ascetic ordeal of the renowned convert as sublimated sensuality, the modern Pan stays within the range of his competence and makes his *self*-portrait acceptable.

(1) *O Assisi, in your profound peace* (2) *the soul (my soul) ever intent on its own aims* (3) *did not relax; but imagined only the anger* (4) *of the Tescio River when its rugged bed overflows.* (5) *The thirsty track of the torrent twists* (6) *white with the fury of its own thirst.* (7) *Like upward-longing flames,* (8) *rise the olive trees from the twisted bank.* (9) *For a long while I saw, whitening in the fresh* (10) *breath of the evening prayer,* (11) *the tortuous windings of desire.* (12) *I also saw the flesh of Francis,* (13) *inflamed by the demon of all flesh,* (14) *bleeding on the thorns of the roses.*

With his soft southern ear for music, d'Annunzio exploited the name of Assisi for all it was worth, placing it in relative isolation at the very beginning. We get an impression of the hill-town rising before us amid hushing whispers, as if we were taking the famous approach from Perugia. Peace, deepened by the pause after *Assisi*, suffuses the restful solemnity of this first line—but the expectation thus aroused is immediately thwarted by the sharp change of tone. The lines that follow gather momentum, and their dizzy career shatters the initial promise and the tranquil vision. The insistence on the verb *torcere* ("to twist") and its derivatives *tòrta* and *tortuosità* conjures up a snakelike image of Eros, caught between the white aridity and the sky. Those olive trees yearning to ascend are not pious, but demoniacal. The refreshing exhalation of evening prayer (10) is convulsed by the speediest and most sinuous of serpentine lines, with *tortuosità desiderose* winding through ten of its eleven syllables—a superb rhythmical find, and one that bears the unique signature of d'Annunzio.

After that climax of fury and rapidity, the torrid final tercet on St. Francis himself is almost a relief, although it naturally springs from the accumulated tension of the preceding lines as an epitome of the landscape seen as quivering libido. But the real recapitulation of the demon's workings has been given in line 11, and now he is going to be subdued, even if painfully: the victory of sainthood is expressed in the final roses that tend to reestablish the earlier mood. Not quite, however. There is a gushing of blood (of which d'Annunzio professed to be fond, in life as well as in poetry) that symbolically repeats the imagined flood of the river. We see and feel the pain of a self-torturing Eros, rather than an achieved peace. Francis is still this side of Paradise. At the same time his offered blood can appease the thirst of the stony landscape, as a ritual of fertility. In his assimilation of the saint, d'Annunzio retained an unusual (for him) amount of taste; and it is to his credit that he addressed only the town in the second person, using the more distant third person for Francis himself. The repetition of *vidi* ("I saw") in the two tercets tilts the poem toward visionary tumult, already anticipated by *si finse* ("imagined," 3), before the fevered but less hallucinatory perceptions of the second quatrain.

[G.C.]

GUIDO GOZZANO

TOTÒ MERÙMENI

I

Col suo giardino incolto, le sale vaste, i bei
balconi secentisti guarniti di verzura,
la villa sembra tolta da certi versi miei,
sembra la villa-tipo, del Libro di Lettura...   4

Pensa migliori giorni la villa triste, pensa
gaie brigate sotto gli alberi centenari,
banchetti illustri nella sala da pranzo immensa
e danze nel salone spoglio da gli antiquari.   8

Ma dove in altri tempi giungeva Casa Ansaldo,
Casa Rattazzi, Casa d'Azeglio, Casa Oddone,

Although in the work of Carducci, Pascoli, and d'Annunzio there are poems in which we can see anticipations of the contemporary achievement, yet the vast bulk of the work of the three titans—Carducci's statuesque oratory, Pascoli's drab sentimentality, d'Annunzio's rapt cult of sensual orgy and the Nietzschean superman—was felt, around 1900, as an oppressive yoke from which poetry had to struggle free if it was to express with any vigor the spirit of the new age. The problem was largely one of language. There has generally been in Italy a gulf between the spoken and the written word; Italy, one young poet had complained, never writes as it speaks. The discrepancy was felt to be especially great in the twentieth century, when new ways of thinking and feeling, a new conscience, could not make themselves heard through the muffled trappings of the old rhetoric.

Poets tried in many ways to escape from Carducci's stucco pantheon, from d'Annunzio's gilded cage. Most pyrotechnic of the new movements was that of the Futurists, who issued their first manifesto in 1909. They acclaimed the machine and the man of the future; they proposed bombing the mausoleum of the muses, as well as libraries, museums, public buildings—the language itself. Abolish adjectives! Abolish punctuation! Abolish syntax! When all these manifolds were exploded, thought and feeling could flow freely through such "liberated" words as those of their leader, Marinetti, in his poem on the bombardment of Adrianople: *Sciumi Maritza o Karvavena ta ta ta ta ta giiitumb giii-tumb ZZZANG-TUMB (280 colpo di partenza) srrrrrrr GRANG GRANG...* Though this school produced no great writer, many men of talent enjoyed brief but exhilarating rides on its rowdy bandwagon. Such a poet as Palazzeschi learned to let the sound of words carry much of the meaning, as in his droll "The Sick Fountain," which begins: *Clof, clop, cloch, | cloffete, | cloppete, | clocchete, | chchch. . . .* The Futurist blast, which aimed at leveling everything in sight, was at least important in clearing the air. Without Marinetti and his Futurism, said Ezra Pound, the movement which he, Joyce, and Eliot initiated in London would have been impossible.

But even earlier and more significant for the real future of poetry were the Crepuscolari, or twilight school (just after the turn of the century), first so called because their verses seemed the last dim flicker of a great day of poetry—though later the name came to suggest the misty grey monotony of their manner. In reaction against the flushed heroics, sexual hysteria, and gaudy optimism of d'Annunzio, they deliberately swung to the other extreme: began to look at life wanly (but with irony) from garret windows, began to loll and droop in withered gardens, to dwell on sickness, and to yearn dolefully for *La belle dame sans merci*. (Corazzini and Gozzano both died young of tuberculosis.) Defiantly, they wrote about familiar matter of today in a colloquial language new to poetry: they flouted the cult of the superman by disclaiming all heroism, by protesting like Prufrock: "I am not Prince Hamlet, nor was meant to be." One of the best, Corazzini, went so far as to appeal, beatnik-fashion, "Why call me a poet? . . . I'm only a little tot in tears."

Guido Gozzano (1883-1916) shared some of these attitudes. But with a superior irony learned partly from Laforgue (who also influenced Eliot), and with a vision of his hollow men as characteristic of his time, he was able to mock both himself and the twilight life. In an age keyed to bardic rant and the operatic gesture, he dared, says the critic Antonielli, to lower his voice; aware that many of the fine words, *patria*, *umanità*, etc., had become nauseous on the lips of the orators, he turned to a direct and different language, enriching it, as Eliot and others were to do, by quotation and parody. Or by flippancy: he has the boy who reads Schopenhauer and Nietzsche meditate on *Arturo e Federico*, just as Eliot has Arnold and Emerson become "Matthew and Waldo, guardians of the faith."

His "*Totò Merùmeni*" (it is no accident that the name sounds like that of Terence's *Heautontimorùmenos*, the self-punisher) appears in his major work, *I colloqui (The Conversations)* of 1911. Patterned in nearly every detail on Gozzano's own life, though artfully exaggerated, this sketch of Totò is like certain characters of the early Eliot and even more the quiet failures of E. A. Robinson: Bewick Finzer, Levi "the inferior wraith," and Miniver Cheevy, "who coughed . . . and kept on drinking."

The quatrains, all but two riming *abab*, are in lines of fourteen syllables, generally broken by a pause after the seventh. The effect, more languid and compulsive than that of the classic line of eleven syllables with varying pause, is appropriate to this atmosphere of moral paralysis. The poem opens against a background of decayed elegance in Piemonte: contrasted with memories of a glamorous past is a present of gardens gone to seed and unkempt tourists with their chugging automobile. (1) *With its untended garden, the spacious rooms, the handsome* (2) *seventeenth-century balconies decorated with greenery,* (3) *the villa seems to be taken from certain of my verses,* (4) *it seems the typical villa, from the Libro di Lettura* [literally a *Book of Readings*, probably here an illustrated reader or anthology designed for use in schools]. There is a curious effect here, like a mirage: having written verses about such villas, the poet finds that the actual one seems almost an imitation of its true exemplar, the villa of the poem. Gozzano frequently judges nature by some work of art— picture, engraving, poem—as if for him these had the greater reality . (5) *The sad villa thinks of better days; it thinks of* (6) *gay companies under the century-old trees,* (7) *dazzling banquets in the immense dining-room* (8) *and dances in the salon [now] stripped by the antique dealers.* (9) *But where in other times the House of Ansaldo came,* (10) *The House of Rattazzi, the House of d'Azeglio, the House of Oddone* [how sonorous the names of the local aristocracy of other days, and with what a racket we are jolted into the

s'arresta un'automobile fremendo e sobbalzando;
villosi forestieri picchiano la gorgóne.   12

S'ode un latrato e un passo, si schiude cautamente
la porta... In quel silenzio di chiostro e di caserma
vive Totò Merùmeni con la sua madre inferma,
una prozia canuta ed uno zio demente.   16

II

Totò ha venticinque anni, tempra sdegnosa,
molta cultura e gusto in opere d'inchiostro,
scarso cervello, scarsa morale, spaventosa
chiaroveggenza: è il vero figlio del tempo nostro.   20

Non ricco, giunta l'ora di « vender parolette »
(il suo Petrarca!...) e farsi baratto o gazzettiere,
Totò scelse l'esilio. E in libertà riflette
ai suoi trascorsi che sarà bello tacere.   24

Non è cattivo. Manda soccorso di danaro
al povero, all'amico un cesto di primizie;
non è cattivo. A lui ricorre lo scolaro
pel tema, l'emigrante per le commendatizie.   28

Gelido, consapevole di sé e dei suoi torti,
non è cattivo. È il *buono* che desidera il Nietzsche
« ...in verità derido l'inetto che si dice
buono, perché non ha l'ugne abbastanza forti... »   32

Dopo lo studio grave, scende in giardino, gioca
coi suoi dolci compagni sull'erba che l'invita;
i suoi compagni sono: una ghiandaia rôca,
un micio, una bertuccia che ha nome Makakita...   36

III

La Vita si ritolse tutte le sue promesse.
Egli sognò per anni l'Amore che non venne,
sognò pel suo martirio attrici e principesse,
ed oggi ha per amante la cuoca diciottenne.   40

Quando la casa dorme, la giovanetta scalza,
fresca come una prugna al gelo mattutino,
giunge nella sua stanza, lo bacia in bocca, balza
su lui che la possiede, beato e resupino...   44

IV

Totò non può sentire. Un lento male indomo
inaridì le fonti prime del sentimento;

present!], (11) *an automobile halts, convulsed and jerking;* (12) *shaggy foreigners set about pounding the door-knocker.* But the old house, shut in itself, observes furtively: (13-14) *Some barking is heard, and a footstep, the door opens warily . . . In that silence of cloister and barracks [barracks:* in the absence of troops] (15) *Totò Merùmeni lives with his ailing mother,* (16) *a great-aunt grey with age, and a crazy uncle.* A depressing household, with even the strangers' automobile strangling as it passes. We are not far here from the world of the early Eliot: "The woman keeps the kitchen, makes tea, / Sneezes at evening, poking the peevish gutter."

II—(17) *Totò is twenty-five, has a scornful disposition,* (18) *has much knowledge and taste in products of the inkwell,* (19) *little common sense, little principle, terrifying* (20) *intuitions: is the true child of our time.* Something of a snob, with literary ability (slightingly referred to, as often in Gozzano), Totò has little practical sense or moral conviction—nothing but the harrowing insights of the neurotic. (21) *Not rich, when the time came to "peddle his little words"* (22) *(there's his Petrarch for you! . . .) and become an embezzler or news-sheet scribbler,* (23) *Totò chose exile. And at liberty reflects* (24) *on his follies it will be handsomer not to speak of.* For any situation in life the literary Totò (again like Prufrock) will have his pat quotation (though here, suspects the critic Mariani, he has imperfectly remembered his Petrarch). Like the last words of the stanza (which echo Dante), this is another example of his seeing life through art. His choice of professions— embezzler or journalist—is of course a dig at what Gozzano considers the moral indifference of the world of business. (25) *He's not bad. He sends help in money* (26) *to the poor man; to his friend a basket of choice fruit;* (27) *he's not bad. The schoolboy appeals to him* (28) *for a theme, the emigrant for a recommendation.* The poet protests too much with his repeated "He's not bad." Totò is easy-going and not averse to doing easy favors, especially of a

sort that flatters his vanity. Here and elsewhere he is like Robinson's Tasker Norcross: ". . . he was not bad; He was not . . . well, he was not anything." (29) *Cold,*—a word Gozzano frequently uses of himself and his counterpart in the poems—*conscious of his nature and its faults,* (30) *he's not bad.* There is no fire in Totò any more, if there ever was; no great good, no great evil. A moral mediocrity; a hollow man. This he knows and accepts; he seems to feel too that what goodness he has is due to the absence in him of the power and energy necessary for real evil. For Gozzano is presumably ironic in saying that Totò (30) *is the* good man *that Nietzsche desires,* and in working two lines of Nietzsche into his stanza: (31) ". . . *in truth I have scorn for the nincompoop who is called* (32) *good [only] because he does not have claws strong enough [not to be] . . .*" (33) *After his hard study, he goes down to the garden, plays* (34) *with his sweet companions on the inviting turf;* (35) *his companions are*—and again the ironic let-down, half in burlesque of those idyllic phrases of the line above—*a croaking jay,* (36) *a pussycat, a pet monkey named Makakita . . .*

III—(37) *Life took back all her promises.* This echo of Leopardi ("A Silvia," p. 278, lines 36-38, and elsewhere) might seem overdramatic; again it is saved by self-irony: (38) *He dreamed for years of Love that never came,* (39) *dreamed, for his torment, of actresses, kings' daughters,* (40) *and has today for his love—the cook, eighteen.* (41) *When the house is asleep, the young girl, barefoot,* (42) *fresh as a plum in the chill of early morning,* (43) *comes into his room, kisses him on the lips, flings herself* (44) *on him who possesses her; [he is] happy and supine.* Totò is the more passive of the two; the healthy peasant girl takes the initiative—she is the only breath of physical life in this lackadaisical world. (Her buxom energy is felt in the bouncing b's of line 43.)

IV—Like Gerontion or Tasker Norcross, *Totò* (45) *is incapable of feeling. Some slow unarrested illness* (46) *dried up the deepest*

l'analisi e il sofisma fecero di quest'uomo
ciò che le fiamme fanno d'un edificio al vento.　　　48

Ma come le ruine che già seppero il fuoco
esprimono i giaggioli dai bei vividi fiori,
quell'anima riarsa esprime a poco a poco
una fiorita d'esili versi consolatori...　　　52

V

Così Totò Merùmeni, dopo tristi vicende,
quasi è felice. Alterna l'indagine e la rima.
Chiuso in se stesso, medita, s'accresce, esplora, intende
la vita dello Spirito che non intese prima.　　　56

Perché la voce è poca, e l'arte prediletta
immensa, perché il Tempo (mentre ch'io parlo!) va.
Totò opra in disparte, sorride, e meglio aspetta.
E vive. Un giorno è nato. Un giorno morirà.　　　60

(*I colloqui.* 1911)

founts of feeling; (47) *analysis and sophistry* [cf. Eliot's "thoughts of a dry brain in a dry season"] *made of this man* (48) *what flames make of a house, with the wind blowing.* (49) *But as the ruins that once knew the fire* (50) *put forth the gladioli with beautiful bright flowers,* (51) *that parched soul puts forth, by dribs and drabs,* (52) *a scattering of wispy consolatory verses. . . .*

V—(53) *So Totò Merùmeni, after sad mischances,* (54) *is almost happy*—a man who "resigns himself with a smile to a mediocre life," as Gozzano said of such characters. *He alternates research, rime.* (Gozzano himself was an entomologist who planned and partly completed a long poem on butterflies.) (55) *Shut in himself, he meditates, expands* [physically too?], *explores, understands* (56) *the life of the Spirit he did not understand before.*

In poetry as slyly ironic as this, it is hard to know what the limits of derision are: is Totò, writing his verses, playing with pets, in bed with the cook, really learning something about the life of the Spirit? And is what we have in the last lines of the poem a commendable adjustment, or mere compliance in futility? Probably the feeling is ambivalent throughout this section. Certainly there is a tone of sadness that precludes sheer mockery: the irony is brooding and rueful. (57) *Because the [single] voice is little, and the treasured art [his poetry]* (58) *immense, because Time (even as I am speaking!) flies.* The *because* goes with no particular sentence, but with the feeling of the whole section; it is why Totò's life—man's life—is as it is. By bringing the "*I*" into the poem again, Gozzano identifies himself more closely with Totò—and at the same time sees his own life, his own poetry, as no more real than that of the world he creates. (59) *Totò works by himself, smiles, and hopes for (awaits) better things.* (60) *And goes on living. One day was born. One day will die.* No grandeur. No heroics. The usual lonely pattern to be endured.

[J.F.N.]

DINO CAMPANA

L'INVETRIATA

La sera fumosa d'estate
Dall'alta invetriata mesce chiarori nell'ombra
E mi lascia nel cuore un suggello ardente.
Ma chi ha (sul terrazzo sul fiume si accende una lampada) chi ha   4
A la Madonnina del Ponte chi è chi è che ha acceso la lampada? — c'è
Nella stanza un odor di putredine: c'è
Nella stanza una piaga rossa languente.
Le stelle sono bottoni di madreperla e la sera si veste di velluto: 8
E tremola la sera fatua: è fatua la sera e tremola ma c'è
Nel cuore della sera c'è,
Sempre una piaga rossa languente.

(*Canti orfici.* 1914)

Typical of the hallucinatory style of Dino Campana (1885-1932), "The Window" expresses the excitement, confusion, and terror with which the poet felt the coming of night. The hazy summer sunset reflected from a window, blending its blood-red brilliance with the gloom, fills the poet's chamber—and his soul—like a brooding red wound. Meanwhile lamps are being lighted in his little town. As the evening is being bewitched by these will-o'-the-wisps, his eye darts restlessly from one to another.

Poe and Whitman were favorites of Campana; here the influence of the first is seen in the macabre vision, of the second in the free-rolling rhythms. Stammering repetition and broken syntax are less a mark of Futurist influence than of Campana's excitable soul. (1) *The summer evening smoke-like* (2) *Mixes dazzling rays from the high window into the gloom* (3) *And leaves in my heart a searing brand.* Then a long tumbling sentence in which punctuation and syntax are disregarded as he questions light after light, one of them before the statue of the Madonna on the bridge near his home. (4) *But who has (on the terrace on the river a lamp is lighted) who has* (5) *To the Madonna of the Bridge who is it who is it who has lighted the lamp?* —*there's* (6) *An odor of rot in the room:*— *there's* (7) *A red wound languishing in the room.* He glances up, distracts himself momentarily with a poetic whimsy: (8) *The stars are buttons of mother-of-pearl and the evening is wearing velvet:* (9) *And it's tremulous* ["tremola" literally means *it shimmers*] *the haunted evening*—here "fatua," which normally means *stupid,* is used because the lights are like the eerie *ignis fatuus,* seen in cemeteries, marshes, etc.—*it's haunted the evening and is tremulous but there is* (10) *In the heart of the evening there is,* (11) *Still a red wound languishing.* At the end everything has dissolved in everything else—everything but the one vivid wound at the heart of the evening, the heart of the poet, the heart of the world. That he looks beyond the wound to a further truth about reality seems to be indicated by the title: not "Sunset" or "Wound" but "The Window."   [J.F.N.]

GIARDINO AUTUNNALE

Al giardino spettrale al lauro muto
De le verdi ghirlande
A la terra autunnale
Un ultimo saluto!   4
A l'aride pendici
Aspre arrossate nell'estremo sole
Confusa di rumori
Rauchi grida la lontana vita: 8
Grida al morente sole
Che insanguina le aiole.
S'intende una fanfara
Che straziante sale: il fiume spare   12
Ne le arene dorate: nel silenzio
Stanno le bianche statue a capo i ponti
Volte: e le cose già non sono piú.
E dal fondo silenzio come un coro   16
Tenero e grandioso
Sorge ed anela in alto al mio balcone:
E in aroma d'alloro,
In aroma d'alloro acre languente,   20
Tra le statue immortali nel tramonto
Ella m'appar, presente.

(*Canti orfici*. 1914)

High over the Futurist bandstands and across the wan sky of the Crepuscolari, the poetry of Dino Campana flashed in 1914 like the wildest of meteors. Driven since he was fifteen by a nervous compulsion, the bronze-haired blue-eyed roustabout had wandered over much of the world, *Leaves of Grass* in his pocket; he had been in and out of jail and of the asylum that finally claimed him, had himself peddled his crudely printed *Canti orfici*—whose very title, *Orphic Songs*, suggested mystery, magic, revelation. Campana lived for poetry; when close to him, said Cecchi, one could feel it like an electric shock or a high explosive. His own work, too idiosyncratic to be imitated, provided the young writers with a new sense both of the freedom poetry might enjoy and of its pictorial and musical possibilities—all richly realized in his "Autumn Garden."

The setting is the Boboli Gardens in Florence. (1) *To the spectral garden to the laurel shorn* (2) *Of the green garlands* (3) *To the autumn earth* (4) *A last greeting!* There should be commas after *garden* and *garlands:* the fever of Campana's thought is frequently impatient of punctuation. In this he resembles the Futurists (whose poetry, he objected, lacked music); but he is unlike them in relying heavily on the adjective, often taking a chance on those that in terms of communication seemed a bad risk in the context. Here *muto* is such a word; it means "silent,' but in the poem, as an earlier version proves, it stands for "pruned" or "shorn." The laurel are *mute* of their garlands because with clipping they have lost some of their murmur or rustle. Campana may have been thinking too of Dante's *luogo d'ogni luce muto*, "a place devoid [mute] of all light." His farewell to the waning garden continues with a violent change of color: from spectral grey to bitter red. (5) *To the dry hillsides*, (6) *Harsh, reddened in the final sunlight* (7-8) *The faraway [sound of] life cries, troubled with gruff rumblings:* (9) *Cries to the dying sun* (10) *That fills with blood the flower-beds*. As the passage is steeped in keener red, emotion goes well beyond literal meaning: the sun is *in extremis*, is a dying sun; its blood is on the place of innocence; and life from the city below, clamorous and confused in its purposes, is invoking a dying god. Shrill color turns to shrill sound, as if for a moment that crimson had a voice: (11) *A brass band is heard* (12) *That lifts ear-splitting*—a single piercing blast, it seems, because all is immediately muted to a twilight silence: *the river vanishes* (13) *Between its gilded sands* ["ne le" for the usual "nelle"—like "de le," etc., above—is a rather literary touch]: *in the silence* (14) *Stand the white statues at the bridgehead* (15) *Turned: and things exist no longer*.

Always fond of studding his poems with references to works of art, Campana makes this the most portentous image of the poem. As everything fades in his evening vista, the statues stand out like illusions on the bridges over the Arno—in their unearthly whiteness, against the russet and dim gold, seeming to belong to another order of reality. Called immortal in

line 21, they are already like gods. *Volte* ("turned") gives them a life and volition of their own: to turn to or away from something is a gesture charged with drama. We are not told what the statues mean in the poem: they impress by their very presence; they seem the tutelary deities of the scene, supreme and unchanging, as everything else loses its form in the gathering darkness. The firm shapes of day no longer exist. (Thought, feeling, and imagery here recall Hopkins' "Spelt from Sibyl's Leaves," also about disintegration at the end of day.) (16) *And from the deep silence, as it were a chorus* [the subject is the phrase "come un coro"] (17) *Tender and vast* (18) *Arises and yearns upward to my balcony*, the rampart or terrace in the park. This chorus is the voice with which the whole scene cries out to him. In the welter of sensations, each flowing into each like the twilight forms, images of color and sound now give way to the more immediate images of smell: (19) *In the [sharp] fragrance of laurel*, (20) *The fragrance of laurel bitter and languorous*, (21) *Among the immortal statues in the sunset*, privileged to survive the day and its undoing, (22) *She appears to me, present*.

The sudden revelation refocuses the entire poem, makes it meaningful in a way we had not previously suspected. This is no farewell to a mere garden, but to a girl he loved—whose apparition, we now see, has been anticipated by the mystic statues over the river: she is the goddess of the scene and the motive of the poem. Appearing so abruptly, for a moment she seems a stranger. But everything the poem has said is about her or the poet's relation to her: the farewell to a ghostly garden, a dying year, a dying sun; the scarlet land, the flower-beds running blood, the music snatched abruptly into silence, the golden river gone, the olympian statues turned, the thrilling cry of all that stricken world, the fragrance sweet and bitter. What they constitute is a definition of lost love.   [J.F.N.]

UMBERTO SABA

LA CAPRA

Ho parlato a una capra.
Era sola sul prato, era legata.
Sazia d'erba, bagnata
dalla pioggia, belava.   4

Quell'uguale belato era fraterno
al mio dolore. Ed io risposi, prima
per celia, poi perché il dolore è eterno,
ha una voce e non varia.   8
Questa voce sentiva
gemere in una capra solitaria.

In una capra dal viso semita
sentiva querelarsi ogni altro male,   12
ogni altra vita.

(*Il canzoniere*. 1921)

Umberto Saba, Giuseppe Ungaretti, Eugenio Montale—these are great names not only of Italian poetry but of world poetry in the twentieth century. Though sometimes thought of as a school, the three are very different: Saba (1883-1957) in particular has little in common with the others. A native not of one of the traditional centers of Italian culture but of the bustling port of Trieste across the Adriatic, where to be born in 1883, he says, was like being born anywhere else a generation earlier, Saba felt himself both *arretrato*, behind the times, and *periferico*, on the periphery of Italian letters. In some ways this was an advantage: he was protected from the hurlyburly of churning values in the Italy of his day and confirmed in his devotion to traditional rhythms, particularly of the hendecasyllable, the standard eleven-syllable line of Italian poetry. He describes himself, a bit tongue-in-cheek, as the least revolutionary of poets, but adds in the next breath that his lines are so individual that one knows at a glance they are not by anyone else. Saba has been far from an isolated poet. Many would agree with G. Titta Rosa, who says that his poetry "has accompanied our generation like a friendly voice: we would even say, the dearest"—though perhaps not always so exciting to the modern ear as the work of his two contemporaries. In his *Storia e cronistoria del canzoniere* (1948) Saba gives a fascinating account, almost poem by poem, of his life work.

"*La capra*" ("The Goat") is one of the best known of modern Italian poems. Belonging to a little collection of 1909-1910 called *Casa e campagna* (*House and Country*), it is part of his monumental *Il canzoniere*. Like most of his poetry, "*La capra*" is lucid and personal. The poem is composed of three *strofette*, or little stanzas. In the first, the poet's tone is casual, almost offhand. (1) *I have spoken with a goat.* (2) *She was alone in the field, she was tethered.* (3) *Satiated with grass, soaked* (4) *with rain, she was bleating.* A simple situation, simple diction. The goat is described in a succession of short phrases, not all of them, it should be noticed, giving a reason for grief. The goat has fed well—the motive of her sorrow must be deeper than physical discomfort. In the first four lines there are twenty-three *a* sounds, enough of them accented to let us fairly hear the blatting animal.

Having set his scene, Saba moves quietly on to the heart of the poem in the second stanza. (5) *That even bleating was brother* (6) *to my grief. And I answered, first* (7) *to make fun, then because grief is eternal,* (8) *has one voice, and does not vary.* (9) *I heard this voice* (10) *lamenting in a goat [left] all alone.* (Note: *Sentiva*, in lines 9 and 12, is the third-person form; in some editions one or both lines have read *sentivo:* "I heard.") The poet's response to the goat's misery is central to the poem and central to his poetry, which gives frequent evidence of what the critic Spagnoletti called his "Franciscan affection for animals" and his "cosmic sense of communion"—his keen feeling for the meaningful community of all living things. Here the poet's first reaction to the scene is a jesting one. It is only with his second thought that he discovers the scene's real significance: all life is sympathetically connected. The quiet sequence in which Saba describes his change of feeling about the goat reflects the unpremeditated manner in which such changes come about and such discoveries are made.

The rest of the poem is an elaboration of the discovery made in the second stanza. Saba reproduces the ruminative quality of his thought in the verse by carrying over key words from one line to the next: *dolore, voce, capra.*

(11) *In a goat with a semitic face* (12-13) *I heard every other ill, every other life, lamenting.* The poet, aware that he is bound to the goat by their common misery, now fully feels the kinship. Saba, whose mother was Jewish, finds the goat's expression "semitic," an identification which is reinforced by his use of *viso* ("face"), ordinarily used only of human faces. That bleating of line 5 has become by line 9 "this voice." Saba admits that this stanza has always made a greater impression than the others, for reasons of content, but he denies that he intended any particular racial reference—racial strains in his work, he says, are far more subtle than in this line, which is "predominantly visual . . . a thumbstroke in the clay to shape the figure."

In the final stanza Saba has so intensified his sympathy that he is able to see, in a goat's solitary misery, all the suffering of all living creatures—and how prominent a part of life he believes suffering to be is shown by the way he equates the two in the last two lines. It is a triumph of his sympathetic imagination that he has been able to do this; a triumph of his poetic power that he has been able to do it simply, making the most general conclusions in the poem seem to evolve naturally from the original situation.   [J.L.]

UMBERTO SABA

MEZZOGIORNO D'INVERNO

In quel momento ch'ero già felice
(Dio mi perdoni la parola grande
e tremenda) chi quasi al pianto spinse
mia breve gioia? Voi direte: « Certa   4
bella creatura che di là passava,
e ti sorrise. » Un palloncino invece,
un turchino vagante palloncino
nell'azzurro dell'aria, ed il nativo   8
cielo non mai come nel chiaro e freddo
mezzogiorno d'inverno risplendente.
Cielo con qualche nuvoletta bianca,
e i vetri delle case al sol fiammanti,   12
e il fumo tenue d'uno due camini,
e su tutte le cose, le divine
cose, quel globo dalla mano incauta
d'un fanciullo sfuggito (egli piangeva   16
certo in mezzo alla folla il suo dolore,
il suo grande dolore) tra il Palazzo
della Borsa e il Caffè dove seduto
oltre i vetri ammiravo io con lucenti   20
occhi or salire or scendere il suo bene.

(Cose leggere e vaganti. 1920)

In few poets have autobiography and poetry been more closely identified than in Saba, whose *Canzioniere* is a record of his life and feelings over about fifty years. "Winter Noon" is one of sixteen poems called *Cose leggere e vaganti*, (*Light and Wandering Things*): images of foam, soap-bubbles, changing clouds, drifting smoke, etc., define the nature of reality as Saba perceives it. The phrase "light and wandering" is used twice in the group, once of a child and once of a girl to whom most of these poems are addressed. Though her name, Paolina, does not occur in "Winter Noon," she is never far from the poet's mind.

Dead set against obscure or "hermetic" poetry (though an admirer of the great poets Ungaretti and Montale, whose work was rarely hermetic in any narrow sense), Saba went so far as to declare that such poets as Mallarmé and Valéry were "impotent" in the presence of the Muse. But his own clarity is deceptive: he himself calls his work "the easiest and most difficult . . . that came out in the first half of the century."

"Winter Noon" is built around his favorite themes: happiness, sorrow, love, desire, childhood, the city (generally his beloved Trieste). The poem finds the poet in one of the coffee-houses he was so fond of, watching the vivid scene through a window, discovering in everything a confirmation of what he had come to know.

(1) *At that moment [of a time] when I was still happy* (2) *(may God forgive me a word [so] great* (3) *and awesome) who [was it who] reduced almost to tears* [4] *my short-lived joy?* As everything here hints, the saddened poet feels that felicity, which never lasts and to which man has little claim, is a thing so tremendous and disproportionate to our nature that he, like a pagan placating his jealous gods, asks forgiveness for using the word. He continues: (4) *You will say, "A certain* (5) *beautiful creature who was passing there,* (6) *and she gave you a smile."* The first guess as to the cause of unhappiness is love, for in their uncertainty the best things (they also "light and wandering") can make us saddest. But no: (6) *A toy balloon, rather* —but the denial is not really total, for although the balloon is a real balloon, the poet sees in it the nature of all light, wandering things— (6) *A balloon, rather* (7) *a turquoise wandering balloon* (8) *in the blue of the air; and the native* (9-10) *heaven never [so] brilliant* ["risplendente," 10] *as on the clear and cold winter noon.* The color of the balloon is very close to the color of the sky: dictionaries sometimes define both *turchino* and *azzurro* as "sky-blue." But Saba, for whom in a later poem *turchino* is "the color of the sea," intended some difference, or he would not have juxtaposed the two colors. No great difference, or he could have made the balloon red or yellow. The balloon is more elusive for being almost the color of the sky, just as the sky becomes a more insubstantial pageant for being so like the lost balloon. One cannot insist that the "native heaven" is more than the sky over Trieste —that it is the proscenium of the human drama wherever played, but there is something of this hint in a sky clear and cold not only because of the calendar but

because of what it is at present saying—so brilliantly—to the poet.

The day itself is all shimmer and drift: (11) *A heaven with some little white clouds* (12) *and the windows of the houses afire in the sunlight,* (13) *and the thin smoke from a chimney or two,* (14) *and over all things, the divine* (15) *things, that globe*—Glancing from heaven to earth, the poet's eye sees the city in all its rich variety, with all the *things* that make it what it is, things so passionate and sad and lovely in the life of man that they become, for the poet, divine. Then back from earth to heaven; and in heaven the balloon, lost, wandering, forever irrecoverable, is more portentous than the sun itself, for it has become the very spirit of things longed for and lost forever. (15)—*that globe escaped* ["sfuggito," 16] *from the heedless hand* (16) *of a boy (he was weeping* (17) *surely in the middle of the crowd [for] his sorrow,* (18) *for his mighty sorrow.)* For the boy this is total grief: as total as any sorrow for the divine things—including that for the girl who did or did not pass. All loss is the lost balloon. And immediately, having intimated his deepest and saddest point—that the boy's tears are the *lacrimae rerum,* "tears for things"—the poet looks back at the real Trieste, where a balloon slipped away (18-19) *between the Exchange Building and the Coffee House,* and returns the poem to where it opened: to himself at a certain moment (19) *where, seated,* (20) *through the window I was gazing in wonder, with shining* (21) *eyes at [how it] now rose now dipped—his treasure.* Saba's strength, he once said, lay in looking at things; but his looking becomes contemplation. Eyes bright with interest and grief, he follows a balloon bobbing across the heavens, but in its wavering flight he is contemplating too the fluctuations of all things human. We may find in the loosely constructed, rather ravelling last sentence, running through eleven lines, some feeling of that haphazard course. [J.F.N.]

UMBERTO SABA

ULISSE

Nella mia giovanezza ho navigato
lungo le coste dalmate. Isolotti
a fior d'onda emergevano, ove raro
un uccello sostava intento a prede,   4
coperti d'alghe, scivolosi, al sole
belli come smeraldi. Quando l'alta
marea e la notte li annullava, vele
sottovento sbandavano piú al largo,   8
per fuggirne l'insidia. Oggi il mio regno
è quella terra di nessuno. Il porto
accende ad altri i suoi lumi; me al largo
sospinge ancora il non domato spirito,   12
e della vita il doloroso amore.

(*Mediterranee*. 1946)

---

(1) *In my youth I have navigated* (2) *along
the Dalmatian shores. Little islands*
(3) *would emerge on the surface of the sea,
where infrequently* (4) *a bird would pause,
intent on prey,* (5) *[they were] covered with
seaweed, slippery, in the sunlight* (6) *beautiful
as emeralds. When the high* (7) *tide and the
night would blot them out, sails* (8) *would
slip off to leeward more to the open* (9) *to
escape their treachery. Now my kingdom* (10) *is
that no man's land. The port* (11) *lights up
its lights for others; me to the open sea* (12)
thrusts still the unconquered spirit, (13) *and
the grief-stricken love for life.*

The reader's appreciation of this poem
will be enriched if he has some awareness
of the autobiographical background and
of the implications of the figure of Ulysses
for an Italian poet. Saba was born in
Trieste, and the Adriatic, with its beautiful
and somewhat lonely sea coast, is a
recurrent memory in his work. Lines 2-6,
the symbolism of which may not be clear

to us until we have read further into the
poem, are noteworthy for the sharpness
with which the *isolotti* (the -*otti* is more
than a diminutive ending; it suggests
"rugged little islands, "sturdy little is-
lands") are brought before us.

The figure of Ulysses lends itself to
many interpretations; no Italian writer
could think of him without recalling
Canto XXVI of the *Inferno*, where the
tale of the Ithacan's last voyage is told.
He is portrayed as seeking, above all,
knowledge of the virtues and vices of
mankind, and as symbolizing the restless
drive of the intellect, in its dedication to
knowledge forgetful even of the limitations
imposed by the Deity. That Saba has
likewise an older Ulysses in mind is
indicated by the reference in line 1 to
a youth already long since passed. The
allusion to the Dalmatian coast identifies
the poet with his subject. The exploration
of these attractive but treacherous islands

is tacitly compared to the youthful experiences of the poet, tentative and cautious. Now in old age it is precisely the unknown which attracts him: like Ulysses (whom, Dante tells us, neither filial piety nor love of family could restrain) the poet refuses to look for security, but resolves, with spirit unbroken and deep sympathy for the human adventure, to enlarge his horizon and seek over a yet wider sea for the ultimate secret. The last lines have again personal overtones; Saba had reason to be conscious of his "unconquered spirit," and to acknowledge grief as an element in his acceptance of life; he said he was, like Ungaretti, a *uomo di pena*, "a man of suffering." He had suffered under the last years of the fascist regime and his bitter experiences are still fresh in his mind ("Ulysses" was written in 1946). But the poem is great not because of what it tells us about the writer (who is indeed very discreet in his allusions) but because of the spirit of affirmation—neither easy optimism nor merely passive acceptance, but an ultimate faith in the destiny of humankind.

Technically the poem is notable for the fusion of imagery with meaning. This is achieved through a perfectly conventional form, almost a sonnet, of thirteen hendecasyllables, unrimed but richly though irregularly linked by assonance (*navigato, raro, alta*, etc.; *isolotti, sole*, etc.). The dramatization of certain key words at the end of a line (2, 3, 7, 9, are good examples) produces a kind of suspense, a momentum that carries us from line to line and stresses, orchestrally, the theme of eager, restless searching. It is probably not accidental that the last word of the poem—of the whole *Canzoniere*—is *amore*.

"*Ulisse*" is the last poem of *Il canzoniere*. For many years Saba had been referring in his work to Homer's hero, notably in another poem of the same title in *Parole* (1933-1934), which addresses an aging Ulysses, *al declino*, who according to Saba is "probably the poet himself." The first "*Ulisse*" refers to one of Saba's oldest and most frequent themes, that of *la brama*, the raging physical desire that is the motive of all life and art. Ulysses, the restless seeker, is for Saba an embodiment of this desire. The world of *brama*, however, is the physical world of adventures among the dangerous but brilliant islands which in youth one left only when they were annulled by night. Now the old Ulysses (Saba was 63 when he wrote the poem) has given them up forever: turned from the bright world of physical desire to a no man's land of the wide night. A no man's land: Saba cannot be mindless of the fact that Ulysses took the name of No One or No Man in his famous adventure with the Cyclops. In age, the little harbor lights are a pallid substitute for the emerald islands of the morning—but even these lights are for others now. *Brama* has become more spiritual, more compassionate—but invincible as ever as the mariner-poet sails forth on his last adventure. Saba died in 1957 at the age of 74.

For a vivid example of the difference between much poetry of our century and of the last, it is interesting to compare "*Ulisse*" with the handling of the same theme in Tennyson's "Ulysses," which, five times as long, has a strong tone of harangue and oratory, of the kind of inspiration and "eloquence" which Saba, and other moderns, pride themselves on avoiding. For the most part Saba lets the imagery speak for him; when he does speak from his own heart, as in the last two lines, it is almost as if the landscape, of whose reality he has now convinced us, had a voice of its own.   [T.G.B.]

GIUSEPPE UNGARETTI

SAN MARTINO DEL CARSO

Di queste case
non è rimasto
che qualche
brandello di muro   4

Di tanti
che mi corrispondevano
non è rimasto
neppure tanto   8

Ma nel cuore
nessuna croce manca

È il mio cuore
il paese piú straziato   12

(*Allegria di naufragi*. 1919)

Ungaretti's poetry, born in the ordeal of World War I and its trenches, where this poem was written, marked a turning point in modern Italian literature. Following so close on the roar of grenades and the sonorous harangues of d'Annunzio, it seemed to have little chance of being heard. Yet the very quality of soft-toned utterance won a growing audience for this unusual poetry. D'Annunzio's claim to modernity had been a dazzle of imagery and a sensual cult of nature and of the super-human ego—to the point of proclaiming Energy the "Tenth Muse." The Futurists, headed by Marinetti (like Ungaretti, born in Egypt and educated in Paris, where Ungaretti spent the significant years of his youth and early manhood), exploded conventional syntax and imagery to celebrate the restless dynamism of the new Muse in the driving tempos of the machine age. Ungaretti (1888-) instead withdrew into the inner sanctum of the contemplative soul, refusing the public myths, to look at the world as a realm of mysterious essences.

(1) *Of these houses* (2) *nothing remains* (3) *but certain* (4) *shreds of wall* (5) *Of so many* (6) *who were close to me* (7) *nothing is left* (8) *not even that* (9) *But in my heart* (10) *no cross is missing* (11) *My heart is* (12) *the most tortured village.*

To capture the pure note, he lowered the tone of his poetry to a bare whisper; slowed down its pace to potentially infinite duration; filled each pause with meaning. It was a real break with the loud heroics then in vogue, this vital Franciscan feeling that focused on existence as wonder and suffering. The suspended syntax and punctuation of "*San Martino del Carso*," which is about a ruined city on the Austrian front and the ruined city of the poet's heart, recall Apollinaire (pp. 82 ff.), whom he had known in Paris. The poem exemplifies perfectly Baudelaire's definition of the modern concept of art as evocative magic containing both the object and the subject, the world external to the artist and the artist himself. [G.C.]

GIUSEPPE UNGARETTI

SENZA PIÚ PESO

Per un Iddio che rida come un bimbo,
Tanti gridi di passeri,
Tante danze nei rami,

Un' anima si fa senza piú peso,   4
I prati hanno una tale tenerezza,
Tale pudore negli occhi rivive,

Le mani come foglie
S'incantano nell'aria...   8

Chi teme piú, chi giudica?

(Sentimento del tempo. 1933)

(1) *For a God laughing like a child, (2) So many cries of sparrows, (3) So much dancing in the branches, (4) A soul is shedding all its weight* [literally *becomes without weight any more*], *(5) The meadows have such tenderness, (6) In the eyes such purity revives, (7) The hands like leaves (8) Are spellbound in the air... (9) Who longer fears, who judges?*

Ungaretti sees his entire work as a unit which he calls *Vita d'un uomo* (*Life of a Man*). The publication of the second main section, *Sentimento del tempo* (*Sense of Time*) shows Ungaretti developing in depth. The reading of Petrarch and Góngora had stimulated a metaphysical bent only latent in the plain diction of the war poems, and had made for a new approach to traditional rhythm. The familiar hendecasyllabic line reappears frequently, as in lines 1, 4, 5, 6; imagery, with piercing oxymoron, takes a turn for the "hermetic." Abstract vision becomes second nature for the poet, who is motivated not only by a will to test and develop the potential of each word as sound and idea (hence such alliterative play as that in lines 4 and 5), but also by a profound Christian insight.

The experience embodied in "Turning Weightless" springs from one of his central themes: the longing for lost innocence. This rare event—the return to Eden—is taking place here in a moment of ecstasy. Not only the soul but words as well shed their weight, to the point of vibrating as pure transparency. The world of history is transcended; hence, as the last line says, fear and judging are abolished. The hands raised in prayer like leaves identify the poet with the tree of line 3, so full of birdsong, as if he were joyfully united with the floral existence of a Terrestrial Paradise—and this, along with the shedding of weight, establishes a close contact with the close of Dante's *Purgatorio*. The *pudore* of line 6 has nothing to do with Adam's shame after the eating of the apple, but implies on the contrary a regained innocence of the eye.   [G.C.]

GIUSEPPE UNGARETTI

ALLA NOIA

Quiete, quando risorse in una trama
Il corpo acerbo verso cui m'avvio.

La mano le luceva che mi porse,
Che di quanto m'avanzo s'allontana.   4

Eccomi perso in queste vane corse.

Quando ondeggiò mattina ella si stese
E rise, e mi volò dagli occhi.

Ancella di follia, noia,   8
Troppo poco fosti ebbra e dolce.

Perché non t'ha seguita la memoria?

È nuvola il tuo dono?

È mormorio, e popola   12
Di canti remoti i rami.

Memoria, fluido simulacro,
Malinconico scherno,
Buio del sangue...   16

More abstruse, constricted, and elliptical than Ungaretti's earlier work, his *Sentimento del tempo* created a furore in the world of Italian letters. Magazines were founded with the express purpose of attacking Ungaretti, who was accused of being a "hermetic" poet and the leader of the "hermetic school." Flung at Ungaretti by the famous critic Francesco Flora in 1936, "hermetic" (*arcane, mysterious*, or, in modern usage, *airtight*) implied that for the uninitiated reader there was no way into this terse, cryptic, densely written poetry, in which so much of the meaning lay not only in the far-ranging metaphors, but even in the arrangement of the lines and in the blank spaces between. Defenders did not hesitate to point out that this kind of poetry was merely a logical consequence of the process of exfoliating the nineteenth-century incrustations of politics, philosophy, oratorical eloquence, etc.—all that heritage of a gaudy romanticism—to get at the *essenzialità* of poetry, and that the conditions of the difficult and bitter '20's, in which so many of the traditional values seemed to have peeled and crumbled, made necessary a speech that would have, in order to be honest, the wry, crabbed, complex tone of the age.

Most difficult in the new poetry was the daring use of analogy, which so characterized some of the new poets that they came to be known as *analogisti*. In its simplest form (as the French critic Pierre-Quint explained) analogy says merely, "My soul is like a bird." The process is carried one step further with "My soul *is* a bird." Difficulty arises with the third step, which omits all reference to the soul and says "This bird . . ."—all the while meaning the soul. The more remote the terms equated (bird-soul, etc.) the more vivid the poetry, provided that it succeeds in making contact with the reader. Hermetic poems are likely to be full of objects that are really untagged metaphors. Obviously a pretentious poet can make this a game in which the reader can never win; the forthright poet will rely on images that have a voice in themselves or in chorus with other images—the key will be somewhere in the poem.

"*Alla noia*," for example, is haunted by the dreamlike figure of an elusive nymph or goddess, always reached for, never caught. *Noia* normally means "boredom," "tedium," "ennui"—as it does in an earlier poem of Ungaretti similarly entitled: *Noia*. In our poem, however, the qualities attributed to *noia* seem to add up to something else: whatever the mysterious figure is, she does not seem to be boring. Vexing in some way, yes; nagging, teasing, tantalizing—and yet associated with dreams and beauty and laughter and song and solace and longing. The *noia* lies largely in the fact that she will not let the poet alone; his quest for her is a vain quest, an exacerbating roundabout (5). In contrasting this poem with the earlier "*Noia*," the critic Spagnoletti suggests that here she is "a seductive figure that dazzles man, relieving him of the burden of humanity" that would be *noia* in the proper sense.

Perhaps there is no difficulty in the poem greater than that of translating the title. It is true there are mysteries, words of ambiguous reference, transitions in the white space between the lines. But if the thought slips out of sight here and there,

we can generally follow it till it reappears, richer than ever. After all, aspects of the very theme, this sad and passionate drama deep in the psyche, are themselves mysterious. Suppose we take *noia* here as some object of desire whose complete possession, in the absence of further longing, would be *ennui*, some desire which memory cannot even reconstruct in all its vividness, except in the spellbound moments between sleep and waking.

(1) *Stillness, when arose intact* [literally *in one weave*] (2) *The unripe body to which I am traveling.* At a quiet hour, then, the phantom arises complete, "in one weave" after being seen partially in the raveled visions of the night and the moments of half-remembrance. Her body, toward which the poet always moves in longing, is young and unripe, unachieved—and therefore (another meaning of *acerbo*) bitter too. The next lines, singled out for praise by even hostile critics, have a visionary loveliness, like passages in Dante: (3) *The hand was radiant that she offered me,* (4) *[The hand] that even as I move recedes.* (5) *So here I am lost in these vain pursuits.* (6) *When the morning was all ripple*—all a sparkle of watery light—*she stretched* (7) *And laughed and stole away before [from] my eyes.* (8) *Handmaid of madness, Noia,* (9) *Not enough, never enough [too little] were you rapt (drunken) and sweet.* His experience of the figure has been maddeningly incomplete, only enough to know that she could offer a delirium of bliss. (10) *Why didn't memory keep step with you?* Like many absent joys, this one cannot be summoned up before the memory in anything like its dazzling actuality. He wonders if she has nothing to offer but mirage and mist: (11) *Is it a cloud, your gift?* No, more than that: a real whisper, real and abundant music—but always far away: (12) *It is a murmuring, and it populates* (13) *The branches with far-away songs.* (14) *Memory, shifting image,* (15) *Melancholy derision,* (16) *Dark of the*

Quale fonte timida a un'ombra   17
Anziana di ulivi,
Ritorni a assopirmi...

Di mattina ancora segreta,   20
Ancora le tue labbra brami...

Non le conosca piú!

(*Sentimento del tempo.* 1933)

---

blood . . . Then the somber lighting fades, and the scene shifts to a pleasant vision of tranquillity, like a little poem from the Greek anthology: (17) *Like a shy fountain in a shade* (18) *An ancient [shade] of olive trees,* (19) *you return to lull me.* This is the comfort she could give, and by that vision he is aroused to a violence of desire: (20) *By morning secret still* (21) *Still may I long for your lips* . . . Again a rending reversal of feeling between that line and the next, as the implications of that utter kiss—rendered here so physically in the very sounds of *labbra brami*—come home to the poet, and he knows that beyond this there could be no further longing: (22) *May I never know them again!*

Perfect for their purpose, the wavering images and rhythms, the pregnant pauses, the very vagueness here and there. But what contributes as much as anything to the success of the poem is the use of sound itself: music as much as imagery becomes a way of communicating the poetic experience. The first lines, which present the still untroubled vision, are in smooth hendecasyllables. One of the purposes of Ungaretti's earlier experimentation, of his breaking down the line into words and syllables for his inspection, was to clean and reassemble this classic rhythm. As the vision fades, the rhythm breaks in line 7 (two syllables short), to return only in line 10. The rest of the lines are shorter, more broken, more fitful, as the poet's thought veers rapidly from side to side. Throughout the poem a musical continuity is preserved or appropriately cut by sequences of sounds or their interruption. Toward the beginning we have a series in *an* or *am: quando, trama, mano, quanto, m'avanzo, s'allontana.* We also have one in *or* or *er: risorse, corpo, acerbo, verso, porse, perso, corse*—such sequences run like bright metallic threads through the tapestry of dream. Particularly meaningful are the *risorse, porse, corse*—the last two providing the only end-rime in the poem, to dramatize the vanity of the pursuit, the endless circling, the return always to the place one started from. There is a kind of ripple of sound in the *and-ond* and even in the elision of *quando ondeggiò,* in a line (6) about the ripple or shimmer of morning light. In line 12 the five *o* sounds fairly populate the teeming line—a sound picked up in the *remoti* that follows, its own *r-m-i* echoed by *rami.* There is a similar effect in 17-19, in which the nine keen *i*'s are spangled like the silver of the olive foliage the lines describe.

We may wonder if poets such as Ungaretti, after a lifetime of labor, bring about any real advance in sensibility among their readers. It is certainly true that a poem which seems easy enough to follow today seemed hermetic and impenetrable thirty years ago.   [J.F.N.]

GIUSEPPE UNGARETTI

MATTINA

M'illumino
d'immenso

(*Sentimento del tempo.* 1933)

(1) *I flood myself with light* (2) *of the immense* This famous little poem, also from *Sentimento del tempo*, is the kind that particularly infuriated the anti-hermeticists. In the battle between *formisti*, the defenders of the primacy of pure form in poetry, and the *contenutisti*, the defenders of content, the new poets would of course be with the *formisti*. But what this little poem lacked, said its opponents, was precisely *form*. They saw it as a mere exclamation on a piece of paper, transforming into poetry neither the morning (*mattina*) nor the immensity. Nor the heaven nor the sea—because elsewhere the poet had called this poem "*Cielo e mare*" ("Heaven and Sea")—a change that seemed to confirm the suspicion that perhaps Ungaretti himself did not know what it was about. If "Morning," they said, why not "Noon?" Or "Night," which with its paradox would be even more striking? Or, best of all, "Death?"

But these strictures all miss the point. It *is* an exclamation, as Valéry says the lyrical basically is. Indeed, much poetic theory since Poe has been impressed by his "I hold that a long poem does not exist"—though Poe was also against "a *very* short poem." "*Mattina*" might have been about any number of other things, in which case it would almost certainly have been a longer poem. But it would not have been *this* poem, and to us as readers *this* poem is our concern.

In fact, it is not about the morning or the sea; the real point of Ungaretti's insight is the effect of any vast reality of the physical universe (seen in morning, sea, or sky) on the human soul. Far from dismaying the poet, as the vastness of space had dismayed Pascal, it leaves him exhilarant, with a sense of expansion, of inner radiance. The poet is not illuminated *from without* by sea or sky; he illuminated himself by the contact: the fire of his own soul burns high and clear in its excitement.

Probably no one would claim that this is one of Ungaretti's greater poems, but it is a memorably noted experience: this sudden realization that, vast and brilliant as the universe may be, it is less so than the soul embracing it. Poetry of this kind, recalling the experiments of Pound and like them owing something to Oriental poetry, has been called *poesia-baleno*, flash-of-lightning poetry. "*Mattina*" has, although in miniature (like a cameo), more form than some have been willing to concede—particularly in the exploiting of appropriate sounds. The most emphatic syllable of the poem prolongs the accented *u* of *illumino*, a long, low, rounded, musing, almost rhapsodic *oooo*—an effect supported by the dwelt-on doubled *l*'s and *m*'s (actually pronounced as double in Italian, like a clearly articulated il*l* *l*uck and di*m* *m*en in English), and the final *o*'s. The lines almost rime (*mino, menso*); probably full rime would be too locked in, too confining for a little poem whose widening circles are off for infinity.   [J.F.N.]

TU TI SPEZZASTI

1

I molti, immani, sparsi, grigi sassi
Frementi ancora alle segrete fionde
Di originarie fiamme soffocate
Od ai terrori di fiumane vergini   4
Ruinanti in implacabili carezze:
— Sopra l'abbaglio della sabbia rigidi
In un vuoto orizzonte, non rammenti?
E la recline, che s'apriva all'unico   8
Raccogliersi dell'ombra nella valle,
Araucaria, anelando ingigantita,
Volta nell'ardua selce d'erme fibre
Piú delle altre dannate refrattaria,   12
Fresca la bocca di farfalle e d'erbe
Dove dalle radici si tagliava:
— Non la rammenti delirante muta
Sopra tre palmi d'un rotondo ciottolo   16
In un perfetto bilico
Magicamente apparsa?

In his earlier work Ungaretti seems to have taken meter apart to look at the single word in its purity. When he returns, as here, to the classical rhythms, he uses them with a strength new in Italian poetry. In much the same way his "hermeticism" might be seen as a necessary stage on the road to a new and meaningful clarity. Certainly his best work, such as "*Tu ti spezzasti*" ("You Were Broken") is in no way forbiddingly hermetic. In 1936 the poet left Italy for several years to serve as professor of Italian literature at the University of São Paulo (Brazil), to return to Italy only when forced by the pressures of the war in 1942. *Il dolore* is concerned with two sorrows: the death of a little son in Brazil and the tragedy of a warring world. "*Tu ti spezzasti*," which reflects the first of these sorrows, opens with glimpses of a terrifying Brazilian landscape: rocky, volcanic, tropical—as if still quivering with the geological convulsions that shook it long ago. Rocks loom against an empty heaven; a wounded and grotesquely twisted tree, turned flinty with age, strains from its stony bed high over an ocean where monster turtles stir darkly in the sea growth. This is not the method of "The soul is a bird" (see p. 309) but of the terser "This bird . . . ." For the landscape, perfectly real in itself, is also the background of human life: man's fate.

The first 18 lines are made up of two questions addressed to the dead boy. The syntax is tormented, as if the speaker, fascinated by the dire vista he remembers, could hardly tear himself away from the contemplation of it to get the questions out. The rhythm of the hendecasyllable hammers on the objects and their qualities, breaking up the line into rhythms more like those of our iambic pentameter (line 1) than those of Dante's or Leopardi's more legato line (line 13 illustrates the traditional pattern).

(1) *The many, monstrous, scattered, grey rocks* (2) *A-tremble yet from the mysterious slings* (3) *Of the primordial conflagrations, banked* [beneath the cooling crust of the earth, but still a threat: not dead] (4) *Or from the terrors of the virgin floods* (5) *Rushing down in inexorable caresses*—floods either of lava or of the primeval rivers that had as yet no beds. There is cruel irony in "virgin" and "caresses": what these rivers embrace they destroy. (*Ruinare*, an old form closer to the Latin than the usual *rovinare*, to "rush down" or "destroy," is appropriate in this vision of vast time.) (6) *—Over the dazzle of sand, set stark* (7) *Against an empty horizon, don't you remember [the rocks]?* Harsh sounds prevail in the opening lines; one should note also the blunt *a*'s of line 5 and the repetition, like a vexing reflection, in *abbaglio della sabbia* (6).

A Dalí landscape still racked with its violent past, this world of space and time seems hardly sympathetic to human life. Or to any life, as we see now. (8) *And the bent-over [Araucaria* of line 10*]*—why is the noun *Araucaria* so far from its adjective? Because, like the tree, the syntax and the reader are left dangling?—*which spread at the only* (9) *Massing of shade [its own] in the valley,* (10) *The Araucaria [a South American pine] gigantic in its yearning*—like an El Greco figure, straining tall with longing— (11) *Changed from its lonely fibers to fierce flint,*

(12) *More resistant than the others* [plants, etc.] *so condemned [to this infernal landscape],* (13) *Its mouth fresh with butterflies and grasses* (14) *Where it was hewn from the roots.* A monstrous and hag-ridden tree, harsh as its name, growing from the side of a rock over the ocean, one side hollowed—cut or blasted from its roots—standing only because it is now petrified, in contortions of agony. More mineral than plant, and hence more resistant than the other plants condemned to exist here. (*Refrattario*, used of bricks, clay, etc., implies particularly resistance to heat.) The mouth of the tree with its greenery and butterflies sounds pleasant; but the mouth is a great wound in the tree, and the only mouths associated with grass and insects are dead mouths— in all this throbbing landscape the only life is a life that feeds on death. (15) *Don't you remember it raving without a sound* (16) *Up over a rounded boulder, three spans wide*—less than a yard; cut off from much of its support, it now seems rooted to a remarkably small rock, where it could never naturally have grown— (17) *In perfect balance* (18) *Magically come forth?*

After 16 lines of the same rhythm, now we have, abruptly, two almost identical short lines, each with accents on the fourth and sixth syllables. With a writer as syllable-conscious, as rhythm-conscious, as Ungaretti, this is not haphazard. A change of rhythm generally dramatizes something in the lines: here it must be the incredible balance of the tree, like a conjurer's illusion. There is in these shorter lines something like an awed catch in the breath, but their more slender balance is also a rhythmical rendering of that incredible poise.

Hitherto, landscape. But landscape which implies a statement about the nature of existence. A poet cannot say outright that life is violent, twisted, and brutal without running the risk of giving us melodramatic or cynical platitudes. Who,

Di ramo in ramo fiorrancino lieve,
Ebbri di meraviglia gli avidi occhi   20
Ne conquistavi la screziata cima,
Temerario, musico bimbo,
Solo per rivedere all'imo lucido
D'un fondo e quieto baratro di mare   24
Favolose testuggini
Ridestarsi fra l'alghe.
Della natura estrema la tensione
E le subacquee pompe,   28
Funebri moniti.

2

    Alzavi le braccia come ali
E ridavi nascita al vento
Correndo nel peso dell'aria immota.   32
Nessuno mai vide posare
Il tuo lieve piede di danza.

3

Grazia felice,
Non avresti potuto non spezzarti   36
In una cecità tanto indurita
Tu semplice soffio e cristallo,

Troppo umano lampo per l'empio,
Selvoso, accanito, ronzante   40
Ruggito d'un sole ignudo.

(*Il dolore.* 1947)

however, can deny the truth of a land-scape? Ungaretti insists on nothing; he merely points at what is there and lets us look.

In the second stanza of the opening section, the dead child appears as he was in life, swarming recklessly up the tree to peer over the cliff into the ocean gulfs below. A light bright darting shape among the branches, the foreign child is seen as a bird foreign to Brazil—one of the smallest, prettiest, and gayest of Italian birds, always in motion, fond of pines. (19) *From branch to branch [like] a light-winged little bird* [the *Regulus ignicapillus* of the ornithologists], (20) *Eager eyes drunken with wonder* (21) *You conquered its mottled top,* (22) *Reckless, musical child*—except for the imagined rumble of ancient telluric chaos and the figurative roaring of a bestial sun (40-41), this human singing is the only sound in the world of the poem: everything else is sunk in a weird and lunar silence, desperation *raving without a sound* (15)— (23) *Only to see again in the luminous depths* (24) *Of a sunk and quiet crater in the ocean* (25) *Fab-*

ulous turtles (26) *Stir to life in the seaweed.*
(27) *The tension of nature [wrought to] extreme[s]* (28) *And the subaqueous pageants* (29) *[Were] funereal warnings.*

The prospect from the treetop is of another nightmare landscape where enormous turtles, monsters of fable, figures of doom, stir in a locked and knotted world where no human life is possible. All nature here is extreme, in a state of tension: the undersea spectacle is ominous with a feeling of doom. (The words *pompe funebri*, though separated, are baleful: the phrase, common on undertaking establishments in Italy, means "funerals.") This section opened (19) with three hendecasyllables of musing remembrance, more lyrical than those at the beginning of the poem. Then an abrupt line—"headless"—lacking a syllable (22). In line 25 the great seamonsters loom in a line of their own, their fabulous bulk (as in 26 and 28) quite filling the shorter measures. Line 29 is curt with warning.

In the second section: a slight little aria —as the child was slight against his formidable world. A brisk dancing rhythm of three accents to the line, with many quick little unstressed syllables. Line 32 is longer, four accents for the boy's long energetic races; line 34 is a little shuffling jig. (30) *You raised up your arms like wings* (31) *And again gave birth to the wind* (32) *Running in the [dead] weight of the motionless air.* (33) *No one ever saw rest* (34) *Your light little foot [made for] dancing.* The child running with arms raised, all life and verve, is a living mockery of the rigid tree. There is no wind in its branches, no wind in the heavy air of the mountain valley, until the child freshens the air, creatively, with his flight. The image of the child recalls also the first image used of

him: the gay little bird in the branches. And some readers have seen in his posture hints of the angelic. The poet certainly does not insist on that suggestion—for to insist would be to risk sentimentalizing the little figure. The aria ends in a vein of fond fatherly exaggeration: the human child becomes, in those affectionate eyes, a more than human Ariel.

In the third section, after an invocation to a being all happiness and grace come two grave hendecasyllables—followed by a third, if one dwells on *tu* or lets it be followed by a meaningful pause. (35) *[O] happy grace,* (36) *You could not not have been broken* (37) *In a blindness so stony,* (38) *You—simple breath and crystal.* The world being as it was, blind and monstrous, the child being as he was, a buoyant breath of life and song, a candor and sparkle of crystal, if things remained true to their nature there was no other outcome for the two incompatibles except the child's destruction. There has been no resentment yet, but now, in the face of the bitter fact, the father strikes out, in lines a bit shorter, brusquer, contracted with anger. His protest becomes poetry in the graphic mythologizing of the sun as a shaggy monster, the lion of the July zodiac or a naked wildman from the woods—a process that recalls Antonio Machado's mighty personifications of the sere Castilian mesa. (39) *A dazzle of light too human for the dire,* (40) *Wild, dogged, and buzzing* (41) *Roar of a naked sun.* A gripping and fearful deity of the blasted landscape: shaggy with glitter, the vibrations of light on the burning stone seen as vibrations of sound, as a roaring vertigo destructive of man and all his values.

[J.F.N.]

MERIGGIARE PALLIDO E ASSORTO

Meriggiare pallido e assorto
presso un rovente muro d'orto,
ascoltare tra i pruni e gli sterpi
schiocchi di merli, frusci di serpi.   4

Nelle crepe del suolo o su la veccia
spiar le file di rosse formiche
ch'ora si rompono ed ora s'intrecciano
a sommo di minuscole biche.   8

Osservare tra frondi il palpitare
lontano di scaglie di mare
mentre si levano tremuli scricchi
di cicale dai calvi picchi.   12

E andando nel sole che abbaglia
sentire con triste meraviglia
com'è tutta la vita e il suo travaglio
in questo seguitare una muraglia   16
che ha in cima cocci aguzzi di bottiglia.

(Ossi di seppia. 1925)

T his poem was published in Eugenio Montale's first book (*Bones of Cuttlefish*). Written, however, nearly a decade before, when Montale was nineteen, it is prophetic of his later career: close to the realities of the vivid Ligurian scene, at once physical and metaphysical—as a stone wall glittering with broken glass becomes an image for the nature of existence.

(1) *To rest at noon, pale and absorbed* (2) *next to a scorching garden wall,* (3) *to hear among the thorns and sticks* (4) *crackle of blackbirds, stir of snakes.* All throughout the poem the infinitives are used absolutely, subject to no verb: to rest, to hear, to spy, to observe, to feel—the order is itself meaningful in terms of degrees of awareness. In the syntax alone then there is something tentative, timeless: not "I rested" but the experience itself, "to rest."

Meriggiare means to spend the noon (*meriggio*) resting in the shade until the intensity of the sun has lessened. The subject of this poem, presumably the poet, rests now by a wall whose stones are scorchingly hot in the sunlight. Though there may be reasons outside the poem for the subject's pallor, it is sufficient to know that it goes with *assorto* ("sunk in thought"): the thinker, withdrawn from the physical, traditionally suffers like Hamlet from the "pale cast of thought." Almost every line provides a physical sensation: the feel or sound or look of something—even by implication the very scent and savor of these salty sun-dried headlands. The young poet resolutely avoids anything "pretty" in either imagery or music; he rests in a place of sticks and stones, listening to sounds not conventionally idyllic. What compensates for the avoidance of melody is the rightness of the rasping language: the equivalent of a landscape dense in sensations that nettle, burn, abrade. Montale would have us feel this in the very way we speak his lines: from far away the blackbird's *cloc cloc cloc*, he says, sounds like Morse code. "*Schiocchi [skee-áwk-kee]* produces a certain *armonia imitativa;* try to produce the sound by making the tongue pop or crackle *(scoppiettare)*."

But the poet's siesta *(siesta* too means "noon") is an observant one: far from bored, his interest bright as a boy's, he misses nothing: (5) *In the cracks of the ground or on the vetch* [a common climbing plant] (6) *to spy on files of red ants* (7) *that now disperse, now interweave* (8) *on summit[s] of the tiny heaps [anthills]*. In the first stanza the rimes were expressively close together *(aabb)*: he was *near* the wall; the sounds were *among* the brambles. In the second, the rimes are separated *(abab)*: more like the raveling ants that scatter and reunite, and the busy eye that follows. The rime with *veccia*, in the middle of *s'intrecciano*, is interwoven with a word that means "they interweave." In the third stanza the rimes are again as in the first, with a similar effect. (9) *To observe through foliage the throbbing* (10) *far away of scales of sea*— The scales make the sea part of this world of things bitter and abrasive: not even its waters are seen as fluid, but as scaly, rugged, tough—akin to the grating snake (like which it "palpitates"), the jeweled red ants, dry sticks, and fiery stone wall. The distant sea is framed in nearby leaves —it is one with their prickly world, the more so because its glitter is the visual equivalent of a shrill monotony ringing from the cliffs. (11-12) *While the quavering screaks of cicadas rise from the bald peaks*—

again in this line a deliberate and appropriate entry of scrannel pipes that affront the flute-loving ear.

His siesta over, the poet rises and resumes his walk. (13) *And passing into the dazzling sun* (14) *to feel with melancholy wonder* (15) *how all life and its laboring (travail) is* (16) *in this following a wall* (17) *that has on top sharp pieces of bottle[s]*. Considerably grimmer than Robert Frost's stone wall, this broken glass embedded in cement glitters in the sunlight like the distant sea —a shrill sparkle in key with the other calculated discords of the poem. This forbidding barrier, the poet feels, is life itself: a monotonous trudging alongside a limit we can never pass. The last stanza too makes full use of the form. Whereas the ear has grown accustomed to a pause after the fourth line, the notion of weary walking forces us through yet a fifth, which, longer than the rhythms we have been paced to, seems interminable. The rimes of the stanza too are significantly different from earlier ones: *abcab*, but the *a* rimes *(-aglia)* are hardly distinct from the *b* rimes *(-iglia)*, and the unrimed *c (-aglio)* is confusingly close to both. In itself ugly, this is here effective: rime and half-rime in a jagged tangle like glass on the wall.

This poem ventures an interpretation of the nature of life that in other contexts might be cynical and depressing. Here it is not—in this verve and brilliance of a landscape vibrant with raw color. *Sentire con triste meraviglia* (14)—the emotional effect of the experience, though deepened with sorrow, has been chiefly that of wonder. We are shown a hard-bitten universe that might well have been dismaying to the querulous Crepuscolari (see p. 293), but Montale meets it with a spirit as tough as its own and with quite other resources of endurance and human courage—so admirably ingrained in the very fiber of his stubborn poem. [J.F.N.]

ARSENIO

I turbini sollevano la polvere
sui tetti, a mulinelli, e sugli spiazzi
deserti, ove i cavalli incappucciati
annusano la terra, fermi innanzi   4
ai vetri luccicanti degli alberghi.
Sul corso, in faccia al mare, tu discendi
in questo giorno
or piovorno ora acceso, in cui par scatti   8
a sconvolgerne l'ore
uguali, strette in trama, un ritornello
di castagnette.

È il segno d'un'altra orbita: tu seguilo.   12
Discendi all'orizzonte che sovrasta
una tromba di piombo, alta sui gorghi,
piú d'essi vagabonda: salso nembo
vorticante, soffiato dal ribelle   16
elemento alle nubi; fa che il passo
su la ghiaia ti scriccioli e t'inciampi
il viluppo dell'alghe: quell'istante
è forse, molto atteso, che ti scampi   20
dal finire il tuo viaggio, anello d'una
catena, immoto andare, oh troppo noto
delirio, Arsenio, d'immobilità...

Ascolta tra i palmizi il getto tremulo   24
dei violini, spento quando rotola
il tuono con un fremer di lamiera
percossa; la tempesta è dolce quando
sgorga bianca la stella di Canicola   28
nel cielo azzurro e lunge par la sera
ch'è prossima: se il fulmine la incide
dirama come un albero prezioso
entro la luce che s'arrosa: e il timpano   32
degli tzigani è il rombo silenzioso.

Discendi in mezzo al buio che precipita
e muta il mezzogiorno in una notte
di globi accesi, dondolanti a riva, —   36
e fuori, dove un'ombra sola tiene
mare e cielo, dai gozzi sparsi palpita
l'acetilene —

finché goccia trepido 40
il cielo, fuma il suolo che s'abbevera,
tutto d'accanto ti sciaborda, sbattono
le tende molli, un frúscio immenso rade
la terra, giú s'afflosciano stridendo 44
le lanterne di carta sulle strade.

Cosí sperso tra i vimini e le stuoie
grondanti, giunco tu che le radici
con sé trascina, viscide, non mai 48
svelte, tremi di vita e ti protendi
a un vuoto risonante di lamenti
soffocati, la tesa ti ringhiotte
dell'onda antica che ti volge; e ancora 52
tutto che ti riprende, strada portico

(1) *The whirlwinds lift the dust* (2) *over the roofs, in eddies, and over the open spaces* (3) *deserted, where the hooded horses* (4) *sniff the ground, motionless in front* (5) *of the glistening windows of the hotels.* (6) *Along the promenade, facing the sea, you go down* (7) *on this day* (8) *now rainy now aglow, in which* (10-11) *a refrain of castanets* (8) *seems [like] bursts* (9) *to shatter its hours,* (10) *even, close-knit.*

(12) *It is the sign of another orbit; follow it.* (13) *Go down towards the horizon, overhung* (14) *by a leaden waterspout, high over the whirlpools,* (15) *more restless then they; a briny stormcloud* (16) *whirling, blown by the unruly* (17) *element against the clouds; let your step* (18) *grate on the shingle, let it catch your feet,* (19) *the tangle of seaweed; that moment* (20) *it may be, long awaited, that will save you* (21) *from pursuing your journey until the end, link of a* (22) *chain, a motion motionless, oh too familiar* (23) *delirium, Arsenio, of inaction.* . . .

(24) *Listen, among the palm-trees, to the tremulous jet* (25) *of violins, quenched when rolls* (26) *the thunder with a quiver of sheet iron* (27) *struck; the tempest is sweet when* (28) *white rushes out the dog-star* (29) *in the blue sky, and distant seems the evening* (30) *which is close at hand: if the thunderbolt cuts it,* (31) *it branches forth like a tree made precious* (32) *within the reddening light; and the kettledrum* (33) *of the gypsies is the silent rumble.*

(34) *Go down amidst the precipitous darkness* (35) *turning the noon into a night* (36) *of kindled globes, which sway along the beach,* (37) *and in the offing, where a solid shadow holds* (38) *sea and sky, from scattered boats there throbs* (39) *the acetylene—* (40-41) *until the sky trickles in trembling drops, the drinking soil steams,* (42) *everything, close by, wallows around you; there flap* (43) *the loose awnings, an immense rustle skims* (44) *the earth, down flop squeaking* (45) *the paper lanterns on the streets.*

(46) *Thus, lost among the wicker and the mats* (47-48) *dripping, a reed (you) that drags its roots along with it, clammy, never* (49) *torn up, you shake with life and strain* (50) *towards a void resounding with laments* (51-52) *choked, the dome [crest] of the ancient wave that rolls you swallows you up again; and again* (53) *all that claims you back, street,*

mura specchi ti figge in una sola
ghiacciata moltitudine di morti,
e se un gesto ti sfiora, una parola   56
ti cade accanto, quello è forse, Arsenio,
nell'ora che si scioglie, il cenno d'una
vita strozzata per te sorta, e il vento
la porta con la cenere degli astri.   60

(*Ossi di seppia.* 1925)

porch, (54) *walls, mirrors, nails you to a lonely* (55) *icy multitude of dead,* (56) *and should a gesture touch you, should a word* (57) *fall at your side, such is perhaps, Arsenio,* (58) *in the dissolving hour, the hint of some* (59) *strangled life which rose for you, and the wind* (60) *carries it off with the ashes of the stars.*

The scene is a seaside resort on the Ligurian coast, the part of Italy where Montale was born (1896) and which supplies the background and imagery of *Ossi di seppia.* This very title hints at the dry, desolate purity of his early inspiration: white cuttlefish bones stranded on the margin of the beach, where the sea casts up all its drift and wreckage. The white cuttlefish bones lie helpless among the sand and weeds; a wave every now and then disturbs and displaces them, giving them a semblance of motion and life. The quality of "motionless motion" thus associated with the bleaching bones is echoed throughout the collection, and particularly in "*Arsenio,*" a name the poet arbitrarily gives to his character.

On a stormy day, while the wind blows threatening clouds across a fitfully appearing sun ("this day now rainy now aglow," 7-8), the poet goes down to a promenade facing the sea. Hansom cabs are stationed in front of a row of hotels, their horses, as usual in such seaside resorts, wearing little white cotton hoods for protection against the sun. A little band plays popular music in front of some café; the wind brings suddenly a refrain of castanets, and this sharp sound seems to upset the close-knit texture of monotonous hours.

The grey lifeless routine of the poet's day is instantly disturbed by this "sign of another orbit." A note is introduced similar to the "dance, and Provencal song, and sunburnt mirth" of Keats, for the castanets suggest intense life, romance, Spanish dancing. The poet feels impelled to follow the other orbit eagerly, as if somehow this new rhythm might offer a possible relief from his stagnation. Its excitement is in keeping with the commotion which now convulses the elements; a waterspout is rapidly travelling across the sky. The poet wants to share this excitement; he makes the gravel crunch under his footstep; he feels alive in overcoming the obstacle the seaweed opposes to his onward tread. Thus, perhaps, he might break the spell that nails him to the monotony of a fictitious life, where his allotted days are like the links of a chain, and where everything is so preordained that, while seeming to move, it actually stands still.

One must refer at this point to what Montale said once in "Intentions: An Imaginary Interview" (*Rassegna d'Italia,* I, 1) in regard to the influence he felt, in the years he was composing *Ossi di seppia,* of the philosophy of Bergson and particularly of Boutroux: "Miracle was for me as evident as necessity." Life may be likened to a link in a chain: a taut chain uncoiling from a windlass toward an inevitable anchorage, death. We seem to move, but in reality we do not act, we are drawn along: ours is a motionless motion, a delirium of inaction. Such is the ultimate meaning of the "even, close-knit hours" of our life. But what if suddenly the rhythm should change? A refrain of castanets, putting a stop to the dead sequence of chained hours—the miracle! This attitude is mirrored also in the words the poet used to define his inspiration (in the same interview): "I obeyed a need of musical expression. I wanted my words to be more fitting than those of the other poets I had known. Fitting what? I seemed to live under a glass-bell, and still I felt I was near something essential. A thin veil, hardly a thread, separated me from the final *quid*. Absolute expression would mean the tearing of that veil, of that thread: an explosion, or else the end of the delusion of the world as representation. But this was an unattainable end."

Is the miracle possible? The expectation of it opens an almost idyllic vista, a "pastoral" interlude: "Listen, among the palm-trees . . ." (24). The scene acquires suddenly the quality of magic. The earth and the sky become peopled with fairylike enchantment. The sound of the violins is like the jet of a fountain; the storm is held at bay by a space of azure sky in which the dog-star twinkles white, the lightning is like a tree of precious metal against a pink light. From a gypsy band playing in front of a café the kettledrums simulate the rumble of the storm; the lines of lights along the shore and the acetylene lamps of the fishing boats at sea seem to belie the threat of an impending storm.

The first drops fall; the immense rustle, usual in these summer storms on the Tyrrhenian sea, precedes the cloudburst; and the awnings, the paper lanterns in front of the cafés (hiding the electric bulbs), which a moment ago gave a festive appearance to the promenade, are torn away; the wicker chairs and screens, the mats that form the usual appurtenances of the beach shops and cafés are scattered here and there; the poet himself is no better than a shaking reed swept away in this general commotion (*tutto d'accanto ti sciaborda*, 42: the verb, perhaps inadequately rendered by "wallows," conveys the characteristic sound of shaken liquids, and is typical of Montale, whose early associations were with the sea), aching down to its loose but (alas) still clinging roots. The surrounding scene (street, walls, porticoes, mirrors of shops and hotels) falls about his ears, and he is aware only of being in the midst of an "icy multitude of dead," painfully alive to this one awareness of death, beyond the reach of any human succor—that faintly heard voice is soon carried away by the wind, and made remote as the memory of a dead universe.

Human destiny has no possibility of salvation nor even of sympathy from the surrounding world, since the poet does not share the pathetic fallacy of the Romantics. His desperate attempt to break away from the deadly sequence of chained hours has failed. The hoped-for miracle is not taking place after all. He has to resign himself to live nailed to a lonely, icy multitude of dead; he cannot be saved from pursuing his monotonous journey to its bitter end.

[M.P.]

LA CASA DEI DOGANIERI

Tu non ricordi la casa dei doganieri
sul rialzo a strapiombo sulla scogliera:
desolata t'attende dalla sera
in cui v'entrò lo sciame dei tuoi pensieri   4
e vi sostò irrequieto.

Libeccio sferza da anni le vecchie mura
e il suono del tuo riso non è piú lieto:
la bussola va impazzita all'avventura   8
e il calcolo dei dadi piú non torna.
Tu non ricordi; altro tempo frastorna
la tua memoria; un filo s'addipana.

Ne tengo ancora un capo; ma s'allontana   12
la casa e in cima al tetto la banderuola
affumicata gira senza pietà.
Ne tengo un capo; ma tu resti sola
né qui respiri nell'oscurità.   16

Oh l'orizzonte in fuga, dove s'accende
rara la luce della petroliera!
Il varco è qui? (Ripullula il frangente
ancora sulla balza che scoscende...)   20
Tu non ricordi la casa di questa
mia sera. Ed io non so chi va e chi resta.

(*La casa dei doganieri e altre poesie.* 1932)

Le occasioni (Occasions), which reprinted "*La casa dei doganieri*" in 1939, gave the fullest measure of Eugenio Montale's genius for nuance and perception through a characteristically quiet diction, in which the sudden cry of the visionary is all the more piercing when it comes. And yet the unearthly revelation is wholly human, springing from the scrupulous attention with which the smallest objects, details, or tones of everyday life have been recorded: in Montale's world the significance of the insignificant may be a poignant discovery.

The troubled climate of the prewar thirties is felt in *Le occasioni*, but instead of dating the poetry it testifies to the broad human scope, the prophetic sensitivity of a writer who had always been close to the imperiled civilization of Europe. Such a prophetic note rings in "*La casa dei doganieri*"—which in imagery and spirit may remind us of the beginning of Yeats's "The Second Coming," with its "Things fall apart...."

(1) *You don't remember the shore-watchers' house* (2) *on the edge of the steep cliff over-*

hanging the reef: (3) *desolate, it awaits you, from [ever since] that evening* (4) *when the swarm of your thoughts entered there* (5) *and paused there, restless.* (6) *The south wind has battered for years the old walls* (7) *and the sound of your laughter is no longer gay:* (8) *the compass turns—a crazy thing—at random* (9) *and the reckoning of the dice doesn't come out.* (10) *You don't remember; another time confuses* (11) *your memory; a thread is slipping from the spool.* (12-13) *I still hold an end of it: but the house recedes—and on the roof the weathervane* (14) *blackened by smoke whirls pitiless.* (15) *I hold an end of it; but you remain alone* (16) *and do not breathe here in the darkness.* (17-18) *Oh the retreating horizon, where the light of the tanker rarely burns!* (19) *This way through? (The breakers seethe* (20) *still on the cliff that falls away . . .)* (21) *You don't remember the house of this* (22) *my evening. And I don't know who leaves and who stays.*

Montale, on his Ligurian Elsinore, has given us a tragic vision of his native Riviera, all rocks and relentless waters. The seascape, suggesting a hard-fought but inevitable victory of the elements ranged against not only the man-built world (the wind against the house, 6) but even the very land that supports it (the breakers against the cliff, 19-20), establishes a mood of lucid despair. Like other pieces from *Le occasioni* and later collections, the poem takes shape as a truncated dialogue with an intensely remembered and (in this case) unremembering person.

A certain place, a certain moment fostered a relationship between the speaker and the absent lady. Separation has intervened; instead of the brief communion there are two solitudes that no longer touch. Time keeps wearing away life, as the assiduous seas undermine the rocks of the coastline (a familiar sight along the Genoese Riviera). The struggle of memory, on the part of man, is as dogged and lost as the lonely resistance of the house

against the wind. Significant human permanence is threatened; the "shore-watchers' house," high on its dominant cliff, is not only a place of control and vigilance, but an emergency shelter as well. Built to protect against human transgression—the activity of smugglers—it cannot prevent, in the long run, the transgression of the elements, nor ultimately of time itself, the natural medium of existence and its deadly foe. A spiritual event, a meeting of souls, once took place here; now it is lost, forever irrecoverable.

The symbolic stressing of the objects actually present at the scene—such as the merciless weathervane of lines 13-14 (which stands for the passing of time), the Rimbaudian compass, the Mallarmean dice—points too toward intimate thoughts of the speaker. Through these objects the reference of the poem spreads to a more than personal horizon, and the strong intimation of loss of sense, loss of direction, madness itself, comes to invest all of the human world; the struggle, in the very decade before World War II, seems desperate—even though in lines 17-18 a glimmer of hope is seen in the light of the faring tanker. Doom impends, reason and life are threatened, for this is a poem not only of memory but of insight and prophecy. The tolling insistence of "You don't remember" (1, 10, 21), three times repeated, is an ironic strand of unity in this crumbling world. The precariousness of memory is well dramatized by the image of the unwinding thread, with its suggestions of the Fates and Ariadne in the labyrinth. At the end the speaker himself becomes a shore-watcher, in a way, taking his post (22) at the house of impermanence. After speculation, in the momentous question of line 19, about a possible breakthrough to a surer reality, the question ends, as it has to, unresolved. Unless we find our answer in the strength of the poem itself.   [G.C.]

L'ANGUILLA

L'anguilla, la sirena
dei mari freddi che lascia il Baltico
per giungere ai nostri mari,
ai nostri estuarî, ai fiumi   4
che risale in profondo, sotto la piena avversa,
di ramo in ramo e poi
di capello in capello, assottigliati,
sempre piú addentro, sempre piú nel cuore   8
del macigno, filtrando
tra gorielli di melma finché un giorno
una luce scoccata dai castagni
ne accende il guizzo in pozze d'acquamorta,   12
nei fossi che declinano
dai balzi d'Appennino alla Romagna;
l'anguilla, torcia, frusta,
freccia d'Amore in terra   16
che solo i nostri botri o i disseccati
ruscelli pirenaici riconducono
a paradisi di fecondazione;
l'anima verde che cerca   20
vita là dove solo
morde l'arsura e la desolazione,
la scintilla che dice
tutto comincia quando tutto pare   24
incarbonirsi, bronco seppellito;
l'iride breve, gemella
di quella che incastonano i tuoi cigli
e fai brillare intatta in mezzo ai figli   28
dell'uomo, immersi nel tuo fango, puoi tu
non crederla sorella?

(La bufera e altro. 1956)

In Montale's great *"L'Anguilla"* ("The Eel"), from *La bufera e altro (The Hurricane and Others)*, the valor which the poet had always shown in the face of a menacing environment is no longer on the defensive; it bursts out in a proud hymn of confidence and joy. Far as the eel (*l'anguilla*) ranges—thousands of sea miles to its river, up torrents in their rage, corkscrewing through rifts in the rock, flopping through puddles or mudflats to its inland pond or well—the poet goes even further: from this will-to-live thrilling as electricity in the million veins of earth, this unquenchable spark of vitality in the mud—in which some say all life began—Montale moves to such love as Dante saw:

My lady carries love within her eyes,
    By love ennobling all she gazes on . . . .

The physical urgency, the human passion

are "arrow of Love on earth." An arrow, it would seem, that comes from other spheres; and Montale, who has used the phrase "religious penetration of the world" in speaking of this poem, here makes his own comment in his own language on Dante's climactic line: "The love that moves the sun and the other stars." But he makes it as a poet today must: not in Dante's manner, which cannot be improved or repeated, not in the all-purpose togas of old rhetoric, but in a kind of speech in which intelligent men can hold communication in our time.

The poem's thirty-line sentence has as determined a drive as the eel itself—the more a single thrust since the first and last words go together, with what is between showing why they do: *"The eel... can you / not believe her [to be your] sister?"* Though the human "you" appears only toward the end, she is in the poet's mind throughout: her presence is glimpsed in the "siren" of line 1—the image of the fabulous enchantress, half-fish, half-woman, is over-glamorous for the eel alone.

The first ten lines are about the eel's stubborn odyssey that ranges space and time: (1) *The eel, the siren* (2) *of freezing seas that leaves the Baltic* (3) *to come to our seas,* (4) *to our estuaries, to rivers* (5) *which it ascends, deep down, against the brunt of the flood,* (6) *from branch to branch and then* (7) *from vein* [literally *hair*] *to vein, [as these are] narrowed,* (8) *ever more inward, ever deeper in the heart* (9) *of the rock, filtering* (10) *through pockets of mud*—a tireless striving, under the water, under the earth. But suddenly, in a glorious burst of airy light from the chestnut foliage, we see the eel for the first time, far from the Baltic, a silver flicker in some tarn or well. (10) *—until one day* (11) *a light shot from the chestnut trees* (12) *catches its glitter in deadwater wells,* (13) *in ditches that run down* (14) *from cliffs of the Apennine to the Romagna*—the fish has crossed the great central mountain ridge of Italy and is descending toward the Adriatic.

Transfigured now, it is more than fish: (15) *the eel, torch, lash,* (16) *arrow of Love on earth*—what an energy of threshing sound in *torcia-terra; frusta-freccia!*—a guiding fire, a spur and fury, an arrow of Love like that which the mystics knew. But a triumph born of anguish, a rebirth from apparent death: (17) *—which only our gullies or dried out* (18) *creeks of the Pyrenees lead back* (19) *to paradises of fertility*—the breeding place of the eel far out at sea. "I put *pirenaici*," the poet declares, "to indicate a possible [*eventuale*] voyage of the eel from the Pyrenees to the hills of the Apennines."

The eel is almost spirit now, its purified and symbolic color the last trace of its physical nature: (20) *the green soul that seeks* (21) *life there where only* (22) *burning drought and desolation gnaw,* (23) *the spark that says* (24) *all begins when all appears* (25) *charred to carbon, a buried stick*—like the eel in drying riverbeds, again buried and again revived—this time by an amazing transfer!—in the brilliance of a woman's eyes: (26) *brief rainbow* ["iride" means also "iris" of the eye and the flower] *twin* (27) *of that* [the twinning rime: *gemella-quella!*] *your eyelashes set [like a jewel]* (28) *and you keep aglow, inviolate, amid the sons* (29) *of man, [who are] steeped in that [life-giving] mire of yours*—the transition from eel to woman is made with that most delicate of bridges, the rainbow: a radiance of passion is their bond.

The vital energy that penetrates the universe is seen best in the eyes of the woman bearing through Yeats's "complexities of mire and blood" her glowing gift among the race that has its life from her. And the final rhetorical question, to which the poem has already made its ringing answer: (29) *—can you* (30) *not believe her [to be your] sister?* [J.F.N.]

DALLA ROCCA DI BERGAMO ALTA

Hai udito il grido del gallo nell'aria
di là dalle murate, oltre le torri
gelide d'una luce che ignoravi,
grido fulmineo di vita, e stormire   4
di voci dentro le celle, e il richiamo
d'uccello della ronda avanti l'alba.
E non hai detto parole per te:
eri nel cerchio ormai di breve raggio: 8
e tacquero l'antilope e l'airone
persi in un soffio di fumo maligno,
talismani d'un mondo appena nato.
E passava la luna di febbraio   12
aperta sulla terra, ma a te forma
nella memoria, accesa al suo silenzio.
Anche tu fra i cipressi della Rocca
ora vai senza rumore; e qui l'ira   16
si quieta al verde dei giovani morti,
e la pietà lontana è quasi gioia.

(Giorno dopo giorno. 1947)

The poetry of Salvatore Quasimodo (1901–1968), hermetic in its earliest phases and given to what the critic Anceschi called "a metaphysic of aridity," did something of an about-face during the bitter experiences of the Second World War. The German occupation of northern Italy in particular did much to shock Quasimodo out of his poetic seclusion: in grief and protest he began to write poetry of wider appeal, its avowed purpose to *rifare l'uomo*, to "remake man," a task for which many of Quasimodo's critics considered his literary talents inadequate. (He was awarded the Nobel Prize in 1959.) But few would question the grace of phrasing and rhythm (which probably owe something to his long self-schooling as a translator of Greek) and the vividness and power of the imagery in such a poem as "*Dalla rocca di Bergamo alta*" ("From the Fortress of Upper Bergamo")—Bergamo, in Lombardy, is built on two levels; on the upper is preserved a picturesque castle of the past. The volume in which this poem appears deals with his "day after day" experiences of the bitterness of war and foreign occupation—often seen, as here, against memories of the poet's idyllic childhood in a Sicilian paradise of fabulous plants and animals.

Like many of Quasimodo's poems, this one is addressed to an unspecified "you." Perhaps for the same reason that other poems were: the device breaks the circle of the poet's loneliness and establishes communication with someone, if only an ideal reader. Or perhaps, like some of the other poems of this series, it is addressed to a lady loved in happier days far away—there is no word that gives a clue as to whether man or woman is addressed. Or perhaps the "you" is one of the victims of the war, one of the young dead whose spirit wanders among the cypresses of the Fortress. Or perhaps the poet is speaking to himself as "you": the theme of escape from a self-centered isolation, so prominent in this poem, might be seen as paralleling Quasimodo's own career as it developed in the war-torn '40's.

The opening lines are rich in sensations of dawn as perceived, or half-perceived, by a person enclosed within walls, somehow cut off from all that urgent and stirring activity. (1) *You heard the cry of the cock in the air* (2) *beyond the walls, beyond the towers* (3) *chill with a light you did not know,* (4) *the lightning-cry of life, and the murmuring* (5) *of voices in the cells, and the call* (6) *of the sentinel bird before dawn.* All is like a summons, thrilling with life, to which the "you" has for some reason made no response. The crowing of a cock may remind us also of Peter's betrayal of Christ and suggest that the impassive "you" has turned his back on suffering humanity. He is now in the circle of the briefest rays of the sun, in some winter season of the soul. (7) *And you said no words for yourself:* (8) *you were by now in the circle of brief ray[s]:* (9) *and the antelope and the heron fell silent* (10) *lost in a gust of malignant smoke,* (11) *talismans of a world just born.* The antelope and the heron, here and elsewhere in Quasimodo's work, are emblems and memories of childhood in Sicily. As childhood memories, in this poem they are like the newly created animals of Thomas' "Fern Hill." Now all their happy world has been expunged by the bitter smoke of war, and they can no longer "speak"—these memories—to the poet. (12) *And the February moon passed* (13) *openly over the world, but to you [it was*

only a] form (14) *in the memory, lighted in its own silence.* Nothing in the real world can shatter the introspection of this isolated "you"; instead of noticing the actual moon, he is sunk in memories of a moon of long ago—a dead cold lunar world of the unfeeling spirit, though the memories themselves may be of warmth.

Then a change: the person addressed is imagined as at least in motion, walking quietly among the cypresses of the fortress grounds, as if beginning to participate, though silently, in a human world so racked with recent death. (15) *You also among the cypresses of the Fortress* (16) *move now without sound . . .* The final lines, preceded by the ominous *ira* ("rage"), give depth and meaning to the quiet picture of early dawn at the Fortress and to all that has preceded: *and here rage* (17) *is quieted by the green of the young dead,* (18) *and the pity [grown] remote is almost joy.* The rage of war has sunk to a numb silence; fresh grass is vivid over the graves of young men dead. The grief of some years past has been softened by time: now there is almost a pleasure—almost a joy—in the memory of what was. The mysteriousness of nature, in its inexorable seasonal changes, has pacified the human heart that was once indignant over a seemingly useless sacrifice. *Pietà* means "pity," "mercy," and "piety"; the possibility of religious overtones in the ultimate *gioia* is not to be disregarded.

This is a poem of two worlds: the fortress world of Bergamo and its winter landscape, and another world, far away and long ago, to which the poet turns in longing. These vistas of death and winter, of silent heraldic animals evoked from the past, of the portentous cry of the cock and the sentinel bird, have something of the feeling of the haunted paintings of Hieronymus Bosch—here, however, all is calmed and reconciled by the green peace of the final phrases. [W.F.]

ALEXANDER BLOK

Черный ворон в сумраке снежном,
Черный бархат на смуглых плечах.
Томный голос пением нежным
Мне поет о южных ночах.

В легком сердце -- страсть и беспечность,
Словно с моря мне подан знак.
Над бездонным провалом в вечность,
Задыхаясь, летит рысак.

Снежный ветер, твое дыханье,
Опьяненные губы мои...
Валентина, звезда, мечтанье!
Как поют твои соловьи...

Страшный мир! Он для сердца тесен!
В нем — твоих поцелуев бред,
Темный морок цыганских песен,
Торопливый полет комет!

Chòrnyi vòron v sùmrake snèzhnom,
Chòrnyi bàrkhat na smùglykh plechàkh.
Tòmnyi gòlos pènyem nèzhnym
Mnè poyòt o yùzhnykh nochàkh.   4

V lèkhkom sèrdze—stràst' i bespèchnost'
Slòvno s mòrya mne pòdan znàk.
Nàd bezdònnym provàlom v vèchnost'
Zàdykhàyas', letìt rysàk.   8

Snèzhnyi vèter, tvoyè dykhàn'e
Op'yanènnye gùby moyì...
Vàlentìna, zvezdà, mechtàn'e,
Kàk poyùt tvoyì solov'yì.   12

Stràshnyi mìr! On dlya sèrdza tèsen!
V nèm tvoyìkh pozelùyev brèd,
Tèmnyi mòrok tzygànskykh pèsen,
Tòroplìvyi polèt komèt!

This untitled work by Russia's great Symbolist poet, Alexander Blok (1880-1921), was written in 1910 and included in his *Harps and Violins* volume as the second part of a three-poem unit. (Typographically the second and fourth stanzas were placed to the right, to align with the last letter of line 4.)

(1) *The black raven in the snowy twilight,* (2) *The black velvet on tanned shoulders,* (3) *A languid voice in tender singing* (4) *Sings to me of southern nights.* (5) *In the light heart —passion and insouciance,* (6) *As if a sign were given me from the sea.* (7) *Over the bottomless pit into eternity,* (8) *Panting flies the racer.* (9) *The snowy wind, your breath,* (10) *My intoxicated lips . . .* (11) *Valentina, the star, the dream!* (12) *How they sing, your nightingales . . .* (13) *The terrible (frightening) world! It is too narrow for the heart!* (14) *It has the delirium of your kisses,* (15) *The dark snare of gypsy songs,* (16) *The swift flight of comets!*

Blok always described external phenomena as signs of spiritual realities and saw mystical visions in his erotic experiences. At its most obvious level, the lines present the poet riding with a woman in a small, narrow sleigh driven by a race horse and guided by a coachman—it was customary in pre-revolutionary St. Petersburg for couples to drive to the outskirts of the city to "the islands" on the shores of the Baltic. Various words and images refer to the realistic details of the ride (snowy wind, panting racer, sea). The poet's companion wears a velvet coat or evening dress on her *smuglykh plechakh* ("tanned shoulders," 2). But whether the black raven is a purely symbolic image or a bird on the woman's hat (as was the fashion at that time), the phrase bears larger connotations in the system of allusions and suggestions on which the poem is based.

The central images—the swift movement, the flight of the sleigh, the coursing of time, the delirium of passion, the gypsy song—are typical of Blok's poetic diction: they appear, with the wind image, in most of his poems of the period. The insistent adjectives *chornyi* ("dark," 1, 2) and *snezhnom* (*snezhnyi*: "snowy," 1, 9) project the contrast of black-white as the main colors of the poem, paralleled, as it were, by another contrast: the song of southern nights in the snowy dusk of a northern night—the nightingales, those birds of spring, in wintry St. Petersburg.

The poet's companion is probably a singer: he calls her "Valentina," the name of the leading lady of Meyerbeer's Romantic opera *The Huguenots*, then extremely popular in Russia. But here again we can merely guess—the ride takes place after a performance, perhaps with the very artist who sang Valentina's part. In any event, music is the underlying reality of the poem: as they speed through "the islands" and across the bridge that evokes the "bottomless pit of eternity," the poet hears the song among the kisses. The song becomes a symbol of intoxication, a departure from reality—it makes nightingales' sound in the night, in the snowy darkness, and it calls forth a vision, a dream—as Valentina, distant as a star, is also a vision, a dream.

The final quatrain contrasts the darkness of the world and the whiteness of the dream. *Strashnyi mir!* ("The terrible" or "frightening" "world"), a simple statement, contains the momentary oblivion and the deceit of passion ("delirium" and "snare," 14, 15)—of all the "comet-like" passions. It holds the allurement of flights; but the game of emotions does not satisfy the human heart, filled with dreams and yearnings. Hence man outgrows his universe. For Blok "the terrible world" encompassed all the phenomena of reality with their contrasts and conflicts. The Romantic in him could never accept it—neither "the bottomless pit of eternity," which the black water reminded him of, nor the windy galloping of time and sensations, which emphasized the frailty of all dreaming and all singing. The "black raven" that opens the poem is the symbol of this frightening universe.

The Russian text embodies not only the swift rhythm of the poem, which corresponds to the driving movement of the sleigh, but also a perfect unity of masculine and feminine rimes, alliteration, and other sounds, with insistence upon *s* and *l* and partial insistence upon *zh* and *ch*. The mark of the Romantic appears in the play on contrasts (noted earlier) and juxtapositions; and it is especially manifest in the rime *bespechnost'* with *vechnost'* ("carelessness" or "insouciance" with "eternity," 5, 7).

The poem begins as incantation: the song the poet hears is within him. Then the passion, of love and of the ride, which has the effect of a spell intoxicating as any dream, is interrupted by his sudden awakening into the "terrible world." And this is the structure of the poem: incantation, motion, leading to the impassioned climax in the exclamatory "Valentina, the star, the dream"—and then the fall into frightening reality.   [M.S.]

A NOTE ON THE PROSODIES

Before venturing into the unfamiliar prosodies of French, Spanish, Italian, German, and Portuguese, it may be useful to look at our own; for all verses are composed of sounds and of silences. To be sure, each of these six languages has evolved a characteristic system, yet all of them have also responded (at an earlier time) to the influence of Greece, Rome, and Provence and (at a later time) to the literary currents of modern Europe. Hence, a widely known element of one of these prosodies may offer the simplest approach to the rest, especially since the terms are quite generally used. We start, then, with a famous fact about English verse—that every line can be scanned, including free verse, with its changing meters and rhythms. It can be scanned into *feet* of stressed and unstressed syllables: iambic ⌣′ , trochaic ′⌣ , anapaestic ⌣⌣′ , dactylic ′⌣⌣ , spondaic ′′ , etc.—and into numbers of feet per line—dimeter, 2; trimeter, 3; tetrameter, 4; pentameter, 5; hexameter, 6, etc. "The cúrfew tólls the knéll of párting dáy" is a perfect iambic pentameter, whereas the first line of *Endymion*—"A thing of beauty is a joy forever"—has an extra last syllable (it is a "feminine" line). The third line of *Endymion*—"Pass into nothingness; but still will keep"—is also pentameter, but the opening foot is a trochee. Thus school children have been taught to scan the body of English poetry; it was all quite simple.

In reality, of course, it is much more interesting. Few lines of English verse are made of syllables that are equally "strong" and equally "weak." Take, for example, Landor's "Ah, what avails the sceptred race": "ah" is perceptibly stronger than the other weak syllables. The line is called a "perfect" iambic pentameter, but the first iamb differs from the others. Similarly, the "is" in the first line of *Endymion* is perceptibly weaker than the other strong syllables. "Stressed and unstressed," then, is not quite an either-or matter. Both have many shadings of strength and of weakness; and this very complexity adds interest and attraction to the gross pattern of emphasis. As much can be said of differences in quantity— that is, in the amount of time it takes to speak a syllable. The word *gloom*, for example, has much greater quantity than *glib*, the word *shade* than *shed, feel* than *fill;* yet all these words, when stressed in a line, bear the same scanning symbol. Only when one recognizes such variation in stress and quantity can he accept the dictum that all English verse is "either strict iambic or loose iambic." Some refer to the "counterpoint" as the difference between the meter and the sonal cadence, an excellent word for suggesting that the iambic is at best a metrical base against which the poet plays his innumerable shadings of stress, quantity, and other sonal instruments.

Though nothing could be gained by graphing such variations, it helps to be reminded of their presence, as it helps to become aware of such other elements as timing and riming. When reading the second line of *Endymion*—"Its loveliness increases; it will never"—one naturally stops after "increases." Such a phrasal pause within a line (*caesura*) is much more apparent than the briefer delays imposed by the meaning of the words. At the end of a line the stop is emphatic when it coincides with a normal speech pause. But an unrelieved sequence of such coincidences (*end-stopped* lines) can be tiring—as it often is with "perfect" heroic couplets. Commonly the last word of a line runs over into the next—as the last of "Its loveliness increases; it will never" runs over into "Pass into nothingness" (line 3). The speed of this *enjambment* depends somewhat upon end-rime, for when it is present, the reader expects to stop, if only for an instant. His actual pause will necessarily be shorter with a masculine rime (*keep-sleep*) than with a feminine (*forever-never*); and it will also be affected by the exactness of the rime and by its quantity. Pauses, then, involve much more than the simple difference between a full stop and none, at the end and within a line. They occur everywhere and in delicate gradations, for the meaning combines and divides the words into breath-groups, which tend to recur in a pattern of pauses. End-stopped lines match sense and stress with bald regularity. But when there is no such coincidence, when the poet plays his meanings against his meter, the sequence of sounds can often be so "musical" as to delight even a person who has no idea of their meaning. (If the word "musical" can ever be applied to verse, it is here: to a sonal pattern with no denotation whatever.)

The pleasure one takes in such verse always depends to some extent on repetitions of identical or similar sounds. For its perfect rime, English rejects *rime riche* (*perceive-receive*—which French admires: beau*té*-san*té*), looking instead to the last accented vowel and what follows (st*ill*-h*ill*, r*ending*-off*ending*—"poor rime" to the French). Yet English is typically lean in rime possibilities, compared to Italian, for example. It will accept consonantal repeti-

tion (*groined-groaned*; a*mple*-si*mple*) as approximate rimes and merely orthographic identities (*above-prove; laughter-slaughter*) as "eye-rimes." It makes no systematic use of assonance or of alliteration, though the first (repetition of identical or similar vowel sounds: sch*e*me-bes*ee*ch; d*aw*n-bl*oo*d) has served excellently in Spanish and the second (repetition of consonants, especially initial: *F*ull *f*a*th*om *f*ive *th*y *f*a*th*er lies) was used regularly in Old English and importantly in Middle English verse. Why? Do preferences inhere in each language? Our greatest achievements (Elizabethan drama, *Paradise Lost*, and so on) are cast in a five-stress line without rime, adopted from a language wealthy in rime (Italian) and imitated in most other literatures with little success. In Greek verse, quantity was primary, stress secondary. In English, the rôles are reversed. In the Romance languages, the line-unit is determined by the number of syllables. One may question the metalinguist's belief that each language shapes the reasoning of its speakers, but one can hardly doubt that a poet's creations are conditioned by the special discriminations, resources, and directions of his language, which are also his to alter and to enlarge.

From the point of view of prosody, all the poems in this book can be measured as sound and silence. Silence has only one dimension (time); sounds have several, the most important of which have been noted. But, as we have found, in English all these dimensions—pause, stress, quantity, sonal repetition—are capable of wonderful range and complexity and variety. We may find no less in the poetry of French, German, Spanish, Italian, and Portuguese. The characteristic flavor of each must, of course, be experienced in order to be known; and the experiencing is available, at least to some degree, to every interested reader. It will be fostered by some knowledge of the essential ways in which each of these prosodies differs from our own.

If we begin with German, it is not only because its prosody still shows, as does our own, the ancestral influences of Old Germanic verse, with its marked alliteration and caesura: virtually all we have said of English prosody can also be said of modern German. Both are governed by the same principle: stress. Both have various shadings in strong and weak syllables—even in single words. (*Hausfrauen*, for example, has two strong syllables, but *frau* is weaker than *Haus*. *Freundlichkeit* has two weak syllables, but *keit* is stronger than *lich*.) The wide range of vowel sounds, many of which are very long or very short, produces rich differences in quantity—which helped Hölderlin, in his passion to emulate the Greek, to try to reconcile classical quantity and German stress (p. 117). But basically German verse is as accentual as English; and its blank verse is sometimes as flexibly accented as our own. "Du schlank und rein," however, is rigorously iambic (in all lines but one, p. 133); so is most of "Jahrestag" (p. 122), whose lines end with consonantal repetitions. Rime in general resembles our own in preferences, though a German poet may acceptably pair an indistinct with a clear vowel (as in Stündlein-Kindlein, Blick-zurück, Verzichtkriegt, etc.).

Most of our German poems are in meter, but "Hyperions Schicksalslied" and "Da ich ein Knabe war" (pp. 114, 120) have the varied rhythms and unequal lines of free verse. But what shall we call Rilke's "Elegie" (p. 150)? Its meters shift, often from iambs to dactyls of varying length; enjambments abound; caesuras, alliteration, and assonance are all evident, along with contrastingly long and short sentences. Is it free verse on a dactylic base? In a very real sense, this poem shows what a modern poet can make of freedom, combining regular with irregular meters, and rime with non-rime and assonance, in a strikingly unified whole.

Spanish, Portuguese, and Italian may be discussed together, for each of their words has its own pattern of stress (mañana, maçã, automobile) and each line is determined by the number of syllables it contains. The verse, therefore, is *both* syllabic and stressed. Once he decides on the number of syllables, the poet can do as he pleases with his patterns of stress; but the number of syllables is controlled by the accent on the final word. In the hendecasyllable there are, of course, 11; but when the accent falls on the final syllable: 10; when it falls on the antepenult: 12. In practice the modern poet obeys not arithmetic but his ear; and it is his ear that overrules the rules when he turns to classic meters ("Motivo," "Preciosa...," "A Silvia," pp. 230, 232, 278), or to blank verse ("L'Infinito," p. 276), or to free verse ("Profundamente," "Pequeño responso...," pp. 194, 226), or to an amalgam of the two.

A few additional matters call for at least passing attention. Italian makes conspicuous use of perfect rime, assonance on the whole being unimportant. But Spanish and Portuguese have greatly preferred assonance and rime mixed with assonance, rime itself being mostly reserved for strict forms.[1] A second difference in inclination has been true of the line itself, the 11-syllable being "characteristically Italian," the 8-syllable "characteristically Spanish and Portuguese." Although the hendecasyllable is indeed important, Italian poets make abundant

---

[1] Italian rimes closed *o* with open *o*. Rimes in Italian, Portuguese, and Spanish are predominantly feminine; in English, with its wealth of monosyllabic words, masculine.

use of the settenario (7) along with other lines. Similarly with the octosyllable, of the popular *romance* tradition: it is still prevalent in Spanish and Portuguese, but so are the hendecasyllable and the heptasyllable (7) and combinations of the two. Partisans of English prosody, to whom syllabic count may seem frightfully mathematical, should remember that these languages also offer the flexibility of elision (non-sounding of a final vowel before an initial vowel—a Portuguese poet, for example, can make 4 syllables of *minha alma* or 3 *minh' alma;* see also "No era nadie," p. 182). Neither Carducci's attempt to use quantity in Italian verse nor his actual disregard of length of syllable in favor of accent (see p. 285) had any altering consequence: one could always find dactyls, trochees, anapaests etc. in the lines. Similarly with the metrical innovations in Spanish proposed by Rubén Darío. For Spanish and Italian have little quantity. Quantity is typical only of Portuguese verse, which uses it quite naturally as a variation in sound.

These three prosodies then, are syllabic—whereas ours is accentual. The distinction is valid so long as it remains a distinction, for all four prosodies also have much in common. In fact, some students argue that our "characteristic line" is not iambic pentameter at all but a decasyllable in rising rhythm. The case can be buttressed with classic examples, such as: "It is the cáuse, it is the cáuse, my sóul"—*Othello;* "But hóld some twó dáys cónference with the déad"—*The Duchess of Malfi;* "Rócks, Cáves, Lákes, Féns, Bógs, Déns, and Shádes of Déath"—*Paradise Lost.* Is English verse, then, syllabic?

The ultimate answer lies in what the poet feels to be the structural unit of his line, and of his language. And in French there can be no question: in ordinary discourse, each syllable is about equally strong, with slight additional stress on the last that is fully pronounced in a word or a group. What, then, holds the line together, in particular the "characteristic" *alexandrin?*[2] Immutable rules, said the classicists: exactly 12 syllables, caesura after the sixth, *rime riche*, no enjambment, etc. ("El desdichado," p. 2, except for the spelling of rimes *Reine-Sirène*). Needless to say, the rules were broken—at first gently, by the Romantics, then violently, by Rimbaud and Verlaine (see p. 41). But it was not till *vers libre* dawned on France (with Rimbaud's "Mouvement," 1886, see p. 33) that all French poets could think of writing by rhythm alone. Battles swarmed between the advocates of rhythm and of syllabic count. But when master enunciators read 1100 Classic and Romantic *alexandrins* for the phoneticians at the Collège de France, photographic recordings showed that less than half actually contained 12 syllables (650 had 9, 10, 13, or 14).[3] What accounts for the pattern of rhythm—the duration, intensity, pitch? Since the stresses in every sentence are dictated by the meaning, we may answer: the *accent of meaning*, a pattern that always varies in accordance with the speaker's intent. In English this accent can be played against the rhythm of stress; in French the two coincide.[4]

As our selection makes apparent, modern French verse ranges from almost classic (Nerval, Mallarmé, Valéry) and

---

[2] For Henri Bremond, the 8-syllable line is the most characteristically French.

[3] Coquelin's reading of "La ballade du duel," a classic pattern of octosyllables with 14 masculine and 14 feminine rimes, showed Rostand's intention to have been carried out only 10 in 28 times (Burnshaw, *André Spire and His Poetry*, 1933, pp. 126-134).

[4] When it occurs at the rime, the final mute *e* may add little more than a liquid prolongation ("d'une nuit d'Idumé*e*," p. 44). But when, within the line, it is followed by a

generally conventional (Baudelaire, Laforgue, Aragon) writing to prose poetry (Rimbaud, Claudel, Perse) and *vers libre*, rimed, mixed, or utterly free (Apollinaire, Éluard, Char). Thus, a French poet may do literally whatever he chooses—with syllabism, rhythm, quantity, rime, assonance, cacophony, etc., etc. He can write child-like songs and philosophic essays, in lucid or impenetrable syntax; he can leave nothing unsaid or everything: he is free.

. A similar choice of possibilities and burdens confronts every other serious writer of verse in our time.   [s.b.]

A NOTE ON THE PRONUNCIATIONS

As anyone who makes the attempt soon knows, it is not possible to learn to pronounce —or to hear—a foreign language merely by obeying written instructions. Thus the notes that follow—obviously rudimentary and over-simple (see "qualification" # 4, p. xiv above) —can be no more than a brief refresher for some and a most elementary guide for others. Yet they may at least lead to an appreciation of the sonal qualities of French, German, Spanish, Portuguese, and Italian, especially when used in connection with good recordings. Listening to sounds is essential in learning to make them. We suggest that the poems be recited aloud, unless the reader knows the languages well enough to hear them in his mind.

Except for instances that are specified, the vowels discussed here are never drawn-out or slurred as vowels often are in English. (Avoid the "glide-off of the final *ee* sound of *day*, for example.) Note also that the omission of a consonant does not mean that it is the same as in English, but that it is merely somewhat similar. Our many "like" and "as" statements are to be taken literally.

Note: "initial" refers to the beginning of a syllable or of a word. The word "consonant" has been abbreviated as "cons."

FRENCH

VOWELS

â, a + **s**—open, as in *father* (âme, basse).

à, a—closed, as in *cat* (là, salle).

è, ê, e + cons., **ei, ai**—all these are open *e*, pronounced as in English *met*.

é, er, es, ez, ai—closed, as in *mate*.

i, î, ie, y—*ee* as in English *thee*.

o—open as in English *for* (homme; *also:* Paul).

ô, o + silent cons., **au, eau**—closed, as in *go* (beau, vos, hôte, l'eau, au).

ou—closed, as in *moon* (fou, vous, trou).

u—say *ee*, then round lips to say *oo* (plume).

eu, œu (often final)—purse lips to say *oo*, then say *ay* as in English *pay* (peu).

eu, œu + pronounced consonant—as in *fur*.

mute e—*a* as in *Louisa:* appears as final *e* (automobile); verb endings *-es*, *-ent*; and end of syllable within a word (petit).

NASALS: **n** or **m**, final or before a cons., combines with preceding vowel:

en, an, em, am—"open *a*" nasalized.

in, im, ain, ein, aim, eim—"open *e*" nasalized (faim, fin, mains, sein).

on, om—"open *o*" nasalized (long, ombre).

un, um—*un* of *lunch* nasalized (lundi).

word that begins with a consonant, it is usually pronounced as a syllable ("Le Prince d'Aquitaine," p. 2). Of interest, in this connection: "Hopkins found evidence for sprung rhythm in Chaucer, but because he read him without pronouncing some final unaccented *e* vowels"—W. H. Gardner, *Gerard Manley Hopkins*, 1949, vol. II, p. 166).

u before vowel—pronounce French *u*, then cut it off sharply, then say the next vowel (lui, nuit), but avoid a *w* sound.

oi—similar to the *wa* sound of English *swat* (loi, mois).

i + vowel, vowel + **ill**, vowel + final **il**—all like the *y* sound in *yet*.

CONSONANTS

c, ç—like *s* in *sew;* but before **a, o, u,** the **c** is pronounced *k* (comme, casse, cuir).

ch—similar to *sh* in English *wish*.

g—"hard" as in *gone* before **a, o, u**; otherwise like the *z* in *azure* (Georges, gîte).

gn—*ni* sound similar to English *onion*.

j—like the *z* in *azure* (je, Jean, jour, joli).

h—is always silent (see "Stress" below).

q, qu—always pronounced *k* (cinq, quand).

r—either "uvular" (made by gentle clearing or upper part of throat) or "trilled" (by vibrating tongue against upper gum).

s—*s* when initial or before or after consonants; otherwise *z* as in *doze* (rose).

t, th—always *t* as in *tin* (ton, théorie).

tion—*s* (edition); but *t* after *s* or *x*.

w—occurs rarely; it has sound of **v**.

x—*ks* (fixe); sometimes *s* (dix); *z* (dixième).

z—*z* as in *doze*.

SILENT CONSONANTS (with some exceptions):

m, p, th in medial groups are sometimes silent (damner, sculpter, asthme).

final consonants are generally silent (les, pots), but **c, f, l, r** are usually pronounced.

STRESS: each syllable is given *almost* equal stress, with slight extra stress on last *pronounced* syllable (présent, automobile). Liaison: an otherwise silent final cons. links with initial vowel of next word (les amis), except before aspirate *h* (les héros) or after the word *et*.

GERMAN

VOWELS: when long, very long; when short, very short. **Long:** doubled (Haar); before *h* or a single cons. (ihn, gut); at the end of a stressed syllable (haben). **Short:** before a double cons. (kommen) or two or more cons.

(oft, Fenster, Nest). Note: there are many exceptions to these rules.

a—long, as in *far;* short, as in *guts*.

e—long, as in *gate;* short, as in *get*.

i—long, as in *machine;* short as in *pin*.

o—long, as in *no;* short as in *nor*.

u—long, as in *rule;* short as in *put*.

e in final syllables—*a* as in *comma*.

ä—long, as in *care* (but sometimes as in *gate*); short, as in *get*.

ö—long: round lips, then pronounce long **e**. short: round lips, then pronounce short **e**.

ü—long: round lips, then pronounce long **i**. short: round lips, then pronounce short **i**.

ei, ai—*i* as in *mine* (ein, Mai, Kaiser).

ie—long, as in *machine* (Tier).

au—*ou* as in *house* (auf, Maus, aus).

äu, eu—round lips, then say *oil* (deutsch).

Note: before initial stressed vowel, stop the breath for an instant and close the glottis. This causes a click, which is heard if the word is whispered ('an, 'ist, 'Apfel).

CONSONANTS (Press tongue against upper teeth to pronounce **d, t, n, l.**)

b—initial: *b;* before **st** and **t** and at end of a word or syllable: *p* (gibst).

c—in foreign words only; generally: *ts* before **ä, e, i, u;** *k* before **a, o, u.**

ch—after **e, i, ä, ö, ü, ei, ie,** and cons.: sound of *h* as in *hew*. After **a, o, u, au**: guttural, as in Scottish *loch*. Initial **ch** is *k* except in foreign words mainly of French origin.

chs—*ks* as in *basks* (Ochs, Fuchs, sechs).

d—initial: *d;* final or in short syllables or before cons.: more like a *t* sound.

g—initial: as in *go;* final word or syllable and before **st** or **t**: *k* (legst, legt).

j—*y* as in English *yes* (ja, Juni, Jahr).

ng—*ng* sound as in English *singer* (lang).

pf—*pf* sound as in English *helpful* (Pferd, Kopf).

ps—*ps* sound as in English *dropsy* (Psalm).

qu—*kv* (Quelle, quer).

r—trilled or uvular, remotely as in French.

s—*z* initial (Sohn); elsewhere *s* (Haus, das).

ß ("scharfes s")—voiceless as in *miss*.

sp, st—initial: *sh* as in *shoe* + *p* or *t*.

sch—*sh* as in *shoe* (Schuh, Fisch).

th—always *t* (Theater, Thron).

v—*f* (vier, Vater), but in words of foreign origin: *v*, except when final (Violine).

w—always *v* (wer, Wasser, Winter, warm).

z—*ts* as in *its* (zwei, Arzt, Zimmer).

STRESS: simple words stress the stem (*Vat*er, *hab*en); compound nouns stress first element (*Haus*tür). Foreign words usually stress last syllable (Stu*dent*). Verbs in -ieren stress *ie* (stud*ie*ren). On verbs, separable prefixes are stressed (*aus*kommen); but inseparable prefixes (be-, ent-, er-, ge-, ver-, zer-) are unstressed (ent*kommen*).

SPANISH

VOWELS: stressed vowels are held longer and pronounced more tensely; unstressed are never slurred or swallowed.

a—as in *father* (casa: sound each clearly).

e—*a* as in *taken* when syllable ends in a vowel; otherwise as in *met* (*pe*so; bel*dad*).

i—*ee* as in English *see* (amigo).

o—as in *go* when syllable ends in a vowel; otherwise: a sound somewhere between *o* in *oat* and in *or*, but unglided.

u—*oo* as in *poodle* (puro, cucú).

DIPHTHONGS: two vowels pronounced as one, a strong (**a, e, o**) + a weak (**i, u**) or a weak + a weak. The **i** gives a *y* sound, the **u** a *w* sound (examples: **ia**—as in *rabia;* **ie**—as in *especie;* **io**—as in *genio;* **ua**—as in *agua*). The **i** is spelled **y** at the end of a word.

CONSONANTS

b and **v** are pronounced alike. Initial or after **m** or **n**: like *b* in *bat* but less explosive. In most other cases: close the lips *almost* and say *b*.

c—*k* before **a, o, u** (casa, como, cucú). Before **e** or **i**: *s* for Spanish Americans; *th* as in *thin* (for Castilian Spaniards).

ch—*ch* as in English *chest* (muchacha).

d—*th* as in *although* between vowels; in most other cases like English *d* but with tongue against upper front teeth (lado; dos).

g—*ch* of German *ach* before **e** or **i**; otherwise similar to *g* in *gun* (giro; gloria).

gua, guo, güi, güe—*g* + *w* + vowel sound.

h—always silent (hombre).

j—same as *ch* in German *ach* (jota, mujer).

ll—in Castilian Spanish: like *lli* in *million;* in Spanish American: like *y* in *yet*.

ñ—*ny* sound as in *canyon* (cañón, niño).

qu—*k*. (Spanish *cu* produces English qu.)

r—vibrate tongue against palate above upper front teeth. Vibrate more strongly for **rr** and when **r** follows **n** or begins word.

s—weak *s*; closer to *z* before a voiced conson. (asbesto, mismo).

w—rare; pronounced like Spanish **b** and **v**.

x—*s* before a consonant, but otherwise *gs* or *ks* as in *digs, asks*. In Spanish America, **x** is regularly like *ks* (texto, extra).

y—consonantal: like the *y* in *yet* (yo).

z—same as Spanish **c** + **e** or **i** (see above).

English sound	Spanish spelling
s or *th* sound	—ce, ci, za, zo, zu.
g as in *go*	—gue, gui, ga, go, gu.
k as in *king*	—que, qui, ca, co, cu.
ch as in *ach*	—ge, gi, ja, je, ji, jo, ju.

STRESS: final syllable when word ends in a cons. except **n** or **s** (habl*ar*) next-to-last, when word ends in **n, s,** or a vowel (*habl*an, *ca*sa). Exceptions are marked with a written accent.

PORTUGUESE

(We offer only the main elements, based on Brazilian usage. For vowel harmony, stress, liaison, metaphony, and for many exceptions to the following, consult a standard textbook.)

VOWELS

a—when stressed: open, like *a* in *part;* otherwise "slurred" sound of *u* in *but*.

e—when stressed: either open, as in *get*, or closed, as in *they;* when unstressed: slurred sound of French mute *e* "combined" with *i* in *dish;* sometimes almost silent.

i—as in *bee* when stressed; but somewhat like the slurred **e** before a stressed **i**; and as in *dish* before *l* or *l* + cons.

o—when stressed: open, as in *raw*, or closed, as in *rote;* when unstressed it is more like *oo* in *room* than *u* in *full*.

u—*oo* as in *room*.

DIPHTHONGS: two vowels pronounced as one. The **i** or **e** gives a *y* sound, **u** a *w* sound: **ai**—as in *die;* **ei**—as in *gay;* **oi**—as in *boy* or *Lois;* **ui**—as in *Louis;* **ia, ea**—as in *yacht, young;* **ie**—as in *yet;* **io, eo**—as in *your, yoke,* *yule;* **au**—as in *cow;* **eu**—as in *get, gate* + *w;* **iu, io**—*ee* + *w;* **ua, oa**—as in *watt;* **ue, oe**—as in *wet, wait;* **ui, oi**—as in *wee.*

TRIPHTHONGS: three vowels pronounced as one: **a, o,** or **e** in the middle and stressed.

CONSONANTS

c, ç—*s* as in *sew;* but before **a, o, u,** and cons. (except **ch**), the **c** is *k.*

ch—as in French (*sh* as in English *shun*).

d—*d* except between vowels; then *th* of *thou.*

g—*g* of *guard* before **a, o, u;** otherwise like *z* in English *azure* (see French *g* above).

j—*z* as in *azure* (see French *j* above).

lh—pronounced *lli* as in English *million.*

n—n; but before *k* or hard *g:* similar to *ng* sound of English *sing.* (banco, frango).

nh—similar to *ni* sound in English *onion.*

qu—*k;* but before **a** or **o:** *kw* (as in *queen*).

r—trilled; strongly when **rr**, at beginning of a word, also sometimes after **l, n, s.**

s—as in *see;* but as in *maze:* between vowels (pesar) and before **b, d, g, l, m, n, r.**

x—like **ch** above; but between vowels it sometimes has the sound of *s* or of *ks.*

NASALIZATION is produced by "til" mark on **ã;** by **m** or **n** + consonant; by vowel + final **m** (lã, longe, longo, fundo, tinta, um, etc.). Nasalized diphthongs: —**ãe:** slurred **a** + slurred **i;** **em, en:** close **e** + slurred **i;** **õe: oi** diphthong + slurred **i;** **ão, am:** slurred **a** + nasalized *w* (mão, falaram).

ITALIAN

VOWELS: always clear-cut and pure:
a—*a* as in English *ah!* (casa, ama, sala).
e—sometimes *e* as in *they*, but unglided; sometimes *e* as in *bet* (bene, vento, è).

i—*i* as in *machine* (libri, vini, Amalfi).
o—sometimes *o* as in English *oh!* (posto); sometimes as in *or* (moda, no, cosa).
u—as in *rule* (luna, uno, uso, studente).

CONSONANTS

c—*k* before **a, o, u;** *ch* in *chest* before **e** or **i** (casa, con; cena, cibo, ciao).

ch—*k* (used only with **e** or **i**).

g—as in *go* before **a, o, u** (diga, gufo); as in *gem* before **e** and **i** (Gina).

gh—as in *go* (used only with **e** or **i**).

gli—similar to *lli* in English *million.*

gn—similar to *ny* in English *canyon.*

qu—always as in English *question.*

r—one flip of the tongue against gums of upper front teeth (Roma, ristorante).

s—sometimes as in *house;* sometimes as in *rose* (always so before **b, d, g, l, m, n, r, v**).

sc—as in *ask* before **a, o,** or **u** (toscano); as in *fish* before **e** or **i** (pesce, sci).

z—sometimes *ts* as in *bets;* sometimes *ds* as in *beds* (grazie; zero).

Note: ci, gi, and **sci** do not pronounce the **i** when next letter is **a, o,** or **u** (unless the **i** is stressed)—mancia, giallo, sciare. (The **i** merely "softens" the **c, g,** or **sc.**)

DOUBLE CONSONANTS are pronounced much more forcefully than single—*ff, ll, mm, rr, ss, vv* are virtually sounded twice. With *bb, cc, dd, gg, pp, tt* the explosion is stronger. However, *zz* is almost the same as **z.**

STRESS: usually the next-to-last syllable (a*mi*co, par*la*re). But many words stress the last syllable (cit*tà*): they are always written with an accent. Some words stress the third-from-last and a few the fourth-from-last.

NOTES ON THE CONTRIBUTORS

THOMAS G. BERGIN   Sterling Professor of Romance Languages, Yale University. Author: *Giovanni Verga.* Translator: *The Divine Comedy; The New Science of G. B. Vico; The Poems of William of Poitou;* etc. Editor: *Liriche di Rambaldo di Vaqueiras;* etc.

CALVIN S. BROWN   Alumni Foundation Distinguished Professor of English, University of Georgia. Author: *Music and Literature; Tones into Words: A Comparison of the Arts;* etc. General Editor: *The Reader's Companion to World Literature;* etc.

STANLEY BURNSHAW   Formerly Lecturer in Literature, New York University. Author: *Caged in an Animal's Mind; The Bridge;* etc. Translator: *André Spire and His Poetry.*

GLAUCO CAMBON   Visiting Lecturer, University of Michigan; Fellow, Indiana School of Letters. Author: *Tematica e sviluppo della poesia americana.*

ERNESTO GUERRA DA CAL   Chairman, Department of Spanish and Portuguese, New York University. Author: *Lengua y estilo de Eça de Queiroz, I; O tema do mar no nosa lírica primitiva; Lua de Alén-Mar;* etc.

DUDLEY FITTS   Cochran Instructor in English, Phillips Academy; Editor, Yale Series of Younger Poets. Author: *Poems, 1929-1936.* Translator: *Poems from the Greek Anthology; Lysistrata; Frogs;* etc.

EUGENIO FLORIT   Professor of Spanish Literature, Columbia University; Middlebury Summer School. (See p. 261.)

WALLACE FOWLIE   Literature Faculty, University of Colorado; Foreign Editor: *Poetry.* Author: *The Age of Surrealism; Mallarmé; Rimbaud; Claudel; Dionysus in Paris;* etc. Translator: *Seamarks* [St.-John Perse].

HOWARD E. HUGO   Associate Professor of English, University of California. Author: *The Letters of Liszt to Marie Wittgenstein; Heinrich Heine;* etc. Editor: *The Romantic Reader;* etc.

ANDREW O. JASZI   Professor of German, University of California. Contributor: *The Germanic Review, The German Quarterly, New Mexico Quarterly, PMLA,* etc.

JOHN W. KNELLER   Chairman, Department of French and Italian, Oberlin College. Co-author: *Introduction à la poésie française.*

JONATHAN LEVY   Graduate Student, Columbia University.

JUAN MARICHAL   Associate Professor of Romance Languages and Literatures, Harvard University. Author: *La voluntad de estilo.* Editor: *Poesías completas; Teatro completo; Volverse sombra y otros poemas* [Salinas].

SOLITA SALINAS MARICHAL   Instructor in Spanish, Simmons College. Author: *Rafael Alberti* [in preparation].

JOHN FREDERICK NIMS   Visiting Professor, University of Madrid; Professor of English, University of Illinois. Author: *The Iron Pastoral; A Fountain in Kentucky; The Knowledge of the Evening* [in press]. Translator: *The Poems of St. John of the Cross;* etc.

JULIAN PALLEY   Department of Spanish, University of Oregon. Contributor: *Hispania, New World Writing, Portfolio,* etc.

HENRI PEYRE   Chairman, Department of Romance Languages, Yale University; President, Modern Language Association. Author: *The Contemporary French Novel; Writers and Their Critics; Hommes et œuvres du vingtième siècle; Les générations littéraires;* etc.

RENATO POGGIOLI   Late Professor of Slavic and Comparative Literature, Harvard University. Author: *Pietre di paragone; Il fiore del verso russo; Teoria dell'arte d'avanguardia; The Phoenix and the Spider;* etc.

MARIO PRAZ   Professor of English Literature, University of Rome. Author: *The Romantic Agony; The Flaming Heart;* etc.

PAUL PATRICK ROGERS   Chairman, Department of Spanish, Oberlin College. Author: *Goldoni in Spain;* etc. Editor: *Escritores contemporáneos de México; Surtidores* [García Lorca]; etc.

GREGOR SEBBA   Visiting Profesor, Graduate Institute of Liberal Arts, Emory University; Professor of Economics and Statistics, University of Georgia. Author: *Descartes and His Philosophy; Nicholas Malebranche; Goethe on Human Creativity;* etc.

MARC SLONIM   Formerly Literature Faculty, Sarah Lawrence College. Author: *The Epic of Russian Literature; The Three Loves of Dostoevsky;* etc.

DORA ALENCAR DE VASCONCELLOS   Consul General of Brazil in New York. Author: *Palavras sem eco; Surdina de contemplado; O grande caminho do Branco* [in press].